Cambridge Studies in Social and Emotional Development

General Editor: Martin L. Hoffman

Advisory Board: Nicholas Blurton Jones, Robert N. Emde, Willard W. Hartup, Robert A. Hinde, Lois W. Hoffman, Carroll E. Izard, Jerome Kagan, Franz J. Monks, Paul Mussen, Ross D. Parke, and Michael Rutter

Conflict in child and adolescent development

Although conflict in human affairs has fascinated theorists and researchers for centuries, this is the first book that focuses on the role of conflict in psychological and social development. Leading scholars in developmental and clinical psychology present findings from psychology, anthropology, sociology, sociolinguistics, and family relations to provide an intriguing picture of what is known about conflict in development and a preview of future research. Conflict is not always a negative, destructive event; the research shows that it has many positive effects in the development of individuals and their interpersonal relationships. A major theme of *Conflict in Child and Adolescent Development* is how the management of conflict can enhance the psychological growth of individuals and strengthen relationships among people.

Conflict in child and adolescent development

Edited by

CAROLYN UHLINGER SHANTZ
Wayne State University

WILLARD W. HARTUP
University of Minnesota

CAMBRIDGE
UNIVERSITY PRESS

Published by the Press Syndicate of the University of Cambridge
The Pitt Building, Trumpington Street, Cambridge CB2 1RP
40 West 20th Street, New York, NY 10011–4211, USA
10 Stamford Road, Oakleigh, Victoria 3166, Australia

First published 1992

Printed in the United States of America

Library of Congress Cataloging-in-Publication Data

Conflict in child and adolescent development / edited by Carolyn
Uhlinger Shantz, Willard W. Hartup.

p.   cm. – (Cambridge studies in social and emotional
development)

Includes indexes.

ISBN 0-521-40416-9

1. Conflict (Psychology) in children.   2. Conflict (Psychology) in
adolescence.   3. Interpersonal relations in children.
4. Interpersonal relations in adolescence.   5. Adjustment
(Psychology) in children.   6. Adjustment (Psychology) in
adolescence.   I. Shantz, Carolyn Uhlinger.   II. Hartup, Willard W.
III. Series.
BF723.C647C66   1992
155.4'18 – dc20   91–43036
                                                            CIP

A catalog record for this book is available from the British Library.

ISBN 0-521-40416-9 hardback

Contents

Part III. Conflict and developmental adaptations

Preface

This book is an attempt to bring together the diverse ideas and findings now available on conflict in the development of children and adolescents, and to formulate the most significant questions that lie ahead. Everyone connected with this volume acknowledges that conflict is a central force in human development, contributing to both successful and unsuccessful outcomes. Convinced that the time is right for a comprehensive examination of conflict in child and adolescent development, the authors assess the current status of our knowledge as well as future prospects.

The editors wish to thank the authors who contributed chapters to this volume. Few had tidy fields with which to work; many were required to take "leaps of faith" that ideas and findings could be woven together. Implications of widely differing studies needed to be identified. We think they succeeded admirably. Further, we enjoyed the lively and thought-provoking exchanges we had in the course of writing and editing. We "agreed to disagree" with our authors at times (quite appropriately for those working on conflict) about some interpretations or viewpoints. But these were easy agreements to make because we think the "conflict of ideas" is as important for scientific growth as for the growth of individuals.

Now, speaking individually, I, Carolyn Shantz, wish to acknowledge my great appreciation to David W. Shantz for starting my interest in conflict a decade ago. From his reading of animal ethological research at that time, he saw the potential for the study of children's conflicts to reveal a much more dynamic picture of social development. Also I thank Bill Hartup for having the initial idea for this book and inviting me to join him in this effort. It has been a rewarding collaboration for me. My gratitude also goes to Barbara Maier for her expert secretarial service, patience, and good humor as this book evolved. And my appreciation, too, to Catherine and Cynthia Shantz and to James and Gladys Uhlinger.

And, I, Willard Hartup acknowledge the many lessons my long-time companion, Rosemary Hartup, has taught me about conflict. I am also deeply indebted to numerous collaborators for their contributions, most notably Carolyn Shantz and Brett Laursen. I am grateful also for the technical assistance rendered by Terri Smith and Lonnie Behrendt. My work on conflict and child development was supported by Grant No. RO1 42888, National Institute of Mental Health, "Conflict and Friendship in Children," and also by my appointment as Rodney S. Wallace Professor for the Advancement of Teaching and Learning at the University of Minnesota.

Carolyn U. Shantz
Willard W. Hartup

Contributors

Frances E. Aboud
Department of Psychology
McGill University
Montreal

Mark Dixon Bailey
Department of Educational
  Psychology
University of Wisconsin
Madison

Robert B. Cairns
Department of Psychology
University of North Carolina
Chapel Hill

Michael Chapman (deceased)
Department of Psychology
University of British Columbia
Vancouver

W. Andrew Collins
Institute of Child Development
University of Minnesota
Minneapolis

Cheryl L. Conant
Department of Psychology
University of Waterloo
Waterloo, Ontario

Judy Dunn
Department of Individual and
  Family Studies
Pennsylvania State University
University Park

Robert E. Emery
Department of Psychology
University of Virginia
Charlottesville

Wyndol Furman
Department of Psychology
University of Denver
Denver, Colorado

Catherine Garvey
Department of Psychology
University of Maine
Orono

John M. Gottman
Department of Psychology
University of Washington
Seattle

Willard W. Hartup
Institute of Child Development
University of Minnesota
Minneapolis

Lynn Fainsilber Katz
Department of Psychology
University of Washington
Seattle

Elizabeth Kennedy
Department of Psychology
Florida Atlantic University
Boca Raton

Laurie Kramer
Department of Psychology
University of Illinois
Champaign

Brett Laursen
Department of Psychology
Florida Atlantic University
Fort Lauderdale

Michelle L. McBride
Department of Psychology
University of British Columbia
Vancouver

Elizabeth L. McQuaid
Department of Psychology
University of Denver
Denver, Colorado

Patricia Minuchin
Family Studies, Inc.
70 East 10th Street
New York

David G. Perry
Department of Psychology
Florida Atlantic University
Boca Raton

Louise C. Perry
Department of Psychology
Florida Atlantic University
Boca Raton

Martha Putallaz
Department of Psychology
Duke University
Durham, North Carolina

Hildy S. Ross
Department of Psychology
University of Waterloo
Waterloo, Ontario

Carolyn U. Shantz
Department of Psychology
Wayne State University
Detroit, Michigan

Blair H. Sheppard
Department of Psychology
Duke University
Durham, North Carolina

Cheryl Slomkowski
Department of Individual and
    Family Studies
Pennsylvania State University
University Park

Jaan Valsiner
Department of Psychology
University of North Carolina
Chapel Hill

Deborah Lowe Vandell
Department of Educational
    Psychology
University of Wisconsin
Madison

Conflict and development: An introduction

Carolyn U. Shantz and Willard W. Hartup

Conflicts occur everywhere in social and mental life. Whenever people interact – and especially when they interact often – disagreements and oppositions are inevitable. People differ in what they believe, what they know, and what they think should be done and how, as well as what they do, and these differences make conflict with others bound to occur. Some conflicts are fleeting and forgettable; some are not: The latter are heavy with meaning and emotions, turning points for individuals and their relationships, highly memorable, and have long-term effects. Further, conflicts occur not only between people, but within individuals. For example, one may learn something that is contrary to one's existing expectations or beliefs, or one's feelings about an event are strangely at odds with what one thinks. Conflicts – between people and within people – are part and parcel of everyday living, and to such an extent that they must be regarded as intrinsic to the human condition.

The "trouble" with conflict is not only that it is unavoidable, but that it is a risky business. One seldom knows when a disagreement will occur, with whom, over what issue, with what tactics, or how it will turn out. These uncertainties and unpredictabilities are discomfiting, as are other uncontrollable experiences, and thus tend to engender strong feelings. What specific emotions occur vary tremendously between individuals, and they vary as well at different points in any given conflict – at its outset, in the middle, and at its end. Apart from common reactions such as uncertainty and anxiety, emotions can be fear, anger, sadness, surprise, perplexity, excitement, satisfaction, or glee. It is seldom the case that conflicts elicit nonchalance or indifference.

Whenever we oppose others, are opposed, or internally experience discordant ideas, one issue arises immediately: How can this disagreement be managed? Will it be or can it be avoided entirely, denied, minimized, confronted, rationalized, or negotiated? Or will it be mismanaged, escalating out of control? Conflict *management* as well as conflict *occurrence*

1

must be accounted for. Current research gives strong credence to the view that how one deals with conflict is every bit as important as how it may have been precipitated. And these twin issues – management and occurrence – are relevant to a wide range of conflicts, extending from everyday, mundane ones to rarer, destructive ones. Conflict management, then, as well as conflict instigation, receives major attention in this book.

But, also in this book, a different question is explored: Can conflict have beneficial effects in psychological and social development? For many people, this is a radical question, in that conflict is commonly regarded as a negative event (Hocker & Wilmot, 1991; Selman, 1980). The question is not radical, however, for many theorists. Quite the opposite, in fact: Conflict has been widely recognized as a central force in developmental change, for both good and ill. Actually, no other single phenomenon plays as broad and significant a role in human development as conflict is thought to. Many different functions – cognition, social cognition, emotions, and social relations – are thought to be formed and/or transformed by conflict. Putting this thesis another way, ontogeny is thought to be impossible without conflict. In this sense, most developmental theories are dialectical ones, with functions ascribed to conflict in ontogeny that are similar to its functions in social and cultural evolution.

Focusing variously on one or more basic functions, developmental theorists have proposed that conflict is a significant force in individual change extending from earliest infancy through adulthood. In the realm of cognitive and social-cognitive development, for example, the major theory of Piaget was built around the internal conflicts that inevitably occur both between appearance and reality, and between rationality and nonrationality, as well as the social conflicts that occur between one's own perspective and those of others. The basic idea is that, through such confrontations, the mind begins to dominate the senses so that one is fooled less and less often by mere appearance, logic evolves gradually from intuition, and one's perspectives become differentiated from those of others as well as coordinated with them. Thus it is from everyday disagreements – both internal and social – that true objectivity and logic emerge.

Likewise, when Freud considered the structures and dynamics of personality, he posited two competing clusters representing, on the one hand, the primary urges, needs, and wishes of the primitive self (the id) and, on the other hand, the obligations, standards, and responsibilities of the self in relation to others (the superego). He further posited a mechanism, the ego, for negotiating and synthesizing id "wants" and superego "oughts" in relation to the dictates of "reality." This delicate balancing of competing forces, Freud posited, affords adaptation or maladaptation to changing circumstance. As the reader will find in the contributions gathered together in this book, other theorists, including Vygotsky, Sullivan, Erikson, Lewin, Reigel, and Miller, also spoke extensively about conflict and its role in human development.

Given this emphasis on intrapsychic and interpersonal conflict in theorizing about child and adolescent development, it might be supposed that there has been extensive study of it. Curiously, there has not. The reasons for this neglect are numerous and are discussed at points in the book. Suffice it to say here, though, that developmental scholars have been required for many decades to confront a major discontinuity between what is believed about conflict and its role in development versus what is known about it.

During the preceding decade, researchers have intensified their efforts to explore conflict and its developmental ramifications. The contributors to this volume, most of whom are developmental and clinical psychologists, ranged through many disciplines to inform their views – anthropology, communication, education, sociology, family relations, social work, and sociolinguistics, as well as psychology. The volume's breadth derives from this disciplinary diversity as well as the variety of developmental theories that embrace the conflict construct.

Changes in developmental psychology

The recent empirical work dealing with conflict in child and adolescent development is embedded in changes occurring within the field of development psychology itself. In order to gain a wider perspective on the "growing points" in conflict research, a few illustrations are in order.

Aggression and conflict

Consider aggression. Hundreds of studies have dealt with the origins, conditions, and effects of child and adolescent aggression – especially with peers – from the 1960s to the 1980s. This emphasis on aggression is a direct reflection of its significance for both society and the individual. The dominant theoretical perspective guiding the earlier work was social learning theory (Bandura & Walters, 1963) in which imitation, rewards, and punishments were explored to explain the acquisition of aggressive behavior, its maintenance, and its extinction. A high proportion of the studies of aggression were done in laboratory settings affording controlled experimental conditions, these controls being essential to investigators in their efforts to better understand the processes underlying aggressive behavior.

As researchers began to observe and describe aggression in natural set-tings in an attempt to verify the experimental results (see Patterson, Littman, & Bricker, 1967), other circumstances became increasingly evident. For example, aggression often occurs during an argument over some object, statement, or action of another person; that is, conflict is commonly the context in which aggression occurs. This means that to understand aggres-sion one must understand social conflict. Additionally, naturalistic obser-vations reveal that, during disagreements, behaviors other than aggression (including prosocial ones) also occur as children try to negotiate their differences. Focusing only on aggression, then, precludes understanding the relation between aggression and other dispositions, that is, the organ-ization and flexibility of social behavior. Finally, naturalistic studies make it clear that the rate of aggression is much lower in most situations than had been assumed (Shantz, 1987). Thus, the salience of aggressive behavior and its social impact seems to have led earlier investigators to overestimate its occurrence. Most conflicts are revealed, in fact, to be accomplished by talk, and nonaggressive talk, at that.

Viewing aggression in the context of conflict has a significant effect on research specifications, as well: Aggression and conflict are different events. Thus, *aggression* is most appropriately specified as behavior aimed at hurting another person or things the other lays claim to (see Parke & Slaby, 1983). *Conflict*, however, is best defined as a state of resistance or opposition between (at least) two individuals. Aggression must be viewed as but one among many tactics for winning a disagreement, and as just noted, conflicts often have no aggression occurring between the individuals involved.

In this volume, Perry, Perry, and Kennedy focus directly on the relation between peer aggression and peer conflict, and that topic enters into sev-eral other chapters: those dealing with sibling conflicts (Vandell and Bailey), peer conflicts among very young children (Ross and Conant), conflicts between friends (Hartup), conflicts in group relations (Aboud), and con-siderations relating to intervention (Furman and McQuaid). The dominant view in these chapters is that aggressive behavior during conflict represents a mismanaged conflict, sometimes a destructive one (i.e., destructive to individuals and their relationships). The story is an intriguing and complex one, as readers will find.

Parent–child relationships

Another example is instructive – the study of childhood socialization through parent–child interaction. Given the view that a major task in every society is the enculturation of the young, an important research topic is the child's compliance with parental directives and teachings aimed toward inculcating socially desirable behaviors and inhibiting undesirable ones. The early behaviorists viewed socialization as "social molding," in which societal (parental) rules and standards are gradually internalized by the child, resulting in a self-regulated, socialized, and moral young member of society. The causal model underlying this approach is a unilateral one in which, essentially, parental teachings and modeling are seen as relevant stimuli and the child's actions are singled out as relevant "outcomes."

But the idea that the child becomes social by the conscious efforts of caretakers and that training is imposed on a highly malleable being began to be questioned. First, Robert Sears (1951) extended the behaviorist socialization model to recognize the dyadic nature of social relationships (including parent–child relations) and the bilateral features of the social transactions occurring within these relationships. This model was a forerunner of subsequent social learning formulations (Mischel, 1973) in that cognitive functions were specified as well as reinforcement functions.

Two decades were required, however, for developmental psychologists to renounce unilateral models of parent–child relations (see Bell, 1968; Rheingold, 1969) and until Martin Richards (1974) would note the following in the introduction to *The Integration of a Child into a Social World*:

Early in the preparation of this volume, one of the publishers' representatives suggested that the word "socialization" should appear in the title. This was rejected – unanimously I think – by the contributors. . . . The word has tended to become the property of psychologists who . . . imply that the child is mere putty to be worked on by external forces. . . . [Instead] in the analysis of an interactive system, as we have with the child and his [*sic*] environment, it is not only necessary to take account of the roles of both sides of the process but also to use a methodology which allows for the richness of the interaction itself. (pp. 4–5)

The transition from unilateral conceptualizations of parent–child relations to bilateral ones remained excruciatingly slow, even then, so that Maccoby and Martin (1983), after reviewing the extensive literature in this area, specifically recommended that compliance by the child cease to be the dominant focus and that researchers examine, instead, *conflictual interactions*, including the give-and-take that goes on between parents and their children and adolescents.

The move toward multilateral models of socialization (including systemic views of families and other social groups) has accelerated over the preceding decade, and the empirical literature reflects this. Conflict is now regarded commonly as an interactive event, and parent–child relations are viewed in terms of arguing and negotiating, teasing and being teased, children asserting themselves and – at times – parents complying with children's demands. While long in coming, this minirevolution in thinking about childhood socialization is reflected throughout this book. Dunn and Slomkowski, for example, document both serious and playful conflicts, with all their emotions and justifications, involving very young children and their parents. A significant question is posed: What are children learning from these events? Katz, Kramer, and Gottman also examine both the direct and indirect impact of spousal conflict on children's functioning. And moving ahead in the life span, Collins and Laursen examine conflict involving adolescents within a relationships perspective that applies to their interactions with both parents and friends.

It is not the case, as might be supposed, that parents' conflicts mainly occur with their toddlers and adolescents, that is, during the so-called terrible twos and adolescent storm and stress. The available evidence does not suggest that the growth function for conflict occurrence is U-shaped but, rather, that conflict in family relations is developmentally relevant across the entire life span. Thus, families must learn to confront important differences among their members, to use conflict to "clear the air," and to settle disputes in satisfying ways. In this book, Emery proposes a general model of the major issues that underlie most family disagreements. At the same time, a dark side to conflict exists between parents and their infants, children, and adolescents, the side assayed by Minuchin in her chapter on abuse and neglect. Remedial and preventive programs directed specifically at the problems faced by parents and children in managing their relationships also are described and evaluated by Furman and McQuaid.

Organization of this volume

To provide a comprehensive and comprehensible overview of conflict in relation to child and adolescent development – its opportunities as well as its hazards – conflict must be considered in many different ways and at many levels of analysis. The complexity of the construct requires this, as do the methodological variations employed by contemporary investigators. Moreover, the diverse interests of our audience demand a volume that is broad rather than narrow in theoretical and methodological perspective. The contributors to this volume thus speak to academicians and researchers (both those established and those as graduate students), clinicians and teachers, and to the public – anyone who wishes to understand better the conditions, correlates, and effects of conflict in the lives of children and adolescents.

Contributors were asked to avoid writing ordinary "reviews of the literature" and, instead, to address central issues with selected findings.

Charged with illuminating "what we currently know" and indicating "what is especially important to learn in the future," each author attempts to outline a research agenda based on existing work. The references attached to each chapter are best regarded as invitations to readers to explore in depth the guiding theories of conflict and findings on both normative issues and individual-to-individual variations among children and adolescents.

Part I. Conflict and the processes of development

To provide some perspectives on conflict in the social sciences, Part I begins with a conceptual and philosophical analysis of conflict, the history of its study, and some concerns about theoretical uses of the concept of conflict (Valsiner and Cairns). Then certain basic processes involved in conflict are summarized and discussed, ranging from the molecular to the molar (in a heuristic sense): physiological (Katz, Kramer, and Gottman), perceptual and cognitive (Chapman and McBride), sociolinguistic and communicative (Garvey and Shantz), and social-cognitive (Dunn and Slomkowski).

Covering a wide range of issues, this listing actually does not do justice to the breadth and richness of the questions addressed in these chapters. For example: (a) How are physiological indexes of emotions among parents related to their behavior, and how is that behavior related to children's social-emotional development? (b) How does conflict in one social domain (with peers) affect conflict management in other domains (with siblings)? (c) What are the roles of cognitive conflict and social argumentation in changing children's concepts about their physical and moral worlds? (d) What can the analysis of turn-by-turn talk between children (from different subcultures or cultures) tell us about the ways differences are negotiated during play, or in a ritual form? (e) What is it that children appear to be learning in their common conflicts with siblings and their mothers? (f) And, from a broader perspective, what are the common as well as the scientific specifications of the conflict construct, and what implications are carried by these meaning variations for understanding and studying conflict in child and adolescent development?

Part II. Conflict and interpersonal relationships

Most social conflict occurs within relationships, that is, between individuals whose lives are intermeshed and whose interactions extend over substantial amounts of time. Conflict-induced violence, for example, is known to occur mostly within close relationships. More than two thirds of the conflicts requiring intervention by law enforcement officials involve people who know one another. Ordinary, garden-variety disagreements, too, occur mostly among people who have some special significance to one another, and disagreements among children and adolescents are not exceptions to this rule.

In Part II, the contributors consider in depth how conflicts appear to function in close relationships, especially those salient in childhood: with mothers and fathers (Emery; Collins and Laursen), with siblings (Vandell and Bailey), and with friends (Hartup). Considered are not only how conflicts affect relationships, but how relationships affect conflicts. Once again, the story is complex: Conflicts within relationships are not entirely destructive; indeed, disagreements seem to be necessary both to establishing ties between individuals and to maintaining them. Because relationships change in important ways as children grow older, their conflicts are considered here in developmental perspective: The changing nature of conflict and its resolution among very young children is analyzed (Ross and Conant) as well as conflict changes occurring across the transition to adolescence (Collins and Laursen). And, finally, the manner in which the social context bears on conflict management within relationships is also scrutinized (Hartup; Emery).

Once again, the range of topics does not reveal the interesting questions raised in the book about conflict and social relationships. Examples are: (a) What are the issues and tactics that arise during the child's earliest encounters with other children and how do these change with age? (b) Do disagreements occur differently in the social exchanges of friends and nonfriends, and does conflict figure differently in children's friendships as these relationships "mature"? (c) What are the unique properties of sibling conflicts, especially as contrasted to conflicts among children and their friends? (d) Do adolescents' conflicts vary according to the individuals involved, and do these conflicts change with age? (e) Granted that family conflicts must be viewed systemically, how do these disagreements differ according to the "depth" of the analysis?

Part III. Conflict and developmental adaptations

Developmental science is marked by two main concerns: (a) *normative issues* specifying age-related transformations in thinking and acting that typify children and adolescents generally and (b) *differential issues* specifying those attributes that determine effective functioning of individual children and adolescents, along with the sources of these variations. Part III of this book is focused on differential issues. Conflict experience, being implicated in the emergence of significant variations among individuals, receives attention. Special attention is also given to individuals having continuing difficulties in managing their conflicts.

Conflict management is now known to differentiate children generally according to their competence in relating to other children, and management of certain specific disagreements (entering a group, obtaining access to scarce resources, and responding to social provocation) are especially important (Putallaz and Sheppard). As mentioned earlier, aggression and conflict need to be distinguished conceptually, and Perry, Perry, and Kennedy demonstrate the far-reaching consequences of reading the developmental research with this distinction clearly in mind. For example, it becomes evident that the quality of the caretaker–child relationship in early childhood predicts conflict involvement and mismanagement rather than aggression. These authors, as well as Minuchin, demonstrate the need for understanding both cognitive and affective concomitants of children's relationships, that is, the transactions and expectations bearing on conflict that characterize both aggressors and their victims. Conflict and its role in group relations are also considered (Aboud), especially the interactions of children and adolescents with peers who differ from themselves ethnically, racially, and socioeconomically.

Because conflict outcomes are especially destructive among certain individuals, many investigators are working to devise ameliorative interventions. Challenges confront them, however. It is not obvious whether intervention should be designed to reduce the occurrence of social conflict, alter conflict management, or some combination of the two. Again, the story, as told by Furman and McQuaid, is a complex and intriguing one.

Within these chapters, a wide range of significant questions is examined: (a) Are conflict attributions and behaviors related to social competence in a similar manner? (b) What is the connection between conflict management in parent–child relations and aggression in peer relations? (c) To what extent are abusive relationships centered in social conflict, and to what extent are neglectful relations based on conflict avoidance? (d) Does racial integration in schools increase social conflict or not? (e) To what extent do conflicts "clear the air" and increase understanding among group members as opposed to "muddy the waters" and magnify group differences? (f) What is the nature of "destructive" conflict, and what are some of the best methods for ameliorating it?

What is not in this book

Because conflict has fascinated scholars, theorists, and researchers from many disciplines, there are voluminous writings that address a wide range of topics relating to this book. It may be helpful to students of conflict to specify some of those areas of scholarly endeavor in order to expand beyond the focus of this book and, in so doing, note its limitations.

Many social scientists have been interested in conflict in institutional and larger social systems, such as industrial/organizational, legal, and international affairs. Although not addressed in this book, there are social scientific studies or theories that occasionally pose developmental issues. For example, Sherif, Harvey, White, Hood, and Sherif (1961) provided ground-breaking work on intra- and intergroup conflicts of children (see Aboud, this volume). Also, some social scientists have addressed conflict in adulthood and between generations of families. Few of them have taken, in our view, a truly life span perspective, and thus, their work is not represented in this volume except as concerns conflict between the generations of parents, children, and adolescents. Because social relationships and the residuals of conflict are carried forward from childhood to adulthood, we hope this book will encourage more study of conflict's role in development across the entire life span.

Interpersonal conflict is dealt with more extensively in these pages than is intrapsychic conflict. Such, however, is the current research imbalance in the field. The imbalance is rather paradoxical. One might expect, given that several major developmental theorists emphasize intrapsychic conflict (e.g., Piaget, Freud, and Erikson), that many researchers would focus on it too. But that is not the case. A notable exception, however, is the extensive work on the role of intrapsychic conflict in cognitive development (see Chapman and McBride). Other types of intrapsychic conflict – those of great interest to many clinicians – are virtually absent from the developmental literature. Further, little information exists on the relation between intrapsychic and interpersonal conflict, intriguing and important though that topic may be. There are, in short, vast terrains to be explored in order to understand how conflict functions in development.

There is yet another anomaly in the relation between developmental theories and research activities concerning conflict. It appears to be a "lack of fit" between what many theorists mean by conflict and how the phenomenon is studied. Perhaps this is because most theorists tend not to be very specific about the processes that conflict involves nor specific about the various effects it has on development at different ages. Thus, researchers have tended to use more inductive processes to describe in detail the whens, whats, wheres, and hows of conflict among people. A focus on description is evident in the following chapters. As in most relatively new fields of research, few explanations are available, and they come slowly and tentatively. By bringing together the current knowledge on conflict and development, as well as delineating future goals, we have tried to assist both theory construction and empirical efforts.

Conclusion

The major premise of this book is that the study of people as they engage one another in opposition or are engaged in internal disagreements is necessary for any clear understanding of social and cognitive development. It is this dynamic – the virtual "dance" of discord and accord, of disaffirmation and affirmation – that is critical to the comprehension of development. We believe that readers will find that conflict, with all its perils and promises, is among the most fascinating phenomena now being studied in child and adolescent development.

References

Bandura, A., & Walters, R. H. (1963). *Social learning and personality development*. New York: Holt, Rinehart, & Winston.

Bell, R. Q. (1968). A reinterpretation of the direction of effects in studies of socialization. *Psychological Review*, *75*, 81–95.

Hocker, J. L., & Wilmot, W. W. (1991). *Interpersonal conflict* (3d ed.). Dubuque, IA: Brown.

Maccoby, E. E., & Martin, J. A. (1983). Socialization in the context of the family: Parent–child interaction. In E. M. Hetherington (Ed.), *Handbook of child psychology: Vol. 4. Socialization, personality, and social development* (4th ed.). New York: Wiley.

Mischel, W. (1973). Toward a cognitive social learning reconceptualization of personality. *Psychological Review*, *80*, 252–283.

Parke, R. D., & Slaby, R. G. (1983). The development of aggression. In E. M. Hetherington (Ed.), *Handbook of child psychology: Vol. 4. Socialization, personality, and social development* (4th ed.). New York: Wiley.

Patterson, G. R., Littman, R. A., & Bricker, W. (1967). Assertive behavior in children: A step toward a theory of aggression. *Monographs of the Society for Research in Child Development*, *32*(5, Serial No. 113).

Rheingold, H. L. (1969). The social and socializing infant. In D. A. Goslin (Ed.), *Handbook of socialization theory and research*. Chicago: Rand McNally.

Richards, M. P. M. (Ed.). (1974). *The integration of a child into a social world*. Cambridge: Cambridge University Press.

Sears, R. R. (1951). A theoretical framework for personality and social behavior. *American Psychologist*, *6*, 476–483.

Selman, R. L. (1980). *The growth of interpersonal understanding*. New York: Academic Press.

Shantz, C. U. (1987). Conflicts between children. *Child Development*, *58*, 283–305.

Sherif, M., Harvey, O. J., White, B. J., Hood, W. R., & Sherif, C. W. (1961). *Inter-group cooperation and competition: The Robbers Cave experiment*. Norman, OK: University Book Exchange.

Part I

Conflict and the processes of development

1 Theoretical perspectives on conflict and development

Jaan Valsiner and Robert B. Cairns

Introduction

It is very appropriate to argue that the notion of conflict is at the heart of the majority of theoretical schemes, not only in developmental psychology (Shantz, 1987), but in the social sciences. In one form or another, conflict has figured importantly in the theoretical models of writers as diverse as Sigmund Freud (1936/1965), B. F. Skinner (1938), Jean Piaget (1962, 1973, 1980, 1985), Donald Hebb (1946), and Kurt Lewin (1926a, 1926b, 1933, 1935). Similarly, the phenomena to which the concept has been applied have been wide ranging, from emotion (Mandler, 1979, pp. 309–315), motivation (Lewin, 1935; Miller, 1948), and thinking (Baldwin, 1902), to psychopathology (Maher & Maher, 1979), and personality assessment (Bandura & Walters, 1959). Obviously, these areas of traditional psychology extend beyond the developmental-theoretic perspectives and beyond those investigators who are concerned with the interpersonal relations of children and adolescents.

Given the multiple theoretical contexts in which the idea of conflict has been employed, we begin this chapter with an overview of its several meanings and applications in different content domains of psychology.

Emotion. Mandler (1979) has tracked the conflict theories of emotion, beginning with classic figures from history, such as Herbart, Dewey, and Freud, and ending with the modern accounts of Hebb (1949) and Mandler (1964). The kernel idea is that "when an important activity of the organism is blocked, emotions follow" (Hunt, 1941, p. 269). The conflict is presumed to arise between the organized activity and the event that blocks or interrupts the activity. One of the insights to emerge from this work has been that conflict may give rise to positive states and outcomes as well as negative ones. The conflict theory of emotion "has been refurbished time and time again" over the past 100 years (Mandler, 1979, p. 306). Yet there is little unanimity on the mediational processes by which interruption acts

15

to arouse emotion or what the dynamics and functions are of emotion thus aroused.

Motivation. Kurt Lewin defined *conflict* as "the opposition of approximately equally strong field forces" (1935, p. 88). He identified three basic cases of conflict, namely, when (a) "the child stands between two positive valences," (b) "the child faces something that has simultaneously both a positive and negative valence," and (c) "the child stands between two negative valences" (pp. 89–91). In a social learning version of this typology, these conflicts have reached psychologists' everyday discourse as *approach–approach, approach–withdrawal, and withdrawal–withdrawal.*

Each of the cases of motivational conflict has distinctive properties. The first case – approach–approach – should be solved with relative ease because "it is usually a condition of labile equilibrium" (Lewin, 1935, p. 123). The solution arises because, all things equal, approach to one of the alternatives should increase its salience and give it predominance over the other. Once the first goal is attained, the other alternative could increase in attractiveness and may lead to an approach to that goal as well. The second case – approach–avoidance – which developed into productive research programs in animal and human behavior, typically leads to behavioral oscillation, where the individual becomes trapped at the intersection between the forces of attraction and avoidance in a type of stable equilibrium. The third case – withdrawal–withdrawal – in which the child is captured between two negative valences, constitutes a special case of entrapment and coercion if it is impossible to escape the field. When the barriers to escape are insurmountable, Lewin (1935) indicates that the child may employ extreme solutions to leave the setting (i.e., escape by redefining reality or by suicide).

Personality and psychopathology. Freud (1936/1965) outlined the basic social-motivational scheme whereby the ego and superego are constructed by a conflict between libidinal sources of energy and societal constraints on how the energy may be expressed. Throughout the course of living, these structures of personality continue to "war." In some conditions (e.g., dreams, hypnosis, intoxication, and stupor) the otherwise inhibited forces break through ego defenses and become expressed in ways that are blatantly asocial, antisocial, or bizarre. Otherwise, the expression of this energy is sublimated and captured in productive ways or appears in subtle and undetected ways in the psychopathology of every life. Failures in intrapsychic management occur when the intrapsychic conflicts become externalized in the form of interpersonal conflicts or serious distortions of reality.

Psychoanalysis was a relevant source of inspiration for learning-theoretic perspectives. For example, the idea that frustration was a necessary and sufficient condition for aggression (Dollard, Doob, Miller, Mowrer, & Sears, 1939) follows the lead of psychoanalytic thought. This proposition may be viewed as a special case of the conflict theory of emotion, in that behavioral interruption (frustration) was presumed to give rise to psychological phenomena of a strongly negative kind. The delineation between "frustration" and "aggression" 50 years ago has a modern parallel in the difference between "conflict" and "aggression," with many of the same issues at stake (see Perry, Perry, & Kennedy, this volume; Shantz, 1987).

Cognitive development. At another level of analysis, conflict has been employed in theoretical models of cognitive development to account for differentiation, reorganization, and hierarchical integration. Piaget (1962, 1973, 1985, and other works), for example, refers to the lack of fit between the existing schemata of the person and the perceptual challenges of external events and objects. Resolution of the "conflict" is presumed to occur when there is a modification of both the new information (assimilation) and the cognitive schema (accommodation). Such is the nature of the continuing dialectic that underlies cognitive modification and growth (see also Chapman, 1988; Chapman & McBride, this volume). By extension, unfamiliar social exchanges may lead to changes in the child's social-cognitive apparatus and in the perceptions of the acts of the other. Piaget was clearly indebted to the genetic epistemology of James Mark Baldwin, on the one hand, and to psychoanalytic thought, on the other. Baldwin (1906) adumbrated the essential genetic-epistemology argument, even in descriptions of the circular reactions of growth and the stages of development. Freud, of course, continued to emphasize intrapsychic conflict in the dynamics of behavior, despite radical changes in motivational structure.

Behavioral biology. Conflict also has been employed in ethology and other models of behavioral evolution. In ethology, displacement occurs when there is a conflict between incompatible behaviors directed at the same object (Hinde, 1966). Displacement would occur, for example, when an animal vigorously grooms itself or digs: It is in a conflict between agonistic behavior (aggression) and fear. Hence, displacement is not unlike the approach–avoidance conflict of the Lewin–Miller model, coupled with the assumption of energy displacement of classical psychoanalytic theory. And, of course, the orthodoxy of evolutionary theorizing accepts competition and conflict between organisms as basic to the processes of natural selection of individuals who are best fitted for survival. This competition, in turn, is assumed to lead to assortative mating and the transmission of distinctive characteristics.

Interpersonal conflict in social and child psychology. In contemporary studies of social development, conflict has generally been restricted to problems of interpersonal relations, either among peers or within families. In this regard, contemporary interest in issues of conflict has been triggered by the negative social interactions of children (Duncan, 1991; Hartup, 1970, 1983; Hartup & Laursen, in press; Kolominskii & Zhiznevskii, 1990; Shantz, 1987), of adults' relations with each other and with themselves (see formalized theory construction efforts by Coombs, 1987, and Lewin, 1948), and of social institutions (Hahn, 1990; Rummel, 1987). Social psychologists have attempted to make sense of the issue of conflict as well (Deutsch, 1969, 1985), and major naturalistic-empirical investigations of the social construction (and reconstruction) of conflict between groups constitute the classics of social psychology (Sherif, Harvey, White, Hood, & Sherif, 1961).

It is remarkable that social scientists' interest in conflict has been paralleled with the interest in conflict *resolution*, rather than by other equally possible outcomes (e.g., conflict *maintenance*, conflict *intensification*). A formidable research literature on the social relations of children has been created in the past few decades (see Asher & Gottman, 1981; Shantz, 1987), with a major focus being the interactional conflict between peers and how these conflicts may be handled by responsible adults. The concerns of social interaction include the developmental trajectory of conflictual interactions; age-related changes in the form of conflict expression, determinants of conflicts among children; and escalation within and between conflict episodes.

Summary: descriptions of perspectives on conflict. Despite competing views, there has been only modest overt conflict among theories of conflict. The lack of confrontation reflects, to a significant extent, the tendency of theorists to talk past each other. Despite apparent similarities, they address different levels of analysis, different phenomena, and/or different constructs. For example, the scholarly review of Mandler (1979) on the conflict theory of emotions does not refer to the problem of interpersonal conflicts, even though social relations are probably the primary area of emotional arousal involving conflict. Similarly, Shantz (1987) restricts her review of conflict to conflicts between children, with only modest reference to the motivational, emotional, and developmental functions of conflict. More broadly, theoretical considerations of interpersonal conflicts, field theory of motivational control, conflict theories of emotion, intrapsychic conflict, and conflict in development seem to dwell in different lands. Although such insulation avoids conflict, it also inhibits the cross-fertilization of ideas and concepts. In the special case of interpersonal conflicts among children, the literature seems to be rich in data and impoverished in theory. This theoretical poverty reflects, in part, the disengagement of child psychology from two broad sources of systematic theory. One source involves the advances made in general psychology; the other involves systematic views of development. Insulation from these two lines of thought has deprived the empirical research on conflict of rich sources of stimulation and direction. In our present chapter, we attempt to fill in the existing gap in the literature by analyzing the metatheoretical underpinnings of the concept of conflict in developmental theorizing.

The semantics of conflict

Language use in culture

The language use of ordinary human beings guides the thinking of social scientists. Noting this channeling of the reasoning of common language users, we need not endorse the naive version of linguistic determination of reasoning often attributed to the Sapir–Whorf hypothesis, but rather recognize the necessary organizing role of language in human reasoning (see Bertalanffy, 1955). The meanings of everyday concepts that have historically come into being within a collective culture tell us how common sense has become semiotically encoded. In case we want to transcend the traps of common language use when we theorize about conflict, the history of the meaning of this term needs to be analyzed.

According to the *Oxford English Dictionary* (1971), the noun *conflict* is derived from Latin root *conflictus* (thrown together, strike together) and meant "striking together, shock, fight." In the order of occurrence, the OED listings are:

1. a. An encounter with arms, a fight, a battle (e.g., "Fightenge with shorte spere in conflictes") [first listed citation in 1440];
    b. A prolonged struggle (e.g., "under menace of all but exterminating conflict") [1835];
    c. Fighting, contending with arms, martial strife (e.g., "the bloody conflicts") [1622];
2. a. Transitive and figurative nuances (e.g., "To note the fighting conflict of her hue, How white and red each other did destroy") [1531];
    b. A mental or spiritual struggle within a man (e.g., "after longe conflyct had within himselfe") [1430];

    c.   The clashing or variance of opposed principles, statements, arguments, etc. (e.g., "there may not be a conflict of principles") [1875];

3.   a.   Dashing together, collision, or violent mutual impact of physical bodies (e.g., "The common Motion of Matter preceding from external Impulse and Conflict") [1555].

A shared notion that characterizes the common language meanings of the term conflict is the emphasis on the *incompatibility* of the opposing aspects. Or, more generally, in none of these dictionary explanations of the meaning of the term do we get a glimpse of the possibility that the opposing entities "in conflict" may be mutually dependent. As we argue later in this chapter, the absence of an interdependency notion in the common language meaning of the term guides the person using the term toward the utilization of "exclusive separation" as a means of cognitively organizing the issues of conflict.

Treating conflict in the social sciences: Between science and culture

Social scientists are members of their collective culture first, and scientists second. Hence, it is not surprising that common language meanings of conflict have their impact on how scientists think about conflict. As the common language meanings carry with them a negative connotation of the term, it is not surprising that the urge to resolve existing conflicts has blinded the scope of theoretical views on conflict in the social sciences of the twentieth century. Among other reasons for the underdevelopment of sociological approaches to conflict, Bernard remarked that sociologists may fear going contrary to their cultural demand system:

We have a – cultural if you wish – policy of hush-hush with reference to many conflicts. In contrast to the Communist policy we believe in "letting sleeping dogs lie," in "not making an issue of it," "not stirring up trouble." As a result we have swung so far away from the subject of conflict that even to mention certain controversial subjects in textbooks has been taboo. That it should be possible to deal with conflict as an objective process without taking sides or becoming a propagandist or protagonist seems so unrealistic that this basic field of human behavior has been almost suppressed, or at least greatly minimized, in favor of a more static approach. This, if less realistic, at least has the merit of emphasizing what people have in common rather than what they have in conflict. (Bernard, 1950, p. 15)

This evaluation of the state of affairs of the post–World War II sociology in the United States is all the more remarkable as it belongs to the time of transition from world war to cold war, with all the ideological polarization of oppositions involved. However, the strategy of avoiding the investigation of particularly feelings-inducing scientific problems is but one of the self-defense strategies of scientists. Devereux (1967) has provided a useful analysis of different ways in which social scientists select and handle different conflicts between their world views and the objects of their investigation. The notion of an "objective and emotionless" social scientist is probably a contradiction in terms. In their activities, social scientists are constantly in ambivalent and conflict-ridden relationships with their subject matter, even if they may publicly deny that. Such denial can be viewed as a part of a wider cultural-historical emphasis on control over the affective sphere of the human psyche and channeling it toward accepted frameworks (Lyman, 1990).

If we look at the study of conflict in sociological literature over time, we can see an interesting change in the ways in which that study has been framed. Whereas, at the turn of the century, the issues of conflict in social entities were viewed as a possible mechanism for development (see Simmel, 1904), by midcentury the focus had reversed to view social conflict as an anomaly to be eliminated or remedied (see Coser, 1964, pp. 15–27). Furthermore, working on conflict after the horrors of the Second World War and under the conditions of the Cold War was shaped by the danger of being outlawed by the dominant ideological trends in the U.S. society (Bernard, 1950).

The history of the study of conflict in sociology seems to be paralleled in psychology. No wonder that psychological perspectives on conflict are narrowly channeled in our present day. Psychologists are employed by the society to maintain the status quo rather than facilitate the promotion of a developmental trajectory by the next generation that may require serious modification of the existing social order – the basis for the social institutions that cater for child development. Consider, for example, the cultural belief that guides us to think that aggressive adolescents ("troublemakers") are rejected by their peers. Researchers of adolescence may be surprised when conclusive evidence appears that demonstrates that a "highly aggressive" adolescent, instead of being rejected among his peers, happens to become a leader in a peer group (Cairns, Cairns, Neckerman, Gest, & Gariépy, 1988). Such findings – contrary to our common sense – occur when psychological research becomes a general science, rather than a mere reiteration of the commonsense knowledge in new terms (Valsiner, 1985).

Psychology has had difficulties transcending the commonsense meanings of the concepts with which it operates (see Smedslund, 1978; Valsiner, 1985). As a result, psychological terminology is notably "elastic" (Hartup & Laursen, in press) and "magic" (Cairns, 1972) in its efforts to maintain commonsense legibility while keeping up an aura of the "scientific nature" of its uses. The term *conflict* seems to be used overwhelmingly in this elastic way. Hence, the task of this chapter is complicated by the danger of the common sense meanings of the term interfering with our understanding of certain positive features of conflicts and conflictual processes.

The general point is that there has been a rather narrow focus in the scientific literature on children's conflicts. The scientific enterprise is not free from socially defined constraints. Likewise, the ways that are considered legitimately "scientific" for the study of particular "sensitive areas" of research are carefully constrained (Cairns, 1986; Sorokin, 1956). At the same time, the theoretical sphere of a given problem – in this case, conflict – requires widening our field of understanding. For instance, there can be a wide range of possible goals that relate to conflicts (e.g., escalation, maintenance, neutralization, resolution) and an equally wide range of possibilities for reaching those goals. Furthermore, the understanding of appropriate time frames for changing a "conflict state" may vary a great deal. It would be unrealistic to assume that participants in a conflict of any kind (and this includes conflicts within a person) are eager to resolve it in the quickest possible way. Instead, although some conflicts are resolved quickly (e.g., the husband and wife handle their children's "fights" with utmost urgency, in an effort to de-escalate the conflict), others may be maintained over a long time (e.g., the wife enhancing the upkeep of a longer-term conflict between her husband and her mother-in-law), whereas still others can be episodically escalated (e.g., the husband who in a momentary spell of patriotic feelings volunteers to join the army to participate in a military conflict with another country). The very same people can act with different strategies and within different time frames upon different conflicts that fill their lives, and no axiomatic assumptions can be made as to the way in which conflicts are dealt with.

A metatheoretical frame for two perspectives on conflict

Analytic efforts to make sense of the world around us necessarily lead us to some form of *partitioning* (dividing, separating) different aspects of our perceived world (see Valsiner, 1987, pp. 16–19). This partitioning starts at the perceptual level (e.g., "figure" versus "ground") and continues at higher levels of cognitive and affective functioning (e.g., the operation of categorization and affective "blocking" of different kinds of traumatic experience). In short, the active person differentiates the knowledge about the world by way of partitioning it into similarity classes and selectively attending to some aspects.

This partitioning can be accomplished in multiple ways. The critical aspect that differentiates two major strategies of partitioning is the question of how the relationship between the partitioned subparts of a whole are viewed. If the results of partitioning are viewed as separate, mutually exclusive entities, then only external characteristics (such as similarity–dissimilarity in form) can be used to describe their relationships.) For example, if a phenomenon is detected to be in state A under the exclusive separation strategy, then the context of state A is either eliminated from the focus of attention or described as a separate entity that may exist in parallel (but whose relationship with the phenomenon is merely formal). In contemporary psychology, we can observe many examples of that kind. For instance, a child psychologist measures some psychological characteristic "in" the child, thus eliminating the intricate interdependence of that characteristic with the child's environment. However, the psychologist need not be blind to the role of the environment and may proceed to measure some relevant characteristic of the environment separately from the one measured "in" the child. By making this measurement decision, the psychologist is intuitively using the framework of exclusive separation (of the child from the environment). As we conceptualize it here, the systemic interdependence of CHILD ⇐ [RELATING WITH] ⇒ ENVIRONMENT is replaced by independent measurement of the CHILD separate from the ENVIRONMENT. The psychologist may subsequently try to recapture that relationship through formal means (e.g., correlating the measured characteristics of the children within a sufficiently large sample and their environments), but the original systemic relatedness is no longer available for his or her analysis. The populational-level generalization that emanates from this exclusive separation of the child from the environment cannot be interpreted as reflecting the original interdependence of CHILD ⇐ [RELATING WITH] ⇒ ENVIRONMENT (see Valsiner, 1984, 1986).

Unreflective use of the exclusive partitioning can lead developmental researchers to the construction of data that have lost relevant information about developmental processes. If we take a consistently developmental perspective, it is exactly the possibility to *trace the emergence* of one psychological phenomenon on the basis of its predecessors of different form that we need to be interested in. Methodologically, coding schemes in observational research that are constructed on the basis of exclusive separation of the target phenomena (e.g., "behavior A" is required to be reliably distinguishable from "behavior B," and both need to be clearly detectable from the background of their contexts) can irreversibly close off access to the developmental processes for the investigator (e.g., if behavior B emerges from behavior A through an intermediate state during which the A vs. B distinction is hard to make, our traditional coding schemes tend to eliminate such fuzzy transitions of the phenomena from our data).

Exclusive partitioning dominates the world of classical logic and the empiricist view of the world. It is thus not surprising that early efforts to classify natural phenomena used that kind of partitioning. This mode of partitioning was obvious in the Linnean classificatory scheme superimposed upon nature. We can see that partitioning at work in any classificatory efforts (uni- or multidimensional) of phenotypic forms that attempt to segregate the phenomena into nonoverlapping categories.

In contrast, another major way of partitioning the world involves *inclusive separation* of the partitioned parts from one another. Its meaning should be quite obvious from the contrast drawn between the exclusive separation and the aspects of phenomena that it misses. Thus, in the case of inclusive separation, contemporary methodology leads the researcher to opt for preserving the interdependence between the phenomenon and its context (or between different aspects of the phenomenon). At the same time, these different (mutually coexisting and linked) aspects are kept differentiated. This strategy allows the investigators to preserve the systemic organization of the phenomena in the data derived from the phenomena and thus retain in the data the processes relevant for development.

Conflict in the case of the exclusive partitioning

The meaning of *conflict* necessarily differs when it is applied to an exclusively or inclusively partitioned world. In the first case, *conflict* can be defined as *mismatch* or *difference* between the separated parts, and conflict resolution becomes synonymous with a choice between different preexisting preference options (see Coombs, 1987, for a formal elaboration of this world view). Thus, A and B (exclusively separated) can be said to be "in conflict" because they are not the same or similar. If by some manipulation one of them is made similar to the other (e.g., when one partner in a long dispute succumbs to the demands of the other partner), conflict between them is solved. Likewise, social psychologists' views on conflict and its resolution can reflect a similar tendency to eliminate differences between opposing parties (Deutsch, 1985).

The exclusive partitioning of the world is the basis for a rather simple view of conflict (and opposition), by redefining it as *difference* and assuming that, by the *elimination of differences*, one resolves conflicts. This classical logic-based world view leads to homogenization of the differentiated world: The world becomes differentiated into a limited number of homogeneous classes of phenomena, in which within each class, the specimens are perceived to be similar to one another (see Valsiner, 1984). In contrast, if the homogenization effort (i.e., "conflict resolution" in this mind-set) fails, the oppositions between the homogeneously perceived classes are viewed as states of conflict.

The mind-set of reducing heterogeneity in order to "resolve conflicts" has wider repercussions for the methodology in psychology. Thus, it is not surprising at all that psychologists often believe in the averaged data that are reported in the literature (despite the presence of variability to an extent that renders the averages meaningless). It is the basic assumption of homogeneity of the exclusively partitioned classes of phenomena that axiomatically guides them to that belief, bypassing the issue of the adequacy of the homogeneity assumption (see Shvyrkov, 1987).

Conflict and the inclusive partitioning of the world

In contrast, the implications of the inclusive partitioning of the world for the issue of conflict are very different. Because inclusive separation preserves heterogeneity, *conflict* can be defined in terms of the *nature of linkages between* the differentiated parts of a whole. These linkages can be viewed as involving *opposition* between the parts. These oppositions (including conflict as a subclass of oppositions) make it possible for the parts to coexist, or temporarily transform into one another. Thus, the "harmonious play" of children may become transformed into a "fight" and vice versa, where *both* states of the children's relationships indicate "friendship" by both children (consider, for instance, an adolescent's claim that she "fights with her brother because we are good friends"). Likewise, well-known opposite concepts of "cooperation" and "competition," "dependence" and "independence" or "rationality" and "irrationality" cease to be mutually exclusive, but rather become interdependent and coexistent. Each of the opposing concepts depends upon the other for its existence, and the elimination of one leads to the elimination of the whole system in which both are parts. The opposites are inseparable as they are functional interdependent parts of the whole. The whole can exist due to the opposition that the relationship between the parts creates, and it ceases to exist when that opposition is eliminated.

As a historical aside, it is worthwhile to remember the intensive disputes in psychology of the 1920s around the question of "units of analysis" appropriate for the study of psychological phenomena. The claims of leading Gestalt psychologists (Köhler) and structural-functional developmentalists (Vygotsky, Basov) about the indivisibility of the "minimal system" that still retains the properties of the whole (see Valsiner, 1988, pp. 173–179) were made along the lines of inclusive partitioning of psychological structures.

The notion of the interdependence of opposite facets of the holistic phenomenon are obvious in the case of some classic treatments of conflict in the social sciences. Thus, Georg Simmel's account of the organization and functions of conflict made use of the inclusive separation framework as it is explained here:

> In every peaceful situation the conditions for future conflict, and in every struggle the conditions for future peace, are developing. If we follow the stages of social development backward under these categories, we can find no stopping place. In historical reality each condition always has the other as its corollary. (1904, p. 799)

The inclusive separation of differentiated parts of a whole operates according to the principles of dialectic logic. Unfortunately, the extensive ideologization of "dialectics" in the political sphere of human social life (e.g., see Bernard, 1950; Sorensen, 1951) has led the social sciences away from efforts to give exact form to the widely declared principles of the "unity of opposites," their "conflict," and that conflict being "overcome" by way of the whole transforming into a new structural state. It is developmental psychology that is obviously in need of such formalization. This need was clearly perceived about a century ago (see Baldwin, 1906; Simmel, 1904) but has been only partially developed (see Vygotsky's quest in Van der Veer & Valsiner, 1991; and also contemporary dialectical psychology, e.g., Dowd, 1990; Kramer & Bopp, 1989; Langer, 1982; Riegel, 1976; Van IJzendoorn & Van der Veer, 1984).

There are good general reasons to insist upon the use of the inclusive separation framework in the methodological discourse of developmental psychology. Development is known to be possible only in the case of open systems (see Valsiner, 1987). Open systems are defined by their exchange relationship with their environments. Thus, it is impossible to study development by eliminating the focal concern – that of the *process of interchange between the developing organism and its environment* (see Dowd, 1990) – from the empirical scrutiny of developmental psychologists.

The core of development: "Goodness-of-misfit"

Goodness-of-fit models

The contemporary know-how in our discipline is remarkably limited in its conceptualizations of developmental change. Van Geert (1988) has analyzed the metatheoretical models by which the developmental transitions have been viewed. First, most of these models are of the *agreeement* type: Development is viewed as *goodness-of-fit* between the parts of the system (see also Lerner, 1984, pp. 149–153). In the case of theoretical models of the agreement type, development takes place when there is agreement between different parts of the system or between the system and its environment.

This goodness-of-fit between the developing organism and the structure of the environmental demands can be viewed as a *harmonious* (well-coordinated) opposition. The agreement between the two parts of the whole (organism and its environment) reflects their mutual links, which are conceptualized as well adapted to each other. Even when rapid "break-downs" or "breakthroughs" occur in the course of development, the theoretical models of the agreement type can be applied in ways that view any conflict as a non-oppositionally definable phenomenon. The possibility of setting up notions of the harmonious opposition type of relationships within a whole provides for the non-conflictful explanation of conflict. For example, the "catastrophe theory" of René Thom (1973, 1976; see also Zeeman, 1981) is an attempt to describe critical breakthroughs in the world by way of smooth nonlinear functions. Knowledge of those functions (if available) is expected to make any "catastrophic change" as predictable as any linear function would afford, making it impossible for any novelty to emerge from a qualitative breakthrough (see Truesdell, 1982). In short, any model of development that emphasizes orderly and predictable change from a previous state to a new one is essentially a conflict-free model.

Goodness-of-misfit models

In contrast to the harmonious opposition models, the conflict type of models entail a different definition of the relationship between the parts of the developing system. According to Van Geert (1988, pp. 233–234), the conflict hypothesis holds that progress occurs as a consequence of the meeting of two opposing strategies or the alteration of opposing tendencies.

The crucial distinction within the class of conflict theories (which we will call *goodness-of-misfit* models of development) is between the (a) conflict maintenance and (b) conflict transformation notions. The former model of development is based on the conflicting oppositions that are maintained as long as the developing system retains its present state (stage). Once the system moves to another state (stage), a new set of oppositions in conflict "takes over" the role of maintaining the progress of the system. The given set of oppositions is not viewed as participating in the process of any qualitatively new reorganization. Rather, it remains unaltered during the given stage and is replaced by another set when the organism passes on to the next stage. Development is thus managed by an eternal maintenance of oppositions, but conflict does not produce anything new (rather it helps to get to the next predetermined state). The oppositional nature of the organization at a given stage is recognized, but it is denied that this nature participates in further developmental transformation. Erikson's (1963, pp. 270–273) description of ego development through an ordered and predetermined sequence of stages, each of which entails their stage-specific "crises" and "critical oppositions," can serve as an example of the conflict maintenance type of the goodness-of-misfit model (see also Geulen, 1986).

In contrast, theories that work along the lines of conflict transformation entail the notion of the *synthesis of a possibly novel state in development*. That novel state is constructed with the help of conflicts that were functioning in the previous state, that brought it to a breaking point, and that reorganized it into a novel set of oppositions. It is not surprising that the dialectical perspectives in psychology try hard to conceptualize the emergence of novel conflicts from the web of the previous ones (Brandstätter, 1984; Riegel, 1976). Obviously, the most extreme emphasis on the conflict transformation model is present in the heritage of Lev Vygotsky, whose consistent call for understanding a synthesis of novel psychological phenomena has not been developed further (Van der Veer & Valsiner, 1991).

Vygotsky's explicit concern about the role that oppositions between the parts of the developing system play in development was profound. Along the lines of German developmental psychology of his time, he conceptualized human ontogeny as proceeding through a series of "crises" (e.g., birth, the first year of life, Vygotsky, 1933/1984a; the third year, Vygotsky, 1933/1984b; and the seventh year, Vygotsky, 1933/1984c). In each of these crisis periods, the dialectically opposing existing psychological functions were thought to come into conflict with one another within the same structural-dynamic whole. An external indication of that state of affairs in a child's development may be a *temporary regression* in his or her observable activities or psychological functions. However, theoretically that regression can be merely a diagnostic sign indicating the construction of a novel psychological organizational form on the basis of previous oppositions.

It is noteworthy that phenomena of temporary regression in child development have been a puzzle for contemporary child psychology (e.g., see specific arguments in Bowerman, 1982; Carey, 1982; Klahr, 1982, pp. 64–68; Mehler, 1982, pp. 146–149; and Strauss, 1982). The maturationist assumptions behind most contemporary empirical research on cognitive development have led to declarations of the obligatory predeterministic unfolding of the regressive phenomena (i.e., an agreement-type model), even by authors who use the "revolution" metaphors for specific transitions in ontogeny (e.g., Mounoud, 1982). Vygotsky's theoretical emphasis on the dialectical synthesis of higher levels of organization as a result of these temporarily regressive periods is shared by few contemporary developmentalists (for an exception, see Langer, 1969, 1982).

Vygotsky's theoretical goodness-of-misfit perspective was highly Piagetian in its nature. However, whereas Vygotsky's emphasis was on the process of disequilibration as the birthplace of novelty, Piaget's ambivalent attitude toward equilibration (a move toward the "restoration of harmony") and the construction of novelty (an emergence of new oppositions) was more complicated. Of course, Piaget's notion of "optimizing equilibration" (*equilibration majorante*; see Chapman, 1988, pp. 280–282; Piaget, 1980, chap. 8, 1985, pp. 25–31) tries to reconcile (create harmony) between the opposing processes of equilibration and disequilibration.

Although seeing the state of equilibrium as positive in itself, Piaget recognized the developmentally relevant movement away from that state and toward another one, one that might never be achieved in reality. The latter notion – the development of novel structures under "far-from-equilibrium" conditions – has become recognized in some "hard" sciences of our time (e.g., in the context of "non-equilibrium thermodynamics"; see Prigogine, 1973, 1976, 1982). The notion of history is entering the otherwise time-dismissing realm of hard sciences. The presence of irreversible changes in our environment reflects the need for time-sensitive physical sciences.

Development and conflict: Phenomena reconsidered

The analysis thus far has indicated that the notion of *development by oppositions* is emerging from different sources of scientific theorizing in its hesitant and tentative ways. On the one hand, there is a movement toward the proposition that an adequate explanation of developmental processes cannot be built along the lines of a coordinated or harmonious view of qualitative "breakthroughs." At the same time, the set of thought models that could be the foundation for construction of conflict-centered theoretical models remains underdeveloped in specifics. Hence, we encounter recurrent general calls for dialectical or contextual approaches to development, that are not elaborated theoretically (e.g., the exact parts of the system between which a conflict or opposition is posited are not specified), and in empirical research, social forces guide investigators to the use of data construction and analysis methods that cannot reveal conflictual aspects of the developmental process.

However, the empirical side of the investigation of social conduct in ontogeny has given solid proof of the robustness of conflict. Virtually all of the studies of interpersonal behavior in infancy and young children, from Maudry and Nekula (1939) to Holmberg (1980) and Eckerman (1979) tell the same story: Peer interactions in the first year of life are likely to show both conflict and nonconflict. It has been known since Goodenough (1931) that the proportion of overt conflicts to total interactions diminishes with age and experience. Why the diminution? Or is it the case that people become more clever about concealing disagreements or recognizing their subordinate status relative to peers and adults? Evidence about different strategies of negotiations of peer relations in boys and girls indicates that the seemingly "peaceful" backbiting of girls in a peer network might be more conflictful in nature than boys' explicit fights, which lead to bloody noses and horrified schoolteachers whose disciplinarian roles seem to be contested (Cairns, Cairns, Neckerman, Ferguson, & Gariépy, 1989; Cairns, Neckerman, & Cairns, 1989).

Much attention has been given recently to the avoidance of conflicts and the promotion of supposedly "healthful" solutions rather than confrontational ones. To make progress toward these goals, it would be informative to ask why there are not more conflicts. From this perspective, it is a minor miracle that mutually supportive interactions between persons occur at any age. A special feature of social behavior is the ability of children to adapt to changing circumstances while simultaneously maintaining internal coherence and dyadic organization in action. With inevitable maturational changes in the internal state and external conditions for individuals in a relationship, it would be remarkable if all persons changed at the same rate. In the case of families, it is clearly not the case that children will change at the same rate as will parents. And in the case of adolescent peers and friendships, there is scant likelihood that maturational shifts will be closely coordinated. Hence, the fickleness of friendships and the reorganization of families in childhood and adolescence. When synchrony becomes difficult or impossible, the ground rules for relationships become redefined, or new relationships are formed and old ones decay. Such is the dynamic of social development whereby conflict is a necessary component of growth and change. From birth to death, individuals are to be biased toward social exchanges.

When children interact, they implicitly provide direction and support for the thoughts and actions of each other (Cairns, 1979). The social actions are thus coordinated with internal direction and goals. When such synchrony fails, the interaction ceases or conflicts arise. These two goals – social synchrony and internal consistency – are simultaneously met when the two individuals in a relationship adopt common directions. By-products of this process include similar patterns of emotional expression, parallel strategies, and/or thinking along the same lines. That is, biases toward synchrony and similarity are built into the structure and dynamics of exchanges. But *similarity* is not sameness: It makes the interacting peers sufficiently alike, sufficiently different, for their mutual construction of new interpersonal and intrapsychological phenomena. Following J. M. Baldwin (1902) and H. S. Sullivan (1940), one cannot hope to understand an individual's behaviors and beliefs independent of the social network in which he or she is embedded.

Our proposition that development can take place through conflict (goodness-of-misfit) implies that attempts to systematically assess any concept (including conflict) presupposes a clear idea of the relationships in which the idea is embedded. Furthermore, it requires clear methodological focus on the temporal organization of both interactive and intrapersonal phenomena. Thus, we suggest three propositions relevant to social conflicts in children and adolescents, namely:

1. Social conflicts are inevitable across development in behavior, in cognition, and in cognitive-social adaptations. The inevitability reflects the essential nature of behavioral organization in the child, as well as in those with whom the child interacts, and the restructuring that necessarily occurs during maturation of the child and others. Hence, the conflictual processes that investigators can observe need to be investigated as value-neutral, rather than value-laden, phenomena.
2. Social conflict may facilitate or retard the course of development. In either case, if may serve important functions for the individual and the relations in which he or she is involved. Hence, our developmental methodology needs to concentrate on the processes of conflict together with their ontogenetic resulting states.
3. Conflicts that occur in one domain should not be divorced from other domains, in that they may provoke corresponding shifts in emotional expression, cognition, and social skills. Hence, the methods used in one area of research (e.g., peer interaction) need to be complemented by others (e.g., investigation of children's understanding of the interactive situations).

Concluding comments

The issues of conflict are as complicated as they are important. We have argued in this chapter that the detection of phenomena commonly labeled "conflict" need not entail conflict as a general mechanism of development. Furthermore, phenomena that can be observed need not involve conflict in everyday terms (i.e., the detection of the absence of conflict) and may actually entail concealed oppositional processes that maintain the appearance of harmony at the given time and prepare for a developmental transition in the future.

Our main concern has been with the idea of goodness-of-misfit. If we try to explain the process of development by way of oppositions (and conflict), the oppositional parts of the same whole need to be related in ways that lead to construction of novel organizational form, rather than to the breakdown of the whole. So we could argue that there are two kinds of conflict (from the perspective of development): good conflict (an oppositional relationship between parts of a developing system that leads to the emergence of novel states of that system) and bad conflict (the clash or war of exclusively competing opposites that devastate each other, thus leading to the extinction of the whole in which they are parts). Even bad interpersonal conflicts may play a useful function for the developing child under some circumstances. They may represent not merely deficiencies or immaturity in interpersonal skills, but equally important, the processes that make for intrapersonal harmony and integrity. Development takes place under conditions of interpersonal relationships that are both harmonious and conflictful. How these two masters of development are simultaneously served remains a compelling yet incomplete story.

References

Asher, S. R., & Gottman, J. M. (Eds.) (1981). *The development of children's friendships* Cambridge: Cambridge University Press.

Baldwin, J. M. (1902). *Development and evolution.* New York: Macmillan.

Baldwin, J. M. (1906). *Thought and things: Vol. 1. Functional logic or genetic theory of knowledge.* London: Swan Sonnenschein.

Bandura, A., & Walters, R. H. (1959). *Adolescent aggression.* New York: Ronald Press.

Bernard, J. (1950). Where is the modern sociology of conflict? *American Journal of Sociology, 56,* 11–16.

Bertalanffy, L. von (1955). An essay on the relativity of categories. *Philosophy of Science, 22,* 243–263.

Bowerman, M. (1982). Starting to talk worse: Clues to language acquisition from children's late speech errors. In S. Strauss (Ed.), *U-shaped behavioral growth.* New York: Academic Press.

Brandstätter, J. (1984). Personal and social control over development: Some implications of an active perspective in life-span developmental psychology. In P. B. Baltes & O. Brim (Eds.), *Life-span development and behavior* (Vol. 6). New York: Academic Press.

Cairns, R. B. (1972). Attachment and dependency: A synthesis of social learning and psychobiology. In J. L. Gewirtz (Ed.), *Attachment and dependency.* Washington, DC: Winston.

Cairns, R. B. (1979). *Social development: The origins and plasticity of social interchanges.* San Francisco: Freeman.

Cairns, R. B. (1986). Phenomena lost: Issues in the study of development. In J. Valsiner (Ed.), *The individual subject and scientific psychology.* New York: Plenum.

Cairns, R. B., Cairns, B. D., Neckerman, H. J., Ferguson, L. L., & Gariépy, J.-L. (1989). Growth and aggression: I. Childhood to early adolescence. *Developmental Psychology, 25,* 320–330.

Cairns, R. B., Cairns, B. D. Neckerman, H., Gest, S., & Gariépy, J.-L. (1988). Social networks and aggressive behavior: Peer support or peer rejection? *Developmental Psychology, 24,* 815–823.

Cairns, R. B., Neckerman, H. J., & Cairns, B. D. (1989). Social networks and the shadows of synchrony. In G. R. Adams, T. P. Gullota, & R. Montemayor (Eds.), *Advances in adolescent development.* Beverly Hill, CA: Sage.

Carey, S. (1982). Face perception: Anomalies of development. In S. Strauss (Ed.), *U-shaped behavioral growth.* New York: Academic Press.

Chapman, M. (1988). *Constructive evolution.* Cambridge: Cambridge University Press.

Coombs, C. (1987). The structure of conflict. *American Psychologist, 42,* 355–363.

Coser, L. A. (1964). *The functions of social conflict.* Glencoe, IL: Free Press.

Deutsch, M. (1969). Conflicts: Productive and destructive. *Journal of Social Issues, 25,* 7–41.

Deutsch, M. (1985). *Distributive justice.* New Haven, CT: Yale University Press.

Devereux, G. (1967). *From anxiety to method in the behavioral sciences.* The Hague: Mouton.

Dollard, J., Doob, L. W., Miller, N. E., Mowrer, O. H., & Sears, R. R. (1939). *Frustration and aggression.* New Haven, CT: Yale University Press.

Dowd, J. J. (1990). Ever since Durkheim: The socialization of human development. *Human Development, 33,* 138–159.

Duncan, S. (1991). Convention and conflict in the child's interaction with others. *Developmental Review, 11,* 337–367.

Eckerman, C. O. (1979) The human infant in social interaction. In R. B. Cairns (Ed.), *The analysis of social interactions: Methods, issues, and illustrations.* Hillsdale, NJ: Erlbaum.

Erikson, E. H. (1963). *Childhood and society* (2d ed.). New York: Norton.

Freud, S. (1965). *The problem of anxiety.* New York: Norton. (Original work published 1936)

Geulen, D. (1986). The conditions of human development. In P. Van Geert (Ed.), *Theory building in developmental psychology.* Amsterdam: North-Holland.

Goodenough, F. L. (1931). *Anger in young children.* Minneapolis: University of Minnesota Press.

Hahn, A. (1990). The sociology of conflict. *Sociologie du Travail, 32,* 375–386.

Hartup. W. W. (1970). Peer relations and social organization. In P. Mussen (Ed.), *Carmichael's manual of child psychology* (Vol. 2). New York: Wiley.

Hartup, W. W. (1983). Peer relations. In E. M. Hetherington (Ed.), *Handbook of child psychology: Vol. 4. Socialization, personality, and social development* (4th ed.) New York: Wiley.

Hartup, W. W., & Laursen, B. (in press). Conflict and context in peer relations. In C. Hart (Ed.), *Children on playgrounds: Research perspectives and applications.* Ithaca, NY: SUNY Press.

Hebb, D. O. (1946). On the nature of fear. *Psychological Review, 53,* 259–276.

Hebb, D. O. (1949). *The organization of behavior: A neuropsychological analysis.* New York: Wiley.

Hinde, R. A. (1966). *Animal behavior.* New York: McGraw-Hill.

Holmberg, M. C. (1980). The development of social interchange patterns from 12 to 42 months. *Child Development, 51,* 448–456.

Hunt, W. A. (1941). Recent developments in the field of emotion *Psychological Bulletin, 38,* 249–276.

Klahr, D. (1982). Nonmonotone assessment of monotone development: An information-processing analysis. In S. Strauss (Ed.), *U-shaped behavioral growth.* New York: Academic Press.

Kolominskii, Ia. L., & Zhiznevskii, B. P. (1990). Social-psychological analysis of conflicts between children in the course of play. *Voprosy psikhologii, No. 2,* 35–42.

Kramer, D. A., & Bopp, M. J. (Eds.). (1989). *Transformation in clinical and developmental psychology.* New York: Springer.

Langer, J. (1969). Disequilibrium as a source of development. In P. Mussen, J. Langer, & M. Covington (Eds.), *Trends and issues in developmental psychology.* New York: Holt, Rinehardt & Winston.

Langer, J (1982). Dialectics of development. In T. G. Bever (Ed.), *Regressions in mental development.* Hillsdale, NJ: Erlbaum.

Lerner, R. M. (1984). *On the nature of human plasticity.* Cambridge: Cambridge University Press.

Lewin, K. (1926a). Vorbemerkungen über die psychischen Kräfte und Energien und über die Struktur der Seele. *Psychologische Forschung, 7,* 294–329.

Lewin, K. (1926b). Vorsatz, Wille und Bedürfnis. *Psychologische Forschung, 7,* 330–385.

Lewin, K. (1933). Environmental forces, In C. Murchison (Ed.), *A handbook of child psychology* (2d ed.), Worcester, MA: Clark University Press.

Lewin K. (1935). *A dynamic theory of personality: Selected papers.* New York: McGraw-Hill, (D. K. Adams & K. E. Zener, Trans.).

Lewin, K (1948). *Resolving social conflicts.* New York: Harper.

Lyman, S. M. (1990). Anhedonia: Gender and the decline of emotions in American film, 1930–1988. *Sociological Inquiry, 60,* 1–19.

Maher, B. A., & Maher, W. B. (1979). Psychopathology. In E. Hearst (Ed.), *The first century of experimental psychology.* Hillsdale, NJ: Erlbaum.

Mandler, G (1964). The interruption of behavior. In D. Levine (Ed.), *Nebraska symposium on motivation* (Vol. 12). Lincoln: University of Nebraska Press.

Mandler, G. (1979). Emotion. In E. Hearst (Ed.), *The first century of experimental psychology.* Hillsdale, NJ: Erlbaum.

Maudry, M., & Nekula, M. (1939). Social relations between children of the same age during the first two years of life. *Journal of Genetic Psychology, 54,* 193–215.

Mehler, J. (1982). Unlearning: Dips and drops – a theory of cognitive development. In T. G. Bever (Ed.), *Regressions in mental development.* Hillsdale, NJ: Erlbaum.

Miller, N. E. (1948). Studies of fear as an acquirable drive: 1. Fear as motivation and fear-reduction as reinforcement in the learning of new responses. *Journal of Experimental Psychology, 38,* 89–101.

Mounoud, P. (1982). Revolutionary periods in early development. In T. G. Bever (Ed.), *Regressions in mental development.* Hillsdale, NJ: Erlbaum.

Oxford English Dictionary (1971). Oxford: Oxford University Press.

Piaget, J. (1962). *Play, dreams and imitation in childhood.* New York: Norton.

Piaget, J. (1973). The affective unconscious and the cognitive unconscious, *Journal of the American Psychoanalytic Association, 21,* 249–261.

Piaget, J. (1980). *Adaptation and intelligence.* Chicago: University of Chicago Press.

Piaget, J. (1985). *The equilibration of cognitive structures.* Chicago: University of Chicago Press. (Original work published 1975)

Prigogine, I. (1973). Irreversibility as a symmetry-breaking process. *Nature, 246,* 67–71.

Prigogine, I. (1976). Order through fluctuation: Self organization and social system. In C. H. Waddington (Ed.), *Evolution and consciousness: Human systems in transition.* Reading, MA: Addison-Wesley.

Prigogine, I. (1982). Dialogue avec Piaget sur l'irreversibilité. *Archives de Psychologie, 50,* 7–16.

Riegel, K. (1976). The dialectics of human development. *American Psychologist, 31,* 689–700.

Rummel, R. J. (1987). A catastrophe theory model of the conflict helix, with tests. *Behavioural Science, 32,* 241–266.

Shantz, C. U. (1987). Conflicts between children. *Child Development, 58,* 283–305.

Sherif, M., Harvey, O. J., White, B. J., Hood, W. R., & Sherif, C. W. (1961). *Intergroup conflict and cooperation: The Robbers Cave experiment.* Norman, OK: University Book Exchange.

Shvyrkov, V. V. (1987). What Harvard statisticians don't tell us. *Quality & Quantity, 21,* 335–347.

Simmel, G. (1904). The sociology of conflict, I, II, III. *American Journal of Sociology, 9,* 490–525, 672–689, 798–811.

Skinner, B. F. (1938). *The behavior of organisms: An experimental analysis.* New York: Appleton-Century-Crofts.

Smedslund, J. (1978). Bandura's theory of self-efficacy: A set of common-sense theorems. *Scandinavian Journal of Psychology, 19,* 1–14.

Sorensen, R. C. (1951). The concept of conflict in industrial sociology. *Social Forces, 29,* 263–267.

Sorokin, P. (1956). *Fads and foibles in modern sociology and related sciences.* Chicago: Regner.

Strauss, S. (1982). Ancestral and descendant behaviors: The case of U-shaped behavioral growth. In T. G. Bever (Ed.), *Regressions in mental development.* Hillsdale, NJ: Erlbaum.

Sullivan, H. S. (1940). *The collected works.* New York: Norton.

Thom, R. (1973). A global dynamic scheme for vertebrate embryology. *Lectures on Mathematics in the Life Sciences, 5,* 3–45.

Thom R. (1976). The two-fold way of catastrophe theory. In P. Hilton (Ed.), *Structural stability, the theory of catastrophes and applications in the sciences.* Berlin: Springer.

Truesdell, C. (1982). Our debt to the French tradition: "Catastrophes" and our search for structure today. *Scientia, 76,* 63–77.

Valsiner, J. (1984). Two alternative epistemological frameworks in psychology: The typological and variational modes of thinking. *Journal of Mind and Behavior, 5,* 449–470.

Valsiner, J. (1985). Common sense and psychological theories: The historical nature of logical necessity. *Scandinavian Journal of Psychology, 26,* 97–109.

Valsiner, J. (1986). Between groups and individuals: Psychologists' and laypersons' interpretations of correlational findings. In J. Valsiner (Ed.), *The individual subject and scientific psychology.* New York: Plenum.

Valsiner, J. (1987). *Culture and the development of children's action.* Chichester: Wiley.

Valsiner, J. (1988). *Developmental psychology in the Soviet Union.* Bloomington: Indiana University Press.

Van der Veer, R., & Valsiner, J. (1991). *Understanding Vygotsky: A quest for synthesis.* Oxford: Basil Blackwell.

Van Geert, P. (1988). The concept of transition in developmental theories. In W. J. Baker, L. P. Mos, H. V. Rappard, & H. J. Stam (Eds.), *Recent trends in theoretical psychology.* New York: Springer.

Van IJzendoorn, M. H., & Van der Veer, R. (1984). *Main currents of critical psychology.* New York: Irvington.

Vygotsky, L. S. (1984a). The crisis of the first year of life. In L. S. Vygotsky, *Sobranie sochinenii: Vol. 4. Detskaia psikhologia.* Moscow: Pedagogika. (Original work dated 1933)

Vygotsky, L. S. (1984b). The crisis of the third year. In L S. Vygotsky, *Sobranie sochinenii: Vol. 4. Detskaia psikhologia.* Moscow: Pedagogika. (Original work dated 1933)

Vygotsky, L. S. (1984c). The crisis of the seventh year. In L. S. Vygotsky, *Sobranie sochinenii: Vol. 4. Detskaia psikhologia.* Moscow: Pedagogika. (Original work dated 1933)

Zeeman, E. C. (1981). Dynamics of the evolution of animal conflicts. *Journal of Theoretical Biology, 89,* 249–270.

2 The education of reason: Cognitive conflict and its role in intellectual development

Michael Chapman and Michelle L. McBride

In Plato's *Meno*, Socrates questions an untutored slave boy about geometry. Shown a 2- by 2-foot square drawn in the sand, the boy confirms that its area is 4 square feet. When asked how long its sides would be if its area was exactly twice as much, the boy affirms that the sides would be twice as long as well. Confronted with an actual 4- by 4-foot square, however, he agrees that its area is 16 square feet. Guessing that the right answer must be somewhere between 2 and 4 feet, he suggests 3 feet, only to retract his answer when shown that the area of a 3-foot square is 9 square feet instead of 8. Urged to try again, he responds, "It's no use Socrates. I just don't know" (Hamilton & Cairns, 1961, p. 368). At this point in the dialogue, Socrates turns to his friend Meno and remarks that, despite appearances, the slave boy is closer to the truth than he was before, because the perplexity resulting from the experience of having his beliefs contradicted has awakened in him a desire to know. In the remainder of the dialogue, Socrates guides the slave boy to the discovery of the answer through a series of strategic questions.

In contrast to Plato, most psychologists have regarded psychological conflict as more disruptive than beneficial. Thus, Freud (1901/1953) explained certain distortions of rational thinking and neuroses as the result of conflict among basic drives, and Luria (1932) described the "disorganization of behavior" that can attend intrapsychic conflict of various kinds (see also Guthrie, 1938; Janet, 1925). Similarly, early learning-theoretic studies of conflict focused on the kinds of "response competition" that lead to such negative outcomes (Miller, 1944). However, other theorists such as Dewey (1910/1933), Festinger (1957), Berlyne (1960), Piaget (1924/

The preparation of this chapter was supported in part by Operating Grant #OG00373334 from the Natural Science and Engineering Research Council of Canada. The authors would like to thank the editors and Jeremy Carpendale for their comments on an earlier draft.

We regret to inform readers that Michael Chapman died prior to the publication of this book. Correspondence concerning this chapter should be addressed to Michelle McBride. – The Editors

1928, 1975/1985), and Riegel (1976) have followed Plato in according conflict a positive role in rational thinking and the genesis of knowledge, arguing that conflict can provide a motivational stimulus for positive adaptations.

This chapter is an exploration of issues raised by the latter position. First, theories in which cognitive conflict plays a positive role in intellectual development are discussed, with special emphasis on issues raised by Piaget's theory of equilibration. Then, research on the effects of cognitive and "sociocognitive" conflict on cognitive development is summarized with respect to those issues. Finally, some unresolved problems are discussed, and potential new directions in the theory of cognitive conflict and its role in intellectual development are proposed.

The role of conflict in cognitive development

The central idea in theories of conflict as a positive factor in cognitive development is that inconsistency among one's currently held beliefs or between one's beliefs and relevant experiences can undermine false certainties and motivate a search for new knowledge. For example, Dewey (1910/1933) stated that the uncertainty that follows the obstruction of everyday activities leads one to seek "a more commanding view of the situation" (p. 14). Among Gestalt psychologists, Köhler (1917/1925) expressed a similar idea with his concept of "*Umweg*" (detour) problems. The conflict that occurs when an organism's movement toward a goal is blocked by a barrier of some kind can result in a search for novel pathways that lead indirectly to the goal. Lewin (1931) generalized and extended such ideas in his theory of environmental "field forces." In a typical *Umweg* situation, children are initially attracted to a goal blocked by some barrier. After they run against the barrier, it acquires a negative valence that repels them from the original field of attraction. When they turn their attention once again to the goal, the experience of having gone out of the field helps them to see their way around the barrier.

A more comprehensive theory of the role of conflict in cognition was provided by Festinger (1957) in his theory of "cognitive dissonance." The central meaning of cognitive dissonance is that of logical inconsistency or contradiction (p. 13), although any two elements are dissonant in a general sense if they do not fit together (p. 12). The "psychological discomfort" (p. 2) caused by dissonance is adaptive insofar as it motivates persons to modify their beliefs so as to bring them into closer correspondence with reality (p. 11).

Cognitive conflict also played a role in the acquisition of knowledge in

Berlyne's (1960) theory of "conceptual conflict." Besides logical contradiction, other types of conceptual conflict included "doubt" as a conflict between the incompatible tendencies to believe or not believe a given statement, "perplexity" as a conflict among tendencies to accept mutually exclusive beliefs, "conceptual incongruity" as an attribution of mutually inconsistent properties to the same object, and "confusion" as resulting from incompatible symbolic responses from ambiguous stimuli (p. 287). Such forms of conflict may lead to *epistemic curiosity*: a motivational state leading to a search for new knowledge.

Berlyne (1960) also argued that Piaget's theory of equilibrium could be reinterpreted as referring to "a class of hitherto overlooked sources of drive and reward" resulting from cognitive conflict. Although some observers (e.g., Mischel, 1971) have argued that Piaget's concept of equilibration cannot be reduced to drive reduction theory, Piaget and Berlyne did agree in according cognitive conflict a significant role in cognitive development. Because much recent reseach on cognitive conflict has been inspired directly or indirectly by Piaget's equilibration theory, that theory is examined in the following section.

Piaget's theory of equilibration

The idea of equilibration as a directing principle in development was among Piaget's most basic intuitions (Chapman, 1988, in press-a). From the beginning, he viewed equilibration as a proces that was fueled by conflict or "disequilibrium," either between the organism and the environment or among the organism's own activities. In his work on children's verbal reasoning during the 1920s, the primary source of disequilibrium in cognitive development was said to be interpersonal conflict. Children's encounters with perspectives that differed from their own were viewed as the primary cause in the development of rational thinking. Later, following his formulation of the theory of concrete operations in the 1940s, Piaget laid more emphasis on intrapsychic disequilibria involving conflicts between children's action schemes and external realities or among different schemes within individual children. However, this shift in emphasis did not reflect an abandonment of his earlier theory that cognitive development was motivated in part by the conflict of perspectives. Instead, he argued that the equilibria among the individual's internal schemes were "identical" in form to those that characterize cooperation between individuals. The form of equilibrium existing in interpersonal exchange was described in a series of sociological essays written concurrently with the development of the theory of concrete operations in the 1940s (Piaget, 1965/1977; described in

Chapman, 1986, 1988). But beyond asserting a formal identity between intrapersonal and interpersonal operations, he did little to describe how social interaction and cognitive development might be related on a functional level.

This focus on intrapsychic processes was reflected in his further efforts to develop equilibration theory. For example, he described equilibration as a probabilistic process of *decentration* (Piaget, 1957). This term was taken from his work on perception, in which it specifically denoted a movement away from isolated acts of perceptual "centrations" toward their intercoordination. In its more general sense, decentration was understood as a movement away from any kind of thought that is narrowly "centered" on particular aspects of a situation. Thus, the polar concept of centration–decentration replaced Piaget's earlier, and easily misunderstood, notion of "egocentrism." Cognitive development was described as progressing to the extent that the probability of centering on two or more aspects simultaneously increased relative to the probabilities of centering on each aspect alone.

Neither in this probabilistic model of equilibration nor in his later reformulations of equilibration theory (Piaget, 1975/1985) did Piaget elucidate the possible role of interpersonal perspectival conflict in creating cognitive disequilibrium. The focus was instead on the coordination of centrations (Piaget, 1957) or on the overcoming of contradictions and gaps in knowledge (Piaget, 1975/1985) within the individual psyche. This is not to say that Piaget ever abandoned his earlier belief in the disequilibrating function of perspectival conflict, but he never explained how such social processes are related to the equilibration of intrapsychic operations that preoccupied him in his later theorizing.

One of the first persons to call for an integration of Piaget's earlier social theory and his later theory of operations was Smedslund (1966). In an essay entitled "The Social Origins of Decentration," he argued that the only factor capable of enticing children out of an egocentric consciousness based on successive centrations on the immediate here and now is a conflict between two or more centrations that bear simultaneously on the same situation. However, two types of cognitive conflict may be distinguished. The first type occurs when children's expectations are disconfirmed by experience, and the second type when children communicate with other persons whose perspectives differ from their own. According to Smedslund, the first type of conflict can lead children to modify their expectations, but only the second can lead them out of the egocentrism of their cognitive system as a whole. He concluded by hypothesizing that communicative conflict "is a necessary condition for intellectual decentration" (1966, p. 166) and called for a return to Piaget's earlier concerns with the social environment as a factor in intellectual development.

This line of thinking was developed further by Doise and his colleagues (summarized in Doise & Mugny, 1984; see also Perret-Clermont, 1980), who criticized Piaget for neglecting the "causal" effects of social context on individual development. To remedy this shortcoming, they sought to integrate Piaget's earlier sociocognitive ideas with the psychosocial theories of Mead (1934/1962) and Vygotsky (1934/1986). According to Doise and Mugny, the three thinkers shared the idea that certain aspects of individual cognition originate in the "internalization" (or in Piaget's terminology, the "interiorization") of social interaction. For Mead, symbolic thought has its origins in the internalization of the exchange of "significant gestures"; for Vygotsky, all higher cognitive processes were said to occur first on the plane of social relations before being internalized by the individual; for the early Piaget (esp. 1932/1965), the internalization of cooperation with other persons was the primary factor in the decline of egocentrism. From these common themes, Doise and Mugny drew their central premise that the coordinations of one's own actions with those of other persons results in the formation of "systems of coordination" that later can be employed on the level of individual cognition in coordinating disparate centrations. The empirical findings generated by this research program are discussd in subsequent sections.

Another kind of criticism of Piaget's emphasis on intrapsychic equilibratory processes was represented in Riegel's (1976) "dialectical psychology." In opposition to Piaget's apparent preference for the balance and stability of equilibrium, Riegel argued that development is more often characterized by "upheaval, conflict, and change." And against the Piagetian focus on subject–object interaction, Riegel emphasized the dialogical interaction between subject and subject. However, Riegel's conception of dialectics was disputed by Tolman (1981), who argued that the dialectical view of development is not one that merely emphasizes "upheaval, conflict, and change" over "balance, stability and rest," but one that recognizes the inherent contradictions involved in all development. In particular, development must be recognized as involving both balance and imbalance, both conflict and equilibrium. In this respect, Tolman concluded that Piagetian theory was truly dialectical in its emphasis on the tendency toward equilibrium coupled with incessant disequilibrating influences.

Because of the central role of disequilibrium in Piaget's account of developmental processes, most research on the effects of cognitive conflict in intellectual development has been conducted against the backdrop of his equilibration theory. Perhaps the central question in this research has been the extent to which cognitive conflict in general promotes progressive cognitive change above and beyond the effects of social learning. A second important question has been the extent to which specifically social interaction is essential in this process. Both of those questions also have been pursued in research on moral development, following Kohlberg's (1969) use of equilibration theory to explain stage transitions in moral reasoning. Because the focus of this chapter is on the role of conflict in cognitive development as such, the research on cognitive conflict and moral development will be considered only insofar as it contributes to an understanding of the equilibratory processes by which conflict is believed to affect development.

Intrapsychic cognitive conflict

A major question in the North American reception of Piaget's theory was whether the ability to solve typical Piagetian reasoning problems could be acquired through learning or instruction (e.g., Bruner, Olver, & Greenfield, 1966). Consistent with Piaget's constructivist orientation, he considered learning as a phenomenon to be subsumed under a more general model of equilibratory processes (Piaget, 1959a, 1959b). One implication of such a view is the idea that what children can absorb through learning is limited by their existing operatory structures. Consistent with that assumption, the research on learning carried out at the Center of Genetic Epistemology during the 1960s appeared to demonstrate that children's learning was constrained by their cognitive-developmental level (Morf, Smedslund, Vinh Bang, & Wohlwill, 1959).

Another approach to the question of learning and cognitive development was taken by Inhelder, Sinclair, and Bovet (1974) in *Learning and the Development of Cognition*. Instead of merely studying cognitive constraints on learning, they sought to determine whether constructive, equilibratory processes in development could be stimulated. By presenting children with problems requiring the use of incompatible schemes, they hoped "to arouse a conflict in the child's mind between these schemes that would lead to new types of coordination between them" (p. 26). In a typical experiment, children were (a) pretested to ascertain their initial cognitive levels, (b) given a training procedure designed to make evident the contradictions inherent in preoperational thinking, and then (c) given two posttests in order to determine the extent and durability of their progress. Tasks studied in this way included the conservation of continuous and discontinuous quantities, the conservation of number, and class inclusion.

In general, the results of these studies indicated that children benefited from the training, but the extent to which they improved depended on their initial level. For example, in the first study reported in the book, 13 of 15 children judged to be nonconservers in the pretest remained nonconservers following two training sessions in which they were provided with experiences contradicting their belief that the amount of water flowing through a series of jars would change as a function of their shapes. In contrast, 7 of the 19 children who pretested at intermediate levels of conservation became full conservers at Posttest 1, and 4 more became conservers at Posttest 2. No children who attained full conservation were observed to regress from Posttest 1 to Posttest 2. Such results were interpreted in accord with the equilibration model: The discrepancy between children's expectations and experience was said to result in equilibration leading to conservation, but only for children who had cognitive structures sufficient to apprehend such a discrepancy to begin with. Evidence for the occurrence of cognitive conflict was taken from children's verbal expressions of conflicting centrations in the training sessions.

These conclusions were crticized by some commentators, for both methodological and theoretical reasons. For example, Lefebvre-Pinard (1976) argued that (a) the procedures used by Inhelder et al. often were insufficient for ensuring that cognitive conflict actually occurred during training or that children progressed as the result of such conflict, and (b) the lack of progress reported by Inhelder for preoperational children may have resulted from the fact that those children simply did not apprehend the conflict presumed to exist in the problem. Evidence for this second point came from a study in which measures of children's ability to apprehend contradiction were found to predict the extent to which they benefited from cognitive conflict (Lefebvre & Pinard, 1974). Similar criticisms were voiced by Zimmerman and Blom (1983a), who attempted to assess the presence of intrapsychic cognitive conflict through response latency and measures of children's certainty and found neither measure to be related to conservation performance. The adequacy of those measures for operationalizing the Piagetian concept of disequilibration was questioned by Cantor (1983) and Murray (1983) (but see Zimmerman & Blom, 1983b).

Studies of "sociocognitive conflict"

Whereas the procedures of Inhelder et al. (1974) were designed to induce conflict between expectations and experience or between schemes that were more or less incompatible with each other within individual children, other researchers set out to study cognitive conflicts arising in the context of communication between individuals as originally suggested by Smedslund (1966). The latter sort of conflict has been termed "sociocognitive conflict" by researchers working in that tradition (e.g., Doise, Dionnet, & Mugny, 1978; Mugny & Doise, 1978). In an early example of research on such conflict, Murray (1972) pretested children on a standard measure of conservation and then grouped them into triads consisting of two conservers and one nonconserver. A week later, they were tested again on the same items plus two parallel tests. All of the nonconservers were found to have progressed from pretest to posttest, a result that Murray interpreted as an effect of social interaction. However, it was unclear (a) whether children's improvements reflected a lasting increase in understanding or merely a temporary increase in correct judgments and (b) whether those improvements occurred as the result of sociocognitive conflict or simply through the imitation of conservers' responses.

Like Murray's (1972) study, subsequent research was framed in terms of an opposition between social learning and equilibration as explanatory models. According to social learning theory, imitation or observational learning should be sufficient to explain the effects of sociocognitive conflict. According to equilibration theory, a residual effect of conflict should be found even when those processes are controlled. Another characteristic of the subsequent research was that it was devoted mostly to studies of conservation or spatial perspective taking. The popularity of these tasks can be attributed to the fact that cognitive conflict was believed to be the product of contradictory centrations. For example, the typical Piagetian conservation tasks involve transformations (e.g., rolling out a ball of clay) resulting in simultaneous and compensatory changes in different physical dimensions (making the clay longer and thinner at the same time). Centration on either dimension separately leads to contradictory affirmations (e.g., the clay becomes "more" in growing longer or "less" in becoming thinner). According to the equilibration model, confrontation with such contradictory affirmations in the context of social interaction can be a stimulus to cognitive development.

The generality and stability of the cognitive changes induced by such sociocognitive conflict was tested by Silverman and Stone (1972). First, they pretested 8-year-olds for conservation; then in an experimental interaction session they paired conservers with nonconservers based on their pretest scores and asked each pair to agree on a single answer to the same conservation problem. Finally, they tested the children again a month later on the same problems plus two different ones. They found that changes from pretest to posttest were more likely to be in the direction of conservation than the reverse and that nonconservers who had interacted with conservers scored higher at posttest than a control group who had experienced no social interaction. They concluded that such results were better explained through equilibration than through social learning; if modeling or imitation alone were at work, then one would have no reason to expect more change in one direction than in the other (Rosenthal & Zimmerman, 1972). The possibility that such results merely reflected an effect of social dominance was ruled out in studies by Silverman and Geiringer (1973) and by Miller and Brownell (1975).

Another possible explanation of such findings is that conservers are more certain of their answers than nonconservers and that less certain interaction partners are more likely to adopt the answer of the more certain partner than the reverse. Part of the initial difficulty of distinguishing between the social learning and sociocognitive conflict hypotheses lay in the procedure of pairing conservers with nonconservers. If nonconservers are exposed to correct responses during the experimental phase of the experiment, then any progress toward conservation might be the simple result of exposure to the correct answer. According to the sociocognitive conflict hypothesis, however, children's confrontations with perspectives that differ from their own should lead them to an understanding of the incompleteness and relativity of their own perspectives, *even when the opposing perspective is equally partial or incomplete.* In such a case, social learning mechanisms presumably could be ruled out in a definitive manner.

Such was the logic of a study of the conservation of length conducted by Mugny, Doise, and Perret-Clermont (1975–1976; described in Doise & Mugny, 1984, chap. 5, exp. 1). Instead of pairing conservers with nonconservers, these investigators paired nonconserving children with an adult confederate who also gave a nonconserving response, but one that contradicted those given by the children themselves. For example, if the children said that stick B was longer than stick A because B protruded beyond A at one end, then the adult confederate would affirm that A was longer because it protruded beyond B at the other end. The conservation performance of children who had interacted with such a nonconserving model was compared with that of groups who had interacted with a conserving model or with no model at all.

In brief, conservation was enhanced in children exposed to both the conserving and nonconserving models, relative to children exposed to no model. Moreover, the effects of sociocognitive conflict were more likely to generalize to a closely related task than the effects of modeling. Although the improvement found in the conserving-model group could have occurred through some combination of modeling and sociocognitive conflict, that observed in the nonconserving-model group was apparently the result of sociocognitive conflict alone. These results were strongly supportive of the hypothesis that social interaction involving a conflict of centrations can result in cognitive development apart from any modeling effects. In three other studies reported by Doise and Mugny (1984), the progress resulting from sociocognitive conflict was found (a) to depend on the intensity of such conflict, (b) to occur as the result of spontaneous conflicts among the responses of nonconserving peers, and (c) to be facilitated by a correspondence between the physical dimensions of the task and relevant social norms. The latter phenomenon Doise and Mugny called "social marking" and is discussed further in later sections of this chapter.

In subsequent research, reports on the effectiveness of such "symmetrical" sociocognitive conflict have been uneven. Perret-Clermont (1980, chap. 3) found no progress among nonconservers paired with other nonconservers at a first posttest (although she reported some progress at the second posttest). However, Ames and Murray (1982) found that second graders paired with peers who had given incompatible nonconserving responses on the pretest items progressed following social interaction to a significantly greater extent than children (a) for whom the opposite of their pretest answers was simply modeled for them, (b) who were asked to pretend that the opposite of their pretest answers was true, (c) who were led to give answers different from their pretest answers, or (d) who simply performed the tasks in front of another child. Children in the social interaction group progressed even when they had not experienced any conservation responses during the interaction phase of the experiment.

In contrast, Russell and his colleagues failed to find that symmetrical sociocognitive conflict facilitated performance in a variety of tasks, including class inclusion (Russell, 1981a), perspective taking (Russell, 1981b), transitivity in measurement (Russell, 1982a), the conservation of length (Russell, 1982b), the understanding of visual illusions (Russell & Haworth, 1988), and the conservation of liquid (Russell, Mills, & Reiff-Musgrove, 1990). As an alternative explanation for the efficacy of symmetrical sociocognitive conflict reported in previous research, Russell et al. (1990) suggested that progress in cognitive performance could result from (a) spontaneous improvement among nonconservers resulting from the experience of being tested, coupled with (b) a tendency for nonconservers to adopt conservation responses when confronted with conservation arguments. In this view, symmetrical dyadic interaction between nonconservers may have been found in previous research (e.g., Ames & Murray, 1982), because (a) the probability that at least one child in a dyad of nonconservers would show spontaneous improvement is twice as great as it would be for one child working alone and (b) the second child in the dyad is likely to adopt the conservation response of the first.

Russell et al. (1990) produced evidence for such an interpretation in the following way: They induced symmetrical sociocognitive conflict in a conservation-of-liquid task among dyads of nonconserving 5- to 7-year-olds by showing each child in a dyad a different view of a display that contained equal quantities of liquid poured into beakers of different shapes. From the top of the display, one child saw that one beaker was wider than another, and from the bottom of the display, the other child saw that the first beaker was shorter than the second. These symmetrical dyads were compared with a "solo" group in which individual children were shown both views of the display and with a group of asymmetrical dyads consisting of a conserver and a nonconserver. Consistent with the hypothesis, (a) some spontaneous improvement was found in the solo subjects, (b) nonconservers in the asymmetric dyads were more likely to adopt the conservation responses of their partners than the reverse, and (c) the rate of improvement in the symmetrical dyads was not significantly greater than that in the solo group. In other words, no evidence was found for a facilitating effect of sociocognitive conflict beyond that which might have resulted from spontaneous improvement by one child whose conservation response was then adopted by the other child in the dyad.

The spontaneous improvement hypothesis of Russell et al. (1990) would appear to provide an alternative explanation for the facilitating effects of symmetrical sociocognitive conflict. However, that hypothesis would not explain the effects of symmetrical sociocognitive conflict reported by Mugny et al. (1975–1976), because in that study children were not exposed to a conservation response at all, but only a different nonconserving response. Such was also the case in a study by McBride (1991) in which children were given conservation-of-length and conservation-of-liquid problems in story form (cf. Russell & Haworth, 1986). Each story involved two nonconserving protagonists with conflicting perspectives on the problem. For example, in the conservation-of-length task two farmhands are asked to go fetch two logs, one longer than the other, in order to fix a fence. In the forest, they discover two logs of the same length lying side by side. One farmhand kicks the end of one of the logs, points at its far end sticking out beyond that of the other log, and asserts that the first log is now longer than the second. The other farmhand disagrees, arguing instead that the second log is longer than the first because it sticks out at the other end. The two farmhands are unable to agree, and the children are asked what they think about the situation. Conservation responses were significantly more frequent in this conflictual story task than in a similar story task involving no conflict or in a standard conservation task. Such results cannot be explained as the result of nonconservers adopting a conservation response that they recognize as being superior, because none of the children in the study were exposed to any conservation responses. Indeed, one interpretation of the results is that cognitive conflict does not have to involve real interaction with another person in order to be effective; fictive sociocognitive conflict would appear to be sufficient for inducing decentration.

These considerations suggest one possible reason why Doise and his colleagues (e.g., Doise & Mugny, 1984, chap. 5) reported symmetrical sociocognitive conflict to be efficacious whereas Russell and his colleagues (e.g., Russell et al., 1990) did not. In both research programs, groups of children exposed to symmetrical sociocognitive conflict were compared to control groups of children working alone. Care was taken in each case to provide children in the solo groups with some possible experience of intrapsychic conflict. Sociocognitive conflict was judged to be effective only if it produced more improvement than that produced by intrapsychic conflict. In such a design, one might obtain null results, not because sociocognitive conflict was ineffective in inducing change, but because intrapsychic conflict was equally effective. Consistent with this interpretation, both Mugny et al. (1975–1976, reported in Doise & Mugny, 1984, chap. 5, exp. 1) and Russell et al. (1990) reported some improvement in their experimental groups following sociocognitive conflict. However, Mugny et al. did not find any improvement in their solo group, whereas Russell et al. did. Thus, only the former investigators found significantly more improvement following sociocognitive conflict than following intrapsychic conflict. Such a result could have occurred if the procedure of Mugny et al. for inducing intrapsychic cognitive conflict in the solo group was less efficacious than the procedure of Russell et al. in the corresponding group.

To summarize the research reviewed so far, some evidence exists for a facilitating effect of both intrapsychic cognitive conflict and sociocognitive conflict on cognitive progress. The two major types of sociocognitive conflict studied have been *symmetrical* conflict between two opposing responses at the same level of development and *asymmetrical* conflict between responses at different levels of development. Of the two, asymmetrical conflict is the more consistently effective, but the fact that symmetrical sociocognitive conflict has proved to be effective at all has been cited as evidence that such effects are mediated by equilibratory processes and not merely by social learning. However, the evidence for a facilitative effect of *intrapsychic* cognitive conflict raises the question once again of whether social interaction is necessary for such effects.

Evidence from other tasks

As mentioned previously, most research on sociocognitive conflict has been focused on studies of conservation, but effects of cognitive conflict have been found for other types of tasks as well. Although the issues involved are similar to those discussed in the previous sections, the results are somewhat less consistent.

Spatial perspective taking

The most commonly used task besides conservation has been some form of spatial perspective taking. For example, Doise and Mugny (1979, 1984, chap. 6) showed children a model village displayed on a table in front of them and asked them to reproduce the village on a second table immediately to one side. Children who failed to preserve the spatial orientation of the model – that is, children who failed to transform left–right and front–back relations when they turned 90 degrees to the side – performed the task again a week later under one of two conflict conditions: Either (a) they reproduced the model individually and then were shown the model and the reproduction from a perspective 180 degrees from their original position or (b) they reproduced the model together with another child who was positioned 180 degrees around the display. Children in both groups progressed beyond their original performance as a result of this conflict of perspectives, but children in the dyadic conflict condition progressed significantly more than children in the individual condition. Thus, an effect of symmetrical sociocognitive conflict was found above and beyond the effects of intrapsychic cognitive conflict.

In other studies, such an effect has not always been found. For example, Emler and Valiant (1982) replicated Doise and Mugny's (1979) procedure and found that children who had experienced *intraindividual* conflict (solving the problem individually, but moving around the display to view it from different perspectives) as well as children who had experienced *interindividual* conflict (solving the problem in dyads, each member of which had a different perspective) progressed more from pre- to posttest than did children who had experienced neither form of conflict. In other words, intraindividual conflict appeared to be sufficient; no effect of interindividual conflict was found beyond that of intraindividual conflict alone.

Emler and Valiant explained the discrepancy between their results and those of Doise and Mugny (1979) in terms of cultural differences; children from more individualistic cultures should benefit more from intraindividual conflict than children from less individualistic cultures, and the culture of their Scottish sample was judged likely to be more individualistic than that of Doise and Mugny's Spanish sample. Further evidence for such an explanation was provided by Mackie (1980), who compared children from a Pacific Island Maori culture with New Zealand children of European backgrounds on the Doise and Mugny (1979) spatial perspective task. The New Zealand sample benefited as much from intraindividual conflict as from interindividual conflict, but the Pacific Island sample benefited more from the interindividual than the intraindividual condition. Mackie interpreted these results in terms of the more individualistic orientation of European culture.

A more radical challenge to Doise and Mugny's conclusions was mounted by Russell (1981b), who found no evidence for sociocognitive conflict in analyzing the interactions of children attempting to reproduce a scene shown in a photograph of a display seen from different perspectives. Instead, children tended not to counter their partner's correct placements nor to resist corrections of egocentric errors. Russell's interpretation of these findings was that most egocentric errors reflect a failure of performance factors such as concentration and reflection rather than a lack of competence in perspective taking as such. Unlike Doise and Mugny (1979, 1984), Russell did not compare the performance of children working in dyads with children working alone. His argument was not that children do not benefit from working together on such tasks, but that any benefits observed from collaboration cannot be attributable to sociocognitive conflict if no evidence for such conflict is observed in their actual interactions.

The picture is complicated further by the results of Bearison, Magzamen, and Filardo's (1986) fine-grained analysis of the disagreements between children solving spatial perspective problems. Both verbal and enactive disagreements (or combinations thereof) were coded, and verbal disagreements accompanied by explanations were distinguished from verbal disagreement without explanations. Significantly, only verbal disagreements accompanied by explanations during the dyadic interaction session were found to be related to improvement in individual task performance. Moreover, the relation between the two variables was found to be curvilinear: More pre- to posttest improvement was found for children who had experienced an intermediate level of verbal disagreements with explanations during the interaction session than for children who had experienced lower or higher levels of such disagreements. In other words, performance appeared to be facilitated by disagreements accompanied by explanations, but beyond a certain point, more disagreements was no longer better.

Consistent with the results of Bearison et al. (1986), Peterson and Peterson (1990) found that pre- to posttest improvement of deaf children's performance on a spatial perspective task was related to the frequency of verbal (i.e., signed) disagreements, but not to the frequency of enactive disagreements. Curiously, verbal disagreements with explanations were found to be negatively related to improvements in performance, a result that Peterson and Peterson interpreted as consistent with the finding of Bearison et al. that a high frequency of verbal disagreements with explanations was negatively related to improvement in performance. The complex nature of the relation between conflict and performance as found in both the Bearison et al. and the Peterson and Peterson studies may explain why a relation between the two variables has not always been found, especially when conflicts are coded only globally (e.g., Azmitia, 1988).

Moral reasoning

Following Kohlberg's (1969) constructivist theory of moral development, a number of theorists have proposed that the development of moral reasoning should be facilitated by cognitive conflict (e.g., Berkowitz & Gibbs, 1985; Turiel, 1974). In most research in this area (reviewed by Walker, 1988), the relation between measures of moral development and experiences presumed to involve cognitive conflict of some kind has been investigated, although the data often have been correlational in nature, and the specific role of cognitive conflict often has been speculative. For simplicity, this discussion will be limited to studies bearing on the processes by which cognitive conflict presumably affects moral reasoning.

Most such studies have involved conflict induced by presenting subjects with a moral dilemma and exposing them to reasoning that involves both sides of the dilemma and is one or more Kohlbergian stages of moral development above their own (e.g., Tracy & Cross, 1973; Turiel, 1966; Walker, 1982). Such manipulations potentially involve conflict in two senses: Conflict exists (a) between the reasons favoring each side of the dilemma (e.g., in the case of Kohlberg's famous Heinz dilemma, the reasons why Heinz should steal a drug to save his wife vs. the reasons why he should not steal the drug) and (b) between the subjects' own developmental levels and the level of reasoning to which they are exposed. Although such manipulations have been found to be effective, it has not always been clear which type of conflict is effective or, indeed, if the results might be attributable instead to some form of imitative learning.

Perhaps the most systematic effort to tease apart the relevant factors to date has been that of Walker (1983), who assigned fifth through seventh graders to one of four conflict conditions: Children were exposed to two adults (a) who respectively defended each side of a moral dilemma with reasoning one stage higher than that of the children themselves, (b) who defended only that side of the dilemma favored by the individual subjects and who reasoned one stage higher than the subjects, (c) who defended only that side of the dilemma not favored by the subjects and who reasoned one stage higher than the subjects, or (d) who defended both sides of the dilemma with reasoning in the same stage as the subjects. Compared to no-treatment and no-conflict control groups (which did not differ from each other), all four of the treatment conditions were found to affect posttest moral reasoning scores positively. However, conditions (a) and (b) (which did not differ from each other) were more efficacious than conditions (c) and (d) (which also did not differ from each other). These results were interpreted as supportive of the efficacy of both sources of cognitive conflict: the conflict between different moral choices within one stage of reasoning and the conflict between reasoning pertaining to different stages. The fact that higher stage reasoning in defense of a choice opposite to that of the subject was effective suggests that equilibration resulting from cognitive conflict and not merely from social learning processes was at play, and the fact that same-stage pro-and-con reasoning was effective suggests that both symmetrical and asymmetrical conflict can lead to progress. The parallels with the research on conservation are manifest.

In other research, the relation between moral development and characteristics of interpersonal interactions involving moral issues has been explored. For example, Berkowitz and Gibbs (1983, 1985) distinguished two modes of dialogical moral discussion. The *representational* mode involved nontransformational references to the other person's statements or opinions (requests for feedback or for justifications, paraphrases, juxtaposition of positions), and the *operational* mode involved some kind of transformational references to the partner's contributions (clarifications, critiques, contradictions). Their basic finding was that improvement in moral reasoning was related to moral discussion in the operational, but not in the representational, mode. On the assumption that the operational mode involves more conflict, that finding is consistent with the hypothesis that the development of moral reasoning is fostered by cognitive conflict. A different conclusion was reached by Damon and Killen (1982), who reported that progress in moral reasoning was unrelated to conflict in children's discussions of a distributive justice situation. Instead, the children showing the most progress were those involved in the reciprocal acceptance of transforming interactions, a result that led Damon and Killen to conclude that the quality of interaction that is most effective in promoting moral development is a process of coconstruction and conciliation rather than conflict. In a study of the effects of group discussions on moral decisions by Berndt, McCartney, Caparulo, and Moore (1983–1984), children's decisions were found to be influenced by both the opinions and the reasons they were exposed to during the group discussions, whether those opinions and reasons were socially desirable or undesirable.

The foregoing studies were placed in perspective by Walker and Taylor (1991), who pointed out that most research on moral reasoning and interaction styles had followed the lead of Piaget (1932/1965) and Kohlberg (1969) in focusing on peer interactions. Instead, Walker and Taylor analyzed the interactions occurring among family members and found, in contrast to Berkowitz and Gibbs, that representational rather than operational interactions were related to progress in moral reasoning. Walker and Taylor speculated that operational interaction coming from parents might be experienced by their children as hostile criticism and that representational interaction might provide a kind of Socratic questioning more favorable to moral development within the parent–child relationship. Although that line of reasoning has not been pursued in the standard literature on sociocognitive conflict, a parallel can be found perhaps in Sigel's (1981, in press) research on parental "distancing strategies" – instructional strategies resembling Socratic inquiry that have the effect of drawing children's attention away from immediate perception and toward "distant" symbolic representations. Briefly, Sigel and his colleagues found that parents' use of such distancing strategies in interacting with their children was related to the development of children's representational competence, a result interpreted as an effect of the "discrepancies" (1981) or "conflicts" (in press) induced in children's minds by the strategies in question.

Another parallel between the research findings in the domains of cognitive and moral development, respectively, involves the question of how *social* the cognitive conflict must be in order to affect development. This question was studied by Roy and Howe (1990) in a study of the effects of different types of conflict on pre- to posttest changes in children's reasoning about legal transgressions. They found that children who had experienced individual cognitive conflict in the form of statements conflicting with their judgments progressed as much as children who had experienced sociocognitive conflict in the context of dyadic discussions relative to a no-conflict control group. Thus, Roy and Howe's results are consistent with those of some studies of cognitive development in which sociocognitive conflict proved to be no more beneficial than individual cognitive conflict (Emler & Valiant, 1982; Mackie, 1980), contrary to the results reported by Doise and Mugny (1979).

Other tasks

In at least two studies (Jahoda, 1981; Ng, 1983), progress in children's thinking about bank profit was produced by means of cognitive conflict induced through a form a Socratic questioning. For example, if children said that a man borrowing $100 would have to repay only $100 at the end of a year, they were asked where the bank would obtain money to pay its employees and to cover its expenses. Under the impact of such questioning, some children were observed to generate conceptions of interest during the course of the interview.

On three tasks drawn from Piaget's late works, Vincenzo and Kelly (1987) found that children working in triads progressed more across three sessions compared to children working alone. The three tasks were the tower of Hanoi problem (Piaget, 1974/1976, chap. 14), relative movements (Piaget, 1974/1980, chap. 15), and transfers from one collection to another (Piaget, 1974/1980, chap. 9). Consistent with the findings of Doise and Mugny (1984) on symmetrical sociocognitive conflict, children were found to progress even if they had interacted with children at their own level.

In at least one instance, however, such symmetrical conflict was found to result in regression rather than progression. Tudge (1989) compared children working alone on Siegler's (1981) balance beam problem with children who interacted with partners at either their own level, a lower level, or a higher level. In contrast to previous research, children interacting with same-level or lower-level partners were found to regress from pre- to posttest, relative to children working individually, and only children interacting with higher level partners were found to progress. This unique result was interpreted in terms of the trade-offs involved in Siegler's (1981) sequence of rules for predicting the behavior of the balance beam given certain configurations of weights placed at varying distances from the fulcrum. In brief, children who initially followed a rule that yielded indeterminate predictions for some weight–distance configurations frequently regressed to rules that always yielded definite predictions, even if those predictions were sometimes false. Tudge interpreted his findings as inconsistent with the hypothesis that sociocognitive conflict is generally beneficial for cognitive development.

An alternative interpretation is that the regressions observed by Tudge represented the initial, disequilibratory phase in a process of disequilibrium followed by reequilibration (see Langer, 1982). In other words, some time might pass between the disconfirmation of a given rule and the construction of a more equilibrated rule, and the interval might be filled with a temporary regression.

Interacting factors

Social factors

One way to address the question of the relative importance between intrapsychic cognitive conflict and sociocognitive conflict is through research on factors that appear to interact with sociocognitive conflict in affecting cognition. The idea is that interactions involving social factors reveal the essentially social character of sociocognitive conflict.

One such social factor is *socioeconomic status*. In the typical sociocognitive conflict paradigm, children from lower social class backgrounds have been found to score lower than middle-class children at pretest, but most of this difference is eliminated through the experience of sociocognitive conflict (Doise & Mugny, 1984; Perret-Clermont, 1980). Such results perhaps can be interpreted in the light of Sigel's (1981, in press) work on the effects of parental "distancing strategies" as described previously. Sigel and his colleagues found not only that parents' use of distancing strategies was related to the children's representational competence, but also that parents from different social class backgrounds differed in their use of such strategies and that social class differences in children's cognitive performance could be explained accordingly.

Such results are significant for several reasons. First, they provide relevant data that must be considered in any general theory of the effects of social inequality on cognitive development. Second, they suggest that sociocognitive conflict training might compensate in part for such effects once they have occurred. Third, they highlight the potential importance for cognitive-developmental psychology of social context in general. Although social class differences in children's cognitive development are quite as marked as age differences, the former have received considerably less attention than the latter (Schröder & Edelstein, 1991; Smith, 1991). As a result, an important dimension of cognitive development may have been overlooked.

A second social factor found to interact with the effects of cognitive conflict is *social marking*, defined as a correspondence between the relationship existing between social partners and the structure of the task in which they are engaged. For example, Doise et al. (1978; described in Doise & Mugny, 1984, chap. 5, exp. 4) provided children with feedback contradicting their nonconservation judgments under two conditions. In the social marking condition, the longer and shorter of two "bracelets" employed in the conservation-of-unequal-lengths task were assigned, respectively, to the adult experimenter and to the children themselves.

The distribution of bracelets was socially marked in this condition, because adults are typically of greater size than children. In the control condition, the bracelets were assigned instead to paper cylinders, likewise differing in size. The authors reasoned that sociocognitive conflict would be more salient in the socially marked condition and accordingly would result in more cognitive progress on the posttest. The results conformed to this hypothesis.

Subsequent research generally has supported the social marking hypothesis (De Paolis, Doise, & Mugny, 1987), although it is not clear whether the observed effects are best explained through a greater salience of social information, a redundancy between social and physical information, or some other factor. Gilly and Roux (1988) found that social marking improved performance on ordering tasks, whether or not such social marking was consistent with the logical structure of those tasks, and Girotto (1987) reported that children performed better on a spatial transformation task when an adult's model was inconsistent with a social norm than when it was consistent with the norm, whether or not the model was objectively correct. This curious result was explained with the hypothesis that the adult's violation of the social norm helped children to ignore the misleading effects of the adult model when the latter was incorrect.

A third potentially important social factor is the *form of reasoning* to which children are exposed in the interactions intended to evoke sociocognitive conflict. For example, Russell (1982b) reported that the ability of conservers to influence the judgments of their nonconserving interaction partners was a function of their relative ability to produce justifications for their judgments. Similarly, Bearison et al. (1986) found that only those verbal disagreements that were accompanied by explanations were related to improvement on spatial perspective problems. As described previously, explanations and performance were curvilinearly related, such that the greatest improvement occurred with an intermediate frequency of verbal conflicts with explanations.

The form of reasoning to which children have been exposed has also been indexed in terms of the cognitive level of the interaction partner. In general, interaction with a cognitively more advanced partner generally has been found to be more effective than interaction with partners of the same or lower cognitive level (Doise & Mugny, 1984, chap. 5; Russell et al., 1990). However, some authors have argued that a moderate discrepancy between levels might be more beneficial than a more extreme discrepancy. For example, Mugny and Doise (1978; also reported in Doise & Mugny, 1984, chap. 6) paired children at various levels in their ability to transform spatial relations. Children who showed a low level of ability to make such transformations at pretest showed more progress following a collaborative interaction session when paired with children of an intermediate level than when paired with another lower level child or with a child at an advanced level. This result apparently occurred because the intermediate partners gave more explanations than the advanced partners, who tended instead merely to issue instructions. Thus, the lower level children tended merely to give in to their advanced partners without experiencing the kind of sociocognitive conflict that might have led to cognitive progress. Consistent with these findings, Tudge (1989) found that only children exposed to higher level reasoning demonstrated progress on the balance beam problem. In contrast, Perret-Clermont (1980, chaps. 4 & 5) reported that conservation and the reproduction of geometric figures were facilitated through interaction even with a less advanced partner, and Weinstein and Bearison (1985) found that intermediate conservers progressed after interacting with nonconservers. These differences across studies can perhaps be explained as a function of the different tasks employed. As mentioned previously, the question of the optimal discrepancy between stage levels of persons engaged in moral discussion also has been a central issue in research on cognitive conflict as a stimulus to moral development. According to Walker's (1988) review, the research suggests that exposure to higher stage reasoning, whether it is one or more Kohlbergian stages higher, is sufficient to foster development of moral reasoning.

A final social factor interacting with effects of sociocognitive conflict is the interaction partner's degree of *social dominance*. In several studies, the possible effects of dominance relations in the interaction between conservers and nonconservers were controlled. In studies by Miller and Brownell (1975), Russell (1982b), and Silverman and Geiringer (1973), nonconservers tended to adopt the conservation responses of their conserving partners regardless of the relative dominance of the individuals involved. However, Russell et al. (1990) reported an interaction between nonconservers' adoption of their partners' conservation responses and the partners' relative dominance; the adoption of conservation responses was more frequent when the partner was socially dominant than otherwise. Social dominance was measured in those studies in terms of one partner's ability to prevail consistently in discussions involving either conservation itself (Silverman & Geiringer, 1973) or matters of preference or opinion unrelated to the conservation task (Miller & Brownwell, 1975; Russell, 1982b; Russell et al., 1990).

In summary, evidence exists that several aspects of children's social interactive context can affect the extent to which sociocognitive conflict facilitates cognitive development. However, such evidence does not provide a definitive answer to the question of whether cognitive conflict must be social in order to facilitate cognition. The fact that intrapsychic cognitive conflict also has been found effective suggests an alternative hypothesis: that sociocognitive conflict facilitates cognition only because it stimulates intrapsychic cognitive conflict to a greater or lesser degree. In this connection, it is significant that characteristics of children as individuals also have been found to mediate the effects of cognitive conflict.

Individual variables

Preeminent among such individual mediating variables have been children's age and cognitive-developmental level. One of the findings that stood out in the research of Inhelder et al. (1974) was that children's progress following various training procedures was highly dependent on their initial levels of competence: Children who were assessed at a transitional level of operational thinking were more likely to progress than children who were assessed as unambiguously preoperational. A similar effect has been reported for sociocognitive conflict: Ames and Murray (1982) found that the conservation performance of second graders improved more following social interaction with a peer than did the performance of first graders, and Perret-Clermont (1980, chap. 4) found nonconservers' performance on a conservation-of-number task to improve more following social interaction if they knew how to count than otherwise. As noted previously, one interpretation of such results is that the experience of sociocognitive conflict is likely to have little effect on children who do not yet comprehend contradiction as such (Lefebvre-Pinard, 1976). Piaget's (1974/1980) observation that preoperational children often affirmed contradictory statements in succession without recognizing the contradiction is relevant in this connection.

Little information on other individual variables mediating the effects of cognitive conflict exist. In a study of contradiction training and cognitive style, Overton, Byrnes, and O'Brien (1985) reported that a reflective cognitive style enhanced the effects of contradiction training for 12th graders, but not for 8th or 10th graders. Their interpretation of this finding was that a reflective cognitive style facilitates the expression of competence once the requisite cognitive structures have developed. Similar findings were reported by Shafrir and Pascual-Leone (1989) in a study of postfailure reflectivity; children who spontaneously tended to pay attention to their performance errors (i.e., the postfailure reflectives) apparently were better able to use that information in reevaluating and correcting their performance on a computer-based inference task than children who tended to ignore their errors (the postfailure impulsives). Such results suggest that individual differences exist in children's ability to benefit from experiences contradicting their expectations.

An epistemological paradox

The fact that children's developmental level appears to mediate the effects of cognitive conflict on cognition presents one with an epistemological paradox. On the one hand, cognitive conflict is believed to be in some sense necessary for cognitive development. On the other hand, children apparently do not fully benefit from cognitive conflict until they reach a level of development sufficient for comprehending the conflict itself. Clearly, cognitive conflict cannot be responsible for the development of the same capacity necessary to apprehend it. But then cognitive conflict would not be a necessary factor in development. The attempt to unravel this paradox provides some insight into the processes by which cognitive conflict may affect cognition.

It is easy to see that Russell's (1981b) argument for the "impossibility" of sociocognitive conflict is a variation on the same kind of epistemological paradox. According to Russell, the failure to comprehend the contradiction between conflicting nonconservation answers is an essential part of the inability to conserve (Russell et al., 1990, pp. 75–76); young children's tendency to center on one aspect of a situation to the exclusion of others prevents them both from attaining conservation and from grasping both sides of a contradiction. If carried to its logical conclusion, Russell's argument would negate equilibration as an explanation for development: If the same lack of competence results in both nonconservation and the egocentric inability to understand perspectives conflicting with one's own, then the confrontation with other perspectives could not be a factor that leads to conservation.

Resolving this paradox involves a reconsideration of the assumptions underlying the concepts in question. For example, one might question the assumption of Russell et al. (1990, p. 75) that lack of insight into the contradiction among possible nonconservation responses is "part and parcel" of nonconservation. Surely it is possible to recognize a contradiction as such without being able to resolve it immediately. Indeed, Piaget (1974/1980) described a transitional stage in the development of the understanding of contradiction in precisely this way. Thus, one must reject the notion that the understanding of contradiction among opposing nonconservation responses is tantamount to conservation. It is possible for children to understand the contradiction involved in stating both (a) that stick A is longer than stick B because it protrudes beyond B to the right and (b) that stick B is longer because it protrudes beyond A to the left, without thereby understanding that the two sticks are of equal lengths. The reverse would also seem to be the case: It is surely possible to understand that sticks A and B are of equal lengths without thereby seeing the potential contradiction involved in centering on the complementary protrusions of each stick beyond the other. In short, the understanding of contradiction would not appear to be "part and parcel" of conservation after all.

To be sure, this reply to Russell's (1981b) argument for the impossibility of sociocognitive conflict does not escape the epistemological paradox entirely. The apprehension of cognitive conflict may contribute to the development of conservation (or other cognitive competencies) once children are able to apprehend that conflict, but it cannot explain how children initially develop the capacity for apprehending that conflict. The latter development must result from some other factor besides equilibration. In this connection, Piaget's (1960) postulation of four major explanatory factors in development – maturation, the material environment, the social environment, and equilibration – becomes relevant. His argument was not that equilibration is the only significant factor in development, but that it is a significant factor in addition to the other three (Chapman, 1988, chap. 7).

Once one admits that multiple factors might exist that interact with one another in producing cognitive development, the epistemological paradox regarding cognitive conflict becomes more tractable. Nonequilibratory factors might be responsible for children's development to the point at which they can apprehend the contradictions characterizing a particular level of understanding, and the apprehension of those contradictions might then set in train an equilibratory process leading to a new level of understanding in which those contradictions are overcome. Thus, equilibration would interact with other factors in determining the course of development. This resolution of the epistemological paradox suggests the following problems for further research: (a) to describe more precisely what equilibration is and how it functions, (b) to identify the nonequilibratory factors relevant for development in particular domains, and (c) to explain how those factors interact with equilibration and with each other in the development of particular abilities.

Contradiction, centration, and conservation

This response to Russell's argument for the impossibility of sociocognitive conflict leaves untouched the questions with which we began, namely,

(a) to what extent cognitive conflict is necessary or sufficient for cognitive development and (b) in what degree social interaction is necessary for apprehending such conflict. We anticipate the conclusions of our argument by answering these questions as follows: (a) Cognitive conflict is neither necessary nor sufficient for cognitive development, but instead is a *facilitative* factor; (b) the cognitive conflict that facilitates cognitive development indeed has roots in social interaction, but not necessarily interaction with respect to the specific tasks that are facilitated.

We begin by examining the concept of cognitive conflict itself. So far, in this chapter, the term has been used very generally to include multifarious types of conflict, from mere impediments to cognitive activity at one extreme to logical contradictions at the other. However, most research on the effects of cognitive conflict has involved *contradictions*, understood in the most general sense as the simultaneous affirmation of contrary propositions. One can further distinguish contradictions between contrary *judgments* from contradictions between the reasons invoked to *justify* those judgments. In most of the research reviewed in this chapter, the second type of contradiction is the more relevant. In regard to the conservation of length, for example, the relevant contradiction is the simultaneous affirmation of contrary judgments with their associated justifications: (a) that stick A is longer than stick B because it protrudes beyond B at one end and (b) that stick B is longer than stick A because it protrudes beyond A at the other end.

The contradiction only arises because contrary propositions involving the asymmetrical relation "longer than" are simultaneously affirmed. The mere observation of A protruding beyond B at one end in no way contradicts the observation of B protruding beyond A at the the other end. These observations conflict only when they are taken as justifications for contrary affirmations of relative length. The concept of centration, with which the Piagetian approach to cognitive conflict generally has been framed, obscures the important distinction between merely observing some feature of the world and affirming some proposition about it.

Moreover, observations as such function as valid justifications for affirmations about the world only within a certain operational context. The observation that stick A protrudes beyond stick B at one end provides a valid justification for the judgment that A is longer than B only if the operation of aligning the opposite ends of the two sticks has first been carried out. In this view, young children's nonconservation involves a neglect of the operational context in which their observations could serve as valid justifications. When the experimenter displaces stick B toward the right in the conservation-of-length task, children's attention typically is drawn to the protrusion of stick B beyond stick A in the direction that B was displaced. Nonconservers take this protrusion as evidence for the judgment that B is "longer than" A, neglecting (at least momentarily) the fact that such a protrusion is evidence for relative length judgments only if the opposite ends of the sticks have been aligned. The displacement of stick B beyond stick A thus serves as a "misleading cue" of the kind that frequently characterizes Piagetian tasks in general (Gold, 1987; Pascual-Leone, 1987); it draws children's attention toward some particularly salient aspect of the situation and away from some other aspect that is essential for fully understanding the problem.

This model of nonconservation provides a context for understanding how the experience of contradiction can facilitate development. Having one's initial judgment and its associated justification (e.g., that B is longer than A because it protrudes beyond A in one direction) confronted with a contradictory judgment and justification (that A is longer than B because it protrudes beyond B in the opposite direction) can facilitate conservation insofar as it helps children overcome the pull of the misleading cue. In effect, the contradiction calls children's attention to the nonalignment of the sticks at the opposite end and ultimately to the fact that the operational precondition for justifying a length judgment with the protrusion of B beyond A has not been fulfilled.

Confronted with such a contradiction, children might react in several possible ways: (a) They might affirm conflicting judgments in turn without noticing the contradiction at all, as in Piaget's (1975/1985) "alpha reaction"; (b) they might notice the contradiction without resolving it, concluding, for example, that "stick A is longer for you, and B is longer for me" (Russell, 1982a, p. 83); or (c) the contradiction might lead to conservation through a *discrediting* of the misleading cue used to justify a judgment of nonconservation. The second of these three possibilities implies that recognition of the relevant contradiction is not a sufficient condition for conservation. As pointed out previously, one must evoke other factors in development besides cognitive conflict to explain how children develop the ability to apprehend that conflict to begin with. For example, the narrowness of young children's attention might prevent them from apprehending both aspects of the contradiction at the same time (Chapman, 1990).

Besides arguing that the experience of contradiction is not sufficient for conservation, we also suggest that it is also not necessary. As described in the preceding paragraphs, nonconservation occurs when children base their judgments of relative length on comparisons between sticks at only one end. The experience of having such nonconservation judgments contradicted can facilitate the development of conservation to the extent that it leads children to compare the sticks at both ends simultaneously. But the experience of contradiction is not the only factor that might lead them to do so. It is at least possible that other developmental factors – the broadening of attention with age or greater expertise in comparing lengths – might lead children to consider both ends to begin with. In that case, children could show conservation without ever having had their conservation judgments explicitly contradicted. For such children, contradiction in the specific context of the conservation problem would not be a necessary condition for the development of conservation.

In summary, specific experiences of contradiction are neither necessary nor sufficient for conservation, but they can facilitate conservation by counteracting misleading cues inhering in the task. Such contradiction may or may not occur in the context of real, interpersonal interaction; to the extent that children develop the capacity for what Piaget (1954/1973, p. 121) called "the precorrection of errors" – the ability to anticipate possible inconsistencies and to correct them in advance – they could develop conservation eventually whether or not anyone ever contradicted their nonconserving judgments. However, for children susceptible to the misleading cues in the conservation problem, the experience of having a nonconserving judgment contradicted by another person might counteract the misleading cue and thereby facilitate the development of conservation. An obvious research problem suggested by this approach is the question of what makes the perceptual cues afforded by particular tasks more or less misleading to children at different points in their development.

New directions in theory and research

The evidence reviewed in this chapter leads us to the conclusion that the experience of cognitive conflict in the form of contradictions can facilitate cognitive development. However, questions remain about how such facilitation actually occurs. As described in the preceding section, we suggest that the experience of contradiction serves, in effect, to counteract premature closure by calling children's attention to possibilities that they otherwise might have overlooked. This interpretation is consistent with both the Vygotskian notion of the social origins of mind and with Piagetian concepts of equilibratory processes in development. In agreement with Vygotsky (1934/1986), it accords an essential place for communicative competence in the development of thought. In agreement with Piaget (e.g., 1975/1985), it acknowledges the fundamental role of operations and their intercoordination in the same process. The capacity for comprehending contradictory propositions develops in the context of communication, and the construction of models of reality that can reconcile contrary propositions based on different perspectives occurs through the coordination of operations.

We believe as well that the evidence reviewed in this chapter suggests several new directions for research. As described previously, the kind of discourse experienced by subjects has been found to affect subsequent cognition in a number of studies. The major problem with such research so far is that it lacks a unifying framework. We would suggest that one possible framework is argumentation theory: the study of *argumentation* as a specific form of discourse, characterized by attempts to justify or refute opinions (Van Eemeren, Grootendorst, & Kruiger, 1984). So defined, argumentation must be distinguished from mere quarrels as expressions of disagreement. To the extent that persons engage in argumentation, they do not merely express their disagreements, but also cooperate in discussing them. Nor is argumentation synonymous with conflict resolution. Although one goal of argumentation might be the resolution of disagreements, another might be a dialectical search for truth, whether or not agreement is attained.

The usefulness of argumentation theory can be seen in interpreting the results of studies in which the discourse of the participants was analyzed. For example, both Russell (1982b) and Bearison et al. (1986) reported that exposure only to conflicting justifications, and not merely to conflicting judgments, appeared to be related to cognitive performance. Similarly, the findings of Berkowitz and Gibbs (1983, 1985) and Damon and Killen (1982) to the effect that transactive, coconstructive argumentation was especially effective in fostering the development of moral reasoning might be interpreted in the same light. Finally, all the research regarding the potential significance of the cognitive- or moral-developmental level of the interaction partner might benefit from more fine-grained analyses of the forms of argumentation employed in the respective interactions. Framing research on the effects of sociocognitive conflict in terms of argumentation theory has the further advantage that it links such research with studies on the structure and development of children's arguments (e.g., Berkowitz, Oser, & Althof, 1987; Corsaro & Rizzo, 1990; Dorval & Gundy, 1990; Garvey, 1984, chap. 5; Hartup & Laursen, in press; O'Keefe & Benoit, 1982; Piaget, 1923/1955; Shantz, 1987). Such research could provide information on the forms of argument that might be effective in promoting cognitive development, under the assumption that children's reasoning develops in part through the interiorization of argumentation (Chapman, in press-b).

This is not to say that argumentation alone is sufficient for the development of the kinds of "logical" thinking characteristic of the concrete-operational tasks featured in studies of sociocognitive conflict. We would agree with Piaget on the importance of operativity in the development of such thinking, but would add that operative and communicative competencies are perhaps more intimately related than he realized. As reported by Schmid-Schönbein (1989), linguistic representation appears to play a role in the interiorization of action, and as argued in this chapter, operations may be implicated in the understanding of the logical concepts typically involved in concrete-operational tasks. Such considerations suggest that the effects of sociocognitive conflict can be understood only in the context of the functional relation between operative and communicative competencies (Chapman, 1991).

References

Ames, G. J., & Murray, F. B. (1982). When two wrongs make a right: Promoting cognitive change by social conflict. *Developmental Psychology, 18,* 894–897.

Azmitia, M. (1988). Peer interaction and problem solving: When are two heads better than one? *Child Development, 59,* 87–96.

Bearison, D. J., Magzamen, S., & Filardo, E. K. (1986). Socio-cognitive conflict and cognitive growth in young children. *Merrill-Palmer Quarterly, 32,* 51–72.

Berkowitz, M. W., & Gibbs, J. C. (1983). Measuring the developmental features of moral discussion. *Merrill-Palmer Quarterly, 29,* 399–410.

Berkowitz, M. W., & Gibbs, J. C. (1985). The process of moral conflict resolution and moral development. In M. W. Berkowitz (Ed.), *Peer conflict and psychological growth.* San Francisco: Jossey-Bass.

Berkowitz, M. W., Oser, F., & Althof, W. (1987). The development of sociomoral discourse. In W. K. Kurtines & J. L. Gewirtz (Eds.), *Moral development through social interaction.* New York: Wiley.

Berlyne, D. E. (1960). *Conflict, arousal, and curiosity.* New York: McGraw-Hill.

Berndt, T. J., McCartney, K., Caparulo, B. K., & Moore, A. M. (1983–1984). The effects of group discussions on children's moral decisions. *Social Cognition, 2,* 343–359.

Bruner, J. S., Olver, R. R., & Greenfield, P. M. (1966). *Studies in cognitive growth.* New York: Wiley.

Cantor, G. N. (1983). Conflict, learning, and Piaget: Comments on Zimmerman and Blom's "Toward an empirical test of the role of cognitive conflict in learning." *Developmental Review, 3,* 39–53.

Chapman, M. (1986). The structure of exchange: Piaget's sociological theory. *Human Development, 29,* 181–194.

Chapman, M. (1988). *Constructive evolution: Origins and development of Piaget's thought.* Cambridge: Cambridge University Press.

Chapman, M. (1990). Cognitive development and the growth of capacity: Issues in neo-Piagetian theory. In J. T. Enns (Ed.), *The development of attention: Research and theory.* Amsterdam: Elsevier.

Chapman, M. (1991). The epistemic triangle: Operative and communicative components of cognitive competence. In M. Chandler & M. Chapman (Eds.), *Criteria for competence: Controversies in the conceptualization and assessment of children's abilities.* Hillsdale, NJ: Erlbaum.

Chapman, M. (in press-a). Equilibration and the dialectics of organization. In H. Beilin & P. Pufall (Eds.). *Piaget in retrospect and prospect*. Hillsdale, NJ: Erlbaum.

Chapman, M. (in press-b). Everyday reasoning and the revision of belief. In J. Puckett & H. W. Reese (Eds.), *Mechanisms of everyday cognition*. Hillsdale, NJ: Erlbaum.

Corsaro, W. A., & Rizzo, T. A. (1990). Disputes in the peer culture of American and Italian nursery-school children. In A. D. Grimshaw (Ed.), *Conflict talk: Sociolinguistic investigations of arguments in conversations*. Cambridge: Cambridge University Press.

Damon, W., & Killen, M. (1982). Peer interaction and the process of change in children's moral reasoning. *Merrill-Palmer Quarterly, 28*, 347–367.

De Paolis, P., Doise, W., & Mugny, G. (1987). Social markings in cognitive operations. In W. Doise & S. Moscovici (Eds.), *Current issues in European social psychology* (Vol. 2). Cambridge: Cambridge University Press.

Dewey, J. (1933). *How we think*. Lexington, MA: Heath. (Original work published 1910)

Doise, W., Dionnet, S., & Mugny, G. (1978). Conflit sociocognitif, marquage social et développement cognitif [Sociocognitive conflict, social marking, and cognitive development]. *Cahiers de Psychologie, 21*, 231–245.

Doise, W., & Mugny, G. (1979). Individual and collective conflicts of centrations in cognitive development. *European Journal of Psychology, 9*, 105–108.

Doise, W., & Mugny, G. (1984). *The social development of the intellect*. Oxford: Pergamon Press.

Dorval, B., & Gundy, F. (1990). The development of arguing in discussions among peers. *Merrill-Palmer Quarterly, 36*, 389–409.

Emler, N., & Valiant, G. L. (1982). Social interaction and cognitive conflict in the development of spatial coordination skills. *British Journal of Psychology, 73*, 295–303.

Festinger, L. (1957). *A theory of cognitive dissonance*. Stanford, CA: Stanford University Press.

Freud, S. (1953). The psychopathology of everyday life. In J. Strachey (Ed.), *The standard edition of the complete psychological works of Sigmund Freud* (Vol. 6). London: Hogarth Press. (Original work published 1901)

Garvey, C. (1984). *Children's talk*. Cambridge, MA: Harvard University Press.

Gilly, M., & Roux, J.-P. (1988). Social marking in ordering tasks: Effects and action mechanisms. *European Journal of Social Psychology, 18*, 251–266.

Girotto, V. (1987). Social marking, socio-cognitive conflict and cognitive development. *European Journal of Social Psychology, 17*, 171–186.

Gold, R. (1987). *The description of cognitive development: Three Piagetian themes*. Oxford: Oxford University Press.

Guthrie, E. R. (1938). *The psychology of human conflict*. New York: Harper.

Hamilton, E., & Cairns, H. (Eds.). (1961). *The collected dialogues of Plato*. New York: Pantheon.

Hartup, W. W., & Laursen, B. (in press). Conflict and context in peer relations. In C. Hart (Ed.), *Children on playgrounds: Research perspectives and applications*. Ithaca: SUNY Press.

Inhelder, B., Sinclair, H., & Bovet, M. (1974). *Learning and the development of cognition*. Cambridge, MA: Harvard University Press.

Jahoda, G. (1981). The development of thinking about economic institutions: The bank. *Cahiers de Psychologie, 1*, 55–73.

Janet, P. M. F. (1925). *Psychological healing* (2 Vols.). New York: Macmillan.

Kohlberg, L. (1969). Stage and sequence: The cognitive developmental approach to socialization. In D. A. Goslin (Ed.), *Handbook of socialization theory and research*. Chicago: Rand McNally.

Köhler, W. (1925). *The mentality of apes* (2d ed.). New York: Harcourt, Brace. (Original work published 1917)

Langer, J. (1982). Dialectics of development. In T. G. Bower (Ed.), *Regressions in mental development: Basic phenomena and theories*. Hillsdale, NJ: Erlbaum.

Lefebvre, M., & Pinard, A. (1974). Influence du niveau initial de sensibilité au conflit sur l'apprentissage de la conservation des quantités par une methode de conflit cognitif [Influence of the initial level of sensitivity to conflict on learning conservation of quantity through a method of cognitive conflict]. *Psychological Journal of Behavioural Science/ Revue Canadienne des Sciences du Comportment, 6*, 398–413.

Lefebvre-Pinard, M. (1976). Les expériences de Genève sur l'apprentissage: Un dossier peu convaincant (même pour un Piagetian) [The Genevan experiments on learning: A rather unconvincing document (even for a Piagetian)]. *Canadian Psychological Review, 17*, 103–109.

Lewin, K. (1931). Environmental forces in child behavior and development. In C. Murchison (Ed.), *A handbook of child psychology*. Worcester, MA: Clark University Press.

Luria, A. R. (1932). *The nature of human conflicts*. New York: Liveright.

Mackie, D. (1980). A cross-cultural study of intra-individual and interindividual conflicts of centrations. *European Journal of Social Psychology, 10*, 313–318.

McBride, M. L. (1991, April). *How social must socio-cognitive conflict be? Effects of fictive conflict on cognitive development*. Poster presented at the meeting of the Society of Research in Child Development, Seattle.

Mead, G. H. (1962). *Mind, self, and society*. Chicago: University of Chicago Press. (Original work published 1934)

Miller, N. E. (1944). Experimental studies of conflict. In J. McV. Hunt (Ed.), *Personality and the behavior disorders* (Vol. 1). New York: Ronald Press.

Miller, S. A., & Brownell, C. A. (1975). Peers, persuasion and Piaget: Dyadic interaction between conservers and nonconservers. *Child Development, 46*, 992–997.

Mischel, T. (1971). Piaget: Cognitive conflict and the motivation of thought. In T. Mischel (Ed.), *Cognitive development and epistemology*. New York: Academic Press.

Morf, A., Smedslund, J., Vinh Bang, & Wohlwill, J. F. (1959). *L'apprentissage des structures logiques* [The learning of logical structures]. Paris: Presses Universitaires de France.

Mugny, G., & Doise, W. (1978). Sociocognitive conflict and structuration of individual and collective performances. *European Journal of Social Psychology, 8*, 181–192.

Mugny, G., Doise, W., & Perret-Clermont, A.-N. (1975–1976). Conflit de centrations et progrès cognitif [Conflict of centrations and cognitive progress]. *Bulletin de Psychologie, 29*, 199–204.

Murray, J. B. (1972). Acquisition of conservation through social interaction. *Developmental Psychology, 6*, 1–6.

Murray, J. B. (1983). Equilibration as cognitive conflict. *Developmental Review, 3*, 54–61.

Ng, S. H. (1983). Children's ideas about the bank and shop profit: Developmental stages and the influence of cognitive contrasts and conflict. *Journal of Economic Psychology, 4*, 209–221.

O'Keefe, B. J., & Benoit, P. (1982). Children's arguments. In J. R. Cox & C. A. Willard (Eds.), *Advances in argumentation theory and research*. Carbondale: Southern Illinois University Press.

Overton, W., Byrnes, J. P., & O'Brien, D. P. (1985). Developmental and individual differences in conditional reasoning: The role of contradiction training and cognitive style. *Developmental Psychology, 21*, 692–701.

Pascual-Leone, J. (1987). Organismic processes for neo-Piagetian theories: A dialectic causal account of cognitive development. *International Journal of Psychology, 22*, 531–570.

Perret-Clermont, A.-N. (1980). *Social interaction and cognitive development in children*. New York: Academic Press.

Peterson, C. C., & Peterson, J. L. (1990). Sociocognitive conflict and spatial perspective-taking in deaf children. *Journal of Applied Developmental Psychology, 11*, 267–281.

Piaget, J. (1928). *Judgment and reasoning in the child.* London: Routledge & Kegan Paul. (Original work published 1924)

Piaget, J. (1955). *The language and thought of the child.* Cleveland: Meridian. (Original work published 1923)

Piaget, J. (1957). Logique et équilibre dans les comportments du sujet [Logic and equilibrium in the conduct of the subject]. In L. Apostel, B. Mandelbrot, & J. Piaget (Eds.), *Logique et équilibre.* Paris: Presses Universitaires de France.

Piaget, J. (1959a). Apprentissage et connaissance: Premiére partie [Learning and knowledge: Part 1]. In P. Gréco & J. Piaget (Eds.), *Apprentissage et connaissance.* Paris: Presses Universitaires de France.

Piaget, J. (1959b). Apprentissage et connaissance: Seconde partie [Learning and knowledge: Part 2]. In M. Goustard, P. Gréco, B. Matalon, & J. Piaget [Eds.), *La logique des apprentissages.* Paris: Presses Universitaires de France.

Piaget, J. (1960). The general problems of the psychobiological development of the child. In J. M. Tanner & B. Inhelder (Eds.), *Discussions on child development* (Vol. 4). London: Tavistock.

Piaget, J. (1965). *The moral judgment of the child.* New York: Free Press. (Original work published 1932)

Piaget, J. (1973). Language and intellectual operations. In J. Piaget (Ed.), *The child and reality.* New York: Grossman. (Original work published 1954)

Piaget, J. (1976). *The grasp of consciousness.* Cambridge, MA: Harvard University Press. (Original work published 1974)

Piaget, J. (1977). *Études sociologiques* [Sociological studies] (3d ed.). Geneva: Librarie Droz. (Original work published 1965)

Piaget, J. (1980). *Experiments in contradiction.* Chicago: University of Chicago Press. (Original work published 1974)

Piaget, J. (1985). *The equilibration of cognitive structures.* Chicago: University of Chicago Press. (Original work published 1975)

Riegel, K. F. (1976). The dialectics of human development. *American Psychologist, 31*, 689–700.

Rosenthal, T. L., & Zimmerman, B. J. (1972). Modeling by exemplification and interaction in training conservation. *Developmental Psychology, 6*, 392–401.

Roy, A. W. N., & Howe, C. J. (1990). Effects of cognitive conflict, socio-cognitive conflict and imitation on children's socio-legal thinking. *European Journal of Social Psychology, 20*, 241–252.

Russell, J. (1981a). Dyadic interaction in a logical problem requiring inclusion ability. *Child Development, 52*, 1322–1325.

Russell, J. (1981b). Why socio-cognitive conflict may be impossible: The status of egocentric errors in the dyadic performance of a spatial task. *Educational Psychology, 1*, 159–169.

Russell, J. (1982a). Propositional attitudes. In M. Beveridge (Ed.), *Children thinking through language.* London: Arnold.

Russell, J. (1982b). Cognitive conflict, transmission, and justification: Conservation attainment through dyadic interaction. *Journal of Genetic Psychology, 140*, 283–97.

Russell, J., & Haworth, H. M. (1986). Answer preference and answer conflict in children's completions of concrete operation stories. *Educational Psychology, 6*, 299–311.

Russell, J., & Haworth, H. M. (1988). Appearance versus reality in dyadic interaction: Evidence for a lingering phenomenism. *International Journal of Behavioural Development, 11*, 155–170.

Russell, J., Mills, I., & Reiff-Musgrove, P. (1990). The role of symmetrical and asymmetrical social conflict in cognitive change. *Journal of Experimental Child Psychology*, *49*, 58–78.

Schmid-Schönbein, C. (1989). *Durch Handeln zum Denken* [Through action to thought]. Munich: Profil.

Schröder, E., & Edelstein, W. (1991). Intrinsic and external constraints on the development of cognitive competence. In M. Chandler & M. Chapman (Eds.), *Criteria for competence: Controversies in the conceptualization and assessment of children's abilities*. Hillsdale, NJ: Erlbaum.

Shafrir, U., & Pascual-Leone, J. (1989, April). *Post-failure reflectivity/impulsivity and spontaneous attention to errors*. Paper presented at the meeting of the Society for Research in Child Development, Kansas City, MO.

Shantz, C. U. (1987). Conflicts between children. *Child Development*, *58*, 283–305.

Siegler, R. S. (1981). Developmental sequences within and between concepts. *Monographs of the Society for Research in Child Development*, *46*(2, Serial No. 189).

Sigel, I. E. (1981). Social experience in the development of representational thought: Distancing theory. In I. E. Sigel, D. M. Brodzinsky, & R. N. Golinkoff (Eds.), *New directions in Piagetian theory and practice*. Hillsdale, NJ: Erlbaum.

Sigel, I. E. (in press). The centrality of a distancing model for the development of representational competence. In R. R. Cocking & K. A. Renninger (Eds.), *The development and meaning of psychological distance*. Hillsdale, NJ: Erlbaum.

Silverman, I. W., & Geiringer, E. (1973). Dyadic interaction and conservation induction: A test of Piaget's equilibration model. *Child Development*, *44*, 815–820.

Silverman, I. W., & Stone, J. (1972). Modifying cognitive functioning through participation in a problem-solving group. *Journal of Educational Psychology*, *63*, 603–608.

Smedslund, J. (1966). Les origins social de la décentration [The social origins of decentration]. In F. Bresson & M. de Montmollin (Eds.). *Psychologie et épistémologie génétiques*. Paris: Dunod.

Smith, L. (1991). Age, ability and intellectual development. In M. Chandler & M. Chapman (Eds.), *Criteria for competence: Controversies in the conceptualization and assessment of children's abilities*. Hillsdale, NJ: Erlbaum.

Tolman, C. (1981). The metaphysic of relations in Klaus Riegel's 'dialectics' of human development. *Human Development*, *24*, 33–51.

Tracy, J. J., & Cross, H. J. (1973). Antecedents of shift in moral judgment. *Journal of Personality and Social Psychology*, *26*, 238–44.

Tudge, J. (1989). When collaboration leads to regression: Some negative consequences of socio-cognitive conflict. *European Journal of Social Psychology*, *19*, 123–138.

Turiel, E. (1966). An experimental test of the sequentiality of developmental stages in the child's moral judgments. *Journal of Personality and Social Psychology*, *3*, 611–618.

Turiel, E. (1974). Conflict and transition in adolescent moral development. *Child Development*, *45*, 14–29.

Van Eemeren, F. H., Grootendorst, R., & Kruiger, T. (1984). *The study of argumentation*. New York: Irvington.

Vincenzo, J. P., & Kelly, F. J. (1987). Perturbations and compensations in social cognitive conflict: A functional analysis of cognitive development. *Psychological Reports*, *61*, 547–556.

Vygotsky, L. (1986). *Thought and language* (rev. ed.). Cambridge, MA: MIT Press. (Original work published 1934)

Walker L. J. (1982). The sequentiality of Kohlberg's stages of moral development. *Child Development*, *53*, 1330–1336.

Walker, L. J. (1983). Sources of cognitive conflict for stage transition in moral development. *Developmental Psychology*, *19*, 103–110.

Walker, L. J. (1988). The development of moral reasoning. *Annals of Child Development, 5,* 33–78.

Walker, L. J., & Taylor, J. H. (1991). Family interactions and the development of moral reasoning. *Child Development, 62,* 264–283.

Weinstein, B. D., & Bearison, D. J. (1985). Social interaction, social observation, and cognitive development in young children. *European Journal of Social psychology, 15,* 333–343.

Zimmerman, B. J., & Blom, D. E. (1983a). Toward an empirical test of the role of cognitive conflict in learning. *Developmental Review, 3,* 18–38.

Zimmerman, B. J., & Blom, D. E. (1983b). On resolving conflicting views of cognitive conflict. *Developmental Review, 3,* 62–72.

3   Conflict and the development of social understanding

Judy Dunn and Cheryl Slomkowski

The idea that social conflict plays a special role in the development of children's understanding of other people, of themselves, and of their social world more generally is taken up in a number of different theoretical accounts of development in childhood (e.g., Erikson, 1959; Piaget, 1932/ 1965; Sullivan, 1953). In this chapter, this idea is examined in the context of two general questions. First, how does the study of children in conflict with their mothers, siblings, friends, and peers illuminate the nature of their social understanding – specifically their grasp of others' feelings and intentions and how these can be influenced, their understanding of social-moral rules, and their developing sense of self and of interpersonal relations? In the first main section we consider this question, initially in light of research on early childhood, then in relation to the developmental changes in social understanding revealed by studies of conflict in older children. In the second main section, a second general question is examined: Does the experience of conflict and dispute foster the development of these capabilities? If so, what aspects of conflict might be important? And do we have grounds for assuming that patterns of both normative development and individual differences in social understanding are influenced by the experience of social conflict?

Conflict and the nature of social understanding

Two broadly differing approaches to the study of the nature of children's understanding of their social world can be distinguished. On the one hand, we have studies that focus on children as reflective observers/commentators by presenting them with hypothetical social situations to consider that are designed to reveal distinctions or differences in their conceptual development. On the other hand, there is research that focuses on children's

This chapter was written while the first author was supported in part by grants from NICHD (HD-23158) and NSF (BNS-8806589).

behavior and conversation in real-life situations or on their responses to questions about their own relationships; inferences are made from observations of that behavior about the nature of their understanding. The distinction between these approaches is what Flavell and Wohlwill (1969) characterized as the difference between a "formal analysis" of children's developing concepts, in which the aim is to describe children's developing understanding in an ordinal developmental scale, and a "functional analysis," in which the level of understanding that is reflected in children's daily life is of relevance. Within this latter approach, studies of conflict have proved particularly illuminating. Children's arguments with their parents, siblings, and peers give us an especially enlightening window on their understanding of the feelings and intentions of others, of categories of interpersonal relations such as friendship and authority, and of the social regulations that establish and maintain such relations. The study of conflict behavior can help us to understand children at any stage of development – in the preschool years, middle childhood, or adolescence; to illustrate, we will consider first the evidence from early childhood and will begin by drawing on data from a series of naturalistic studies of children with their mothers and siblings (Dunn, 1988).

Conflict in early childhood

Within the family, children begin to confront their parents and siblings with increasing frequency and increasing emotion during the second year. For example, these conflicts between children and their mothers, which extended beyond simple prohibitions or refusals, doubled in frequency between ages 18 and 24 months in one recent study (Dunn & Munn, 1987), and Goodenough's (1931) classic study showed angry outbursts doubled in frequency between ages 6 and 18 months. During the third and fourth years, such confrontations become increasingly verbal. The significance of this opposition to others has been given, of course, a central place in some psychoanalytic accounts of development. Thus, Spitz (1957) comments on the second-year confrontations with the mother:

The acquisition of the "No" is the indicator of a new level of autonomy, of the awareness of the "other" and of the awareness of the self; it is the beginning of the restructuring of mentation on the higher level of complexity; it initiates an extensive ego development, in the framework of which the dominance of the reality principle over the pleasure principle becomes increasingly established. (p. 129)

Spitz's emphasis on the developmental significance of opposition to others is well in tune with recent interest in children's developing sense of autonomy during the second and third years, yet it is interesting to note that, in the past 20 years, the great number of studies on parent–child conflict conducted have chiefly focused on *compliance* to parental demands, not on the significance of children's increasing assertion of control (Maccoby & Martin, 1983). That is, rather than examining conflict as a context in which both mother and child influence one another, and in which children's increasing self-assertion reflects a positive developmental change, the attention was on parental influence as a matter of socialization. The shift toward seeing parent–child conflict as a dyadic matter reflects a major change in our perspective on parent–child relations, from a socialization framework to a relationships framework.

In recent observational studies of children's behavior in conflict with family members during the toddler and preschool years, one theme stands out, a theme that is echoed in the studies of preschool children in dispute with their peers and friends. It is the growing understanding of their social world that is evident in the children's behavior as shown, strikingly, in four domains: in their understanding of the feelings and intentions of others, of the social rules of the children's worlds, in their increasing grasp of social strategies, and of categories of both interpersonal relations and personal identity.

Understanding feelings, intentions, and social rules. One of the earliest signs of the growth of children's grasp of others' feeling states evident during conflict is their teasing behavior (often nonverbal, in the second year) that reveals some grasp of what will annoy or upset another. This is frequently seen in the course of conflict with a sibling. As early as age 16–18 months, the following teasing acts were observed in one of our studies in Cambridge: removing the sibling's comfort object in the course of a fight, leaving a fight in order to go and destroy a cherished possession of the sibling, holding a desired object just out of reach of the sibling, pulling the sibling's thumb (sucked in moments of stress) out of his or her mouth during a dispute, and pushing a toy spider at a sibling (following the mother's comment that the sibling was afraid of spiders). Such acts became more frequent, more elaborate, and more verbal during the course of the second and third year; 36 of the 40 children we studied were observed to tease by age 24 months (Dunn, 1988).

Once children can talk, they begin to refer to feelings – their own and other people's – in justifying their own behavior in conflict or in attempting to excuse themselves. In the example that follows, the 28-month-old, in a dispute with his older brother, attempts to "sort him out" (physically subdue him) in a fight using boxing gloves, with his father's encouragement. As he gets the worst of the fight, he uses the excuse of a headache to leave the battlefield and complains that his brother has hurt him:

1. Child and sibling are in conflict.
Father to child: Sort him out.
Sibling to child: Oh no!
Child to sibling: Len! (hits him).
Sibling to child: Oh no!
Child to sibling: Biff him now (hits him again).
Child to mother: Hitting it. Mum look. Do Len fight. Enough. Got headache (takes boxing gloves off). Len hurt me. Len hurt me. He biff me.

Accusing the sibling of causing hurt, reporting such hurt to the parent, and blaming the sibling for hurting another are all common occurrences in the third year. Such accusations reflect not only an increasingly articulate grasp of the causes and consequences of feeling states, but also the children's understanding that hurting others is a transgression of acceptable behavior.

It is on this matter of children's grasp of social rules that naturalistic study of conflicts has proved particularly interesting. The justifications and excuses children give during family conflict, in attempts to get out of trouble, to redirect parental blame to a sibling, or to gain their own ends provide a remarkably rich source of data on their understanding of social rules. In disputes with both mother and sibling, the rules most commonly referred to, after the issue of the child's own feelings or needs, were rules of possession and sharing, or taking turns, and of damage to material goods (Dunn & Munn, 1987). Their attempts to enlist adult help in conflicts with siblings also highlights their growing grasp of what is sanctioned behavior within the family, and what is not. For example, the studies we conducted in Cambridge showed that there was a notable difference in the probability of appealing to a parent for help, depending on who had initiated aggression or teasing. In 66% of sibling conflicts in which the older sibling had been the initial aggressor, the younger siblings appealed to their mothers for help. In contrast, in only 3% of the incidents in which they themselves had acted in this way did they appeal for help (Dunn & Munn, 1985). The differences in their attempts to get adult aid in the face of their own or another's breach demonstrate in children as young as 18–24 months both an anticipation of how the parent is likely to behave and a practical grasp of what is acceptable behavior.

Three features of children's use of justifications and excuses in these family conflicts deserve further comment. First, by the third year children understand that rules can be questioned and applied differently to separate categories of persons. This appreciation that rules apply differently to babies, to the sick or fatigued, or to those who are only pretending is used as a weapon in the armory that is brought to bear in arguments by children who are not yet 3 years old. Second, by age 36 months children understand that rules concerning, for instance, positive justice or harm to others, can be applied with reference to the rights, needs, or feelings of others yet also in the interests of self. In the example that follows, the 36-month-old child attempted to keep his older sister Chrissie from joining the game of soccer that he was playing with his mother, with an insistence that his sister was taking his mother's turn:

> 2. *Child and mother are playing with soccer ball. Sibling attempts to join game by kicking ball when it comes near her.*
> Child to sibling: No! It's Mummy's go again. No! It was Mummy's go again.
> Mother to child: Chrissie did it for me.
> Child: I'll put this ball away. I'm going to put it away if Chrissie's going to spoil it for Mummy.

Third, although the majority of children's justifications and excuses referred to their own wishes and needs or rules of positive justice, on occasion a number of other justifications or excuses were also made that have special interest for the developmentalist. Excuses of intent (claims such as "I don't mean to," "All I'm trying to do is . . . ," "He [the sibling] did mean to do it!") were occasionally made by children of age 36 months and younger. Now, although as adults we see as crucial the distinction between acts intended to harm other people and those that are accidental, this is a distinction that Piaget believed children make relatively late. He commented that there is "some reason to doubt whether a child of 6–7 could really distinguish an involuntary error from an intentional lie . . . the distinction is, at the best, in the process of formation" (1932/1965, p. 145). In the context of family conflict and real life disputes in a preschool setting (Schulz, 1980), it appears that such distinctions are made much earlier, a point to which we will return.

Children are not only directly involved in conflicts with others; they also witness arguments and confrontation between others, both at home and in preschool settings. Studies of their reactions to such disputes reveal how salient such conflicts are to young children: It is relatively rare for children to ignore them. Their reactions, moreover, provide us with more evidence concerning the children's grasp of the emotions expressed by the antagonists and the topic of the disagreement. For example, to mother–sibling disputes in which the sibling or mother expressed intense negative emotion, the children were most likely to respond by watching soberly (50% of such disputes) or attempting to support the sibling (18%). To mother–sibling disputes in which the sibling was laughing, the children were most likely to respond by laughing (33%) and/or by imitating the sibling (34%). Their response also varied according to the topic of the dispute (Dunn & Munn, 1986). A series of studies by Cummings and his colleagues (Cummings, Zahn-Waxler, & Radke-Yarrow, 1981) has shown that young children are considerably disturbed by witnessing such exchanges: Their play is suppressed, and heightened aggression may be shown toward peers later. Such reactions confirm the salience to young children of the expression of intense negative emotion.

Studies of slightly older children's conflicts in preschool settings give converging evidence for children's understanding of social rules to that provided by the research within the family. Much and Shweder (1978), for example, analyzed children's excuses in naturally occurring "situations of accountability" in nursery school and kindergarten, that is, when they were accused of wrongdoing. The researchers classified the episodes as breaches of five kinds of rules: morals, conventions, school regulations, instructions, and truths (beliefs). The children excused and justified their behavior differently for violations of each type of rule. This research and a number of related studies have shown that the accounts children give in the context of moral transgressions "imply a perception of moral rules as unalterable, intrinsically valid, beyond negotiation. . . . The lack of reference to consequences and competing precepts also suggests the unconditional authority and respect that moral rules command" (p. 202).

Developments in social strategies. The close analysis of the arguments between preschool children in such settings has highlighted another aspect of their differentiated social knowledge, paralleling the findings on children's understanding of others' intentions and feelings referred to earlier. This is the examination of social strategies, notably in the study by Eisenberg and Garvey (1981) of children between ages 2 and 7 years. Here, analysis of the sequential dependencies in speakers' contributions within episodes of conflict demonstrates how closely children in arguments react to the intentions and strategies of their opponents. "The successful resolution of an adversative episode is a mutual endeavor: a child is more likely to win if he considers his opponent's intentions *and* more likely to concede if his own desires are taken into account" (p. 168; see also Putallaz & Gottman, 1981).

In summary, from these observational studies we see that young children reveal, as Shantz (1987) notes in her review of the literature, "an impressive degree of knowledge about social rules, people's intentions, and social strategies" (p. 299). Whether they employ their powers of understanding to manage or resolve the conflict depends importantly on the quality of the relationship they have with their opponent. Hartup and his colleagues showed, for instance, that conflicts between 4-year-old friends were resolved more frequently with disengagement and more frequently resulted in equitable outcomes than conflicts with nonfriends (Hartup, Laursen, Stewart, & Eastenson, 1988). Research within the tradition of studying children as reflective commentators on conflict gives us a picture that parallels the results from observational studies in many respects. Turiel, Nucci, Smetana, and their colleagues for example, have directly questioned children about whether moral rules, in contrast to conventional rules, are considered to be external, unalterable, and serious (e.g., Smetana, 1983; Turiel, 1980, 1983). This work has demonstrated that preschool-age children are capable of making such conceptual distinctions (Smetana, 1981, 1985) between these two "domains of social knowledge" (Turiel, 1983) and do not view transgressions globally, as some models of moral development would predict (e.g., Kohlberg, 1969). Furthermore, these findings converge with evidence for differential responses of toddlers to moral and social-conventional transgressions observed in the day-care setting (Smetana, 1984).

Concepts of conflict and relationships. A second, and flourishing research approach within the child-as-commentator tradition is the investigation of children's concepts of conflict and conflict resolution, studied in relation to their developing understanding of individuals and relationships. This work has chiefly focused on children in middle childhood and adolescents (as we discuss later), but it should be noted that recent work has shown that even young children can take into account the interpersonal bond of friendship when evaluating transgressions that could lead to conflict. In one study (Slomkowski & Killen, in press), preschoolers were asked to judge and evaluate the permissibility of two commonly occurring transgressions: taking a toy and making a mean face. Questions were asked with respect to a friend and a nonfriend (e.g., "If a friend took a toy away from you that you were playing with, would that be okay or not okay? Why [or why not]?" "If a nonfriend made a mean face . . ." and so on). In addition, the role of the child being interviewed was presented both as victim and as violator (e.g., "If you took a toy away from a friend, would that be okay or not okay?"). Although a majority of the children judged acts to be wrong whether committed by a friend or nonfriend, self or other, a significant number shifted their response from "not okay" for a nonfriend to "okay" for a friend, for most transgressions. Importantly, children who shifted their judgments cited the friendship bond as the reason for transgression being permissible for friends (e.g., "It's okay for Katie to take a toy from me because she's my friend."), whereas they made reference to social conventions and moral issues when evaluating transgressions with nonfriends.

It cannot be discerned at present from these findings whether children would go on to evaluate these transgressions in terms of norms for friendly relations (e.g., "That's not how you act when someone's your friend.") or in terms of moral reasons (e.g., "It's not fair to take a toy from your friend."). More detailed work involving further probes of children would be a useful and interesting direction to take in future work. However, a number of inferences can be made from these results as they stand. First, as children of this age did not discriminate between the wrongfulness of acts committed by the self and by the other, they are perhaps less completely egocentrically oriented than earlier views would have predicted. Second, the results suggest that the differential meaning of relationships (friend vs. nonfriend) bears significantly upon the child's evaluation of transgressions leading to conflict. In general, then, conflictual events are perceived differently depending upon the nature of the child's relationship with the other child. We noted earlier that children are observed to manage conflict differently with friends and nonfriends (Hartup et al., 1988). The results of the Slomkowski and Killen study (in press) parallel these findings with the demonstration that the quality of the relationship between children is also important in their reflective comments concerning transgressions. Direct examination of links between young children's developing conceptions of conflicts in close relationships (e.g., with friends and siblings) and their conflict behavior in those relationships undoubtedly will be an important area for future research.

Children as participants in conflict or as commentators. As Pool and her colleagues point out (Pool, Shweder, & Much, 1983), the two methods of studying children in conflict – interview and observation – give us a picture of different aspects of children's knowledge of rules and relationships, and each is useful. It is, of course, hazardous to draw inferences about what children understand from their talk and behavior in conflict. In part, this is a sampling-of-behavior problem. Conclusions about what a child understands about others' emotions will be much more firmly based if we have evidence not only from their response to others' distress, but also from their attempts to provoke upset, their jokes about emotions, their conversations about causes of emotions, their questions and comments about why people express emotion, their pretend play about inner states, and so on. In addition to these 'sampling' issues, there are other difficulties in making inferences about children's understanding from discourse (see

Scholnick & Wing, 1992). One is that there is another speaker involved in the dispute, and we do not know if the child would demonstrate the same capabilities independently; another is that conversational data are so often incomplete, and much is left unsaid; another is that we cannot always be sure that what the coder deduces a child means is what the child actually means. It is especially important for those studying very young children to be cautious about drawing grand conclusions from isolated examples, to use multiple observations, and to examine the children's behavior in a variety of social settings with different social partners (see Dunn, 1988). However, while acknowledging these difficulties, a number of particular strengths to the direct observation of children in conflict should be noted.

First, with very young children such as those in their second year, direct questioning presents obvious problems, and more importantly, children of this age may well not yet be able to reflect on social rules or moral issues. This does not mean that they do not make relevant distinctions in their social behavior. With reference to this point, Pool et al. (1983) make a powerful case for an ethnographic approach to studying children's social understanding as revealed in children's arguments:

> Young children cannot necessarily tell us about their knowledge of the formal criteria of validity that distinguish morality, convention, and prudence. They simply "know more than they can tell" (Nisbett & Wilson, 1977), and they display this knowledge in ways that are available to ethnographers of any primitive society, that is, vis-a-vis excuse patterns, ordinary language applications of adjectives of appraisal, and so on. . . . What the savage knows he may not be able to tell us, but what the savage himself is unable to say about what he knows is not necessarily a secret and is certainly not beyond our deliberate grasp. (p. 212)

Second, even with older children, there is some evidence that children show developmentally mature behavior before they reflect and comment upon it. Rubin and Pepler (1980), for instance, in a study of play and social perspective taking found that the behavioral analogues of social perspective taking appeared before the ages at which the children generally articulated the corresponding level of perspective taking in a reflective interview. Flavell and Wohlwill (1969) take up the Piagetian position that knowledge occurs first at the level of action and then on the plane of reflective thought in their argument that conceptions begin to develop as the child implements them in action, even if they are not yet consciously understood. It is through their continuous use, according to this view, that conceptions become consolidated and then eventually reflected upon (see Selman, Schorin, Stone, & Phelps, 1983, for further discussion of this point). Such a position fits well, of course, with a Vygotskian view that developmental advances first take place in the context of social interaction, and only later become "internalized."

Third, and particularly important, it is only by observing children in conflict that we will begin to understand the significance of *affect* in children's developing social understanding. The role of emotion in conflict is a neglected topic, as Shantz (1987) noted in her review. Yet in those studies of conflict in which it has been included, the results have been provocative, as we will discuss in the second main section of the chapter. The neglect of the topic of affect brings us to the matter of developmental changes in the social understanding revealed by children's behavior in conflict – what we know and what issues stand out for further investigation.

Conflict in middle childhood

These studies of conflict in early childhood and interviews with children concerning transgressions have given us a window on their grasp of the cause and consequence of feelings, their use of justification and excuse, the distinctions they make between breaches by friends and nonfriends, and their notions of moral breaches as importantly different from conventional transgressions. What developmental changes in the nature of social understanding are evident from studying conflict in older children?

First, it is highly likely that the nature of social rules referred to when children justify or excuse their actions will change as their social knowledge base increases; thus, conflict continues to be potentially very illuminating as a context of study in middle childhood and adolescence. It is probable that, around 4–6 years of age, major changes begin in the breadth of children's social knowledge, their curiosity about the workings of the social world, and its sanctions and expectations (see, for instance, the study by Tizard & Hughes, 1984). It is likely too that children's understanding of what will upset or comfort another – clearly evident in disputes – will become more elaborate in middle childhood, as their comprehension of complex social emotions increases. Consider the following examples, quotations from four different 6- to 7-year-olds studied at home (Bretherton, Fritz, Zahn-Waxler, & Ridgeway, 1986).

Statement	Context
"Now come on, Mom. If Dad says that you never say you're sorry, then it's your turn to say you're sorry."	To parents who are making up after a fight on the previous day.
"And I tried to go up to Jim to play with him again, but he won't come near me. And he's not . . . when a kid isn't really your friend yet, they don't know you didn't mean to do it to them."	Explaining to mother about an incident at school where he accidentally hit another boy.

"Well that's all right. Sometimes when I hit you and then I want to comfort you, you push me away because you're still angry."

Explaining to a friend why another child did not respond to friend's efforts to comfort her.

"Do you know that when you get mad at me, I go to my room and I think, and you know what I think about? I think I'm no good and I think no one loves me."

To mother, after a reprimand in the car for not doing what she was asked to do.

"If you can't remember to kiss me, then you're not thinking about me enough."

When mother forgot to kiss her goodnight.

The sophistication of these children's grasp of the emotions of others, their understanding of appropriate strategies for resolving conflict, and their ability (see the last example) to use these capabilities to gain their own ends is remarkable.

It is notable, however, that little systematic research has focused on documenting such developmental changes within the family, even though these issues are of immediate practical concern to parents and, as the examples just quoted indicate, the findings would be interesting to developmental psychologists. There is some evidence that, during middle childhood, children become better able to read social cues of hostility or exclusion in conflict situations with their peers (Dodge, 1985; Putallaz, 1983). The increase of such skills by no means, of course, guarantees kinder behavior toward others; rather, skills at reading others' intentions can be used for good or evil! The focus of the developmental research on conflict in middle childhood, however, has been chiefly on how concepts of conflict and resolution change, on children's changing notions of individuals and relationships (especially friendship), and on the changes in how they interact with others: Of primary interest has been children's conceptions of interaction between peers and friends.

Concepts of conflict and relationships. A notable example is Selman's (1980, 1981) five-stage developmental theory of interpersonal understanding and conflict. Selman focuses on the process of conflict resolution (as a crucial part of friendship maintenance) to delineate a developmental pattern in which young children move from conceptions of conflict resolution as momentary and physicalistic to more sophisticated conceptions of mutual and symbolic solutions later in adolescence and adulthood. A significant contribution of this theory is the explicit recognition that the development of conceptions of conflict resolution entails changing conceptions of individuality and interpersonal relationships (e.g., friendship). Hence, conceptions of conflict resolution emerge with, and are dependent on, developments in the social understanding of individuals' motives or intentions, as well as with conceptions of relationships.

Selman initially used interviews based on hypothetical, open-ended dilemmas with children, adolescents, and adults to formulate the developmental model; later, he included natural settings (Selman et al., 1983). Children at the lowest level of the model (level 0, including children through about 8 years of age) conceive of individuals as physical entities and conceptualize friendships as momentary physical interaction. Hence, their conceptions of conflict resolutions at this stage involve, according to the model, physical solutions such as force. In contrast, at the fourth level (level 3; later adolescence) in Selman's model, children recognize individuals as stable personalities, and their conceptions of friendship include intimacy and mutual sharing. Core conceptions of conflict resolution at this level include mutual solutions to conflict such as active discussion of any problem between friends. In addition, there is a growing recognition that some conflicts could strengthen a friendship. In this model, then, conflict clarifies both the development of social understanding about individuals and relationships and the role of conflict in relationships. Although the model has been extremely productive in generating research (as will be discussed), it should be noted that in light of the recent work on conflict between friends and nonfriends in the preschool period, the lowest level of the model does need revision.

A related fusion of social reasoning about conflict and conceptions of friendships is proposed by Damon (1977), who focuses on the development of positive justice, rather than conflict per se. This topic, which includes notions of sharing and the distribution of resources, is clearly fundamental in children's conflicts, as the observational work on preschool children has emphasized. The developmental progression of reasoning about positive justice in Damon's six-level model, which was based on both interview and observational data, begins in early childhood with reasoning based on children's own desires. It is an account that clearly fits well with the findings of the recent observational research on young children's conflicts, which highlights the centrality of self-interest in those disputes (Dunn, 1988). Reasoning, according to Damon, then develops to a level at which it is recognized that conflicts about distributions of resources may arise from differing desires of individuals. A milestone at this level is that the basis for each person's claim may be evaluated, so that the most "deserving" claims should be rewarded. Yet more advanced reasoning about positive justice involves further differentiation of ideas about the bases for justice, so that adolescents may recognize that people can have different but equally deserving reasons for their claims to justice and that the distribution of resources should be based on the coordination of principles of equality and reciprocity. Thus, in the Damon model, the progression through the different levels of positive justice involves the development of new conceptions of the desires of the self and other and advanced reasoning about the coordination of different perspectives.

How does a consideration of the friendship bond enter into reasoning about positive justice? Damon argues that ideas of positive justice arise in part through early friendship relationships and that conceptions of friendship and positive justice may be fused through development. It must be stressed that Damon does not argue that the two conceptions are isomorphic; rather, the position is that it is important to recognize that they co-occur and that ideas of justice may arise and mature within developing friendship relationships.

The strongest link between friendship and conceptions of positive justice may be present in early childhood. As Damon suggests, a major part of early friendships is sharing; thus, a close association exists between positive justice and early notions of friendship relations. For example, at the earliest levels of ideas about positive justice, young children report that liking a friend is a reason to share with them, whereas disliking a child is a basis for not sharing or for being unfair to that child. Damon further argues that notions of positive justice characteristic of later levels – such as equality and reciprocity – emerge in part from the development of friendships and conceptions of friendship. Thus, within this framework, concepts of fairness, sharing, and not sharing are tightly tied to defining features of the friendship bond. Interestingly, Damon also suggests that the fusion between friendship and justice becomes weaker as children enter adolescence because they are able to disentangle notions of fairness from considerations of the friendship bond.

Our first general question concerned what light is shed on the nature of social understanding by a focus on conflict: What is implied by these models of the development of conflict resolution and notions of positive justice? Both the Damon and the Selman models suggest that by examining the level or stage of children's conflict resolution, we would gain insights into the nature of their grasp of the perspective of others, their powers of self-reflexive thought and "understanding of reciprocity of thoughts, feelings, and expectations between persons" (Selman et al., 1983). What empirical evidence is there for connections between children's level of reasoning about conflict, and (a) their actual behavior in conflict or (b) other aspects of social understanding, in terms of formal assessments?

Selman and his colleagues here make a useful distinction between expressing social understanding (communicative competence) and using social understanding to achieve a goal (social negotiation strategies). Both functional aspects of social understanding will be related, they propose, to the level of thought attained in the Selman model. In a study that focused on children in three contexts – one-to-one interviews, group discussions, and observations of an activity group – associations were found between the level of social understanding reflected in the interview and both the communicative competence and strategies for negotiation used by the children. However, a difference was found in the pattern of results for communicative competence and social negotiation strategies. It was only among the older children that differences in communicative competence were found to be related to the level of reflective understanding from the interview. For the social negotiation strategies, the differences related to level of reflective thought were found only in the younger subjects.

The researchers interpret this difference in the following way: The expression of social understanding in discourse, which depends on the verbalization of thoughts and feelings, requires that the social understanding is mastered at the level of reflection. If, as they argue, reflexive knowledge follows "active" knowledge developmentally, it is only among the older children that such reflective understanding has been consolidated. In contrast, the social understanding involved in social negotiation strategies is reflected in direct interaction about relationships without requiring the reflective thought implicated in the verbalization of thoughts and feelings. Indeed, the children's level of behavior sometimes exceeded their level of reflective understanding, a finding that is quite compatible with the argument that unconscious use of a concept in action precedes children's ability to reflect on and articulate their thoughts concerning that concept.

Such findings show how useful empirical comparisons of children as participants and children as reflective commentators can be, as in the study by Shantz and Shantz (1985) of first and second graders that related social-cognitive conceptions and conflict behavior. Here, the social-cognitive conceptual level was related to the *issues* over which the children quarreled and their success in resolving conflict. What we particularly need is more study of natural behavior in situations of real emotional significance to the participants and, especially, studies of older children within their families. One small-scale study of siblings in middle childhood is pertinent here. It focused on the associations between children's level of reasoning about conflict on the Damon model, a range of formal assessments of sociocognitive development, and children's conflict behavior with their siblings. Links were reported between the Damon level of reflective thought about conflict and a number of aspects of real-life conflict behavior (Beardsall,

1986). Conflict behavior that reflected understanding of the other sibling was more frequent in the children who scored higher on the Damon model, but interestingly, this included both "nice" actions (conciliation), and "nasty" behavior (teasing). Indeed, the most powerful associations were between high scores on the "formal" assessment and teasing, unkind behavior. The results imply that children who understand what upsets their sibling use this knowledge in different ways: Their motivation to use their social understanding changes in different relationships, and a high degree of understanding by no means guarantees a less conflicted relationship.

Developmental changes in social understanding have been further illuminated by other studies of conceptions of conflict and their links to changes in social relationships in middle childhood, beyond the theoretical models already considered. But again, there are inconsistencies between what children are observed to do in conflict with friends and nonfriends and their reflective accounts. For example, the distinctions that children make between conflict and support in friendship change between middle childhood and adolescence: Berndt and Perry (1986), in a study of second-, fourth-, sixth-, and eighth-grade children, found that younger children did not believe that they could engage in conflict with their friends and, at the same time, be in a supportive relationship with them. However, by adolescence the two are deemed compatible. Yet studies of children's behavior and conversations with friends and nonfriends show, as we have seen, that, even in early childhood, there is more disagreement between friends than between nonfriends (Gottman & Parkhurst, 1980), and more criticism of friends than nonfriends (Nelson & Aboud, 1985). Some studies report that conflicts occur just as frequently with friends as nonfriends, although they are resolved more equitably (Hartup et al., 1988) or even occur more frequently with friends (Green, 1933), and that children display more hostility to strong associates than to nonassociates (Hinde, Titmus, Easton, & Tamplin, 1985).

What is clear from the interview studies is that there are indeed changes in conceptions of conflict within relationships from middle childhood to adolescence. For example, Youniss and Volpe (1978) report that when asked to tell a story in which a friend did something that the other friend did not like, younger children (ages 7 and 8) cited specific acts (e.g., hitting, taking a toy, name calling), whereas older children referred to violations of friendship principles (e.g., breaking a promise). In addition, younger children suggested specific, rule-abiding actions as the basis for conflict resolution, whereas older children included an explicit acknowledgment of violation along with reparative actions.

Summary. The developmental studies of middle childhood have delineated the close connections between changes in the nature of children's relationships and their strategies for resolving conflict, and have described their developing conceptions of conflict. To examine children's most mature powers of resolving conflict, arguments between friends may prove to be the context that is particularly revealing – rather than conflict between less involved associates. The study of very young children in their close relationships have shown that their powers of understanding in situations of real emotional significance are greater than was evident in the test situations devised by psychologists. It is not clear to what extent the familiarity with the other participants in the disputes, versus the emotion involved, contributes to the sophistication that children show in such disputes, but the general pattern is that they marshal their arguments and reasoning in those situations that touch their interests most closely (Dunn, 1988; see also Stein & Miller, 1990).

The studies of disputes in middle childhood have shown, moreover, that conflict plays a changing role in friendship with other children. Gottman and Mettetal (1986) propose that conflict management between friends in the 3- to 7-year-old age range is in the service of coordinating play; in middle childhood, it is in the service of ensuring peer acceptance and avoiding rejection. As children grow toward adolescence, it is increasingly about self-exploration in the context of developing intimacy. In a parallel way, the topics over which children fight change (Shantz & Shantz, 1985), and this too can illuminate changes in what matters to children and thus reveal their changing social knowledge and conception of self.

In the host of developmental issues that remain in need of investigation, two in particular stand out. First, what happens in parent–child conflict as children develop? How do children's strategies and their grasp of the use to which social rules can be put both change? Until now, the bulk of systematic research has focused on peers and friends. Yet understanding family conflict is both socially important and likely to be very revealing. Second, what role does emotion play in the developmental changes in social understanding outlined and in the sophistication (or lack of maturity) with which children perform in the context of conflict? This brings us to the second general question raised in the introduction: Does conflict foster development of the capabilities that are clearly highlighted in disputes? If so, what features of conflict exchange are key to its developmental significance?

Conflict as a developmental context

The view that conflict with others plays a special part in the development of social understanding is taken in several different theoretical approaches, notably those of Piaget (1932/1965) and Sullivan (1953). Much of the emphasis in such accounts is on the "cognitive conflict" the child experiences when faced with another mind – an opposing view of the world. According to Piaget, this experience is especially formative when that other perspective that the child begins to glimpse belongs to a peer, whose status in relation to the child means that argument and discussion can take place more freely (and by implication more fruitfully, developmentally speaking) than with an adult.

However attractive this is as an account of why conflict is formative, it leaves a centrally important theme unexplored. The conflict that a child experiences with family and friends involves far more than an opposition of cognitive perspectives on the world. First, it involves the experiencing, expression, and witnessing of emotions. It is, as we noted, only with young children that the emotional experiences in conflict have been systematically studied. However, these studies have provided intriguing results.

Consider the emotions expressed by children in the course of their second year (when their goals are frustrated) in conflict with their mothers. The displays of anger documented by Goodenough in the 1930s increase in frequency over the period when children make astonishingly rapid developments in their sense of self and understanding of others (Dunn, 1988). Could these emotional experiences themselves contribute to what children are learning in conflict – to the cognitive changes in children's growing ability to tease, manipulate, justify, and excuse? We know from experimental studies that the emotional context of an experience profoundly affects the way in which it is remembered and affects current functioning (Bower, 1981; Maccoby & Martin, 1983). For example, one study of first and third graders' conceptions of moral issues showed that the emotion that children experienced in connection with particular events was clearly related to their memory of such events and to the way they differentiated such events (Arsenio & Ford, 1985). And in a longitudinal study of children observed in conflict at ages 18, 24, and 36 months, we found that it was in those contexts in which children most frequently expressed anger and distress that they, 18 months later, were likely to reason rather than simply protest (Dunn, 1988). The association raises the possibility that it was in part because of the emotion experienced in these encounters that the children were especially attentive to the other's behavior; they remembered, reflected on, and learned from the memories of those particular exchanges. The notable growth of social knowledge reflected in the reasoning of the 36-month-olds was demonstrated in just those conflict exchanges in which the children had earlier expressed anger and distress. Such findings raise yet more questions concerning emotion and learning in conflict. What, for instance, are the effects of different emotions on what children remember or learn?

Conflict not only involves children's experience, expression and observation of emotions. It involves, as we have described, the experience of manipulating, comforting, amusing, and frustrating others with whom children have significant close relationships. It exposes children to experiences of bargaining, threats, compromise, and concessions, not only the articulation of social rules and excuses, but how these are used against themselves, all within the context of relationships that matter deeply to the child. There are three themes here that weave together to make conflict experiences potentially powerful learning situations. First, children's self-interest is centrally engaged and threatened. Second, their emotional state is aroused; we should acknowledge here not only the guilt and anxiety stressed in other models of moral development (Hoffman, 1983; Kagan, 1984), but the complex emotions involved in children's close relationships. The affective tensions in the relationships between child and sibling and between child and parents provide one important impetus for the child to understand others and the social world. In this model, the child's motivation to understand the world stems not solely from a wish to allay guilt or to conform, as in the accounts offered by Hoffman and Kagan, but also from the child's role in the complex pattern of family power relations. Third, social rules, justification, and excuses are articulated for and by the child in conflict; they are explicitly articulated, disputed, and discussed. Such a model gives weight to the cognitive changes that lead to children's ability to argue and reason, to the developing sense of self, and to the emotional significance of the tension between this self-concern and the relationships with family and friends.

In terms of our general question concerning the developmental significance of conflict, such an account suggests that conflict is indeed a context in which understanding can be fostered. It emphasizes the powerful combination of emotional arousal and cognition that makes disputes and confrontation between children and their family and friends potentially important. But what grounds do we have for concluding that conflict does, in fact, play a special role in normative development, in terms of the findings of systematic research?

First, we should acknowledge that all theories about the normative development of social understanding, however plausible, remain theories. It is extremely difficult to establish firmly the special significance of conflict as a context for normative development. It is clear, for example, that with children of age 4 years and beyond, conversations reflecting intellectual search into the social world often take place in contexts that do not involve conflict (see Tizard & Hughes, 1984). The features of human development that we are considering are so important that they are likely to be achieved in a variety of contexts. Although there may indeed be special potential in the emotionally urgent situations of conflict within the family and between friends (the situations that are, of course, particularly difficult for psychologists to study), we are far from having established this for normative development.

Evidence for the developmental impact of conflict on individual differences in outcome is, in contrast, clearer. Here, progress may be made by focusing the inquiry with some specificity – asking, for example, whether certain aspects of social cognition are influenced by particular features of conflict experiences: We can, for instance, explore the question of whether the understanding of emotions is influenced by (a) the frequency of conflict experiences, (b) the articulation of the causes and consequences of emotions in the course of conflict in discourse, (c) the affective messages accompanying the conflict, or (d) some particular combinations of such features. Approaches of this sort are beginning to delineate the unique importance of discourse (Dunn, Brown, Slomkowski, Tesla, & Youngblade, 1991) and the affective message a parent conveys (Cummings, Hollenbeck, Iannotti, Radke-Yarrow, & Zahn-Waxler, 1986). With such studies, we gain insights about the development of individual differences and the significance of particular aspects of conflict in these developments; there is, however, no necessary connection between the processes that influence such individual differences and the processes affecting normative development of social understanding. The significance of the affective, social, and cognitive experiences in the setting of conflict for normative development remains extremely plausible – but unconfirmed.

Conclusion

The study of children in conflict with their mothers and siblings has considerably clarified our views of the nature of children's understanding of the causes and consequences of others' feelings and their grasp of social rules and strategies. It has raised further questions about the role of affective experience in the development of this social understanding. Paralleling this *functional* analysis of their behavior in conflict, *formal* analysis of their reflections and judgment concerning conflict in interview settings has highlighted changes in conceptual development and linked these changes to developments in the nature of their close relationships. In closing, we emphasize two questions that the recent research on conflict suggests will be particularly illuminating to pursue in relation to the issue of conflict as a developmental context.

First, how does the developmental significance of conflict differ in the context of relationships of different quality? Does confrontation within a best friendship carry very different implications than does confrontation with a parent? It may be, for example, that conflict within a sibling relationship fosters understanding of manipulative, teasing strategies and devious ways of undermining another child, because, even in the warmest sibling relationship, argument and teasing are frequent. Conflict with a close friend about whom the child really cares may provide more frequent opportunities to learn the arts of compromise and conciliation, of comforting and consolation (although of course, some friendships include much competition and manipulation). The key point is that the quality of the particular relationship may affect the kind of social understanding that it fosters. For young children, conflict with their mothers is likely to provide a forum for the articulation of rules, for talk about cause. But how does the significance of such conflict change as children grow up? This is the second question for which developmental research would be especially welcome and illuminating. For example, do best friendships – and therefore conflict within best friendships – become more salient in adolescence, whereas conflict with parents and siblings is more important to younger children? When the two general questions we posed at the start of the chapter are set within a differentiated developmental framework that takes into account both the qualities of relationships and the developmental stage of the child, the prospect of making progress in understanding the significance of conflict appears both practical and exciting.

References

Arsenio, W. F., & Ford, M. E. (1985). The role of affective information in social-cognitive development: Children's differentiation of moral and conventional events. *Merrill-Palmer Quarterly, 31*, 1–17.

Beardsall, L. (1986). *Conflict between siblings in middle childhood.* Unpublished doctoral dissertation, University of Cambridge.

Berndt, T. J., & Perry, T. B. (1986). Children's perceptions of friendships as supportive relationships. *Developmental Psychology, 22*, 640–648.

Bower, G. (1981). Mood and memory. *American Psychologist, 36*, 129–148.

Bretherton, I., Fritz, J., Zahn-Waxler, C., & Ridgeway, D. (1986). Learning to talk about emotions: A functionalist perspective. *Child Development, 57*, 529–548.

Cummings, E. M., Hollenbeck, B., Iannotti, R., Radke-Yarrow, M., & Zahn-Waxler, C. (1986). Early organization of altruism and aggression: Developmental patterns and individual differences. In C. Zahn-Waxler, E. M. Cummings, & R. Iannotti (Eds.), *Altruism and aggression.* Cambridge: Cambridge University Press.

Cummings, E. M., Zahn-Waxler, C., & Radke-Yarrow, M. (1981). Young children's responses to expressions of anger and affection by others in the family. *Child Development, 52*, 1274–1282.

Damon, W. (1977). *The social world of the child.* San Francisco: Jossey-Bass.

Dodge, K. (1985). A social information processing model of social competence in children. In M. Perlmutter (Ed.), *Minnesota symposium on child psychology* (Vol. 18). Hillsdale, NJ: Erlbaum.

Dunn, J. (1988). *The beginnings of social understanding.* Cambridge, MA: Harvard University Press.

Dunn, J., Brown, J., Slomkowski, C., Tesla, C., & Youngblade, L. (1991). Young children's understanding of feelings and beliefs: Individual differences and their antecedents. *Child Development, 62,* 1352–1366.

Dunn, J., & Munn, P. (1985). Becoming a family member: Family conflict and the development of social understanding in the second year. *Child Development, 56,* 764–774.

Dunn, J., & Munn, P. (1986). Siblings and the development of prosocial behavior. *International Journal of Behavioral Development, 9,* 265–284.

Dunn, J., & Munn, P. (1987). The development of justification in disputes. *Developmental Psychology, 23,* 791–798.

Eisenberg, A. R., & Garvey, C. (1981). Children's use of verbal strategies in resolving conflicts. *Discourse Processes, 4,* 149–170.

Erikson, E. H. (1959). Identity and the life cycle. *Psychological Issues,* Monograph 1. New York: International Universities Press.

Flavell, J. H., & Wohlwill, J. F. (1969). Formal and functional aspects of cognitive development. In D. Elkind & J. H. Flavell (Eds.), *Studies in cognitive development: Essays in honor of Jean Piaget.* Oxford: Oxford University Press.

Goodenough, F. L. (1931). *Anger in young children.* Minneapolis: University of Minnesota Press.

Gottman, J., & Mettetal, G. (1986). Speculations about social and affective development: Friendship and acquaintanceship through adolescence. In J. M. Gottman & J. G. Parker (Eds.), *Conversations of friends: Speculations on affective development.* Cambridge: Cambridge University Press.

Gottman, J. M., & Parkhurst, J. T. (1980). A developmental theory of friendship and acquaintanceship processes. In W. A. Collins (Ed.), *Minnesota symposium on child psychology* (Vol. 13). Hillsdale, NJ: Erlbaum.

Green, E. H. (1933). Friendships and quarrels among preschool children. *Child Development, 4,* 237–252.

Hartup, W. W., Laursen, B., Stewart, M. I., & Eastenson, A. (1988). Conflict and the friendship relations of young children. *Child Development, 59,* 1590–1600.

Hinde, R. A., Titmus, G., Easton, D., & Tamplin, A. (1985). Incidence of "friendship" and behavior with strong associates versus nonassociates in preschoolers. *Child Development, 56,* 234–245.

Hoffman, M. L. (1983). Affective and cognitive processes in moral internalization. In E. T. Higgins, D. N. Ruble, & W. W. Hartup (Eds.), *Social cognition and social development.* Cambridge: Cambridge University Press.

Kagan, J. (1984). *The nature of the child.* New York: Basic.

Kohlberg, L. (1969). Stage and sequence: The cognitive-developmental approach to socialization. In D. A. Goslin (Ed.), *Handbook of socialization theory and research.* Chicago: Rand McNally.

Maccoby, E. E., & Martin, J. A. (1983). Socialization in the context of the family: Parent–child interaction. In E. M. Hetherington (Ed.), *Handbook of child psychology: Vol. 4, Socialization, personality, and social development* (4th ed.). New York: Wiley.

Much, N. C., & Shweder, R. A. (1978). Speaking of rules: The analysis of culture in breach. In W. Damon (Ed.), *Moral development: New directions for child development.* San Francisco: Jossey-Bass.

Nelson, J., & Aboud, F. (1985). The resolution of social conflict between friends. *Child Development, 56,* 1009–1017.

Nisbett, R. E., & Wilson, T. D. (1977). Telling more than we can know: Verbal reports on mental processes. *Psychological Review, 84,* 231–259.

Piaget, J. (1965). *The moral judgment of the child.* London: Routledge & Kegan Paul. (Original work published 1932)

Pool, D. L., Shweder, R. A., & Much, N. C. (1983). Culture as a cognitive system: Differentiated rule understandings in children and other savages. In E. T. Higgins, D. N. Ruble, & W. W. Hartup (Eds.), *Social cognition and social development.* Cambridge: Cambridge University Press.

Putallaz, M. (1983). Predicting children's sociometric status from their behavior. *Child Development, 54,* 1417–1426.

Putallaz, M., & Gottman, J. (1981). An interactional model of children's entry into peer groups. *Child Development, 52,* 986–994.

Rubin, K. H., & Pepler, D. J. (1980). The relationship of child's play to social growth and development. In H. C. Foot, A. J. Chapman, & J. R. Smith (Eds.), *Friendships and social relations in children.* London: Wiley.

Scholnick, E. K., & Wing, C. S. (1992). Speaking deductively: Using conversation to trace the origins of conditional thought in children. *Merrill-Palmer Quarterly, 38,* 1–20.

Schulz, T. R. (1980). Development of the concept of intention. In W. A. Collins (Ed.), *Minnesota symposium on child psychology* (Vol. 13). Hillsdale, NJ: Erlbaum.

Selman, R. (1980). *The growth of interpersonal understanding: Developmental and clinical analyses.* New York: Academic Press.

Selman, R. (1981). The child as friendship philosopher. In S. R. Asher & J. M. Gottman (Eds.), *The development of children's friendships.* Cambridge: Cambridge University Press.

Selman, R. L., Schorin, M. Z., Stone, C. R., & Phelps, E. (1983). A naturalistic study of children's social understanding. *Developmental Psychology, 19,* 82–102.

Shantz, C. U. (1987). Conflicts between children. *Child Development, 58,* 283–305.

Shantz, C. U., & Shantz, D. W. (1985). Conflict between children: Social-cognitive and sociometric correlates. In M. W. Berkowitz (Ed.), *Peer conflict and psychological growth: New directions for child development.* San Francisco: Jossey-Bass.

Slomkowski, C., & Killen, M. (in press). Young children's conceptions of transgressions with friends and nonfriends. *International Journal of Behavioral Development.*

Smetana, J. G. (1981). Preschool children's conceptions of moral and social rules. *Child Development, 52,* 1333–1336.

Smetana, J. G. (1983). Social-cognitive development: Domain distinctions and coordinations. *Developmental Review, 3,* 137–147.

Smetana, J. G. (1984). Toddlers' social interactions regarding moral and conventional transgressions. *Child Development, 55,* 1767–1776.

Smetana, J. G. (1985). Preschool children's conceptions of transgressions: The effects of varying moral and conventional domain-related attributes. *Developmental Psychology, 21,* 18–29.

Spitz, R. A. (1957). *No and yes: On the genesis of human communication.* New York: International Universities Press.

Stein, N. L., & Miller, C. A. (1990). The process of thinking and reasoning in argumentative contexts: Evaluation of evidence and the resolution of conflict. In R. Glaser (Ed.), *Advances in instructional psychology.* Hillsdale, NJ: Erlbaum.

Sullivan, H. S. (1953). *The interpersonal theory of psychology.* New York: Norton.

Tizard, B., & Hughes, M. (1984). *Young children learning.* London: Fontana.

Turiel, E. (1980). Domains and categories in social cognitive development. In W. Overton (Ed.), *The relationship between social and cognitive development.* Hillsdale, NJ: Erlbaum.

Turiel, E. (1983). *The development of social knowledge: Morality and convention.* Cambridge: Cambridge University Press.

Youniss, J., & Volpe, J. (1978). A relational analysis of children's friendships. In W. Damon (Ed.), *Social cognition: New directions for child development.* San Francisco: Jossey-Bass.

4   Conflict talk: Approaches to adversative discourse

Catherine Garvey and Carolyn U. Shantz

Children's verbal conflict behavior is more diverse than might be supposed from the majority of studies on disputes. The diversity is particularly evident in turn-by-turn talk in different activities, in different speech communities, and at different ages. Yet at the same time, there appear to be patterns within this diversity. Examination of these patterns can broaden our understanding of conflict behavior and social competence, provide some bases for research decisions for studying adversative episodes, and suggest new goals for future research.

The objective of this chapter is to review evidence on the variations in verbal conflict behavior. Further, based on that evidence from children's everyday disputes, we propose a conceptual framework for examining children's practical knowledge and experience of social conflict and their competence in conducting it. This framework derives from the extraction of certain common properties, or dimensions, that appear to have heuristic value in organizing the diversity of adversative talk.

Conflict is considered here as a social activity, created and conducted primarily by means of talking. As such, it may be expected to show variations in its forms and relations to other social activities according to the goals of the participants, both within and across speech communities. As used here, the terms *diversity* and *variations* relate more closely to the perspectives of sociolinguistics than to those of developmental psychology. The claims and methods of those in the sociolinguistic traditions will be briefly discussed.

Variations in conflict behavior, both verbal and behavioral, have been studied in developmental psychology, usually within a single speech community and in a single type of situation, as a function of individual differences of the participants: social relations, such as friendship (Gottman, 1986) and peer social status (e.g., Dodge, 1983; Ladd, 1983); gender (e.g., Miller, Danaher, & Forbes, 1986); age; level of sociocognitive development (e.g., Shantz & Shantz, 1985); and parent–child interaction, including child compliance and parental discipline techniques (e.g., Patterson, 1982). Whether natural or experimental situations are employed, the common focus is explicitly or implicitly on "serious" conflict (i.e., not playful conflict) and its outcomes or correlates. A major concern has been the process of conflict resolution or problem solving, often seen as a goal to which most conflict exchanges are directed. As will be discussed shortly, there is evidence that serious conflict can be differentiated from somewhat similar behavior such as mock fighting, teasing, and thematic conflict in dramatic play.

Sociolinguistic perspectives on variations in conflict

The sociolinguistic perspectives (herein broadly construed to include work in ethnography, anthropology, discourse analysis, communication, sociology, and some work in psychology, as well) comprise investigations into conflict behavior both within and across speech communities. It is beyond the scope of this chapter to attempt to summarize the range of these literatures. See Brenneis (1988) for a broad review and van Dijk (1985) for a discussion of differences in approaches to the analysis of talk that characterize some of these disciplines.

For the most part, sociolinguists emphasize the interactive processes through which actual conflicts emerge and develop in order to study conflict as a skilled and differentiated communicative behavior. Few of these investigations deal directly with developmental trends. Their potential relevance for development, however, lies primarily in the detailed analyses of conflict interactions that arise spontaneously in an array of both everyday and more formal interactions in different groups. Among the diverse conflict interactions that have been analyzed are those that appear to be playful or teasing, conflicts that conform to a prescribed format, and conflicts that appear to avoid or preclude resolution without, however, leading to interpersonal agonism. These various disputing activities share a broadly accepted defining feature of verbal conflict, that is, explicit expression of mutual opposition by a minimum of two speakers (e.g., Shantz, 1987; Vuchinich, 1984). Therefore, consideration of the ways in which the disputes differ may contribute to a broader conceptualization of the development and uses of conflict as a ubiquitous and versatile human activity.

Process of conflict talk

Certain fundamental insights into the nature of interactive talk can contribute to an understanding of conflict. Four major claims advanced, in particular, by conversation analysts and ethnomethodologists (e.g., Levinson, 1983) are pertinent to a process-focused analysis of conflict talk. First, both participants in verbal interactions and the analysts seeking to understand those interactions are utilizing the same verbal (and nonverbal) data and the same sets of conventional interpretive procedures for deriving the significance and function of the talk and the social moves realized in that talk. Second, the data of talk are minutely and sensitively configured not only to fit into the external social context (e.g., a classroom setting or a family dinner), but actually to create a context of interaction as one speaking turn follows another. Third, at the same time participants process these context-dependent *tokens*, or single instances, as socially available *types*, or categories, of actions (e.g., insult, refusal) and at different levels of organization (e.g., a clarification sequence embedded in a conflict, a narrative told to support an opposing position).

Fourth, speech and nonverbal gestures are continuously subject to re-interpretation as an interaction evolves. At any point, the meaning of an utterance may be ambiguous to one or more of the participants and only subsequently understood or reassessed. Further, turns may realize more than one social act (e.g., apology, refusal, and explanation for the refusal) and may be analyzed as functioning simultaneously at more than one level of structural or functional organization. For example, a "justification" may be at the same time an answer to a question, a defense in response to a challenge, and a counterchallenge. Conversation analysts rely on the interpretations of participants *as revealed in their responses* to determine the meanings and functions of an utterance – just as a speaker determines from an interlocutor's response whether his or her utterance was interpreted as meant (and can institute repair immediately if a "misreading" is detected).

Despite these complications, speakers, both in conversations and in conflicts, exchange turns (and social acts) rapidly and for the most part smoothly and coherently, making instantaneous judgments of relevance, appropriateness, and significance. The fact that these judgments may be revised as the interaction proceeds or that two participants may not concur on the meaning of what is transpiring does not vitiate the claim that such judgments of "what we are doing now" must be made constantly if the participants are to continue to respond to one another (Goffman, 1976). How children engage in verbal conflicts may be viewed, then, as a special aspect of how they learn to use language with increasing skill and versatility for interactive purposes. Indeed, Goodwin (1983) has shown how verbal techniques used to aggravate or mitigate corrections in conversations are related to the techniques used to exacerbate or downplay disagreements or other opposing moves in conflicts.

Conflict as conversation

Sociolinguistic studies employ descriptive analyses of the structural and/or functional properties of conflicts as verbal activities serving a number of roles in the construction and maintenance of social order and personal status and, thus, potentially displaying both affiliative as well as dispersive properties (Simmel, 1955). Most important, however, is the view of conflicts as conversational phenomena that necessarily utilize the linguistic and pragmatic resources of interactive talk (O'Keefe & Benoit, 1982). As such, conflict interactions, their verbal social moves, and the speech acts comprising them are often analyzed in considerable linguistic detail. These analyses provide descriptive bases on which to compare different adversative exchanges (a) within the unfolding of a single conflict interaction, (b) across focal participants' interactions, and (c) potentially within and across social groups. Such analyses typically are concerned with the sequencing of oppositional moves and may incorporate data from different levels of linguistic, or communicative, organization (e.g., lexicon, syntax, intonation, response timing, and nonverbal gestures). Any of these may function as "contextualization cues" (Gumperz, 1982) by which the opposing speakers create the very context to which their behavior subsequently adapts and which it confirms. And as in any type of conversational interaction, it is, to a considerable extent, precisely in the form, manner, and timing of the talk itself that a speaker displays an understanding of the activity and, thereby, also displays competence as a knowledgeable and accountable actor (Goffman, 1971).

Conflict behavior as commonly viewed from the sociolinguistic perspectives is a product of interactive, interpretative work on the part of the disputants. Thus, the major concern is to identify *in the talk itself* those features that give the interaction "the character that it so manifestly has for the participants themselves" (Drew, 1985). Of course, participants may have several concurrent goals and motives in an interaction (e.g., to persuade another to carry out an action, to affirm a relationship, and/or enhance personal status). The goals may shift during an interaction as may the verbal strategies and the affect displayed by the participants. Often, too, the manifest issue of the conflict may differ from the latent issue that sustains the oppositions, and/or the initial topic may shift as the dispute progresses (O'Keefe & Benoit, 1982).

The boundaries of a conflict episode, thus, are identified by the onset and the termination of oppositional exchanges and are not determined by topic, issue, number of participants, or strategy (Maynard, 1985, 1986; Vuchinich, 1984, 1990). For example, what appears to begin as an argument about the use of an object may evolve into a contest of personalities that affects the status of the contestants in their group (Emihovich, 1986; Goodwin & Goodwin, 1990).

Situation and activity factors. Conflict behavior also may be constrained or supported by situational factors; participants act in specialized social roles as they follow, for example, an institutional agenda or uphold the standard operating procedures in a meeting or classroom. Disputants, of course, may occupy simultaneously several social roles (e.g., personal, institutional, activity-based) even as they take on the discourse-specific roles that have been designated variously as opposer–opposee (Eisenberg & Garvey, 1981) or accuser–defender (Walton & Sedlak, 1982). Also, changes may take place in the participant structure of a dispute as alliances are sought or rejected (Coulter, 1990; Maynard, 1986), and disputants may shift from, for example, a direct exchange of opposing moves to a series of offensive stories about a copresent antagonist without relinquishing the basic conflict activity (Goodwin & Goodwin, 1990). Conversational resources themselves may be deployed in complex moves so that two "messages" are sent simultaneously (e.g., one critical and one playful).

Cultural factors. At the same time, both the forms that conflicts take and the functions they serve are viewed as part of the value systems of the culture. For example, in respect to the processes of socialization, the way a child learns to argue, with whom, where, over what issues, and with what kind of expressed affect may vary not only with personality, development, and relationships (Dunn & Munn, 1987), but also with the emphases of her or his community on self-assertion, group consensus, or verbal skill (Eisenberg, 1986; Miller & Sperry, 1987). When and how justifications are required and what is an acceptable basis for accounting for "untoward" behavior (Scott & Lyman, 1968) is also part of what is learned and displayed in many conflict interactions. Young children will learn and elaborate the forms and styles of conflicting preferred by (and modeled by) those in their changing and expanding social groups.

Adults in different speech communities value and elaborate various types of conflict. For example, confrontational insult exchanges occur among speakers of black English (Kochman, 1970; Labov, 1972), whereas "friendly," sociable bickering occurs in urban Jewish families (Schiffrin, 1984). These are likely to be found in less mature forms (and perhaps with different social functions) in the conflicts of those communities' children. Indeed, the lengthy, rather legalistic *discussione* of Italian school children reported by Corsaro and Rizzo (1990) prefigure a style of argument common among Italian adults. Thus, the types and styles of conflict that children witness and in which they engage may vary according to cultural beliefs and values concerning, inter alia, competitiveness, child compliance, and differentiation of gender roles.

In summary, the sociolinguistic perspectives provide evidence on the diversity of conflict behavior within and across groups. This diversity may be related to structural features of the conflict such as the participant structure of the activity (e.g., among persons in symmetrical vs. asymmetrical status relationships, or those based on power vs. solidarity), to the inter-personal history of a relationship (e.g., familiarity), and to the shifting goals of the participants. So, too, conflicts may vary among social groups depending on the situation in which the conflict arises or the task at hand (e.g., a factual dispute between children working on a school assignment, a contest between a parent and a child over bedtime).

The importance of variations in verbal conflicts

Central to the thesis of this chapter is that even among peer groups of children within the same community and within similar activity settings, marked differences in conflict behavior have been observed (Corsaro & Rizzo, 1990; Emihovich, 1986; Garvey, 1987; Goodwin & Goodwin, 1990; Maynard, 1985). These differences seem to be salient and meaningful to the children themselves. That is, the differences in the communicative forms of conflict are reacted to by the participants, may even be explicitly commented on after an interaction (e.g., "We were just play fighting"), or may be noted in a metacommunication during the conflict, as when a girl, evaluating a cutting remark she had just made, says "That was a good one" (Eder, 1990, p. 75). Children appear to be able to manipulate actively their communicative resources to fine tune their conflicts in a variety of ways and to signal a variety of meanings.

Our justification for examining the sociolinguistic research is the relevance of the descriptions of variations to an understanding of the diversity of children's behavior and the scope of their repertoire for engaging in conflict. We would claim, in particular, that it is important to identify and describe the distinctions made by participants themselves as they encode and in-terpret oppositions. Insofar as children can manipulate and respond to meaningful variations in formulating oppositions in conflict behavior, such variations may be as important as the more commonly studied "strategies" for handling opposition (e.g., compromise offers, insistence) and may even help to explain how such social moves actually operate in interactions. It is our claim that the various types of conflict behavior that children display are related by means of their common reliance on the communicative resources that the children command.

Commonly observed differences in conflicts

Looking across studies embodying the sociolinguistic perspectives and those more central to psychological approaches, we can see that what has been described as interesting variations in the former have often been seen as problematic in the latter. Given the focus of most psychological research on serious conflicts, on the outcomes of those conflicts (e.g., conciliation, stalemate), or on their longer term effects on relationships, many other kinds of conflict have been excluded from investigation. In this section, we will illustrate the diverse and contrasting forms that children's mutual oppositions can take. As the participants interact, they establish some common ground as to "what we are doing." Their definitions of the interaction are displayed in their behavior and, thus, are available to researchers as well. It is the salient features of these definitions that we will attempt subsequently to organize into dimensions of variations in the verbal conflicts.

Serious and nonserious conflicts

A fundamental decision for interactants is whether what they are doing is serious or not. *Serious* here means that the participants understand one another as currently being in earnest and meaning what they say and do. Examples of serious conflicts abound in the literature. To illustrate, two boys, A and B, argue about the use of a toy truck (italics in examples indicate emphasis):

1.
A: It's mine. (looks at B, who has started to play with the truck)
B: Well, I'm using it. I'm using it. (continues to move the truck)
A: Could I take it home?
B: No, it's the school's.
A: Yes, I *am* take it home.

(Discourse excerpt, Garvey, 1984, p. 128)

In contrast, there are also nonserious conflicts, that is, ones marked by disclaimers of serious intent and that have a playful and sometimes teasing quality. For example, Davies noted the joking, teasing tone among three Australian boys (A, B, C) who were friends. D was interviewing them and had asked A if he had a girlfriend:

2.
A: No I haven't got one.
B & C: Aw Patrick!

A: No, I haven't. (laughing)
D: Did you used to have?
A: I didn't used to have no one.
C: Aw, don't gimme that, Patrick, 'cos you used to like Mandy (Patrick laughs). No, you did Patrick, don't give me that.
A: She's got freckles all over.
C: Oh, you used to like her.
A: No I didn't.

(Davies, 1982, p. 109)

What participants say to one another and their demeanor (sober vs. smiling or laughing) are indexes of their definitions of what is going on between them. Interestingly, researchers have differed as to whether they make a distinction between serious and nonserious conflict, and if so, how it is coded. Two examples in the literature, rough-and-tumble and teasing, illustrate the implications of this distinction for research endeavors.

Rough-and-tumble. The wrestling, chasing, and punching that often define *rough-and-tumble* have the topography of aggressive interactions, that is, the very behavior that occurs when one is trying seriously to wrestle another into submission or hurt another. Yet also present are laughing, giggling, happy shrieking, or exaggerated gestures that serve as disclaimers of serious intent, that is, serve as signals to participants that "this is play" (Bateson, 1956). The combination of the two types of behavior in rough-and-tumble make it potentially ambiguous for observers (and sometimes for the children themselves). That ambiguity is reflected in the research literature: Sometimes rough-and-tumble is defined as "play fighting" and is clearly differentiated from "serious fighting" (e.g., Humphreys & Smith, 1987), and sometimes it is not so differentiated. For example, rough-and-tumble has been coded as "aggressive play" (Dodge, 1983) and as "fights or mock fights" (Ladd, 1983), or quite to the contrary, as "physical prosocial behavior" (Coie & Kupersmidt, 1983). More recently, "rough play" has been coded and subdivided into "rough-and-tumble play" where "everyone appeared to enjoy the activity" versus "ambiguous rough play" where "it was not clear whether the participants viewed the activity as fun, play, or aggression" (Dodge, Coie, Pettit, & Price, 1990, p. 1294).

The coding of some types of verbal behavior that occurs along with rough-and-tumble also seldom directly reflects the distinction between serious and playful forms. For example, "argue" has been defined as hostile talk, which includes "insults, threats, contentious remarks" (Ladd, 1983, p. 291); or a category, "hostile verbalizations," has included "insults, threats, and contentious statements" (Dodge, 1983, p. 1388). No mention is made of co-occurring vocal or verbal qualifiers to physical acts (or to verbal ones) that may signal "this is play." In contrast, sociolinguistic reports of children's conflicts frequently document the playful use of insults, threats, or challenges (Boggs, 1978; Goodwin, 1982). Further, Maynard (1985) has shown how children can use "nonserious" cues to shift a serious conflict to a playful one and thereby defuse or terminate a dispute.

The point of this discussion is to highlight the importance of the differentiation of serious and playful behavior, not only for participants, but for those who study children's conflict behavior, verbal or nonverbal. It bears noting that serious conflict is not equated here with aggressive conflict; although serious conflicts can include aggressive ones, most serious conflicts do not involve any aggressive behavior (Shantz, 1987).

Teasing. A second problematic behavior is *teasing*, a kind of verbal analog to rough-and-tumble. It, too, can be serious and hurtful, or it can be playful and good natured. In the research literature, teasing, like rough-and-tumble, has been coded in diverse ways (e.g., as "antisocial" [Dodge, 1983] or as "playful behavior" [Dunn, 1988]). Dunn, for example, described confrontations between a mother and her younger children and their siblings that "had a deliberate teasing quality" in which the children "smiled and laughed" (pp. 15–16).

Ritual conflicts

Conflicts also differ by the extent to which they are routinized, that is, display a repeatable, prescribed format. Examples are the "verbal dueling" observed in Turkish communities (McDowell, 1985); the "contradicting routine," a favorite type of verbal adversative activity among Hawaiian children (Boggs, 1978); and the *cantilena*, a singsong, "mocking" procedure used by Italian children (Corsaro & Rizzo, 1990). These contrast with the free form of most other conflicts, which may vary in structure from turn to turn. Interestingly, the rituals may be identified as either playful or serious. For example, Dunn (1988) noted activities called "ritual insults" between siblings and contradicting routines, all of which were broadly grouped as "joking and humor." Gottman (1986) observed "squabbling" by two children that "had a teasing, insulting quality similar to the ritual insult exchanges that can be found among young preadolescent black children" (p. 189).

Ethnographers and sociologists have provided extensive descriptions of ritual insult exchanges in black speech communities and, more recently, have begun to trace their incidence and use among white females (Eder, 1990) and white working-class males (Leary, 1980). Labov (1972), in a study of black working-class communities, proposed a format for a common type of ritual insult: "Your (relative) is so (insult term) that (extremely negative outcome or state of affairs)." This format organizes such insult moves as "Your family so poor they hafta paint the furniture on the walls." The respondent is expected to counter with a different but parallel and equally devastating insult (e.g., "Your family so hard-up the cockroaches use food stamps"). Kochman (1983) has shown that the interpretation of such insults as serious or playful is often problematic for the participants themselves and may depend on subtle deviations from the linguistic–pragmatic formula prescribed in a given speech community for producing personal challenges or insults.

What all these ritual conflicts share in common – whether they are serious or playful – are the requirements that they be produced according to certain formal rules for style of production, class of content, semantic, and/or syntactic structure; and they are marked often by stereotyped openings and closings. Further, such conflicts are usually performed in the presence of an audience (who may determine the "winner" and "loser"), and their production is often evaluated explicitly as a poor or excellent exemplar of the genre (Davies, 1982; Mitchell-Kernan & Kernan, 1975).

Pretend conflicts

Whether conflicts might occur in the context of pretend activity or whether a conflict might be "reframed" (Goffman, 1974) as make-believe are questions that have rarely been raised. Cummings, Iannotti, and Zahn-Waxler (1989) count as instances of aggression between peers cases in which "pretend themes of aggression" are verbally described. Gottman (1986), however, noted an interaction in which children were "making fun of each other" within the context of a pretend engagement. Procedures used by preschoolers for responding to oppositions produced within the pretend frame were proposed by Garvey (1987) for U.S. children and by Ditchburn (1988) for Canadian children. Although Hartup, Laursen, Stewart, and Eastenson (1988) included as conflicts in their analyses those "concerning role assignments in dramatic play," they excluded "thematic conflicts emerging in this context" on the grounds that the "determinants of these conflicts may differ from others" (p. 1593). Conflicts arising with siblings and mothers in "play," which presumably included those in pretend play, were excluded from analysis by Dunn and Munn (1987). Goodwin (1988), however, stresses that, for urban black girls, confrontative types of conflict occur in pretend play, often as the children enact mother–child compliance disputes, whereas their disputes about planning or executing games and tasks are more "cooperative."

From a longitudinal study of nine mothers' and their children's pretend play (Haight & Miller, in press), Haight and Garvey (1991) found that eight of the pairs conducted conflicts in pretend scenarios and roles. Conflicts enacted in a pretend frame are common, too, among preschoolers; they include confrontations between the roles of good guys and bad guys as well as between those of mother and child. Heath (1983) gives an example of a 3-year-old rural black girl who created a pretend conflict, speaking as both the accuser (herself as adult) and the defendant (represented by a doll as child). She composed the accusations, counter-accusations, and denials normally provided by different persons. Her performance, which was free of support by an actual agonist, displays an ability to manipulate alone a "real" and seemingly "hostile" conflict form while engaging in make believe. She enacted anger, but presumably did not actually experience it:

3.
Girl: You done eat my dinner.
Doll: I ain't, you did.
Girl: You all time eatin'; you took it.
Doll: Ain't, I saw you eat it.
Girl: Set better on me den on you, but I ain't eat it.
Doll: You did.

(Heath, 1983, pp. 98–99)

This example suggests that competence at a learned form of conflict (perhaps one following a "conflict script") may be explored and consolidated in the pretend frame as well as in real-world engagements.

Mitigated and aggravated conflicts

Another family of descriptors, such as "hostile" and "aversive," has been used to characterize verbal conflicts. Grimshaw (1990) proposed a dimension of conflict, "intensity-tone-direction," claiming that "conflict talk can be seen, both by participants and non-participants (including analysts) as being in some general sense more or less benign or malign" (p. 294). D'Andrade and Wish (1985) identified a factor in interactive talk that they labeled "supportive/hostile." It reflects the degree of force or demand, and clusters separately from a factor of *assenting/dissenting*.

As there are different terms that refer to these phenomena, we will use the term *mitigated/aggravated* to designate this "basic interactive dimension" (Labov & Fanshel, 1977, pp. 84–85) of interactive speech. It is an important source of variation in conflict talk and has been shown to be a major factor in judging remedial moves such as excuses and justifications

(Holgraves, 1989). Other terms referencing attitude or the probable effects of conflict also may tap this dimension: "cooperative/competitive" (Schiffrin, 1984) or "constructive/destructive" (Deutsch, 1973). In many cases, researchers' classifications of conflict behavior as "hostile" appear to be based on the use of aggravated speech variants; in other cases, the observation that conflict has "escalated" refers to a shift toward increasingly aggravated speech forms and/or physical force. Boggs (1978) observed, in the verbal disputing of Hawaiian children, a tendency for disputes to escalate from contradiction to challenge, insult, counterinsult, and threat or trial.

Using linguistic-pragmatic criteria, it may be possible to disentangle the confounding of serious (i.e., nonplayful) and aggravated (i.e., nonmitigated) conflict. First, however, it is necessary to show that a serious conflict can be conducted in a mitigated or in an aggravated manner. In Example 4, the children do not appear to be joking or even teasing good-naturedly; each seems to mean seriously what he or she says ("I want to play with it"). Yet their speech is polite: Their oppositions are not aggravated in respect to linguistic form. Further, they are not speaking in a pretend framework and are not following a ritualized format. Two 4-year-olds, a Scottish boy and girl, argue about which would play with a toy car they had just found:

4.
J: I want to play with it!
L: I . . . You played with it at home!
J: No! No! It was a different one. And I never played with this one.
L: But I want to play with it! I've never played with one of this!
J: Nor have I, 'cos I only found it today.

(Discourse excerpt, Logothetis, 1990)

In the contrasting Example 5, the participants also appear seriously to mean what they say and wish to convey the social acts (e.g., commands, refusals) that their speech directly represents. That is, they are not joking. But what they say is produced in aggravated form, that is, a form that is used conventionally to enhance disagreement (Goodwin, 1983). A 5-year-old girl (N) tries to dislodge her young brother (L), who has climbed onto the girl's tricycle:

5.
N: Git away. (pushing him and tugging at the tricycle)
L: I'm a ride dis.
N: No you ain't, you too li'l.
L: I show ya.
N: No you ain't, git off, yo' ugly head don't know how.
L: Git outa, outa (interrupted)

(Discourse excerpt, Heath, 1983, p. 99)

The turns in serious conflicts can be formulated in ways designed to maintain the "face" of participants (Example 4) or to exacerbate differences on the interpersonal level as well as the level of the ostensible issue at hand (Example 5). These alternatives are built into the linguistic, pragmatic, and social organization of talk. Language provides an array of techniques for delicately adjusting talk along a mitigated–aggravated continuum.

Four dimensions of conflict talk

The sociolinguistic perspectives emphasize the actual conversational procedures by which conflicts are conducted, that is, how speakers produce and interpret linguistic-pragmatic behavior as social moves. This focus complements the concern, common in the developmental literature, with interactants' intentions or attitudes, situational influences on outcomes, and the psychological correlates or determinants of conflict.

In this section, we describe the classes of evidence for communalities among conflicts. From the evidence we propose four linguistic and pragmatic dimensions of conflict talk that, together, may account for many of the differences in conflicts observed across disciplines. The bases for the poles of the dimensions will be discussed in the following section.

Four types of evidence form the bases for abstracting dimensions. First, there are the characterizations provided by the analysts who recorded the interactions and who, in some cases (e.g., Boggs, 1978; Schiffrin, 1984), questioned the participants about their assessment of the conflicts. Second, there are the spontaneous metacommunications of the disputants on the meaning or nature of the conflict (e.g., "I was just kidding"; "You don't have to be rude"). Third, certain formal linguistic or communicative features occur that, considered in their sequential context, contribute to the identification of a dimensional value in a particular engagement (e.g., derogatory terms of address, politeness markers, tone of voice, nonverbal gestures). Fourth, and most critical, however, are the interpretations of the participants themselves as revealed in their responses to one another's moves. We will argue that all four dimensions have the potential to be operative simultaneously, that is, any conflict can be analyzed as a particular pattern of the four dimensions. Examples will be given later of this multidimensional feature.

Orientation

This dimension taps a fundamental decision for participants: Is this social act intended as serious or not serious (i.e., as a joke, just kidding, play)?

Sacks (1975) claims that the determination of a statement (serving, for example, as a complaint) as "serious" brings into conditional relevance the contrast class "true–false," whereas that contrast class is not relevant in the case of the determination "joke." The criticality of this dimension can be seen in the ritual insult exchanges known as "the dozens" or "sounding" (Kochman, 1983); departure from the prescribed semantic content may result in a shift from a playful to a serious orientation and lead, thereby, to hurt feelings and anger.

Similarly, Leary (1980) points out how a stranger to a group of working-class white male friends takes as serious several insults that the group treats as nonserious. But even in mother–child compliance disputes, the issue of serious versus nonserious can arise and can be made explicit, as when a mother rejects a child's teasing disobedience with "I'm not joking!" or asks the teaser "Are you pulling my leg?" (Haight & Garvey, 1991). The opposite (or marked) pole of the dimension is indicated by cues to a nonserious orientation. Paralinguistic or prosodic features, smiles, an exaggerated straight face as well as outlandish claims, and abrogation of a precondition on the performance of a speech act (e.g., requesting an action that already has been carried out) are ones that commonly occur.

Format

In this dimension, one pole represents normal conversational sequencing, whereas the other represents ritualized procedures. The defining feature of ritual conflicts is formally constrained elements in repeated or regulated sequential patterns. The formal constraints can include classes of lexical, syntactic, phonological, or prosodic features. The sequential patterning of exchanges (e.g., insult–insult) is itself usually repeated in formal units, or rounds. Two subtypes of ritualized conflicts are recognized, the *conventional* and the *spontaneous*. Each will be defined and illustrated later.

Frame

This dimension concerns participants' attitudes and behavior toward reality and nonreality. One pole, *real*, concerns the here-and-now reality of the place and time of speaking. Representations are read as veridical within a "standard scheme of interpretation" (Goffman, 1976). If some other frame is selected, then this departure from the standard scheme would have to be marked in some way. The other pole of this dimension is labeled *nonreal*, or pretend. There are a variety of linguistic and nonverbal cues that indicate a pretend transformation or invention of objects, settings, actions, and roles (Garvey & Kramer, 1989; Giffin, 1984), and children can explicitly indicate this dimension (e.g., "Don't really eat it, just pretend eat it").

Mode

This final dimension captures linguistic and pragmatic mitigation at one pole and aggravation at the other pole. When disagreements, refusals, or corrections are done, they are performed normatively in mitigated fashion (Levinson, 1983), that is, in turns that display deference and preserve "face" by postponing, hedging, or accounting for the negative component. There are numerous techniques for mitigating social acts, especially in disagreement-relevant moves. As Vuchinich (1984) puts it, "Linguistic devices have evolved to constrain by degrees the hostility conveyed in an oppositional move" (p. 220). Aggravated turns, in contrast, are designed not to soften or delay, but rather to highlight the oppositional component. Thus, returning a reciprocal action (e.g., a threat to a threat, a challenge to a challenge), increasing volume, interrupting a turn, and using direct commands and derogatory descriptors of the opponent occur in many communities (Boggs, 1978; Brenneis & Lein, 1977; Goodwin, 1982). When such interpersonally threatening behaviors occur, it is critical that participants monitor the context to ascertain whether the speaker is being serious (or playful), acting for real (or pretending), and following a ritual format (or not).

Preference organization and conflict talk

Mitigation and aggravation are techniques that function in a broad system in the social use of language, that of preference organization, as described by Levinson (1983) and others within the framework of ethnomethodology. There exist institutional preferences resting on social organizational principles that are built redundantly into the structure of language use. Consider where alternative responses are available: One can either agree or disagree with an assertion; one can comply with or refuse a request; or one can invite a speaker to correct a flawed utterance or correct the error oneself. Of these alternatives, one is said to be preferred; in each case, the former alternative is preferred and the latter dispreferred. The preferred alternative is more usual, more widely acceptable, and generally expected (in the absence of other indications). There are also preferential rankings of possible responses. For example, one can strongly or weakly agree with an assessment and weakly or strongly disagree.

Preference is indicated in the form of the turn itself. According to Levinson (1983), dispreferred actions such as refusals and disagreements "tend to occur in a marked format and they tend to be avoided" (p. 333). They are avoided by postponing the dispreferred response element in the turn by the use of some delay or preface. For example, whether one really wants to accept an invitation or not, when declining (a dispreferred action) one is expected to display awareness of the standard by prefacing the refusal with an apology and/or providing an account for the delict (e.g., "I'm sorry, but I can't because I have a class tonight"). In contrast, the preferred action, an acceptance, can be done directly and without justification (e.g., "Sure, what time?).

The preference systems reflect a normative aspect of conversational usage. Conflict talk, with its disagreements, refusals, and denials, will be a natural site for the varied manifestations of preference organization. In some conflicts, dispreferred alternatives will be handled normatively, that is, will be mitigated in some way – delayed, hedged, prefaced, accounted for – as the children do in Example 4 and to a lesser degree in Example 1. Another possibility, however, is that speakers may choose to exacerbate the conflict by flouting the norm. They will select aggravated forms and avoid the normatively mitigated forms of dispreferred responses. They may use insults and threats as the children do in Examples 2, 3, and 5. Any accounts for opposing will be couched as insults or challenges (e.g., "You ugly head don't know how").

Thus, the preference organizations can be flouted or exploited for communicative purposes without invalidating the fundamental norms. The aggravated speech forms, here considered as representing one pole of the mode dimension may be favored, in fact, in certain types of interactions in some speech groups. Their distribution and use warrant further research as do their history of acquisition and developmental change. Variation along the dimension of mode is theoretically and empirically independent of whether the participants intend that their messages be taken seriously (vs. playfully), and ritualized conflicts may employ either aggravated or mitigated speech forms.[1] Further, children can enact a pretend conflict in either mitigated or aggravated form. Example 3 is in aggravated form. In Example 6, however, the oppositions are mitigated. Two 5-year-old girls were enacting the roles of two women; one (E) was busy baby-sitting, but the other (M) wanted her to go for a drive:

6.
M: You come here, the babies are sleeping now.
E: No, they'll cry when I leave 'cause they'll hear the car.
M: No, the car is broken. *I* have the car.
E: Awright, but one baby will take care of these little babies.
                                    (Discourse excerpt, Kramer, in preparation)[2]

In refusing the request (a dispreferred action), E provided a reason for her refusal, and although M indirectly reinstated the initial request (thus opposing the prior opposition), she also provided a reason for not accepting the account. The reasons, however, were valid only in the pretend world.

Patterns of dimensions in conflict

Co-occurrence of dimensions

As noted earlier, all four dimensions have the potential to be operative simultaneously. However, in any interaction, the setting, the history and usual activities of the individuals, and the nature of the prior interaction may predispose the participants to attend to one or two dimensions as those more likely to be relevant. Conflicts, as we have shown, can be conducted in the pretend framework, as in Examples 3 and 6, or as "real," that is, referencing the "paramount reality of everyday life" (Schutz, 1962), as in Examples 1, 2, 4, and 5. This dimension of frame is likely to be more salient to children and their parents than, say, to the representatives of management and labor in a bargaining session.

Poles of dimensions

The dimensions are described in terms of their extreme, dichotomous poles, although, as was indicated earlier in respect to the poles of mitigation and aggravation, the dimensions actually may be continua. Following a principle of linguistic structure, we will treat these poles as representing unmarked and marked variants. Similar to the preference systems, the alternatives of which Levinson (1983) characterizes as unmarked (preferred) and marked (dispreferred), we consider the *unmarked pole* as the conversationally normative, or expected, pole. The *marked pole*, in contrast, requires some special indication to identify its occurrence. For example, in respect to the dimension of frame, speakers normally expect that assertions refer to the real world, not an imaginary or hypothetical one. Thus, even preschoolers may misunderstand an assertion and need to clarify explicitly the intended interpretative frame. Such behavior indicates their sensitivity to that dimension.

In the following example, then, a verbal conflict arises about frame (i.e., whether an assertion is to be interpreted as referring to the real or pretend world). One 4-year-old boy (S) has shown another (D) his (actually) muddy pants; shortly after that, D held up his leg and pointed to the knee of his pants:

7.
D: I got dirty pants . . . see I got dirty pants.
S: (looking at D's pants) No you don't.
D: Yes I do . . . I'm pretending they're dirty pants.
S: No. (1.0 second silence) No, no you don't.
D: Dirty . . . I'm pretending they're *dirty pants*.
S: (direct gaze, no response)
D: 'Cause I . . . I worked in the mud.

(Discourse excerpt, Kramer, in preparation)

D intended his initial claim to be interpreted in a nonreal framework, as is made clear by his subsequent remarks and his provision of an imaginary account for his pretend claim. But S challenged this claim by insisting on real world facts (perhaps because his own prior claim about dirty pants was made and interpreted in the real frame).

Although disagreements on a dimensional value may be infrequent, such instances reveal the importance of the dimension to the speakers. The dispute of Example 7 appears to be serious on the dimension of orientation as neither child gives signs of teasing or joking, and it is somewhat mitigated on the dimension of mode as D first explains the nature of his claim and then attempts an imaginary justification for it. As the dispute does not conform to a preestablished procedure, it is nonritual on the dimension of format. But in respect to the frame dimension, the children disagree; D chooses a marked (pretend) and S the unmarked (real) interpretation.

Examples of the assembled dimensions

In further discussing a dimensional analysis of conflicts, we adopt the following procedures and notation: (a) The unmarked pole of a dimension will be indicated as (−), the marked as (+). Finer gradations in continua will not be indicated. (b) If participants indicate that they disagree on the value of a dimension, that value is indicated as (!). (c) Conflict episodes may be described as having the same dimensional profile throughout their course. In the prior examples, we have used only excerpts that were relatively homogenous with respect to the dimension under discussion. Changes can occur, however, in midconflict (Maynard, 1985), and they can do so abruptly and clearly. Thus, only the profile for homogenous conflict episodes is indicated unless changes occur within the episode, at which point the changed dimensional value is shown at the point at which it appears to become clear to the speakers. The primary unit for analysis, the conflict episode, begins with mutually expressed opposition (Shantz, 1987) and ends with mutual abstinence from opposing moves (Vuchinich, 1990). (d) At certain points in an episode, however, the speakers (and probably the analyst as well) may be uncertain as to the value to be assigned. The value may emerge only gradually. In such cases, the indeterminate turn or exchange is indicated as (?) for the value of the dimension(s) in question. (See Example 9 for an emerging value.) (e) As all four dimensions are potentially relevant in determining the profile of a conflict, all are indicated in the order of orientation, format, frame, and mode.

Thus, Examples 1 and 4 can be described as (–), (–), (–), (–) as they are serious, nonritual, real, and mitigated. Example 5 is (–), (–), (–), (+), that is, serious, nonritual, real, and aggravated; it contrasts with Examples 1 and 4 only on the mode dimension. Example 2 is indicated (+), (–), (–), (+); it is nonserious, nonritual, real, and aggravated. Example 7 is indicated as (–), (–), (!), (–): serious, nonritual, speakers disagree on frame, and mitigated. The provisional description of Example 6 is (–), (–), (+), (–), that is, (probably) serious, nonritual, nonreal, and mitigated. (Although the children were pretending, the request "you come here" appeared to be meant and interpreted sincerely, and indeed, it eventually received compliance.) Empirical work must establish how independent or interdependent certain values may be. For example, do conflicts conducted in the nonreal value of frame vary systematically on the orientation dimension, that is, can they be either serious or nonserious? The present proposal raises, but does not answer, that question. We have presented examples that suggest the independence of the orientation dimension from that of frame – Examples 3 and 6. The question remains, however, whether the two dimensions are bilaterally independent.

Because all multidimensional scoring examples thus far presented are of nonritualized conflicts, we turn to those that are marked on format. Ritualized conflicts, as noted earlier, may be conventional or spontaneous. An example of the conventional type (a black English ritual insult sequence) in a relatively immature form as performed by preschoolers is provided next. Two boys initiated a conflict about block-building; M had knocked down R's blocks but denied having done so:

8.
R: I know you did that Mark. I know your sneaky – I know your sneaker tricks.
M: Sucker.
R: So are you. So . . . I know your Mama was. (begins rebuilding)
M: Your mother was sucker.
R: I know you. Your Mama was
M: Yeah. Your Daddy was.
R: Yeah. So was your –

(Discourse excerpt, Emihovich, 1986, pp. 492–493)

The investigator, questioning the children after the conflict, learned that the two were not in agreement on whether they were playing ("jiving," as M, a black child called it) or "arguing" (as R, a white child, thought); thus the orientation dimension is indicated as (!). Neither child, however, was unclear about how to proceed with the ritual, although both were unable to construct formally complete insults. The example, composed of rounds (here the repeated units of reciprocal insult exchanges) is further identified as (+), ritualized format; (–), real frame (not pretend); and (+), aggravated mode. The "dozens" format used here is abbreviated and highly stereotypic, which is characteristic of younger children's attempts at ritual insult exchanges (Labov, 1972).

The spontaneous type of ritual conflict probably appears more often in the interactions of young children. It evolves from an ongoing interaction, taking some prior exchange as the format model for the ad hoc ritual (Garvey, 1977). Virtually any kind of exchange can be ritualized by repeating formally constrained items in the exchange and by sequencing the exchanges in rounds. In the next example, two preschoolers, engaged in pretend play, evolved a complex ritual conflict from their prior exchanges. A format shift from nonritual to ritual may have been realized only gradually by the participants, a possibility we have indicated by (?) for format at the onset of the conflict. As the oppositions began, the children also may have been unsure of the orientation. Thus, this example illustrates that dimensional value may emerge only gradually. (In this example the final rounds are separated by lines.) A boy (B), acting as father, drove off on a car; he waved, saying "Goodbye." The girl (G) replied, "Bye." Then:

9.

B: See you tomorrow. (still "driving" car)
G: Okay.
B: I have to go to school.
G: You're already at school.　　　　(1st opposition)
B: No I'm not.　　　　(2d opposition)
G: Yes, you are.　　　　(orientation ?; format ?; frame +;
　　　　mode +)

B: No, I'm not.
G: You are too!
B: No, I'm not! (1.0 second silence)
_____

B: I have to go to work.　　　　(Social act disjunction;
G: You're already at work.　　　　repetition in turn patterns,
B: No I'm not.　　　　rhythm, and intonation suggest
　　　　nonserious and ritual values have
　　　　become clear to both children.)
_____

G: But you're not going to the party.　　　　(Episode continues, marked on
B: Yes, I am.　　　　all dimensions: +; +; +; +)
G: You're already at the party.
B: No, I'm not.

(Discourse excerpt, Garvey, 1977, p. 116)

Because this example is playful, utilizes pretend references, and evolves into a spontaneous ritual with round structure, the question must be addressed as to whether it should be considered a conflict at all. The same question, of course, arises in relation to the other examples that are marked as nonserious, ritualized, and/or nonreal.

Significance of varieties of conflict

There are a number of rationales underlying the premise of this chapter that varieties of disputes not only qualify as conflicts but also illuminate some fundamental developmental competencies, both linguistic and social. Four of those rationales will be presented here. Then attention will be given to some limitations of the sociolinguistic approaches.

Understanding children's conflict repertoires

We suggest that by considering Example 9 (as well as the other nonserious, ritualized, and/or nonreal examples) as a variety of conflict, we may better understand the scope of the repertoire that children draw on in adversative interactions and better detect the sources of their capabilities. First, the episode is built on the essential principle of conflict, that is, mutual verbal opposition, as each child contradicts the assertions of the other. That the conflict form may be used also for other purposes, such as play, or draw on a particular referential frame, such as pretense, does not detract from the fact that the children are using direct and indirect opposing arguments to negate one another's assertions. They have learned the linguistic-pragmatic forms and content employed in their speech community for opposing and can use these techniques in serious interactions, as well as in playful, but nonreal, or nonritualized ones. And they are beginning to learn the verbal devices through which oppositions can be mitigated or aggravated to various degrees. Considering the different kinds of conflict interactions in which children engage allows us to assess the scope and flexibility of their repertoire.

Further, as easily as this ritualized conflict (Example 9) evolved from an initially nonadversative pretend interaction, so can a serious, nonpretend (or nonritualized) conflict erupt among children and become increasingly aggravated, or an initially serious conflict can be changed to a playful one. It would be difficult to arrive at a principled basis for excluding the proposed varieties from the construct of conflict. In addition to their immediate interaction functions, moreover, the playful, ritualized, or pretend conflicts may provide opportunities for practice and consolidation of children's adversative discourse skills.

Documenting changes within episodes

A second reason for incorporating these different varieties of conflicts in research is that interactions can change on any of these dimensions in midcourse. Two important questions for study emerge. (a) Are there any intrinsic directions of change as is suggested by Boggs's (1978) observation that a switch to aggravated values predicts further and increasingly aggravated ("escalated") conflict? (b) At what age and how do children begin to use strategically changes in dimensional values (e.g., introducing a nonreal frame, a signal of a nonserious orientation, or a ritualization cue to deal with opposition)?

Revealing socialization

A third reason is to elucidate the processes of skills acquisition in conflicting. Parents may initiate or support particular kinds of "practice" conflicts, either primarily for play or to model and encourage self-assertive and self-defensive strategies and the appropriate conditions for their use in their speech communities (Eisenberg, 1986; Miller & Sperry, 1987). Further, it is likely that some parents use shifts on one or more of the dimensions to manage their children's noncompliance. Haight and Garvey (1991) identified episodes in which a child's (C) refusal to pick up his toys was met by his mother's (M) shift to a playful, ritualized contradicting, with the result of finally enlisting his cooperation. (In the next example, colons mark the lengthening of the vowel with high-falling pitch):

10.
M: I will be first. I will be first to pick up all the leggos. (2.0 second silence) I'm first, not yo:u.
C: *I'm* first. (both pick up leggos)
M: *I'm* first.
C: *I'm* first. (after a few minutes, child wanders away)
M: I am fi:rst (singsong; child returns and begins again to pick up toys). Jason is not fi:rst.

                        (Discourse excerpt, Haight & Garvey, 1991)

This conflict is notated as +, +, −, +. Although this mother may have sincerely wanted to influence the child's behavior, she selected playful behavior with which to do so – a patterned, challenging "tease" with which the child was familiar, apparently.

Specifying changes with age and differences across groups

Finally, a fourth reason for investigating varieties of conflict is the evidence that several of the varieties become more complex or elaborated with age. A variety may have a developmental history. In particular, the ritualized formats of certain speech communities or the aggravated styles favored by some groups must be learned over a period of years, as must be the appropriate conditions of use and the conventional meanings their use invokes. Precursors and subsequent elaborations of some types of ritual insult sequences (Labov, 1972); the contradicting routines of Hawaiian children (Boggs, 1978), which were conducted playfully in parent–child interactions but more often seriously in child–child ones; and the *discussione* of Italian children (Corsaro & Rizzo, 1990) all deserve examination from a developmental perspective.

Comparisons across groups may profit from a consideration of variations on dimensional values. For example, Sheldon (1992) has observed differences in both mode and frame dimensions in same-sex groups of preschool boys and girls. Mitigated oppositions were favored by the girls, who used a variety of linguistic techniques (e.g., modality expressions: "Maybe you could just...."; request-for-agreement tags: "isn't it?"). But another characteristic of the girls' disputes was the tendency to use frame as a resource for negotiating differences, that is, to reframe an opposition into the pretend realm.

Both within and across those groups whose members frequently come into contact, there are sometimes subtle but socially significant variations in conflict form that members must learn to distinguish and interpret correctly if interpersonal misunderstanding is to be avoided. In particular, the cues that signal playful rather than serious orientation, especially when combined with aggravated forms, appear to require an extended course of learning and experience in their use. (See Aboud, this volume, for additional discussion of this point.)

It is possible also that a dimensional approach can provide a basis for linking differently oriented research findings. Several researchers from different disciplines have examined the emergence and uses of elaborated discourse negation. That is the use of what have been called reasons, justifications, explanations, accounts (e.g., "I can't 'cause I'm too tired") or alternatives (e.g., "This is not [big], it's small"). Children begin to use these patterns with caregivers in contexts in which the caregiver probes the child's simple negative response (asking, for example, "Why not?") or elaborates such a response (e.g., "It's not a goose? What is it then?") (Keller-Cohen, Chalmer, & Remler, 1979). These linguistic patterns also underlie the development of mitigated responses in conflicts, responses often viewed as evidence of social rule acquisition that is displayed in "situations of accountability" (Much & Shweder, 1978), as developmentally more advanced strategies of noncompliance (Kuczynski, Kochanska, Radke-Yarrow, & Girnius-Brown, 1987), and as evidence of the child's increasingly differentiated understanding of the social world (Dunn & Munn, 1987). The provision of accounts in contexts of refusal or disagreement is also evidence of the acquisition of normative techniques for handling dispreferred responses, as discussed previously.

Some limitations of the sociolinguistic perspectives

The contributions of sociolinguistic perspectives are embedded in fields with characteristic goals, methods, and styles of data presentation. Some of the limitations these characteristics produce, although perhaps evident to the reader by this time, are specified briefly here in order to clarify the nature of the research cited.

One factor that limits the utilization of sociolinguistic research by other disciplines is the nature of the linguistically focused procedures themselves. Seldom are raw data reduced by means of coding systems, as the objective is either to explicate the very judgments that coding systems necessarily take for granted or to describe in depth the exchange sequences. Analytic procedures are infrequently subjected to reliability checks, and results are rarely quantified; often raw data on the frequency of occurrence of the linguistic patterns are not provided.

Emphasis on sequential contingencies and the adaptations of turns at speaking to their particular environments is not compatible with the aggregation of data across individual speakers. Research reports in these literatures generally rely on explication by means of example. That is, the data are transcripts of episodes or sequences that contain particular features or patterns, which are then interpreted and discussed in detail. Often, too, in focusing on patterns of conflict talk that are strikingly distinctive of a particular community, the occurrence and distribution of less salient forms are not provided. Also, systematic sampling of groups is not characteristic of many studies that detail variations in conflict behavior, and the representativeness of the variations is not statistically documented. Often, however, conflict interactions are extracted from many hours of recordings of a small group of subjects' diverse activities (e.g., Goodwin, 1983; Miller & Sperry, 1987) for which extensive ethnographic data have been collected in ecologically valid situations.

Finally, in few studies, even those investigations of children's conflicts, are developmental changes examined in any systematic way. Few researchers have attempted to relate conflict behavior to cognitive or sociocognitive factors that may enable certain skills involved in interpersonal conflict activities. Rather, studies embodying the sociolinguistic approaches have been searches for correlates of conflict variations in features of social role relationships, group dynamics, institutional structures, or cultural value systems (see Grimshaw, 1990, for a discussion of such foci).

Conclusions

The sociolinguistic perspectives on conflict talk invite a consideration of conflict as a special aspect of communicative competence and, thereby, social competence. Children employ the distinctions provided by their linguistic-pragmatic systems to initiate, conduct, modulate, and terminate conflicts. They may choose to exacerbate rather than resolve disputes, and they may utilize conflict forms for a variety of purposes and may achieve, thus, a variety of effects on group and interpersonal relationships. We have proposed several dimensions on which conflict behavior can vary, attempting to incorporate distinctions about aspects of conflicts made in both the sociolinguistic and psychological research literatures. We have attempted to show that even young children's conflict talk can be surprisingly diverse and versatile, far more so than the consideration of serious conflicts alone would suggest.

The dimensions tap conflict-internal variables, ones we believe are monitored by the participants themselves even when they are unsure of a particular value in the interaction. The dimensions do not directly index the influence of exogenous variables such as the relative status of the participants or their relationships, ethnicity, gender, object or opportunity resources, or "open" or "closed" situations (Hartup & Laursen, in press). Rather, some of the effects of these exogenous variables on conflict behavior should be manifested by changes on the dimensions of orientation, frame, mode, and format. Examination of the alternative responses suggested by the poles and gradations of these dimensions may provide a means to examine the microgenesis of conflict episodes and to track developmental changes in children's conflict talk within and across speech situations.

Notes

1. The ritualized disputes illustrated in this chapter are, to greater or lesser degrees, aggravated in respect to mode. Mitigated, ritualized formats, however, can occur also. An example would be formal debates (e.g., between high school debating teams or in Parliament) in

which turns at speaking are preallocated, and procedural steps (e.g., rebuttal) and role terms (e.g., "my Honorable Colleague") are prescribed.
2. We thank Thayer L. Kramer for her permission to use the videotapes and scripts collected as part of her doctoral work in progress (*The Relation between Conflict Management and Liking during the Initial Interactions of Preschool Children*) at the University of Maine. Also, the first author is grateful to the Spencer Foundation for supporting her work with these materials.

References

Bateson, G. (1956). The message "this is play." In *Group processes: Transactions of the second conference*. New York: Josiah Macy, Jr. Foundation.

Boggs, S. (1978). The development of verbal disputing in part-Hawaiian children. *Language in Society, 7*, 325–344.

Brenneis, D. (1988). Language and disputing. *American Review of Anthropology, 17*, 221–237.

Brenneis, D., & Lein, L. (1977). "You fruithead": A sociolinguistic approach to children's dispute settlement. In S. Ervin-Tripp & C. Mitchell-Kernan (Eds.), *Child discourse*. New York: Academic Press.

Coie, J. D., & Kupersmidt, J. B. (1983). A behavioral analysis of emerging social status in boys' groups. *Child Development, 54*, 1400–1416.

Corsaro, W., & Rizzo, T. (1990). Disputes and conflict resolution among nursery school children in the U.S. and Italy. In A. Grimshaw (Ed.), *Conflict talk*. Cambridge: Cambridge University Press.

Coulter, J. (1990). Elementary properties of argument sequences. In G. Psathas (Ed.), *Interaction competence*. Lantham, MD: University Press of America.

Cummings, E. M., Iannotti, R. J., & Zahn-Waxler, C. (1989). Aggression between peers in early childhood: Individual continuity and developmental change. *Child Development, 60*, 887–895.

D'Andrade, R. G., & Wish, M. (1985). Speech act theory in quantitative research on interpersonal behavior. *Discourse Processes, 8*, 229–259.

Davies, B. (1982). *Life in the classroom and playground: The accounts of primary school children*. London: Routledge & Kegan Paul.

Deutsch, M. (1973). *The resolution of conflict*. New Haven, CT: Yale University Press.

Ditchburn, S. (1988). Conflict management in young children's play. *International Journal of Early Childhood, 20*, 62–70.

Dodge, K. A. (1983). Behavioral antecedents of peer social status. *Child Development, 54*, 1386–1399.

Dodge, K. A., Coie, J. D., Pettit, G. S., & Price, J. M. (1990). Peer status and aggression in boys' groups: Developmental and contextual analyses. *Child Development, 61*, 1289–1309.

Drew, P. (1985). Analyzing the use of language in courtroom interaction. In T. van Dijk (Ed.), *Handbook of discourse analysis: Discourse and dialogue* (Vol. 3). New York: Academic Press.

Dunn, J. (1988). *The beginnings of social understanding*. Cambridge, MA: Harvard University Press.

Dunn, J., & Munn, P. (1987). Development of justification in disputes with mother and sibling. *Developmental Psychology, 23*, 791–798.

Eder, D. (1990). Serious and playful disputes: Variation in conflict talk among female adolescents. In A. Grimshaw (Ed.), *Conflict talk*. Cambridge: Cambridge University Press.

Eisenberg, A. (1986). Teasing: Verbal play in two Mexicano homes. In B. Schieffelin &

E. Ochs (Eds.), *Language socialization across cultures*. Cambridge: Cambridge University Press.

Eisenberg, A., & Garvey, C. (1981). Children's use of verbal strategies in resolving conflicts. *Discourse Processes*, *4*, 149–170.

Emihovich, C. (1986). Argument as status assertion: Contextual variations in children's disputes. *Language in Society*, *15*, 485–500.

Garvey, C. (1977). *Play*. Cambridge, MA: Harvard University Press.

Garvey, C. (1984). *Children's talk*. Cambridge, MA: Harvard University Press.

Garvey, C. (1987, April). *Creation and avoidance of conflict*. Paper presentation at the meeting of the Society for Research in Child Development, Baltimore.

Garvey, C., & Kramer, T. L. (1989). The language of social pretend play. *Developmental Review*, *9*, 364–382.

Giffin, H. (1984). The coordination of meaning in the creation of a shared make-believe reality. In I. Bretherton (Ed.), *Symbolic play: The development of social understanding*. New York: Academic Press.

Goffman, E. (1971). *Relations in public*. New York: Harper & Row.

Goffman, E. (1974). *Frame analysis*. New York: Harper & Row.

Goffman, E. (1976). Replies and responses. *Language in Society*, *5*, 257–313.

Goodwin, C., & Goodwin, M. (1990). Interstitial argument. In A. Grimshaw (Ed.), *Conflict talk*. Cambridge: Cambridge University Press.

Goodwin, M. (1982). Processes of dispute management among urban black children. *American Ethnologist*, *9*, 76–96.

Goodwin, M. (1983). Aggravated correction and disagreement in children's conversations. *Journal of Pragmatics*, *7*, 657–677.

Goodwin, M. (1988). Cooperation and competition across girls' play activities. In S. Fisher & A. Todd (Eds.), *Gender and discourse: The power of talk*. Norwood, NJ: Ablex.

Gottman, J. (1986). The world of coordinated play: Same- and cross-sex friendship in young children. In J. Gottman & J. Parker (Eds.), *Conversations of friends: Speculations on affective development*. Cambridge: Cambridge University Press.

Grimshaw, A. (1990). Research on conflict talk: Antecedents, resources, findings, directions. In A. Grimshaw (Ed.), *Conflict talk*. Cambridge: Cambridge University Press.

Gumperz, J. (1982). *Discourse strategies*. Cambridge: Cambridge University Press.

Haight, W. L., & Garvey, C. (1991, April). *Caregiver–child interaction and the emergence of young children's conflict repertoire*. Poster presentation at the meeting of the Society for Research in Child Development, Seattle, WA.

Haight, W. L., & Miller, P. (in press). *The ecology and development of pretend play*. New York: SUNY Press.

Hartup, W. W., & Laursen, B. (in press). Conflict and context in peer relations. In C. Hart (Ed.), *Children on playgrounds: Research perspectives and applications*. Ithaca: SUNY Press.

Hartup, W. W., Laursen, B., Stewart, H. I., & Eastenson, A. (1988). Conflict and friendship relations of young children. *Child Development*, *59*, 1590–1600.

Heath, S. (1983). *Ways with words: Language, life, and work in communities and classrooms*. Cambridge: Cambridge University Press.

Holgraves, T. (1989). The form and function of remedial moves: Reported use, psychological reality and perceived effectiveness. *Journal of Language and Social Psychology*, *8*, 1–16.

Humphreys, A. P., & Smith, P. K. (1987). Rough and tumble, friendship, and dominance in school children: Evidence for continuity and change with age. *Child Development*, *58*, 201–212.

Keller-Cohen, D., Chalmer, K., & Remler, J. (1979). The development of discourse negation in the nonnative child. In E. Ochs & B. Schieffelin (Eds.), *Developmental pragmatics*. New York: Academic Press.

Kochman, T. (1970). Toward an enthnography of behavior. In N. E. Whitten, Jr. & J. F. Szwed (Eds.), *Afro-American anthropology*. New York: Free Press.

Kochman, T. (1983). The boundary between play and nonplay in black verbal dueling. *Language in Society*, 12, 329–337.

Kuczynski, L., Kochanska, G., Radke-Yarrow, M., & Girnius-Brown, O. (1987). A developmental interpretation of young children's noncompliance. *Developmental Psychology*, 23, 799–806.

Labov, W. (1972). Rules for ritual insults. In D. Sudnow (Ed.), *Studies in social interaction*. New York: Free Press.

Labov, W., & Fanshel, D. (1977). *Therapeutic discourse: Psychotherapy as conversation*. New York: Academic Press.

Ladd, G. W. (1983). Social networks of popular, average, and rejected children in school settings. *Merrill-Palmer Quarterly*, 29, 283–307.

Leary, J. P. (1980). White ritual insults. In H. Schwartzman (Ed.), *Play and culture*. West Point, NY: Leisure Press.

Levinson, S. (1983). *Pragmatics*. Cambridge: Cambridge University Press.

Logothetis, K. (1990). *Preschool children in communication with their peers*. Unpublished doctoral dissertation, Edinburgh University.

Maynard, D. (1985). How children start arguments. *Language in Society*, 4, 1–30.

Maynard, D. (1986). Offering and soliciting collaboration in multi-party disputes among children (and other humans). *Human Studies*, 9, 261–285.

McDowell, J. (1985). Verbal dueling. In T. van Dijk (Ed.), *Handbook of discourse analysis* (Vol. 3). London: Academic Press.

Miller, P., Danaher, D., & Forbes, D. (1986). Sex-related strategies for coping with interpersonal conflict in children aged five and seven. *Developmental Psychology*, 22, 543–548.

Miller, P. J., & Sperry, L. (1987). The socialization of anger and aggression. *Merrill-Palmer Quarterly*, 33, 1–31.

Mitchell-Kernan, C., & Kernan, K. T. (1975). Children's insults: America and Samoa. In M. Sanches & B. Blount (Eds.), *Sociocultural dimensions of language use*. New York: Academic Press.

Much, N., & Shweder, R. (1978). Speaking of rules: The analysis of culture in breach. In W. Damon (Ed.), *Moral development: New directions in child development*. San Francisco: Jossey-Bass.

O'Keefe, B. J., & Benoit, P. J. (1982). Children's arguments. In J. R. Cox & C. A. Willard (Eds.), *Advances in argumentation theory and research*. Carbondale: Southern Illinois University Press.

Patterson, G. R. (1982). *Coercive family processes*. Eugene, OR: Castalia.

Sacks, H. (1975). Everyone has to lie. In M. Sanches & B. Blount (Eds.), *Sociocultural dimensions of language use*. New York: Academic Press.

Schiffrin, D. (1984). Jewish argument as sociability. *Language in Society*, 13, 311–335.

Schutz, A. (1962). *Collected papers: The problem of social reality* (Vol. 1). The Hague: Martinus Nijhoff.

Scott, M., & Lyman, S. (1968). Accounts. *American Sociological Review*, 33, 46–62.

Shantz, C. U. (1987). Conflicts between children. *Child Development*, 58, 283–305.

Shantz, C. U., & Shantz, D. W. (1985). Conflict between children: Social-cognitive and sociometric correlates. In M. W. Berkowitz (Ed.), *Peer conflict and psychological growth: New directions for child development*. San Francisco: Jossey-Bass.

Sheldon, A. (1992). Conflict talk: Sociolinguistic challenges to self-assertion and how young girls meet them. *Merrill-Palmer Quarterly*, 38, 95–117.

Simmel, G. (1955). *Conflict and the web of group affiliation*. New York: Free Press.

van Dijk, T. (Ed.). (1985). *Handbook of discourse analysis*. London: Academic Press.

Vuchinich, S. (1984). Sequencing and social structure in family conflict. *Social Psychology Quarterly*, *47*, 217–234.

Vuchinich, S. (1990). The sequential organization of closing in verbal family conflict. In A. Grimshaw (Ed.), *Conflict talk*. Cambridge: Cambridge University Press.

Walton, M. D., & Sedlak, A. J. (1982). Making amends: A grammar-based analysis of children's social interaction. *Merrill-Palmer Quarterly*, *28*, 389–412.

5   Conflict and emotions in marital, sibling, and peer relationships

Lynn Fainsilber Katz, Laurie Kramer, and John M. Gottman

Children are exposed to conflict in their families on a regular basis (Cummings, Zahn-Waxler, & Radke-Yarrow, 1981, 1984). They encounter conflict as their mothers angrily tell them to go to their room, their siblings get upset with them over a game, or they hear their parents quibble about how to spend money. It is important to understand what these experiences with conflict are like for youngsters, as their future social adjustment may depend, in part, on how they comprehend and cope with these early experiences (Emery, 1982). It is also important to advance our understanding of conflict within the family context because of its potential to negatively affect the quality of family life. Because mutual interdependencies within the family function to further the goals of individual members, the challenge for families is to manage conflict in such a way as to maintain the cohesion of the family unit and, at the same time, allow for individuals' needs. Indeed, the very survival of the family unit may depend on their ability to express negative affect while ensuring that any subsequent conflict does not become divisive.

The study of conflict within families requires careful attention to decisions about what unit of analysis is to be examined. Whereas conflicts can occur among any combination of family members, most research has focused on dyadic (e.g., marital, parent–child, sibling), or triadic subsystems. Each subsystem has a unique power and dominance relationship and also differs in terms of the accessibility members have to each other. As a result, it is important to recognize that the form and frequency of conflict may vary considerably from dyad to dyad (or triad). Moreover, the effects of the conflict on other family members will be different depending on who the active participants in the dispute happen to be.

It is also the case that conflict within one subsystem of the family can have effects on other individuals, both within and external to the immediate family. For example, conflict within the marital relationship may influence the quality of parent–child and sibling relationships. These effects are likely to be bidirectional, so that conflict in the parent–child or sibling relationships may also influence marital interactions. Furthermore, relationships with other significant individuals, such as peers and co-workers, may also influence and/or be influenced by family conflict. Both the intrafamilial and the extrafamilial effects of family conflict need to be understood in order to fully elucidate the functions of conflict in families.

In this chapter, we will explore conflict within two sets of family dyads: the marital and sibling subsystems. These two sets of relationships, at the heart of our research efforts, will be used to illustrate our thinking. First, we address how conflict in the marital relationship is associated with the quality of children's relationships with their parents and peers. In the Family Psychophysiology Project at the University of Washington, Gottman and Katz have conducted research on the links between marital conflict, parent–child interaction, and child behavior. In addressing this problem, we have applied psychophysiological methods and theory to understand how conflict and affective expression in the marital subsystem have an impact on the child's socioemotional development. In most conceptualizations of emotion, physiology is considered, at minimum, an important component (see, e.g., Lyons, 1980; Schwartz, 1982). Psychophysiological processes are not viewed in a reductionist sense as more primary or fundamental than psychological processes, but as additional tools with which to understand the richness and complexity of human behavior. A psychophysiological approach, with its unique theoretical perspective and concepts, may provide a small increment of understanding that will ultimately help in the final goal of building theory. In our data, we will see that psychophysiological processes help us better understand how marital satisfaction is associated with the quality of children's peer relations.

We will then turn our attention to examine how conflict within the peer relationship is related to children's adjustment to becoming a sibling. In the "Becoming a Sibling" project, at the University of Illinois at Urbana-Champaign, Kramer and Gottman have studied how the process of becoming a sibling is influenced by the relationships young children have with their peers and parents. This research has highlighted the importance of conflict and conflict management as interpersonal processes that influence the quality of relationships children develop with others. Particular attention will be paid to the specific conflict management processes children use with their peers that predict their adjustment to becoming a sibling. We will examine how being a good conflict manager, even before a sibling is born, predicts the quality of a child's sibling relationship.

A central methodological approach in our research is the detailed description of microsocial processes that occur during family conflict. We believe that description of family interaction is critical for the production of working hypotheses, which ultimately contribute to the development of theory. Ethologists' and primatologists' work is replete with examples of the usefulness of descriptive research (see Darwin's classic work on emotional expression, for example). Our efforts have focused also on the description of affective processes within families. This is because studies of family process have pointed to the primacy of affective communication (particularly the communication of negative affect) in functional and dysfunctional family interaction (see Gottman, 1979, for a review). We will begin with a discussion of our research on how conflict within the marital system is related to children's socioemotional development.

Marital conflict and child outcomes

For the past 6 years, Gottman and Katz have studied the processes by which marital and family conflict affects children's peer relationships and physical health. This approach has called for an integration of psychophysiological theorizing and methods with more traditional observational and self-report methods to advance our understanding of social behavior.

A psychophysiological approach to the study of conflict

The application of psychophysiological methods to the study of social behavior and interpersonal processes is in its infancy. Cacioppo and Petty's (1983) book on social psychophysiology provided the first forum for psychologists whose work integrated social and biological thinking, and encouraged continued research on the psychophysiology of emotion, interpersonal attitudes and processes. Most recently, psychophysiological theorizing and methods have been extended to the developmental study of humans (Fox, 1989; Kagan, Reznick, Clarke, Snidman, & Garcia-Coll, 1984) and primates (Suomi, 1990). Let us briefly review the historical context of such an integration.

Historical context: Arousal theory. Early psychophysiological writing considered arousal to be a unidimensional continuum ranging from a state of deep sleep to one of extreme effort or excitement (e.g., Duffy, 1957). Increases in arousal were believed to reflect an increase in "excitation" or "energy mobilization" (Cannon, 1929), which was presumed to be indexed by a massive and diffuse autonomic response. Cannon's (1929) famous "fight or flight" reaction, representing the organism's adaptive preparation for emergency and the mobilization of the body's fuels, is an example of the focus of arousal theory on the intensity of behavior. The particular form in which arousal was manifested – be it autonomic, overt behavioral, or cortical – was not considered to be theoretically meaningful.

Remnants of classic arousal theory can be found in more recent theories of emotion. For example, the idea of diffuse, general arousal was adopted by Schachter and Singer (1962) in their proposal that this type of physiological arousal was the underlying substance for all emotions. They suggested that discrete emotions, such as joy and anger, differed only by the cognitive labels individuals use to explain their perceptions of their own bodily cues of arousal. This view has been elaborated as a cognitive theory of emotion by Mandler (1975) and has recently been applied by Berscheid (1983).

John Lacey's (1967) influential paper called for a revision of arousal theory. Electrocortical, autonomic, and overt behavioral arousal, Lacey argued, are different forms of arousal and are imperfectly coupled. He argued against the notion of generalized arousal by pointing out that dissociations between somatic and behavioral measures are quite common. He also introduced the concept of "directional fractionation" to explain these dissociations among different physiological indices. Briefly, *directional fractionation* refers to instances when increases in one physiological system (e.g., heart rate) are accompanied by decreases in another (e.g., skin conductance). Lacey recognized that, under many conditions, the autonomic nervous system is capable of acting as a whole, with increments in a wide range of physiological systems. However, his main contention was that different types of somatic responses play different roles in the execution of different behaviors. Research should be addressed not only to questions about the magnitude of the response, he thought, but also to questions about its specific form.

Psychophysiological researchers have adopted Lacey's call recently for specificity in response patterning across and within different physiological and behavioral systems. In a search for emotion-specific patterning in physiological responses, Ekman, Levenson, and Friesen (1983) found evidence for an "autonomic signature" for each emotion. They documented that heart rate decreases with facial expressions of disgust, but increases with anger, fear, joy, and sadness. Anger and fear are differentiated by the fact that hands become hot in anger but cold in accordance with fear facial expressions. This work has been replicated now several times, including in a cross-cultural study of tribesmen in Sumatra (Levenson, personal communication).

Specificity in physiological response patterning also has been proposed in research on endocrine functioning. It is well known that the autonomic and endocrine systems are sensitive to stresses such as bereavement or coping with chronic illness of offspring (see Temoshok, Van Dyke, & Zegans, 1983, for a review). An important model linking endocrine functioning and emotional reactions was advanced by Henry and Stephens (1977). They proposed that specific emotional states are connected to the two adrenal endocrine stress systems. According to their model, the sympathetic-adrenomedullary system is activated during active coping and the affective responses of anger and hostility. This biological system is responsible for the secretion of the catecholamines (norepinephrine, epinephrine, and dopamine), which in normal functioning, accelerate metabolic rate and the expenditure of energy in the body. The second adrenal endocrine stress system, the pituitary-adrenocortical system, is proposed to be activated during chronic stress and engages a passive coping response, such as depression, helplessness, or withdrawal. This biological system is responsible for the secretion of the glucocorticoid cortisol, which is related to glucose metabolism and the maintenance of metabolic processes during normal functioning. There is also some evidence that the chronic activation of both of the axes in the model of Henry and Stephens is related to tissue damage, for example, plaque formation in arteries related to atherosclerosis (Taggart & Carruthers, 1971).

To summarize, movement in the field of psychophysiology has been away from the conceptualization of arousal as a simple unidimensional manner and toward the identification of specific physiological processes accompanying different psychological events. This trend is consistent with the central fact that biological processes reflect changes in the metabolic needs of the organism. To the extent that different interpersonal behaviors require the support of different combinations of bodily functions, there may be specificity in linkages between interpersonal behaviors and physiological events. In terms of our thinking about conflict, this approach highlights the importance of specificity in describing different forms of conflict. In addition, it cautions against the broad use of the term *arousal* because the meaning of arousal depends on the physiological system being described. This thinking is just beginning to be applied to the interpersonal context.

Psychophysiology and interpersonal interaction. A growing body of evidence supports the idea that interpersonal interactions can affect the autonomic nervous system (ANS) of the actors and that this effect is related to the emotional qualities of the interaction (DiMascio, Boyd, & Greenblatt, 1957; Kaplan, Burch, & Bloom, 1964; Malmo, Boag, & Smith, 1957). For example, Kaplan et al. (1964) found that individuals who disliked each other were more likely to show correlations in skin conductance than dyads who liked each other. Thus, among relatively unacquainted dyads, interpersonal interactions can influence the physiological responses of the participants.

Recent studies of marital interaction suggest that interpersonal interactions within close relationships also can strongly affect the ANS. Levenson and Gottman (1983) studied couples during natural interactions to investigate the degree to which variation in marital satisfaction could be explained by physiological patterns between the spouses. Couples engaged in a high-conflict discussion while physiological and observational data were collected. Using a measure of "physiological linkage," Levenson and Gottman were able to account for 60% of the variance in marital satisfaction. Greater physiological linkage during a high-conflict discussion was associated with lower levels of marital satisfaction. Levenson and Gottman's (1985) 3-year follow-up of these same couples revealed that high arousal during the original laboratory discussions predicted a decline in marital satisfaction over 3 years.

Taken together, these studies suggest that the affective climate of interpersonal interactions can influence the ANS. Although this remains true regardless of whether the people have recently met or have a long interaction history, the most careful and systematic studies have been conducted with people who know each other well – the marital dyad. Given these findings, it is reasonable to hypothesize that emotional interactions within the family also influence the autonomic nervous activity of the child. We have begun to address this question in our research on the effects of marital discord on young children's socioemotional development.

Marital discord, parenting, and children's emotional development

Self-report, observational, and physiological measures were obtained within a natural social-interactive context to examine the marital and parent–child processes predictive of risk and psychopathology. Couples ranging in marital satisfaction were videotaped during a high-conflict marital discussion and during a parent–child interactive teaching task with their 4- to 5-year-old child. In the parent–child interaction task, parents obtained information about a story the child had previously heard and attempted to teach their child to play a videogame. Physiological measures were obtained from the husband and wife during the marital session and from the child during the parent–child interaction. All physiological indexes were synchronized in time with behavior (for a more detailed discussion of procedures, see Gottman & Katz, 1989; Katz & Gottman, 1991a).

Families also were recontacted 3 years later for an assessment of marital and child functioning. Couples completed marital satisfaction questionnaires and were interviewed regarding their considerations of separation and divorce and actual incidences of separation and divorce. Children's adjustment was assessed using parent and teacher ratings of behavior problems, an observational sample of peer interaction, and an assessment of children's academic achievement.

Preliminary results suggest that children from maritally distressed homes do not display the social processes necessary for managing interpersonal conflict. Gottman and Katz (1989) reported that children from maritally distressed homes have higher levels of urinary dopamine (a stress-related hormone), and that this, in turn, is related to their tendency to play at a lower, potentially conflict-free level with their best friends. That is, these children tended to engage in more solitary play or parallel play rather than develop imaginative fantasy activities with their friends. Because engagement in nonstereotyped fantasy play runs a heightened risk of conflict, we reasoned that children from maritally distressed homes are either unable to manage or wish to avoid potential conflict with their peers. The findings of high levels of stress-related hormones in children from maritally distressed homes supports the hypothesis that these children may choose to play at lower levels of engagement with their friends as a way of regulating their experience of stress.

We have found also that physiological underarousal in both husband and wife is related to the ways in which these couples interact with their child and with the child's behavior with both their parents and their friends (Gottman & Katz, 1989). Specifically, couples who were physiologically underaroused when resolving a marital conflict were more negative as parents, tending to be cold and unresponsive, and failed to set limits with their child during parent–child interaction. Negative parenting was related to a cluster of variables we interpreted as indexing anger and noncompliance by the child. This cluster included a measure of finger pulse amplitude, which was targeted in our research because there is some support for an interpretation of emotion specificity in this measure. For example, Ekman et al. (1983) found that hands are hotter in anger than in fear. Given the positive relationship between finger temperature and finger pulse amplitude, we hypothesized that anger is associated with higher finger pulse amplitude. In our research, children's finger pulse amplitude was positively associated with negative parenting and with the other variables in the anger/noncompliance cluster, lending some support to our interpretation of this cluster as tapping the child's anger. The cluster of anger/noncompliance variables also was related to negative interaction with a best friend. Thus, couples who are underaroused during marital conflict resolution are more negative as parents, and this, in turn, is related to their children being angry and noncompliant with parents and peers.

Although these preliminary findings suggest a possible link between conflict in both the marital system and the peer system, much remains to be understood about the nature of these effects. For example, we do not know which specific marital behaviors are related to anger and noncompliance in the child. This question must be addressed to begin to tease apart the mechanisms underlying the relationship between marital interaction and anger and noncompliance in children. If children learn angry behaviors through modeling, one would expect that children who are often angry with parents and peers have parents who also are angry when resolving marital conflict. To test these notions, it is necessary to examine the specific affective patterns couples display when resolving marital disputes.

There is some evidence relating different forms of marital conflict with child behaviors. For example, Rutter et al. (1974) found a stronger relation between child behavior problems in unhappy marriages that were characterized as "quarrelsome" than in those characterized as "apathetic." However, Cummings and his colleagues have found that exposure to angry interactions between adults (be they parents or strangers) leads children to respond behaviorally with distress (Cummings et al., 1981), to identify these events as eliciting negative emotions (Cummings, 1987), and to show increased aggressiveness in subsequent play with friends (Cummings, Iannotti, & Zahn-Waxler, 1985). Although these results suggest that children are highly sensitive to the type of conflict expressed between adults, these reports make it difficult to predict exactly how children may respond to different types of interparental conflict.

These findings have led us to wonder about the associations of child behavior problems and the longitudinal health of the marriage. Children may react not only to the specific behaviors that their parents use to resolve marital conflicts, but also to more global interaction patterns that bode ill for the long-term stability of the marital relationship. To test this hypothesis, marital interaction was coded using Gottman's Specific Affect Coding System (SPAFF; Gottman, 1990; Version 2.0). In this system, positive and negative emotions are identified (such as anger, contempt, and sadness) as well as emotional behavior patterns (such as validation, domineering, and belligerence). We then asked whether marital interaction patterns obtained when children were 5 years old were related to child outcomes in predictions of teachers' ratings of internalizing and externalizing behaviors when the children were 8 years old. We found that a hostile pattern of marital interaction, as indexed by the wife's contempt, was correlated with externalizing difficulties in the child at follow-up but not with internalizing difficulties (Katz & Gottman, 1991b). In our coding system, contempt has a distant, "icy" quality that suggests superiority, moralistic disapproval, and smugness. The variables that correlated with wives' contempt included their anger, defensiveness, and sadness and their husbands' belligerence and contempt. Thus, we suggested calling this pattern of marital interaction, indexed by wife contempt, a *mutually hostile conflict resolution style*.

Why would children with hostile parents be more likely to be described 3 years later as externalizing? Although our data are consistent with a modeling hypothesis, we do not find this explanation very satisfying. This is because our externalizing variable encompasses a wide range of behaviors, including distractibility, hyperactivity, rule-breaking behavior, and the tendency to get easily bothered when faced with a challenging situation. Parents may not be modeling all of these types of behaviors in their hostile marital interactions.

An alternative explanation is that these children may be sensing that this kind of marriage is headed toward dissolution. Previously we found (Gottman & Levenson, 1991) that the particular quality of negative affect communicated by couples during conflict resolution differentially predicted whether couples would separate or divorce 4 years later. In particular, contempt by the wife was predictive of marital dissolution, whereas anger was unrelated to marital dissolution (Gottman & Levenson, 1991). This result was replicated with the current sample. Given this prediction of marital dissolution, we think that the wife's contemptuous affect is interpreted by the family as a rejection of both the husband and the marital relationship. Children may react to this threat of a dissolving marriage with increased externalizing behaviors. This interpretation is consistent with Patterson and his colleagues' observations of a high rate of marital dissolution in families with children classified as aggressive (G. R. Patterson, personal communication).

We found that anger and withdrawn behaviors in marital interaction among husbands predicted both internalizing and externalizing difficulties in children at follow-up. This prediction was much stronger for internalizing than externalizing behaviors (Katz & Gottman, 1991b). In the coding system, husbands who were angry ranged from showing milder forms of anger, such as annoyance, irritation, and impatience, to more intense forms, such as yelling, raising their voice, and righteous indignation. However, the other SPAFF variables that correlated with the husband's anger suggested a pattern of a whiny and withdrawn husband with a belligerent and highly engaged wife. Thus, to the extent that husbands are angry and withdrawn when resolving marital conflict, their children (as seen by their teachers) show signs of depression, act in a schizoid or anxious manner, and have somatic complaints. These children may be modeling their fathers' withdrawal as a listener in the face of their wives' relentless confrontation. This appears to be a rich climate for fostering internalizing behavior patterns among children 3 years later.

It is important to note that children's behavior patterns could not be predicted from self-reports of marital satisfaction collected at the initial assessment. We found it necessary to directly observe marital interaction to ascertain the specific marital processes that predict externalizing and internalizing behaviors in children over the long term.

To summarize, psychophysiological concepts and measures are useful in understanding some relationships between marital discord and children's peer interaction. We also have begun to elucidate the specific marital inter-action patterns that are related to children's externalizing and internalizing behavior patterns. Yet there remains a need to clarify the mechanisms by which marital interaction patterns predict such behavior patterns of children. One potential candidate is parenting behavior. The importance of parenting practices in mediating between marital quality and child outcomes also has been identified by Emery (1982) and Easterbrooks and Emde (1988). Briefly, the hypothesis (usually called the *socialization hypothesis*) proposes that parents experiencing marital discord will engage in more inconsistent, less sensitive, or otherwise less optimal socialization practices than do happily married couples, and that these differences in parenting behaviors affect children. An alternative hypothesis is a *stress model*, in which the active ingredient of the marital effect on children is that the ambient environment in the home may be tense with unresolved or continued conflict, and that this acts as a continuous chronic stressor. These hypotheses need to be tested (preferably, using longitudinal methods) to obtain a clearer understanding of how the marital relationship influences children's socioemotional development.

Conflict in the sibling and peer systems

Children learn about conflict and conflict management through various sources. Parents demonstrate through conflict interaction with their spouses not only how to engage in conflict with others, but also how to regulate the negative affect that accompanies conflict and how to resolve conflicts. Having the opportunity to observe parents manage or resolve disputes may be beneficial for children if it leads to the acquisition of conflict management skills. In fact, Cummings, Ballard, El-Sheikh, and Lake (1991) have shown that children's responses to interadult anger are less negative when they view the resolution to a conflict. In general, siblings relate more positively to one another when parents report greater marital happiness and less conflict (Brody, Stoneman, & Burke, 1987; Kramer & Gottman, (in press); MacKinnon, 1989; Stoneman, Brody, & Burke, 1989). Similarly, more positive peer interaction is associated with more positive marital relationships (Gottman & Katz, 1989). It seems likely, then, that children may adopt some of their parents' conflict management strategies in subsequent conflict exchanges with peers and siblings.

However, parents are not the only source of information children have for learning about conflict, its management, and the regulation of negative affect. Because children are most likely to engage in conflict with other children, their early conflictual interactions with siblings and peers also may be helpful to them in learning how to manage conflict. In the following sections, we will examine some ways in which children's experiences in child-based relationships contribute to the mastery of conflict management skills. This will lead to a discussion of the complementary contributions of family and peer relationships to children's social adaptation.

Conflicts in the sibling relationship

Sibling relationships offer children unique opportunities for learning about conflict. This is true for two reasons. First, due to greater accessibility of siblings and asymmetries in power and dominance, conflicts are reported to occur very frequently in these relationships (Felson, 1983; Gelles & Straus, 1979; Raffaelli, 1990; Steinmetz, 1978). Second, conflicts with siblings tend to involve a great deal of negative affect. These conflicts, then, may help children learn to tolerate negative affect in ways that conflict with other significant individuals do not. We will discuss later how experiences with conflicts in sibling relationships may facilitate the acquisition of conflict management strategies.

Although it is not clear at present whether children have more conflicts with siblings or peers (Shantz & Hobart, 1989), children do spend a fair amount of time in these exchanges. Children as young as 18, 24, and 36 months have been observed to engage in an average of 4 to 9 conflicts per hour with their older siblings (Dunn & Munn, 1987). Older children in fourth and fifth grade report an average of 4.7 fights per day with siblings (Prochaska & Prochaska, 1985). The mean duration of fights was 8 minutes, with bad feelings lasting about 6 minutes after the fight was over. Greater involvement in conflict should provide children with greater opportunities to experience some of the constructive outcomes associated with managed conflicts. To be sure, frequent disputes can have deleterious outcomes for children. This should not be overlooked as we emphasize, in this portion of the chapter, the constructive outcomes that are associated with conflict.

The contribution of conflict in social development has been proposed by others (Eisenberg & Garvey, 1981; Gottman, 1983; Piaget, 1932/1965; Shantz, 1987; Shantz & Hobart, 1989). To briefly summarize, a likely major benefit of engaging in conflict is that children acquire conflict management skills. For example, as children engage in conflicts, they learn to negotiate, compromise, take turns, as well as how to pursuade another to adopt their point of view. In this way, engagement in conflict provides children with experiences in which they can attempt to coordinate their activities and viewpoints with another. They learn through conflict that others can have divergent opinions, feelings, and intentions with which they can agree or dispute. Through this process, children enhance their understanding of social rules, social strategies, and the intentions of others (Shantz, 1987). The process of accentuating differences between individuals in conflict also can lead to better understanding of oneself and to identity formation. Shantz and Hobart (1989) have described how conflict may assist in developing an individuated sense of self as well as a sense of belonging with others.

Conflicts among siblings involve impressive amounts of negative affect and often include physical aggression (Felson, 1983; Gelles & Straus, 1979; Steinmetz, 1978). Conflicts may be most intense and severe when they occur in sibling relationships rather than in other relationships in which children participate. This may be due in part to the greater familiarity and access siblings have to one another, as well as to parental expectations that conflicts among siblings are "normal" and to be expected (Steinmetz, 1978).

It is very difficult to "escape" from the negative interactions and emotions experienced in sibling conflicts. Berscheid and Graziano (1979) have emphasized the importance of understanding the conditions under which a social relationship is initiated in order to truly appreciate the qualities of the relationship. For example, children's peer relationships are "voluntary" in the sense that they are formed and maintained on the basis of free choice. High frequencies of conflict in peer interactions can lead to lowered interest in continuing the friendship and, ultimately, dissolution of the relationship (Gottman, 1983, 1987; Hartup, Laursen, Stewart, & Eastenson, 1988). In contrast, brothers and sisters cannot choose to discontinue the relationship despite high levels of conflict or negative affect. However, being "stuck for life" with a sibling may lead children to develop greater capacities for modulating the expression of negative affect and to tolerate negative affect when it is directed at them by another.

The involuntary nature of sibling relationships may have particular effects on the strategies children use to manage conflict. Using self-reports, Raffaelli (1990) explored the different ways conflict occurs and is managed in adolescents' relationships with peers and siblings. The adolescents reported that they were more likely to allow disputes with their siblings to escalate but were more likely to avoid engaging in conflict with their friends, instead working to quickly curtail the escalation of conflict. Male friends tended to resolve the dispute rapidly, whereas female friends were more likely to separate and to later use formal strategies to repair the relationship. Siblings, however, were less likely to formally repair their relationship after a dispute, often simply resuming interactions without any reference to the dispute. Raffaelli concluded that siblings, compared with peers, are more able to tolerate conflict when it occurs and see it as less detrimental to their relationship. Although very interesting, acceptance of these results is limited by the exclusive use of self-report data and the fact that the perception of only one participant in the conflict was assessed. Observational methods may reveal other dimensions of how conflict occurs and is managed in various child-based relationships.

In summary, the sibling relationship may be a prime context for learning how to oppose another and how to tolerate negative affect. Because conflict is not a threat to the continuance of a relationship with a sibling, children may be freer to explore those aspects of themselves that contribute to their individuality and personal development in this context. In addition, being able to tolerate the negative affect that often accompanies conflictual interactions with siblings conceivably may lead to skills in negotiating conflict with significant others and in handling difficult emotions in intimate interpersonal relationships.

Significance of sibling conflict for peer relationships

Given that conflict appears to foster children's social development, we might expect that enhanced abilities in managing sibling conflict have positive implications for subsequent interpersonal relationships, such as with peers. However, the results from relevant studies have been mixed.

Patterson's (1986) observational studies of antisocial boys and their families have shown a link between repetitive patterns of irritable exchanges between siblings and peer rejection. Similarly, Hetherington (1988) reported that children (age 9 to 15) who had hostile and aggressive relationships with siblings had less satisfactory relationships with schoolmates in addition to more behavior and academic problems.

However, several studies have failed to demonstrate reliable associations between the quality of sibling and peer interactions. Berndt and Bulleit (1985) found that most of the correlations between measures of preschoolers' sibling and peer interactions were nonsignificant, with the exception of onlooking/unoccupied behaviors and aggression. However, Abramovitch, Corter, Pepler, and Stanhope (1986) were unable to obtain significant correlations for frequencies of agonistic behaviors (e.g., directive commands, insults, disapproval, threats) across the peer relationships of siblings. They concluded that there is little evidence that aspects of sibling interaction carry over into children's relationships with peers. The work of Brody, Stoneman, and MacKinnon (1982; Stoneman, Brody, & Mackinnon, 1984) also suggests that children behave differently when interacting with their siblings than with their friends. Brody et al. demonstrated that role asymmetries were quite apparent in sibling relationships but were virtually absent in peer relationships. For example, children assume more dominant roles (e.g., as a manager or a teacher) when interacting with a younger sibling but take a more egalitarian role (e.g., as a playmate) when interacting with a peer.

More recent research by Stocker (1991) identified links between sibling and friend relationships, but not between sibling and peer relationships. In this case, children who had more negative sibling relationships (by their mothers' reports and through observations) reported having closer friendships. This counterintuitive finding should be replicated, given that the supporting correlations were relatively small, ranging from .26 to .34 ($p < .05$), and that measures of friendship quality were based exclusively on self-report.

Clearly, the investigation of linkages between sibling and peer relationships is a complex endeavor. A variety of factors are likely to play mediatory functions, such as the age span of siblings (Berndt & Bulleit, 1985), the quality of the friendship relationship (Stocker, 1991), and individual characteristics of the children themselves (Brody et al., 1987). These should be investigated in future research.

Significance of peer conflict for sibling relationships

Although we have few demonstrations of extensions from sibling relationships to the peer world, Kramer and Gottman (in press) have found evidence for the opposite pattern. That is, children who had more positive relationships with peers before their siblings were born had more positive relationships with their siblings when the latter were 6 and 14 months old.

Thirty families with children age 3 to 5 years and who were expecting a second child participated in the Becoming a Sibling research project.

Parents in these predominantly white, middle-class families were in their early thirties and were married 7.5 years on the average. Eighteen (60%) of the firstborn children were females. Once their siblings were born, the following older–younger sibling dyads were formed: 11 female–female, 7 female–male, 7 male–male, and 5 male–female. In addition, the best friends of the firstborn children also participated. These friends were identified by the child and his or her mother as being the peer they liked the most and with whom they had the most contact. The best friends were similar to the focal firstborn children in terms of gender and demographic characteristics, but tended to be older.

The families were visited in their homes every 2 to 3 weeks from the last trimester of pregnancy to when the second child was 6 months old. An initial follow-up assessment was conducted when the second child was 14 months of age. A second follow-up is now being performed as each of the younger children reaches the age that their older sibling was when they were born.

Observational and self-report methods were used to assess the quality of the developing sibling relationships, parent–child relationships, marital relationships, and the older children's relationships with their best friends. The quality of the sibling relationship was assessed by videotaping interactions in the home when the baby was age 1, 3, 6, and 14 months. A second measure of sibling relationship quality was mothers' appraisals of the quality of this relationship, ascertained through interviews. Mother–child interaction was evaluated using videotaped home observations. Mothers' reports were used to estimate marital satisfaction (using the Marital Adjustment Test, Locke & Wallace, 1959) and fathers' involvement in child care. Finally, friendship quality was assessed by audiotaping the free play interactions of the firstborn children and their self-selected best friends in five 30-minute play sessions across the transition. The conversations were coded for instances of conflict, conflict management, engagement in fantasy play, and a broader set of positive and negative activities and affects.

Before presenting the results of this study, it is important to highlight some of the unique aspects of this sample. First, the volunteer families were relatively well educated (almost all held at least bachelor's degrees) and highly motivated to participate in this research. Second, we elected to study firstborn children between the ages of 3 and 5 years, because children in this age range are relatively articulate when conversing with their friends and display a range of play behaviors. However, most children in the United States become siblings when they are between the ages of 18 months and 3 years. As a result, the findings of this study may be most applicable to families with relatively older firstborn children. Despite these characteristics of the sample, many of the findings are in line with those reported in other longitudinal samples (Dunn & Kendrick, 1982; Stewart, Mobley, Van Tuyl, & Salvador, 1987).

The quality of children's sibling relationships, we found, at 6 and 14 months postbirth, is strongly predicted by the quality of the firstborn child's relationship with a best friend. This result was particularly robust as statistical significance was obtained after controlling for the effects of age, gender, social competence, and quality of parent–child and marital relationships. Correlation and multiple regression analyses revealed that the effects were attributable to several aspects of the best friend relationship: the abilities to play interactively and engage in extended fantasy play, the management of conflicts and negative affect, and reciprocity in best friend selection. Children whose play with their best friend included more positive affect and activities and fewer unmanaged conflicts also engaged in more positive interactions with their 6- and 14-month-old siblings. Extended fantasy play with the best friend was strongly positively correlated with more harmonious sibling interactions at the 14-month follow-up. Firstborn children who were in reciprocal best friendships tended to have more positive interactions with their siblings when the infants were 6 months old.

Unmanaged conflicts and relationships with peers and siblings

The frequency of conflicts children had with their best friends did not distinguish between children who got along well versus poorly with their siblings. Both groups of children experienced similar levels of conflict in their friendships. This is consistent with previous studies that failed to obtain significant associations between the frequency of conflicts and the closeness of children's friendships (Green, 1933; Hartup et al., 1988).

A major predictor of sibling relationship quality was the frequency of *unmanaged* conflicts: times when the dyads did not manage conflicts, were ineffective in implementing management techniques, or relied on others (usually parents) to resolve conflicts for them. Conflict management behaviors included (a) referring to a rule to resolve the argument, (b) giving a reason for the disagreement, (c) making an offer or compromise, (d) exploring the feelings of the child who was upset, (e) using a weakened form of the demand that permits "face saving," and (f) making a humorous or self-deprecating statement. These were based on categories developed by Eisenberg and Garvey (1981) and Gottman (1983). Behaviors of both children were taken into account when evaluating whether a conflict had been managed or not. That is, a conflict was considered as being managed when at least one child in the dyad performed one of the management strategies listed earlier; unmanaged conflicts were coded when neither child used one of these strategies.

These results suggest that learning how to manage conflicts with a peer is one of the most effective ways children prepare for becoming a sibling. What follows are some findings and speculations about how the social processes and affects associated with unmanaged conflicts in peer relationships may be associated with variations in the quality of sibling relationships. The play interactions of two 4-year-old girls with their best friends will be used to illustrate some of these findings and speculations.

Difficulty sustaining play and positive interactions. Difficulties in sustaining play were characteristic of many peer dyads who engaged in higher frequencies of unmanaged conflicts. The level of unmanaged conflicts was strongly associated with lower percentages of positive interaction among friends. These children engaged in fewer sustained positive play activities and were less able to repair and maintain positive interactions in their play. Coordinating joint play was particularly difficult for these children. They played independently rather than jointly, had difficulty sharing resources and taking turns, and often communicated unclearly or disconnectedly. Furthermore, their attempts to increase the level of social engagement were often unsuccessful (Gottman, 1983, 1987).

Several of these interpersonal processes are illustrated in the following encounter between Shelley (4 yrs., 2 mos.) and her best friend, Candace (5 yrs., 8 mos.). Shelley had demonstrated significant difficulties in adjusting to her sister's arrival. Videotaped observations consistently revealed few interactions between the siblings, as well as a great deal of negative affect and verbal and physical prohibitions. As suggested in the following excerpt, Shelley and Candace's interactions were marked with frequent and unmanaged conflict, and uncoordinated play:

> S: I know where the, I know, I know. Let me do it – the rest. Let me do the rest. Let me do the rest! All right? Cause I know how to do it. Uh . . . Is it good?
> C: Then can I do it by myself?
> S: No. Just me can do it.
> C: Stop it. I can I can do it Shelley, I can.
> S: No you can't. Uh uh (cough).
> C: That, how bout turning it around Shelley? (pause)
> S: You shouldn't do be in the puzzle with somebody else not looking else you have a bad too.

Escalation of negative affect and inhibition of positive affect. When conflict is repeatedly not managed, children become frustrated, angry, and impatient.

An escalation of negative affect often occurs where negative statements are contingently reciprocated and unpleasant feelings intensify. The interaction becomes progressively more disagreeable for both children. For example:

S: Candace, I'm gonna tell on you.
C: What?
S: If you don't stop whining.
C: What?
S: Whining. You say "Can I beg, uh, please have some paper?" and last time you don't ask, people if you, won't give you anything if you e-ever want to come back and say those things to people.
C: Oh, that's not a bad word.
S: Yes it is! If you whine, that's a bad word.
C: No it's not.
S: Yes it is! I mean it. I'll be nice to you if you don't say any bad words to me, and not whine.

Children who engaged in higher levels of unmanaged conflict also experienced less positive affect. For example, statements reflecting affection, approval, sympathy, consideration, sharing, and validating the relationship were strongly negatively correlated with frequencies of unmanaged conflict. In addition, children who experienced relatively more unmanaged conflicts were highly likely to be in unilateral rather than reciprocal friendships. After experiencing conflict after conflict, without effective management strategies, it appears quite difficult for children to reciprocate positive affect. The combination of low levels of positive affect and high levels of negative affect may lead children to express little preference for playing with one another. If this continues, they will no longer choose each other for friends and ultimately will avoid seeing each other.

Conflict management and relationships with peers and siblings

There are some attributes of children's responses to conflict situations that are associated with more constructive outcomes. Children who are able to manage conflicts play at higher levels of social engagement, and their interactions with peers and siblings also suggest greater social understanding.

Quality of social play. Conflict management in the present study was strongly correlated with episodes of sustained play and communication, and overall positive interaction. In addition, children who demonstrated greater competence with conflict management often used play, especially fantasy play, to manage disagreements.

Rose's (4 yrs., 7 mos.) relationship with her friend Andrea (4 yrs., 2 mos.) provides some good examples of how competencies in conflict management are associated with other prosocial behaviors. Their interactions were more positive and entailed higher levels of sustained play and conversation, positive affect, and dimensions of social understanding. These positive attributes appeared to generalize to the sibling relationship. Rose's relationship with her newborn sister was described by their mother as quite positive at age 6 and 14 months. The videotaped observations of the siblings also revealed relatively high levels of mutual attention and interaction, positive affect, and low frequencies of prohibitions, threats, object struggles, and negative affect.

In the following episode, Rose and Andrea use fantasy play to reach a mutually satisfying resolution to a disagreement. They have different ideas of what to play – Andrea wants to pretend they are caring for a baby, while Rose wants simply to play ball. Conflict is averted (at least for the moment) as they create a fantasy in which each gets to play what they want. Andrea becomes the mother, while "son" Rose is playing ball:

> R: I know what I want to play. I wanna play this. Ball and bat. Wanna play ball and bat? Do ya? You *never* want to.
> A: I wanna play babysitter.
> R: Okay. I'm the baby and you're the mom, and I'm out playing ball by myself . . .
> A: Just pretend-end, you are my little boy.
> R: I will and I'm playing basketball, kay?
> A: Let's pretend when you came home I, that I was, I was, that I told you to be quiet because the baby was sleeping.

Social understanding. Through conflict, children broaden their perspectives about their social worlds and develop greater understanding of others. Young children demonstrate a surprising level of social-cognitive competence as they use their understanding of others' intentions and motives to persuade others to adopt their point of view. These ideas echo those of Selman (1980), who used children's reports on the qualities of their friendships to demonstrate that competence in perspective taking and social understanding are related to competence in conflict resolution. (See also Dunn & Slomkowski, this volume).

In the following excerpt, Rose uses her understanding of the role of mother to alleviate conflict. In this exchange, Andrea is motivated to change the focus of their play so that it centers more on taking care of a baby and less on playing ball with an older child (as Rose desires). The conflict occurs within the frame of the pretend play: "Mom" is too busy with the baby to play ball:

R: Mommy, will you play ball and bat with me?
A: No, I have to get to work.
R: No! Please play bat and ball with me.
A: I can't!!
R: Yes you can.
A: No, I can't honey!
R: No.
A: Can't you see I'm busy!
R: Yes after you get the baby in there can ya?
A: Yes.
R: Okay!

By citing the rule that mothers must first attend to the needs of their babies before they can play with their older children, Rose not only resolves the conflict, but also demonstrates that she understands some important elements of the role of mother. Her ability to appreciate the functions and obligations of mothers within the fantasy play allows her to view the interaction from Andrea's perspective. She then can understand what is motivating her behavior and use this information to propose a mutually satisfying solution. The level of social understanding that is evident in these 4-year-olds' conversation leads us to conclude that competence in perspective taking and social understanding go hand in hand with the development of skills in conflict management.

In summary, good conflict managers approach conflictual situations with imagination. They demonstrate creativity, flexible thinking, and humor as they respond to social dilemmas. In the process of conflict management, they reveal a sophisticated understanding of social roles and relationships. Children can play at higher levels of social engagement when conflicts are managed. As a result, they are more able to share positive feelings, engage in positive activities, and have fun with one another. Not surprisingly, conflict management is associated also with reciprocated friendship status. All of these attributes should facilitate greater capacities for social understanding.

It is this capacity for greater social understanding that we believe helps children to develop more positive relationships with their siblings. In the present study, children who managed disagreements and who were better able to tolerate frustrations and deescalate negative affect with a friend were more likely to perform these behaviors with a younger sibling. Furthermore, as the ability to manage conflicts also is associated with enhanced social understanding, we see more positive interactions among these children and their younger siblings. For example, these children are likely to show affection and humor, help, share, validate, and support one another. Similarly, as good conflict managers are better able to sustain play and communication in their interactions with friends, they are better able to establish prosocial interaction sequences with a younger, more dependent child.

Directionality of effects

The question must be addressed of whether conflicts create a negative emotional climate in which positive interaction is difficult to sustain or if the conflicts are an outcome of suppressed positive interaction. Similarly, we need to know if children's experiences with peers – and in particular, conflict experiences – directly influence the quality of sibling relationships or simply occur concomitantly. Of course, there is are no clear answers to these chicken-and-egg problems because reciprocal influences are likely. However, we conducted some exploratory analyses using structural equation modeling techniques to begin to address some questions about which variables had direct effects upon sibling interaction and which performed more mediatory functions. We found support for the contention that the frequency of unmanaged conflicts is directly associated with the overall quality of peer play. By direct we mean that no other variables mediate this relationship. Furthermore, the quality of peer interaction was found to be directly related to the quality of the sibling relationship. This supports our view that the prevalence of unmanaged conflicts either influences or is an indication of the overall climate of a relationship. Because peer relationships were studied before the sibling was born, these results suggest that the quality of peer interaction does have some influence on sibling relationships.

Influences of family and friends

It is important to consider additional factors that may influence children's adaptation to becoming a sibling. Besides the friendship variables, other factors were associated with disparities in the quality of sibling relationships. These bring our attention back to the ways in which conflict in one subsystem of the family influences the quality of other social relationships both within and outside of the family. (See Vandell & Bailey, this volume, for a discussion of some of these points.)

Several dimensions of parent–child and marital relationships were important in predicting the quality of the sibling relationship. The quality of mother–firstborn interaction and mothers' reports of their marital satisfaction were both moderately associated with the quality of their children's sibling relationship. For example, more positive sibling interaction was correlated with more positive marital relations. However, structural equation modeling indicated that the effects of these family variables were indirect effects, that is, each was mediated by the quality of play children achieved with their friends. For example, the measures of parent–child interactions and marital satisfaction were directly associated with higher qualities of peer play, which in turn, had direct effects on the quality of sibling interactions. These results suggest that whereas peer relationships may lead to the development of social and emotional competencies that are directly relevant for sibling interaction, the contribution of parent–child and marital relationships may be more indirect.

In summary, the friendship relationship may be a unique context for developing competencies relevant for sibling interaction. Our results suggest that what children learn from their friends about relating to other children may be even more important than what they learn from their parents. This is because parents usually adapt to the needs of children in ways that peers do not. Compared with parent–child relationships, the peer system demands more advanced interpersonal behaviors from children in order to sustain a relationship. As younger siblings are even less likely to adapt their behaviors to the firstborn child, experiences with friends may provide excellent preparation for becoming a sibling.

In contrast, parents may contribute indirectly to children's relative success in relating to their sibling by providing them with opportunities for peer contact, as well as monitoring, coaching, and directly teaching social skills relevant for social interaction. Furthermore, parents influence sibling behaviors indirectly through their beliefs, attitudes, and expectations for their children's relationship (Howe & Ross, 1990; Rubin, Mills, & Rose-Krasnor, 1989) and by the way conflict is handled in the marital relationship (Cummings et al., 1991; MacKinnon, 1989). Additional research is needed to further understand the relative contributions of peers and parents in the establishment of sibling relationships.

Final comments

In this chapter, we have tried to identify some of the interpersonal processes and affects that are associated with conflict and conflict management in the family and with peers. We have also begun to explore the impact these have on children's functioning. Our studies suggest that the strategies that parents use during marital conflict do contribute to children's social adjustment. In a reciprocal fashion, the quality of children's extrafamilial experiences, such as with friends, also appear to influence the relationships they have with family members – in this case, their siblings. These methodologies, then, support the approach of looking for linkages across relationships as a way to better understand the functions of conflict in child and family development.

Specifically, we have found that a psychophysiological approach has added to our understanding of how marital distress affects children's socio-emotional development. Children from maritally distressed homes had higher levels of urinary dopamine, which in turn was related to their playing at a low, potentially conflict-free level with their best friend. Although a direct pathway from marital distress to children's level of play also existed in the data, without the addition of a mediating variable, an explanation for the relationship between marital distress and peer play would have been lacking. In this case, the inclusion of the biological variable of urinary dopamine led to the hypothesis that children from maritally distressed homes may structure their play to avoid episodes of conflict in order to modulate their level of stress. Psychophysiological research demonstrating high levels of finger pulse amplitude during anger also helped clarify the relationship between negative parenting and a cluster of variables relating to child's anger and noncompliance. In this instance, the addition of a psychophysiological variable helped in the interpretation of the construct as relating to anger and noncompliance.

The importance of conflict resolution is attested in these data. In the Becoming a Sibling project, unmanaged conflict with a best friend, rather than the amount of conflict per se, predicted more negative engagement with siblings. Thus, it is not simply the fact that conflict exists, but it is the way in which conflict is handled that is the important predictor of sibling relations. In the Family Psychophysiology project, those marital processes (i.e., mutually hostile interactions) that predicted marital dissolution were associated with externalizing behaviors in children 3 years later. To the extent that couples who separate and/or divorce have difficulty resolving conflict, we have evidence of long-term effects of unmanaged marital conflict on children. Our results support those of Cummings et al. (1991), who reported that children's responses to interadult anger are less negative when they view the resolution to a conflict. In the context of marital and peer interaction, dysfunctional child behavior patterns were associated with unmanaged conflict.

The approach that we have taken to describe specific microsocial processes during conflict highlight the benefits of detailed recording of behavior. On the descriptive level, we were able to identify the behavioral components of unmanaged conflict in two interpersonal contexts. During peer play, we found that dyads who engage in higher frequencies of unmanaged conflict have difficulties sustaining play and positive interaction, escalate negative affect, inhibit positive affect, and do not use fantasy play to manage disagreements. In marital interaction, conflict that eventually undermines the integrity of the marital relationship was found to be mutually hostile, with the wife being contemptuous, angry, defensive, and sad, and the husband being contemptuous and belligerent. It is hoped that the detailed description of microsocial processes associated with unmanaged conflict can help build therapeutic programs aimed at teaching couples and children those specific conflict management skills that are constructive to interpersonal interaction.

The results of the detailed description of the interpersonal processes associated with conflict also should engender better theories. Several different theoretical mechanisms were alluded to in this chapter about the ways marital, parent–child, sibling, and peer systems may be linked. Social learning theory and the socialization hypothesis are just two of many possible explanations of how these systems may influence each other. Unfortunately, little evidence exists at present for confirming or disconfirming any of these theories. It is hoped that other investigators will begin to struggle with the theoretical issues faced in this complex area.

The results of these two studies differed in terms of the direct and indirect pathways of influence, linking marital, parent–child, sibling, and peer relationship systems. The results appeared to depend on which family subsystem was selected as the outcome variable. When the sibling relationship was targeted, marital and parent–child relationships appeared to be linked with sibling interaction only indirectly, through their effects on peer relations. When the child's peer relations or long-term adaptation was isolated as the outcome variable, the marital and parent–child relationships were found to be directly linked to these child outcomes (Gottman & Katz, 1989). This suggests that the decision about which subsystem is to be targeted as the outcome variable is very important when identifying pathways of influence within families.

Additional work is needed to clarify the mechanisms by which dysfunctional conflict in the marital relationship is related to children's interpersonal difficulties with siblings and peers. Given the reported results, the quality of parent–child interaction probably plays an important mediatory role. For example, it is possible that couples with different conflict management techniques have distinct parenting styles that are, in turn, predictive of conflict in the peer and sibling systems. Efforts to typologize marital and parenting conflict resolution styles may help elucidate such potential pathways.

Some of the more immediate effects of marital conflict on child behavior also need clarification. Connections between coercion, punitiveness, and aggressiveness in the parent–child relationship and poor peer relations have been documented consistently (e.g., Attili, 1989; Dishion, 1990; Kolvin et al., 1977; Parke et al., 1989; Pettit, Dodge, & Brown, 1987; Snyder, 1989). But there is only preliminary evidence that conflict between parents either in front of their children or over parenting issues has negative effects on peer relationships (Cummings et al., 1981, 1984). Nor do we understand how such conflict between parents affects sibling interaction. It is our hope that future researchers will address these issues by attending to the behavioral aspects of families' functioning.

As noted earlier, conflict is an integral part of daily living. Although it is customary to address the negative consequences of conflict, it is also the case that the ability to manage conflict effectively is an integral skill that we teach our children and that they learn from one another. The ways in which children may benefit from constructive or functional marital, family, and friend conflict also need to be articulated before a full picture emerges of how conflict functions, for better or worse, within families.

References

Abramovitch, R., Corter, C., Pepler, D. J., & Stanhope, L. (1986). Sibling and peer interaction: A final follow-up and a comparison. *Child Development, 57*, 217–229.

Attili, G. (1989). Social competence versus emotional security: The link between home relationships and behavior problems at school. In B. H. Schneider, G. Attili, J. Nadel, & R. P. Weissberg (Eds.), *Social competence in developmental perspective*. London: Kluwer Academic Publishers.

Berndt, T. J., & Bulleit, T. N. (1985). Effects of sibling relationships on preschoolers' behavior at home and school. *Developmental Psychology, 21*, 761–767.

Berscheid, E. (1983). Emotion. In H. H. Kelley, E. Bersheid, A. Christensen, J. Harvey, T. L. Huston, G. Levinger, E. McClintock, A. Peplau, & D. R. Peterson (Eds.), *Close relationships*. San Francisco: Freeman.

Berscheid, E., & Graziano, W. (1979). The initiation of social relationships and interpersonal attraction. In R. L. Burgess & T. L. Huston (Eds.), *Social exchange in developing relationships*. New York: Academic Press.

Brody, G. H., Stoneman, Z., & Burke, M. (1987). Family system and individual child correlates of sibling behavior. *American Journal of Orthopsychiatry, 57*, 561–569.

Brody, G. H., Stoneman, Z., & MacKinnon, C. (1982). Role asymmetries among school-aged children, their younger siblings, and their friends. *Child Development, 53*, 717–720.

Cacioppo, J. T., & Petty, R. E. (Eds.). (1983). *Social psychophysiology: A sourcebook*. New York: Guilford Press.

Cannon, W. B. (1929). *Bodily states in anger and fear*. New York: Appleton.

Cummings, E. M. (1987). Coping with background anger in early childhood. *Child Development, 58*, 976–984.

Cummings, E. M., Ballard, M., El-Sheikh, M., & Lake, M. (1991). Resolution and children's responses to interadult anger. *Developmental Psychology, 27*, 462–470.

Cummings, E. M., Iannotti, R. J., & Zahn-Waxler, C. (1985). Influence of conflict between adults on the emotions and aggression of young children. *Developmental Psychology, 21*, 495–507.

Cummings, E. M., Zahn-Waxler, C., & Radke-Yarrow, M. (1981). Young children's responses to expressions of anger and affection by others in the family. *Child Development, 52,* 1274–1282.

Cummings, E. M., Zahn-Waxler, C., & Radke Yarrow, M. (1984). Developmental changes in children's reactions to anger in the home. *Journal of Child Psychology and Psychiatry, 25,* 63–74.

DiMascio, A., Boyd, R. W., & Greenblatt, M. (1957). Physiological correlates of tension and antagonism during psychotherapy: A study of "interpersonal physiology." *Psychosomatic Medicine, 19,* 99–104.

Dishion, T. J. (1990). The family ecology of boys' peer relations in middle childhood. *Child Development, 61,* 874–892.

Duffy, E. (1957). The psychological significance of the concept of "arousal" or "activation." *Psychological Review, 64,* 265–275.

Dunn, J., & Kendrick, C. (1982). *Siblings: Love, envy and understanding.* Cambridge, MA: Harvard University Press.

Dunn, J., & Munn, P. (1987). Development of justification in disputes with mother and sibling. *Developmental Psychology, 23,* 791–798.

Easterbrooks, M. A., & Emde, R. N. (1988). Marital and parent–child relationships: The role of affect in the family system. In R. A. Hinde & J. Stevenson-Hinde (Eds.), *Relationships within families: Mutual influences.* Oxford: Oxford University Press.

Eisenberg, A. R., & Garvey, C. (1981). Children's use of verbal strategies in resolving conflicts. *Discourse Processes, 4,* 149–170.

Ekman, P., Levenson, R. W., & Friesen, W. V. (1983). Autonomic nervous system activity distinguishes between emotions. *Science, 221,* 1208–1210.

Emery, R. E. (1982). Interparental conflict and the children of discord and divorce. *Psychological Bulletin, 92,* 310–330.

Felson, R. B. (1983). Aggression and violence between siblings. *Social Psychology Quarterly, 46,* 271–285.

Fox, N. (1989). Psychophysiological correlates of emotional reactivity during the first year of life. *Developmental Psychology, 25,* 364–372.

Gelles, R. J., & Straus, M. A. (1979). Determinants of violence in the family. In W. R. Burr, R. Hill, F. I. Nye, & I. R. Reiss (Eds.), *Contemporary theories about the family: Vol. I. Research-based theories.* New York: Free Press.

Gottman, J. M. (1979). *Marital interaction: Experimental investigations.* New York: Academic Press.

Gottman, J. M. (1983). How children become friends. *Monographs of the Society for Research in Child Development, 48*(3, Serial No. 201).

Gottman, J. M (1987). The observation of social process. In J. M., Gottman & J. G. Parker (Eds.), *Conversations of friends: Speculations on affective development.* Cambridge: Cambridge University Press.

Gottman, J. M. (1990). *Manual for the Specific Affect Coding System.* Unpublished manuscript. University of Washington.

Gottman, J. M., & Katz, L. (1989). Effects of marital discord on young children's peer interaction and health. *Developmental Psychology, 25,* 373–381.

Gottman, J. M., & Levenson, R. W. (1991). *Toward a typology of marriage based on affective behavior: Preliminary differences in behavior, physiology, health and risk for dissolution.* Unpublished manuscript, University of Washington.

Green, E. H. (1933). Friendships and quarrels among preschool children. *Child Development, 4,* 237–252.

Hartup, W. W., Laursen, B., Stewart, M. I., & Eastenson, A. (1988). Conflict and the friendship relations of young children. *Child Development, 59,* 1590–1600.

Henry, J. P., & Stephens, P. M. (1977). *Stresss, health and the social environment.* New York: Springer-Verlag.

Hetherington, E. M. (1988). Parents, children, siblings: Six years after divorce. In R. Hinde & J. R. Stevenson-Hinde (Eds.), *Relationships within families: Mutual influences.* New York: Oxford University Press.

Howe, N., & Ross, H. S. (1990). Socialization, perspective-taking, and the sibling relationship. *Developmental Psychology, 26,* 160–165.

Kagan, J., Reznick, J. S., Clarke, C., Snidman, N., & Garcia-Coll, C. (1984). Behavioral inhibition to the unfamiliar. *Child Development, 55,* 2212–2225.

Kaplan, H. B., Burch, N. R., & Bloom, S. W. (1964). Physiological covariation and sociometric relationships in small peer groups. In P. H. Leiderman & D. Shapiro (Eds.), *Psychobiological approaches to social behavior.* Stanford: Stanford University Press.

Katz, L. F., & Gottman, J. M. (1991a). Marital discord and child outcomes: A social psychophysiological approach. In J. Garber & K. Dodge (Eds.), *The development of emotion regulation and dysregulation.* Cambridge: Cambridge University Press.

Katz, L. F., & Gottman, J. M. (1991b, April). *Marital interaction patterns and children's peer relationships and emotional development.* Paper presented at the meeting of the Society for Research in Child Development, Seattle, WA.

Kolvin, I., Garside, R., Nicol, A., MacMillan, A., Wolstenhollme, F., & Leitch, I. (1977). Familial and sociological correlates of behavioral and sociological deviance in 8-year-old children. In P. Graham (Ed.), *Epidemiology of childhood disorders.* New York: Academic Press.

Kramer, L., & Gottman, J. M. (in press). Becoming a sibling: "With a little help from my friends." *Developmental Psychology.*

Lacey, J. I. (1967). Somatic response patterning and stress: Some revisions of activation theory. In M. H. Appley & R. Trumbell (Eds.), *Psychological stress: Issues in research.* New York: Appleton-Century-Crofts.

Levenson, R. W., & Gottman, J. M. (1983). Marital interaction: Physiological linkage and affective exchange. *Journal of Personality and Social Psychology, 45,* 587–597.

Levenson, R. W., & Gottman, J. M. (1985). Physiological and affective predictors of change in relationship satisfaction. *Journal of Personality and Social Psychology, 49,* 85–94.

Locke, H. J., & Wallace, K. H. (1959). Short marital-adjustment and prediction tests: Their reliability and validity. *Marriage and Family Living, 21,* 251–255.

Lyons, W. (1980). *Emotion.* Cambridge: Cambridge University Press.

MacKinnon, C. E. (1989). An observational investigation of sibling interactions in married and divorced families. *Developmental Psychology, 25,* 36–44.

Malmo, R. B., Boag, T. J., & Smith, A. A. (1957). Physiological study of personal interaction. *Psychosomatic Medicine, 19,* 105–119.

Mandler, G. (1975). *Mind and emotion.* New York: Wiley.

Parke, R. D., MacDonald, K. B., Burks, V. M., Carson, J., Bhavnagri, N., Barth, J. M., & Beitel, A. (1989). Family and peer systems: In search of the linkages. In K. Kreppner & R. M. Lerner (Eds.), *Family systems and life-span development.* Hillsdale, NJ.: Erlbaum.

Patterson, G. R. (1986). The contribution of siblings to training for fighting: A microsocial analysis. In D. Olweus, J. Block, & M. Radke-Yarrow (Eds.), *Development of antisocial and prosocial behavior.* New York: Academic Press.

Pettit, G. S., Dodge, K. A., & Brown, M. M. (1987). Early family experience, social problem-solving patterns, and children's social competence. *Child Development, 59,* 107–120.

Piaget, J. (1965). *The moral judgment of the child.* Glencoe, IL: Free Press. (Original work published 1932)

Prochaska, J. M., & Prochaska, J. O. (1985). Children's views of the causes and "cures" of sibling rivalry. *Child Welfare, 65,* 427–433.

Raffaelli, M. (1990). *Sibling conflict in early adolescence*. Unpublished doctoral dissertation, University of Chicago.

Rubin, K. H., Mills, R. S. L., & Rose-Krasnor, L. (1989). Maternal beliefs and children's competence. In B. H. Schneider, G. Attili, J. Nadel, & R. P. Weissberg (Eds.), *Social competence in developmental perspective*. Dordrecht: Kluwer Academic Publishers.

Rutter, M., Yule, B., Quinton, D., Rowlands, O., Yule, W., & Berger, M. (1974). Attainment and adjustment in two geographic areas: Some factors accounting for area differences. *British Journal of Psychiatry, 126*, 520–533.

Schacter, S., & Singer, J. E. (1962). Cognitive, social and physiological determinants of emotional state. *Psychological Review, 69*, 379–399.

Schwartz, G. E. (1982) Psychophysiological patterning and emotion revisited: A systems perspective. In C. E. Izard (Ed.), *Measuring emotions in infants and children*. Cambridge: Cambridge University Press.

Selman, R. (1980). *The growth of interpersonal understanding: Developmental and clinical analyses*. New York: Academic Press.

Shantz, C. (1987). Conflicts between children. *Child Development, 58*, 283–305.

Shantz, C., & Hobart, C. J. (1989). Social conflict and development: Peers and siblings. In T. J. Berndt & G. W. Ladd (Eds.), *Peer relationships and child development*. New York: Wiley.

Snyder, J. J. (1989, May). *The family's role in early peer relationships*. Paper presented at the NIMH Family Research Consortium, Harwich Port, MA.

Steinmetz, S. K. (1978). Sibling violence. In J. M. Eekelaar & S. N. Katz (Eds.), *Family violence: An international and interdisciplinary study*. Toronto: Butterworth.

Stewart, R. B., Mobley, L. A., Van Tuyl, S. S., & Salvador, M. A. (1987). The firstborn's adjustment to the birth of a sibling: A longitudinal assessment. *Child Development, 58*, 341–355.

Stocker, C. M. (1991, April). *Sibling relationships in middle childhood: Links with friendships and peer relationships*. Paper presented at the meeting of the Society for Research in Child Development, Seattle, WA.

Stoneman, Z., Brody, G. H., & Burke, M. (1989). Sibling temperaments and maternal and paternal perceptions of marital, family, and personal functioning. *Journal of Marriage and the Family, 51*, 99–113.

Stoneman, Z., Brody, G. H., & MacKinnon, C. (1984). Naturalistic observations of children's activities and roles while playing with their siblings and friends. *Child Development, 55*, 617–627.

Suomi, S. (1990, May). *Heart rate variability and behavioral inhibition in primates*. Paper presented at the Summer Institute of the Family Research Consortium, Monterey, CA.

Taggart, P., & Carruthers, M. (1971). Endogenous hyperlipidemia induced by emotional stress of race driving. *Lancet, 1*, 363–366.

Temoshok, L., Van Dyke, C., & Zegans, L. (1983). *Emotions and health illness: Theoretical and research foundations*. New York: Grune & Stratton.

Part II

Conflict and interpersonal relationships

6   The social structure of early conflict: Interaction, relationships, and alliances

Hildy S. Ross and Cheryl L. Conant

A marked achievement of social life occurs when young children who hold divergent positions on an issue recognize the existence of their differences, justify their own stands while taking account of the opponent's views, and compromise to arrive at a mutually satisfactory outcome. Through such conflicts, young children encounter overt opposition on issues of central concern. As they debate, children evaluate and interpret the experience. They expose their own arguments to the scrutiny of their opponents and, in turn, question the validity of justifications proposed by others. Cultural principles related to the fair treatment of others are applied to specific situations, and goals are modified to preserve ongoing relationships. Conflict creates its own social structure, both between opponents and through the support of third parties, and has implications for the social order of the group that extend beyond the boundaries of any specific altercation. Conflict thus holds great potential both for individual development and for the social organization of relationships and group structure. Contrast this image of conflict with scenes of acrimonious physical combat that also characterize disputes between young children, with moral principles overcome by power, and with interpersonal relationships built on bullying and intimidation. Along with the potential for individual and group development, conflict carries the risk of disruption and serious personal harm. These dual faces of conflict make it all the more important to understand the development and structure of early conflict and the place that early conflict holds in the social lives of young children.

Our goal in this chapter is to describe how young children fight with their peers. We place major emphasis on the structure of conflict, which can be examined at several different levels. Conflicts among young children are structured *events* that extend over time (Hay, 1984; Shantz, 1987). As such, one may ask how conflicts begin, how they progress, and how they

Work on this chapter was supported by a grant from the Social Sciences and Humanities Research Council of Canada.

153

are resolved. Conflicts are also structured *interactions*, in that each child's actions are constrained by the prior actions of the opponents as they take account of one another's behavior in the conduct of their disputes. Moreover, conflicts influence *group structures*: Asymmetries in conflict outcomes and alliances formed among group members during conflicts partially determine the social structures of groups (Maynard, 1986; Strayer, 1980). The structures of the events, the interactions, and the relationships within groups will thus guide our explorations of early conflict. We argue that the unfolding of conflict structure depends upon the meaningful interpretation of behaviors. At each stage of a conflict, a child's actions alter the probability of the opponent's response and affect the future of the interaction. Meaningful interpretations of behaviors may be influenced by the focus of the conflict, the age of the children, and the context of the dispute. In the review that follows, we shall emphasize the structure of conflict, the meaning of the actions that constitute interpersonal conflict, and the interface of culturally derived principles and enduring relationships in the conduct and outcome of conflicts between young children.

The structure of early conflict

If conflict between children is a structured interactive event, then opposition provides the foundation of that structure. Conflict begins with overt opposition between individuals and continues until opposition ceases. Moves within conflict either continue the opposition or address it with attempts at conciliation or resolution. Whether two children are fighting over toys or space or arguing over facts, rights, or opinions, opposition has been critical both in definitions of conflict and in examinations of the progress of conflict in time (e.g., Eisenberg & Garvey, 1981; Hartup & Laursen, in press; Hay, 1984; Maynard, 1985b; O'Keefe & Benoit, 1982; Shantz, 1987; Shantz & Hobart, 1989). According to Eisenberg and Garvey (1981), opposition has a powerful influence on ensuing peer interaction, in that "opposing a partner's linguistic or gestural move . . . creates a 'public' event calling for resolution" (p. 151). Opposition creates an obligation for a response or remedy from whomever is challenged (Walton & Sedlak, 1982). Because of this, it may be a fairly simple organizing principle. Children drawn into opposition with one another may be able to maintain meaningful interaction through sustained opposition more frequently, or at an earlier age, than they do through most other forms of interchange (Bronson, 1981). Nevertheless, in all cases opposition immediately establishes a relationship between combatants – both the individuals and the positions they espouse stand in opposition to one another. When disputants introduce new and seemingly incongruous elements into a debate, the oppositional relationship they have established maintains the coherence of the interchange (O'Keefe & Benoit, 1982). Thus, opposition is a powerful relationship that directs interaction.

As conflicts between children extend over time, they move through stages that begin before the establishment of opposition and progress to its resolution (Hay, 1984; Shantz, 1987). Stage 0 concerns the arguable event. The *arguable event* is generally the behavior, request, or statement that is challenged. Although it does not determine the occurrence of conflict, it provides the focus and directs the content of the dispute. Eisenberg and Garvey (1981) aptly number this move "0" in the unfolding of verbal quarrels. At Stage 1, *initial opposition* occurs. Conflicts begin when opposition becomes apparent, generally when one child protests, resists, disagrees with, or otherwise challenges another. Based on the initial opposition, one can identify the antecedent, arguable event (Eisenberg & Garvey, 1981; Maynard, 1985a). At Stage 2, *mutual opposition* occurs. The child whose behavior is opposed may in turn resist the influence of the other, in which case opposition has become mutual. Alternatively, the child's behavior may be conciliatory, which results in either the continuation of unilateral opposition or the resolution of conflict. Stage 3 continues the use of a wide variety of *oppositional strategies* as in the first two stages. Interpersonal influence is evidenced as children modify their actions in relation to the strategies of their peers throughout the conflict episode. Stage 4 consists of the *conflict ending*. Conflicts end when opposition ceases, either because it has been resolved by the participants or because it has been dropped by one or both of them. We follow Hay (1984) and Shantz (1987) in using these temporal stages to organize our review of the progress of conflict. We shall explore the characteristics and development of conflict in the first 6 years of life and the evidence of meaningful interactions and interpersonal influence in the behavior of young combatants within and across stages of conflict.

The arguable event

Opposition establishes the conflict, but it is not the first relevant move in a dispute. One also must look backward in time to see what it is that the opposition addresses, and that could be almost any action or statement (Garvey, 1984; Maynard, 1985a). As Maynard states, "any move, claim, stance, or position that one person takes explicitly or implicitly, verbally or nonverbally, can become part of an argument if it is opposed" (p. 23). Even seemingly positive moves (hugs, offers) lead to conflict (Hay & Ross, 1982; Russell, 1981; Shantz, 1987). One consequence of this diversity is the difficulty in predicting the onset of conflict from the move that precedes it (Eisenberg & Garvey, 1981). Determining the probability that particular actions lead to opposition rather than to peaceful interaction is the key to predicting conflict from the antecedent event. It seems likely that different types of antecedents would influence peer objection. Nevertheless, we have found only one such estimate of the probability of conflict. Russell (1981) observed toddlers in mixed-aged dyads of either 12- and 18-month-olds or 18- and 24-month-olds. She found that 15% of all social overtures resulted in conflict; in contrast, 26% of attempts by one child to take a toy that the other was currently playing with or had just abandoned were protested by the companion. Thus, taking a toy was more likely than other social overtures to be challenged by a peer.

The arguable event influences the progress of the ensuing conflict. If the initial influence attempt is aggressive, conflicts are more often about behavioral issues, more often involve further aggression, and are more likely to end in compromise than are conflicts begun without aggression (Laursen & Hartup, 1989). Verbal arguments begun with possession claims, name calling, and statements about procedures are overwhelmingly opposed by simple counterassertions; oppositions to factual statements are elaborated more often with reasons or countersuggestions (Phinney, 1986). The beginnings of arguments thus determine the issues, set the tone, and influence the strategies and outcomes of disputes.

Opposition between young children seems most often to focus on proximal moves, such as reaching for or taking a toy as arguable events. Forceful beginnings, as in tugging a toy or assaulting the peer, begin a minority of conflicts, although inclusion of verbal aggression increases that proportion (Caplan, Vespo, Pederson, & Hay, 1991; Laursen & Hartup, 1989; Russell, 1981). Killen (1989) classified conflicts in relation to the moral or social conventional rules that are violated in an initiating transgression. She found that physical and psychological harm and disruptions of social order were more likely to be sources of conflict in preschool classrooms than in play involving twosomes; possession was a more common theme when two children played together.

As children grow older, conflict is more likely to begin with distal events and verbal categories become more important. Camras (1984) studied object conflicts between preschool, kindergarten, and second-grade children. Two children played with a pair of gerbils placed in a box so that only one of them could play with it at a time. The box had to be pushed or pulled through an opening in a Plexiglass barrier to be exchanged between the pair. When these children attempted to get the gerbils from their peers, they usually requested, demanded, or hinted that they wanted a turn. They also attempted to pull the box from their peers. Older children were slightly more likely to ask, and younger ones more likely to pull. In another study of purely verbal disputes, the kindergarten children challenged the statements of their peers, especially those concerning procedures such as what is going on, how something is to be done, and who shall do it. Facts were disputed far more often than opinions, with statements of possession, intention, and attribution falling between (Phinney, 1986).

Children's objections are not always to arguable events in the form of overt actions or statements. Children can oppose the *presupposition* of an action or statement, as well as its manifest content (Maynard, 1985a; O'Keefe & Benoit, 1982). An example helps illustrates this possibility (Maynard, 1985a):

> M: Where's my—where is my folder? *Arguable event*
> J: How'm I sposed to know? *First objection*
> Mi: M, waddiya expect us to do, find everything for ya. *Second objection*

In this conflict, it is not the semantic content but presuppositions of the arguable event that are challenged. The first objection is to the presupposition by M that those addressed will know the answer and the second to the presupposition attributed to M that others should find things for her. Similarly, on the nonverbal level, an offer presumes that the other person wants the object involved; when an offer is resisted, as it sometimes is among young children, this presupposition is challenged. Presuppositions become apparent as arguable events when they are explicitly challenged.

Initial opposition

Not only do arguable events vary, but children initiate opposition in many different ways. Age-related changes in the means of opposition reflect changes in the nature of arguable events and development in the ability to oppose. Children of 1 or 2 years of age have been described as physically resisting, trying to regain objects, forcefully retaliating or counterattacking, and protesting vocally and verbally. They fuss, protest "No," and claim objects as "mine" (Caplan et al., 1991; Hay & Ross, 1982; Russell, 1981). Preschoolers resist the attempts of others to take their possessions by pulling, moving objects out of reach, leaving the area, grabbing, offering reasons, telling others to wait, and interjecting verbally with nonspecific imperatives (Camras, 1984; Weigel, 1984). During verbal quarrels, usually among older children, the forms of opposition become even more differentiated. Children challenge the assertions and requests of others with simple negative statements of protest, denial, disagreement, or refusal;

they also reason, contradict, offer counterproposals, postpone, dismiss, propose means to repair a breach, express rule violations, insult, and threaten (Eisenberg & Garvey, 1981; Genishi & DiPaolo, 1982; Maynard, 1985b, 1986; Phinney, 1986). Despite this wide variety of forms, opposition to others, to their behavior or ideas, is generally fairly easy to discern. Although the importance of this initial moment of opposition to the establishment of conflict is clearly recognized, relatively few researchers have examined first oppositions in detail. Diverse forms of opposition are often merged in analyses of conflict in order to distinguish conflict from other encounters. But some notable exceptions exist to this generalization, and they begin to tell the story of the forms of initiating opposition, the development of means of opposing, and the relation of the initial opposition to ensuing conflict events.

The object conflicts of 1- and 2-year-olds are begun most often with physical resistance to an agemate's attempts to take a toy and with attempts to regain the toy if the initial take has been successful (Caplan et al., 1991). Physical resistance can be divided into behaviors directed toward the object (such as tugging or moving a toy) and behaviors directed toward the opponent (such as pushing, pulling, hitting, or kicking the peer). Among these children, most resistance involves object-directed behavior; peer-directed retaliation is rare. Vocal and verbal protests occur more often, and 2-year-olds are more likely than 1-year-olds to voice their opposition (20% vs. 11% of the time; Caplan et al., 1991).

As was the case for attempts to obtain an object, purely physical resistance declines after 2 years of age. Recall that Camras (1984) studied children fighting over possession of two gerbils in a box. Although those children physically resisted the attempts of their peers by pulling the box toward themselves a majority of the time, they also expressed their opposition verbally. They protested ("no," "hey," or "watch it") or demanded that the other child give up the gerbils. Altogether, these simple verbal oppositions were found in 28% of the conflicts. More often, children asked their opponents to wait or offered a reason that justified their resistance. Younger children were less likely to protest verbally (80% vs. 86% of the time) and to temporize (17% vs. 39% of the time) than were older children. They were not less likely to offer reasons for resistance, however (25% of the time). Older girls were less likely to pull on the box as they resisted (35% vs. 55–67%) but were more likely to protest verbally (91% vs. 79–81% of the time) than the other children.

Reasoning, when used as part of initial opposition, is a most effective means of avoiding further conflict. Phinney (1986) found that 5-year-old children used reasoning in 25% of their initial oppositions in classrooms, whereas Eisenberg and Garvey (1981) found reasoning within nearly half of the oppositions voiced by preschoolers in dyadic play sessions. These investigators agree, however, on the effect of reasoned opposition: When children justify their initial objections, their partners do not pursue the conflict as often.

Parental reasoning does not seem to have the same immediate effects as peer reasoning. Goodenough (1931) was the first to note that although parental reasoning is associated with the development of cooperation in the long run, it does not lead to immediate child compliance. Others have since confirmed that parental reasoning does not foster immediate child compliance (Chapman & Zahn-Waxler, 1982; Lytton & Zwirner, 1975). The discrepancy in the effects of parental and peer reasoning could be explained in terms of the distinction that Piaget proposed between the moral authority of parents and reciprocity between peers. Between peers, compliance depends upon understanding and accepting the position of the other child, and the literature reviewed earlier indicates that reasoning seems to make the other's position clearer and more compelling. Parents, however, may rely on their authority to gain immediate compliance. When parents reason, this may encourage negotiation and counterproposals rather than compliance from their children (Kuczynski, Kochanska, Radke-Yarrow, & Girnius-Brown, 1987). One exception exists to this generalization, however: When parents intervene in peer disputes, reasoning enhances child compliance (Ross, Tesla, Kenyon, & Lollis, 1990). The fact that parental justifications concerned issues that arose between agemates may make reasoned objection pertinent.

In sum, physical aggression is rare as an initial opposition, even among very young children, although taking, tugging, and pulling objects are frequent means of beginning an object struggle. Verbal protests occur among 1-year-olds and grow more frequent with age until few disputes begin without a verbal objection. Finally, reasoning and other elaborated conciliatory moves effect immediate acquiescence more readily than do simple objections or orders. As Eisenberg and Garvey (1981) state, "most children will not accept a simple *No* from a peer as a sufficient form of opposition. The Opposer is expected to give an accounting for most non-positive responses" (p. 159).

Mutual opposition

The move immediately after the initial opposition has a special place in the structure of conflict. Shantz (1987) and Maynard (1985a) both argue forcefully that opposition is transformed into conflict when it becomes mutual – when the objection of one child is in turn challenged by the child whose actions were first protested. Otherwise, objections that are immediately remedied, challenges that are dropped, denied permissions that are accepted, and aggression that receives no response would all be classed as conflicts, when the quality of such events makes them seem mild in comparison with longer disputes. Nonetheless, some researchers have classified unrefuted objections or protests as conflicts (Eisenberg & Garvey, 1981; Hay & Ross, 1982; Phinney, 1986; Weigel, 1984).

In fact, unilateral oppositions are more likely to be embedded in the midst of positive interactive exchanges; they are preceded by affiliative interaction, and after they end, children are likely to remain near one another and to continue interaction. Conflicts with only two moves are more likely than longer disputes to be low in affective intensity and to be terminated by insistence rather than negotiation (Laursen & Hartup, 1989). Looking back at the characteristics of initial opposition, we know that reasoning and counterproposals (both elaborated moves) are more likely to end the conflict without arousing mutual opposition, whereas a simple No is more often challenged (Camras, 1984; Eisenberg & Garvey, 1981; Phinney, 1986). Characteristics of the children also influence whether a conflict move results in continued opposition. Weigel (1984) examined possession disputes of preschool children in which an initiator requested an object from a peer, a defendant resisted that attempt, and the initiator then resisted or yielded the object. The initiator's resistance determined whether the conflict was mutual or unilateral. Initiators were more likely to resist if they still had possession of the object as a result of their initial attempt and if they generally won as initiators in other object conflicts. As possessors often win, resistance was more likely when children had a good chance of emerging victorious.

Clear differences exist, then, between short and longer conflicts in the attributes of the children, the relation to prior and subsequent interaction of the children, the nature of initial opposition, and the affective quality of the dispute. It seems that a distinction based on the mutuality of opposition is clearly warranted. Nonetheless, whether we call them conflicts or not, brief oppositional encounters should continue to be studied along with longer disputes. We still have a great deal to learn about the determinants of extended conflict and the ways in which potential issues of dispute are resolved. Brief oppositional encounters are occasions when contentious issues are raised and then quickly put to rest; they are a most apt contrast to conflicts, in which contentious issues are raised and disputed. The more we understand about the factors that differentiate brief and sustained opposition, the more we will know about the determinants,

issues, and effective strategies of conflict, as well as the individual characteristics and relationships between combatants.

Oppositional strategies

During the initiation and ongoing mutual opposition that constitute conflict, children use a vast array of strategies to further their goals. Shantz
(1987) described the variety of conflict strategies as "limitless." Nevertheless, the choice of a strategy by one child encourages certain types of
responses rather than others from the peer and so may radically alter the
conflict. Most common is the repetition of oppositional acts focused on the
arguable event. During the object conflict of toddlers, a common meaningful sequence is that of a behavior directed toward the object leading to a
similar object-directed behavior, such as grab toy, tug toy, tug toy (Conant,
1987). During the verbal arguments of preschoolers, insistence on a previous utterance is common and most often leads to further insistence by
the partner (Eisenberg & Garvey, 1981). Reasoning and conciliation are
also reciprocated among peers (Eisenberg & Garvey, 1981; Phinney, 1986).
Generally, researchers do not differentiate between the use of various
strategies as initial or as subsequent oppositional moves, and so in this
section we shall review what is known about the use and consequences
of different strategy choices at any point in a conflict. The emphasis that
researchers have placed on physical aggression and communicative strategies will be reflected here. The impact of one child's choice of strategies
on the partner's moves will be considered for both the short, primarily
object-oriented toddler conflicts and the much more complex, primarily
verbal conflicts of older children.

Physical aggression has been found to be relatively rare in conflict, among
both toddlers and older children. Physical aggression is negative physical
contact and includes pushing, hitting, and kicking. Generally, fewer than
20% of conflicts include physical aggression – 17% among 21-month-olds
(Hay & Ross, 1982), 9% among 12-month-olds and 10% among 24-month-
olds (Caplan et al., 1991), and 14% among 3-to 5-year-olds (Eisenberg &
Garvey, 1981). Similarly, relatively few physical attacks or threats are
resisted by young peers (Strayer & Strayer, 1976), supporting the view that
conflict should be distinguished from aggression (e.g., Hay, 1984; Shantz,
1987). A minority of conflicts thus contain aggression, and a minority of
aggressive assaults result in retaliation.

Despite its rarity, aggression is a salient event in peer interaction and has
been divided into instrumental and hostile subtypes according to the intentions of the aggressor (Hartup, 1974). Bronson (1981) divided aggressive

conflict moves into instrumental assaults, which aimed to gain an object or otherwise control a peer's physical movements, investigatory assaults, which appeared to be accidental side effects of exploring the other person, and belligerent assaults, which had been prohibited by a parent or protested by a peer. Observations showed that younger toddlers' conflicts involved relatively more investigatory assaults than those of older toddlers (35% vs. 2% of the time), whereas the conflicts of older toddlers contained relatively more instrumental assaults (67% vs. 36% of the time).

Different types of hits have also been identified: Brownlee and Bakeman (1981) considered the effects of three types of hitting on the affective quality of the interactions of boys aged 1, 2, and 3 years. They distinguished between open-handed low-intensity swipes to the body (*open hit*), low-intensity hits with an object (*object hit*), and high-intensity hits or hits to the head (*hard hit*). Children's fights rarely involved hard hits (about 10% of the time), although these almost always resulted in negative affect (14 of 17 incidences). Consequences of the other two types of hitting were only predictable among 2-year-olds. For them, object hits were associated with positive or neutral interaction, whereas open hits often resulted in no interaction. The investigators interpreted the different types of hits as especially communicative among the 2-year-olds: 1-year-olds were thought to be too young to share an understanding of hitting, whereas 3-year-olds were expected to use more precise verbal communication. Only among 2-year-olds did the type of hitting aid in predicting the subsequent affective tone of the interaction. Thus, physical aggression consists of several types of strategies, some having predictable consequences for the conflict, if not by pure forcefulness, then by the communication of oppositional intent.

Oppositional intent may also be communicated by means of aggressive facial expressions (Camras, 1977). Aggressive expressions include at least one of the following: lowered brow, stare, face thrust forward, lips pressed together or thrust forward, lips pressed together with tightened mouth corners, and nose wrinkled. Kindergarten children, observed as they shared control of the gerbil box, used these types of threatening gestures during 25% of the occasions that they resisted their peers. When the children used aggressive expressions, their partners waited longer before next attempting to get the gerbils, and they, in turn, were more likely to resist this subsequent attempt. In another study of facial expression during conflict, a somewhat different, perhaps milder, threat display was found to have an impact on conflict outcome (Zivin, 1977a). Resistance attempts of preschoolers accompanied by a *plus face* (raised brows, eyes wide open in apparent direct eye contact, and raised chin) and a *minus face* (gently furrowed brows, eyes dropped, broken eye contact, and lowered chin) were noted. The plus face was found in a third and the minus face in a fifth of the resistance attempts observed. Children won 66% of the conflicts in which resistance included a plus face; they lost 85% of their conflicts in which a minus face was part of the initial resistance. Facial expressions were thus highly effective in predicting conflict outcome. In addition, the plus face was less likely to be used when the children could not see one another than when they could, which suggests that this expression may sometimes be used as part of a deliberate strategy to influence conflict outcome.

Not surprisingly, a variety of verbal communicative strategies influence the progress of conflict sequences. Reflecting language development, the incidence of verbalizations during conflict increases during the second year and beyond (Brownell & Brown, 1985; Green, 1933b). In one study, Conant (1987) observed that up to 33% of all strategies employed by 15- to 24-month-olds were actions accompanied by either words or nonword vocalizations and that 12% of the 24-month-olds' strategies consisted of words or phrases alone. Furthermore, among 21- and 24-month-olds, verbal strategies tend to elicit verbal strategies from the partner and to inhibit more object-oriented strategies. These sequences reflect the children's emerging abilities to converse and negotiate, which, with age, become predominant in conflict and allow for a broad array of new conflict strategies. In addition to verbal communication, gestures influenced the conflict sequences observed in this study. At all ages, gestural strategies, such as pointing and reaching, tended to lead to protective responses from the partner. Partners evidently interpreted these gestures as threats to the possession of their toys and responded accordingly.

Young toddlers vary the content of their verbal communications according to their goals. Hay and Ross (1982) noted that verbal remarks occurred more often when speakers tried to gain possession of toys than when they protected toys in their possession. Negatives such as "No" and "Don't!" were used most frequently to protect toys, whereas possessive statements such as "Mine" and "My toy!" were used to gain and to maintain possession of toys. Naming the toy also was used differentially: Fifty percent of verbal attempts to gain possession included the name of the toy, whereas only 16% of protective statements included toy names. Using somewhat different distinctions, Brownell and Brown (1985) found that verbal mediation, possession assertion, and positive negotiations all increased in frequency over the second year. In these ways, very young combatants use communication in attempts to influence the progress of conflict.

In contrast to toddlers' arguments, preschoolers' disagreements can be quite elaborate in their verbal structure. Phinney (1986) provided typical examples: Conflicts among 5-year-olds, she observed, often begin with one child denying or contradicting the partner's assertion, which is then met with a denial or counterassertion by the child who is opposed. This type of turn sequence is common in conflicts and has been noted by other conflict analysts, such as Eisenberg and Garvey (1981), who reported that insistence reliably leads to counter insistence by the partner, and Boggs (1978), who identified a sequence of assertion, claim, or allegation followed by contradiction. These sequences have been called "simple" (Genishi & DiPaolo, 1982; Phinney, 1986) because of their relative lack of information from which compromise and conciliation can derive. Moreover, these sequences are generally escalatory in nature: They are less likely to lead to resolution than are other moves (Eisenberg & Garvey, 1981).

More elaborate conflict moves that include reasoning and attempts at compromise have been considered unique because of the information they contain: These strategies give the partner more detail about the perspective of the speaker and what resolutions the speaker may find reasonable. Eisenberg and Garvey (1981) identified four elaborated moves, each of which increased the likelihood that the conflict would be resolved. Compromise in the form of turn talking, sharing, conditional agreements, and suggestions of alternatives were all likely to end the conflict. Reasoning, whether in support of assertions or requests, or to explain noncompliance, more often led to compromise than to other moves. According to Eisenberg and Garvey, these four elaborated moves are high in their adaptive value in that hearers can easily respond to them. Such responses show some acceptance of the partner's perspective and, in the case of compromise, some understanding of fairness between the disputants. Within object disputes, justifications also seem to have an impact on conflict outcome: Children who justify their resistance are more likely to retain possession of disputed objects than those who merely demand their turns (Camras, 1984).

The relative frequency of elaborated reasoning and simple insistence seems to be influenced by the context of the conflict. Genishi and DiPaolo (1982) noted that far more of the conflicts that they observed in nursery school classrooms were simple in contrast to the conflicts that Eisenberg and Garvey (1981) studied in preschool-age dyads in the laboratory. They felt that the presence of teachers could have inhibited elaborated moves in the nursery school. In addition, children in dyadic settings have only one another with whom to interact. Their greater interdependence increases the importance of resolving disagreements so that play can resume. Within the nursery school, however, disputes may occur between children who are not necessarily interacting and who are not as dependent on interacting together after conflict ceases. Accordingly, the interdependence of the children fosters the use of reasoning in disputes because reasoning is more effective and less divisive than other conflict strategies. Also, disputes are less likely to end after a first objection in the dyadic setting than in the group setting, regardless of what form the objection takes. Children who are playing together, and who depend on one another alone for continued play, also have to resolve their disagreements rather than drop them; in group settings, however, children can simply drop their opposition and move on to other partners. In apparent contradiction to this explanation, Camras (1979) observed children in dyads and also found less reasoning than did Eisenberg and Garvey (25% vs. 48% of initial oppositional moves included reasoning). Recall, however, that the children studied by Camras did not play together but played independently and one at a time with a desirable resource: Interdependence within play was not a factor in this context.

In considering the variety of strategies that have been observed in conflicts between young children, we have reviewed the form and consequences of the use of aggressive and communicative strategies. In numerous ways, the interactive structure of conflict reflects the dependencies existing among the strategies of children. Often the strategies of one child are reciprocated by the other, such as physical, object-directed strategies following physical, object-directed strategies, or verbal strategies following verbal strategies. Some types of physical aggression, however, tend to end interaction or to produce negative affect more than others. Clearly, children make some interpretations of their young opponents' behaviors: Facial expressions can communicate aggressive intent, and gestures can communicate threats to possessions. Whereas simple verbal messages tend to escalate conflict, more elaborate reasoning tends more often to lead to resolution. Especially in their reasoning and conciliations, children take account of the needs of their adversaries and the context in which they are interacting. Thus, young children are not blind opponents but interpret their partners' actions and respond accordingly. Next, we consider the manner in which arguable events and strategy use influence conflict outcomes.

Conflict endings

Over 50 years ago, Anderson (1937a, 1937b) emphasized the distinction between submissive and conciliatory outcomes in conflict. According to this investigator, a child may submit to a dominant partner in ending a conflict or declare a truce such that differences in viewpoints remain. But it is only when children reach a common goal and integrate positive behavior with one another that growth appears. Ideally, opposition ends with compromise, reconciliation of opposing views, or the acceptance of one view based on established standards such as truth or fairness (Garvey, 1984). Such endings lead to continuing social exchange between former adversaries, whereas submission of one child to the will of another often ends the interaction along with the conflict (Laursen & Hartup, 1989; Sackin & Thelen, 1984). But despite their advantages, most conflicts are not resolved with conciliatory endings. In fact, some claim that children typically fail to resolve their disputes (Boggs, 1978; Maynard, 1985b): "Once a dispute has begun it is rarely resolved to the mutual satisfaction of the participants" (Boggs, 1978, p. 333).

The types of resolutions children create – indeed, the types of resolutions that are possible – depend upon the issues in dispute. Arguments over facts or opinions can end with the children arriving at a common position, dropping the topic, shifting the basis of their opposition, or turning the opposition into a game. In such instances, one child's view cannot conquer the other's view by force; agreement is necessary if one position is to prevail. In contrast, conflicts over possessions, over the inclusion or exclusion of children from the play group, or over the control of behavior can lead to clear winner–loser outcomes. When conflicts end, one child generally has possession of the disputed object, has been included or excluded from joint play, or has behaved or failed to behave in the prescribed way. Some of these outcomes are cooperative, as when a child is accepted into a play group, complies with another child's requests, or apologizes for past actions.

Despite the interconnections between issues and conflict outcomes, only two studies of preschool children have addressed this question directly. Killen and Turiel (1991) contrasted conflicts resolved by the children through bargaining, compromising, transforming the conflict into a game, and reconciliation with those in which the issue was unresolved. Overall, more conflicts remained unresolved than were resolved, particularly for issues of psychological harm and the disruption of social order. In comparison, when issues of physical harm, distribution of resources, and rights arose, children resolved their conflicts nearly as often as they dropped the issue. Similarly, Laursen and Hartup (1989) found that conflicts instigated by aggression led to eventual compromise more often than did conflicts begun by other means; however, they did not find a relation between their major categories of conflict issues – behavior versus object possession – and the prevalence of either winner–loser or compromise outcomes.

Although examples of conciliation can be found in the object disputes of toddlers, these disputes are far more likely to end with a clear win for one of the children than in conciliation. Over 80% of object conflicts among toddlers end when one of the children gains possession of the toy (Caplan et al., 1991; Conant, 1987). When that happens, the loser tends to initiate the next conflict between the pair (Hay & Ross, 1982). Other object conflicts end when children split a set of multiple objects (10% of the time in Conant, 1987) or when one child offers or gives a toy to the other (7% of the time in both Caplan et al., 1991, and Conant, 1987). These latter endings mark the beginnings of conciliation. Children as young as 12 months of age have been observed giving toys to a companion at the conclusion of conflict, and these prosocial appeasement gestures increase in frequency over the second year of life. Conciliatory endings have been reported for 5% of object conflicts among 1-year-olds and for 10% or 14% of such conflicts among 2-year-olds (Caplan et al., 1991; Conant, 1987).

Conciliation is a more frequent conflict outcome among preschool children than among toddlers. Both Laursen and Hartup (1989) and Sackin and Thelen (1984) found evidence of compromise and conciliatory outcomes in one of every three conflicts using observations of preschool conflicts that did not include adult intervention. A substantial and growing minority of children's disputes are thus resolved in a way that reconciles the views of two children and satisfies both with a mutually agreeable outcome. The issues involved in these conflicts mainly included physical aggression, territorial and possession disputes, and control (Laursen & Hartup, 1989; Sackin & Thelen, 1984). The possibility exists, then, that the absence of clear resolutions noted in other studies (Boggs, 1978; Maynard, 1985b) applies mainly to verbal disputes over fact or opinion, rather than to conflicts involving aggression, possession, or behavioral control.

Nonetheless, a majority of verbal arguments end after moves that are adaptive, in that they contain new information, propose a remedy, and recognize the perspective of the other child (among preschoolers, Eisenberg & Garvey, 1981; and among elementary school aged children, Walton & Sedlak, 1982). Such moves include reasoning and proposals of conditions or alternative plans (Eisenberg & Garvey, 1981) and denials, excuses, justifications, apologies, and other compliant actions that are called "remedies" (Walton & Sedlak, 1982). A small number of disputes end with clear acceptance of these remedies (Walton & Sedlak, 1982) or with explicit compromise (Eisenberg & Garvey, 1981), but in other cases, it is not possible to tell whether both parties freely accept the reasoning, conditions, or remedies, or whether the dispute is merely dropped. In these instances, though, the additional information provided just prior to the end of the dispute makes implicit conciliation a good possibility.

Children thus win some conflicts with their peers, lose others, leave issues unresolved, and compromise in order to arrive at mutually satisfactory resolutions. Reasoning seems to promote relatively rapid and conciliatory outcomes, but little is known about the arguments children use to justify their own actions or to persuade others. Do principles of justice or standards of truth help children resolve disagreements? Furthermore, we may ask how social relationships influence the ways in which conflicts end. Considerations of issues of justice or social relationships take conflict out of the confines of transitory interaction between two individuals and place it within the broader social domains having to do with group relationships and cultural standards. Furthermore, what is fair may not always coincide with relational considerations; these factors may compete with one another in both the conduct and the outcome of conflict. Consequently, in the next sections we will explore the origins and development of relationships and principles of justice as these are related to early conflict.

Conflict and enduring relationships

Enemies and friends

One characteristic of relationships is that individuals come to treat one another in special and distinct ways. A child who has a relationship with another treats that special peer in ways that are not found in the behavior of the same child in other social contexts (Ross & Lollis, 1989). With respect to conflict, children who are especially prone to fight with one another in ways that cannot be predicted from their interactions with others could be considered enemies. However, relationships based solely on enmity have not been found in the interactions of young children (Green, 1933a; Hayes, Gershman, & Bolin, 1970; Ross, Conant, Cheyne, & Alevizos, 1992; Ross & Lollis, 1989). In one investigation dealing with the unfolding of children's relationships, 1- and 2-year-olds played with agemates (previously strangers) over a 3-month period. Positive behavior toward one another came gradually to reflect reciprocal relationships developed between them; in contrast, their conflicts continued to reflect individual characteristics (Ross & Lollis, 1989). That is, the children differed from one another in the conflicts that they initiated with their peers and in the conflict moves that they elicited from them, but these characteristics were the same from partner to partner. Consistent with this, one can predict the rate of conflict initiation with one partner from the frequency of conflict initiated earlier with others (Hay & Ross, 1982). But we have also studied kibbutz toddlers in their peer groups, and in this context, relationships seemed to influence child–child conflict, though not in ways that allow us to define children as enemies. That is, the children in these groups picked out particular peers with whom they participated most often in conflict, but they typically chose the same children for friendly interaction. These children were more often "fighting friends" than "enemies" (Ross et al., 1992). We explain the differences between these studies in terms of the contrasting demands of the dyadic versus the group setting. In the group setting, friends were more often together than were nonfriends, and conflict issues arose in the normal course of play; in the dyadic setting, children had only one play partner, and friendships were not associated with an increase in the amount of time the children spent together. As a consequence, the social relationships existing between the children had less impact on conflict in the dyadic setting than in the group context.

Children in preschool groups also have more conflicts with friends than with other children, a circumstance that is related to their spending more time together (Green, 1933a; Hartup, Laursen, Stewart, & Eastenson, 1988; Hinde, Titmus, Easton, & Tamplin, 1985). In addition, preschool children can select others on sociometric tests whom they dislike, but these choices are rarely reciprocal (Hayes et al., 1970). Moreover, the reasons children give for disliking someone differ from their reasons for liking someone. Children cite individual characteristics of others in relation to disliking (aggression, rule violation, and aberrant behavior); reasons for liking another child often involve the relationship between the children ("He lives near me," "We do things together," "We like each other," and so on). So, if mutual enemies exist in this age period, they have yet to be found by researchers, and further research on this issue is clearly warranted. However, mutual friends do fight. Fights between friends may not be the same as those between children who do not mutually like one another, even though they begin in the same way, last as long, and involve the same issues of possession and behavioral control. Conflicts between friends are less hostile, less likely to terminate with one child standing firm and one child losing, and as a result, are more likely to be followed by proximity and interaction (Hartup et al., 1988). The evidence thus suggests that young children depend on their good friends for play and support; they seem able to mitigate the jeopardy that conflict poses while, at the same time, hazarding to disagree.

Dominance relationships

Friendships are egalitarian and reciprocal relationships; other stable relationships that emerge within nursery school groups are asymmetrical – these are relationships based on dominance. Dominance relationships are dyadic too, in that they are based on interactions during which one child typically submits to the attacks and threats of another (La Freniere & Charlesworth, 1983; Strayer & Strayer, 1980). Dominance hierarchies, consisting of the ordered arrangement of these dyadic relationships in a group, are transitive: If A is dominant in relation to B, and B is dominant in relation to C, then A is also dominant in relation to C. Dominance hierarchies, based on submission to initiated threats and aggression, and also at times object losses, have been found in children's groups from the second year on, although these hierarchies are more stable within groups of older children than within groups of younger ones (Frankel & Arbel, 1980; LaFreniere & Charlesworth, 1983; Missakian, 1980; Sluckin & Smith, 1977; Strayer & Strayer, 1976; Strayer & Trudel, 1984). According to ethological theory, established dominance should minimize aggressive conflicts within groups by establishing priorities and allowing group members to anticipate when their aggressive initiations will result in harmful consequences for themselves. And indeed, some evidence suggests that physical aggression declines with the establishment of dominance hierarchies in preschool and toddler groups (Frankel & Arbel, 1980; La Freniere & Charlesworth, 1983). For example, top-ranking nursery school children in one study (La Freniere & Charlesworth) were very aggressive in the fall but became notably less so in the winter and spring, while at the same time maintaining their dominant status. Although much work on dominance can be criticized because verbal threats and quarrels are not measured, these investigators constructed dominance hierarchies based on verbal measures and found them to correlate highly with hierarchies based on submission to physical attacks, threats, and object acquisition.

Established dominance relations have an impact on the conduct of conflict. In object conflicts, initiators who typically win are more likely than those who do not win as often to persist in their attempts to get objects from resisting opponents (Weigel, 1984). Dominance relations also influence the outcome of object disputes. Charlesworth and La Freniere (1983) introduced a movie viewer to groups of preschool children: Only one child could view a cartoon at a time, but in order to do so, a second child had to press a button to keep a light on, and a third had to operate a crank. Dominant children always succeeded in getting the most viewing time and did so largely through conflict. Children low on the dominance hierarchy were more likely to be bystanders, neither viewing, illuminating, nor cranking the machine. Moreover, the children seemed to know their own prerogatives when this highly attractive toy was introduced: "When first faced with the situation, subordinate children frequently moved into the crank and light positions rather than deal with the dominant who immediately took over the viewing position" (p. 184). In Camras's (1984) study, perceived dominance (based on ratings of who is tougher) was associated with time in possession of the gerbils, and dominant boys used less polite strategies to wrest the gerbils from their peers than did other children. Dominant children are also more likely to use the plus face in conflict situations than are subordinate children (Zivin, 1977b). Finally, dominant children use more aggressive facial expressions when in conflict with a nonfriend than with a friend, whereas submissive children use these expressions more often with friends (Camras, 1979, 1984).

Nonetheless, dominant children are not always winners. For example, dominant children do not totally monopolize the toys that they win but also let others have them and sometimes organize the distribution of turns (Camras, 1984; Charlesworth & La Freniere, 1983). Moreover, children low in the dominance hierarchy do not stop attacking or threatening their dominant peers even though these threats are not likely to meet with submission. In addition, when dominant children resist other children or themselves counterattack, the dominance hierarchy does not do well in predicting the eventual outcome of the dispute (Strayer & Strayer, 1976). Considerations of rights and fairness may override dominance in this event. Entitlement to an object, as established by prior possession, often accounts for conflict outcomes in these instances, dominance relations notwithstanding (Bakeman & Brownlee, 1982; Frankel & Arbel, 1980; Russon & Waite, 1991).

Justification, entitlement, and conflict

By the time children have reached 3 or 4 years of age, they attempt to justify their viewpoints during conflict using rights of entitlement. Corsaro (1985) described the types of justifications that preschoolers use to keep other children from joining their ongoing play and found that 47% of all resistance takes the form of some type of claim to entitlement of objects or space. Current or prior use ("I was here first"), school rules ("That's not allowed"), and social rules for role playing ("Babies need to sleep") are examples of such claims. Other, less frequent justifications include resistance attempts referring to overcrowding ("There's not enough room for you"), to friendship ("If you do that, I can't be your friend"), and to arbitrary rules made during the course of play ("Wagons are for dump trucks only"). Only 15% of the time, and only during initial opposition, did these preschoolers use verbal protest without some form of justification. The use of these justifications suggests considerable sophistication in these children's knowledge of their social setting (Corsaro, 1985). From this study, we know little about the validity of the justifications, however, or about the effect of entitlement on the outcome of conflict. Other studies have examined the impact of entitlement on those conflicts that are most easily observed – disputes over objects. The three principles of entitlement that have been considered most frequently, possession, prior possession, and ownership, are the focus of the following discussion.

In our Western culture, current possession is one justification for entitlement to an object, and indeed, it is a factor that influences the outcome of object conflicts among even very young children. The majority of object disputes among both toddlers and preschoolers are won by the initial possessor of the object; challengers are more likely to lose (Conant, 1987; Ramsey, 1980; Weigel, 1984). The rates reported in observational studies range from 65% for children 15 to 24 months of age (Conant, 1987) to 56–66% (Ramsey, 1980) and 75% (Weigel, 1984) for children between ages 3 and 5 years. One-year-olds also win conflicts over toys they initially possess even against challengers who are otherwise more dominant group members (Russon & Waite, 1991). It should be noted that, among such young children, winning by possessors may not be due to felt entitlement; rather, possessors may win these disputes because the object is of higher value to them than to the challenger or because it is physically easier to keep an object than to take it away from someone else (Weigel, 1984). Nevertheless, there is evidence that felt entitlement may emerge early: In one instance, toddler possessors who were successful in keeping their toys were more likely than successful challengers to show negative affect (Conant, 1987). Quite possibly these winners became upset at the attempted intrusion on their possessions and violation of their possession rights.

Justifications of entitlement based on possession are strengthened by a history of possession. Among young children, the probability of resistance to a peer's attempt to take an object and conflict outcome are influenced by the length of time the possessor has had the disputed object. Both toddlers and preschoolers who have had a toy for several minutes prior to a challenge are more likely to resist the challenger (Bronson, 1981; Winegar & Renninger, 1989; but not Brownell & Brown, 1985, for resistance). Furthermore, possessing an object for some time decreases the probability of losing it to a challenger. In one observational study (Bronson, 1981), toddlers who had just picked up their toys lost 55% of the challenges against them, but toddlers who had had the toy for some time lost disputes only 38% of the time. Concordantly, the nursery school children observed by Winegar and Renninger lost conflicts 81% of the time over toys they had just acquired but lost conflicts over toys they had had for more than 2 minutes only 29% of the time.

Thus, current possession and length of possession influence conflict outcome in favor of possessors. Challengers, however, also gain an advantage if they have possession of the object prior to the current possessor. Indeed, prior possession by the challenger influences both the probability that the challenge will be resisted and the probability that the challenger will regain possession of the object. Bakeman and Brownlee (1982) found, among preschoolers but not among toddlers, that resistance was more likely when the challenger had not had prior possession. Brownell and Brown (1985) also found this effect for children 18 and 24 months of age but not for 1-year-olds. Furthermore, these investigators found that 24-month-olds' resistance to challengers was more likely to be intense if the challenger had not played with the toy previously. Conflict outcomes were also influenced by prior possession in these groups; children older than 12 months were more likely to win objects that they had just possessed (Bakeman & Brownlee, 1982; Brownell & Brown, 1985). Thus, the influence of prior possession by the challenger may become stronger with age and (presumably) with the children's increasing abilities to monitor other children's activities with toys. Children may begin then to behave in accordance with the principle that possession grants entitlement to a past possessor in situations in which their own current possession is threatened.

That young children have some understanding of rights of entitlement granted through ownership is suggested by their peer interactions involving toys. Conant (1991) had mothers give toys to 2-year-olds in a laboratory setting and found that the children won more conflicts over these toys than over other ones. Children also were more likely to claim "owned toys." Ownership claims during conflict were used both as assertions of control over toys and attempts to gain access to them. In another study, Eisenberg-Berg, Haake, and Bartlett (1981) gave individual preschool children a toy (soap liquid for blowing bubbles), told some that the toy belonged to them and that they could take it home, and told others that the toy belonged to the nursery school and had to remain there at the end of the day. In dyadic encounters, the children who were owners were observed to possess the toy longer than children who were not. Owners were also more likely to defend their toys from challengers than were nonowners and were more likely to make ownership claims. Nonowners, however, were more likely to give up the toys in response to a peer's attempts to get it. Children also are more likely in a group setting to defend toys that they are told belong to them (Eisenberg-Berg, Haake, Hand, & Sadalla, 1979).

In conflicts between even very young children, then, resistance and outcome are related to principles of possession, prior possession, and ownership. Possessors are more likely to win, and this probability is strengthened when length of possession increases. The probability that challengers will not be resisted and will win possession of a toy increases when the challenger has had the toy prior to the possessor. These effects are stronger among older toddlers and preschoolers than among 1-year olds, suggesting that children become better at monitoring their partners and utilizing possession rights in conflict situations. Ownership also influences the conflicts of 2-year-olds and preschoolers who claim, defend, and win "owned toys" more than other toys. In these ways, young children appear to recognize their rights of entitlement and incorporate them into their ongoing disputes. The effects of many other rights and the effects of established principles for valid argument are not known. Although reasoning and justification are good strategies for resolving conflicts between preschoolers (Eisenberg & Garvey, 1981), they have not been assessed in detail. Do children recognize some types of justifications as more legitimate than others? How and when do children contest the validity of an opponents' justifications, and what responses do opponents make? How do rights and feelings of entitlement contrast with established dominance and friendship relations in influencing children's decisions within conflict? How do these considerations influence the configuration of conflicts involving third parties?

Third parties to conflict

Alliances, interventions, and collaborations embroil third parties in disputes that they do not initiate, and these have a major impact on conflict activity and outcome. When two people share a common conflict position, their strength doubles and their arguments are bolstered by agreement and extension. Even if they do not prevail, the supportive relationship between allies creates at least one positive outcome of conflict. In considering third-party disputes, we place conflict in a new social context – one that involves cooperation, support, altruism, and enduring social relationships. Both adults and peers enter conflicts started by others, and we shall divide consideration of third-party intrusions accordingly.

Adult intervention

Of all the social exchanges that children have with their peers, conflicts are the most likely to prompt adult intervention (Lollis, Ross, & Tate, in press; Russon, Waite, & Rochester, 1990). The mere presence of a passive adult increases the amount of aggression, both verbal and physical, between children; that is, aggression increases over time when a passive adult is present, whereas it decreases when the adult remains absent (Besevegis & Lore, 1983; Siegel & Kohn, 1959). In the absence of an adult, children may moderate their aggression, taking more responsibility for the quality of their interactions with their peers. When an adult is present but passive, children may expect that aggressive overtures are acceptable to this authority and, at the same time, that they are protected from intense peer retaliation by the adult. Children also seem better able to generate their own resolutions to conflicts in dyadic play sessions in which adults typically do not intervene than in preschool groups in which adult interventions are frequent (Killen & Turiel, 1991). Moreover, teachers are more likely to be present during long conflicts between nursery school children and to be absent during shorter ones (Laursen & Hartup, 1989).

The rate of adult intervention seems to vary dramatically between settings: Reports range from only 9% (Killen, 1989) to 44% (Russon et al., 1990) of conflicts within group settings, varying within a single study by as much as 29% across different preschool classrooms (Killen, 1989). Adults intervene more with younger children than with older ones (Bakeman & Brownlee, 1982; Russon et al., 1990), intervene in conflicts over physical or psychological harm, distribution of resources, and rights more than over issues of social order (Killen & Turiel, 1991), and intervene when they are nearby, when infants solicit intervention, or when crying or the severity of the dispute draws their attention (Russon et al., 1990). Adult intervention tends to promote adult-generated solutions, especially for conflicts involving physical harm and social order (Killen & Turiel, 1991); adult interventions also promote greater equality between combatants than might otherwise obtain (Lollis et al., in press).

When adults intervene in children's conflicts, their goals are frequently to redistribute resources and to discourage inappropriate behavior (Lollis et al., in press). Such goals are accomplished through commands, clarifying statements, and physical interventions. Reasoning, suggestions of alternatives, and bargaining are also used. Russon et al. (1990) report that even infant daycare teachers justify their interventions with moral rules ("We don't hit people," "CT, that was LE's book, give it back") and point out the consequences of the children's actions for others ("No. That hurts him"). The teachers seem to be attempting to generate fair or equitable solutions, though they occasionally make errors including supporting the wrong child, scapegoating, and acting inconsistently.

Inconsistency and bias in supporting one child more than the other is a greater problem with maternal interventions. For example, we examined mothers' interventions in the object disputes of their 20- and 30-month-old children with their peers (Ross et al., 1990). Both mothers were present for play sessions that alternated between the two homes. When mothers intervened in conflicts, they addressed their own child almost exclusively and supported the rights of the other child 90% of the time. We also assessed whether the mothers consistently enforced principles of entitlement by intervening only when the other children's rights were violated: Neither possession nor ownership guided the mothers' interventions. Although mothers endorsed these principles some of the time, they also argued against ownership ("Let her play with it because she doesn't have one like that at home") and possession ("You've had it long enough. Give him a turn") as they justified their positions. Generally, rights of ownership or possession were enforced by the mothers only when the other child's rights were violated; mothers seldom supported their own children in similar circumstances but intervened, nonetheless, in support of the other child. Thus, although mothers justified their interventions by reference to principles that might help children understand how to resolve disputes fairly, these women were inconsistent in endorsing those same rights in their own judgments.

Adult interventions in children's conflicts, then, do not always realize their potential for generating fair solutions or for promoting an understanding of self and other. Adults present relevant principles for solving disputes but may be inconsistent in their application and also interfere with children's own efforts to control aggression and resolve disputes. In the case of mothers with their own children, the parent–child relationship is a far more powerful determinant of how mothers intervene, as well as what resolutions and justifications they offer, than any principles of entitlement that might apply.

Alliances with peers

Although alliances have been found to determine outcome in studies of conflict and dominance among nonhuman primates, few investigators have focused on alliances and interventions in children's conflicts. Existing studies show that a substantial number of conflicts draw more than two peers into combat. Strayer and Noel (1986), for example, reported that one in every five or six conflicts among 4- to 6-year-old preschoolers included third-party participation, whereas Maynard (1986) found that more than half of the verbal arguments observed within first-grade reading groups involved more than two children.

Multiparty disputes are structured similarly to dyadic conflicts between peers (Maynard, 1986). That is, an arguable event is opposed by a second party who either contradicts the original position or offers a counterposition.

A reaction then occurs in which the opposition is countered in some way. Third parties then can align themselves relative to the position, its contradiction, or a counterposition. Third parties may propose counterpositions in support of either of the original antagonists. Third parties can offer their support spontaneously, or it can be solicited by one of the combatants. If solicited, support can be offered or withheld, and once offered, support can be accepted either explicitly (by some form of action) or implicitly (by not contravening) or be rejected by the party supported.

Several additional types of triadic conflict can be distinguished, based on whether the third party is the source or the target of agonism and whether the alliance is made with the child who originally attacked or was attacked: Defense, alliance, generalization, and displacement occur at similar rates (Strayer & Noel, 1986). If A and B are the original conflict partners, and A has attacked B, then, if C attacks A, C is *defending* B. If, instead, C also attacks B, then an *alliance* has formed between A and C. If A attacks B and then attacks C, the attack has *generalized*. If B rather than A attacks C, then *displacement* has occurred.

The patterns that Strayer and Noel (1986) observed between children are at once complex and interesting. In most cases, for example, original aggressors tend to emit aggression frequently and to be dominant in relation to other conflict partners. This is not the case for defense, however. In these encounters, the dominant child is the defender, and this child does not limit his or her defense to friends but defends others against attackers who are themselves frequently attacked. The dominance of defenders is confirmed by evidence from grade school boys as well (Ginsberg & Miller, 1981). Dominant children also tend to attract allies from among their friends and to generalize and displace aggression to their friends who are subordinate to them. Subordinate children do not form alliances to defeat jointly those who generally dominate, but rather, dominant children offer and receive support from one another.

A curious absence from these studies is an evaluation of the immediate effect of alliances on conflict outcomes. The presumption is that collaboration within conflict greatly enhances the likelihood of a favorable outcome. This has been amply demonstrated in the nonhuman literature (e.g., de Waal, 1984; Goodall, 1986), and the dominance of both allies and defenders (as shown by Strayer & Noel, 1986) seems to support the proposition that collaboration is associated with winning. However, Maynard's (1986) observations show that children continue to fight even in the face of joint opposition: Thus, the power of collaboration is not automatic.

To obtain a preliminary indication of the effects of collaboration on conflict outcome, we have analyzed a number of conflicts cited by Corsaro

(1985, chap. 4) that focus on the problem of group entry. In this investigation, preschool children were intensively observed and videotaped over a 10-month period. Children often found themselves alone and, in such circumstances, sought to enter an ongoing group. Such entries often involved conflict (half of the entry attempts met with resistance) and sometimes exclusion (half of the resisted entries resulted in exclusion). According to Corsaro, the children sought and received support from their peers, but neither the analysis nor the selection of illustrative transcripts was centered on this event. Each conflict ends, however, with a more or less definite outcome regarding group entry, and so the transcripts are useful for examining the relation between collaboration and conflict outcome. These data are limited and selected, of course; even their generalization within the original data set cannot be assumed. Nevertheless, because there is so little information on the structure of multiparty conflicts, a preliminary analysis is useful.

Nine conflicts were described over social participation and the protection of interactive space. In all cases, two or more children were playing together, and one other child sought entry to the group. Collaboration occurred in eight of the nine transcribed conflicts, probably because the children already playing together had a joint investment in their ongoing play. Indeed, alliances were most often formed between the original players, who jointly excluded the child who sought entry (eight times), although these players sometimes defended the entering child, as did bystanders (six times in all). Collaboration was more often spontaneous (nine times) than solicited (five times); six of the eight collaborations among original group members were spontaneous and two solicited, whereas three of the six defensive collaborations were solicited. Alliances were always between the original group members, and when they occurred, they always resulted in the exclusion of the entering child. The following transcript illustrates this process (Corsaro, 1985, p. 124):

Two girls, B and Be, are constructing a zoo, building enclosures, and placing animals in them. L is watching from a distance. After a few minutes L approaches, sits beside B, and picks up some of the animals.
    B–L: You can't play.
    L–B: Yes, I can. I can have some animals, too.
    B–L: No, you can't. We don't like you today.
    Be–L: You're not our friend.
    L–B, Be: I can play here, too.
    B–Be: No, her can't—her can't, right Be?
    Be–B: Right.

Defensive collaborations with the child who sought entry occurred with bystanders half the time and with original group members half the time.

When bystanders supported group entry attempts, they were not successful if opposed by an alliance between original group members; children were only successful in overcoming opposition to their attempted entry when their efforts were supported by members of the original group. The power of collaboration among original group members is illustrated further by the inability of adults to overcome easily such united opposition (observed in three instances).

The prevalence of collaboration in these episodes is striking. Furthermore, for group entry, support from the original group members seems to be critical to the success or failure of the attempt. Alliances between the original players always resulted in exclusion, and entering children were successful only with the support of one of the original group members. Neither adult nor bystander support was effective. These results, however, might be peculiar to the particular problems that the entering children were facing. To enter an ongoing play group, one needs the cooperation of the original group members; if they cannot be convinced to welcome one's participation, peer play will soon disintegrate. Bystanders might be more effective in successfully defending others from attack or restoring toys to a victim where continued good will is not essential. The content of conflict, then, seems critical for establishing the effect of differences in conflict structure.

We have given considerable attention to the relatively few studies of collaborative conflict that have been reported. Just as it was important to consider conflict as structured dyadic interaction, so is it important to expand our vision still further. We must learn how conflict draws in other group members and how it influences and is influenced by enduring social relationships. The study of multiparty conflict, in our view, is essential for understanding the place of conflict in children's social lives. Many exciting questions arise, including those related to conflict issues and the existence or establishment of relationships between the children as described earlier. Standards of validity and moral principles as well as established relationships between children should influence the alliance and defense processes, and as in dyadic conflict, these forces may sometimes oppose one another.

An additional question concerns the developmental origins of collaborative efforts in conflict. Although we have no systematic data to speak to this issue, we offer the following example of conflict in kibbutz toddlers, in which support is offered spontaneously and is elicited in a dispute. Three children, T, U, and M, are playing on the porch of their children's house. T runs up the stairs and closes the balcony gate, leaving U and M outside. She smiles:

U–T: The door! The door!

M–T: To come in! (Note that this infinitive form is a one-word utterance in Hebrew, expressing the child's desire to come in.)

U–T: The door!

T–U & M: (Does not respond.)

U–M: M, M, M. (U calls to M.)

M–T: To come in! (M supports U.)

T–U & M: (Does not respond.)

U–M: M, M.

M–U: (Does not respond.)

U–T: To come in! To come in!

With M's first spontaneous request "To come in," an alliance is established between U and M. U then elicits further support from M, who asks again "To come in." T does not respond, and U's second attempt to gain support from M also fails to elicit a response. After the cited excerpt the conflict continues between U and T, with M watching, until a caregiver opens the gate. This example shows that alliances contribute to conflict even among children as young as 2 years of age.

Interpretations and future directions

Despite the dramatic changes in conflict activity between 1 and 6 years of age, a basic continuity exists in this form of interaction. Toddlers, as well as preschoolers, appear to recognize the appropriateness of reasoned argument when they claim toys, and they appear to know something of the basis for such arguments when conflict outcomes follow principles of entitlement to objects. Even very young children sometimes yield to their peers with what seem to be conciliatory gestures. Groups of 2-year-olds, as well as 6-year-olds, are organized in stable dominance hierarchies, where power is based on social relationships. Furthermore, toddlers are quite capable of collaborating within conflict and can acknowledge the existence of alliances with their agemates. Even though the more sophisticated aspects of conflict that are based on reasoning are infrequent in the second year and are far more developed in older children, continuity in the form of conflicts is striking. Thus, conflict provides at least one context for the development of some important social abilities.

Opposition and its resolution between individuals provides a very powerful structure for interpersonal disputes, and our review has revealed consistency in the structure of early conflict. Conflict moves from an arguable event, to initial and subsequent oppositional moves and toward the resolution or abandonment of a dispute. Opposition and responses to it that include compromise and conciliation are actually quite easily discerned within conflict; even when issues change or when third parties enter disputes, the oppositional structure continues to constrain interaction. Although researchers have explicitly emphasized the role of oppositional structure in conflict, they have generally failed to acknowledge the extent to which their analyses also depend upon understanding the meaning of conflict as it unfolds in a social and cultural context. A dispute between young children, we feel, is an "act of meaning," that aptly exemplifies Bruner's (1990) recent discussions of the term. Bruner argues forcefully that the creation of meaning and its negotiation within a cultural community must be central to psychology: "Given that psychology is so immersed in culture, it must be organized around those meaning-making and meaning-using processes that connect man to culture" (p. 12). Moreover, meaning is generally public and shared within a culture, which also provides the means for recognizing incoherence and renegotiating meanings. Meaning is interpreted as sequences of events unfold, in narrative form, over time; the overall configuration of an interactive sequence gives meaning to its constituent events.

Interpretations of early conflicts as meaningful narrative sequences have been implicit in much recent developmental work. For example, the concept of *opposition* is clearly based on an interpretation of the meaning of events in relation to cultural standards. We and others have emphasized the wide variety of ways in which opposition may occur, and it is only by interpreting the relations among the actions of young children that we judge them to be opposed to one another. Moreover, disputes have a narrative structure of antecedent, opposition, and resolution; these elements are meaningful only in relation to the whole conflict. We understand and analyze early conflict in this way. Conflict issues are identified and differentiated because we infer the intentions of the protagonists. We interpret differentiating characteristics in the form or outcome of conflicts between friends and acquaintances in terms of our cultural understanding of friendship. Bruner (1990) himself briefly discusses the character of justification in children's early arguments. He describes justifications as narrative accounts that tell the story of a conflict in terms that legitimize the actions of the narrator. A child can convincingly place a conflict within a context that justifies his or her goals by telling the right story. Presumably, resolutions that may emerge from such negotiations depend upon the antagonists reaching some form of agreement on the narrative that best describes their conflict.

Although Bruner (1990) recognizes language and its acquisition as the principal means whereby children enter into meaning, he acknowledges that interpretable narrative structure is expressed through social interaction before it can be expressed linguistically. In this chapter, we have reviewed many ways in which children show their cultural knowledge and shared interpretations of events within conflict. Oppositional strategies are recognized, and meaningful relations are uncovered between the strategies selected by each antagonist in turn. Reasoning is effective and increases with development. Aggressive intent is communicated through facial expression and style of aggression, and the content of verbal utterances is related to goals in property disputes even among toddlers. Culturally based principles such as ownership or prior possession influence the characteristics and outcome of conflict, and children justify their positions with arguments that clearly reflect understanding of cultural values. Dominance relations contribute to the organization of children's groups, and group members appear to recognize their own positions and prerogatives within their preschool cultures.

Whereas much has been learned by researchers who implicitly consider the meaning of actions within conflict, an explicit recognition of the role of meaning could extend dramatically our understanding of conflict. For example, a direct and detailed study of the young children's justifications in conflict narratives could reveal important elements in the negotiation of shared meaning. Further attention to meaning may reveal the contexts in which specific culturally based principles for the resolution of conflict develop. If researchers narrow their focus to specific conflict issues and interpret conflict as it unfolds in narrative fashion, we may be able to apply standards of truth, coherence, and validity to children's arguments. The influence of these features of the interactive exchange on third-party interventions and the influence of friendship or dominance on these features of conflict will expand our knowledge of the interface between conflict and relationships. Explicit analyses of early conflicts as acts of meaning will enhance, in time, our understanding of human culture and children's entry into it.

References

Anderson, H. H. (1937a). An experimental study of dominative and integrative behavior in children of preschool age. *Journal of Social Psychology, 8,* 335–345.

Anderson, H. H. (1937b). Domination and integration in the social behavior of young children in an experimental play situation. *Genetic Psychology Monographs, 19,* 343–408.

Bakeman, R., & Brownlee, J. R. (1982). Social rules governing object conflicts in toddlers and preschoolers. In K. H. Rubin & H. S. Ross (Eds.), *Peer relations and social skills in childhood.* New York: Springer.

Besevegis, E., & Lore, R. (1983). Effects of an adult's presence on the social behavior of preschool children. *Aggressive Behavior, 9,* 243–252.

Boggs, S. T. (1978). The development of verbal disputing in part-Hawaiian children. *Language and Society, 7,* 325–344.

Bronson, W. C. (1981). Toddlers' behaviors with agemates: Issues of interaction, cognition, and affect. In L. P. Lipsitt (Ed.), *Monographs on Infancy* (Vol. 1). Norwood, NJ: Ablex.

Brownell, C. A., & Brown, E. (1985, April). *Age differences in object conflicts and possession negotiations during the second year.* Paper presented at the meeting of the Society for Research in Child Development, Toronto, Ontario.

Brownlee, J. R., & Bakeman, R. (1981). Hitting in toddler peer interaction. *Child Development, 52,* 1076–1079.

Bruner, J. (1990). *Acts of meaning.* Cambridge, MA: Harvard University Press.

Camras, L. (1979, April). *Peer relations and facial communication in a conflict situation.* Paper presented at the meeting of the Society for Research in Child Development, San Francisco.

Camras, L. A. (1977). Facial expressions used by children in a conflict situation. *Child Development, 48,* 1431–1435.

Camras, L. A. (1984). Children's verbal and nonverbal communication in a conflict situation. *Ethology and Sociobiology, 5,* 257–268.

Caplan, M., Vespo, J. E., Pederson, J., & Hay, D. F. (1991). Conflict and its resolution in small groups of one- and two-year-olds. *Child Development, 62,* 1513–1524.

Chapman, M., & Zahn-Waxler, C. (1982). Young children's compliance and noncompliance to parental discipline in a natural setting. *International Journal of Behavioral Development, 5,* 81–94.

Charlesworth, W. R., & La Freniere, P. (1983). Dominance, friendship and resource utilization in preschool children's groups. *Ethology and Sociobiology, 4,* 175–186.

Conant, C. L. (1987). *Toddler sociability in object conflict with peers.* Unpublished master's thesis, University of Waterloo, Waterloo, Ontario.

Conant, C. L. (1991). *The influence of toy ownership on toddler peer interaction.* Unpublished doctoral dissertation, University of Waterloo, Waterloo, Ontario.

Corsaro, W. A. (1985). *Friendship and peer culture in the early years.* Norwood, NJ: Ablex.

de Waal, F. B. M. (1984). Sex differences in the formation of coalitions among chimpanzees. *Ethology and Sociobiology, 5,* 239–255.

Eisenberg, A., & Garvey, C. (1981). Children's use of verbal strategies in resolving conflicts. *Discourse Processes, 4,* 149–170.

Eisenberg-Berg, N., Haake, R. J., & Bartlett, K. (1981). The effects of possession and ownership on the sharing and proprietary behaviors of preschool children. *Merrill-Palmer Quarterly, 27,* 61–67.

Eisenberg-Berg, N., Haake, R., Hand, M., & Sadalla, E. (1979). Effects of instructions concerning ownership on preschoolers' sharing and defensive behaviors. *Developmental Psychology, 15,* 460–461.

Frankel, D. G., & Arbel, T. (1980). Group formation by two-year-olds. *International Journal of Behavioral Development, 3,* 287–298.

Garvey, C. (1984). *Children's talk.* Cambridge, MA: Harvard University Press.

Genishi, C., & DiPaolo, M. (1982). Learning through argument in a preschool. In L. C. Wilkinson (Ed.), *Communicating in the classroom.* New York: Academic Press.

Ginsberg, H. J., & Miller, S. M. (1981). Altruism in children: A naturalistic study of reciprocation and examination of the relationship between social dominance and aid-giving behavior. *Ethology and Sociobiology, 2,* 75–83.

Goodall, J. (1986). *The chimpanzees of Gombe: Patterns of behavior.* Cambridge, MA: Harvard University Press.

Goodenough, F. (1931). *Anger in young children.* Minneapolis: University of Minnesota Press.

Green, E. H. (1933a). Friendships and quarrels among preschool children. *Child Development, 4,* 237–252.

Green, E. H. (1933b). Group play and quarreling among preschool children. *Child Development, 4,* 302–307.

Hartup, W. W. (1974). Aggression in childhood: Developmental perspectives. *American Psychologist, 29*, 336–341.

Hartup, W. W., & Laursen, B. (in press). Conflict and context in peer relations. In C. Hart (Ed.), *Children on playgrounds: Research perspectives and applications*. Ithaca: SUNY Press.

Hartup, W. W., Laursen, B., Stewart, M. I., & Eastenson, A. (1988). Conflict and the friendship relations of young children. *Child Development, 59*, 1590–1600.

Hay, D. F. (1984). Social conflict in early childhood. In G. Whitehurst (Ed.), *Annals of child development* (Vol. 1) Greenwich, CT: JAI.

Hay, D. F., & Ross, H. S. (1982). The social nature of early conflict. *Child Development, 53*, 105–113.

Hayes, D. S., Gershman,. E., & Bolin, L. T. (1970). Friends and enemies: Cognitive bases for preschool children's unilateral and reciprocal relationships. *Child Development, 41*, 1276–1279.

Hinde, R. A., Titmus, G., Easton, D., & Tamplin, A. (1985). Incidence of "friendship" and behavior with strong associates versus non-associates in preschoolers. *Child Development, 56*, 234–245.

Killen, M. (1989). Context, conflict, and coordination in social development. In L. T. Winegar (Ed.), *Social interaction and the development of children's understanding*. Norwood NJ: Ablex.

Killen M., & Turiel, E. (1991). Conflict resolution in preschool social interactions. *Early Education and Development, 2*, 240–255.

Kuczynski, L., Kochanska, G., Radke-Yarrow, M., & Girnius-Brown, O. (1987). A developmental interpretation of young children's noncompliance. *Developmental Psychology, 23*, 799–806.

La Freniere, P., & Charlesworth, W. R. (1983). Dominance, attention, and affiliation in a peer group: A nine-month longitudinal study. *Ethology and Sociobiology, 4*, 55–67.

Laursen, B., & Hartup, W. W. (1989). The dynamics of preschool children's conflicts. *Merrill-Palmer Quarterly, 35*, 281–297.

Lollis, S. P., Ross, H. S., & Tate, E. (in press). Parents' regulation of children's peer interactions: Direct influences. In R. D. Parke & G. W. Ladd (Eds.), *Family-peer relationships: Modes of linkage*. Hillsdale, NJ: Erlbaum.

Lytton, H., & Zwirner, W. (1975). Compliance and its controlling stimuli observed in a natural setting. *Developmental Psychology, 11*, 769–779.

Maynard, D. W. (1985a). How children start arguments. *Language and Society, 14*, 1–29.

Maynard, D. W. (1985b). On the functions of social conflict among children. *American Sociological Review, 50*, 207–223.

Maynard, D. W. (1986). Offering and soliciting collaboration in multi-party disputes among children (and other humans). *Human Studies, 9*, 261–285.

Missakian, E. (1980). Gender differences in agonistic behavior and dominance relations of Synanon communally reared children. In D. O. Omark, F. F. Strayer, & D. G. Freedman (Eds.), *Dominance relations: An ethological view of human conflict and social interaction*. New York: Garland.

O'Keefe, B. J., & Benoit, P. J. (1982). Children's arguments. In J. R. Cox & C. A. Willard (Eds.), *Advances in argumentation theory and research*. Carbondale: Southern Illinois University Press.

Phinney, J. (1986). The structure of 5-year-olds' verbal quarrels with peers and siblings. *Journal of Genetic Psychology, 147*, 47–60.

Ramsey, P. G. (1980, August). *Ownership behaviors in young children's social interactions*. Paper presented at the meeting of the American Psychological Association, Montreal.

Ross, H. S., & Lollis, S. P. (1989). A social relations analysis of toddler peer relationships. *Child Development, 60,* 1082–1091.

Ross, H. S., Conant, C. L., Cheyne, J. A., & Alevizos, E. (1992). Relationships and alliances in the social interaction of kibbutz toddlers. *Social Development, 1,* 1–17.

Ross, H. S., Tesla, C., Kenyon, B., & Lollis, S. P. (1990). Maternal intervention in toddler peer conflict: The socialization of principles of justice. *Developmental Psychology, 26,* 994–1003.

Russell, V. (1981). *The influence of age and sex on conflict episodes among toddlers.* Undergraduate honors thesis, University of Waterloo, Waterloo, Ontario .

Russon, A. E., & Waite, B. E. (1991). Patterns of dominance and imitation in an infant peer group. *Ethology and Sociobiology, 12,* 55–73.

Russon, A. E., Waite, B. E., & Rochester, M. I. (1990). Direct caregiver intervention in infant peer social encounters. *American Journal of Orthopsychiatry, 60,* 428–439.

Sackin, S., & Thelen, E. (1984). An ethological study of peaceful associative outcomes to conflict in preschool children. *Child Development, 55,* 1098–1102.

Shantz, C. U. (1987). Conflict between children. *Child Development, 58,* 283–305.

Shantz, C. U., & Hobart, C. J. (1989). Social conflict and development: Peers and siblings. In T. J. Berndt & G. Ladd (Eds.), *Peer relationships in child development.* New York: Wiley.

Siegel, A. E., & Kohn, L. G. (1959). Permissiveness, permission, and aggression: The effect of adult presence or absence on aggression in children's play. *Child Development, 30,* 131–141.

Sluckin, A. M., & Smith, P. K. (1977). Two approaches to the concept of dominance in preschool children. *Child Development, 48,* 917–923.

Strayer, F. F. (1980). Social ecology of the preschool peer group. In W. A. Collins (Ed.), *The Minnesota symposia on child development* (Vol. 13). Hillsdale, NJ: Erlbaum.

Strayer, F. F., & Noel, J. M. (1986). The prosocial and antisocial functions of preschool aggression: An ethological study of triadic conflict among young children. In C. Zahn-Waxler, M. Cummings, & R. Iannotti (Eds.), *Altruism and aggression.* Cambridge: Cambridge University Press.

Strayer, F. F., & Strayer, J. (1976). An ethological analysis of social agonism and dominance relations among preschool children. *Child Development, 47,* 980–989.

Strayer, F. F., & Strayer, J. (1980). Preschool conflict and the assessment of social dominance. In D. O. Omark, F. F. Strayer, & D. G. Freedman (Eds.), *Dominance relations: An ethological view of human conflict and social interaction.* New York: Garland Press.

Strayer, F. F., & Trudel, M. (1984). Developmental changes in the nature and function of social dominance among preschool children. *Ethology and Sociobiology, 5,* 279–295.

Walton, M. D., & Sedlak, A. J. (1982). Making amends: A grammar-based analysis of children's social interaction. *Merrill-Palmer Quarterly, 28,* 389–412.

Weigel, R. M. (1984). The application of evolutionary models to the study of decisions made by children during object possession conflicts. *Ethology and Sociobiology, 5,* 229–238.

Winegar, L. T., & Renninger, K. A. (1989, April). *Object conflict and sharing in the preschool: Further evidence for a prior possession rule.* Poster presented at the meeting of the Society for Research in Child Development, Kansas City, MO.

Zivin, G. (1977a). Facial gestures predict preschoolers' encounter outcomes. *Social Science Information, 17,* 715–730.

Zivin, G. (1977b). On becoming subtle: Age and social rank changes in the use of facial gesture. *Child Development, 48,* 1314–1321.

7 Conflict and friendship relations

Willard W. Hartup

Becoming friends and maintaining these relationships are among the most significant achievements of childhood and adolescence. Both children and teenagers spend much time with their friends, and these relationships are transcendentally important to the youngsters themselves. Friendship relations, however, are developmentally significant for reasons other than their ubiquity: Friendships furnish children with socialization opportunities not easily obtained elsewhere, including experience in conflict management as well as in cooperation and sharing.

Conflict is considered in this essay as both a determinant and an outcome of children's interactions with their friends. That is, conflict management is believed to determine whether or not children become friends and what their friendships may be like but also to determine the residual derived from these relationships by individual children. The work that undergirds this essay is about equally divided between studies based on "insider" views of conflict and its implications and those based on "outsider" views. Children's own views (the insiders) are usually established through talking with them or through the use of questionnaires; the views of others (the outsiders) are established using a variety of methods. Both insider and outsider views of conflict and friendship relations are examined here.

Conflict and friendship relations cannot be discussed without considering them in temporal perspective. Disagreements, for example, have beginnings, middles, and ends – causes, instigating and oppositional tactics, resolution attempts, and outcomes (Peterson, 1983; Shantz, 1987). Friendships also have beginnings, middles, and ends – formative, maintenance, and termination "stages" (Levinger, 1983). Separate consideration is thus given in this essay to conflict and its role in friendship formation, maintenance, and termination.

Support in the completion of this manuscript was provided by the Rodney S. Wallace Endowment, College of Education, University of Minnesota, and Grant No. RO1 42888, National Institute of Mental Health.

186

Conflicts also differ between friends and between nonfriends according to the contexts in which the disagreements occur (Hartup & Laursen, in press). Disagreements differ, for example, according to the settings in which they occur, the tasks (issues) confronting the disagreers, and the interpersonal relations existing between the parties. Both contextual variations and individual differences are therefore considered in this commentary and a contextual theory of conflict and friendship relations is outlined.

Conflict: Its nature and implications

The nature of conflict

Conflicts consist of *oppositions* between individuals: "when one person does something to which a second person objects" (Hay, 1984, p. 2). Oppositions, however, differ enormously from one another, and some seem not to be conflicts. Both children and adults, for example, usually think about conflicts in terms of fighting and quarreling rather than in terms of fleeting disagreements (Selman, 1980). And, indeed, short two-turn disagreements differ from longer ones. Among nursery school children, short disagreements arise most commonly in ongoing interaction, are not very intense, are resolved mainly by insistence rather than negotiation, and usually end with the children staying together (Laursen & Hartup, 1989); these exchanges seem to be compliance episodes rather than conflicts. Longer disagreements, being more intense and consequential, conform more closely to ordinary notions about conflict.

Conflict and aggression are not always clearly differentiated. Many writers regard them as virtually synonymous. Aggressive conflicts command attention, however, because the excessive use of aggressive tactics in conflict resolution is a risk marker in child and adolescent development (Parker & Asher, 1987). Nevertheless, many disagreements among children are neither instigated nor resolved aggressively. Many are benign, some are even humorous. Considerable confusion results, then, when aggressive and nonaggressive conflicts are not differentiated.

Conflict and competition also need to be differentiated from one another. Competition usually refers to situations in which the interdependencies existing between two individuals constrain their access to rewards (e.g., the zero-sum or winner–loser situation). Competitive contingencies, in this sense, certainly elicit disagreements, but not always. Also questionable is the assumption that interpersonal disagreements are inherently competitive, that is, constrain access to rewards.

Conflict, then, requires continuing and careful specification, especially in relation to compliance, aggression, and competition. Whether one can identify any social condition beyond opposition that specifies conflict is doubtful. Opposition remains the word that most commonly defines the term conflict in English and remains the operational term most commonly employed in child development research.

Conflict episodes

Most investigators use disagreement *frequencies*, as these occur in the interaction between individuals, as criterion measures. The validity of frequency measures has been studied most extensively in relation to marital satisfaction. Considerable evidence shows that nondistressed married couples are more positive and less negative in their interactions than are distressed couples (Gottman, 1979), with both verbal and nonverbal measures discriminating in this manner. Agreements and disagreements discriminate separately between nondistressed and distressed couples, and agreement–disagreement ratios are similarly effective (Markman, 1981).

The validity of these measures in discriminating the interactions of friends from those of nonfriends has also been studied, and these results are summarized in the section entitled "Conflict and established friendships." Before examining them, however, one needs to consider the possibility that the frequency with which conflicts occur may not be the only metric that ought to be used in assessing interpersonal relations. Conflicts vary in content or issue, and conflict rates are known to vary with relationship "closeness" depending only on what the disagreements are about (Surra & Longstreth, 1990). Conflicts vary, too, in resolution strategies employed and outcomes obtained. Rate measures actually reveal a relatively small amount about the disagreements occurring between children, and yet, time and again, these measures are the only criterion variables used.

Recognition also needs to be given to the interior dynamics of the conflict episode. Existing evidence, for example, shows that children's activities after a disagreement relate to whether they were interacting before the disagreement started. When conflicts arise within ongoing interaction rather than from outside intervention, disagreements are less likely to involve aggression and will be shorter as well as involve continued interaction afterward. In fact, what occurs after a disagreement is determined as strongly by predisagreement conditions as by the conflict behaviors that actually occur (Laursen & Hartup, 1989).

When "insistence" is actually used in conflict resolution, though, a common consequence is reactive insistence as well as reduced likelihood that the conflict will end in compromise (Eisenberg & Garvey, 1981; Laursen

& Hartup, 1989). When disagreements are not aggressive, when affective intensity is low, and when conciliation rather than dominance occurs, interaction between the children tends to continue after the conflict – whether or not interaction was occurring earlier (Sackin & Thelen, 1984).

Configurations such as these have been documented among mainly nursery school children in open-field situations. Intraconflict dynamics, however, may vary with the children's ages and the social context. Numerous methodological and conceptual constraints thus need attention in assessing conflict and its role in friendship relations.

Conflict and close relationships

Close relationships are more or less enduring ties between individuals marked by interdependence between them. Behaviorally, a relationship is a series of interactions between two individuals occurring over time, each interaction being relatively limited in duration but affected by past interactions and affecting future ones (Hinde, 1979).

Close relationships begin with propinquity (i.e., physical proximity). Consequently, every demographic and sociological force that brings two individuals together is relevant to their relationship experience. Among the events that then determine whether a close relationship emerges are the benefits each individual perceives as deriving from interaction with the other, especially as related to the costs involved. The so-called "exchange theories" argue that relationships emerge only to the extent that the tie or bond is in the mutual interest of the individuals involved (Kelley & Thibaut, 1978).

Our understanding remains limited concerning how individuals evaluate what is "received" from a social exchange, why we are so strongly motivated to make social comparisons and to concern ourselves with "fairness," how information about self and other is integrated in determining social interaction, and which commodities, resources, and rewards are significant in these exchanges (see Graziano, 1984; Hinde, 1979). Nevertheless, exchange theory (and its variants) has considerable validity in accounting for the emergence and maintenance of close relationships, including the relationships that children construct with their friends.

Two kinds of social events would seem to supply most of the basic information that individuals need about exchange outcomes: agreements and disagreements. Agreements provide us with a sense of what is correct and workable (i.e., rewarding) in an exchange and provide us with a basis to use in estimating the likelihood that the relationship will "work" or "pay off" in the future. Agreements, especially when their occurrence coincides with conditions of either uncertainty reduction or anxiety reduction, also establish other individuals as "secure bases" (Ainsworth & Wittig, 1969). And, finally, agreements establish that exchanges with individuals who are similar to ourselves are likely to be more favorable than exchanges with individuals who are not.

Disagreements, in contrast, create doubt about what has been assumed to be correct and workable, thereby motivating change in modes of thinking and acting. Disagreements assist in establishing relationships by documenting the "fit" between individuals, that is, by demonstrating when the skills, interests, and goals of two individuals are not concordant, as well as by marking relationship boundaries, that is, behavioral limits that can be exceeded only at the risk of separation. Stated another way, conflicts assist children, even in the early stages of interacting with one another, in recognizing whether common ground exists between them. Other conflict derivatives that contribute to relational development include perspective taking ("To argue necessitates taking the attitude of the other at the same time one contradicts it" [Maynard, 1986, p. 252]) and individuation ("When children are at odds, they are tacitly affirming that one another's behavior is of significance" [Shantz & Hobart, 1989, p. 88]). Disagreements, that is, are sometimes affirming.

Close relationships actually require more than experience with agreements and disagreements separately; a continuous dialectic is needed to support these ties or bonds. Affirmations, alone, carry little information about exchange possibilities except in contrast with disaffirmations. Similarly, disaffirmations carry information about common ground only in contrast with affirmations. Disagreements and agreements *in tandem* are therefore essential to the construction of close relationships in the same manner that ego development requires a continuing dialectic involving both gratification and frustration or that cognitive development requires continuing tension between assimilation and accommodation.

Beyond suggesting that agreement–disagreement ratios must be "favorable," exchange theory does not specify the "climate of agreement" needed in order for close relationships to emerge or endure. Different relationships may well require different climates. As for children's friendships, the evidence shows that these ratios must exceed unity, even though agreement and disagreement base rates are very low. Gottman (1983), for example, observed children interacting with friends, finding that agreement–disagreement ratios averaged somewhat less than 2 to 1. Because both agreements and disagreements were greater among friends than among nonfriends, agreement–disagreement ratios did not differ.

Disagreements obviously vary considerably in their significance to the individuals involved – both from conflict to conflict and child to child. Little is known, however, about conflict issues and their relationship implications except that such variations are important. Adolescents, for example, compete with friends more intensively than with nonfriends when task performance is "relevant" (i.e., relevant to self-regard) but less intensively when task performance is nonrelevant (Tesser, Campbell, & Smith, 1984). Generally, though, the motivational conditions that differentiate constructive (ego-enhancing) from destructive (ego-debilitating) disagreements between children and their friends cannot be specified. Context variations differentiating constructive from destructive disagreements similarly cannot be specified, although differences between open-field and closed-field situations are discussed in the section entitled "Friendship and context."

Overall, exchange theory furnishes a good general accounting for the manner in which disagreements and agreements affect relational development. Much needs elaborating in extending these notions to children's behavior with their friends. Disagreement–agreement ratios need to be specified; motivational and contextual conditions need to be taken into account. Disagreements and their role in friendship relations, though, can be understood only in relation to these variations.

Friendship: Its nature and implications

The nature of friendship

The essentials of friendship are reciprocity and commitment between individuals who see themselves more or less as equals. Children's friendships are not as exclusive as parent–child relations; interaction between friends also has a more equal power base than interaction between parents and children. Recognizing this egalitarian structure, some writers regard friendships as "affiliative" relationships rather than "attachments" (e.g., Weiss, 1986). Nevertheless, friendships serve some of the same functions in socialization as other close relationships. They are *contexts* in which social skills are acquired or elaborated, *information sources* for acquiring self-knowledge as well as knowledge about others, *emotional and cognitive resources* to be used in everyday problem solving, and *forerunners* of subsequent relationships – especially those requiring mutually regulated activity and intimacy.

Some children behave preferentially toward their associates as early as the second year of life. Others do not behave this way until later. By 4 and 5 years of age, the following are evident: (a) Best friends can be identified by the children themselves; (b) parents and teachers identify these same children as the child's best friends; and (c) children spend more time with associates who are designated as friends than with other children (Hartup, Laursen, Stewart, & Eastenson, 1988; Howes, 1983, 1988).

Children and their friends are concordant in age (a reflection of the egalitarian nature of these relationships) from early childhood on. These are mainly same-sex relationships. Although friendships are not strongly same-race in early childhood, same-race individuals are chosen as best friends with increasing frequency through middle childhood and adolescence (Singleton & Asher, 1979). Behavioral concordances are not as great as the similarities between friends in age, sex, and race. Concordance in two areas, however, is evident by early adolescence: (a) school attitudes and aspirations; and (b) orientation toward certain normative behaviors in the contemporary teen culture, for example, sports, drinking, and criminal activity. Relevant studies show both that normatively similar individuals choose one another as friends more commonly than dissimilar individuals and that friends become more similar to one another over time (Kandel, 1978). These conclusions cannot be drawn with the same degree of certainty about younger children owing to the lack of evidence.

Behavioral markers indicate that friendship relations are based in reciprocity.[1] Among preschool children, early indications of social attraction are sustained social exchanges, complementarities in social play, and mutually directed affect; other reciprocities (e.g., cooperation) are also evident (Howes, 1983). Among older children, friends cooperate more extensively than nonfriends while working on tasks that require turn taking and mutually regulated effort. Friends are more interactive than nonfriends, smile and laugh more, pay closer attention to equity rules in their conversations, and direct their conversations toward mutual rather than egocentric ends (Newcomb & Brady, 1982).

Seemingly, then, equity and reciprocity can be regarded as basic conditions of children's friendships: Children are cooperative with one another in order to become friends as well as to remain friends. In early childhood, these reciprocities mainly involve common activities, whereas by early adolescence, they also include intimacy and sharing. But the weight of the evidence suggests that, at all ages, friendship relations are based in equitable exchanges between individuals who see themselves as sharing an equal power base.

Friendship stages: Formation, maintenance, termination

Beginning with first meetings, the developmental course of child–child relations varies widely. Some relationships do not progress beyond beginnings; they proceed from acquaintanceship to termination without "middles" or "consolidation." Some children build relationships with one another that are sustained endlessly; they never deteriorate or end. These variations, however, are more widely recognized than studied.

Relationship development is generally conceived in commonsense terms. Beyond recognizing that relationships have beginnings, middles, and endings, social scientists have centered their attention on five general phases or "stages": meeting (acquaintance), build-up, continuation or consolidation, deterioration, and termination (Levinger, 1983). As mentioned, not many relationships move through every one of these stages, and the theoretical utility of these demarcations is not well established. Nevertheless, existing studies give no reason to doubt that friendship beginnings are not the same as friendship continuations or endings and that some kind of developmental progression must be recognized. Conflict, for example, probably serves different functions during the formative and consolidation stages of children's friendships, and its functions may vary still further as friendships deteriorate. To illustrate: Certain evidence suggests that quarreling occurs more or less universally during friendship "build-up" or "intensification" – among previously acquainted children as well as unacquainted ones. At the same time, quarreling during early interaction is inversely related to children's subsequent satisfaction with their associates in terms of companionship, intimacy, affection, and support (Furman, 1987).

Such results suggest that children's friendships must be examined temporally and underscore the need for longitudinal studies. At this time, such studies of children's friendships (apart from studies of individual development) are almost nonexistent. Certain investigators have examined the stability of friendship choice across time (e.g., Berndt, Hawkins, & Hoyle, 1986), but friendship development remains largely unstudied. And there is no substitute for longitudinal analysis in this area, just as there is no substitute for such analysis in understanding ontogeny.

Friendship and context

Virtually everything about children's friendships varies according to context. Children's first encounters are different in *closed* situations (in which two children are forced together and cannot determine for themselves with whom and how long to interact) and *open* ones (in which many alternative partners are available). For example, one's behavioral distinctiveness plays a more important role during first encounters in open situations than in closed ones (e.g., Berscheid & Graziano, 1979). Subsequently, the interaction of friends and nonfriends differs according to whether the situation is cooperative or competitive and whether or not the children are ego invested in the activity. These setting effects may be especially significant in relation to conflict management. In some settings, for example, children may seek to minimize the impact of conflict with their friends to a greater extent than with nonfriends. In other settings, children may have more frequent conflicts with their friends than with nonfriends – for example, during activities in which they are ego invested.

Friendship and its developmental significance

Considerable evidence demonstrates that children who have difficulties in social and emotional development also have difficulties in forming and maintaining friendships. Among school-age children, friendship troubles are more common among children referred to child guidance clinics than among nonreferred children (Achenbach & Edelbrock, 1981). Generally, troubled children have fewer friends and less contact with them; these relationships are less stable over time (Rutter & Garmezy, 1983); and understanding of the reciprocities and intimacies involved in friendships is less mature (Selman, 1980).

These results, however, are not easy to interpret. Being without friends seems to be a risk marker, but the developmental necessity of friendship relations is difficult to establish. Good developmental outcome may not require "best friends" in the same way that these outcomes require stable relationships with caretakers. Quite possibly, friendships are developmental advantages rather than developmental necessities. These relationships may constitute optimal settings in which to gain experience in cooperation, self-disclosure, and conflict resolution, experiences that might also be obtained, but with greater difficulty, with other individuals (Hartup & Sancilio, 1986).

According to this reasoning having friends should predict good developmental outcome. Supporting this contention, Ladd (1990) found that kindergarten children's friendships helped to predict their school adjustment over time, above and beyond what could be accounted for by their personal attributes (including their sociometric status). Moreover, the children's friendships forecast both adjustment during the early weeks of kindergarten and changes in adjustment during the school year. Most important, several different dimensions in friendship relations turned out to be significant: having friends in one's classroom to begin with, keeping them, and making new ones.

Other evidence shows that the benefits deriving from friendship (at least among adolescents) may depend on the nature of the relationship (Berndt & Keefe, 1991). Friendships are not all alike: Some are secure and smooth sailing; others are rocky with disagreement and contention. In this instance, teenagers were asked, in the fall and the spring, about both positive and negative aspects of their friendships – that is, emotional support and intimacy, on the one hand, and conflicts, rivalry, and unpleasant competition, on the other. School involvement and misbehavior were rated by both the children and their math and English teachers; grades were also studied. Although friendship attributes were not related to academic achievement, students whose friendships were more intimate and supportive in the beginning became increasingly involved in school, whereas those whose friendships were marred by conflict and rivalry became more disruptive and progressively less involved.

The weight of the evidence, then, suggests that children's friendships have considerable significance as socialization contexts. One can assume that conflicts make both positive and negative contributions to these relationships, although the nature of these contributions has not been clearly specified.

Conflict and friendship formation

Insider views

Children's own views concerning conflict and friendship relations need to be studied for several reasons. First, one can use these notions to validate standardized observations. Second, insiders and outsiders conceivably use different frames of reference in assessing conflicts and their implications, and these must be documented. Outsiders, for example, are known to interpret events by making cross-relationship comparisons (i.e., by contrasting the actions of different dyads in similar situations). Insiders, however, are likely to make comparisons within relationships as well as across them (Furman, 1984; Olson, 1977).

Rate of occurrence. When asked why children do not become friends, youngsters between the ages of 6 and 10 mention disagreements more frequently than anything else. Personality differences rather than conflicts are commonly mentioned by 12- and 13-year-olds (Smollar & Youniss, 1982). A climate of disagreement, then, is clearly believed by children to interfere with friendship formation. Conflicts probably discourage friendship formation mainly because outcomes are not equitable.[2] One must consider also that conflicts elicit noxious emotions: Children describe the circumstances associated with "not becoming friends" in such ways as "We call each other names," "We fight." Thus, conflicts may discourage friendship formation both through reduced equity within the social interaction between individuals and through reduced propinquity established by conditioned avoidance.

Objective self-report methods have been used only once to assess conflict and its role in friendship formation. Furman (1987) administered questionnaires to preadolescents and adolescents who attended a 1-week summer camp, asking them to rate their relations with cabin mates in various respects, including their quarreling. Ratings were made on Days 2, 5, and 7. Cross-sectional contrasts were made between children who were acquainted with one another when they came to camp and those who were strangers: Acquainted children reported themselves as quarreling with one another more frequently than the nonacquainted children throughout the week. Longitudinal contrasts revealed that, as the strangers became acquainted, quarreling increased significantly; quarreling remained stable, though, among the previously acquainted children. Both cross-sectional and longitudinal contrasts, then, suggest that acquaintanceship is accompanied by increasing disagreements. Whether conflicts increase indefinitely with progress toward friendship is not likely, but the results are straightforward: As children come to know one another, they increasingly disagree, however much they engage one another amicably.

Disagreements throughout the week also varied inversely with friendliness rated at the end of the week. Quarreling was greater, the children reported, with "low" friends than with "medium" or "high" friends on Day 2 as well as on Days 5 and 7. Quarreling increased significantly among low and medium friends during the week, but not among high friends. Quarreling during these early encounters, then, predicted progress toward friendship among these children.

Other dimensions. Some writers (e.g., Rizzo, 1987, 1989) argue that the conflicts that occur while children are becoming friends are constructive and that children even initiate them in an effort to change their companions so they better fit friendship expectations. Other investigators (Renshaw & Asher, 1983) suggest that conflicts are used more amicably by older than by younger children in establishing relations between them. In any event, a dialectic involving both agreements and disagreements seems necessary to becoming friends. Additional insider studies, however, are needed to test this notion.

Outsider views

Rate of occurrence. One observational investigation deals with conflict and its role in friendship formation. Gottman (1983) used conversational analysis to study a small and select sample of children between the ages of 3 and 9, initially strangers, who were brought together three times in one of the children's homes. The children were confined to a playroom, and their conversations were recorded (for as long as 90 minutes). Two months later, the children's mothers were asked to estimate the extent to which the children were becoming friends: how often they spoke positively about one another, asked to see one another, telephoned, visited, and so on. Across the three sessions, the number of conversational agreements registered either by the "host" child or the "guest" was consistently correlated with friendship outcome (between .38 and .59), and the number of disagreements was less consistently related to outcome (correlations ranged between .09 and −.43). Only one measure of conflict resolution (weak host demands followed by guest agreement in the third session) significantly entered into the multiple regression predicting the progress toward friendship. Consequently, the occurrence of agreements rather than the occurence of disagreements seems most closely related to friendship progress (see also Gottman & Parker, 1986).

Patterns. Process-oriented analyses of these data (Gottman, 1983) revolved around seven conversational characteristics: communication clarity and connectedness, information exchange, exploration of similarities and differences, establishing common ground, resolution of conflict, reciprocity, and self-disclosure. Considering each measure, session by session, in relation to "hitting it off," the results show the following: (a) Communication clarity and connectedness in the first session was the best predictor. Information exchange, conflict resolution, and common play activities also were significantly correlated with hitting it off, although these variables accounted for relatively small amounts of variance. (b) Communication clarity and connectedness in the second and third sessions were even more closely related to the criterion. Information exchanges, conflict resolution, and common ground also were related to hitting it off, and in addition, self-disclosure and attention to similarities and differences appeared during these sessions on the roster of significant correlates. (c) Regression analyses showed that this combination of variables accounted for more than 80% of the variance in becoming friends.

On the basis of this evidence, Gottman (1983) speculates that the scenario unfolds in this way: Friendship formation begins with success in information exchange and requires that children communicate clearly and connectedly. Children then shift to common ground activities and talk about play and play materials. Should this move not meet with success, the children must return temporarily to exchanging information – otherwise, conflict will ensue. Once common ground is achieved, the task is to strike a balance between the social demands of an activity and conflict; the children must work continually to clarify messages as well as avoid and resolve conflicts (see also Gottman & Parker, 1986). Other studies are needed, though, to establish the generality of this scenario.

Summary. Although the empirical evidence is not extensive, outsider views support several hypotheses about friendship formation: (a) Qualitative dimensions of conflict may be more relevant to becoming friends than quantitative ones. The sheer number of disagreements occurring in these conversations was not closely related to hitting it off, whereas the use of "softer" modes of conflict management was. (b) Agreements (or the ratio of agreements to disagreements) may be more important than disagreements in becoming friends. (c) In any event, a dialectic involving agreements and disagreements is necessary to establishing the common ground that friendships require, and children must work continually to resolve conflicts in order to ensure their continued interaction. These conclusions need to be buttressed with a data base that extends beyond conversations recorded in the children's homes and with enough subjects to enable investigators to examine age differences. Existing results tell us, however, that conflicts function both constructively and destructively in friendship formation.

Conflict and established friendships

Insider views

Several studies, using interviews and questionnaires, demonstrate that children consider conflicts between friends to be significant social events. Furman and Buhrmester (1985) asked fourth and fifth graders to rate the extent to which conflict was involved in their relationships with various individuals including parents, siblings, friends, and teachers. Relations with nonfriends were not studied, but it is noteworthy that relations with friends were characterized by the children as moderately contentious, about the same as were parent–child relations. Friendships were regarded as significantly less contentious than sibling relations.

Rate of occurrence. Disagreements between friends and between nonfriends were compared in two instances. Berndt and Perry (1986) interviewed children and young adolescents, asking them "Do you ever get into fights or arguments with (a best friend or an acquaintance)." Children between 7 and 11 years of age said they engaged in fewer conflicts with friends than with acquaintances, whereas 13-year-olds indicated they engaged in about the same number. Note that these comparisons involved intense conflicts (fighting and arguing). Laursen (1989) administered questionnaires to a large number of 15- and 16-year-olds, asking them to record every conflict (i.e., differences of opinion, objections, quarrels, or arguments) that occurred the day before. Conflicts with friends were reported as occurring nearly four times more often than conflicts with nonfriends; differences were significant even when the total time spent with these individuals was taken into account. Setting differences were also evident: Conflicts with friends occurred mainly during free time, whereas conflicts with nonfriends occurred mostly during task time, that is, at school (once again with total time taken into account).

Methodological variations make it difficult to reconcile these results. One can probably conclude that (a) big fights occur less frequently between friends than nonfriends although total altercations may occur more frequently, (b) significant changes in the relation between conflict and friendship occur across the transition to adolescence, and (c) disagreements between friends occur mostly while the children are "on their own," whereas disagreements between nonfriends occur mostly during schoolwork and while the children are engaging in other assigned tasks.

Memory for conflicts. What conflicts are recalled by children? Shantz (in press) asked 7-year-olds to "tell about an argument, fight, or disagreement with any child in your class." Roughly two thirds of the disagreements that were recalled involved the child and an adversary who was especially liked or disliked. Because most of these conflicts involved friends rather than enemies, it appears that conflicts between the former are more likely to be recalled than conflicts with the latter. It is not known whether this is because arguments and fights occur more frequently between friends than nonfriends (thereby being available for recall in greater numbers) or because conflicts with friends are more salient than conflicts with nonfriends. Nevertheless, three quarters of these same children indicated that they "learned a lesson" from the conflicts recalled, thereby suggesting that conflict interactions with friends contribute something lasting to the child's socialization.

Conflict issues. According to the insiders, conflicts with friends and non-friends differ generally in what they are about (Shantz, in press). More than 50% of the disagreements recalled by the 7-year-olds mentioned earlier involved behavioral issues: teasing, name calling, psychological harm (20%); physical harm (20%); social or friendship rules (16%); and facts and opinions (10%). Social rules, including sanctions relating to friendship, are clearly major issues in the conflicts that children recollect. Similar results were obtained with adolescents' self-reports (Laursen, 1989): Major conflict issues with friends included (in order of mention) friendship, ideas and opinions, teasing and criticism, and annoying behaviors; heterosexual issues and behavioral standards were also mentioned. Each of these issues occurred more often between friends than between nonfriends, indicating a direct relation between conflict issue and relational closeness.

Resolution tactics. Children's views about resolution tactics have not been studied extensively. Selman (1980) examined children's comments about a single social dilemma dealing with a friendship commitment. Developmental issues were highlighted in the analysis. Young school-age children regarded conflict causes as unilateral (i.e., one person acts in a way that causes a problem for the other). Somewhat older children recognized that these conflicts are dyadic and that solutions must be equitable. Still older children regarded these conflicts more abstractly, believing them to be inevitable between friends and, when resolved, to strengthen these relationships. Older children and adolescents also distinguished between minor conflicts (ones that friendships ameliorate) and those that threaten the existence of the relationship (usually violations of trust). Older adolescents also recognized that, when a friend is having trouble, it may be difficult to relate to him or her. In other words, the necessity to resolve conflicts mutually, using insight and self-reflection, is understood.

A basis exists, then, for considering friendship and conflict resolution in developmental terms. Other studies have shown that contentiousness is differentiated from the supportive dimensions of friendship relations by preadolescents but not by younger children (Berndt & Perry, 1986). Generally, though, we know little about age and friendship as these interact in determining conflict tactics, resolution strategies, and outcomes.

Summary. Although the insiders have not been completely consistent in what they have told us, a friend is clearly viewed as "someone whom you fight with, but not forever" (Goodnow & Burns, 1988). School-age friends report that they have fewer arguments with friends than with nonfriends, although time spent together has not always been taken into account.

Conflict definitions also vary among investigations. Conflicts with friends may be more frequent and salient in adolescence than in middle childhood. A developmental perspective is thus needed to evaluate insider views about conflicts in established relationships.

Outsider views

Contextual considerations. Outsider views concerning conflict and friendship cannot be summarized without considering the settings in which the disagreements occur. One recent analysis (Hartup & Laursen, in press) shows that, when many children occupy small spaces, when resources are limited, when play equipment requires coordinated use, and when play partners cannot be changed, conflict occurs more frequently and more intensively than in other circumstances. Occasional exceptions exist, but in general, conditions that heighten social interdependence increase social conflict.

One can distinguish two types of social interdependence: (a) *setting interdependencies*, which are created by environmental conditions necessitating that children interact with one another and not change companions or activities, and (b) *relational interdependencies*, which exist when two individuals, on the basis of earlier experience, expect their interaction to be mutually regulated.

Setting interdependencies are most extensive in closed-field situations: When two children are asked to sit at a table, for example, and play a game for a specified time, the situation is "closed" or "constrained." Social interaction is required. Individual children cannot choose with whom and where their interaction will occur, what to do, nor how long their interaction will last. Children, of course, can make certain choices about what is said and done in these situations, but nevertheless, the social interdependencies between them are extensive. Under open-field conditions, however, children are not so interdependent. On playgrounds or in "free play," for example, children can choose whether to interact or not, with whom to interact, what to do, where to do it, and how long to engage in it.

Children are relationally interdependent with their friends, that is, they expect to spend time with one another and to engage in mutuality, reciprocity, and equity in their social interactions (Bigelow & LaGaipa, 1975). Actually, relational interdependencies are the conditions or necessities of being friends; children can neither become nor remain friends unless these interdependencies are established and maintained.[3] Strangers and acquaintances, in contrast, are not relationally interdependent – in any sense.

Relational interdependencies are likely to interact with setting interdependencies in conflict instigation and management. Under closed-field conditions (i.e., extreme setting interdependence), disagreements carry relatively little risk that interaction will be broken off. Children cannot "pick up their marbles and go home" in closed settings but must continue to interact. Under these conditions, friends may disagree more frequently and more intensely than nonfriends because they are "freer" and more secure with one another than are nonfriends and know one another better. In these situations, children may also wish to avoid the negative self-evaluations that result when important arguments are lost to a friend (Tesser et al., 1984). Under open-field (noninterdependent) conditions, however, disagreements carry considerable risk that interaction will be terminated; other alternatives are available. One assumes that friends, as compared with nonfriends, are more motivated to continue their interaction, and that disagreements between them are more threatening. Stated another way, friends have a greater investment in one another than do nonfriends, an investment that leads them to minimize their conflicts and/or the ensuing damage when continued interaction is at risk.

In the next section, studies conducted in open situations are contrasted with ones conducted in closed situations. According to the arguments stated here, conflicts in open situations should occur less frequently and be less intense between friends than between nonfriends. Conflicts in closed situations, however, should occur more frequently and be more intense between friends than between nonfriends. Separate consideration in this analysis is given to conflict rates and conflict management.

Rate of occurrence. In open situations, results vary according to whether adjustments are made for the time that children spend together. Green (1933) found that nursery school friends quarreled more than nonfriends in relation to the opportunities children had to interact but quarreled less than nonfriends when the amount of time the children actually played together was taken into account. Strong friends quarreled only one fourth as much as "weak friends" (i.e., acquaintances), using a quarrel–playtime ratio.[4] More recent studies confirm these early results: In observations among nursery school children (Hinde, Titmus, Easton, & Tamplin, 1985), the stronger the association between the two children (i.e., the more time spent together), the smaller the number of aggressive conflicts that occurred. The conflict measure was restricted to "reactive hostility" (i.e., refusals and resistance), but, nevertheless, friends engaged in fewer conflicts than nonfriends, taking time spent together into account. Masters and Furman (1981) reported that friends engaged more frequently in "punitive" exchanges than did "unselected" associates, but no adjustment was made for the time that the friends and the unselected associates spent together; proportions of punitive exchanges observed actually did not differ. Observations of nursery school children in two other studies – both controlling for the amount of time that the children spent together – show conflicts occurring at about the same rate between friends as between acquaintances (Hartup et al., 1988; Vespo & Caplan, 1988).

In closed-field situations, the situation is mostly different. Disagreements occur *more* frequently between friends than between nonfriends. Preschool children disagree with their friends more frequently than do nonfriends in their rooms during home visits (Gottman, 1983). School-age children have been shown to disagree more frequently during discussions of social issues (Nelson & Abound, 1985) and during a board game about which they had learned different rules (Hartup, French, Laursen, Johnston, & Ogawa, 1991). These differences do not trace to the greater amounts of social interaction occurring between friends than between nonfriends because the differences remain when this variable is partialled out. In only one closed-field situation, involving academic conversations, were friends and nonfriends observed not to differ in the frequency of their disagreements (Berndt, Perry, & Miller, 1988).

Generally, then, the evidence squares relatively well with our hypotheses: In open-field situations, friends engage in disagreements less frequently (or no more frequently) than do nonfriends, whereas in closed situations, they generally engage in them more frequently.

Conflict management. Conflicts occurring between friends in open-field situations are also resolved differently than are conflicts between nonfriends. In one investigation (Hartup et al., 1988), conflicts arising between nursery school friends were compared with those between acquaintances. The friends' conflicts did not arise in different activities from the nonfriends' conflicts. Moreover, friends' and nonfriends' disagreements did not differ in what they were about (i.e., possession of objects vs. behavioral control). Conflicts between friends, however, were less intense than those involving acquaintances. Resolution strategies were different: Friends mutually disengaged from their disagreements more readily than did nonfriends and "stood firm" proportionally less often. Equal or near equal outcomes, as compared to winner–loser outcomes, were more common between friends than between acquaintances. Finally, subsequent events differed: Following conflict resolution, friends, in contrast to nonfriends, were more likely to remain together and interact. Confirmation of these results with nursery school children has been reported (Vespo & Caplan, 1988), although no open-field studies of school-age children or adolescents deal with these issues.

In closed-field situations, conflicts are actually more intense between friends than between nonfriends, and assertive exchanges are more common. One investigation (Hartup et al., 1991) shows that friends disagreed at greater length during a board game than did nonfriends. Nelson and Aboud (1985) observed that criticisms and explanations were exchanged more frequently between friends than between nonfriends while they discussed a series of social issues. Finally, friends have been observed to refuse persuasive appeals from one another using more extensive rationales than did nonfriends (Jones, 1985).

Although this evidence suggests generally that friends' conflicts are more numerous and more intense than those of nonfriends', in closed-field situations two studies suggest that children also yield more readily with friends. In a modified prisoner's dilemma, for example, the incidence of defaults (clear winners and losers in conflict resolution) was negatively correlated with the friendliness existing between the children (who were preschoolers) (Matsumoto, Haan, Yabrove, Theodorou, & Carney, 1986). And, in a persuasion task, appeals were granted more frequently by school-age friends than by nonfriends, with friendship relations cited as the reason in postsession interviews (Jones, 1985). Friends and nonfriends did not yield differentially in one other instance (Morgan & Sawyer, 1967), although information about one another's expectations was related to outcome. That is, friends who thought their companions expected them to yield would sometimes do so; nonfriends, however, were sticklers for equity regardless of circumstance.

Methodological variations among these closed-field studies are too numerous for readers to sort out completely the inconsistencies in results. Neither conflict nor friendship is defined similarly across these studies. At the moment, it seems that conflicts between children and their friends in closed situations are especially vigorous and their actions extensively rationalized. Conflict outcomes, however, may or may not vary: The evidence is thin.

Summary. The weight of the evidence supports the hypothesis that setting interdependencies (situational openness or closedness) and relational interdependencies (friendship relations) interact as determinants of children's disagreements. Conflicts are more frequent between friends than between nonfriends in closed-field situations, but not in open ones. Conflicts in closed-field situations are more intense between friends than between nonfriends, but the evidence is not consistent concerning yielding. Conflicts in open-field situations, however, seem clearly to be less intense between friends than between nonfriends and to be resolved with "softer" tactics.

The interaction between setting and relational conditions has never been examined directly (i.e., within a single experiment). New investigations must redress this omission. Interaction effects may not be inferred from univariate results even though current evidence suggests that one exists. At this time, the notion that children's conflicts vary according to setting as well as friendship status is a challenging hypothesis, not an established fact.

Conflict and friendship termination

Friendship endings have not been studied extensively among either children or adolescents. The most interesting evidence comes from insider accounts and ethnographic observations. Observational methodologies are relatively limited in what can be gleaned from them, of course, because the events that incite friendship endings are oftentimes inaccessible to outsiders.

Insider views

Occurrence and issues. Although young children (6- and 7-year-olds) know when interaction with a friend ceases and sometimes regret it, they are not very articulate about why this occurs. Disagreements are not often cited in interviews with them (Rizzo, 1989). Somewhat older children (i.e., 9- and 10-year-olds) in both written (Bigelow & LaGaipa, 1980) and oral accounts (Berndt et al., 1986), cite disloyalty and betrayals as reasons for terminating friendships.

Conflicts are also cited in the written accounts, and interviews reveal that conflicts do not differentiate between stable and unstable friendships. Rather, disloyalty and lack of intimacy differentiate relationships that are stable from those that are not. Children's comments about lack of intimacy differentiate stable and unstable friends both before and after the break up, but comments about disloyalty do so only afterward (Berndt, Hawkins, & Hoyle, 1986). Reports about disloyalty and unfaithfulness may sometimes, of course, refer to conflicts, but this has not been established.

Other data also indicate that commitment expectations and their violation are significant in friendship termination. Cabral, Volpe, Youniss, and Gellert (1977) interviewed children and adolescents, asking them questions about three stories in which a child shares confidential information with either a parent, friend, or an acquaintance and then discovers that the confidence has been breached. Those interviewed thought that parents sometimes had the right to break confidences, especially for the child's own good, and that these relationships usually recover. Friends and acquaintances, however, were not regarded as having these same rights. Broken commitments were thought to violate the reciprocal contracts existing between friends and to affect these relationships adversely.

Summary. Loyalty, trust, and intimacy are known to assume significance in friendship relations as middle childhood advances and adolescence approaches (Bigelow & LaGaipa, 1975; Youniss, 1980). One would expect, then, that preschoolers would not consider commitment violations to be reasons for "breaking it off" with a friend but that such violations would be salient among older children. The evidence corroborates these notions. At the same time, overt contention and disagreement in children's talk about their friends are not common concomitants of termination. Alienation rather than argument marks these endings.

Outsider views

Occurrence. Friendships observed in one first-grade classroom ended simply because the children stopped interacting (Rizzo, 1989). Neither emotional outbursts nor arguments forecast their demise, nor were overt declarations made. Similar ethnographic work has not been executed among older children.

Laboratory observations relating to friendship termination have been devoted only to competition for a scarce resource. In this instance (Berndt, Hawkins, & Hoyle, 1986), 9- and 13-year-olds were observed with another child who was either a "best friend" at both the beginning and end of the school year (stable friends) or a best friend at the beginning but not the end (unstable friends). Younger children were expected to be more competitive with stable than unstable friends because self-esteem among younger children depends on performing as successfully as one's friends (see Tesser et al., 1984). Older children, however, were expected to be less competitive with stable friends owing to growing preferences for mutuality and equity in friendship relations.

Results supported these hypotheses: Competition was more extensive between stable than unstable friends among the younger children but less extensive between stable friends among the older ones. Both younger and older children indicated (after the session) a greater concern for equality in reward distribution between themselves and stable friends in constrast to the situation with unstable friends. Only the older children, however, believed their partners had these same concerns. Once again, the data suggest that developmental issues in conflict and friendship relations are significant.

Summary. Friendship endings are seldom observed. Naturalistic observations are difficult to obtain for older children and adolescents, except to chart the time they spend together and certain salient behaviors (e.g., fighting). Nevertheless, systematic observations could be used more extensively to chart the disintegration of these relationships. Children's conversations also can be examined and interaction observed in the laboratory. Such studies should be encouraged because unstable friendships are risk markers among school-age children and adolescents (Rutter & Garmezy, 1983).

Individual differences: An array of understudied issues

Sex differences

Boys' and girls' conflicts differ in numerous ways: During early childhood, disagreements occur more frequently among boys than among girls (Dawe, 1934; Shantz, 1986). Sex differences also emerge relatively early in what children disagree about: Boys' disagreements are more likely to involve power issues than are girls' disagreements; girls are more likely to disagree about interpersonal matters (Maltz & Borker, 1982; Raffaelli, 1990). Conflict tactics differ, too. Boys use power assertion more often than do girls, who use indirect tactics more frequently than do boys as well as bargaining and negotiation (Selman, Beardslee, Schultz, Krupa, & Podorefsky, 1986). Girls also employ strategies and tactics in conflict management that differ according to their companions' sex; boys are less discriminating (Miller, Danaher, & Forbes, 1986).

Sex differences such as these may typify both friends and nonfriends. Most investigators, however, have not examined sex differences among friends and nonfriends separately, nor specified whether the sex differences obtained refer to friends or nonfriends. Naturalistic studies usually involve children who spend time together, and thus one can assume that the reported differences were obtained mostly with friends. Because considerable importance attaches to it, more systematic analysis of this issue is needed: For example, male adolescents are more likely than females to report that disagreements do not affect their relationships. Females, however, more often see long-term implications, both positive and negative (Laursen, 1989; Raffaelli, 1990). And, in a closed-field situation (Hartup et al., 1991), friends did not talk more during their conflicts than nonfriends but assertions were used selectively according to friendship and sex: With friends, girls used assertions accompanied by rationales more frequently than boys, whereas boys used assertions without rationales more frequently than girls. These sex differences were not evident during conflicts between nonfriends.

Although sex differences in conflict management need further exploration separately among friends and nonfriends, attention also should be given to the dimensions of conflict management that may *not* differ between boys and girls. Both preschool-age boys and girls, for example, prefer "softer" modes of conflict resolution with friends than with nonfriends and more readily continue their interaction afterward (Hartup et al., 1988). In addition, both school-age boys and girls are less likely to seek third-party assistance when disagreement involves a friend than a nonfriend (Rizzo, 1989).

Developmental issues

Only three or four investigations, with subjects extending mainly from 8 years of age to 13 or 14, tell us in developmental terms what children understand about conflict and friendship relations. Only one investigation (Berndt et al., 1986) encompasses observations of children across this age range. Unfortunately, comparing results across studies is dangerous owing to a confound between age and methodology in the empirical literature: What is known about conflict and friendship among older children and adolescents is derived mostly from self-reports, whereas most of what we know about younger children comes from observations. Conflicts are also defined differently among investigations.

These methodological conflations are serious. The existing data suggest, for example, that major changes occur in conflict and its role in friendship relations across the transition to adolescence. School-age children report fewer conflicts with friends than with nonfriends (and observations confirm this), but adolescents report more conflicts. (These results emanate from open-field, noncompetitive situations.) In contrast, school-age children engage in more frequent conflicts with friends than with nonfriends in closed-field, competitive situations, whereas adolescents are not as competitive in these same situations with friends as with nonfriends (Berndt et al., 1986).

Sketchy though these results are, they suggest that the contextual theory of conflict and friendship relations outlined earlier needs developmental extension. That is: (a) Among children, closed-field, interdependent situations may elicit more conflicts among friends than among nonfriends because self-esteem depends on performing as successfully as their friends (Tesser et al., 1984). (b) Among adolescents, closed-field situations may promote fewer conflicts among friends than among nonfriends because most adolescents believe that friends must behave equitably. (c) Among children, open-field conditions may promote fewer conflicts with friends than with nonfriends because friends do not want their interaction with one another to cease. (d) Among adolescents, more frequent bickering is expected between friends than between nonfriends in open situations because their worries about the equality (or the lack of it) existing between themselves and their friends are pervasive.

Developmental studies, using methods appropriate for both children and adolescents, are urgently needed to test and refine these hypotheses. Also needed are developmental studies examining conflict strategies and tactics across the various stages of friendship, from beginnings to endings.

Individual differences

Children vary in the number of friends they have, the stability of these relationships, and their behavioral organization. Sometimes children's friendships can be identified as strong or weak; otherwise, pair–pair variations are almost never studied.

Mutual friends have sometimes been compared to unilateral friends (unreciprocated friendship choices), and the results are intriguing: First, unilateral friendships are not very stable, and children do not know these companions as well as they know mutual friends (Ladd & Emerson, 1984). Second, similarities as well as differences exist between these two kinds of "friends" in the ways conflicts are managed (Hartup et al., 1988). During conflict, unilateral associates differ from mutual friends but not from neutral associates: Conflicts between unilateral associates are more intense, more likely to involve standing firm, and more likely to result in winner–loser outcomes than will conflicts between mutual friends. In contrast, unilateral associates commonly remain together after the conflict, as will mutual friends though not neutral associates. One-sided relationships, then, are not different from "no relationship" during disagreement. Once the disagreement ends, though, a one-sided attraction has considerable value in determining whether interaction between the children will continue.

Other variations among children and their friends need to be recognized – variations in intensity, exclusivity, and security, as well as in the normative activities that govern them, the commitment of the children to one another, and the extent to which reciprocity and complementarity are salient issues. Whether a child has a friend or not may account for relatively little in terms of developmental outcome. Whether an infant has a mother does not tell us much, either. But the quality of the relationship that the infant constructs with his or her mother accounts for considerable variance in developmental outcome (Sroufe & Fleeson, 1986), and friendship variations may account for significant outcome variance, too.

Conclusion

Close relationships arise through a continuing dialectic between affirmations and conflict. Common ground between individuals cannot be illuminated through agreements or disagreements separately, but only through the contrast between them. Ordinarily, affirmations must outweigh conflicts in friendship formation and maintenance. Variations among friendships, however, are enormous. Conflicts are not as salient in friendship termination as might be supposed, because older children and adolescents regard disloyalty and violations of trust as the main causes of these terminations.

Insider and outsider accounts dealing with conflict and friendship relations are concordant in many ways but frequently deal with different issues. Outsider observations indicate that, while children are becoming friends, a dialectic involving agreements and disagreements is necessary to establishing the common ground and relational "limits" that friendships require. Observations have not been extensive enough, however, to determine the long-term consequences of these early conflicts. Children themselves report that quarreling during early encounters with one another prevents them from becoming friends. Moreover, they recognize that quarreling is inversely related to the closeness of these relationships as acquaintanceship progresses. In this instance, the insiders and the outsiders illuminate complementary rather than similar issues.

Insider and outsider accounts are sometimes difficult to reconcile unless contextual and developmental variations are taken into consideration. Children are motivated by an overriding desire to remain in the company of their friends: Much energy and time are devoted to this end. When continued interaction is at risk, children and their friends reduce their disagreements, both in numbers and intensity. When continued interaction is not at risk, children and their friends disagree relatively freely, more so than do nonfriends. Adolescents, I argue, are motivated by strong desires to achieve equality in their social interactions, especially with friends. When other companions are available, adolescents disagree more frequently with friends than with nonfriends, so as to continuingly affirm their common ground. When constrained in closed-field settings, however, adolescents avoid conflicts with their friends, believing they should behave equitably with them rather than competitively. Support for these notions exists in no single experiment: A synthesis of differing studies, however, supports them.

Among the most important issues needing examination in this area are variations: First, conflict variations need to be examined. Disagreements differ tremendously in what they are about, their emotional concomitants, and their resolution. Second, the organization of behavior between children and their friends needs attention: Friendship relations vary widely among dyads, and differences among dyads in conflict and conflict management may be related to developmental outcome. Third, developmental variations must be scrutinized closely. Older children have different notions about conflict management than do younger children, and equity expectations may be involved differently in their social relations.

Current evidence strongly suggests that these issues belong on the contemporary research agenda. Troubled children experience difficulty and unhappiness in friendship relations, both in establishing and maintaining them. Only glimmers exist to support the thesis that conflict socialization is constrained in these circumstances, but these glimmers are persuasive.

Notes

1. *Social reciprocity* is not a construct that is easy to define, and consensus about the best way to define it does not exist. *Temporal reciprocity* usually refers to the contingent occurrence of the same actions during social interaction (e.g., talk followed by talk). Such reciprocities are common, and may be especially visible among relationships in the making. These same reciprocities, however, may indicate "enmeshed" functioning later. Indeed, Gottman (1979) reported that dissatisfied married couples evidenced more negative affect in their interactions with one another than did satisfied couples, but also greater reciprocity in their displays of positive affect. The construct also extends to behavioral *complements* (e.g., chase–being chased) and *extensions* (e.g., behavioral strings used in joking, fantasy play, or nattering). (See Foot, Chapman, & Smith, 1980; Gottman, 1983).
2. Children are known to view "fairness" in conflict resolution in terms of equality (Morgan & Sawyer, 1967).
3. Relational interdependencies also exist between children who dislike one another. Relatively little is known about "enemies," but their interactions are clearly mutually regulated, and their relations cannot be regarded as independent. My arguments, however, do not extend to enemies.
4. Green's (1933) report contains a discrepancy between the data reported in the text and that in a table; a decimal point seems to have been misplaced in the table. My account is based on the text.

References

Achenbach, T. M., & Edelbrock, C. S. (1981). Behavioral problems and competencies reported by parents of normal and disturbed children aged 4 through 16. *Monographs of the Society for Research in Child Development, 46* (1, No. 188).

Ainsworth, M. D. S., & Wittig, B. A. (1969). Attachment and the exploratory behavior of one-year-olds in a strange situation. In B. M. Foss (Ed.), *Determinants of infant behaviour* (Vol. 4). London: Methuen.

Berndt, T. J., Hawkins, J. A., & Hoyle, S. G. (1986). Changes in friendship during a school year: Effects on children's and adolescents' impressions of friendship and sharing with friends. *Child Development, 57,* 1284–1297.

Berndt, T. J., & Keefe, K. (1991, April). *How friends influence adolescents' adjustment in school*. Poster presented at the meeting of the Society for Research in Child Development, Seattle, WA.

Berndt, T. J., & Perry, T. B. (1986). Children's perceptions of friendships as supportive relationships. *Developmental Psychology, 22,* 640–648.

Berndt, T. J., Perry, T. B., & Miller, K. E. (1988). Friends' and classmates' interactions on academic tasks. *Journal of Educational Psychology, 80,* 506–513.

Berscheid, E., & Graziano, W. G. (1979). The initiation of social relationships and social attraction. In R. L. Burgess & T. L. Huston (Eds.), *Social exchange in developing relationships*. New York: Academic Press.

Bigelow, B. J., & LaGaipa, J. J. (1975). Children's written descriptions of friendship: A multidimensional analysis. *Developmental Psychology, 11,* 857–858.

Bigelow, B. J., & LaGaipa, J. J (1980). The development of friendship values and choice. In H. C. Foot, A. J. Chapman, & J. R. Smith (Eds.), *Friendship and social relations in children*. New York: Wiley.

Cabral, G., Volpe, J., Youniss, J., & Gellert, B. (1977). *Resolving a problem in friendship and other relationships*. Unpublished manuscript, Catholic University of America, Washington, DC.

Dawe, H. C. (1934). An analysis of two hundred quarrels of preschool children. *Child Development, 5,* 139–157.

Eisenberg, A. R., & Garvey, C. (1981). Children's use of verbal strategies in resolving conflicts. *Discourse Processes, 4,* 149–170.

Foot, H. C., Chapman, A. J., & Smith, J. R. (Eds.). (1980). *Friendship and social relations in children*. New York: Wiley.

Furman, W. (1984). Some observations on the study of personal relationships. In J. C. Masters & K. Yarkin-Levin (Eds.), *Boundary areas in social and developmental psychology*. New York: Academic Press.

Furman, W. (1987). Acquaintanceship in middle childhood. *Developmental Psychology, 23,* 563–570.

Furman, W., & Buhrmester, D. (1985). Children's perceptions of the personal relationships in their social networks. *Developmental Psychology, 21,* 1016–1024.

Goodnow, J., & Burns, A. (1988). *Home and school: Child's eye view*. Sydney: Allen & Unwin.

Gottman, J. M. (1979). *Marital interaction: Experimental investigations*. New York: Academic Press.

Gottman, J. M. (1983). How children become friends. *Monographs of the Society for Research in Child Development, 48*(2, Serial No. 201).

Gottman, J. M., & Parker, J. G. (Eds.). (1986). *Conversations of friends*. Cambridge: Cambridge University Press.

Graziano, W. G. (1984). A developmental approach to social exchange processes. In J. C. Masters & K. Yarkin-Levin (Eds.), *Boundary areas in social and developmental psychology*. New York: Academic Press.

Green, E. H. (1933). Friendships and quarrels among preschool children. *Child Development, 4,* 237–252.

Hartup, W. W., French, D. C. Laursen, B., Johnston, M. K., & Ogawa, J. R. (1991). *Conflict and friendship relations in middle childhood: Behavior in a closed-field situation*. Unpublished manuscript, University of Minnesota, Minneapolis.

Hartup, W. W., & Laursen, B. (in press). Conflict and context in peer relations. In C. Hart (Ed.), *Children on playgrounds: Research perspectives and applications*. Ithaca: SUNY Press.

Hartup, W. W., Laursen, B., Stewart, M. I., & Eastenson, A. (1988). Conflict and the friendship relations of young children. *Child Development, 59,* 1590–1600.

Hartup, W. W., & Sancilio, M. F. (1986). Children's friendships. In E. Schopler & G. B. Mesibov (Eds.), *Social behavior in autism*. New York: Plenum.

Hay, D. F. (1984). Social conflict in early childhood. In G. Whitehurst (Ed.), *Annals of child development* (Vol. 1). Greenwich, CT: JAI.

Hinde, R. A. (1979). *Towards understanding relationships*. New York: Academic Press.

Hinde, R. A., Titmus, G., Easton, D., & Tamplin, A. (1985). Incidence of "friendship" and behavior with strong associates versus nonassociates in preschoolers. *Child Development, 56*, 234–245.

Howes, C. (1983). Patterns of friendship. *Child Development, 54*, 1041–1053.

Howes, C. (1988). Peer interaction of young children. *Monographs of the Society for Research in Child Development, 53*(1, Serial No. 217).

Jones, D. C. (1985). Persuasive appeals and responses to appeals among friends and acquaintances. *Child Development, 56*, 757–763.

Kandel, D. B. (1978). Homophily, selection, and socialization in adolescent friendships. *American Journal of Sociology, 84*, 427–436.

Kelley, H. H., & Thibaut, J. W. (1978). *Interpersonal relations: A theory of interdependence*. New York: Wiley-Interscience.

Ladd, G. W. (1990). Having friends, keeping friends, making friends, and being liked by peers in the classroom: Predictors of children's early school adjustment? *Child Development, 61*, 1081–1100.

Ladd, G. W., & Emerson, E. S. (1984). Shared knowledge in children's friendships. *Developmental Psychology, 20*, 932–940.

Laursen, B. (1989). *Interpersonal conflict during adolescence*. Unpublished doctoral dissertation, University of Minnesota, Minneapolis.

Laursen, B., & Hartup, W. W. (1989). The dynamics of preschool children's conflicts. *Merrill-Palmer Quarterly, 35*, 281–297.

Levinger, G. (1983). Development and change. In H. H. Kelley, E. Berscheid, A. Christensen, J. H. Harvey, T. L. Huston, G. Levinger, E. McClintock, L. A. Peplau, & D. R. Peterson (Eds.), *Close relationships*. New York: Freeman.

Maltz, D., & Borker, R. (1982). A cultural approach to male–female miscommunication. In J. J. Gumperz (Ed.), *Communication, language and social identity*. Cambridge: Cambridge University Press.

Markman, H. J. (1981). Prediction of marital distress: A 5-year follow-up. *Journal of Consulting and Clinical Psychology, 49*, 760–762.

Masters, J. C., & Furman, W. (1981). Popularity, individual friendship selections, and specific peer interaction among children. *Developmental Psychology, 17*, 344–350.

Matsumoto, D., Haan, N., Yabrove, G., Theodorou, P., & Carney, C. C. (1986). Preschoolers' moral actions and emotions in prisoner's dilemma. *Developmental Psychology, 22*, 663–670.

Maynard, D. W. (1986). The development of argumentative skills among children. In P. A. Adler & P. Adler (Eds.), *Sociological studies of child development* (Vol. 1). Greenwich, CT: JAI.

Miller, P. M., Danaher, D. L., & Forbes, D. (1986). Sex-related strategies for coping with interpersonal conflict in children aged five and seven. *Developmental Psychology, 22*, 543–548.

Morgan, W. R., & Sawyer, J. (1967). Bargaining, expectations, and the preference for equality over equity. *Journal of Personality and Social Psychology, 6*, 139–149.

Nelson, J., & Aboud, F. E. (1985). The resolution of social conflict between friends. *Child Development, 56*, 1009–1017.

Newcomb, A. F., & Brady, J. E. (1982). Mutuality in boys' friendship selections. *Child Development, 53*, 392–395.

Olson, D. H. (1977). Insiders' and outsiders' views of relationships: Research studies. In G. Levinger & H. L. Raush (Eds.), *Close relationships: Perspectives on the meaning of intimacy.* Amherst: University of Massachusetts Press.

Parker, J. G., & Asher, S. R. (1987). Peer relations and later adjustment: Are low-accepted children "at risk"? *Psychological Bulletin, 102,* 357–389.

Peterson, D. R. (1983). Conflict. In H. H. Kelley, E. Berscheid, A. Christensen, J. H. Harvey, T. L. Huston, G. Levinger, E. McClintock, L. A. Peplau, & D. R. Peterson (Eds.), *Close relationships.* New York: Freeman.

Raffaelli, M. (1990). *Sibling conflict in early adolescence.* Unpublished doctoral dissertation, University of Chicago.

Renshaw, P., & Asher, S. R. (1983). Children's goals and strategies for social interaction. *Merrill-Palmer Quarterly, 29,* 353–374.

Rizzo, T. A. (1987). *Disputes among friends.* Unpublished manuscript, Northwestern University, Evanston, IL.

Rizzo, T. A. (1989). *Friendship development among children in school.* Norwood, NJ: Ablex.

Rutter, M., & Garmezy, N. (1983). Developmental psychopathology. In E. M. Hetherington (Ed.), *Handbook of child psychology: Vol. 4. Socialization, personality, and social development* (4th ed.). New York: Wiley.

Sackin, S., & Thelen, E. (1984). An ethological study of peaceful associative outcomes to conflict in preschool children. *Child Development, 55,* 1098–1102.

Selman, R. L. (1980). *The growth of interpersonal understanding.* New York: Academic Press.

Selman, R. L., Beardslee, W., Schultz, L. H., Krupa, M., & Podorefsky, D. (1986). Assessing adolescent interpersonal negotiation strategies: Toward the integration of structural and functional models. *Developmental Psychology, 22,* 450–459.

Shantz, C. U. (1987). Conflict between children. *Child Development, 58,* 283–305.

Shantz, C. U. (in press). Children's conflicts: Representations and lessons learned. In R. R. Cocking & K. A. Renninger (Eds.), *The development and meaning of psychological distance.* Hillsdale, NJ: Erlbaum.

Shantz, C. U., & Hobart, C. J. (1989). Social conflict and development: Peers and siblings. In T. J. Berndt & G. W. Ladd (Eds.), *Peer relationships and child development.* New York: Wiley.

Shantz, D. W. (1986). Conflict, aggression, and peer status: An observational study. *Child Development, 57,* 1322–1332.

Singleton, L. C., & Asher, S. R. (1979). Racial integration and children's peer preferences: An investigation of developmental and cohort differences. *Child Development, 50,* 936–941.

Smollar, J., & Youniss, J. (1982). Social development through friendship. In K. H. Rubin & H. S. Ross (Eds.), *Peer relationships and social skills in children.* New York: Springer-Verlag.

Sroufe, L. A., & Fleeson, J. (1986). Attachment and the construction of relationships. In W. W. Hartup & Z. Rubin (Eds.), *Relationships and development.* Hillsdale, NJ: Erlbaum.

Surra, C. A., & Longstreth, M. (1990). Similarity of outcomes, interdependence, and conflict in dating relationships. *Journal of Personality and Social Psychology, 59,* 501–516.

Tesser, A., Campbell, J., & Smith, M. (1984). Friendship choice and performance: Self-evaluation maintenance in children. *Journal of Personality and Social Psychology, 46,* 561–574.

Vespo, J. E., & Caplan, M. Z. (1988, March). *Preschoolers' differential use of conflict resolution strategies with friends and acquaintances.* Paper presented at the Conference on Human Development, Charleston, SC.

Weiss, R. S. (1986). Continuities and transformations in social relationships from childhood to adulthood. In W. W. Hartup & Z. Rubin (Eds.), *Relationships and development.* Hillsdale, NJ: Erlbaum.

Youniss, J. (1980). *Parents and peers in social development: A Piaget–Sullivan perspective.* Chicago: University of Chicago Press.

8 Conflict and relationships during adolescence

W. Andrew Collins and Brett Laursen

"Adolescence" and "conflict" have been considered virtually synonymous terms both in formal theory and in popular stereotypes. Indeed, intensified conflicts in adolescents' interpersonal relationships have been viewed as a hallmark of the extensive and rapid changes in individuals during this period. The focus of this chapter is the nature of conflict in social relationships during adolescence and its linkages to individual development.

Conflicts in social relations have been emphasized in the study of adolescence since the "Sturm and Drang" formulations advanced by G. Stanley Hall (e.g., 1904) and Sigmund Freud (e.g., 1949). Although viewed as intrapsychic in origin, the perturbations of this period were considered especially pertinent to primary relationships: "Although freeing the self from dependency on parents, loosening the libidinal attachments to them, and modifying the superego for adult living are largely intrapsychic tasks, they are usually carried out via alterations in behavior toward the parents whose directives were the original sources of the superego" (Lidz, 1969, p. 108).

Most contemporary views place less emphasis on intrapsychic disruption than this but recognize that transitory perturbations in interpersonal relationships are normative, particularly in early adolescence. *Conflicts*, defined as oppositional interactions, are seen as natural interpersonal sequelae of shifts in role expectations associated with age-graded transitions and maturational changes. Anxiety and accumulation of stress from multiple transitions may increase the likelihood both that conflicts will be initiated and that they will be ineffectively managed (see reviews by Collins, 1990, in press-b; Hill, 1987; Steinberg, 1991). A distinctive feature of these views is the implication that the importance of conflict is tied less to its frequency than to its management (Grotevant & Cooper, 1985, 1986; Hartup, 1989; Shantz, 1987).

Support in the completion of this chapter was provided by a grant from the National Institute of Mental Health to W. Andrew Collins.

The significance of conflicts to the development of individual adolescents can be seen in both personal and interpersonal realms. Many of these outcomes are positive. Qualities of family conflict resolution have been linked to aspects of psychosocial development including indentity formation, the development of social-cognitive skills, and ego development (e.g., Grotevant & Cooper, 1985, 1986; Hauser et al., 1984). Effectively managed conflict also fosters interpersonal adaptations necessitated by the physical, social, and cognitive changes of adolescence (e.g., Collins, 1990; Cooper, 1988; Paikoff & Brooks-Gunn, 1991; Steinberg, 1991).

Outside of the family, conflicts help to determine whether and with whom new relationships will be formed and whether these relationships will be maintained. Conflicts provide an opportunity for both participants to distinguish areas of agreement from disagreement (Braiker & Kelley, 1979; Hartup, this volume). Continuously high levels of conflict, however, are associated with psychosocial problems during adolescence and in later life (Montemayor, 1983; Patterson, DeBarsyshe, & Ramsey, 1989; Steinberg, 1991). Conflicts also may lead to continued perturbations within relationships and even deterioration of relational bonds (Hartup & Laursen, in press).

Whether conflicts are functional or dysfunctional in adolescent development depends, in part, on the characteristics of the relationships in which they occur. Constructive engagement and communication in response to conflicts may foster positive adaptive outcomes. Parent–adolescent relationships in which interactions are marked by responsiveness to the adolescents' expressions of discrepant opinions are associated with sense of identity among the adolescents, as well as social perception skills (Grotevant & Cooper, 1985, 1986). Longitudinal research (Walker & Taylor, 1991) reveals that a parental discussion style that involves supportive, but challenging, discussions of issues is linked to relatively advanced reasoning (Walker & Taylor, 1991). In peer relations, constructive conflict resolution has been linked to short-term outcomes among both children (Eisenberg & Garvey, 1981; Laursen & Hartup, 1989) and adolescents (Laursen, 1990). Thus, the significance of conflicts derives from a variety of constituent processes beyond the occurrence of conflict itself (Perry, Perry, & Kennedy, this volume; Shantz, 1987).

This chapter begins with the view that the developmental significance of conflicts is integral to the larger social interaction patterns characteristic of individuals and their relationships (Shantz & Hobart, 1989). The central contention is that conflicts are microcosms of the linkages between adolescents' social relationships and their development as individuals.

The chapter is divided into three major sections. The first section is devoted to an overview of distinctive characteristics of close relationships in adolescence and a discussion of some central issues in the empirical study of conflict in these relationships. In the second section, the nature and significance of conflict in adolescents' relationships is examined in light of empirical evidence. The third section outlines an agenda for future research on conflicts in adolescence. Particular attention is given to understanding relationships as significant contexts in human development generally, and to conflict as a mechanism for change and adaptation in adolescent relationships particularly.

Relationships and conflict during adolescence

Relationships, regardless of the persons involved, are comprised of frequent, highly interdependent action sequences occurring over time and across diverse settings and tasks (Kelley et al., 1983). In both familial and close extrafamilial relationships (e.g., friendships), these interdependencies are natural products of shared histories and complementary roles that emerge over time. During adolescence, rapid and extensive physical, cognitive, and social changes necessitate interpersonal adjustments in order to maintain these functional interdependencies, and conflicts often occur in this realignment process. This section first addresses the question What are the distinctive characteristics of adolescents' relationships? The second question to be considered is What is the nature and significance of conflicts as integral aspects of these relationships?

Relationships during adolescence

Relationships in adolescence are more extensive and diverse than those of childhood (Blyth, 1982; Csikszentmihalyi & Larson, 1984). Familial relationships remain salient in adolescence, despite the increasing proportion of time devoted to extrafamilial interactions. Adolescents establish a wider range of casual friendships than children do, perhaps because of the more numerous possibilities available in school and at work. Furthermore, romantic relationships become common. Adolescent relationships thus vary in the frequency and diversity of interactions occurring within them, the degree of mutual impact experienced by the participants, and their likely endurance. These diverse relationships have different characteristics that serve both complementary and overlapping functions (see Collins & Russell, 1991; Hartup, in press).

Adolescent relationships are similar in many ways to their childhood counterparts. In Europe and North America, parents and adolescents alike are commonly found to perceive their relationships with one another as warm and pleasant. Of the families that encounter difficulties in this period, a large proportion appear to have had a history of problems (e.g., Kandel & Lesser, 1972; Offer, Ostrov, & Howard, 1981; Rutter, Graham, Chadwick, & Yule, 1976).

Although specific extrafamilial relationships would scarcely be expected to be stable across long periods, several findings imply continuity from childhood to adolescence in capabilities for forming and maintaining friendships. Stable friendships may be neither typical nor required during adolescence (Epstein, 1986; Savin-Williams & Berndt, 1991), but some evidence implies that stability with a "best" friend is more common than instability over the course of a school year (Berndt, Hawkins, & Hoyle, 1986; Berndt & Hoyle, 1985). Of adolescents who experience peer difficulties, most have exhibited similar difficulties in their relationships during childhood (Patterson et al., 1989; Rubin, LeMare, & Lollis, 1990).

Although relationships show important common features from early to later adolescence, significant changes occur in the amount, content, and perceived meaning of the interactions occurring with them, expressions of positive and negative affect, and interpersonal perceptions of the interactors (for reviews, see Collins & Russell, 1991; Parker & Gottman, 1989). Feelings of closeness increase toward parents, especially mothers; perceptions of reciprocity with and acceptance by parents become more frequent (Youniss & Smollar, 1985); and intimacy is increasingly reported in relations with friends (Sharabany, Gershoni, & Hofmann, 1981; for a review, see Savin-Williams & Berndt, 1991). Perceptions of self and others converge with those of parents (Alessandri & Wozniak, 1987) and friends (Furman & Bierman, 1984). These changing patterns of interaction, coexisting with continued connections with significant others, imply that close relationships undergo transformations that permit changes toward appropriate levels of individuation and autonomy as adolescents mature (Grotevant & Cooper, 1986; Wynne, 1984).

Conflict in adolescent relationships

Conflicts are precipitated when behavior by one member of a dyad is incongruent with the goals, expectations, or desires of the other member, resulting in *mutual opposition* (Shantz, 1987). These oppositions may engender perturbations in both interactional (e.g., conflict) and emotional (e.g., decreased relationship satisfaction) aspects of relationships (Kelley et al., 1983). Dyads marked by interdependency, a defining characteristic of relationship closeness (Berscheid, Snyder, & Omoto, 1989; Kelley et al.,

1983), have been found generally to show higher rates of conflict than less interdependent pairs (Hartup & Laursen, in press).

As integral elements of relationships, adolescent conflicts reflect differences among the dyads in which they occur (Csikszentmihalyi & Larson, 1984; Laursen, 1989). Conflicts are presumed to be more common in relationships with family members, especially parents, on the premise that autonomy issues are central to individual development during this period, and these must be dealt with primarily in parent–adolescent relations (Hill, 1987; Steinberg, 1991).

The distinction between familial and extrafamilial relationships has another basis, as well. Relationships with family members, for example, may be described as *closed-field*, in that they are partly defined and constrained by kinship or legal definitions and associated norms and environmental pressures (Berscheid, 1985). Closed-field relationships entail long interaction histories and extensively routinized interactional scripts; consequently, conflicts may stimulate adaptation of interactions and expectancies to altered capabilities and predilections of adolescents and changes in relative power and autonomy within families. Outside of the family, adolescents participate in *open-field* interactions and can form and dissolve relationships without biological or legal constraints, such as those that apply to familial dyads. In these less constrained circumstances, the occurrence of conflicts affects whether and with whom new relationships are formed and whether these relationships will be maintained. Thus, the dyadic variability in conflicts may serve social as well as psychosocial functions.

Conflict variations also may reflect developmental changes associated with adolescence. Several reasons have been advanced as to why conflicts should be more frequent in some periods of preadolescence and adolescence than in others. Psychoanalytic and ethology-oriented writers identify hormonal surgence as the primary reason for intensification of conflicts in early adolescence (e.g., A. Freud, 1969; Steinberg, 1987, 1988). Neopsychoanalytic theorists (e.g., Blos, 1979; Lidz, 1969; Steinberg & Silverberg, 1986) construe these difficulties as reflecting adolescents' modification of parental images, rather than emotional distancing, while adapting to the anticipated role demands of adulthood. Other views imply that conflicts become increasingly likely as adolescents develop cognitive competencies that permit them to recognize inconsistencies and imperfections in others (e.g., Elkind, 1967) and to view many issues as matters of personal concern, rather than as legitimate areas of parental authority (e.g., Smetana, 1988). Formulations loosely grouped under the rubric of biopsychosocial approaches (e.g., Brooks-Gunn & Zahaykevich, 1989; Collins, 1990, in press-b; Lerner, 1987; Petersen, 1987; Simmons, Burgeson, & Reef, 1988) attribute heightened perturbations to violations of expectations and accumulation of stressors associated with multiple personal and social transitions.

Issues in research on adolescent conflicts

Understanding the role of conflicts in adolescents' relationships thus requires attention to two issues: (a) how conflicts are differentiated across the dyads in which adolescents are involved and (b) how conflicts change over time during the adolescent years. Research methods, first of all, must be sensitive to variability across both dyads and time. The studies now available have not always met this criterion, and four methodological issues, to be discussed next, remain important.

Operationalization of conflict. Measures and procedures are needed that provide uncontaminated information about oppositions or disagreements. Measures that conflate conflict with affect (e.g., fighting, arguing) underestimate the incidence of disagreement or opposition occurring in everyday life, yet much existing research relies on such measures. As an instance, the widely used Issues Checklist (Prinz, Foster, Kent, & O'Leary, 1979; Robin & Foster, 1984) requires family members to indicate how frequently during the past 2 weeks each of 44 topics were discussed by parents and adolescents and then to report the average intensity or anger of discussions over each issue. Thus, the measure yields an indication of the extent to which a particular topic arose and the heatedness of the discussion(s), but the incidence of disagreement or opposition, whether heated or not, cannot be estimated.

Other measures may overestimate the incidence of conflict. For example, conversational interruptions are commonly used as an indicator of conflict in observational studies (Hill, 1988; Steinberg, 1981; Steinberg & Hill, 1978). Interruptions, however, may or may not indicate opposition between participants (Hill, 1988). Within some long-term dyads in which partners habitually "finish each others' thoughts," for example, interruptions are more appropriately taken as signs of closeness, not conflict.

The issue of validity arises with regard to conflict analogs used in the laboratory. When seated in a small room and asked to resolve a recent disagreement, parents and adolescents are much more likely to negotiate than in real life; furthermore, the demands of the analog task severely constrain disengagement as a resolution tactic. Robin and Foster (1989) found that 50% of adolescents and 25% of mothers indicated that these discussions were either "somewhat" or "very" different from those at home. Furthermore, conflict behaviors in these settings appear to be highly constrained by the issue selected for discussion (Smetana, 1991) and by context or setting (see Hartup, this volume; Hartup & Laursen, in press).

A related threat to validity comes from the use of hypothetical conflicts to elicit preferences for different modes of resolution. As with research on correlations between social-cognitive competence and social behavior (e.g., Rest, 1983; Shantz, 1983), studies show that constructive resolutions are more readily endorsed in interviews about hypothetical conflicts than they are practiced in face-to-face oppositions (Sternberg & Dobson, 1987; Youniss & Smollar, 1985). Consequently, measures based on hypothetical instances must be used with caution as indicators of typical behavior.

Analysis of conflict processes. To date, most research on adolescent conflicts has focused on the rate of occurrence, neglecting the related processes that often determine the impact of conflict interactions. Among these are the issue(s) being addressed, the circumstances of initiation, the behaviors associated with resolution, and the outcomes of the episode (Shantz, 1987). Research designs are needed in which indicators of the full conflict process are included.

Dyadic perspectives on conflict. Most research on conflict concerns the actions of one person, without regard to the implications for the other or for their conjoint functioning. Consequently, implications of conflict within relationships are often difficult to assess.

This point has two important corollaries. One is that information is needed from both insiders and outsiders (Hartup, this volume). Yet information about adolescents' relationships comes preponderantly from "insider" reports. Researchers have used questionnaire and interview self-reports more extensively than other techniques. Outsider, or observer, information is needed to provide relatively disinterested accounts of conflicts involving adolescents. Because outsiders can attend to conjoint behavior patterns of the two interactors more readily than either of the participants themselves, outsider data are particularly important to assessing conflict as a distinctive element of relationships. For example, coding observed *reciprocal* interruptions and disagreements provides a more clearly dyadic assessment than either frequency counts obtained from each participant separately (Holmbeck & Hill, 1991) or separate insider reports.

The second corollary is that, when insider views are needed, information should come from both members of the dyad. Concordance between parents' and children's reports of conflict is low in most studies, with correlations typically less than .50 (Montemayor & Hanson, 1985; Robin & Foster, 1989). To address the relational significance of conflicts, techniques are needed to make use of the data from both insiders (e.g., Holmbeck & Hill, 1991).

Comparability of measures. Among studies using self-report measures, little consistency has emerged in the factor structure of instruments intended to assess similar phenomena. It is difficult to make generalizations about the frequency of parent–child disagreements about school, for example, when school issues emerge as a separate factor in some studies but are combined with household responsibilities or autonomy issues in others. Factor analysis may clarify the results of independent investigations, but the larger picture remains confused because items tapping diverse behaviors and settings are combined in different ways from one study to the next. Similar difficulties arise when observations of conflicts are coded at different levels of analysis.

Research is, thus, at an early stage with respect to identifying and assessing the aspects of conflict that vary across dyads and across the course of development during adolescence. In the next section, the results of previous studies are reviewed in order to assess the status and future directions of research in this area.

Differentiation and change in adolescent conflicts

Viewing conflicts as significant relational processes in adolescent development raises two questions: whether conflicts, like other processes in relationships during adolescence, are differentiated across dyads; and whether and how conflicts are related to adolescent developmental transitions. In two upcoming subsections, we consider these questions in light of the existing evidence. Because answers to these two questions are often conditional on the specific aspects of conflict being examined, each subsection is further subdivided to give separate attention to five conflict processes (Shantz, 1987): incidence and intensity, issues, initiation, resolution, and outcomes.

Differentiation across relationships

Differentiation in the constituent processes and developmental significance of familial and extrafamilial relationships is now well established (see reviews by Hartup, 1983, 1989). Conflicts with parents, siblings, and peers are, doubtless, similarly differentiated. Most evidence on this point concerns the relative incidence and intensity of conflicts across relationships, but differentiation is increasingly being examined with respect to other aspects of conflict.

Incidence and intensity. Reports of daily conflicts vary considerably depending upon how conflict is defined, which relationship is being assessed, and who is doing the reporting. Adolescents themselves report an average of seven disagreements daily (Laursen, 1989). Most conflicts, regardless of age, involve mothers, followed in descending order by siblings, friends, romantic partners, fathers, and other peers and adults (Csikszentmihalyi & Larson, 1984; Laursen, 1989; Montemayor & Hanson, 1985).

Conflict intensities are also differentiated across relationships, with the most intense affect being expressed in familial, rather than extrafamilial, relationships. Negative affect is not characteristic of disputes with friends or boy/girlfriends (Laursen, 1989; Raffaelli, 1990). Whether these contrasts are attributable to the closed nature of familial relationships, as compared to extrafamilial dyads, is not known.

Issues. Conflict issues have been studied most often with respect to adolescents and their parents. Conflicts in these dyads arise in connection with a wide variety of issues, ranging from mundane disputes over household chores and proper attire to matters of potentially greater consequences for health and well-being (see Montemayor, 1983).

Theoretical views of adolescence imply that conflicts should be most likely and most intense in connection with issues pertaining to psychosocial development, especially autonomy in parent–adolescent relationships and management of extrafamily affiliations (Savin-Williams & Berndt, 1991; Steinberg, 1991). An array of findings from both familial and extrafamilial relationships accords with this prediction. Between parents and adolescents, the most commonly reported conflict issues involve authority, autonomy, and responsibilities (Carlton-Ford & Collins, 1988; Smetana, 1989). Disputes with siblings are equally divided between interpersonal concerns and issues of authority, property, and responsibilities (Hobart, 1991; Raffaelli, 1990). Disagreements with friends and boy/girlfriends reflect issues of interpersonal behavior and relational difficulties (Hobart, 1991; Youniss & Smollar, 1985). As noted earlier, these findings indicate that certain topics commonly evoke discussion but do not reveal their relative salience.

Initiation. Initiations of conflicts commonly reflect distinctive features of the particular relationship in which the violation arises. Conflicts are especially likely when behavior in parent–adolescent dyads violates expectations that are particularly salient to the other (Carlson, Cooper, & Spradling, 1991; Collins, 1990; Holmbeck & O'Donnell, 1991; Smetana, 1991).

The onset of peer disputes also typically reflects violations of expected or desired behavior. Conflict between adolescent females, for example, often begins with one party confronting another about past behavior, especially when the behavior may have violated expectancies of intimacy or trust (Eder, 1990). Because reports of such violations often come second-hand, ancillary disputes frequently arise over the accuracy of information (Goodwin & Goodwin, 1987). Males are more likely to confront immediately behavior that deviates from expectations, especially when the behavior challenges established patterns of dominance. Disagreements of this kind may be common during the early stages of a romantic relationship, because of the different expectations held by males and females about behavior in such relationships.

Although adolescents perceive that most disputes are started by the other party (Laursen, 1990), naturalistic observations indicate otherwise. Parents and their children are equally likely to initiate conflicts, but mothers are the more likely and fathers the less likely targets when conflicts are initiated by adolescents (Vuchinich, 1987).

Little is known about the conditions under which individuals detect and respond to violations. One hypothesis for further investigation is that conflict initiations may be moderated by beliefs about the implications of violated expectations for optimal individual development or for the future of the relationship itself (Collins, in press-a; Goodnow & Collins, 1990).

Resolution. Conflict resolution refers to actions that terminate an oppositional exchange. Commonly used strategies (Vuchinich, 1987) include "submission" (one person accedes to the demands of the other), "compromise" (both make concessions), "third-party intervention" (both accept a solution proposed by a previously uninvolved person), "stand-off" (shift in the topic of speech or focus of activity), and "withdrawal" (one person refuses to continue the exchange). The latter two are often lumped together under the rubric "disengagement." Naturalistic observations, experimental analogs, and self-reports with both peers (Goodwin, 1982; Youniss & Smollar, 1985) and family members (Montemayor & Hanson, 1985; Raffaelli, 1990; Schoenleber, 1988; Smetana, 1991) show clearly that adolescents' conflicts are most commonly resolved through power assertion and disengagement, rather than through negotiation. Half or more of all conflicts are resolved by stand-off or withdrawal, followed in frequency by unilateral power assertion and only then by negotiation (Vuchinich, 1990).

Resolution studies are divided between those focusing on resolution of actual conflicts and those seeking preferred responses. As noted earlier, these two methods often yield different estimates. For instance, Sternberg and Dobson (1987) found a clear preference for compromise and mutual discussion in hypothetical disagreements, with disengagement (e.g., wait and see, avoidance) being infrequently endorsed. The same subjects, however, reported that recent, real-life conflicts are resolved with disengagement as often as with negotiation. Similarly, Youniss and Smollar (1985) found that adolescents offered negotiated solutions for hypothetical situations twice as often as they reported actually using them.

Differentiation across dyads is evident, nevertheless. In disputes with parents, adolescent termination strategies are equally divided between stand-offs and power assertions; negotiation is extremely rare (Montemayor & Hanson, 1985). Resolutions with friends generally involve more explicit efforts to maintain amity than do resolutions with siblings (Hobart, 1991). Raffaelli (1990) found that, in descriptions of conflict with friends, resolution involved disengagement in 54% of the cases, submission in 31%, and compromises in 13%. Among sibling conflicts, 34% were terminated by disengagement, 30% by submission, 27% through third-party intervention, and 9% through compromise.

Diverse findings now indicate that adaptive, well-functioning relationships are marked not by the absence of conflicts, but by responsive engagement in resolving them (Grotevant & Cooper, 1985; Kelley et al., 1983). Little is known, however, about the range of resolution behaviors that function adaptively or the conditions under which particular resolutions are perceived as desirable.

Outcomes. Conflict may temporarily disrupt interactions between adolescents and others, although this is less likely with peers than with parents. With friends and boy/girlfriends, social interaction usually continues following disputes, unlike those with siblings, other peers, and adults. With parents, continued interaction and disengagement are equally likely as outcomes of conflicts (Laursen, 1989). Concordantly, friends and romantic partners are more likely than family members to report positive feelings after a conflict (Laursen, 1989; Raffaelli, 1990), perhaps reflecting an awareness that, in these relationships, mutually satisfactory resolutions are necessary in order to maintain the relationships themselves. Conflict rarely has a detrimental impact, however, on future relations with parents and siblings.

Both adolescents and parents generally feel less satisfaction with their relationships if conflict is frequent than when it is not. Conflict is a primary complaint of parents about their relations with their adolescent children. Rates of parent–adolescent conflict have been linked to parents' life satisfaction and self-esteem, as well as to adolescent attitudes toward parents and family life (Montemayor, 1986; Olson et al., 1983; Schoenleber, 1988; Silverberg & Steinberg, 1990).

Little is known about outcomes of peer conflicts, although research with younger children indicates that contentiousness and poor management of conflicts are associated with peer rejection (Patterson et al., 1989; Shantz & Shantz, 1985). These difficulties in peer relations are interrelated with family patterns of conflict and conflict resolution. Adolescents from families that engage openly and constructively in disagreement, for example, are better able to resolve conflict with peers productively than adolescents whose parents cut off disagreement unilaterally (Cooper, 1988; Cooper & Ayers-Lopez, 1985).

Comment. The pervasive differentiation of conflicts across dyads raises further doubts about the stereotype of adolescence as a time of general contentiousness. It seems more likely that the observed conflict distinctions parallel the different functions served by different relationships in adolescent development, although additional research is needed to examine the implications of this dyadic variability.

Relation to individual change

The hypothesis that conflicts are more probable at some periods of adolescence than others has been tested separately with respect to both pubertal maturation and age. Most theoretical views hold that the likelihood and intensity of conflict are greatest in early adolescence, because of the combination of pubertal changes and age-graded social transitions at this time (for reviews, see Hill, 1987; Steinberg, 1991). Writers in both the psychoanalytic and sociobiological traditions (see review by Steinberg, 1991) have repeatedly identified pubertal maturation as the primary correlate of increases in parent–child conflict. Social-psychological views (e.g., Simmons & Blyth, 1987) give equal emphasis to age as a correlate, because of stressors experienced in age-graded social transitions. Studies of neither pubertal status nor age differences alone, however, have yielded reliable associations with changes in conflict.

Incidence and intensity. A curvilinear relation between pubertal maturation and conflict incidence has emerged in a single laboratory study of parent–adolescent discussions about hypothetical joint decisions, such as where to go on a family vacation (Hill, 1988; Holmbeck & Hill, 1991). Seventh-grade girls who had experienced menarche most recently (within 6 months of the time of the study) showed higher and more sustained levels of reciprocal disagreement and interruptions with parents, especially mothers, than did girls whose menarche either had not yet occurred or had occurred less recently. Positive affect also diminished in connection with interruptions and disagreements in the months just following menarche. Studies involving adolescent sons (Steinberg, 1981; Steinberg & Hill, 1978) offer only equivocal evidence of an association between conflict and maturational status, owing perhaps to reliance on frequency of interruption as a conflict indicator.

Insider reports are inconsistent with these outsider data. As an instance, Steinberg (1987, 1988) reported both cross-sectional and longitudinal comparisons of Issues Checklist reports from 10- to 15-year-olds and their parents. Neither parents' nor adolescents' reports of conflict were consistently related to pubertal maturation. It should be noted, however, that both Steinberg and later researchers (e.g., Flannery & Montemayor, 1991) report significant correlations between pubertal status and reports of behavioral and emotional distance in parent–adolescent relationships. That is, positive affect and subjective closeness, as reported by both parents and adolescents, were negatively related to pubertal status, whereas negative affect in their interactions was directly related to pubertal maturation (Flannery & Montemayor, 1991; Steinberg, 1987, 1988). The implications of these correlations for the occurrence of conflict are not clear, because studies of distance do not report instances of opposition separately from those of negative affect and communication.

Although only limited evidence now links incidence and intensity of disagreements to differences in pubertal status generally, individual adolescents clearly vary in likelihood of being involved in conflicts, and these personal differences may be associated with puberty. For example, levels of certain pubertal hormones appear to be correlated with individual differences in the intensity of conflicts (Inoff-Germain et al., 1988). Individual variations in pubertal timing also may be tied to the incidence of adolescent conflicts with parents. Conflicts over family rules in early adolescence, for example, have been found to be especially likely in families with early maturing offspring, both male and female (Hill, 1988; Hill & Holmbeck, 1987). Other findings indicate that the association between pubertal timing and conflicts may differ for males and females (Steinberg, 1987, 1988).

Thus, the evidence implying that the frequency and intensity of parent–adolescent conflicts peak during the period of most rapid pubertal change rests largely on cross-sectional evidence with girls. The alternative hypothesis that conflicts during adolescence are a function of age, rather than pubertal maturation, has not been satisfactorily addressed in research because of measurement procedures in which instances of conflict are contaminated with other indicators of interpersonal distance (Flannery & Montemayor, 1991; Steinberg, 1987, 1988).

Comparisons of physically heterogeneous age groups, like pubertal-status comparisons, have yielded mixed results. Offer (1969; Offer & Offer, 1975) reported that retrospective accounts of "arguments and fights" were more frequent for 7th and 8th graders than for high school students, and Furman (1989) found that global perceptions of conflict with parents and siblings was greater for both 7th and 10th graders than for 4th graders or college undergraduates. Other studies (Douvan & Adelson, 1966; Moore & Holtzman, 1965; Smetana, 1988) showed no differences across age groups in reported frequency of disagreements. These disparities among studies are difficult to interpret because of differences in measures and small sample sizes.

Similar limitations mark research on age-related patterns of conflict with siblings and peers during adolescence. In one instance (Buhrmester & Furman, 1990), respondents in grades 3, 6, 9, and 12 reported progressively lower incidences of conflicts with older siblings, whereas the incidence of conflicts with younger siblings was similar across grades. Other studies provide a less clear picture, perhaps because older and younger siblings were not considered separately. Furman (1989) and Raffaelli (1990) found negligible differences across ages.

With respect to the incidence of conflicts with peers, few age-related differences have emerged in either observational (Barker & Wright, 1955; Fawl, 1963) or interview studies (Raffaelli, 1990). Incidence may vary with age, however, within certain subgroups. In an ethnographic study of disputes between female adolescent peers in grades five through eight (Eder, 1990), older girls exhibited more frequent conflicts than younger ones. Also, among older children, conflicts with same-sex friends have been found to decline late in adolescence, whereas conflicts with romantic friends increase (Furman, 1989).

Neither age nor pubertal status alone, then, is unequivocally associated with incidence and intensity of conflicts. To date, the strong interest in physical development as the primary correlate of changes in the incidence and intensity of adolescents' conflicts has distracted researchers from examining the combined and interactive effects of age-graded social changes in the occurrence of conflict. Several other research lines suggest, in fact, that multiple changes, both personal and environmental, may better account for functioning in relationships during adolescence than do single salient events. For example, the effects of pubertal changes are exacerbated by other circumstances of early adolescence, such as shifting from elementary to junior high school and beginning to date. This effect appears to be a function of the number of changes impinging on an adolescent at a given time, rather than the source of the change per se (Simmons & Blyth, 1987;

Simmons et al., 1988). Research is now needed that considers the linkage between conflicts in diverse dyads and the multiplicity of changes facing adolescents, as well as the specific changes commonly associated with social and physical development during the period.

Issues. Topic variations among parent–child conflicts appear to be more strongly age related than the incidence and intensity of conflicts (Douvan & Adelson, 1966). Both parents and adolescents indicate that daily hassles (e.g., taking out the garbage, wearing proper attire) decrease with age from 5th to 11th grades, whereas alcohol and dating become increasingly likely issues (Carlton-Ford & Collins, 1988). Papini and Sebby (1988) studied conflicts over four different issues (school, household behavior, self-responsibility, and general matters), finding that conflicts over autonomy were most likely in families with prepubertal adolescents and least likely in those with postpubertal adolescents. Conflicts over household chores and school were unrelated to pubertal status.

Parent–adolescent conflicts sometimes arise because parents and adolescents disagree about which of them properly exercises jurisdiction over the adolescents' behavior, thus raising issues of autonomy. Smetana (1988), for example, reported incongruencies between mothers and children across ages 10 to 18 in the tendency to view issues of conventional behavior (e.g., chores, curfew) as within the realm of appropriate parental influence. Across this age range, adolescents increasingly viewed these issues as matters of personal choice and, thus, under the jurisdiction of the adolescent alone, whereas mothers maintained that the issues carried ramifications beyond personal preference and, thus, were properly within parental jurisdiction. It seems likely that jurisdictional disputes vary more clearly as a function of age than disputes that arise from simple substantive disagreements, but differentiations of this type have not been examined.

The topics of sibling disagreements appear to change little from the preschool years through adolescence, being consistently dominated by disputes over possessions (Hartup & Laursen, in press). Between friends, however, the focus of conflicts shifts from possessions during early childhood to trust and interpersonal concerns during middle childhood and adolescence. This shift appears to be part of a general social reorientation to relational, rather than individual, concerns in friendship between childhood and adolescence (Bigelow & LaGaipa, 1975; Reisman & Shorr, 1978).

In parent–child and peer relationships alike, then, the topics around which conflicts occur increasingly reflect psychosocial issues such as autonomy from parents and affiliation with peers. These topics vary among relationships, however, reflecting the different functions of cross-generational and same-generational relationships in psychosocial development (Hunter, 1984; Youniss & Smollar, 1985).

Initiation. Little is known about variability in the initiation of conflicts during adolescence. It may be that initiations, particularly unprovoked initiations, are largely a function of individual differences in assertiveness (for a review, see Perry et al., this volume) and the initiator's relative dominance in the dyad. On this premise, several hypotheses about temporal patterns might be tested. One is that, as relationships with siblings (Buhrmester & Furman, 1990) and parents (Youniss & Smollar, 1985) become less asymmetrical in adolescence, intrafamilial conflicts may be initiated somewhat more frequently. A second is that, increasingly from middle to late adolescence, relatively more conflicts may be initiated in interactions involving peers who have become less well integrated into mixed-gender crowds than have their agemates. Both hypotheses imply that variability in initiation processes may be relative to other aspects of the different relationships of interest.

Resolution. Abilities for resolving conflicts are believed to be based in capacities for reasoning and self-regulation. Departing from cognitive-developmental formulations (e.g., Selman & Schultz, 1989), various investigators have predicted that knowledge of appropriate skills and strategies for negotiated resolutions increases linearly from middle childhood to late adolescence, on the assumption that logical competence, including understanding of interpersonal relationships, is more advanced among older individuals than younger ones.

Indeed, age-related improvements are evident in studies in which adolescents have been asked to indicate appropriate strategies for responding to hypothetical conflicts. Findings typically indicate a strong emphasis on negotiation as compared with submission, power assertion, or disengagement. Moreover, endorsement of and skill at negotiation varies as a function of social-cognitive abilities within adolescence (Levya & Furth, 1986; Selman, Beardslee, Shultz, Krupa, & Podorefsky, 1986). Such results may indicate an increase in adolescents' expectations that relationship partners will show greater reciprocity toward them and may also be related to the development of competence for maintaining relationships over long periods. Responses to actual conflicts in adolescence, however, show neither a dominant tendency toward negotiation overall nor a gradual shift toward negotiated resolutions during adolescence (Youniss & Smollar, 1985).

An especially strong age-related trend is a decline from early to late adolescence in the use of power assertion for resolving conflicts. Observational studies of parent–adolescent conversations indicate that power assertions, as evidenced by interruptions, decline after the peak period of pubertal changes (Steinberg, 1981; Steinberg & Hill, 1978). In peer interactions, conflict resolution decreasingly involves power assertion at the same time that friendship expectations increasingly concern trust and reciprocity (Bigelow, 1977; Hartup & Laursen, in press). Evidence to date implies gender differences in the degree to which this age-related pattern is manifested. During early and middle adolescence, emphasis on friendship reciprocity is especially evident among females (Youniss & Smollar, 1985), and females become more skilled than males at reaching amicable resolutions (Eder, 1990; Goodwin & Goodwin, 1987; Youniss & Smollar, 1985). Males generally are more likely to resort to power assertion than are females, a pattern that only changes slowly with age. Styles of conflict resolution among girls may depend on the sex of the other party. In interactions with males, preadolescent girls frequently resort to the power-assertive tactics typically used between males at this age; with other girls, however, more conciliatory styles prevail (Miller, Danaher, & Forbes, 1986). It remains to be seen whether this carries over to interactions during adolescence.

Thus, conflict resolution competencies generally become more adult-like during adolescence. This transition is marked more by a declining preference for power-assertive techniques than for more complex interpersonal techniques such as negotiation.

Outcomes. Although frequent intense conflicts generally have been found to be dysfunctional contexts for adolescents, the impact of normative conflicts appears to be moderated by the manner and adequacy of the resolution effected (Grotevant & Cooper, 1985, 1986; Walker & Taylor, 1991). This finding implies that the developmental impact of conflict largely depends on the quality of the relationship in which the disagreement arises. Some promising predictions can be drawn from this implication. In close, trusting relationships, conflict can be a nonthreatening, beneficial experience that prompts growth and insight (Cooper, 1988). Negative consequences may ensue, however, if conflict is perceived as a hostile attack to be countered in one's own defense. The sequelae of conflict also are likely to vary as relationships themselves change. As closeness in a relationship declines, for example, the impact of disagreements may be decreased. A disagreement with a parent or friend that might previously have been devastating (or serious enough to promote reflection) might now be shrugged off as unimportant because a romantic partner has assumed a preeminent position among relationship partners.

Conflict and developmental processes in relationships

Viewing conflict as one aspect of changing relationships during adolescence leads to several propositions about the nature and significance of interpersonal conflict in development. In this section, three of these propositions are singled out. First, conflict provides a perspective on both the distinctions among the multiple relationships in which adolescents participate and the functional interrelations between them. Second, conflict processes are integral to developmental adaptations both by individual adolescents and by the dyads in which they are involved. Third, conflict in close relationships may contribute directly, as well as indirectly, to the development of competence and psychosocial health during adolescence.

Differentiation and interrelations among relationships

Adolescent relationships can be differentiated in several ways. In terms of the distribution of power and authority between participants, adolescents typically depict peer relationships as horizontal and adult–child relationships as vertical (Hunter, 1984). In terms of the presence or absence of mutually rewarding (equitable) exchanges, adolescents invariably mention family members, friends, and romantic partners as their closest, most important relationship partners (Berscheid et al., 1989; Blyth, Hill, & Thiel, 1982). Different patterns of social interaction exist between close, interdependent relationships and those that are not (Berscheid et al., 1989), as well as between dyads that vary in terms of the relative power of the participants (Hunter, 1984; Youniss & Smollar, 1985).

The patterning of conflict across dyads and across time captures the distinctiveness and social significance of the multiple relationships in which adolescents participate. Conflict episodes are more likely to arise in close relationships than in other dyads, regardless of the age of relative power of the participants (Hartup & Laursen, in press; Laursen, 1989). Modes of resolution and the aftermath of disagreements also denote distinctiveness among relationships. Increasingly greater likelihood of conflict with romantic partners over time signifies the gradual incorporation of extrafamilial relationships into the social world of adolescence.

Research on variation among relationships could provide information on the meaning and significance of conflict episodes. The complementary perspective that the interrelations among distinctive relationships may be significant in adolescents' lives is equally promising as an outlook on the role of conflict. One possible benefit is greater understanding of the significance of having multiple close relationships. The construct of social support is one vantage point on conflict in the context of multiple relationships. An adolescent experiencing conflicts in some relationships may find an *arena of comfort* in other relationships (Hetherington, Cox, & Cox, 1985; Simmons et al., 1988). Studies of the interrelations among relationships could address conflict processes not only in close relationships, but also in the expanding social networks of adolescents and their implications for individual development.

Conflict and relationship change

The hypothesis that conflict stimulates dyadic adaptation to changing characteristics of individuals is thus far consistent with findings on change in parent–adolescent relationships (e.g., Collins, 1990, in press-b; Steinberg, 1991). An emphasis on adaptation and mutual realignment may account for change in other relationships, as well. To date, however, the significance of conflict in producing change has not been documented empirically in research on adolescent relationships. Indeed, little research has been devoted to relationship change, whether or not conflict is assigned a central role.

One impetus for examining the role of conflict in changing relationships comes from correlational studies of family problem solving (Grotevant & Cooper, 1985, 1986; Hauser et al., 1984). In these studies, adolescents' scores on measures of identity and social competence were positively associated with family conflict resolution marked by openness to the adolescents' views, facilitation of communication, and warm engagement. These characteristics of family conflicts reflect common dimensions of variation in child-rearing patterns (Maccoby & Martin, 1983). A significant question is whether and how families that vary on these dimensions adapt to conflicts associated with early adolescent transitions.

Similarly, little is known about how transformations in stable friendships occur across time: To what extent and in what ways do conflicts between friends arise as a result of developmental changes? How are these resolved so as to permit friendships to change as well as to continue?

Longitudinal studies are essential in both cases. The model of expectancy formation and change proposed by Collins (1990, in press-b) provides one guide for determining the elements of individual and relational functioning that might be assessed in research on relationship change. In this view, the interdependencies of ongoing relationships form the basis for *expectancies* that affect the perceptions and interpretation of other persons' behavior and, therefore, guide their actions and reactions toward one another. During the transition to adolescence, discrepancies between expectancies and perceptions of actual behavior are especially likely to occur (a) because multiple, rapid changes during adolescence make past behavior an unreliable basis for predicting actions and responses and (b) because these changes elicit new expectancies that may not yet be appropriate. Research is needed in which transformations in adolescents' relationships are tracked in conjunction with significant life events and individual changes.

Interpersonal conflict and individual development

Interpersonal conflict has been repeatedly invoked as a factor in cognitive change (e.g., Berkowitz, 1985; Doise, Mugny, & Perret-Clermont, 1975, 1976), but ramifications for social development have been addressed less frequently. Conflicts and conflict resolution, however, potentially influence several aspects of social competence that are especially significant for adolescents.

First, when conflicts occur in close relationships, adolescents have the opportunity to learn about the dynamics of relationships as they assume new roles within them. Perceptions of mutuality and reciprocity in conversations increase during the adolescent years, especially with mothers; and although there is considerable individual variation in mutuality of influence and self-disclosure (Miller, 1989), adolescents generally perceive that others understand them better over time (Youniss & Smollar, 1985).

Second, as in earlier years, social development in and beyond adolescence requires the continuation of bonds between adolescents and their close relationship partners. Managing conflict appropriately is an essential aspect of maintaining functionally significant relationships across time. Collins (in press-a) has recently proposed that parent–child relationships that facilitate adaptive adolescent psychosocial growth may be characterized by a capacity for discriminating among instances of violated expectancies. Of special concern are instances in which violations signify problems in the socialization of appropriate values or disruptions of the relationship, rather than more superficial differences in style or personal preferences. In addition, responses to conflict that are attuned to the nature of the relationships, as well as to the content of violated expectancies, may be critical to relationship continuity. These points are similar to Elder's (1963) observation that democratic child-rearing methods combine appropriate regulation of adolescents' behavior with attention to preserving a warm, positive teaching atmosphere between parent and child.

Conclusion

In contrast to the popular impressions of disruption and perturbation, adolescence is a period in which conflict becomes more sensitively modulated and more intricately embedded in social bonds that support development toward adult relationships and competences. The distinctiveness of conflicts during adolescence derives primarily from two sources: (a) the increasing differentiation and interrelations among relationships in which conflicts occur and (b) the greater potential for effective resolution strategies. Better understanding of conflict processes in adolescence thus can illuminate the adaptation of relationships to individual change, as well as the development of skills for managing conflicts.

References

Alessandri, S. M., & Wozniak, R. H. (1987). The child's awareness of parental beliefs concerning the child: A developmental study. *Child Development, 58,* 316–323.

Barker, R. G., & Wright, H. F. (1955). *Midwest and its children.* New York: Harper & Row.

Berkowitz, M. W. (Ed.). (1985). *Peer conflict and psychological growth: New directions for child development.* San Francisco: Jossey-Bass.

Berndt, T. J., Hawkins, J. A., & Hoyle, S. G. (1986). Changes in friendship during a school year: Effects on children's and adolescents' impression of friendship and sharing with friends. *Child Development, 57,* 1284–1297.

Berndt, T. J., & Hoyle, S. (1985). Stability and change in childhood and adolescent friendships. *Developmental Psychology, 21,* 1007–1024.

Berscheid, E. (1985). Interpersonal attraction. In G. Lindzey & E. Aronson (Eds.), *Handbook of social psychology* (3d ed.). New York: Random House.

Berscheid, E., Snyder, M., & Omoto, A. M. (1989). The Relationship Closeness Inventory: Assessing the closeness of personal relationships. *Journal of Personality and Social Psychology, 57,* 792–807.

Bigelow, B. J. (1977). Children's friendship expectations: A cognitive developmental study. *Child Development, 48,* 246–253.

Bigelow, B. J., & LaGaipa, J. J. (1975). Children's written descriptions of friendship: A multidimensional analysis. *Developmental Psychology, 11,* 857–858.

Blos, P. (1979). *The adolescent passage.* New York: International Universities Press.

Blyth, D. A. (1982). Mapping the social world of adolescents: Issues, techniques, and problems. In F. Serafica (Ed.), *Social cognitive development in context.* New York: Guilford Press.

Blyth, D. A., Hill, J. P., & Thiel, K. S. (1982). Early adolescents' significant others: Grade and gender differences in perceived relationships with familial and nonfamilial adults and young people. *Journal of Youth and Adolescence, 11,* 425–450.

Braiker, H. B., & Kelley, H. H. (1979). Conflict in the development of close relationships. In R. L. Burgess & T. L. Huston (Eds.), *Social exchange in developing relationships.* New York: Academic Press.

Brooks-Gunn, J., & Zahaykevich, M. (1989). Parent–daughter relationships in early adolescence: A developmental perspective. In K. Kreppner & R. M. Lerner (Eds.), *Family systems and life-span development.* Hillsdale, NJ: Erlbaum.

Buhrmester, D., & Furman, W. (1990). Perceptions of sibling relationships during middle childhood and adolescence. *Child Development, 61,* 1387–1398.

Carlson, C. I., Cooper, C. R., & Spradling, V. Y. (1991). Developmental implications of shared versus distinct perceptions of the family in early adolescence. In R. L. Paikoff (Ed.), *Shared views in the family during adolescence: New directions for child development.* San Francisco: Jossey-Bass.

Carlton-Ford, S. L., & Collins, W. A. (1988, August). *Family conflict: Dimensions, differential reporting, and developmental differences.* Paper presented at the meeting of the American Sociological Association, Atlanta, GA.

Collins, W. A. (1990). Parent–child relationships in the transition to adolescence: Continuity and change in interaction, affect, and cognition. In R. Montemayor, G. Adams, & T. Gullotta (Eds.), *From childhood to adolescence: A transitional period?* Beverly Hills, CA: Sage.

Collins, W. A. (in press-a). Parents' cognitions and developmental changes in relationships during adolescence. In I. Sigel, A. McGillicuddy-deLisi, & J. J. Goodnow (Eds.), *Parental belief systems* (rev. ed.). Hillsdale, NJ: Erlbaum.

Collins, W. A. (in press-b). Relationships and development: Dyadic adaptation to individual change. In S. Shulman & S. Strauss (Eds.), *Relationships and socioemotional development.* New York: Ablex.

Collins, W. A., & Russell, G. (1991). Mother–child and father–child relationships in middle childhood and adolescence: A developmental analysis. *Developmental Review, 11,* 99–136.

Cooper, C. R. (1988). The role of conflict in adolescent–parent relationships. In M. R. Gunnar & W. A. Collins (Eds.), *Development during the transition to adolescence: Minnesota symposia on child psychology.* Hillsdale, NJ: Erlbaum.

Cooper, C. R., & Ayers-Lopez, S. (1985). Family and peer systems in early adolescence: New models of the role of relationships in development. *Journal of Early Adolescence, 5,* 9–22.

Csikszentmihalyi, M., & Larson, R. (1984). *Being adolescent.* New York: Basic.

Doise, W., Mugny, G., & Perret-Clermont, A.-N. (1975). Social interaction and the development of cognitive operations. *European Journal of Social Psychology, 5,* 367–383.

Doise, W., Mugny, G., & Perret-Clermont, A.-N. (1976). Social interaction and cognitive development: Further evidence. *European Journal of Social Psychology, 6,* 245–247.

Douvan, E., & Adelson, J. (1966). *The adolescent experience.* New York: Wiley.

Eder, D. (1990). Serious and playful disputes: Variation in conflict talk among female adolescents. In A. D. Grimshaw (Ed.), *Conflict talk: Sociolinguistic investigations of arguments in conversations.* Cambridge: Cambridge University Press.

Eisenberg, A. R., & Garvey, C. (1981). Children's use of verbal strategies in resolving conflicts. *Discourse Processes, 4,* 149–170.

Elder, G. H., Jr. (1963). Parental power legitimation and its effect on the adolescent. *Sociometry, 26,* 50–65.

Elkind, D. (1967). Egocentrism in adolescence. *Child Development, 38,* 1025–1034.

Epstein, J. L. (1986). Friendship selection: Developmental and environmental influences. In R. C. Mueller & C. R. Cooper (Eds.), *Process and outcome in peer relationships.* New York: Academic Press.

Fawl, C. L. (1963). Disturbances experienced by children in their natural habitats. In R. Barker (Ed.), *The stream of behavior.* New York: Appleton-Century-Crofts.

Flannery, D. J., & Montemayor, R. (1991, April). *Impact of puberty versus age on affective expression, negative communication, and problem behavior in parent–adolescent dyads.* Paper presented at the meeting of the Society for Research in Child Development, Seattle, WA.

Freud, A. (1969). Adolescence as a developmental disturbance. In G. Caplan & S. Lebovici (Eds.), *Adolescence: Psychological perspectives*. New York: Basic.

Freud, S. (1949). *The infantile genital organization of the libido*. Collected Papers (Vol. 2). London: Hogarth Press. (Original work published 1923)

Furman, W. (1989). The development of children's networks. In D. Belle (Ed.), *Children's social networks and social supports*. New York: Wiley.

Furman, W., & Bierman, K. (1984). Children's conceptions of friendship: A multimethod study of developmental changes. *Developmental Psychology, 21*, 1007–1015.

Goodnow, J. J., & Collins, W. A. (1990). *Development according to parents: The nature, sources, and consequences of parents' ideas*. London: Erlbaum.

Goodwin, M. H. (1982). Processes of dispute management among urban black children. *American Ethnologist, 9*, 76–96.

Goodwin, M. H., & Goodwin, C. (1987). Children's arguing. In S. Philips, S. Steele, & C. Tanz (Eds.), *Language, gender, and sex in comparative perspective*. Cambridge: Cambridge University Press.

Grotevant, H., & Cooper, C. (1985). Patterns of interaction in family relationships and the development of identity exploration in adolescence. *Child Development, 56*, 415–428.

Grotevant, H., & Cooper, C. (1986). Individuation in family relationships. *Human Development, 29*, 82–100.

Hall, G. S. (1904). *Adolescence*. New York: Appleton.

Hartup, W. W. (1983). Peer relations. In E. M. Hetherington (Ed.), *Handbook of child psychology: Vol. 4. Socialization, personality, and social development* (4th ed.). New York: Wiley.

Hartup, W. W. (1989). Social relationships and their developmental significance. *American Psychologist, 44*, 120–126.

Hartup, W. W. (in press). Peer relations in early and middle childhood. In V. B. Van Hasselt & M. Hersen (Eds.), *Handbook of social development: A lifespan perspective*. New York: Plenum.

Hartup, W. W., & Laursen, B. (in press). Conflict and context in peer relations. In C. Hart (Ed.), *Children on playgrounds: Research perspectives and applications*. Ithaca: SUNY Press.

Hauser, S., Powers, S., Noam, G., Jacobson, A., Weiss, B., & Follansbee, D. (1984). Familial contexts of adolescent ego development. *Child Development, 55*, 195–213.

Hetherington, E. M., Cox, M., & Cox, R. (1985). Long-term effects of divorce and remarriage on the adjustment of children. *Journal of American Academy of Psychiatry, 24*, 518–530.

Hill, J. P. (1987). Research on adolescents and their families: Past and prospect. In C. E. Irwin, Jr. (Ed.), *Adolescent social behavior and health: New directions for child development*. San Francisco: Jossey-Bass.

Hill, J. P. (1988). Adapting to menarche: Familial control and conflict. In M. R. Gunnar & W. A. Collins (Eds.), *Development during the transition to adolescence: Minnesota symposia on child psychology*. Hillsdale, NJ: Erlbaum.

Hill, J. P., & Holmbeck, G. N. (1987). Disagreements about rules in families with seventh-grade girls and boys. *Journal of Youth and Adolescence, 16*, 221–246.

Hobart, C. J. (1991, April). *Preadolescents' and adolescents' conflicts with siblings and friends*. Paper presented at the meeting of the Society for Research in Child Development, Seattle, WA.

Holmbeck, G. N., & Hill, J. P. (1991). Conflictive engagement, positive affect, and menarche in families with seventh-grade girls. *Child Development, 62*, 1030–1048.

Holmbeck, G. N., & O'Donnell, K. (1991). Discrepancies between perceptions of decision making and behavioral autonomy. In R. L. Paikoff (Ed.), *Shared views in the family during adolescence: New directions for child development*. San Francisco: Jossey-Bass.

Hunter, F. T. (1984). Socializing procedures in parent–child and friendship relations during adolescence. *Developmental Psychology, 20,* 1092–1099.

Inoff-Germain, G., Arnold, G. S., Nottleman, E. D., Susman, E. J., Cutler, G. B., Jr., & Chrousos, G. P. (1988). Relations between hormone levels and observational measures of aggressive behavior of young adolescents in family interactions. *Developmental Psychology, 24,* 129–139.

Kandel, D., & Lesser, G. (1972). *Youth in two worlds.* San Francisco: Jossey-Bass.

Kelley, H. H., Berscheid, E., Christensen, A., Harvey, J. H., Huston, T. L., Levinger, G., McClintock, E., Peplau, L. A., & Peterson, D. R. (1983). *Close relationships.* New York: Freeman.

Laursen, B. (1989). *Relationships and conflict during adolescence.* Unpublished doctoral dissertation, University of Minnesota, Minneapolis.

Laursen, B (1990, March). *Contextual variations in adolescent conflict.* Paper presented at the meeting of the Society for Research on Adolescence, Atlanta, GA.

Laursen, B., & Hartup, W. W. (1989). The dynamics of preschool children's conflicts. *Merrill-Palmer Quarterly, 35,* 281–297.

Lerner, R. M. (1987). A life-span perspective for early adolescence. In R. M. Lerner & T. T. Foch (Eds.), *Biological–psychosocial interactions in early adolescence.* Hillsdale, NJ: Erlbaum.

Levya, R. A., & Furth, H. G. (1986). Compromise formation in social conflicts: The influence of age, issue, and interpersonal context. *Journal of Youth and Adolescence, 15,* 441–452.

Lidz, T. (1969). The adolescent in his family. In G. Caplan & S. Lebovici (Eds.), *Adolescence: Psychosocial perspectives.* New York: Basic.

Maccoby, E. E., & Martin, J. A. (1983). Socialization in the context of the family: Parent–child interaction. In E. M. Hetherington (Ed.), *Handbook of child psychology: Vol. 4. Socialization, personality, and social development* (4th ed.). New York: Wiley.

Miller, M. M. (1989). *Intimacy between adolescent girls and their mothers: Grade-related differences in self-disclosure and relations to psychosocial development status.* Unpublished doctoral dissertation, University of Minnesota, Minneapolis.

Miller, P. M., Danaher, D. L., & Forbes, D. (1986). Sex-related strategies for coping with interpersonal conflict in children aged five and seven. *Developmental Psychology, 22,* 543–548.

Montemayor, R. (1983). Parents and adolescents in conflict: All families some of the time and some families most of the time. *Journal of Early Adolescence, 3,* 83–103.

Montemayor, R. (1986). Family variation in parent–adolescent storm and stress. *Journal of Adolescent Research, 1,* 15–31.

Montemayor, R., & Hanson, E. (1985). A naturalistic view of conflict between adolescents and their parents and siblings. *Journal of Early Adolescence, 5,* 23–30.

Moore, B. M., & Holtzman, W. H. (1965). *Tomorrow's parents.* Austin: University of Texas Press.

Offer, D. (1969). *The psychological world of the teenager.* New York: Basic.

Offer, D., & Offer, J. B. (1975). *From teenage to young manhood: A psychological study.* New York: Basic.

Offer, D., Ostrov, E., & Howard, K. (1981). *The adolescent: A psychological self portrait.* New York: Basic.

Olson, D., McCubbin, H., Barnes, H., Larsen, A., Muxen, M., & Wilson, M. (1983). *Families: What makes them work.* Beverly Hills, CA: Sage.

Paikoff, R. L., & Brooks-Gunn, J. (1991). Do parent–child relationships change during puberty? *Psychological Bulletin, 110,* 47–66.

Papini, D. R., & Sebby, R. A. (1988). Variations in conflictual family issues by adolescent pubertal status, gender, and family member. *Journal of Early Adolescence, 8,* 1–15.

Parker, J. G., & Gottman, J. M. (1989). Social and emotional development in a relational context: Friendship interaction from early childhood to adolescence. In T. J. Berndt & G. W. Ladd (Eds.), *Peer relationships in child development*. New York: Wiley.

Patterson, G. R., DeBarsyshe, B. D., & Ramsey, E. (1989). A developmental perspective on antisocial behavior. *American Psychologist, 44*, 329–335.

Petersen, A. C. (1987). The nature of biological–psychosocial interactions: The sample case of early adolescence. In R. M. Lerner & T. T. Foch (Eds.), *Biological–psychosocial interactions in early adolescence*. Hillsdale, NJ: Erlbaum.

Prinz, R. J., Foster, S. L., Kent, R. N., & O'Leary, K. D. (1979). Multivariate assessment of conflict in distressed and non-distressed mother–adolescent dyads. *Journal of Applied Behavior Analysis, 12*, 691–700.

Raffaelli, M. (1990). *Sibling conflict in early adolescence*. Unpublished doctoral dissertation, University of Chicago.

Reisman, J. M., & Shorr, S. I. (1978). Friendship claims and expectations among children and adults. *Child Development, 49*, 913–916.

Rest, J. R. (1983). Morality. In J. H. Flavell & E. Markman (Eds.), *Handbook of child psychology: Vol. 3. Cognitive development* (4th ed.). New York: Wiley.

Robin, A. L., & Foster, S. L. (1984). Problem-solving communication training: A behavioral family systems approach to parent–adolescent conflict. In P. Karoly & J. J. Steffen (Eds.), *Adolescent behavior disorders: Foundations and contemporary concerns*. Lexington, MA: Lexington Books.

Robin, A. L., & Foster, S. L. (1989). *Negotiating parent–adolescent conflict*. New York: Guilford Press.

Rubin, K. H., LeMare, L. J., & Lollis, S. (1990). Social withdrawal in childhood: Developmental pathways to peer rejection. In S. R. Asher & J. D. Coie (Eds.), *Peer rejection in childhood*. Cambridge: Cambridge University Press.

Rutter, M., Graham, P., Chadwick, O., & Yule, W. (1976). Adolescent turmoil: Fact or fiction? *Journal of Child Psychology and Psychiatry, 17*, 35–56.

Savin-Williams, R. C., & Berndt, T. J. (1991). Friendship and peer relationships. In S. Feldman & G. Elliot (Eds.), *At the threshold: The developing adolescent*. Cambridge, MA: Harvard University Press.

Schoenleber, K. L. (1988). *Parental perceptions and expectations and their relationship to parent–child conflict and parental satisfaction during the transition to adolescence*. Unpublished doctoral dissertation, University of Minnesota, Minneapolis.

Selman, R. L., Beardslee, W., Shultz, L. H., Krupa, M., & Podorefsky, D. (1986). Assessing adolescent interpersonal negotiation strategies: Toward the integration of structural and functional models. *Developmental Psychology, 22*, 450–459.

Selman, R. L., & Schultz, L. H. (1989). Children's strategies for interpersonal negotiation with peers: An interpretive/empirical approach to the study of social development. In T. J. Berndt & G. W. Ladd (Eds.), *Peer relationships in child development*. New York: Wiley.

Shantz, C. U. (1983). Social cognition. In J. H. Flavell & E. Markman (Eds.), *Handbook of child psychology: Vol. 3. Cognitive development* (4th ed.). New York: Wiley.

Shantz, C. U. (1987). Conflicts between children. *Child Development, 58*, 238–305.

Shantz, C. U., & Hobart, C. J. (1989). Social conflict and development: Peers and siblings. In T. J. Berndt & G. W. Ladd (Eds.), *Peer relationships in child development*. New York: Wiley.

Shantz, C. U., & Shantz, D. W. (1985). Conflict between children: Social-cognitive and sociometric correlates. In M. W. Berkowitz (Ed.), *Peer conflict and psychological growth: New directions for child development*. San Francisco: Jossey-Bass.

Sharabany, R., Gershoni, R., & Hofmann, J. (1981). Girlfriend, boyfriend: Age and sex differences in intimate friendship. *Developmental Psychology, 17*, 800–808.

Silverberg, S. B., & Steinberg, L. (1990). Psychological well-being of parents with early adolescent children. *Developmental Psychology, 26*, 658–666.

Simmons, R. G., & Blyth, D. A. (1987). *Moving into adolescence: The impact of pubertal change and school context.* New York: Aldine de Gruyter.

Simmons, R. G., Burgeson, R., & Reef, M. J. (1988). Cumulative change at entry to adolescence. In M. Gunnar & W. A., Collins (Eds.), *Development during the transition to adolescence: Minnesota symposia on child psychology.* Hillsdale, NJ: Erlbaum.

Smetana, J. G. (1988). Concepts of self and social convention: Adolescents' and parents' reasoning about hypothetical and actual family conflicts. In M. R. Gunnar & W. A. Collins (Eds.), *Development during the transition to adolescence: Minnesota symposia on child psychology.* Hillsdale, NJ: Erlbaum.

Smetana, J. G. (1989). Adolescents' and parents' reasoning about actual family conflict. *Child Development, 60*, 1052–1067.

Smetana, J. G. (1991). Adolescents' and mothers' evaluations of justifications for conflicts. In R. L. Paikoff (Eds.), *Shared views in the family during adolescence: New directions for child development.* San Francisco: Jossey-Bass.

Steinberg, L. (1981). Transformations in family relations at puberty. *Developmental Psychology, 17*, 833–840.

Steinberg, L. (1987). Impact of puberty on family relations: Effects of pubertal status and pubertal timing. *Developmental Psychology, 23*, 451–460.

Steinberg, L. (1988). Reciprocal relation between parent–child distance and pubertal maturation. *Developmental Psychology, 24*, 122–128.

Steinberg, L. (1991). Interdependency in the family: Autonomy, conflict and harmony in the parent–adolescent relationship. In S. Feldman & G. Elliot (Eds.), *At the threshold: The developing adolescent.* Cambridge, MA: Harvard University Press.

Steinberg, L., & Hill, J. P. (1978). Patterns of family interaction as a function of age, the onset of puberty, and formal thinking. *Developmental Psychology, 14*, 683–684.

Steinberg, L., & Silverberg, S. B. (1986). The vicissitudes of autonomy in early adolescence. *Child Development, 57*, 841–851.

Sternberg, R. J., & Dobson, D. M. (1987). Resolving interpersonal conflicts: An analysis of stylistic consistency. *Journal of Personality and Social Psychology, 52*, 794–812.

Vuchinich, S. (1987). Starting and stopping spontaneous family conflicts. *Journal of Marriage and the Family, 49*, 591–601.

Vuchinich, S. (1990). The sequential organization of closing in verbal family conflict. In A. D. Grimshaw (Ed.), *Conflict talk: Sociolinguistic investigations of arguments in conversations.* Cambridge: Cambridge University Press.

Walker, L. J., & Taylor, J. H. (1991). Family interactions and the development of moral reasoning. *Child Development, 62*, 264–283.

Wynne, L. (1984). The epigenesis of relational systems: A model for understanding family development. *Family Process, 23*, 297–318.

Youniss, J., & Smollar, J. (1985). *Adolescent relations with mothers, fathers, and friends.* Chicago: University of Chicago Press.

9   Conflicts between siblings

Deborah Lowe Vandell and Mark Dixon Bailey

For better or worse, relationships with siblings form one of our most enduring social bonds. By virtue of the amount of time they spend together
and the quality of their interactions, siblings can be important sources of
companionship, emotional support, help, and affection. Siblings can set a
standard for aspirations and serve as a ready source for social comparison.
But there is another critical component to many sibling relationships. More
than 90% of school-age siblings cite agonism and 79% cite quarrels as
important parts of their relationships (Furman & Buhrmester, 1985a). Adult
siblings also acknowledge the importance of conflict, especially when they
live in geographic proximity or when they are forced to resolve joint dilemmas such as the care of aging parents or the distribution of family
property (Cicirelli, 1982).

  Conflicts between siblings that reverberate with emotional intensity are
a recurring theme in literature. For example, the Book of Genesis features
stories of intense sibling conflict as when Cain kills his brother, Joseph is
sold into slavery by his brothers, and Jacob steals his brother's inheritance.
Shakespeare's *King Lear* focuses on the rivalry between sisters for their
father's favor, while Ibsen's play *Enemy of the People* highlights two
brothers destructively vying for honor and control of a community. Fairy
tales such as Cinderella and The Three Pigs also center on competition,
jealousy, and rivalry between siblings. Similar themes are reflected in recent stories written for children. Beverly Cleary's *Ramona: The Pest* and
Judy Blume's *Tales of a Fourth Grade Nothing* are two popular books for
elementary school children that describe conflicts from the perspectives of
both the younger and older siblings within the family. *The Berenstain Bears*
and *The Care Bears* series portray children's feeling during conflicts with
siblings as well as illustrate for young readers productive ways by which
children can resolve these conflicts. Across these various works is a contrasting portrayal of conflicts as productive and growth enhancing versus
destructive and debilitating.

242

The purpose of this chapter is to explore the issues of constructive versus destructive conflict between siblings within the psychological literature. Empirical research shows some sibling conflicts to be emotionally intense and destructive, whereas other conflicts involve a give-and-take between participants that seems to spur psychological development (Bank & Kahn, 1982; Dunn, 1988; Faber & Mazlish, 1987; Hartup & Laursen, in press). Here, we examine the characteristics of these different types of sibling conflict within a developmental framework. In order to provide a baseline from which the quality and quantity of sibling conflicts can be evaluated, we first examine normative patterns of sibling conflicts from infancy through adolescence. We then explore forces and factors contributing to differences in the intensity and frequency of these conflicts. A central question for families and researchers alike is why some siblings engage in destructive conflicts and others do not. We conclude the chapter by reviewing the research literature concerning when (and how) to intervene in sibling conflicts.

Sibling conflict: A definition

Considerable progress has been made in defining what is meant by "social conflict" and in conceptualizing the developmental functions of conflict. Conflicts are social events involving opposition and disagreement (Hartup & Laursen, in press; Shantz, 1987). Marked behaviorally by actions such as quarreling, fighting, resisting, opposing, refusing, denying, objecting, and protesting, conflict occurs whenever two or more individuals engage in oppositional behavior. If only one person opposes, objects, or protests, and the partner submits, then compliance rather than conflict is said to occur.

Unfortunately, this distinction has not been consistently applied to the examination of siblings. Most sibling researchers have not focused explicitly on *mutual* opposition. Instead, investigators have tended to record instances of physical and verbal aggression without determining if there is mutual opposition. Consequently, in this review, we describe sibling behaviors like aggressing, teasing, and arguing without always knowing the extent to which they involve mutual opposition.

Shantz and Hobart (1989) have argued convincingly that conflict and aggression are not one and the same. Aggression can be unidirectional, whereas conflicts are not. Conflicts *can* include instances in which participants physically aggress against others as in shoving matches, fistfights, and brawls; but conflicts also refer to verbal altercations, arguments, teasing, and debates. Within the current review, we adopt a broad view of sibling conflicts. Here, conflicts between siblings are not restricted to physical or verbal aggression intended to inflict damage on the other but include arguments about the use of family resources like the car, TV, or telephone as well as teasing taunts about boyfriends or girlfriends.

We distinguish, along with others (Coser, 1967; Deutsch, 1973), between destructive and constructive conflicts. Destructive conflicts are character-ized by high negative affect; they spread beyond the initial issue to other issues, and they escalate to intrusive and insistent coercion. Destructive conflicts end with one or both parties being dissatisfied. Constructive con-flicts, in contrast, focus on the issue at hand. During constructive conflicts, affective intensity is not high. And these conflicts, unlike destructive ones, are likely to be resolved by means of negotiations in a way that is accept-able to both parties.

The impact of constructive and destructive conflicts is different. Whereas relationships are undermined by destructive conflicts, especially when such conflicts accumulate over time, most individuals believe that their relation-ships are enhanced by constructive ones (Gottman, 1979). Constructive conflicts also are believed to enhance social understanding and problem-solving skills, whereas destructive conflicts are not associated with these developmental outcomes (Bank & Kahn, 1982; Dunn, 1988; Shantz & Hobart, 1989).

In this chapter, the distinction between constructive and destructive conflicts is applied to disagreements between siblings. Research suggests that both types of conflicts occur within the context of sibling relation-ships. In one longitudinal investigation (Dunn & Munn, 1985a, 1985b, 1986, 1987; Dunn, 1988; Munn & Dunn, 1989), 43 children were observed at ages 18, 24, and 36 months during two 1-hour sessions in their homes as they interacted with their mothers and their preschool-age siblings. Some sibling conflicts were marked by intense distress and anger, whereas others in-cluded the use of conciliation and justification. These differences were as-sociated with other differences in the siblings' interactions (Dunn & Munn, 1986). For example, intense negative affect displayed by toddlers during conflicts with their older siblings was correlated negatively with coopera-tive interactions with the older sibling ($r = -.30$) and with the older siblings' helping, sharing, and comforting of the younger one ($r = -.41$) and co-operating with him or her ($r = -.30$). These patterns of interaction are consistent with the notion that destructive conflict, defined in part by in-tense negative affect, undermines sibling relationships.

Other early sibling conflicts appear more constructive. These investiga-tors found that some toddlers and preschoolers attempt to reconcile their conflicts with siblings and to justify their positions. These types of conflict behaviors were positively correlated with 24-month-olds' sharing, helping, and comforting of their older siblings ($r = .30$, $p < .05$). Similarly, preschoolers who engaged in proportionally more conciliations ($r = .42$, $p < .05$) and justifications ($r = .36$, $p < .05$) were likely to cooperate during pretend play with their 18-month-old younger siblings.

Both constructive and destructive encounters have been observed between older school-age and adolescent siblings. As part of a study of 9- to 15-year-old children from divorced, stepparent, and nondivorced families, Hetherington (1988) obtained parents' and children's reports of sibling relationships. Some siblings (22%) had hostile, alienated relationships characterized by high coercion and aggression as well as low warmth and communication – behaviors indicative of destructive conflicts. Siblings in these relationships reported actively avoiding each other. Other children (33% of the sample) had companionate-caring sibling relationships that were high on warmth and communication as well as moderately low on aggression and rivalry. Most importantly, the quality of the siblings' relationships was related to other aspects of the children's development. In contrast to those children with companionate-caring sibling relationships, siblings who had hostile and aggressive relationships evidenced more behavior problems, poorer peer relationships, and greater difficulties at school. An important issue not resolved in this instance is the extent to which positive child outcomes are the direct or indirect result of the children's sibling relationships. One research task, now, is to determine whether siblings' constructive conflict resolutions contribute to successful peer interactions and academic achievement or if the associations are the result of other "third" variables.

Conflicts between siblings may also be important because they provide a mechanism by which children can differentiate themselves from other members of their family (Shantz & Hobart, 1989). If sibling conflicts facilitate the development of individuation, then it becomes important to consider what happens when conflict is completely absent from sibling interactions. Hetherington (1988) observed that about 10% of the children studied did not appear to have conflicts with siblings. These siblings spent most of their time together, sought each other's advice and support, and were fiercely protective of each other. They were not, however, concerned about or sensitive to others, either peers or adults, tending to be neglected by other children and to lack affectionate and caring relationships with adults. These results suggest that these children have pathologically intense, symbiotic, and restrictive sibling relationships. Others have also identified the absence of sibling conflict as indicative of problematic development (Bank & Kahn, 1982; Schave & Ciriello, 1983). Whether the absence of conflict contributes to problematic relationships or is simply a symptom of other problems has not been determined.

Regardless, these studies argue for the importance of considering both the quality and quantity of sibling conflicts in relation to developmental outcomes. In the following section, we examine sibling conflicts normatively from infancy through adolescence. A central issue is whether there are general developmental changes in the frequency, organization, and topics of conflicts between siblings. These normative patterns then provide a framework for assessing and understanding the considerable variations existing among sibling conflicts.

Sibling conflicts: Normative patterns

Early sibling conflicts

Newborns are not capable of mutual opposition with their older siblings. They do not have fights, and they cannot take toys from their older brothers and sisters. But babies are in opposition with their older siblings in one way: They require considerable maternal attention. Thus, children may feel themselves to be in opposition with their infant siblings, even if the babies do not feel similarly (Vandell, 1987). Older children manifest this opposition through increased behavior problems related to sleeping, eating, and temper tantrums as well as frequent confrontational behaviors with their mothers, especially when mothers are with siblings. Dunn and Kendrick (1982) found that children were three times more likely to do something deliberately "naughty" when their mothers were caring for their infant siblings as opposed to when the mothers were not involved with the babies. Such naughtiness is the epitome of what is meant by sibling *rivalry*, a term derived from the Latin *rivalis* meaning "having rights to the same stream."

Over the course of the first year, as babies become capable of manipulating objects and moving about their homes, they are perceived by their older siblings as becoming more directly oppositional. When preschoolers were interviewed, for example, only 5% reported that their newborn siblings interfered with their ability to play freely, whereas 50% considered 8-month-olds and 85% considered 12-month-olds as interfering with their toys and play abilities (Stewart, Mobley, Van Tuyl, & Salvador, 1987).

When one examines the behavior of infants toward their siblings, these reports are supported. From the first to the second year, infants become more assertive with their older siblings and conflicts increase. In one longitudinal study of early mother–child and sibling interaction, Dunn and Kendrick (1981a, 1981b) observed 40 families shortly after the second child's birth, again when the second child was 8 months old, and finally when the second child was 14 months old. During these home observations, the approaches of the 8-month-olds to their older siblings were overwhelmingly friendly (on average, 15 positive overtures vs. 2 hostile overtures within one thousand 10-second periods). By 14 months, however, toddlers directed a higher proportion of negative overtures to their older siblings (10 negative vs. 20 positive overtures). Parallel changes were observed among the older siblings: Whereas 30% of the overtures made by the preschoolers to their 8-month-old siblings were negative or hostile, this figure increased to 44% of the overtures made to the 14-month-old siblings.

Early sibling conflicts often revolve around toys and objects (Abramovitch, Corter, & Lando, 1979; Dunn & Munn, 1985b; Lamb, 1978). The typical pattern is for older children to try to take toys from their infant siblings who then submit to the older children's demands. By the second year, however, toddlers begin actively resisting the older siblings' attempts to control resources. These active oppositions result in considerable conflict during the second half of the second year. In their longitudinal study of 43 families observed when the younger siblings were 18 and 24 months old, Dunn and Munn (1985b; 1986) recorded an average of eight sibling conflicts per hour. Parallelling Dunn and Kendrick's observations during the first half of the second year, these conflicts involved issues of positive justice and the equal distribution of goods. Or, put another way, the toddlers struggled with their older siblings over objects and toys. Similar types of conflicts have been recorded between toddler twins. In Wilson's (1987) observations of 32 sets of twins at 18 and 24 months of age, the single most common shared meaning was "struggle over objects." And the twins demonstrated another related theme as well: They tussled over their mothers.

Qualitative changes occur in sibling conflicts between 18 and 24 months. Dunn and Munn (1985b) observed that almost half of their 2-year-olds teased their older siblings. Over one third explicitly referred to social rules and almost one quarter tried to reconcile. These relatively sophisticated examples of social understanding were less apparent in 18-month-olds. Interestingly, 2-year-olds in Kenya (Harkness & Super, 1985) demonstrate behaviors similar to the English 2-year-olds observed by Dunn and Munn. During conflicts, they were observed to deny their own misdeeds, blame their siblings, and draw their mothers' attention to their siblings' misdeeds. Dunn (1988; Dunn & Slomkowski, this volume) argues that these types of cognitively sophisticated behaviors during conflict provide a context in which children can both demonstrate and develop social understanding.

Developmental changes in toddlers' emotions during their sibling conflicts suggest an increasing potential for conflicts to become constructive. At age 18 months, Dunn and Munn (1987) observed that toddlers were distressed during 25% of their disputes with older siblings. By age 24 months, intense distress occurred in about 16% of the children's disputes with siblings. By age 36 months, only 9% of the disputes were accompanied by distress. Other changes occurring between ages 24 and 36 months also point to conflicts becoming more constructive. Sibling conflicts become more verbal, and children increasingly try to justify their actions. These justifications focus on the children's own feelings and wishes, but they also refer to social rules and material consequences.

Nevertheless, to portray young siblings' quarrels as virtuoso performances demonstrating sophisticated logic would be erroneous. Phinney (1985) observed that many conflicts between preschool-age siblings are relatively simple exchanges consisting of simple assertions that are not amicably resolved. Indeed, 70% of the quarrels of 5-year-olds observed by this investigator consisted of simple assertions as opposed to elaborated arguments composed of rationales and justifications. These simple assertions usually elicited simple responses from the partner, thereby resulting in chains of simple claims. In comparison with quarrels between friends, quarrels between siblings were more likely to be chains of these simple assertions. Preschool friends conducted more elaborated arguments than children and their siblings.

Even as there are developmental changes in sibling conflicts during the first 5 years of age, other aspects of early sibling conflicts appear to be stable. Although the proportion of conflicts involving distress was observed to decline, there appears to be no decline in the proportion of conflicts involving intense anger. Preschoolers display intense anger in about 10% of their disputes with siblings, a proportion comparable to that observed between younger siblings (Dunn & Kendrick, 1981b; Dunn & Munn, 1987). The topics of the sibling quarrels also remain the same. Like toddler siblings, conflicts between preschool-age siblings center on struggles over objects and possessions (Dunn & Munn, 1987; Steinmetz, 1977). Fully 50% of the preschooler conflicts reported by Dunn and Munn (1987) revolved around rights, possessions, and property. Another similarity is that both toddler-age and preschool-age siblings' conflicts focus on social intrusiveness, personal space violations, and family rules.

Conflicts during middle childhood

During middle childhood, conflicts with siblings remain a salient part of children's everyday lives. When Furman and Buhrmester (1985b) asked fifth and sixth graders about their social networks, the children cited conflict as being more important to their relationships with siblings than to their relationships with parents, teachers, or friends. Although sibling conflicts remain salient events for children, the frequency of these conflicts actually appears to decrease from preschool- to school-age periods. Based on interviews with 62 sibling pairs, McHale and Gamble (1989) report between one and two "serious" conflicts per day in contrast to Dunn and Munn's (1987) observations of about eight disputes an hour between preschool-age siblings. Even if more mundane conflicts between school-age siblings are considered, the sheer frequency of conflicts still seems to decline. The 149 fourth and fifth graders interviewed by Prochaska and Prochaska (1985) reported between four and seven conflicts per day. The average duration of these fights was about 8 minutes, with reported "bad" feelings persisting another 6 minutes.

An important issue is the extent to which the decline in sibling conflicts reflects an overall decrease in siblings' interactions with one another. To address this possibility, Brody, Stoneman, MacKinnon, and MacKinnon (1985) observed preschool-age and school-age sibling pairs in their homes during 30 minutes of unstructured play. Both the proportions and frequencies of agonistic interactions were smaller between school-age than between preschool-age siblings.

Most conflicts between school-age siblings are verbal, but other tactics include physical force, bullying, harassing, and crying (Sutton-Smith & Rosenberg, 1970). In Steinmetz's (1977) survey of school-aged siblings, 68% reported physical aggression against a sibling during the previous year. School-age siblings report fighting for many reasons: getting even, controlling possessions and space (such as who gets to watch which TV show and who gets to sit where in the car), and teasing ("you 'love' Jenny") (Prochaska & Prochaska, 1985). The most common reasons children give for fighting, however, are their own "bad moods." Interestingly, these children rarely saw their fights as bids for parental attention.

With age, sibling conflicts increasingly reflect multiple layers of contention rather than a single cause. Bank and Kahn (1982) propose three such layers. On the surface is the immediate issue. Just below the surface is an unending struggle for status within the family. Beneath them both may be an undercurrent of resentment that is produced by years of conflict and rivalry. These multiple layers make it difficult for parents and the siblings themselves to know sometimes what conflicts and fights are actually about (see Garvey & Shantz, this volume).

School-age children's conflicts with siblings and friends have important similarities and differences. Conflicts between siblings are more common than those between friends (Abramovitch, Corter, Pepler, & Stanhope, 1986; Furman & Buhrmester, 1985b), but the eliciting circumstances are similar. Like siblings, school-age friends have conflicts involving taking toys, name calling, and hitting (Youniss & Volpe, 1978). Unlike school-age friends, whose conflicts show considerable give-and-take, siblings do not actively resolve their conflicts. Instead, siblings report simply withdrawing or ignoring one another (Sutton-Smith & Rosenberg, 1970). Withdrawing and ignoring also have long-term consequences. In one longitudinal study, Wilson (1987) observed that twins who were frequently in conflict as toddlers were more likely than those twins with a history of cooperative play to avoid interacting with each other as 5-year-olds.

Adolescent sibling conflicts

Sibling disputes during adolescence involve some of the same issues that characterize school-age sibling conflicts in middle childhood: control of the television, telephone, behavior, and personal possessions (Felson, 1983; Hobart, 1991; Laursen, 1989; Raffaelli, 1990). These disputes between adolescent siblings are quite different from the adolescents' conflicts with friends. Unlike siblings, friends quarrel over violations of trust and friendship, not control of resources.

　　Many sibling conflicts during early adolescence involve coercion (Felson, 1983; Hobart, 1991). Seventh graders report yelling, threatening, teasing, and name calling as well as physical force (Roscoe, Goodwin, & Kennedy, 1987). Over 60% of the adolescents interviewed by Steinmetz (1977) and Straus (1973) reported hitting a sibling during the previous year. Markers of constructive conflicts such as discussion, compromise, and verbal give-and-take are often absent from these disagreements. Only one quarter of the seventh graders interviewed by Felson (1983) reported resolving their conflicts with siblings in these ways. Whereas adolescent friends attempt overtly to repair their relationships, siblings usually ignore or withdraw from each other following their conflicts (Hobart, 1991; Montemayor & Hanson, 1985; Raffaelli, 1990; Roscoe et al., 1987).

　　Conflicts between adolescent siblings tend to be brief. Young adolescents report that 42% of their arguments with siblings are resolved within 5 minutes and that an additional 46% are resolved within 1 hour (Raffaelli, 1990). Although brief, these disagreements are often accompanied by intense affect. Only 13% of the young adolescents interviewed by Raffaelli (1990) said that they were indifferent during sibling disagreements, while over two thirds reported anger. Twenty-one percent reported being unhappy during sibling conflicts. These patterns of behavior (intense negative affect, high coercion, minimal compromise) are consistent with the argument that a residual core of destructive conflicts exists between many young adolescent siblings.

By middle and late adolescence, disagreements between siblings are relatively rare. When Laursen (1989) questioned 742 high school students, they reported, on average, less than one disagreement with a sibling in one day's time. In contrast, the students reported 2.4 disagreements with their mothers, although free time spent with mother and siblings during the day were comparable (about 80 minutes). In comparison to their disputes with friends or romantic partners, conflicts with siblings were (a) affectively intense and (b) tended to end with simple disengagements and nonresolution – events that are not conducive to psychological growth.

Summary

Observations of sibling conflicts from the second year through adolescence suggest remarkable consistencies. Who is to control resources and possessions is a salient issue – one that is apparent at every age surveyed. Other conflicts focus on rights and responsibilities within the family. Intense affect characterizes a substantial number of conflicts with siblings, regardless of the siblings' ages. Conflicts with siblings are emotionally charged events from early childhood through adolescence. At the same time, important developmental changes occur: most notably, the overall frequency of sibling conflicts decreases. Social cognitive skills, the potential for sophisticated logic, social problem solving, and compromise increase. These developments, however, are sometimes not realized because siblings tend to withdraw from conflicts rather than seek resolutions.

Origins of sibling conflicts

In addition to understanding normative patterns, it is important to note that there are substantial variations in the quantity and quality of sibling conflicts. Some siblings rarely fight, while others fight almost all the time. Some siblings have minor disagreements, while others have physically or emotionally damaging altercations. A critical issue for parents, clinicians, and researchers is the source of these variations. Two different sources are portrayed in the literature. First, sibling conflicts are believed to be based in children's relationships with their parents, especially their mothers. Implicit in this view is a belief that, if parents acted differently, siblings would fight less. Second, sibling conflicts are thought to be outgrowths of the characteristics of individual children and their relationships with each other. Thus, individual characteristics such as temperament and gender as well as dyadic concordances are seen as affecting the quality and quantity of conflict. Both views of the origins of sibling conflict are explored in the following sections.

Parents as sources of sibling conflict

The belief that sibling conflict is rooted in children's relationships with their mothers is suggested by several theories. Freud (1916–1917), for example, argued that "the motives for these [violent conflicts] are rivalry for parental love, for common possessions, for living space" (p. 205). Within most psychoanalytic theories, conflicts between siblings are seen as emerging in reaction to parents' failures to meet individual children's needs for love. Equity theory (Adams, 1965), in contrast, leads one to focus on the relative amounts of attention and love that siblings receive from their parents as sources of conflict. In this case, it is not the child's absolute need for parental attention but how much attention the child gets vis-à-vis the sibling that is important. Social learning theory offers yet another perspective on parental contributions to sibling conflict. Parents can be viewed as models and reinforcers of their children's prosocial and antisocial interactions with siblings (Brody, Stoneman, & Burke, 1987a; Bryant & Crockenberg, 1980; Patterson, 1980). From these diverse theoretical perspectives, then, various processes and mechanisms can be identified through which parents influence their children's conflicts with one another. These processes are (a) differential treatment, (b) inadequate parental attention, (c) the emotional climate of the family, (d) parental modeling and reinforcement, and (e) reasoning.

Differential treatment. A recurring theme in the literature is that differential parental treatment increases conflicts between siblings (Bank & Kahn, 1982; Brody, Stoneman, & Burke, 1987b; Stocker, Dunn, & Plomin, 1989). Differential treatment can take many forms: One child may receive parental affection while the other child is ignored or chastised; one child may receive privileges or possessions while another does not.

Parents, though, are faced with a dilemma. Some differential treatment is appropriate and inevitable. Siblings are usually at different points in their development. It is neither feasible nor desirable for a parent to treat an infant and preschooler the same. Likewise, expectations and privileges for school-age children and adolescents necessarily must vary. Differential treatment also is elicited by the children's behaviors and abilities (Scarr & McCartney, 1983). For example, temperamentally difficult children "pull" different behaviors from their parents than do temperamentally easy children (Webster-Stratton & Eyberg, 1982), and children who can sustain attention for long periods elicit different parental behaviors than do more distractable children (Landry & Chapieski, 1990).

These inevitabilities lead some authors (Faber & Mazlish, 1987; Katz,

1981) to recommend that parents treat their children "fairly" rather than equally. But this recommendation has its own problem, namely, determining what is fair. Parents typically intervene in the name of fairness but are actually more likely to intervene when (a) one of the parties is an infant (Dunn & Kendrick, 1982), (b) age differences between the children is considerable (Raffaelli, 1990), or (c) physical aggression is involved (Steinmetz, 1977). Parents try especially to keep one child (typically the younger one) from being victimized by the other. Nevertheless, although parental interventions may be attempts to make things fair, they may be viewed by older siblings as evidence of parental favoritism (Furman & Buhrmester, 1985b). And, to the extent that children are concerned about parental favoritism and believe that it has occurred, more negative relationships between the siblings are recorded (McHale, Sloan, & Simeonsson, 1986).

Our own observations suggest that there may be perceptions of differential treatment even when more objective measurements fail to detect one. As part of a longitudinal study of twins (Vandell & Beckwith, 1989), one observer rated the mother's behavior with one twin, while another observer rated the mother's behavior with the other twin. In general, there was consistency in the degree to which mothers affirmed the twins' behaviors, taught the twins, and entertained them, but the observers' perceptions did not reflect this consistency. During the observations, raters came to identify with "their" twin, and both observers reported that they thought the mother preferred "the other" twin.

Thus far, the perception and actuality of differential treatment have been portrayed as inescapable. One insidious form of differential treatment, however, is avoidable. In these instances, one child is favored and loved, while the other one is viewed as "the bad seed." Mothers may reserve their prohibitions, reprimands, and disparagements for one child and praise for the other (Bryant & Crockenberg, 1980; Dunn & Munn, 1986). Adults' memories of such differential treatment as children are especially keen (Faber & Mazlish, 1987). A classic example is provided in Anna Bernays's memoir (1940) of her childhood as Sigmund Freud's younger sister. Bernays recalled how the family's physical and emotional resources were showered on her brother to the neglect of the other children.

The effects of differential treatment on both siblings have been documented. In one of the first systematic observational studies in the area, Bryant and Crockenberg (1980) observed 50 pairs of female school-age siblings with their mothers during 2-hour visits to a laboratory playroom. Mother and sibling behaviors during cooperative and competitive tasks were recorded. Some mothers were responsive to the needs of both daughters, whereas other mothers were responsive to neither daughter's needs. Still other mothers were responsive to one daugther and not the other. When mothers were responsive to both daughters' needs, the girls were likely to behave prosocially toward each other. When mothers met one daughter's needs and not the other's, both girls evidenced discomfort and were disparaging toward one another. Differential treatment, then, had negative effects on favored as well as unfavored children.

Other work also suggests that differential parental love and acceptance negatively affects both favored and nonfavored siblings. Stocker et al. (1989) observed 96 families that included young school-age children. During 2-hour home visits, the siblings were audiotaped and videotaped during structured probes and nonstructured interaction. Differential maternal attention and responsiveness were positively correlated with sibling competition, and differential maternal affection was related to attempts by the children to control one another. Hetherington's observations (1988) of adolescent siblings yielded similar results. When one sibling was treated with less warmth and affection as well as more coercion and punitiveness than the other, both the favored and nonfavored siblings were likely to behave in aggressive, rivalrous, and unaffectionate ways toward the other.

These results concerning differential treatment may mean that parental inequities result in increased conflict between the children. Another possibility, however, should also be considered. Differential treatment may be a result of sibling conflicts, as parents try to rectify what they perceive as inequities or victimization. Until longitudinal observations of differential treatment and conflict are obtained, this possibility cannot be ruled out.

Another form of differential treatment also should be considered within the context of longitudinal research. Differential treatment can refer to changes in parental behavior toward the same child over time. One example of such differential treatment is the change in mothers' behaviors toward their older children following the births of their second children. Mothers devote considerable time and energy to their newborn infants, and with attention to their older children often declining markedly following the second birth, prohibitions and admonitions increase (Dunn & Kendrick, 1980; Vandell, 1987). Based on observations made shortly before and after the birth of the second child, Dunn and Kendrick (1980), for example, noted significant decreases in the frequency with which mothers helped, demonstrated, and suggested activities to their firstborn children even as confrontations, prohibitions, and negative looks increased.

These changes in mother–child interaction may be linked to the quality of subsequent sibling interactions. In fact, Dunn and Kendrick (1981a) observed that children whose interactions with their mothers were particularly warm and involved prior to the birth of the sibling evidenced more negative interactions and conflicts with their 14-month-old siblings in comparison with children whose earlier interactions had been less warm and involved. Apparently, children who experienced a marked decline in the quality of their interactions with their mothers then reflected these changes in their interactions with their siblings.

Need for parental attention. Sibling conflict may also arise from inadequate or insufficient parental attention. In this case, conflicts are not viewed as the result of differential treatment and relative deprivation but derive from parents' absolute failures to meet children's emotional needs (Faber & Mazlish, 1987). Some of Bryant and Crockenberg's (1980) observations are consistent with this explanation. Disparagement and discomfort were significant issues between siblings not only when there was differential treatment, but also when mothers failed to meet either daughter's needs. When both daughters' needs were met, then sibling disparagement and discomfort were unlikely.

The best evidence that sibling conflict is linked to inadequate parental attention and warmth is found in work on infant attachment. In this regard, Bosso (1985) observed that toddlers and preschoolers who were insecurely attached to their mothers reacted more negatively to the birth of a sibling than did their securely attached counterparts. In comparison to securely attached children, insecurely attached children directed fewer positive and more negative behaviors to their newborn siblings. Similar results have been obtained with somewhat older children. In observations of 47 sibling pairs (Teti & Ablard, 1989), toddlers who were insecurely attached to their mothers were more likely than securely attached toddlers to aggress against their older siblings and their mothers. Furthermore, conflicts were most frequent when both siblings were insecurely attached to their mothers. Securely attached children, in contrast, were more likely to comfort and soothe their distressed younger siblings even as securely attached younger siblings were less likely to cry when left with their older siblings. Another study (Volling, 1990) suggests that linkages between infant–mother attachment and sibling relationships are long lived. Six-year-olds who had been insecurely attached to their mothers as 1-year-olds were more likely to have aggressive interactions with their younger siblings than were 6-year-olds who had secure attachment histories. Furthermore, children who had been insecurely attached to both mother and father displayed the most frequent and intense sibling conflicts. These observations also demonstrate that it is the quality of the children's interactions with their parents that mediates the associations between attachment and sibling conflict. When mothers were intrusive and insensitive with their children at age 3 years, conflicts between siblings were common at age 6 years. When children had playful interactions with their fathers at age 3 years, prosocial behaviors were observed between siblings 3 years later.

Emotional climate of the family. Another way in which parents influence their children's sibling relationships is through the general emotional climate created within the family. Components of this emotional climate include parents' psychological states and the parents' relationships with each other. When parents are depressed, unhappy, or fighting, the general emotional climate in the household is stressed, and such stressors affect the quality of children's relationships with their siblings.

Most commonly, measures of family stress and conflict are positively correlated with sibling conflict. Young school-age siblings (e.g., see Brody et al., 1987a) were videotaped in their homes as they played a board game and built with Lego blocks. Maternal depression and the quality of the marital relationship also were measured. Both marital quality and maternal depression were positively associated with sibling conflict during these tasks and negatively correlated with prosocial behavior. Rather than using each other for emotional support, the children's interactions with their siblings directly mirrored the negative spousal and parent–child interactions occurring in these families. MacKinnon (1989) obtained similar observations from 96 siblings from divorced and nondivorced families. Positive marital relationships were associated with positive sibling relationships, but conflicted relationships between the parents were related to conflict between siblings. Boys' relationships with their siblings appeared particularly vulnerable to the effects of divorce and marital hostility. In comparison to other mothers and children, divorced mothers reported their sons to be particularly negative, argumentative, and competitive with their siblings.

Sibling relationships are also affected by remarriage. In the first 2 years following remarriage, Hetherington (1988) observed high levels of conflicts between children and their mothers and between children and their stepfathers. These interactions are mirrored in the children's sibling relations. Unprovoked negative start-ups, reciprocated aggression, and reciprocated coercion were more common between siblings in stepfamilies than in the nondivorced families. Boys, in particular, engaged in aversive behaviors with their siblings and stepsiblings in the remarried families. Fortunately, these sibling relationships improved among longer remarried families; the children apparently adjusted to their new life situations.

Although family stress and conflict are commonly mirrored in sibling conflict, this is not always the case. Under some circumstances, family stress and conflict appear to increase closeness, cooperation, and protection (Bank & Kahn, 1982; Hetherington, 1988). In these families, conflicts between siblings occur, but they are resolved with understanding and forgiveness. Bank and Kahn have argued that these sibling relationships and constructive resolution of conflicts within the context of a generally poor family environment only occurs (a) if the children's early emotional needs were met, (b) if the emotional climate changed for the worse after the preschool years, and (c) if one of the siblings was not favored over the other.

Parental modeling and reinforcement of conflict. Social learning processes also help to explain how sibling conflicts emerge from children's interactions with their parents. For example, children who experience hostile or negative interactions with their parents may imitate these exchanges during their interactions with siblings (Kendrick & Dunn, 1983). Consistent with this view, sibling interactions between school-age children were actually observed to be more hostile and antagonistic when mothers reported themselves as using punitive disciplinary techniques than when they did not (Brody & Stoneman, 1986; Hetherington, 1988). Likewise, the frequency and intensity of mother–child conflicts are positively correlated with conflicts between siblings (Hetherington, 1988; Patterson, 1976; Volling, 1990).

As was the case with the reported associations between family stress and sibling conflicts, the associations between maternal disciplinary strategies and sibling conflict are actually concurrent correlations. Consequently, it is not possible to determine the direction of effects. Parents' coercive and punitive behaviors may elicit children's fights with siblings. Alternatively, parental coercion may be elicited by sibling conflicts. One longitudinal investigation suggests that maternal discipline may contribute to sibling difficulties. Kendrick and Dunn (1983) observed that maternal prohibitions when infants were 8 months old were positively correlated with hostile, unfriendly sibling relationships 6 months later with concurrent maternal behavior partialled out.

In addition to modeling conflict behaviors, parents may directly reinforce or encourage sibling conflict. By responding inconsistently to their children's conflicts with siblings, mothers may increase the occurrence of sibling conflict (Grossman, 1986). Consistent discipline, in contrast, seems to be associated with infrequent conflicts between adolescent siblings (Skinner, Elder, & Conger, 1990). These results are consistent with learning theory predictions that variable reinforcement schedules increase the likelihood and persistence of a behavior.

Reasoning. Dunn (1988) has been instrumental in describing yet another way in which mothers modulate and influence conflicts between their young children. Some mothers regularly refer to the feelings and needs of their children. They attempt to explain their younger children's behavior to the older siblings and suggest ways to conciliate conflicts. They talk about social and moral rules within the family. These maternal behaviors were positively related to the children's interactions with their siblings. For example, mothers who mediated conflicts of 18-month-old siblings by referring to rules and to children's feelings had children who showed mature conflict behaviors such as teasing and conciliating at 24 months of age (Dunn & Munn, 1986). Similarly, Howe and Ross (1990) found maternal references to infants' feelings to be positively associated with the occurrence of sibling play.

Parental reactions to sibling conflicts may foster the growth of social understanding in school-age and adolescent siblings as well. Bank and Kahn (1982) observed that by adopting consistent moral principles and communicating them clearly to quarreling siblings, parents minimize the likelihood of one sibling victimizing or abusing the other. At the same time, these investigators argued that parents must have a finely tuned sense of when not to intervene in sibling conflicts. Premature mediation of conflicts that children can resolve by themselves deprives them of the opportunity to learn how to solve problems and resolve conflicts.

Summary. Empirical studies support the folk wisdom that parents play an important role in mediating the quality of sibling relationships. Punitive parental actions and negative parent–child interaction are associated with high levels of sibling conflict. In contrast, when children's emotional needs are met by their parents and when there is no favored child in the family, sibling conflicts are minimized. When parents act as mediators of sibling conflicts by referring to moral principles as well as the children's feelings, young children engage in relatively mature forms of conflict, using justification and moral reasoning themselves. But parents must be sensitive in their interventions. Parental involvement in constructive sibling conflicts may deprive children of the opportunity to develop necessary social problem-solving skills.

Children themselves as sources of sibling conflict

Conflicts between siblings are not derived solely from the children's relationships with their parents. To understand their origins, we must turn to the characteristics of the children themselves for an explanation of why some children fight more than others. Variations in conflict appear to be related to children's individual characteristics as well as to characteristics of the sibling dyad. In this section, conflicts are related to factors such as the siblings' relative ages, age spacing, gender, and temperament. The effects of the match or mismatch between the siblings in terms of gender and temperament on the quality and quantity of conflicts are examined also.

Relative age of the siblings. Several observational studies reveal that sibling conflicts are influenced by the children's relative ages. Regardless of their absolute ages, the older of two siblings is more likely to be the aggressor, and the younger is more likely to be the recipient of the older child's aggression. In both home and laboratory observations, older siblings (preschoolers) were more likely to hit and to take toys from their toddler siblings, while the toddlers tended to watch and submit (Abramovitch et al., 1979; Lamb, 1978; Pepler, Abramovitch, & Corter, 1981). Observations and interviews of school-age children likewise show them being the aggressors during sibling conflicts, whereas their preschool-age siblings are more likely to comply (Berndt & Bulleit, 1985; Sutton-Smith & Rosenberg, 1970). Interviews with adolescents and college students describe a similar pattern in which the older of two siblings initiates more conflicts than the younger one (Felson, 1983).

But it would be inaccurate to portray younger siblings as being solely at the mercy of their older brothers and sisters. Younger siblings develop their own strategies for controlling conflicts. Fifth and sixth graders interviewed by Sutton-Smith and Rosenberg (1970), for example, reported that the younger of two siblings often resorted to crying, pouting, and seeking parental interventions "to get their way." Dunn and Munn (1985a) observed similar strategies among toddlers, who went to their mothers during 36% of their conflicts with older siblings. The mothers then usually supported the toddlers. Whether this maternal support subsequently leads to further sibling conflict, however, is a question for future research.

Age spacing. In a review published in *Child Development*, Dunn (1983) argued that the age spacing between siblings is a less important determinant of the quality of early sibling relationships than either differential maternal treatment or the quality of the mother–child relationship. Importantly, however, Dunn did not conclude that age spacing is unimportant, only that parental factors are more important. In fact, there is evidence that the quality and quantity of sibling interactions (including conflicts) are related to the gap in sibling ages, especially if sufficiently wide age spacings are contrasted. For example, children who are more than 6 years older than their infant siblings evidence minimal negative reactions to the younger child's birth (Henchie, 1963; Nadelman & Begun, 1982). Similarly, observations and interviews with school-age and adolescent siblings indicate that siblings less than 2 years apart have more quarrels than those who are more than 4 years apart (Felson, 1983; Furman & Buhrmester, 1985a; Koch, 1960; Minnett, Vandell, & Santrock, 1983; Raffaelli, 1990). In addition, closely spaced siblings are more likely to use physical aggression, whereas verbal aggression is more common between wider spaced siblings (Felson, 1983; Raffaelli, 1990).

Child gender. Gender differences are also apparent. Boys have more disagreements with their siblings than do girls. Several researchers (Brody et al., 1985; Hetherington, 1988; Miller, Danaher, & Forbes, 1986; Volling, 1990) have noted that boys are more likely than girls to direct hostile acts toward their siblings in the form of threats, physical force, and negative start-ups.

Given the higher incidence of negative behaviors from boys, one might predict the highest levels of sibling conflict between brothers. This is not the case. Studies examining relations between the sexual composition of the sibling dyads and conflict report that opposite-sex siblings actually have more conflicts than do same-sex ones (Dunn & Kendrick, 1981b; Patterson & Cobb, 1971; Pepler et al., 1981; Skinner et al., 1990). Conflicts are especially common between older brothers and their younger sisters. Interestingly, during these conflicts, girls are not simply helpless victims. For example, Patterson and Cobb (1971) described a pattern in which older brothers aggress against their younger sisters who act as agents provocateurs.

Child temperament. Another factor contributing to sibling conflicts is child temperament. During videotaped observations of same–sex sibling pairs, Brody Stoneman, and Burke (1987b) found that physically active, emotionally intense, and nonpersistent children (as determined by maternal questionnaires) initiated more conflicts with their older siblings than did temperamentally easy children. Similarly, Stocker et al. (1989) found that younger siblings who were emotionally intense were more competitive with their older siblings than were less emotionally intense children. Agonistic behaviors are related to the older siblings' temperament as well (Brody et al., 1987b; Munn & Dunn, 1989). Older siblings who were emotionally intense as well as active engaged in more conflicts than did those older siblings who were less intense and active. In contrast, shyness in the older siblings predicted less frequent sibling conflicts (Stocker et al., 1989). The match between siblings' temperament must also be considered. Using their home observations, Munn and Dunn (1989) found conflicts were greater at both 24 and 36 months of age when siblings were mismatched in terms of their adaptability, negative mood, and emotional intensity than where they were better matched.

In these cross-sectional studies, it is impossible to determine whether conflicts between siblings are an outgrowth of children's difficult temperaments or if experiencing frequent conflicts makes children difficult. One longitudinal study (Volling, 1990) suggests the former. Children who were perceived as fussy and difficult by their mothers at age 9 months had more conflicts with their siblings at age 5 years than did children who were initially seen as temperamentally easier. Otherwise, causal direction is difficult to infer from the existing data.

Handicapped siblings. Because handicapped children require substantial parental attention and energy, concern has been expressed about the development of nonhandicapped children in the family. The research reviewed in this chapter on parental contributions to sibling conflict would suggest varying patterns of conflict depending on familial reactions to the handicapping condition. Research on the effects of differential treatment and inadequate parental attention would predict substantial sibling conflicts if children perceive parental favoritism and inequitable treatment in favor of their handicapped siblings. Alternatively, sibling conflicts might be less common in families with a handicapped child if the presence of a handicap provides a context for talking about the feelings and needs of others or if the handicapped siblings are perceived by the nonhandicapped children as less of a threat to dominance.

Research consistent with each of these predictions has been reported. McHale et al. (1986) observed negative sibling interactions when children reported being bothered by parental favoritism of their handicapped siblings. More commonly, however, fewer conflicts and less physical aggression are reported to occur between handicapped children and their nonhandicapped siblings than in families in which neither child is handicapped (McHale & Gamble, 1989). Children report that they get along well with and enjoy helping their handicapped siblings. The reduced conflicts in these families, however, may come about partly because handicapped siblings are more likely to submit to the demands of their nonhandicapped siblings and are less likely to counterattack than a nonhandicapped child would (Abramovitch, Stanhope, Pepler, & Corter, 1987). Disparities in abilities may also be important. For example, when handicapped children are not very skilled, relatively few conflicts with nonhandicapped siblings ensue (McHale & Gamble, 1989).

Interaction history. Sibling conflicts also reflect the children's prior histories of interacting with each other. In microanalytic observations of aggressive boys and their families, for example, Patterson and Cobb (1971) found that sibling conflicts follow predictable patterns. "Hits" from one child were the most likely elicitor of "hits" from the sibling. Coercive cycles were created in which hostile behaviors escalated into even greater hostilities. In the same vein and based on observations of families during their evening meals, Vuchinich (1987) reported that behaviors tend to be returned in kind. Most often, hostile behaviors are the result of ongoing conflicts. Dunn and Kendrick's observations (1981a) suggest that even young infants' negative behaviors are correlated with their older siblings' negative behaviors ($r = .58$ at age 8 months and $r = .54$ at age 14 months).

In addition to reflecting ongoing social interactions, sibling conflicts can reflect long-term family histories. Anecdotal reports from adult siblings reveal that difficult and conflictual relationships initiated during childhood continue in the siblings' relationships as adults (Faber & Mazlish, 1987). Systematic studies reveal similar stabilities. For example, Abramovitch et al. (1987) reported a significant correlation ($r = .72$) over a 1-year period in the frequencies of siblings' agonistic behaviors. Sibling dyads who frequently initiated agonistic interactions during two 1-hour visits frequently engaged in agonistic interactions 1 year later. Stillwell and Dunn (1985) have reported other significant relations over time. Positive approaches by older siblings during observations when the younger children were 14 months old were negatively correlated with maternal reports of sibling aggression at age 6 years ($r = -.55$). And, in Wilson's longitudinal observations (1987), toddler twins who tussled over objects and mothers to the exclusion of positive exchanges also were likely to ignore each other during free play as 5-year-olds.

Situational context. Finally, it appears that the quality and quantity of sibling conflicts vary as a function of the situational context. Conflicts are more common when siblings are in competitive situations such as board games or sports and less common when siblings are watching TV or doing crafts (Brody & Stoneman, 1986). Also, as parents who have traveled by car on long vacations will attest, siblings are likely to fight when they are bored or have nothing else to do (Prochaska & Prochaska, 1985).

Summary. Significant variations in the quality and quantity of sibling conflicts are associated with the characteristics of the children such as their relative ages, age spacing, gender, handicapping condition, and temperament. In addition, the children's histories of interaction and the specific situational context are related to differences in the frequency and intensity of their disagreements.

Intervention strategies for sibling conflict

Parents are bothered by and worry about sibling conflicts. Bookstores and libraries are filled with self-help manuals suggesting ways to reduce the intensity and frequency of sibling conflicts. In the same vein, parent educators (Calladine, 1983; Jalongo, 1985) note that "Dealing with Sibling Conflict" is one of their most requested classes. The literature reviewed in this chapter suggests that, prior to instigating any intervention, it is important for parents to distinguish between constructive and destructive conflicts.

Some sibling conflicts are not aggressive; affective intensity is low. Conciliation and negotiation strategies are employed. Parents probably should ignore these sibling disagreements (Bank & Kahn, 1982; Faber & Mazlish, 1987), because parental intervention can produce winners and losers, thereby increasing the likelihood of subsequent sibling quarrels (see Furman & McQuaid, this volume). Parental intervention in these disagreements also may deprive children of an opportunity to resolve their quarrels on their own (Bank & Kahn, 1982; Deutsch, 1973; Dunn, 1988; Shantz & Hobart, 1989).

For those conflicts characterized by physical or verbal abuse, intense negative affect, and victimization, however, more active parental interventions are recommended. What form, though, should this intervention take? Some interventions within the literature take a proactive stance and are grounded in general advice about parenting (Katz, 1981). These general parenting interventions are seen as affecting children's overall development, including interactions with siblings. Thus, parents are urged to spend "quality" time alone with each child, to avoid comparing siblings, to express pride in each child's accomplishments, and to treat each child uniquely (Faber & Mazlish, 1987; Jalongo, 1985; Katz, 1981).

In addition, specific parental interventions designed to reduce destructive sibling conflicts have been proposed. Drawing on Haim Ginott's work, Faber and Mazlish (1987) outlined four steps for parents to follow when intervening in sibling conflict: (a) Acknowledge children's feelings, (b) reflect each child's point of view, (c) describe the problem, and (d) leave the room to allow the children to resolve the problem. Parents are advised not to lecture, nag, or become emotionally involved in the conflicts. Adopting a similar set of recommendations, Calladine (1983) has suggested drawing up contracts and taking away privileges as ways of dealing with persistent conflicts.

Interestingly, school-age children's suggestions for lessening conflicts between siblings both agree and disagree with these recommendations (Prochaska & Prochaska, 1985). When asked what parents can do to minimize sibling conflicts, the children outlined a three-pronged behavioral approach in which (a) treats and rewards would be given for getting along, (b) discipline would be used for fighting, and (c) children would be kept busy doing "fun things." According to the children, their sibling conflicts were likely to continue or escalate if parents either ignored or joined in the conflicts.

Although these recommendations are grounded in empirical research linking parent–child and sibling relationships described earlier in this chapter, there is little empirical research investigating the effectiveness of these specific recommendations as intervention programs. That is, we do not know if changes in the intensity or frequency of destructive sibling conflicts occur as a result of compliance with any or all of these recommendations. There is, however, some support for the recommendations. Olson and Roberts (1987) contrasted the effectiveness of two interventions designed for clinic-referred aggressive siblings. Training for all families included parent education, and all children participated in role play, verbal rehearsal, and social skills training centered on conflict issues. In addition, time-out following conflict was used with one group. Decreases in sibling aggression occurred when time-out was added to the other interventions but not with the other interventions alone. Others (see Furman & McQuaid, this volume) have also demonstrated that reinforcing children for cooperative play and sending them to time-out for fighting reduce the amount of sibling conflict.

Conclusion

Conflicts with siblings are a fact of life for most children. Children are freer to disagree with siblings than with other people in their social networks. Friendships, for example, can be terminated by repeated disagreements; conflicts with parents are usually unwinnable. But children can disagree with their siblings with some impunity. These conflicts often grow out of the children's need to share common resources including household possessions as well as the love and attention of their parents. The conflicts reflect the children's immediate emotional states as well as their needs to establish separate and individual identities within the family.

Unfortunately, some sibling conflicts are physically or emotionally destructive. They hamper children's relationships with their siblings as well as relationships with others. But other conflicts are contexts for psychological growth and emotional expressions. They allow children an opportunity to develop an understanding of others' wishes, needs, and desires. During these conflicts, children can learn ways of opposing, disagreeing, compromising, and conciliating within the safety of one of their most durable social relationships – the sibling relationship.

Substantial evidence shows that parents play an important role in determining the quality and quantity of sibling conflicts. Parental favoritism, differential treatment, and family stress are associated with destructive conflicts marked by hostility and anger between siblings. Insecure mother–child attachment relationships and punitive disciplinary methods also are linked to destructive sibling conflicts. Reasoning and discussions about feelings and family rules, in contrast, are associated with constructiveness in sibling conflicts and the occurrence of justification and conciliation.

Prior to intervening in sibling conflicts, parents and others must consider the nature of the conflict. Intervention in constructive conflicts may deprive siblings of an opportunity to develop problem-solving skills. It also may increase the likelihood of subsequent conflicts because it may set up situations of winners and losers. Intervening in more intense siblings conflicts, however, is appropriate. Various strategies, including social problem-solving instruction, time-out, and deprivation of privileges have been proposed.

References

Abramovitch, K., Corter, C., & Lando, B. (1979). Sibling interactions in the home. *Child Development, 50,* 997–1003.

Abramovitch, K., Corter, C., Pepler, D. J., & Stanhope, L. (1986). Sibling and peer interaction: A final follow-up and a comparison. *Child Development, 57,* 217–229.

Abramovitch, K., Stanhope, L., Pepler, D., & Corter, C. (1987). The influence of Down's syndrome in sibling interaction. *Journal of Child Psychology and Psychiatry, 28,* 865–879.

Adams, J. S. (1965). Inequity in social exchange. In L. Berkowitz (Ed.), *Advances in experimental social psychology* (Vol. 2). New York: Academic Press.

Bank, S. P., & Kahn, M. D. (1982). *The sibling bond.* New York: Basic.

Bernays, A. (1940). My brother Sigmund Freud. *American Mercury* (November), 334–340.

Berndt, T. J., & Bulleit, T. N. (1985). Effects of sibling relationships on preschoolers' behavior at home and at school. *Developmental Psychology, 21,* 761–767.

Bosso, R. (1985). Attachment quality and sibling relations: Responses of anxiously attached/avoidant and securely attached 18- to 32-month-old first borns toward their second born siblings. *Dissertation Abstract International, 47,* 1293B.

Brody, G. H., & Stoneman, Z. (1986). Contributions of maternal child-rearing practices and play contexts to sibling interactions. *Journal of Applied Developmental Psychology, 7,* 225–236.

Brody, G., Stoneman, Z., & Burke, M. (1987a). Family system and individual child correlates of sibling behavior. *American Journal of Orthopsychiatry, 57,* 561–569.

Brody, G., Stoneman, Z., & Burke, M. (1987b). Child temperament, maternal differential behavior, and sibling relationships. *Developmental Psychology, 23,* 354–362.

Brody, G. H., Stoneman, Z., MacKinnon, C. E., & MacKinnon, R. (1985). Role relationships and behaviors between preschool-aged and school-aged sibling pairs. *Developmental Psychology, 21*, 124–129.

Bryant, B., & Crockenberg, S. (1980). Correlates and dimensions of prosocial behavior: A study of female siblings with their mothers. *Child Development, 51*, 529–544.

Calladine, C. E. (1983). Sibling rivalry: A parent education perspective. *Child Welfare, 62*, 421–427.

Cicirelli, V. G. (1982). Sibling influences throughout the lifespan. In M. E. Lamb & B. Sutton-Smith (Eds.), *Sibling relationships: Their nature and significance across the lifespan.* Hillsdale, NJ: Erlbaum.

Coser, L. A. (1967). *Continuities in the study of social conflict.* New York: Free Press.

Deutsch, M. (1973). *The resolution of conflict.* New Haven, CT: Yale University Press.

Dunn, J. (1983). Sibling relationships in early childhood. *Child Development, 54*, 787–811.

Dunn, J. (1988). *The beginnings of social understanding.* Cambridge, MA: Harvard University Press.

Dunn, J., & Kendrick, C. (1980). Caring for a second baby: Effects on interaction between mother and firstborn. *Developmental Psychology, 16*, 303–311.

Dunn, J., & Kendrick, C. (1981a). Interactions between young siblings: Associations with the interactions between mother and first born child. *Developmental Psychology, 17*, 336–343.

Dunn, J. & Kendrick, C. (1981b). Social behavior of young siblings in the family context: Differences between same sex and different sex dyads. *Child Development, 52*, 1265–1273.

Dunn, J., & Kendrick, C. (1982). *Siblings: Love, envy, and understanding.* Cambridge, MA: Harvard University Press.

Dunn, J., & Munn, P. (1985a). Becoming a family member: Family conflict and the development of social understanding. *Child Development, 56*, 480–492.

Dunn, J., & Munn, P. (1985b). Siblings and the development of prosocial behavior. *International Journal of Behavioral Development, 9*, 265–284.

Dunn, J., & Munn, P. (1986). Sibling quarrels and maternal intervention: Individual differences in understanding and aggression. *Journal of Child Psychology and Psychiatry, 27*, 583–595.

Dunn, J., & Munn, P. (1987). Development of justifications in disputes with mother and sibling. *Developmental Psychology, 23*, 791–798.

Faber, A., & Mazlish, E. (1987). *Siblings without rivalry.* New York: Norton.

Felson, R. B. (1983). Aggression and violence between siblings. *Social Psychology Quarterly, 46*, 271–285.

Freud, S. (1916–1917). Introductory lectures on psycho-analysis. Translated and edited by J. Strachey (1977). New York: Liveright.

Furman, W., & Buhrmester, D. (1985a). Children's perceptions of the qualities of sibling relationships. *Child Development, 56*, 448–461.

Furman, W., & Buhrmester, D. (1985b). Children's perception of the personal relationships in their social networks. *Developmental Psychology, 21*, 1016–1024.

Gottman, J. M. (1979). *Marital interaction: Experimental investigations.* New York: Academic Press.

Grossman, K. E. (1986). From ideographic approaches to nomothetic hypotheses: Stern, Allport, and the biology of knowledge, exemplified by an exploration of sibling relationships. In J. Valsiner (Ed.), *The individual subject and scientific psychology.* New York: Plenum.

Harkness, S., & Super, C. M. (1985). Child–environment interaction in the socialization of affect. In M. Lewis & C. Saarni (Eds.), *The socialization of emotion.* New York: Plenum.

Hartup, W. W., Laursen, B. (in press). Conflict and context in peer relations. In C. Hart (Ed.) *Children on playgrounds: Research perspectives and applications.* Ithaca: SUNY Press.

Henchie, V. (1963). *Children's reactions to the birth of a new baby.* Unpublished master's thesis, Institute of Education, University of London.

Hetherington, E. M. (1988). Parents, children, siblings: Six years after divorce. In R. Hinde & J. Stevenson-Hinde (Eds.), *Relationships within families: Mutual influences.* New York: Oxford University Press.

Hobart, C. J. (1991, April). *Preadolescents' and adolescents' conflicts with siblings and friends.* Paper presented at the meeting of the Society for Research in Child Development, Seattle, WA.

Howe, N., & Ross, H. (1990). Socialization, perspective taking, and the sibling relationship. *Developmental Psychology, 26,* 160–165.

Jalongo, M. R. (1985). Siblings: Can they, will they ever get along? *PTA Today, 10,* 16–18.

Katz, L. (1981). Brotherhood/sisterhood begin at home: Notes on sibling rivalry. *Journal of the Canadian Association for Young Children, 2,* 20–22.

Kendrick, C., & Dunn, J. (1983). Sibling quarrels and maternal responses. *Developmental Psychology, 19,* 62–70.

Koch, H. (1960). The relation of certain formal attributes of siblings to attitudes held toward each other and toward their parents. *Monographs of the Society for Research in Child Development, 25*(4, Serial No. 78).

Lamb, M. E. (1978). Interactions between eighteen-month-olds and their preschool-aged siblings. *Child Development, 49,* 51–59.

Landry, S. H., & Chapieski, M. L. (1990). Joint attention of six-month-old Down syndrome and preterm infants: Attention to toys and mother. *American Journal of Mental Retardation, 94,* 488–498.

Laursen, B. (1989, April). *Conflict and social interaction in adolescent relationships.* Paper presented at the meeting of the Society for Research in Child Development, Kansas City, MO.

MacKinnon, C. E. (1989). An observational investigation of sibling interactions in married and divorced families. *Developmental Psychology, 25,* 36–44.

McHale, S. M., & Gamble, W. C. (1989). Sibling relationships of children with disabled and nondisabled brothers and sisters. *Developmental Psychology, 25,* 421–429.

McHale, S. M., Sloan, J., & Simeonsson, R. J. (1986). Sibling relationships of children with autistic, mentally retarded, and nonhandicapped brothers and sisters. *Journal of Autism and Developmental Disorders, 16,* 399–413.

Miller, P. M., Danaher, D. L., & Forbes, D. (1986). Sex related strategies for coping with interpersonal conflict in children aged five and seven. *Developmental Psychology, 22,* 543–548.

Minnett, A. M., Vandell, D. L., & Santrock, J. W. (1983). The effects of sibling status on sibling interaction: Influence of birth order, age spacing, sex of child, and sex of sibling. *Child Development, 54,* 1064–1072.

Montemayor, R., & Hanson, E. (1985). A naturalistic view of conflict between adolescents and their parents and siblings. *Journal of Early Adolescence, 5,* 23–30.

Munn, P., & Dunn, J. (1989). Temperament and the developing relationship between siblings. *International Journal of Behavioral Development, 12,* 433–451.

Nadelman, L., & Begun, A. (1982). The effect of the newborn on the older sibling: Mothers' questionnaires. In M. E. Lamb & B. Sutton-Smith (Eds.), *Sibling relationships: Their nature and significance across the lifespan.* Hillsdale, NJ: Erlbaum.

Olson, R. L., & Roberts, M. W. (1987). Alternative treatments for sibling aggression. *Behavior Therapy, 18,* 243–250.

Patterson, G. R. (1976). The aggressive child: Victim and architect of a coercive system. In L. A. Hamerlynck, L. C. Handy, & E. J. Mash (Eds.), *Behavior modification and families: Vol. 1. Theory and research.* New York: Brunner/Mazel.

Patterson, G. R. (1980). Mothers: The unacknowledged victims. *Monographs of the Society for Research in Child Development, 45*(5, Serial No. 186).

Patterson, G. R., & Cobb, J. A. (1971). A dyadic analysis of "aggressive" behaviors. In J. P. Hill (Ed.), *Minnesota symposia on child psychology* (Vol. 5). Minneapolis: University of Minnesota Press.

Pepler, D., Abramovitch, R., & Corter, C. (1981). Sibling interaction in the home: A longitudinal study. *Child Development, 52,* 1344–1347.

Phinney, J. S. (1985). The structure of 5-years-olds' verbal quarrels with peers and siblings. *The Journal of Genetic Psychology, 147,* 47–60.

Prochaska, J. M., & Prochaska, J. O. (1985). Children's views of the causes and cures of sibling rivalry. *Child Welfare, 64,* 427–433.

Raffaelli, M. (1990). *Sibling conflict in early adolescence.* Unpublished doctoral dissertation, University of Chicago.

Roscoe, B., Goodwin, M. P., & Kennedy, D. (1987). Sibling violence and agonistic interactions experienced by early adolescents. *Journal of Family Violence, 2,* 121–137.

Scarr, S., & McCartney, K. (1983). How people make their own environments: A theory of genotype-environment effects. *Child Development, 54,* 424–435.

Schave, B., & Ciriello, J. (1983). *Identity and intimacy in twins.* New York: Praeger.

Shantz, C. U. (1987). Conflicts between children. *Child Development, 58,* 283–305.

Shantz, C. U., & Hobart, C. J. (1989). Social conflict and development: Peers and siblings. In T. J. Berndt & G. W. Ladd (Eds.), *Peer relationships in child development.* New York: Wiley.

Skinner, M. L., Elder, G. H., Jr., & Conger, R. C. (1990, March). *Family predictors of sibling conflict.* Paper presented at the Conference on Human Development, Richmond, VA.

Steinmetz, S. K. (1977). The use of force for resolving family conflict: The training ground for abuse. *The Family Coordinator, 26,* 19–26.

Stewart, R. B., Mobley, L. A., Van Tuyl, S. S., & Salvador, M. A. (1987). The firstborn's adjustment to the birth of a sibling: A longitudinal assessment. *Child Development, 58,* 341–355.

Stillwell, R., & Dunn, J. (1985). Continuities in sibling relationships: Patterns of aggression and friendliness. *Journal of Child Psychology and Psychiatry, 26,* 627–637.

Stocker, C., Dunn, J., & Plomin, R. (1989). Sibling relationships: Links with child temperament, maternal behavior, and family structure. *Child Development, 60,* 715–727.

Straus, M. A. (1973). Leveling, civility, and violence in the family. *Journal of Marriage and the Family, 36,* 13–29.

Sutton-Smith, B., & Rosenberg, B. G. (1970). *The sibling.* New York: Holt, Rhinehart, & Winston.

Teti, D. M., & Ablard, K. E. (1989). Security of attachment and infant sibling relationships: A laboratory study. *Child Development, 60,* 1519–1528.

Vandell, D. L. (1987). Baby sister/baby brother: Reactions to the birth of a sibling and patterns of early sibling relations. In F. F. Schachter & R. K. Stone (Eds.), *Practical concerns about siblings: Bridging the research–practice gap.* New York: Haworth Press.

Vandell, D. L., & Beckwith, S. (1989, April). *Maternal styles of interaction with infant twins.* Paper presented at the meeting of the Society for Research in Child Development, Kansas City, MO.

Volling, B. L. (1990). *Mother–child and father–child relationships as contemporaneous correlates and developmental antecedents of sibling conflict and cooperation.* Unpublished doctoral dissertation, Pennsylvania State University, University Park.

Vuchinich, S. (1987). Starting and stopping spontaneous family conflicts. *Journal of Marriage and the Family, 49,* 591–601.

Webster-Stratton, C., & Eyberg, S. M. (1982). Child temperament: Relationship with child behavior problems and parent–child interactions. *Journal of Clinical Child Psychology,* *11*, 123–129.

Wilson, K. S. (1987). *Social interaction in twins: Relations between the second and fifth years of life.* Unpublished doctoral dissertation, University of Texas, Dallas.

Youniss, J., & Volpe, J. (1978). A relational analysis of children's friendships. In W. Damon (Ed.), *Social cognition: New directions for child development.* San Francisco: Jossey-Bass.

10 Family conflicts and their developmental implications: A conceptual analysis of meanings for the structure of relationships

Robert E. Emery

Family conflict may begin as a dispute between siblings, parents and children, spouses, or former spouses. The conflict may be confined to one of these dyads, or it may involve other family members. The content of family conflict ranges from siblings arguing over the relative size of two desserts to spouses debating whether or not to end their marriage. Family conflicts vary in emotional and physical intensity from mock disputes to extreme acts of violence. Finally, family conflict ranges in frequency from rare disagreements to near constant bickering.

The extreme variability in the potential participants, contents, intensity, and frequency of family conflicts greatly complicates the analysis of their developmental functions and effects. The complexity becomes overwhelming from a purely empirical and atheoretical perspective, yet the study of family conflict has been driven largely by empirical rather than theoretical rationales. This is particularly surprising, because conflict plays a central role in a number of theories of development (Shantz, 1987; Valsiner & Cairns, this volume).

The present chapter reflects the author's desire to promote more conceptualization in family conflict research. A complicated argument is presented here, but it leads to assertions that, correctly or incorrectly, greatly simplify the interpretation of some normative developmental functions of family conflict. Specifically, it is suggested that conflict serves the normative functions of testing (or asserting) and changing (or resisting change in) the structure of family relationships. Intimacy and power are argued to be the basic dimensions around which relationships are structured. Thus, dyadic family conflicts are held to be intimacy struggles or power struggles in terms of their *deep meaning*. Conceptualizing conflicts as power struggles or intimacy struggles leads to predictions about the content, intensity, and frequency of family conflicts during the course of development and especially during normative or nonnormative developmental transitions.

270

The search for simplicity in conceptualizing the normative functions of dyadic conflict is followed by an argument for complexity. It is suggested that triadic or systemic processes are essential to understanding family conflict. This is true for the analysis of conflict as a microsocial process and, more generally, for interpreting the deep meaning of alliances and loyalties in the structure of family relationships.

The greatest complexity comes from speculations about individual differences in the developmental effects of family conflict. When conflict results in the successful negotiation of a developmental transition, most of the effects on individuals are due to developmental change, not conflict. However, conflict seems to have powerful, often maladaptive, effects on individuals when it becomes an obstacle rather than a vehicle for change. In the final section of this chapter, some implications of the present analysis are drawn for research on individual differences as well as on normative development. Before addressing these broad issues, it is important to be clear about the present definition of conflict, especially within the family context.

Definition of conflict

Contemporary investigators commonly define "conflict" as goal incompatibility occurring between two or more individuals or groups (Fincham & Bradbury, in press; Shantz, 1987). According to some interpretations of this definition, conflict can exist in the absence of its expression. Two individuals who have opposing goals but who do not act on or express their opposition, nevertheless are considered to be in conflict. The definition of conflict as goal incompatibility also allows conflict to be one-sided. When one person views his or her goals as being in opposition to another's, conflict exists even if the second person does not share the perception (Fincham & Bradbury, in press).

A more restrictive definition of conflict lies behind the conceptualizations outlined in this chapter. *Conflict* is defined here as mutual opposition, the overt expression of differences between two or more individuals or groups. According to this definition, conflict must be expressed in order to be present, although both verbal and nonverbal (e.g., the "silent treatment") expressions of opposition qualify as conflict. The definition of conflict as opposition eliminates one-sided disputes. A confrontation by one individual does not constitute conflict unless it is opposed by someone else. That is, a conflict does not begin until two opponents "square off." What is most important about the definition of conflict as opposition is that it restricts the construct to being an interpersonal process. Although cognitive appraisals and especially emotion regulation are central to understanding conflict processes, the present view is interpersonal not intrapsychic.

Anger and aggression often accompany conflict (see Katz, Kramer, & Gottman, this volume; and Perry, Perry, & Kennedy, this volume), but conflict is a broader construct that is not limited to harmful intentions or outcomes. Conflict frequently includes anger and aggression, but positive emotions (e.g., excitement) and cooperative goals (e.g., mutual problem solving) are characteristic of other conflicts (Shantz, 1987). "Mock battles" also qualify as conflicts because they involve opposition, and such ritualized conflicts can serve important functions (see Garvey & Shantz, this volume). Finally, it is clear that conflict is inevitable in interpersonal relationships (Coombs, 1987), particularly within dynamic systems like the family. Thus, conflict is neither inherently good nor bad. Healthy conflict is distinguished from pathological conflict by its form, function, and management, as well as its effects.

Family conflicts

Family conflicts have the same basic structure as other forms of social conflict. In fact, much can be learned from drawing analogies between family disputes and such seemingly unrelated conflicts as dominance rituals or formalized dispute resolution procedures, as is noted in subsequent sections. Such analogies not only allow for the application of theories and findings from other realms of study, but also offer a perspective on a subject matter that is rife with both personal and professional bias.

Family conflict is distinct from many other forms of conflict in at least three major respects, however. First, because of physical proximity, shared tasks, and long-term commitments, family conflict is both frequent and difficult to escape. This makes the management of conflict in families particularly important. Second, because change is central to the development of individual family members, family relationships are dynamic and often must be reconfigured. Family conflict is a common consequence of transitions in individual development. Third, conflict in the family carries added importance because of the essential social, emotional, and practical functions that Western families serve (Emery, 1988). Thus, family conflicts can carry great consequences for individuals, relationships, and society.

Deep meanings of conflict: Power struggles and intimacy struggles

Conflict can serve a number of functions for individuals, dyads, and triads, a fact that creates tremendous difficulties in conceptualization and research.

For example, conflict can be a means of releasing anger or relieving boredom from the perspective of the individual. From a dyadic view, conflict can have such purposes as resolving differences or gaining autonomy. In triads, conflict can serve complex functions, such as uniting opponents in their opposition against a "common enemy."

The issue is obscured further because the functions of conflict are not revealed simply by its content, intensity, or frequency. Instead, the functions of conflict are determined by the larger interpersonal and developmental context. Further layers of complexity are added because conflict can serve multiple functions simultaneously, some of which may be outside of the intention or awareness of the disputants. Despite these intricacies, it is asserted that a simple distinction can clarify the functions of conflict and thereby facilitate its interpretation within the developmental context.

Surface and deep meanings of conflict

The assertion is that family conflicts (or any social conflicts) carry at least two levels of meaning. The first level is the *surface meaning* of the conflict, that is, its literal content. Surface family conflicts can be minor, such as a disagreement about what television show to watch, or they can be major, as in a disagreement about sexual values. Irrespective of their intensity, frequency, or content, however, the function of conflict is relatively simple when analyzed on its surface. Surface conflicts are straightforward because they are caused by disagreements about a particular issue (content), and their function is clear (to attempt to settle a disagreement) even if the issue is very complicated or impossible to resolve.[1] This problem-solving function of conflict is ubiquitous in daily family life, and many forms of relationship therapy have the goal of teaching troubled families how to solve problems more effectively.

Conflict has another level of interpretation, which is referred to here as its *deep meaning*.[2] The deep meaning of conflict is a metacommunication about what its process of resolution or its outcome conveys about the broader structure of relationships. In terms of deep meaning, conflicts serve the functions of asserting (or testing) and changing (or resisting change) in the structure of relationships. Because it is difficult to view family conflict in perspective, the distinction between surface and deep meanings is best illustrated with some examples from other forms of social conflict.

According to the analysis of ethologists, a given conflict between two male animals may relate at the surface level to the immediate opportunity to mate with a female. The single mating is the content of the conflict, and this constitutes the conflict's surface meaning. At the deep level, however, the same conflict concerns the much broader issue of dominance, that is, the power structure of the relationship between the two males. Winning or losing a given conflict is important not only because of its immediate consequences (surface function), but also because the outcome determines relative male dominance (deep function). For a time, the winner assumes a more dominant role that entitles him to other privileges in the herd. Not every mating is contested because specific surface conflicts resolve broader deep conflicts and determine the (temporary) structure of the relationship between the disputants. Such dominance relations may have been selected through evolution because structural organization holds survival value for the group (Omark, 1980).

The analogy to dominance rituals applies to many other social conflicts. When a less powerful nation challenges the position of a more powerful nation in an international dispute, part of the conflict concerns its surface meaning, that is, the particular challenge. The more important deep meaning, however, relates to the structure of international relations. Leaders feel they must meet a challenge precisely because it is a challenge. That is, the deep issue is one of dominance. Similarly, any reader who is a member of an academic department knows that professorial conflicts about research space also concern underlying issues of dominance, not just space needs. Space is one factor that denotes the dominance hierarchy of an academic department.

The important point in the present context is that family conflicts also have surface and deep meanings. When an abusive husband berates his wife about a bland meal, the deep issue of dominance is essential. Cooking, the surface issue, is minor. Similarly, when early adolescents argue with their parents about dating, the surface issue may be plans for a given Saturday night, but the deep issue is adolescent autonomy and the changing structure of parent–child relationships. Even a minor sibling dispute about who chooses a television show has elements of a dominance ritual: "I'm older. I get to decide."

The assertion that the manner in which surface conflicts are resolved carries deep meaning about the structure of relationships holds implications for family dispute resolution. The most important benefit of problem-solving family therapies, for example, may not be the resolution of specific disputes, but the meaning these resolutions carry for the structure of family relationships. The process of resolving a given dispute may help to define roles and relationships in the family unit, which make future conflicts both less likely to occur and more easily resolved. Because of its deep meaning, conflict both reveals information about the current structure of family relationships (assessment purpose) and is a vehicle for changing that structure (treatment purpose). Dominance or power is only one of two basic dimensions around which relationships are hypothesized to be structured. The second dimension concerns affiliation, or what is referred to here as *intimacy*.

Intimacy and power as basic relationship dimensions

Despite the great number of variables that could be used to characterize relationship structure, it is asserted that intimacy and power are the two most basic dimensions.[3] Much discussion could be devoted to supporting this assertion. However, space allows for only a few observations about its heuristic value and the frequency with which it has been applied in a wide range of subdisciplines of psychology.

The present emphasis on intimacy and power corresponds with the analyses of ethologists who focus on dominance and affiliation in defining the structure of relationships in groups of animals (Omark, 1980). It also is similar to the dimensions used by many organizational psychologists in describing the structure of businesses and variations in leadership styles (e.g., Fielder, 1967). More to the point, the focus is consistent with the theories and research of many personality and developmental psychologists. Among personality theorists, ego psychologist Harry Stack Sullivan (1953) and his followers (e.g., Leary, 1957) focused most sharply on intimacy and power in relationships, as they constructed much of their theory of personality around these dimensions. Some factor analytic research supports the validity of their two, primary relationship constructs (Kiesler, 1983; Orford, 1986). A metaphoric interpretation of Freudian theory also yields these same two dimensions. Freud's basic intrapsychic instincts can be reinterpreted in the interpersonal context as representing intimacy (sex) and power (aggression). In developmental work, Baumrind (1971) has used these two dimensions of relationships in creating her highly regarded classification of parenting styles, which has been effectively used in organizing research on parenting (Maccoby & Martin, 1983). Finally, many family therapists have pointed to similar dimensions, making implicit assumptions about family power hierarchies and explicit statements about an enmeshment–disengagement continuum (e.g., S. Minuchin, 1974).

As used here, the terms *intimacy* and *power* are intended to have broad meaning. *Intimacy* refers to emotional closeness in general and applies to business-like relationships that are low on intimacy as well as to loving relationships that are high on the dimension. *Power* refers not only to designated authority, but also to actual social influence. A parent has legitimate authority in the family, but a difficult, coercive child also holds much power.

The recognition of reciprocal influences in relationships greatly complicates the definition of power, but the ethological concept of dominance is perhaps the closest analogy. In this sense, power involves entitlements, that is, unchallenged or rarely challenged privileges. Parents have more entitlements than children, but the range of entitlements always can be expanded or contracted. Children's power in the family increases as they grow older, and they expand their entitlements by winning key battles, such as keeping uninvited family members out of their own room. A victory in such a conflict is more than a single triumph. The winner gains a new and wider range of uncontested privileges.

Both intimacy and power hold special importance for family relationships. The study of parent–child attachments and parental discipline form the basis of much contemporary research on the development of emotion, socialization, and self-system in children (see Hetherington, 1983). Warm, sensitive parenting and firm, reasoned discipline are basic to children's healthy social and emotional development (Maccoby & Martin, 1983). That is, ideal parent–child relationships in contemporary Western culture are characterized by a high degree of both reciprocal intimacy and developmentally appropriate parental power.

Ideal spousal relationships also are characterized by a high degree of reciprocal intimacy, but the appropriate distribution of power between husbands and wives is a matter of choice according to contemporary, pluralistic views of Western marriage. Ideal sibling relationships are particularly difficult to describe in terms of optimal degrees of either intimacy or power. At least a moderate degree of closeness generally is expected, but there is no consensus about the appropriate power structure of sibling relationships. Despite the lack of consensual values, efforts to create classifications of marital and sibling relationships comparable to Baumrind's (1971) categories of parenting hold much potential for the nomothetic understanding of families.

Conveying deep meaning during dyadic conflicts

Although every conflict is assumed to have both surface and deep meanings, some conflicts and some aspects of conflict resolution are hypothesized to be particularly important to relationship structure. In particular, control over outcomes is asserted to be most important to the power structure of relationships, whereas the type and extent of affect expressed during a conflict are hypothesized to be critical to intimacy structure. Both process and outcome are expected to carry significantly greater deep meaning during what will be called *boundary conflicts*.

Boundary conflicts. Before boundary conflicts can be described, the concept of boundary must be defined. An *interpersonal boundary* is a stated or unstated rule that defines the territory of an individual or a relationship. The concept is akin to the boundary that divides the territory of two animals or two nations, but interpersonal boundaries are more subtle, flexible, and complex.

Interpersonal boundaries often are not apparent until one's territory is invaded. The violation of the boundary creates discomfort and perhaps conflict, which generally makes people aware of the existence of a rule. A straightforward example is the boundary of interpersonal space. Unstated social rules dictate acceptable physical proximity, but the rules are not obvious until they are violated. Discomfort is immediate when a stranger stands too close, however. Bringing up unacceptable topics of conversation is another violation that exposes the existence of a boundary. Asking a 10-year-old about "going potty" or commenting on marital intimacies in front of a child both are violations of intimacy boundaries in families.

Relationships often have multiple boundaries, particularly in relation to interpersonal power. For example, husbands and wives frequently develop specialized family roles, dividing their duties into different realms of responsibility. With role specialization, couples may have one boundary that defines areas of child-rearing power, for example, and another that defines areas of financial power. In an ethological sense, each partner has different territories of dominance.

Boundary conflicts are disputes that occur near the border of intimacy or power territories. For example, being allowed to date is a normative boundary conflict for parents and 14-year-olds, but not for parents and 10-year-olds or parents and 18-year-olds. Unless family circumstances are dramatically atypical, the conflict lies well within the parent's territory in the second case and well within the teenager's in the third case.

It is hypothesized that the nearer a conflict is to a boundary, the more deep a meaning it contains for the structure of relationships. Boundary conflicts are critical because winning or losing serves to reassert or redefine the boundary. If a 14-year-old wins the right to start dating, the parent–child relationship structure is changed, and a new set of privileges becomes available to the adolescent. Not surprisingly, boundary conflicts are hypothesized to be more common during developmental transitions.

Deep meaning conveyed by conflict processes and outcomes. Surface conflicts are resolved by a substantive outcome – such things as where the family goes for a vacation and what clothes are worn to school. It is proposed here, however, that control over outcomes is what conveys deep meaning in terms of the power structure of relationships. Control over the outcome of a conflict, that is, winning or losing, is especially important during boundary conflicts because of their added meaning for relationship power. Compromises or stand-offs also are important outcomes because they re-assert an existing power boundary. Outcome is less important to conflicts that lie well within the territory of one party, however, because the winner is predictable.

The deep meaning for the intimacy structure of relationships is hypothe-sized to be conveyed by the expression of emotions. Emotional expression serves interpersonal signaling and regulatory functions in general (Campos, Barrett, Lamb, Goldsmith, & Stenberg, 1983), and it is asserted that the intensity of affect expressed during conflicts marks the degree of intimacy in a relationship irrespective of the valence of the affect.[4] In any given dispute, for example, intense anger conveys far greater intimacy than does mild anger. The expression of specific emotions (e.g., caring vs. anger) obviously carries meaning, but the degree of intimacy is more accurately indexed by the intensity of emotions than by their valence.

The deep meaning of conflict in terms of intimacy and power, in part, explains why many family conflicts are unresolved in terms of content (Vuchinich, 1986), as well as why mock conflicts and conflicts of mild intensity are meaningful. A conflict that is unresolved on the surface still carries deep meaning, and mock conflicts can serve as tests or affirmations of a relationship (Schiffrin, 1984).

Power struggles and intimacy struggles in dyads

If conflict conveys meaning about the structure of relationships and if intimacy and power are the basic dimensions of relationships, then all conflicts are power struggles or intimacy struggles at their deep level of meaning.[5]

Power struggles. The analogies to dominance rituals discussed earlier illustrate the present view of how conflict is a power struggle at its deep level of meaning. In the family context, the conflicts that accompany parental discipline offer a clear example of a continual, if often mild, power struggle. Parents are not expected to dominate children, but they are expected to remain dominant. Within a child's territory of autonomy, self-regulation is allowed and expected. Parents cross a child's power boundary if self-regulation is not exercised, but the most significant conflict occurs near the expanding boundary between a child's autonomy and a parent's authority. Child development follows a course of ever increasing territories of autonomy for the child and ever decreasing territories of authority for the parent. Conflict occurs at the boundaries of these territories, as children gradually test and increase their autonomy within developmental phases. Conflict escalates during developmental transitions such as the "terrible twos" and early and late adolescence because these are times of rapid acceleration in children's assumption of independence.

This conceptualization suggests predictions related to the content, frequency, and intensity of parent–child conflicts. The content of the most frequent conflicts should follow a pattern of age-graded autonomy issues, such as preschoolers' selection of clothes, school-age childrens' homework, and adolescents' curfews. Once a boundary is expanded, conflict over the former boundary issue is much less likely. More frequent and intense conflicts are expected when the boundaries depart significantly from development norms (restrictiveness or permissiveness is great), when boundaries are deeply penetrated (parents attempt to regulate behavior that has long been in a child's control or the converse), when boundaries are unclear (discipline is inconsistent), when parental dominance is in doubt (parents hold little authority), and during developmental transitions (because of sudden jumps in children's struggles for autonomy).

Power struggles in marital dyads are expected to be less frequent than in parent–child relationships because there is no underlying developmental process that creates constant boundary conflict. Like parent–child relationships, however, power struggles are expected to be more frequent and intense during developmental transitions in the marriage (e.g., into marriage, parenthood, the "empty nest," and retirement). Similarly, power struggles in the marital relationship are predicted to be more serious and common when boundaries are dramatically unequal, when one partner's territory is deeply penetrated, when boundaries are inconsistent, or when dominance is in doubt (i.e., there is role conflict). The contents of marital conflicts are more difficult to predict than are those of parent–child disputes because marital roles (areas of relative autonomy) are defined idiographically across marriages.

Of all dyadic family conflicts, sibling power disputes are predicted to be the most frequent, intense, and all encompassing (provided that there are opportunities for conflict). This is because the normative power structure of sibling relationships is the least clear of all family relationships. Thus, power struggles among siblings often remain unresolved. Siblings may develop their own power structures (e.g., dividing territory in a shared room), but they often are tenuous due to a lack of normative guidance. This means that power struggles in sibling relationships often must be resolved by parents on a dispute-by-dispute basis (Dunn & Munn, 1986).

Intimacy struggles. The dominance construct helps to convey how conflict carries deep meaning as a power struggle, but there is no ready ethological analogy for intimacy struggles. Perhaps they are uniquely human. Intimacy struggles result from an unbalanced intimate relationship according to the perceptions of or desires for closeness on the part of one or both members of a dyad. Each member may want to be closer in the relationship, each may want greater distance, or one may want more intimacy while the other wants more separateness.

This last circumstance is referred to as the "pursuer–pursued" relationship in the popular psychology literature, and it offers a clear example of an intimacy struggle. The pursued partner distances; the pursuer chases. The problem is that the two lovers do not want the same degree of intimacy. Frequent boundary conflicts erupt around issues such as spending time together, affection, and commitment. In part, these are surface conflicts ("You didn't call me!"), but the deep conflict concerning an unbalanced intimate relationship is more important ("You don't love me!").

Unlike the aim in a power struggle, the pursuer is not trying to win a dispute. Rather, he or she is seeking symbols of intimacy. The most important symbol is the degree of emotional intensity expressed during the conflict, as noted earlier. The expression of more intense emotions, even negative ones, conveys a greater degree of intimacy than does the expression of less intense emotions.[6] For example, when a pursuer threatens to end a relationship, the response "I hate you!" conveys much more emotional investment than does "Let's be friends." In fact, the pursuing partner in an intimacy struggle often utilizes this same, indirect strategy of emotional expression. Hope for love and hurt at rejection are converted into expressions of anger. Rather than saying "I feel unloved when you don't call," the pursuing partner casts accusations about the loved one's character flaws in the hope of getting an emotional reaction.

Many chronic conflicts in the family can be conceptualized as intimacy struggles. For example, prolonged conflicts between divorced spouses, even conflicts that extend into legal contests over child custody, often seem senseless in terms of their content. When viewed as intimacy struggles, however, extended, irrational disputes in divorce can be comprehended. One partner (or both) does not want the relationship to end, and areas of potential conflict (e.g., the children) are used to maintain contact with the former spouse. The degree of angry affect expressed during these conflicts/ contacts indicates the strength of the lingering attachment felt by one or both former spouses (Emery, Matthews, & Wyer, 1991; Somary & Emery, 1991).

Another chronic family conflict is coercive or "negative attention-seeking" behavior on the part of difficult children (Patterson, 1982). In the behavioral family therapy literature, coercion and negative attention seeking are conceptualized in operant terms. The disruptive child's misbehavior is viewed as being reinforced by a parent's "negative attention" (e.g., screaming) or by a parent's capitulation to obnoxious demands. An obvious operant solution to this power struggle is to place the child on an extinction schedule.

Part of the difficulty in these types of interactions can be viewed as stemming from intimacy struggles, however. What the operant analysis overlooks is why negative attention is reinforcing to the child or why coercive cycles begin in the first place. Conceptualizing these interactions as intimacy struggles provides a potential answer to both questions. Like a spouse who does not want a divorce, the "attention-seeking" or coercive child may be seeking signs of caring. The expression of intense negative emotions such as anger signals greater affective involvement than does inattention. This is not to say that parents should not discipline obnoxious behavior. Rather, the intimacy struggle analysis suggests that providing the coercive child with more positive attention should both decrease the frequency of negative attention seeking and make necessary discipline more effective. Although many behavioral family therapists advocate using reinforcement, it is not obvious why this approach is preferred from an operant perspective. Perhaps children seek negative signals of affective involvement because of inattention or insecure parent–child attachments, and reinforcement techniques offer emotional reassurance as well as socialization.

Intimacy struggles between siblings are expected to be relatively rare, primarily because closeness between siblings is less important than in other family dyads. Sibling intimacy struggles usually are limited to such circumstances as younger siblings pestering older brothers and sisters to include them in their activities. In such circumstances, the younger child creates conflicts as a means of being included in the older sibling's activities, not as means of controlling them.

Because the desire for greater intimacy often is expressed indirectly during conflict, the present analysis suggests that intimacy struggles have few predictable contents. The analysis does predict that intimacy struggles are intense, however, because of the signaling function of emotional intensity. Finally, intimacy struggles are expected to be chronic within a dyad that has an ill-defined boundary of intimacy. In fact, perhaps the best marker of an intimacy struggle is frequent, intense conflict that seems to serve no substantive purpose.

Confusion between intimacy struggles and power struggles

A thorny problem is that conflict sometimes is a method of maintaining cohesion, and other times it is a means of achieving independence (Shantz & Hobart, 1989). That is, intimacy struggles and power struggles often are intertwined. Conflict may involve a struggle for changes in both intimacy and power; one partner may be struggling for intimacy while the other is struggling for power, or the intentions of the opponents may be misinterpreted. This confusion about the deep meaning of conflict creates difficulties both for the participants in a conflict and for outside observers who are attempting to understand the relationship.

One important confusion of functions arises when the other's intentions are misconstrued. A power struggle can easily be misinterpreted as a threat to intimacy, for example. The strong negative emotions that often accompany power struggles frequently are misinterpreted as a sign of rejection, when, in fact, they convey greater intimacy. As one illustration of this, most theorists conceptualize the successful transition to adolescence as involving significant changes in parent–child power relationships but consistency in intimacy. That is, a loving and supportive parent–child relationship facilitates development even as the teenager assumes increased autonomy (Bengtson & Black, 1973; Fisher & Johnson, 1990; Steinberg, 1981). However, the anger expressed during what is essentially a power struggle can be misconstrued as indicating a desire for less intimacy. More specifically, both parents and children can feel rejected and unloved as they attempt to renegotiate their boundaries of power during the transition to adolescence. Such confusion likely arises in all normative developmental transitions. The dyad benefits from maintaining a consistent intimacy boundary in the face of changes in power, yet conflict in the power structure of relationships is interpreted as threatening their intimacy structure.

Intimacy struggles also can be misconstrued as power struggles. The earlier discussion of coercive behavior is one example of this confusion. Traditionally viewed as a power struggle, part of the conflict may be an intimacy struggle. Difficult children who "test the limits" constantly may be seeking more love, not more autonomy.

An even more subtle confusion results when the parties in conflict have different agendas in terms of intimacy and power. This may be a particularly frequent problem in marriage. Conflicts over issues like spending more time together may reflect a desire for greater intimacy on the part of one partner but a desire for greater power on the part of the other. One partner feels rejected, while the other feels controlled. That is, the conflict is construed as an intimacy struggle by one member of the dyad and as a power struggle by the other.

Summary

To this point, a number of assertions have been offered about the functions of family conflict. These include the hypotheses that (a) conflict has both surface and deep meanings; (b) the deep meaning of conflict concerns the functions of testing or asserting, altering or resisting change in the structure of family relationships; (c) intimacy and power are the basic dimensions around which relationships are structured; (d) boundaries separate the territory of an individual's or a group's intimacy and power, and conflict that occurs at these boundaries carries the most significant deep meaning; (e) control over the outcome of a conflict is most important to the power structure of a relationship, whereas the process of emotional expression signals its intimacy structure; (f) all family conflicts therefore contain elements of power struggles, intimacy struggles, or a combination of the two; and (g) these assertions lead to predictions about the participants, content, frequency, and intensity of dyadic family conflict within phases of child and family development, and especially during developmental transitions. Having sketched this series of hopefully provocative proposals about dyadic family conflict, let us complicate the issue by considering triadic family processes.

Conflict and systemic relationship structure

Most research in clinical and developmental psychology focuses on dyadic family conflict, particularly as it occurs between mothers and children and between marital partners. It has been suggested, however, that researchers increasingly must focus on triadic conflict, which is both empirically frequent and theoretically challenging (Vuchinich, Emery, & Cassidy, 1988). Much of the theoretical challenge comes in the application of the constructs of general systems theory to the family context (P. Minuchin, 1985). Let us briefly examine some basic propositions from a systems perspective.

Concepts from family systems theory

The first and most basic point of systems theory is that the family is a system, a unit that is greater than the sum of its component parts. This is an antireductionist view that emphasizes the importance of wholeness and *interdependency*. The family is neither a collection of individuals, nor a collection of dyadic relationships. It is a functioning whole, a unit that contains interdependent individuals and relationships. The systems perspective therefore holds that individuals are affected not only by conflict in their own relationships, but also by conflict in the relationships between other family members.

A second position of systems theory is that causality is reciprocal. Although causes and effects can be isolated using the experimental method, in natural chains of interaction, cause and effect are a matter of perspective. For example, from one point of view, it can be argued that parental discipline causes children's compliance. From another perspective, however, children's compliance can be said to cause parental discipline (Bell, 1968). In relation to triadic conflict, *reciprocal influence* means that individuals not only are affected by others' family conflicts, but also affect the process and outcome of those conflicts.

A third relevant systems concept is homeostasis, an idea that is familiar throughout the sciences and that carries a similar meaning here. *Homeostasis* refers to the tendency to maintain a steady state by balancing the distribution of essential properties. Homeostatic processes in families are much discussed, but family theorists often fail to delineate the "essential properties" of family relationships that set homeostatic processes into motion. That is, the process of homeostasis is acknowledged, but the content of what is being balanced is not made clear. It is asserted here that families maintain homeostasis around intimacy and power. That is, family homeostasis involves the process of maintaining a balance of intimacy and power in the system of family relationships. This suggests that triadic conflict is both a cause and an effect of the activation of homeostatic processes. On the one hand, substantive disagreements (surface conflicts) activate homeostatic processes because of their potential threat to relationship structure. On the other hand, when relationship structure is changing for other reasons (e.g., a developmental transition), conflict can be a part of a homeostatic process to resist change.

Triadic family conflict as a microsocial process

These broad systems concepts are difficult, if not impossible, to test directly, but they are useful generalities that can guide the development of more specific hypotheses. The concepts of interdependency, reciprocal influence, and homeostasis are evident in the following propositions about triadic conflict as a microsocial process.

Three subprocesses have been hypothesized to comprise the larger microsocial process that describes the role of third family members in what begins as dyadic conflict (Emery, 1989). The first is the emotional *arousal* that conflict creates for participants and for third parties. Empirical evidence clearly documents that family conflict causes psychophysiological arousal among disputants (Levenson & Gottman, 1983, 1985) and among third parties to disputes (El-Sheikh, Cummings, & Goetsch, 1989; Gottman & Katz, 1989). Because of its deep meanings, emotional arousal experienced by participants and third parties is hypothesized to be greater when it occurs between members with an intimate and powerful position in the family (e.g., between parents).

Arousal is hypothesized to motivate participants and third parties to attempt to control their affect, and the second component of the microsocial process focuses on attempts at emotional *regulation*. Such attempts may involve internal coping responses such as calming, rationalization, and so forth, but the instrumental actions of third parties to control, reduce, or resolve the conflict are most relevant to the present analysis. Third parties frequently do become involved in the conflict of others, as is evidenced by the long series of social psychological studies on the "bystander effect," as well as more recent developmental work on children's reactions to parental conflict in mild (Cummings, Zahn-Waxler, & Radke-Yarrow, 1981, 1984) and extreme (Christopoulos et al., 1987) marital disputes. Most directly, observational research on natural family conflict occurring around the dinner table indicates that third family members frequently become involved in what begins as dyadic family conflict (Vuchinich et al., 1988).

Because conflict is distressing to both third parties and disputants, the final component of the microsocial model suggests that the instrumental actions of third parties that reduce conflict (and negative emotional arousal) are likely to be maintained as action extends over time. It does not matter whether the third party's actions are direct problem-solving maneuvers or indirect distraction strategies. As long as conflict and negative emotional arousal are reduced, the triadic interaction pattern should be maintained by negative reinforcement. Different third-party strategies may be linked to individual differences in the effects on disputants and third parties, however, as discussed in the final section of this chapter.

The role of family members as third parties to conflict. The term *third party* connotes the more formal intervention in conflict that occurs in advocacy, mediation, and adjudication. This connotation is a useful one in conceptualizing the third party's role in family conflict. Family members who are not immediately involved in a dyadic conflict are in a position similar to that of formal third-party intervention agents in that they may (a) directly enter or avoid an ongoing conflict; (b) if they enter, ally with one side or maintain a neutral position; and (c) adopt intervention strategies that are direct or indirect, using tactics that vary in intimacy and power.

An example helps to illustrate these points. A common triadic dilemma in family conflict is a parent's potential involvement in a dispute between two siblings (Dunn & Munn, 1986). When two children are arguing, the first choice that a parent faces is whether or not to intervene in the dispute. This decision is influenced by a number of factors including the parent's current mood, their child-rearing goals, and the intensity and history of the conflict. Whether or not the parent does intervene, both the children and the parent are affected by the choice.

If the parent does intervene, the next choice is whether or not to take sides during the intervention. This decision is affected by such factors as which child is judged to be right or wrong, parental rules about appropriate sibling roles (e.g., older children should defer to younger siblings), or parental favoritism. Whatever the circumstances, the decision about taking sides is crucial. It can greatly affect the outcome of the specific conflict, and it holds more general implications for systemic relationship structure. It is hypothesized that the decision about "taking sides" carries deep meaning both about family *alliances* (a power issue) and about family *loyalties* (an intimacy issue). Alliances and loyalties may be particularly meaningful in the family context (to be discussed shortly), but their importance also is evident in formal dispute resolution. For example, the roles of lawyers and judges are defined with great care with respect to alliances and neutrality because of the substantive (surface meaning) and symbolic (deep meaning) effects of taking sides in a conflict.

Once a third party intervenes either as an advocate or a neutral, there are many potential variations in intervention style. Three of the most important variables, especially for neutral third parties, are whether the intervention is direct or indirect, the extent of power that is exercised by the third party, and the intimacy of the third party's relationship with the disputants. For example, a parent's neutral intervention in a sibling dispute can come from a stance of greater authority and lesser intimacy ("You two stop fighting!") or lesser authority and greater intimacy ("Let's talk about what happened"). Metaphorically, a neutral parent can be a police officer, a judge, an arbitor, a mediator, or a therapist. A neutral parent need not be so direct, however. Sibling disputes and many other family conflicts often are ended by a common, indirect third-party intervention strategy: distraction (Dunn & Munn, 1986; Vuchinich et al., 1988).

Alliances, loyalties, and the power of third parties. Third-party choices about intervening, taking sides, and using different strategies are assumed both to affect and to reflect family structure. Two family members siding together against a third is, in part, a power issue. The move may enable two less powerful family members to win a victory over a more powerful third member. It is an alliance. However, taking sides also carries deep meaning in terms of intimacy. It is a demonstration of loyalty. As a loyalty issue, taking sides conveys the third party's relative preferences. A child's complaint to a parent "You always take (sibling's) side" can be a protest about losing a battle, but it also can mean "You love (sibling) more than you love me." Even loyalties that are expressed during mock conflicts like those created during games carry deep meaning. For example, in the card game "hearts," a parent must be careful to distribute the queen of spades equitably among the children in order to avoid the appearance of playing favorites.

As with dyadic conflict, control over outcomes is predicted to convey deep meaning about power in a system of relationships. In triadic conflict, however, power is not only determined by winning or losing. It also is vested in third parties who control the process of dispute resolution. The person who directs the conflict resolution process from a neutral position is in a powerful position (as is a judge or a mediator). Thus, when a third family member does enter a dyadic conflict from a neutral position, this is an index of their power.

Examples of family alliances and loyalties. The importance of choices about taking sides and whether and how to intervene become clear when some common family disputes are considered. In dyadic conflicts between a parent and a child, the normative role of the second parent is clear. If the second parent enters the dispute, they are expected to ally with (and be loyal to) the other parent. Reflecting the importance of parental alliances and loyalties, interparental inconsistency has been linked with both difficult child behavior and subsequent divorce (Block, Block, & Morrison, 1981).

The role of other siblings as third parties to a parent–child dispute is less clearly prescribed, but consideration of the issue suggests the importance of the third party's role. What is the deep meaning if a second child enters a dispute between a sibling and a parent? What if he or she sides with the parent, the sibling, or remains neutral? What power is invested in this child as a third party?

The involvement of children in their parents' conflict is a particular concern because frequent or intense parental conflict is associated with behavior problems among children (Emery, 1982; Grych & Fincham, 1990). Parental conflict creates a difficult loyalty dilemma. Children can attempt to reduce or control their parents' conflict by mediating, distracting, or otherwise addressing the dispute, but they must be especially careful about maintaining neutrality. Their relationship with one parent may be threatened if they takes sides. Entering a conflict between parents also puts children in a position where they assume developmentally inappropriate power in the family. That is, a burden of responsibility falls on a child who mediates conflict between his or her parents.

In addition to the distress associated with encountering conflict, balancing loyalties, and assuming responsibility for others' relationships during routine family disputes, dysfunctional family conflict can create nonnormative family structures. In order to understand these nonnormative structures, it is necessary to introduce some assumptions about the systemic structure of normative family relationships.

Perspectives on the systemic structure of family relationships

Families may be viewed as social organizations that contain characteristic structures. As such, families share features in common with other social organizations like businesses and academic departments. The structure of formal social organizations usually may be diagramed with an organizational chart, and similar charts may be used to detail the structure of a family. Organizational charts of businesses generally note job responsibilities within the hierarchical power structure of a business. Job responsibilities and organizational hierarchies, in turn, determine the formal communication patterns or information flow in a business.

Like most businesses, families typically are structured hierarchically according to the relative power of individual members. Family members also have designated "job responsibilities," or what are more commonly thought of as family roles. The basic family roles are those of mother/father, daughter/son, wife/husband, and sister/brother. As with the structure of business organizations, power hierarchies and family roles determine the formal communication patterns in a family.

Like an analysis of the organization of a given business, however, what is of most interest about families is not their formal (hypothetical) structure, but their informal (actual) structure. A simple chart that ranks two parents as being in charge of 2.3 children conveys little information about the structure of a given family. Similarly, a designated family role as father, for example, provides little detail about a family member's actual role. The organization of families is further complicated because the intimacy structure of family relationships holds importance equal to or greater than their power structure.

Most conceptualizations of relationship intimacy and power offered in clinical and developmental psychology focus on dyadic family relationships and index the relationships on continua (or categories) of intensity. Discipline varies from being strict to lax. Attachments are secure or insecure. However, when one considers such issues as triadic family relationships or within-family differences (Plomin & Daniels, 1987), relative levels of intimacy and power become the focus of interest. Such a consideration of relative intimacy and power is essential to understanding the present views on the structural organization of families.

The normative structure of Western families may be outlined with a few basic, but important, assumptions about relative intimacy and power. Parents are expected to remain considerably more powerful than children, although there are many adaptive individual differences in the degree of parental authority. A related assumption is that differences in power between spouses or between siblings are expected to be small relative to those found between parents and children. This is true despite the power differentials that accompany specialization in marital and parental roles and birth order or other sibling dominance hierarchies. When a parent is *infantilized* or a child is *parentified*, the power structure of the family is nonnormative.

Normatively, more intimate relationships are found between spouses and between both parents and all of the children than between one parent and one child or between two siblings. The emphasis on a happy, loving marriage is obvious. It is almost as obvious that the most intensely felt love among parents and children is expected to be the parents, as a dyad, loving the children, as a group. Parents are not expected to "have favorites" (or at least not to reveal or act on their preferences). Even allowing for some normative differentiation in the intimacy of parent–child relationships, such as greater closeness in same-sex dyads, the differences are expected to be small in comparison to the much stronger love between parents and between parents as a dyad and children as a group.

Developmental transitions and normative and nonnormative family structure

Despite normative social prescriptions, each family must negotiate its unique relationship structure. The most crucial negotiations typically take place during transitions in family development. It is asserted here that the manner in which family members organize their roles and relationships during a developmental transition parallels microsocial family organization during episodes of conflict. That is, alliances and loyalties that develop during transitions determine the structure of family relationships during the next stable phase of development. The transition to parenthood and the divorce transition provide two substantively important examples of this renegotiation of intimacy and power in the system of family relationships.

The birth of a first child forces the renegotiation of both intimacy and power boundaries in a marriage, as many couples adopt more specialized roles during the transition to parenthood. Each spouse typically assumes more or less power in a particular domain, such as child-rearing or financial responsibilities (Emery & Tuer, in press). Because of this developing role specialization, boundary conflicts over such issues as who misses work when the infant is ill carry particularly deep meaning. How the conflict is resolved during the transition sets a pattern that is likely to be maintained during the next developmental stage.

The birth of the first child also challenges intimacy in the marriage. Couples may struggle to maintain continuity in intimacy, but boundaries are tested by practical demands and changes in the demonstrations of affection, for example, time together and sexuality (Belsky, Lang, & Rovine, 1985; Cowan et al., 1985). Although the birth of the first child threatens dyadic intimacy, it also provides an opportunity to form a new loyalty. When parents resolve dyadic intimacy conflicts by sharing together in their love for their child, the loyalty creates a new boundary that unites them in their new roles as parents. They have established the normative pattern of relative intimacies discussed earlier. The shared love for children can create new intimacy for the couple, whereas jealousies result when parental love is highly individualized, that is, when a parent–child intimacy boundary excludes one of the parents.

Divorce offers a poignant illustration of dyadic power and intimacy struggles, as well as the problems posed by alliances and split loyalties in family triads. In contrast to normative transitions in which social prescriptions are relatively clear, nonnormative transitions like divorce are complicated by the absence of widely accepted norms for reorganizing the family relationship structure.

The central dyadic conflict in the divorce transition often is the renegotiation of the intimacy boundary between the parents (Emery, 1988). This task is greatly complicated by the partners' differing desires. Most divorces are not mutual, a circumstance that makes prolonged intimacy struggles likely. The spouse who leaves the relationship may hope to "be friends," while, for the partner who was left, the choice may be to be lovers or to be enemies.

As parents struggle with redefining the boundary of intimacy, children are confronted with loyalty dilemmas and may be drawn into alliances. Even in friendly divorces, the emotional distancing that naturally takes place between parents upsets the homeostatic balance in family relationships. Initially, chidren may feel disloyal to one parent simply by maintaining a relationship with the other. If parents cannot renegotiate their relationship, the loyalty pressures children feel can become unremitting, and pulls to form alliances can be direct and manipulative. Often the withdrawal of one parent, or a child, from the family is the only way in which the transition is completed and a new and stable relationship structure is established.

Summary

Several additional hypotheses have been offered in this section that extend the analysis of the deep meanings of conflict to systemic interaction. The major assertions are as follows: (a) Family conflict inevitably affects others in addition to the dyad in dispute; (b) the microsocial involvement of third family members in dyadic conflict involves the three components of affective arousal, attempts to regulate affect by reducing the conflict, and the maintenance of successful interventions through negative reinforcement; (c) the essential variations on third-party intervention style involve whether to intervene or take sides and what intervention strategy to adopt; (d) third-party intervention carries deep meaning for systemic relationship intimacy (loyalties) and power (alliances); (e) the principal normative loyalty/alliance in families is between spouses/parents; and (f) developmental transitions involve conflicts that create new relationship structures that are sustained during the stable developmental stage that follows.

Implications for research on normative processes and individual differences

The principal goal of the present chapter has been to offer conceptual perspectives on the normative functions of conflict in family dyads and triads. In this final section, some implications of this analysis for research on both normative processes and individual differences are considered.

Research on microsocial processes

Most contemporary research on microsocial conflict is focused on aggressive, dyadic exchanges. One of the major contributions of this research has been the identification of patterns in chains of interaction, a contribution that may be best represented by the concept of coercion (Patterson, 1982). The analysis presented here holds implications for constructs like coercion and suggests new directions for the microsocial analysis of conflict. With respect to coercion, the analysis raises at least three substantive issues. First, it explicitly outlines assumptions about normative family power structures that are implicitly made in defining coercion. The coercion construct implicitly assumes a hierarchical structuring of parent–child relationships. Traditionally, it is considered to be coercive when children use aversive behavior to control parents, but it is not coercive when threats of discipline are removed by parents contingent upon child compliance. The present analysis explicitly points to this normative parent–child power hierarchy. More generally, the broad consideration of normative family power structures should aid in the analysis of coercion in more egalitarian family relationships, specifically relationships between siblings, parents and adolescents, and spouses.

Second, a related implication is that children should win some conflicts with their parents, even through aversive actions. According to the present analysis, parents are not expected to be omnipotent. The child's developmental stage and the topic of dispute determine when parents should win and when they should give in during conflicts. For example, the parents of 2-year-olds need not prevail over every temper tantrum. Children should win some disputes because of the normal expansion of their boundaries of autonomy and because of the sense of mastery and control that accompanies the assumption of increased independence. In particular, parents need not emerge as the victors in tantrums over issues that appropriately lie within the 2-year-old's existing or soon to be acquired area of autonomy. A parent of a 2-year-old should never capitulate to a tantrum over wanting to play in a busy street, but giving in to a tantrum over food preferences may have healthy effects on the toddler's emerging sense of control. When conflicts that are appropriately regulated by parents are met with firm and consistent authority, parental capitulation to tantrums over minor issues is not coercion. Instead, the tantrum may be seen as the 2-year-old's means of assuming independence.

Third is the implication that some coercive exchanges are usefully conceptualized as intimacy struggles. Insecurity about relationship intimacy or unequal desires for closeness in dyadic relationships may explain why coercive cycles develop initially and why negative attention is reinforcing to some children and some adults.

The present analysis also suggests new directions for microsocial research on conflict. Among the most important needs is further study of affect during interaction, because much conflict is hypothesized to involve attempts at emotional regulation. Clever techniques have been developed for assessing affect during episodes of conflict (e.g., Levenson & Gottman, 1983, 1985), and these methods could be applied to the study of both dyadic and triadic conflicts. The direct assessment of the type and intensity of affect experienced by third parties to conflict also is of considerable theoretical interest and empirical potential (El-Sheikh et al., 1989; Gottman & Katz, 1989). Affective intensity may prove to be most important in normative conflict processes, but the valence of affect may be more relevant to individual differences (e.g., whether the disputant responds to conflict with sadness or anger).

Another area ripe for research concerns the broader roles and strategies employed by disputants and third parties to conflict. The analysis of the behavior of disputants need not be limited to calculating the conditional probability of reciprocating aggression in chains of conflictual interaction. Instead, disputant behavior also can be conceptualized as comprising a broader strategy that is influenced by the response of the opponent and extends over time. "Tit for tat" is one such simple and powerful strategy (Axelrod, 1984). Someone who uses the tit for tat strategy begins by cooperating, but always reciprocates either conflict or cooperation depending on the opponent's prior move. The strategy has been demonstrated to be successful in competing against and cooperating with other, more complex strategies (Axelrod, 1984).

Research on roles also holds potential for improving the understanding of both normative conflict processes and individual differences among third parties to disputes. As noted earlier, the major variables that need to be considered involve whether or not third parties enter the dispute, form alliances, or remain neutral, and the type of intervention tactics that they employ. The analysis of both third-party roles, and disputant strategies requires the development of coding systems that rate interaction at a higher level of abstraction than is typically used in microsocial observational coding (Vuchinich et al., 1988).

Research on the meaning of conflict

The present analysis also suggests the need for research on the meaning of conflict. One issue related to meaning concerns the frequency of specific contents of conflict, particularly as they occur in different dyads or triads at various stages of individual and family development. It should be possible, for example, to document age-graded boundary conflicts in parent–child interaction. Such normative information would improve the understanding of nonnormative disputes, as well as the difficulties in individual and family adjustment.

The present analysis also suggests the further study of the meaning that participants assign to their conflicts. In studying the transition to adolescence, some investigators have found that autonomy themes run through the meanings that parents and adolescents attribute to their disputes (Smetana, 1988, 1989). Such analyses could be expanded to other family transitions such as divorce. A valuable addition would be to analyze the intimacy, as well as the power, meanings that conflict holds for disputants.

Another suggestion is to study conflict during developmental transitions because of the added deep meaning it carries during these times. If alliances and loyalties that develop during conflict episodes predict the structure of subsequent family relationships, such research would hold important implications for both assessment and intervention.

Research on individual differences and psychopathology

A final implication relates to individual differences in the effects of conflict, a topic that has been largely ignored in this chapter. Research on conflict and individual adjustment could be improved by new approaches to analyzing conflict such as those suggested in the preceding paragraphs. Research on family alliances and loyalties may be an important avenue to understanding within-family differences, which, in turn, may predict individual differences in development. The question may not be whether mother has loved you, but whether she has loved you best. A much more important implication follows from the present analysis, however. If intimacy and power are basic dimensions of relationships, each also must have an intrapsychic representation. If there are structures that represent intra-individual constructions of love and power and if interpersonal conflict carries deep meaning for relationship structure, then much of the effects of conflict on individuals should occur within these metaphoric structures.

How might intimacy and power be psychologically represented within the individual? This is an issue that was of great concern to ego psychologists (Erikson, 1959/1980; Horney, 1939; Sullivan, 1953). In more contemporary work, attachment theorists have grappled with defining the internal representation of love and have presently settled on the "working model" construct. Internal representations of interpersonal power have been argued to encompass a sense of efficacy (Bandura, 1977), perhaps efficacy in multiple role identities (Erikson, 1959/1980). Whatever their internal representation, the point is that conflict can be analyzed from the perspective of the individual, as well as that of the relationship.

This is a complicated point that may perhaps be made more clearly with a brief example. Conflict frequently accompanies the breakup of close relationships, as in marital separation. At least some of this conflict can be conceptualized as stemming from the anger that is a part of the process of grieving (Bowlby, 1973; Weiss, 1988). When viewed as an intimacy struggle, conflict is an attempt to achieve a reunion, or at least to discover whether the other still cares. From the individual perspective, intensely expressed anger therefore is a sign of hope. Conflict is not bad from the perspective of the grieving party. Rather, a lack of conflict or emotional intensity is bad. The absence of conflict therefore may cause depression because of the deep meaning for the relationship, namely, rejection. Intra-individual anger/hope may be converted into anger/sadness if it does not provoke the desired interpersonal response.

Unfortunately, the present author cannot offer a method for distinguishing conflict stemming from grief/anger from conflict that serves other functions. Fortunately, such knotty specifics have not been the goal of this chapter. Rather, the intention has been to offer a series of fairly specific, hopefully testable, hypotheses and, more generally, to encourage conceptualization in a field that is in need of more theory.

Notes

1. Many conflicts involve strategic distractions or other types of maneuvers that make the stated surface meaning different from the actual surface meaning. Although acknowledged, this complexity is not addressed here. However, it is important to note that the "real" conflict, that is, the conflict that is being avoided, is still considered to be a surface conflict in the present analysis. The deep meaning of conflict always relates to metacommunications about the structure of relationships, and deep meanings remain the same even when "real" surface conflicts are avoided.
2. The use of the psycholinguistic terms to distinguish levels of semantic meaning is intentional.
3. The issue of whether relationship intimacy and power are dimensional or categorical is not addressed here. The term *relationship dimension* is used as a matter of convenience.
4. The notion that the intensity of affect, not necessarily its valence, communicates the degree of intimacy in relationships assumes that much emotional expression is indirect during conflicts. A relevant area of research that supports this assumption is the grieving literature, where emotions of positive valence (love) are hypothesized to be converted into emotions of negative valence (anger and sadness). A specific example of the indirect expression of affect in grieving that is frequently discussed in the clinical literature concerns the expression of anger among divorced partners. Divorced spouses who have prolonged battles are thought to be overly intimate (enmeshed), not overly distant (disengaged) in their relationships, unlike what some casual observers might conclude and unlike what the partners are likely to assert. The notion that hurt over rejection often is expressed as anger also underlies the truism "Love and hate are not far apart."
5. It is intentionally stated that all conflicts involve power or intimacy struggles in order to

avoid making a distinction between those conflicts that do or do not contain these deep meanings. Some conflicts may carry little or no deep meaning, but the strongest hypothesis is put forward here in order to provide clarity and avoid a distracting, if important, side issue.

6. This analysis departs from the Sullivanian view of intimacy as a relationship dimension. Sullivan viewed love and hate as being opposite poles on the continuum, whereas the present analysis places these two intense feelings next to one another. The endpoints of the intimacy continuum in the present analysis would be love/hate at one pole and indifference at the opposite extreme.

References

Axelrod, R. (1984). *The evolution of cooperation.* New York: Basic.

Bandura, A. (1977). Self-efficacy: Toward a unifying theory of behavioral change. *Psychological Review, 84*, 191–195.

Baumrind, D. (1971). Current patterns of parental authority. *Developmental Psychology Monograph, 4*(1, Pt. 2).

Bell, R. Q. (1968). A reinterpretation of the direction of effects in studies of socialization. *Psychological Review, 75*, 81–95.

Belsky, J., Lang, M. E., & Rovine, M. (1985). Stability and change in marriage across the transition to parenthood: A second study. *Journal of Marriage and the Family, 47*, 855–865.

Bengtson, V. L., & Black, K. (1973). Intergenerational relations and continuities in socialization. In P. B. Baltes & K. W. Schaie (Eds.), *Life-span developmental psychology: Personality and socialization.* New York: Academic Press.

Block, J. H., Block, J., & Morrison, A. (1981). Parental agreement–disagreement on child-rearing orientations and gender-related personality correlates in children. *Child Development, 52*, 965–974.

Bowlby, J. (1973). *Attachment and loss* (Vol. 2). New York: Basic.

Campos, J. J., Barrett, K. C., Lamb, M. E., Goldsmith, H. H., & Stenberg, C. (1983). Socioemotional development. In M. Haith & J. J. Campos (Eds.), *Handbook of child psychology: Vol. 2. Infancy and developmental psychobiology* (4th ed.). New York: Wiley.

Christopoulos, C., Cohn, D. A., Shaw, D. S., Joyce, S., Sullivan-Hanson, J., Kraft, S., & Emery, R. E. (1987). Children of abused women: 1. Adjustment at time of shelter residence. *Journal of Marriage and the Family, 49*, 611–619.

Coombs, C. H. (1987). The structure of conflict. *American Psychologist, 42*, 355–363.

Cowan, C. P., Cowan, P. A., Heming, G., Garrett, E., Coysh, W. S., Curtis-Boles, H., & Boles, A. J. (1985). Transitions to parenthood: His, hers, and theirs. *Journal of Family Issues, 6*, 451–481.

Cummings, E. M., Zahn-Waxler, C., & Radke-Yarrow, M. (1981). Young children's responses to expressions of anger and affection by others in the family. *Child Development, 52*, 1274–1282.

Cummings, E. M., Zahn-Waxler, C., & Radke-Yarrow, M. (1984). Developmental changes in children's reactions to anger in the home. *Journal of Child Psychology and Psychiatry, 25*, 63–74.

Dunn, J., & Munn, P. (1986). Sibling quarrels and maternal intervention: Individual differences in understanding and aggression. *Journal of Child Psychology and Psychiatry, 27*, 583–595.

El-Sheikh, M., Cummings, E. M., & Goetsch, V. (1989). Coping with adults' angry behavior:

Behavioral, physiological, and verbal responses in preschoolers. *Developmental Psychology, 25*, 490–498.

Emery, R. E. (1982). Interparental conflict and the children of discord and divorce. *Psychological Bulletin, 92*, 310–330.

Emery, R. E. (1988). *Marriage, divorce, and children's adjustment.* Beverly Hills, CA: Sage.

Emery, R. E. (1989). Family violence. *American Psychologist, 44*, 321–328.

Emery, R. E., Matthews, S., & Wyer, M. M. (1991). Child custody mediation and litigation: Further evidence on the differing views of mothers and fathers. *Journal of Consulting and Clinical Psychology, 59*, 410–418.

Emery, R. E., & Tuer, M. (in press). Parenting and the marital relationship. In T. Luster & L. Okagaki (Eds.), *Parenting: An ecological perspective.* New York: Guilford Press.

Erikson, E. H. (1980). *Identity and the life cycle.* New York: Norton. (Original work published 1959)

Fielder, F. E. (1967). *A theory of leadership effectiveness.* New York: McGraw-Hill.

Fincham, F. D., & Bradbury, T. N. (in press). Marital conflict: Towards a more complete integration of research and treatment. In J. Vincent (Ed.), *Advances in family intervention, assessment, and theory* (Vol. 5). Greenwich, CT: JAI.

Fisher, C. B., & Johnson, B. L. (1990). Getting mad at mom and dad: Children's changing views of family conflict. *International Journal of Behavioral Development, 13*, 31–48.

Gottman, J. M., & Katz, L. F. (1989). Effects of marital discord on young children's peer interaction and health. *Developmental Psychology, 25*, 373–381.

Grych, J. H., & Fincham, F. D. (1990). Marital conflict and children's adjustment: A cognitive-contextual framework. *Psychological Bulletin, 101*, 267–290.

Hetherington, E. M. (Ed.). (1983). *Handbook of child psychology: Vol. 4. Socialization, personality, and social development* (4th ed.) New York: Wiley.

Horney, K. (1939). *New ways in psychoanalysis.* New York: International Universities Press.

Kiesler, D. J. (1983). The 1982 interpersonal circle: A taxonomy for complementarity in human transactions. *Psychological Review, 90*, 185–214.

Leary, T. (1957). *Interpersonal diagnosis of personality.* New York: Ronald Press.

Levenson, R. W., & Gottman, J. M. (1983). Marital interaction: Physiological linkage and affect exchange. *Journal of Personality and Social Psychology, 45*, 587–597.

Levenson, R. W., & Gottman, J. M. (1985). Physiological and affective predictors of change in relationship satisfaction. *Journal of Personality and Social Psychology, 49*, 85–94.

Maccoby, E. E., & Martin, J. A. (1983). Socialization in the context of the family. In E. M. Hetherington (Ed.), *Handbook of child psychology.* New York: Wiley.

Minuchin, P. (1985). Families and individual development: Provocations from the field of family therapy. *Child Development, 56*, 289–302.

Minuchin, S. (1974). *Families and family therapy.* Cambridge, MA: Harvard University Press.

Omark, D. R. (1980). The group: A factor or an epiphenomenon in evolution? In D. R. Omark, F. F. Strayer, & D. G. Freedman (Eds.), *Dominance relations: An ethological view of human conflict and social interaction.* New York: Garland.

Orford, J. (1986). The rules of interpersonal complementarity: Does hostility beget hostility and dominance, submission? *Psychological Review, 93*, 365–377.

Patterson, G. R. (1982). *Coercive family processes.* Eugene, OR: Castalia.

Plomin, R., & Daniels, D. (1987). Why are children in the same family so different from one another? *Behavioral and Brain Sciences, 10*, 1–16.

Schiffrin, D. (1984). Jewish argument as sociability. *Language in Society, 13*, 311–335.

Shantz, C. U. (1987). Conflicts between children. *Child Development, 58*, 283–305.

Shantz, C. U., & Hobart, C. J. (1989). Social conflict and development: Peers and siblings. In T. J. Berndt & G. Ladd (Eds.), *Peer relationships and child development.* New York: Wiley.

Smetana, J. G. (1988). Adolescents' and parents' conceptions of parental authority. *Child Development*, *59*, 321–335.

Smetana, J. G. (1989). Adolescents' and parents' reasoning about actual family conflict. *Child Development*, *60*, 1052–1067.

Somary, K., & Emery, R. E. (1991). Rational and emotional anger in divorce mediation. *Mediation Quarterly*, *8*, 185–198.

Steinberg, L. (1981). Transformations in family relations at puberty. *Developmental Psychology*, *17*, 833–840.

Sullivan, H. S. (1953). *The interpersonal theory of psychiatry*. New York: Norton.

Vuchinich, S. (1986). On attenuation in verbal family conflict. *Social Psychology Ouarterly*, *47*, 281–293.

Vuchinich, S., Emery, R. E., & Cassidy, J. (1988). Family members as third parties in dyadic family conflict: Strategies, alliances, and outcomes. *Child Development*, *59*, 1293–1302.

Weiss, R. S. (1988). Loss and recovery. *Journal of Social Issues*, *44*, 37–52.

Part III

Conflict and developmental adaptations

11 Conflict and the development of antisocial behavior

*David G. Perry, Louise C. Perry, and
Elizabeth Kennedy*

In this chapter we discuss the role of conflict in the backgrounds and current functioning of children who are frequently involved in aggressive encounters, especially with their peers. Some children who often participate in aggression serve primarily in the role of aggressor, others serve primarily as victims, and still others switch back and forth between these two roles. Many of these children not only have experienced conflictful interactions with their families and peers in the past, but bring forward into new interactions certain styles of thought, feeling, and action that cause them to enter additional conflicts and to escalate these conflicts into aggression. What is known about these links between conflict and aggression is summarized in this chapter.

Progress in understanding aggressive behavior requires maintaining a clear distinction, both conceptually and operationally, between the constructs of conflict and aggression. *Aggression* is behavior aimed at harming another person, whereas *conflict* is a state that exists when one person opposes another. For example, if A does something that B resists (by refusing, denying, disagreeing, etc.), conflict exists. Most conflict does not involve aggression, but most aggression involves conflict (Shantz, 1987). In conflict, the interactants' goals are to overcome one another's opposition and resistance by arguing, persuading, bargaining, aggressing, and so on. Harm to the other is not necessarily an objective, though it may be one. Although most aggression involves conflict, considerable aggression occurs without conflict. For example, when a victim fails to resist a bully's demands or blows, aggression without conflict has transpired.

Unfortunately, assessments of aggression and conflict are often confused, as when peer nomination scales purporting to measure aggression

Preparation of this chapter was facilitated by a grant from the National Science Foundation (BNS 89-07558) to the first and second authors.

301

include items that measure conflict (e.g., "always argues") or when assessments of family conflicts fail to take into account the extent to which the conflicts involve aggression. The failure to distinguish aggression from conflict is unfortunate for several reasons. First, some theories of aggressive development emphasize such a distinction. For example, although certain parameters of family conflict have been hypothesized to cause aggressive development (e.g., Patterson, 1982), assessments of family conflict are often confounded with levels of child aggression, making correlations between the family conflict measures and child aggression exceedingly difficult to interpret.

Second, in the few studies in which rates of conflict and aggression have been kept distinct, the two variables have not been found to relate identically to third variables. For example, D. W. Shantz (1986) found that peer rejection is better predicted by children's participation in conflict than by their aggressiveness.

Third, treating conflict and aggression as similar events obscures the fact that conflict often serves as a broader context in which aggression occurs. Recognizing that aggression is often a response made during a more extended conflict has research implications. For example, it directs researchers' attention to the things children do wrong in the early stages of a conflict and that cause the conflict to escalate into aggression.

Fourth, maintaining the distinction between conflict and aggression has permitted the discovery of individual differences among children in the extent to which their aggression occurs in the context of conflict. Some children are aggressive primarily in the context of heated conflicts, whereas other children aggress mainly in the absence of conflict. Moreover, these two types of children differ in important ways, including emotion regulation and social cognition. Clearly, respecting the distinction between conflict and aggression is essential.

This chapter has four main sections. The first deals with conflict and aggression in the family and the second with conflict and aggression in the peer group. The focus in both sections is on how the conflict construct helps us understand the development of stable individual differences in children's aggression. The third section deals with the relation of conflict to children's tendencies to serve as victims of peer aggression. A brief final section summarizes recent work on aggressive relationships. Keeping clearly in mind the distinction between conflict and aggression helps to organize current data on aggressive behavior, to identify serious shortcomings in existing work, and to suggest directions for future research.

The aggressive child: Family conflict

Two rather distinct, but not incompatible, theoretical approaches have guided research on the relation of family conflict to the development of aggressive behavior. The first emphasizes that the disposition to initiate conflicts, to oppose others, and to escalate conflicts to the point of aggression emerges as a reaction to unsatisfactory and frustrating relationships with significant others, especially the attachment object. The other approach, grounded largely in learning theory, suggests that the ways that parents manage conflict in the home contribute to children's dispositions to participate in conflict and to enact aggression.

The relationship approach

Theory. According to attachment theory (Ainsworth, 1979; Sroufe, 1983), children who experience histories of inconsistent and insensitive caregiving develop insecure attachments and come to believe that others will treat them unfairly and unpredictably. These feelings presumably cause the children to develop dispositions (a) to initiate conflicts (i.e., perform responses that are opposed by others), (b) to oppose the actions of others, and (c) to behave aggressively. Conflict initiations are thought to represent strategies for gaining the attention, proximity, or synchronous responding of caregivers who are unresponsive to the child's other signals. When others try to influence them, insecurely attached children presumably suspect exploitation and therefore resist. Regardless of who initiates a conflict, insecure children's desires for control motivate them to escalate the conflict, resorting to aggression when attempts at lower levels of influence fail.

Two patterns of insecure attachment have been identified – resistant and avoidant. Resistant infants are clingy, easily distressed, and not easily soothed; avoidant infants show little emotion and avoid their caregivers. Avoidant infants have presumably experienced more consistent caregiver neglect or rejection and consequently are angrier. Their anger is masked by avoidance but nonetheless is thought to cause them greater problems with conflict and aggression.

In contrast, securely attached children are expected to have little difficulty with conflict and aggression. Because their caregivers have been empathetically responsive, these children expect others to treat them fairly and to take their needs into account, and therefore they have little need to force their will upon others or to defy the attempts at reasonable, low-pressure influence directed toward them by others.

Evidence. Insecurely attached children, when considered as a group (i.e., when the two subtypes are combined), are indeed more disposed toward conflict than securely attached children. In most studies, attachment classifications have been made at either 18 or 24 months of age, and the children have been assessed for conflict with mothers or peers either contemporaneously or in longitudinal follow-ups several years later. Children with insecure attachments emit more responses that are perceived as aversive by the target and therefore bring opposition. That is, they display more negative affect, whine more, and are more attention seeking, restless, and disruptive with both caregivers and peers (Arend, Gove, & Sroufe, 1979; Waters, Wippman, & Sroufe, 1979). Not only do insecure children initiate more conflicts, but when faced with a request or influence attempt from another, they are less compliant and cooperative, regardless of whether the other is the mother, another adult, or a peer (Bates, Maslin, & Frankel, 1985; Matas, Arend, & Sroufe, 1978).

The link between insecure attachment and aggression is less clear cut. Some studies have found more physical or verbal aggression among insecurely attached children (Lieberman, 1977; Londerville & Main, 1981; Matas et al., 1978; Renken, Egeland, Marvinney, Mangelsdorf, & Sroufe, 1989; Sroufe & Egeland, 1989; Troy & Sroufe, 1987), but other studies have not found securely and insecurely attached children to differ in aggression (Bates et al., 1985; Bates & Bayles, 1988; Fagot & Kavanagh, 1990; LaFreniere & Sroufe, 1985; Lewis, Feiring, McGuffog, & Jaskir, 1984). The hypothesis that avoidantly attached children are especially aggressive also fails to receive consistent support. Some studies confirm the hypothesis (Erikson, Sroufe, & Egeland, 1985; Sroufe & Egeland, 1989; Troy & Sroufe, 1987), whereas others do not (Fagot & Kavanagh, 1990; LaFreniere & Sroufe, 1985).

That insecure attachments are linked to conflict but not necessarily to aggression is interesting because it confirms that children can develop problems with conflict without necessarily also becoming aggressive. The hallmark of the conflict-prone child is a stubborn persistence in trying to influence others against their will, and aggression need not be a part of this effort (D. W. Shantz, 1986). Perhaps insecurely attached children are most likely to develop aggressive habits if both (a) the children develop dispositions toward conflict and (b) the parents mismanage family conflicts (e.g., allow the children to escalate coercive behavior). Indeed, children who are extremely noncompliant and whose parents intermittently reward such defiance are likely to develop aggressive habits (Forehand, 1977).

Although some insecurely attached children may develop aggressive habits, insecure attachments are more clearly associated with children's tendencies to serve as victims of peer aggression than with their tendencies to perform aggression. As we shall see later, many victimized children mismanage conflict and are manifestly anxious. Insecure attachments may contribute to these problems.

Attachment theory is not the only guiding force behind research linking the parent–child relationship to children's conflict and aggression. The work of a number of other, more eclectic, relationship theorists points to another theme in the development of a disposition toward conflict. These theorists emphasize that parents who are willing to give their child control during playful interactions will establish in their child the motivation to reciprocate the parent's cooperative stance and reduce the child's inclination toward noncompliant and coercive behavior (Parpal & Maccoby, 1985; Pettit & Bates, 1989; Rocissano, Slade, & Lynch, 1987). The evidence confirms that mothers who happily comply with their child's initiatives and requests and refrain from making intrusive demands during play reduce their child's inclination toward both conflict and aggression.

Critique. That children with insecure attachments and other relationship difficulties develop problems with conflict and sometimes with aggression is consistent with relationship theories. Two questions, however, can be raised about this work.

First, the relation of conflict to aggression is not well articulated by relationship theorists. Dispositions toward conflict and aggression are considered simply to be two coincident consequences of relationship difficulties. The fact that relationship problems predict conflict better than aggression, however, suggests that relationship theories are not, by themselves, especially good theories of aggressive development. To account adequately for aggressive development, these theories must specify under what conditions difficulties with conflict are and are not also associated with aggressive tendencies. Also, the theory does not tell why some children become aggressive without showing a penchant for conflict.

Second, the work on relationship factors in conflict needs to recognize that not all conflict is maladaptive. Kuczynski's work shows that some forms of child noncompliance (e.g., defiance) are predictive of psychopathology and aggression, whereas other forms (e.g., negotiation) are healthy expressions of autonomy (Kuczynski, Kochanska, & Maguire, in press). Moreover, some children of abusive parents become compulsively compliant, which may dispose the children toward victimization by others (Crittenden & DiLalla, 1988). Such findings caution against assuming that low rates of conflict are necessarily desirable and underscore the importance of assessing the quality of children's conflict management.

The conflict management approach

Theory. How parents manage the numerous and inevitable everyday conflicts both between themselves and their children and between their children and siblings has been postulated to be important in the development of a disposition to initiate and escalate coercive conflicts into aggression. The most comprehensive theory and data within this perspective come from Patterson (1982), who believes that aggressive habits develop when parents are unable to stop their children from escalating the intensity of coercive behavior during family conflicts.

In Patterson's theory, family conflicts begin when one family member directs noxious behavior toward another. Many of the aversive responses that start conflicts are seemingly trivial and mild, such as expressing disapproval of the other, asking the other to do something, or asking the other to stop doing something, whereas other provocations are more severe, such as teasing, laughing at, or pushing someone. If the recipient opposes the move with an aversive response of his or her own (e.g., noncompliance, whining, or reciprocated insult), the initial provocateur may respond with another, intensified aversive behavior, and a cycle of mutually escalating hostility may ensue. Aggressive responses are a subset of aversive responses to which a participant may resort when lower key aversives fail. The cycle continues until one person "gives up" by withdrawing his or her aversive behavior. The person who withdraws is usually rewarded by the other person also retreating, but the person who gives up first is rewarding the other for using high-intensity coercive behavior and therefore increases the chance that the other will use force again in the future. This is known as the "coercion model" of aggression.

Patterson hypothesizes that aggressive development is likely if the parents permit conflicts to escalate and at least intermittently reinforce the child's coercive behavior by being the first to withdraw from aversive responding. This contingency teaches children that it is worthwhile to escalate their negativism, whining, and yelling into aggressive behavior when they wish to ward off the noxious demands and intrusions of other people or when they wish to impose their will on a resisting other. Once children learn aggressive tactics at home, they can generalize their coercive tendencies to interactions beyond the home (e.g., to the peer group).

Evidence. Patterson's (1982) comparisons of aggressive and normal boys' interactions with family members support his theory. The frequency and duration of aversive exchanges are exceptionally high in distressed families (those with an aggressive child), and parents of aggressive children, especially mothers, handle these conflicts less competently than parents of nonaggressive children. To begin with, mothers of aggressive children start more conflicts: They present the initial aversive responses that begin conflicts ("start-ups") at high rates. (A *start-up* is defined as an aversive response that follows neutral or prosocial behavior by the other party.) Many mother–child conflicts begin with a maternal command followed by child noncompliance. Other aversive responses favored by mothers of problem children are disapproval, negativism, and yelling. Mothers of aggressive children not only provide more start-ups, but also respond to aversive behavior from other family members with aversive responses of their own ("counterattack"). Moreover, these aversive responses tend to take the form of ineffectual nattering (empty threats, pleading, nagging, and scolding) that serves to escalate the conflict. After allowing a conflict to escalate, mothers may abruptly stop responding aversively (e.g., cease placing demands on the child), thereby reinforcing the child's coercion, or they may explode with anger and physically assault the child. The result is that conflict produces inconsistent and unpredictable outcomes for the child.

Patterson (1982) has found substantial correlations among parental tendencies (a) to present start-up stimuli for conflict, (b) to counterattack the child's aversive overtures, and (c) to continue being aversive given a counterattack by the child. Thus, mothers of aggressive children possess a trait of "irritability," or an unpleasant style of interaction that involves a willingness to engage in, prolong, and escalate hostilities.

Mothers of aggressive children also mismanage sibling conflicts. They intervene inconsistently in sibling fights, and when they do intervene, they often fail to limit the bickering (Loeber & Tengs, 1986). Thus, sibling conflicts also serve as a fertile breeding ground for aggressive habits.

In contrast to parents of aggressive children, parents of normal children present fewer of the initial aversive behaviors (e.g., commands) that start conflicts, and they are less likely to counterattack aversive behavior from the child. That is, they are more likely to ignore or overlook a child startup and thereby prevent a conflict. If they do decide to punish a child's aversive responding, they do not natter but stop whatever they are doing and punish until coercive behavior stops.

Patterson's work also reveals important differences between aggressive and nonaggressive children's behavior during family conflicts. Aggressive children present more start-ups and also counterattack others' aversive initiatives more than normal children do. They are noncompliant and have trouble coping with noxious intrusions from other family members. Moreover, once a conflict is under way, aggressive children are far more likely than nonaggressive children to persist in aversive behavior, thereby escalating the conflict. Patterson (1982) reports substantial correlations among children's tendencies to provide start-ups, to counterattack, and to prolong coercive behavior, indicating a general dimension of deviance analogous to the parental trait of irritability.

Other researchers besides Patterson have studied parents' conflict management. Most studies have focused specifically on how parents can best minimize child noncompliance. Several themes emerge. First, skillful parents recognize in advance the contexts likely to elicit aversive child behaviors that spark conflict, and they proactively take steps to reduce the risk of conflict. For example, mothers who entertain and distract their toddlers while shopping for groceries reduce the chance of conflict (Holden, 1983). Second, parents who synchronize their demands with the child's readiness to receive them are more successful at gaining compliance than those who do not. For example, mothers who make sure they have their child's attention, who precede their requests with a display of affection, and who adjust their requests to fit the child's immediately preceding behavior (e.g., by giving more specific instructions when the child looks baffled) achieve the most compliance (Lytton & Zwirner, 1975; Westerman, 1990). Finally, although parents sometimes need to resort to power assertion (force) to curtail the child's noncompliance and coercion, it is clear that parental force should be no more intense than that necessary to achieve compliance: Abusive use of force is associated with noncompliant and aggressive behavior in children (George & Main, 1979; Walker, Downey, & Bergman, 1989).

Critique. The Patterson work, in particular, provides a vivid and detailed picture of what goes awry in the family conflicts of aggressive children. Two questions, however, can be raised about this work.

First, there is some question as to whether the family conflict variables stressed by Patterson contribute to the acquisition of aggressive habits or only to the maintenance of the child's existing aggressive tendencies. In Patterson's theory, aggressive development results when parents allow children to escalate coercive behavior during family conflicts. However, the research designs are correlational, and therefore it is impossible to discern the direction of the causal arrow between the family conflict variables hypothesized to cause aggressive development (the parent's ability to stop the child's aversive behavior, parental irritability, etc.) and the child's deviant tendencies. We saw that aggressive children are disposed to present start-ups, to counterattack, and to persist with coercion in conflicts with parents; these child tendencies obviously contribute to the frequency and duration of family conflicts and very likely also affect the measures of parental conflict management, including parental irritability and parental ability to stop child aversive responding. Longitudinal research showing that family conflict variables at one time predict child aggression at a later time beyond the simple stability of children's aggression over the two time points is required to confirm the acquisition hypothesis.

Of course, even if aggression is not originally acquired in the context of mismanaged family conflicts but stems from other sources, there remains the possibility that family conflicts serve to maintain or allow child aggression. Indeed, Patterson's (1982) clinical work indicates that when parents are taught to manage family conflicts more effectively (e.g., by punishing child coercion with time-out), child aggression is lessened. This suggests that, at the least, ill-managed family conflict helps to maintain aggressive responding.

Second, the Patterson work might profit from a clearer differentiation between conflict and aggression. Aggression is considered a subset of aversive responses that can be emitted during conflict, but data analyses tend not to distinguish aversive responses that are aggressive from those that are not. Differentiating aggressive from nonaggressive aversive responses would allow additional questions to be asked: How much of children's aversive behavior during family conflict must actually escalate to the point of aggression (and what forms must this aggression take) before children will develop aggressive dispositions? Do some parents allow conflicts to escalate as long as the conflicts remain nonaggressive but swiftly punish aggressive responding, and do their children become contentious but not aggressive? Do the parent management variables thought to cause aggressive development lead to an increase over time in the proportion of children's aversive behaviors that are aggressive? Does mismanagement of conflict lead children to escalate their aversive responding to the level of aggression at increasingly earlier points during conflicts or to display aggression even outside the context of conflict? Until aggressive responses are measured independently of other conflict responses, it will be difficult to conceptualize and evaluate interesting linkages between conflict and aggression.

Parent–parent conflict

Children whose parents often engage in angry fights are more noncompliant (conflict prone) and aggressive at both home and school than children with more peaceful parents (MacKinnon, 1989). Feuding parents are both less able to promote secure attachments (Howes & Markman, 1989) and less able to manage parent–child conflicts effectively (Patterson, 1982), and these parenting deficiencies may mediate the link between marital discord and child deviance. Of course, children can also directly imitate parental conflict and aggression (Bandura, 1986; Steinmetz, 1977). Chronic exposure to angry adult conflicts, especially unresolved conflicts, may also dispose children to become emotionally disregulated during their own conflicts (Cummings, Vogel, Cummings, & El-Sheikh, 1989). Emotional disregulation (especially the inability to soothe oneself during heightened emotional responding) may promote the escalation of conflict into aggression, possibly by interfering with cognitive processes that ordinarily inhibit aggressive responding.

The aggressive child: Peer conflict

Children who receive "basic training" in conflict and aggression at home transfer their antisocial response tendencies to new contexts, including peer groups, the school, and the community (Patterson, 1982). In addition, noncompliant and aggressive youngsters elicit from new people in new settings (e.g., teachers and peers) the aversive start-ups that trigger conflict and aggression, further ensuring the transfer of aggression from family to peers (Dodge, Pettit, McClaskey, & Brown, 1986).

The ways in which conflict and aggression are linked in peer interaction are examined next. We begin by pointing out that aggressive children differ in the extent to which their aggression is embedded in conflict. The ways that aggressive children mismanage conflicts are then discussed. Finally, we review the role of cognition in conflict and aggression.

Individual differences among aggressive children

Aggressive children differ in the extent to which their aggression occurs in the context of extended conflicts. Some aggressive children apply force swiftly and unemotionally to gain what they want. Because these children encounter little resistance from their victims, their aggression is relatively conflict free. We call these children *effectual aggressors*. Most playground bullies qualify for this designation. Other aggressive children perform aggression primarily in the context of extended and emotionally heated conflicts. Regardless of who starts a fight, these children prolong the battle, become emotionally aroused, escalate the conflict into aggression, but, importantly, usually end up losing the battle amid exaggerated displays of frustration and distress. We call these children *ineffectual aggressors*.

A simple way to tell the extent to which an aggressive child embeds aggression in extended conflict (i.e., is an effectual vs. ineffectual aggressor)

	Victimized children	Nonvictimized children
Aggressive children	High-conflict or ineffectual aggressors (also called high-conflict victims)	Low-conflict or effectual aggressors
Nonaggressive children	Low-conflict victims	Nondeviant children

Figure 11.1.   Combinations of aggressor and victim roles

is by noting where the child falls on the dimension of victimization, or the tendency to serve as a target of peer attacks. Aggressive children who are rarely victimized by peers tend to be effectual, low-conflict aggressors, whereas aggressive children who often serve as victims of peer attacks tend to be ineffectual, high-conflict aggressors. Because aggression and victimization are orthogonal dimensions (Kupersmidt, Patterson, & Eickholt, 1989; Olweus, 1978; Perry, Kusel, & Perry, 1988), it is possible to conceptualize the combinations of aggressor and victim roles in a 2 × 2 factorial scheme, as depicted in Figure 11.1. The effectual and ineffectual aggressor subtypes occupy the upper two cells of this configuration.

That ineffectual aggressors have considerably more trouble with conflict than effectual aggressors is confirmed by peer and teacher descriptions of the two kinds of children. Compared to effectual aggressors, ineffectual aggressors are perceived as more disruptive, attention seeking, hyperactive, dishonest (prone to lie and steal), abrasive in peer group entry style, angry in response to teasing, deficient in conflict management skills (argumentative and persistent in attempts to influence others against their will), prone to hostile attributional bias (likely to blame others for things they do not do), likely to lose their fights amidst exaggerated displays of pain and suffering, anxious, depressed, and rejected by peers (Kupersmidt et al., 1989; Perry, Williard, & Perry, 1990; Pierce, 1990). Clearly, ineffectual aggressors are more disposed toward protracted conflict and conflict mismanagement than their more effectual counterparts.

Patterson (1982) observed that the problem child referred to clinics and involved in family conflicts usually is not a highly skilled aggressor who is an effective competitor in peer conflicts: "On the contrary, the problem child is usually unskilled at fist fighting or wrestling; he tends to be an inept competitor" (p. 36). Patterson also noted that these children ignore the metastructure in groups, behaving as if the dominance hierarchy that influences their peers does not exist. These observations suggest that children who are involved in many poorly managed conflicts at home are also contentious with peers: They enter numerous heated conflicts, deploy aggression, but lose. Clearly these children qualify for the label of ineffectual, high-conflict aggressors. Perhaps extensive experience with prolonged coercive conflict in the family disposes children to display emotionally disregulated forms of aggression with peers rather than to become effectual bullies.

The marked differences between effectual and ineffectual aggressors suggest that it will be useful to maintain the distinction between these two kinds of aggressors in future research. Throughout this chapter, we propose hypotheses regarding possible differences between the two types of aggressors in etiology, social cognition, emotion regulation, and prognosis for developmental outcomes.

Distinguishing among aggressive children on the basis of whether their aggression is embedded in extended conflict (the effectual–ineffectual distinction) is, of course, not the only way to subdivide aggressive children. Dodge and Coie (1987) propose a distinction among aggressive children based on whether their aggression is primarily proactive (motivated by future reward) or reactive (motivated by prior provocation). The proportion of a child's aggression that is reactive rather than proactive probably is somewhat higher for ineffectual, high-conflict aggressors than for effectual, low-conflict aggressors. However, the correlation between children's rates of proactive and reactive aggression is very high ($r = .76$; Dodge & Coie, 1987), as is the correlation between children's rates of start-up and counterattack (Patterson, 1982). This indicates that a distinction among children in terms of whether their aggression is primarily proactive or reactive is of limited utility. We believe that aggressive children are better distinguished in terms of the duration, emotional intensity, and outcomes of their conflicts than by whether their aggression is mainly proactive or counterattack.

Aggressive children's management of conflict

Studying when and how conflict does and does not evolve into aggression would allow one to identify not only the mistakes that aggressive children make that cause conflicts to turn violent but also the skillful, peaceful moves that children can make that lead to conflicts being resolved non aggressively. Naturalistic and laboratory comparisons of the conflict management of effectual aggressors, ineffectual aggressors, and nonaggressive children would be informative. Also, because aggressive children selectively direct their attacks toward a minority of peers who serve consistently as victims, comparisons of aggressive and nonaggressive children's handling of conflict with both victimized and nonvictimized partners are needed. Aggressive and nonaggressive children's conflicts need to be compared on at least three dimensions – contexts, tactics, and outcomes. Each is discussed in turn.

Contexts. What are the contexts for aggressive children's conflicts? Some of the contexts for aggressive conflicts can be inferred from research on the stimuli that provoke aggression. For example, much aggression involves object disputes and ego-threatening provocations (Hartup, 1974). Other situations found to cause problems for many children are exclusion by peers, social comparison, peer group entry, and peer persuasion and manipulation (Dodge & Feldman, 1990). Another context for aggressive conflicts is rough-and-tumble play (Humphreys & Smith, 1987; Pellegrini, 1988), which tends to deteriorate into aggression among unpopular aggressive boys but not among popular nonaggressive ones.

Although research confirms that much aggression is a reaction to provocation, an important but often overlooked fact is that aggressive children also are disposed to start conflicts "out of the blue" or in the absence of discernible provocation. Rausch (1965) found that although highly aggressive boys were slightly more likely than nonaggressive boys to respond to an unfriendly act by a peer with an unfriendly act of their own (conditional probabilities of .80 vs. .77), the highly aggressive boys were much more likely than the nonaggressive ones to respond in an unfriendly way to prosocial behavior by a peer (.45 vs. .80). This finding is reminiscent of Patterson's (1982) finding of more aversive start-ups by aggressive children. Tremendous research effort has been expended to determine why aggressive children react adversely to provocation, but equal attention should be paid to the conditions that cause aggressive children to initiate conflicts out of the blue.

In actuality, many of the conditions that elevate children's dispositions to deliver an aversive start-up may be the same conditions that lower children's thresholds for responding to provocations from others with counterattack. We say this because we suspect that the disposition to initiate conflict and the disposition to counterattack are often simply two manifestations of a common underlying state of irritability, or a "readiness to engage in conflict." In an insightful paper, Garvey (1984) pointed out that almost anything said by another individual can be opposed (and therefore be grounds for conflict) if a child is "looking for a fight." It is time to look for the conditions that make children eager for conflict. In addition to observing and interviewing children about the precursors of their conflicts, it might be useful to design experiments in which rates of conflict of aggressive and nonaggressive children are examined as a function of manipulations expected to affect a readiness for conflict (e.g., mood induction, threat, positive and negative social comparisons, exposure to modeled aggression or conflict, and opportunity for angry rumination). Identifying the factors that make a child look for a fight in the first place is probably at least as important as studying the events that occur during conflicts once they have begun.

Tactics and strategies. There is astonishingly little research on what happens during aggressive children's conflicts that causes the quarrels to escalate into aggression. Comparisons of aggressive and nonaggressive children's conflicts are needed and should include assessments of (a) the ways they initiate conflicts, (b) the ways they oppose their partner's startups, and (c) the other tactics, strategies, goals, and roles they assume during quarrels. Existing studies of children's conflicts could serve as a source of hypotheses about differences between aggressive and nonaggressive children's conflict management (see Shantz, 1987, for a review of research on children's conflicts).

Certain moves during conflict escalate the battle, whereas other moves decelerate conflict, and it would seem worthwhile to see if these accelerating and decelerating events function in the same way in the conflicts of aggressive and nonaggressive children. For example, "standing firm" or insisting on having one's way is usually matched by insistence from the partner and therefore escalates a conflict, whereas giving a reason for disagreeing tends to be followed by a proposal for compromise and usually ends the conflict (Eisenberg & Garvey, 1981; Walton & Sedlak, 1982). Other conciliatory moves that slow conflict include apologizing, proposing cooperation, offering an object or sharing, offering something not immediately available, friendly touching, negotiating, bargaining, changing the topic, and clarifying the other's feelings (Hartup, Laursen, Stewart, & Eastenson, 1988; Miller, Danaher, & Forbes, 1986). Perhaps aggressive children fail to make these moves toward peace or fail to respond appropriately when these moves are offered by a partner.

Nonverbal behavior of aggressive and nonaggressive children during conflict also deserves more research attention. Aggressive children are less likely than nonaggressive children to tone down an aggressive attack when a victim shows signs of pain and suffering (Perry & Bussey, 1977; Perry & Perry, 1974). Aggressive and nonaggressive children may differ in production of, or reaction to, other nonverbal signals.

Outcomes. How a conflict ends depends in part on the tactics used during the conflict, and therefore the outcomes of conflicts are likely to differ for aggressive and nonaggressive children. Tactics that are most successful (i.e., that lead to winning) are not coercive ones but, instead, are those that acknowledge the other's perspective and reflect sensitivity to the other's interests and needs (Shantz, 1987). The least successful tactics are sheer insistence on one's way and the use of either physical or verbal aggression (Eisenberg & Garvey, 1981; Shantz & Shantz, 1982). This important finding shatters the myth that aggression generally gets children what they want, but it is consistent with our earlier point that children who enact aggression primarily in the context of heated conflicts (ineffectual or high-conflict aggressors) also are victimized by peers and are generally unsuccessful in their aggression.

Cognitions about conflict and peer aggression

Children's perceptions of events that unfold during conflict almost certainly affect the probability that the conflict will escalate into aggression. In this section, we review two theoretical models concerning the role of cognition in conflict and aggression. We also discuss four additional issues – the cognitions conducive to starting a fight, the relation of affect to cognition, the target specificity of social cognitions, and the origins of social cognitions.

Dodge's social information-processing model. Dodge (1986) has proposed that competent responding to a social cue (e.g., provocation from a peer) occurs only if the child skillfully processes the cue through the five cognitive steps of encoding, interpretation, response search, response evaluation, and enactment. Research confirms that aggressive children possess deficits or biases at these processing steps that lead them to react aggressively to provocation. For example, aggressive children are inclined to interpret ambiguously motivated provocations as acts of deliberate hostility (Dodge, 1980; Slaby & Guerra, 1988), and they expect and value the various rewards that aggression has to offer (control over a victim, tangible rewards, etc.) more than nonaggressive children do (Boldizar, Perry, & Perry, 1989; Perry, Perry, & Rasmussen, 1986; Slaby & Guerra, 1988).

Dodge's model helps explain aggressive children's reactions to a single precipitating provocation. Much aggression occurs, however, not as a direct reaction to a single provocation but as a response to events that unfold during conflict, many of which are quite removed from the original provocation. It would therefore be worthwhile to compare aggressive and nonaggressive children's cognitive processing of cues that occur once conflict is underway, especially cues that research has shown to increase or decrease the chance that conflict will escalate into aggression. That is, aggressive and nonaggressive children might be compared for interpretation, response search, and response evaluation in reaction to a partner's conflict-escalating tactics, such as making strong demands, ignoring the other, defiant noncompliance, simple refusal, and standing firm, but also in reaction to a partner's conflict-decelerating moves, such as offering reasons for disagreeing or suggesting compromises.

Dodge's model also might be used to address some compelling questions about differences between effectual and ineffectual aggressors. The fact that ineffectual aggressors continue to attempt aggressive solutions to conflicts even though these efforts are generally unsuccessful is interesting because it poses a problem for theories emphasizing that action choices are a function of anticipated consequences and perceptions of self-efficacy (e.g., Bandura's social-cognitive theory). Perhaps ineffectual aggressors make unrealistic assessments of outcomes and competencies, or perhaps they attach such great value to dominating an adversary that they persevere in aggression despite failure. Also, a low threshold for extreme affective excitation or an inability to calm themselves when aroused may prevent them from rationally processing information about likely consequences. Our hunch is that both ineffectual and effectual aggressors place great value on controlling their adversaries (see Boldizar et al., 1989) but that ineffectual aggressors also have low thresholds for sensing that they are losing control over an adversary during conflict. This sensed loss of control may lead to arousal that preempts aggression-inhibiting cognitions, much in the same way that parents who feel that they are losing control over a difficult child sometimes forget about the consequences of their actions and resort to abusive behavior (Bugental, Blue, & Cruzcosa, 1989).

Selman's model of negotiation strategies. According to Selman (1980; Selman & Demorest, 1984; Yeates & Selman, 1989), the tactics children use to resolve the inner and interpersonal disequilibrium that arises during conflict can be called "interpersonal negotiation strategies." These strategies can be aimed at transforming the self (e.g., withdrawing or conceding), transforming the other (e.g., asking or aggressing), or both (e.g., suggesting a compromise or an alternative joint activity). A child's selection of a given tactic is thought to rest on social-information-processing steps similar to those proposed by Dodge, but Selman also believes that strategy selection is constrained by the child's underlying capacity for perspective taking. Four developmental levels of perspective taking are identified, and interpersonal negotiation strategies are classified according to the perspective-taking level they reflect. From least to most sophisticated, the four strategy levels are impulsive (nonreflective attempts to influence or to resist influence), unilateral (strategies reflecting the belief that the conflict is caused by and solvable by one person), reciprocal (strategies appreciating that conflicts involve two parties and that resolution requires the agreement of both), and collaborative (attempts to change both oneself's and the other's wishes in pursuit of a mutual goal).

Tests of Selman's model have involved comparing aggressive and nonaggressive children on two measures of strategy usage: the modal developmental level of a child's strategies and the percentage of a child's strategies that are other-transforming rather than self-transforming. As predicted, aggressive children's strategies represent lower developmental levels and are more other-transforming than are less aggressive children's strategies (Leadbeater, Hellner, Allen, & Aber, 1989; Yeates, Schultz, & Selman, 1991). However, combining diverse strategies into global categories by developmental level or by self- versus other-transforming orientation contributes little to our understanding of the specific strategies or sequences of strategies that escalate or deescalate conflict. Consequently, Selman's model is of little utility for elucidating the processes by which aggressive children's conflicts degenerate into aggression.

Cognitions conducive to start-ups. As noted, aggressive children present many aversive start-ups and begin conflicts out of the blue. Consequently, research on cognition in aggression must be expanded to elucidate conditions that make children cast the first stone. Interviewing children about their thoughts, plans, goals, and concerns prior to beginning a conflict might be informative. Also, finding out what aggressive and nonaggressive children worry and ruminate about during recess, lunch, and other free periods at school should be helpful (Parkhurst & Asher, 1985). A child who has been ruminating about a real or perceived humiliation, for example, might be vigilant for an opportunity to reassert control, restore his or her position in the status hierarchy, or otherwise right the wrong by initiating and prevailing in conflict. Also, conflicts may be reactions to internal, fantasized events. For example, aggressive children may imagine approaching play partners but may do so with expectations of rebuff, opposition, or unfair treatment that, although not strong enough to deter them from approaching at all, may cause them, nonetheless, to interact as if a conflict were already underway.

Affect and cognition. How emotional arousal interacts with cognitive factors to influence the escalation of conflict into aggression deserves greater study. Arousal depends partly on cognition. For example, realizing that one is losing control can increase arousal, and awareness of another's pain and suffering can arouse empathic distress. Arousal, however, also affects the cognitions that encourage or discourage aggression. Zillmann (1988) suggests that arousal preempts much cognitive processing that ordinarily serves to deter aggression (e.g., consideration of the negative consequences of aggressing). Arousal also may exaggerate certain of the cognitive deficits and biases associated with aggressive responding, for example, by increasing attributions of hostile intent (Dodge & Somberg, 1987) or by increasing the subjective importance of gaining control over an adversary (Boldizar et al., 1989; Bugental et al., 1989). Of course, arousal need not always have the net effect of increasing aggression. In fact, for some children, arousal may elicit cognitions that encourage flight rather than fight. This may be true of certain victimized children. We imagine that affect–cognition linkages differ markedly for the four groups of children who occupy the different cells of Figure 11.1. Therefore, we recommend using this fourfold classification scheme in research on this issue.

Specificity of cognitions. Often overlooked is the fact that a child's social cognitions are dependent on the identity of the specific peer the child is thinking about (i.e., the "target" of the cognitions). For example, children are more likely to excuse the provocative behavior of a well-liked peer than of a disliked peer (Hymel, 1986), and they are more likely to attribute hostile intent to a peer known to have been aggressive in the past than to a peer whose record is clear (Waas, 1988). Also, the outcomes that children expect for aggressing and the importance they attach to those outcomes depend on target factors such as the sex of the target (Boldizar et al., 1989; Perry, Perry, & Weiss, 1989), the aggressiveness of the target (Perry et al., 1986), and whether the target is a habitual victim of peer aggression (Perry et al., 1990). We shall see later that most aggression is enacted in the context of specific aggressor–victim relationships. It is important, therefore, to investigate how aggressive children's cognitions vary according to whether the target is or is not a preferred victim.

Origins of cognitions. According to social-cognitive theory (Bandura, 1986), the cognitions governing aggression (e.g., outcome expectancies and values) represent mental integrations and summarizations of critical social learning experiences, especially direct feedback from socializing agents (e.g., parents and peers) and exposure to real-life and media models. Relationship theorists (e.g., Sroufe & Fleeson, 1988) emphasize cognitive representations of relationship experiences as important. Children who lack a representation of their caregiver as responsive and empathic or who experience an exploitative aggressor–victim relationship at home are thought to expect others to be hostile and unfair and to believe that aggression and victimization are normal components of a relationship.

Too little research has examined the origins of social cognitions. One finding consistent with both social-cognitive and relationship theories is that maternal hostility and irritability are associated with deviant social information processing by the child: Mothers who state a preference for aggressive solutions to conflict (Keane, Brown, & Crenshaw, 1990; Pettit, Dodge, & Brown, 1988), who are prone to attribute hostility to their children (Pettit et al., 1988), or who are disagreeable and aggressive (Hart, Ladd, & Burleson, 1990; Putallaz, 1987) have children who also show hostile attributional biases and/or endorse aggressive solutions to conflict.

More research on linkages between the home environment and child cognition is needed. One hypothesis is that experience with coercive cycles in the home contributes to the great value that aggressive children assign to achieving control over an adversary (Boldizar et al., 1989). Escalating conflicts are times of intense emotion, especially frustration over not being able to exert control and anxiety over the unpredictability of the outcome. Such experiences may render children hypervigilant for situations offering possible loss of control and raise the value they place on dominating an adversary.

According to attachment theory, securely and insecurely attached children differ in their confidence that other people will take their needs into account and treat them fairly when planning joint activities or negotiating conflicts. Questionnaire and interview instruments tapping these cognitions need to be developed and related to children's penchants for conflict and aggression. Children who lack confidence that others will treat them fairly when planning an activity or settling a dispute may suspect exploitation (when others try to influence them) and obstinately resist. Whether such children escalate the resistance into aggression, however, may depend on additional aggression-specific cognitive mediators such as beliefs that aggression will succeed and that the self is capable of enacting the requisite aggressive responses.

The victimized child and conflict

Little is known about the backgrounds and behavior of children who serve habitually as targets of peer attacks. The scant research suggests, however, that victimized children have as much trouble managing conflicts as aggressive children do, although their specific difficulties with conflict management are not necessarily the same as those of aggressive children.

Individual differences among victimized children

As a group, victimized children share certain characteristics. They use ineffectual persuasion tactics and reward their attackers by losing disputes. They lack humor, self-confidence, self-esteem, and prosocial skills. They cry easily and are anxious, physically weak, disliked by peers, depressed, and lonely (Kupersmidt et al., 1989; Olweus, 1978; Patterson, Littman, & Bricker, 1967; Perry et al., 1988, 1990; Pierce, 1990; Schwartz & Dodge, 1990). Peer, teacher, and self-reports are concordant in revealing these characteristics.

Victims, however, vary in the degree to which their victimization occurs in the context of conflict (Pierce, 1990). Some victims are high-conflict victims. These children are aggressive as well as victimized. They provoke other children and they counterattack when provoked. They angrily persist in trying to influence others against their will or in warding off the influence attempts of others, but they usually end up losing their battles amidst displays of distress and frustration. This description should sound familiar; it is the same as our earlier description of high-conflict, ineffectual aggressors. Indeed, high-conflict, ineffectual aggressors and high-conflict victims are one and the same children: They are children who score high on both aggression and victimization. Low-conflict victims, in contrast, score high on victimization but low on aggression. These children yield quickly and passively to aggressors' demands, so their victimization tends not to occur in the context of extended conflicts. The submissiveness of these children, however, surely must be considered a form of conflict mismanagement.

Pierce (1990) compared peers' perceptions of victims who are either aggressive (high-conflict victims) or nonaggressive (low-conflict victims). High-conflict victims were seen as argumentative, always having to have their own way, ready to blame others for things they did not do, persistent in attempts to enter peer groups that did not want them, disruptive, prone to lie and steal, and likely to respond to teasing with anger. Low-conflict victims, however, were seen as withdrawn, avoidant of conflict, and likely to "hover" rather than to try to enter peer groups. In addition, high-conflict victims were considerably more disliked than were low-conflict victims.

Direct observations of high- and low-conflict victims and nonvictimized children in both natural and structured settings are needed to answer several questions: Do the contexts for conflict differ for these children? Do the groups differ in rate or style of provocation, counterattack, resistance, persistence, persuasion, and conflict resolution? Perhaps one or both types of victims fail to produce the conciliatory responses (suggestion of compromise, offering an explanation for disagreement, etc.) that usually elicit a peaceful move from a partner, or perhaps they fail to move toward peace when a conciliatory response is offered by a partner.

Studies of the social cognitions conducive to victimization are also needed to understand differences between high- and low-conflict victims. Do low-conflict victims yield quickly to aggressors' demands because they fail to consider, or are afraid to perform, assertive and other adaptive responses? What distortions of thought are responsible for high-conflict victims' use of aggressive and other coercive tactics even though they are likely to lose their fights? Do both high- and low-conflict victims possess a hostile attributional bias (a reasonable outcome if this bias is caused by a history of aversive treatment by others), or do only the more aggressive, high-conflict victims possess the bias? Do victimized children experience the cognitions conducive to victimization only when interacting with specific peers that pick on them or when interacting with any peer?

The roles of temperament and emotion regulation in high- and low-conflict victims' mismanagement of conflict also need to be explored. Gottman and Katz (1989) suggest the existence of two adrenal endocrine stress systems – one associated with anger, the other with helplessness and withdrawal. Perhaps the anger system is activated in high-conflict victims, and the fear/withdrawal system in low-conflict victims.

Developmental outcomes for both kinds of victims require study. Low-conflict victims may be at risk for depression and suicide. High-conflict victims may persist in their ineffectual aggression for years to come. Indeed, if they have a strong need to control an adversary but also have a low threshold for sensing that they are losing control during conflict (as we surmised earlier), then we might expect these children to grow up to behave abusively toward their own offspring. Bugental et al. (1989), for example, report that abusive parents are prone to perceive the balance of power and control during conflict to shift in favor of their children, and the parents' abusive behavior is a reaction to this perception.

Backgrounds of victimized children

Children with histories of conflictful, insecure attachments are more likely to develop problems of victimization than children whose attachments were more secure (Jacobson & Wille, 1986; LaFreniere & Sroufe, 1985; Troy &

Sroufe, 1987). Moreover, resistant attachments are more closely linked to victimization than are avoidant attachments. Resistantly attached children are manifestly anxious, cry easily, and explore little, and this cluster of attributes may promote their victimization.

Parental mismanagement of family conflicts also may contribute to a disposition to be victimized. We speculated earlier that parents who allow family conflicts to escalate and who inconsistently reward and punish their children's coercion may cause their children to value control over an adversary. The high value placed on control may cause the child to use force during conflict, but if the child is not a skilled fighter, a high-conflict victim (or ineffectual aggressor) may result. In contrast, parents who avoid family conflict at all costs or who refuse the child any degree of assertion or self-expression during conflict may engender guilt feelings in the child over the thought of opposition or noncompliance, thereby creating the low-conflict victim who compulsively submits to the demands of stronger others. Parental overprotection may also shield the child from conflict and prevent the child from learning the skills necessary to avoid exploitation (Olweus, 1978). In addition, marital conflict may lead to the child's victimization by peers, especially if the marital discord causes the child to become emotionally disregulated (Gottman & Katz, 1989) or to develop internalizing disorders (depression, anxiety) that signal the child's vulnerability to aggressive peers.

Finally, continuity between child abuse and peer victimization should be explored. Victims of child abuse and victims of peer aggression share certain qualities, especially irritability, intractability, and proneness to cry (deLissovoy, 1979; Gil, 1970). It may be that certain child properties that contribute to abuse by parents also contribute to abuse by peers, but the possibility that the experience of being abused by parents also contributes to victimization by peers needs to be explored. Of course, the fact that child abuse has been implicated also in aggressive development means that attention must be paid to discovering moderator variables that govern when child abuse promotes aggression, victimization, or both. Child temperament, child physical strength, and whether the abusive parent intermittently permits child coercion may be important.

Aggressive relationships

Recent studies indicate that most peer aggression occurs in the context of specific dyadic "aggressive relationships" (Coie & Christopoulos, 1989; Dodge & Coie, 1989). Two types of aggressive relationships have been observed. In one type, the "high-conflict" or "symmetrical" relationship, both members aggress against and are victimized by the other member. In contrast, in the "low-conflict" or "asymmetrical" relationship, one member fairly reliably serves as the aggressor and the other as the victim. We suspect that both children in high-conflict aggressive relationships are usually ineffectual aggressors (or high-conflict victims). We suspect further that low-conflict dyads may be composed ordinarily of one low-conflict aggressor and one low-conflict victim. These hypotheses, though, require verification.

How do aggressive relationships evolve? It is fairly easy to understand how low-conflict, asymmetrical (bully–victim) aggressive relationships develop: A skilled aggressor tries out aggressive actions toward a variety of targets and eventually settles on victims who do not resist (Dodge & Coie, 1989; Olweus, 1978; Patterson et al., 1967). Understanding the evolution of high-conflict dyads, however, is more difficult. Sroufe and Fleeson (1988) suggest that children with histories of insecure attachments or abuse have internalized the roles of both exploiter and exploitee and seek out peer interaction partners who allow them to enact both of these familiar roles. Coie and Christopoulos (1989) speculate that there is something about the interactive mix of high-conflict dyads that makes each member highly sensitized to the possibility of hostile intentions on the part of the other, causing aggression to flow in both directions. These authors note that children who are members of a high-conflict dyad often interact with other children in nonaggressive, highly cooperative ways. This substantiates the relationship specificity of the children's difficulties and demonstrates a social flexibility not commonly attributed to aggressive children.

Some victimized children do not dislike their attackers and may even seek them out for social interaction. Dodge and Coie (1989), for example, found that victims in low-conflict relationships did not dislike their bullies and sometimes mimicked or followed them. Troy and Sroufe (1987) also reported that some victimized children even invite a bully to aggress (e.g., "Aren't you going to tease me today? I won't get mad."). The dynamics responsible for such behavior merit study. Of course, because both aggressive and victimized children are rejected by the peer group, the two kinds of outcasts may seek each other for contact simply because no one else will.

Perhaps the most important contribution of the relationship perspective to the study of aggression is a shift away from a traitlike conceptualization of aggression as something that resides strictly within the individual. Clearly, much aggression is the product of the unique interactive chemistry between two people in an enduring relationship. Serious aggression among adults (murder, rape, and spousal and child abuse) is often embedded in relationships. Recognizing the relationship dependency of childhood aggression not only suggests a point of conceptual continuity between child aggression and adult aggression, but also suggests certain developmental hypotheses worthy of test. For example, children who exercise aggression primarily in high-conflict relationships may grow up to exercise aggression in adulthood also mainly in conflictful relationships.

Conclusion

Theory and research on aggression will advance only if a clear distinction is maintained between the constructs of conflict and aggression. Most aggression occurs in the context of broader conflicts, but aggression is not an inevitable response during conflict. Therefore, it is essential to study the patterns of moves that children make during conflict that produce or circumvent aggression.

Children who participate frequently in aggressive encounters with peers display stable individual differences in conflict management style. A child's scores on the two orthogonal dimensions of aggression and victimization usually provide a good picture of how the child manages conflict. Children who are aggressive but rarely victimized (effectual aggressors) swiftly and skillfully use aggression to settle conflicts in their favor, whereas children who are both aggressive and victimized (ineffectual aggressors) become embroiled in extended, emotionally heated conflicts that they tend to lose. Children who are nonaggressive but frequently victimized mismanage conflict by quickly acquiescing to demands. Additional research on the four kinds of children who occupy the cells of Figure 11.1 is needed in order to illuminate the social cognitions, affective difficulties, backgrounds, and developmental outcomes characterizing these different types of children.

Although individual differences in conflict management styles should continue to be a focus of study, most aggression occurs in the context of specific dyadic relationships and is the product of unique interactive chemistries. This means that our research agenda must be expanded to include attention to questions such as these: What are the dynamics that attract and bind children to relationships that are characterized by violence? Why and how do the social cognitions, affective reactions, and conflict management styles of children vary according to whether they are interacting with a partner in an aggressive relationship or with some other child? Aggression is not only a trait within individuals, but also a behavioral process sensitive to relationship parameters.

Attachment theory and social-cognitive theory are often viewed as alternative, competing explanations for developmental phenomena. This is unfortunate because, in fact, these two perspectives are complementary, and progress in understanding aggression will come from exploiting this complementarity. Both theories emphasize that children's mental representations of social experiences mediate aggressive behavior and development, but the theories differ with respect to the classes of social experiences and social cognitions considered to be influential. Social-cognitive theorists emphasize that children acquire action scripts, outcome expectancies and values, and perceptions of self-efficacy through personal interactions with socializing agents, especially during conflict, and through observation. Attachment theorists stress that children acquire expectations about their emotional needs being met and about the empathy and fairness of others primarily on the basis of caregiver availability and sensitivity at times of stress. There is no reason to exclude, a priori, either of these two classes of experiences or cognitions as potentially influential. Indeed, answers to certain puzzling issues may come from drawing on both perspectives. For example, anxious attachments may dispose children to engage in conflict, but whether anxiously attached children also will be aggressive may depend on whether the children develop the specific aggression-encouraging cognitions stressed by social-cognitive theorists.

References

Ainsworth, M. D. S. (1979). Infant–mother attachment. *American Psychologist, 34*, 932–937.

Arend, R., Gove, F., & Sroufe, L. A. (1979). Continuity of individual adaptation from infancy to kindergarten: A predictive study of ego-resiliency and curiosity in preschoolers. *Child Development, 50*, 950–959.

Bandura, A. (1986). *Social foundations of thought and action: A social cognitive theory.* Englewood Cliffs, NJ: Prentice-Hall.

Bates, J. E., & Bayles, K. (1988). Attachment and the development of behavior problems. In J. Belsky & T. Nezworski (Eds.), *Clinical implications of attachment.* Hillsdale, NJ: Erlbaum.

Bates, J. E., Maslin, C. A., & Frankel, K. A. (1985). Attachment security, mother–child interaction, and temperament as predictors of behavior-problem ratings at age three years. In I. Bretherton & E. Waters (Eds.), *Growing points of attachment theory and research. Monographs of the Society for Research in Child Development, 50*(1–2, Serial No. 209).

Boldizar, J. P., Perry, D. G., & Perry, L. C. (1989). Outcome values and aggression. *Child Development, 60*, 571–579.

Bugental, D. B., Blue, J., & Cruzcosa, M. (1989). Perceived control over caregiving outcomes: Implications for child abuse. *Developmental Psychology, 25*, 532–539.

Coie, J. D., & Christopoulos, C. (1989, April). *Types of aggressive relationships in boys' groups.* Paper presented at the meeting of the Society for Research in Child Development, Kansas City, MO.

Crittenden, P. M., & DiLalla, D. L. (1988). Compulsive compliance: The development of an inhibitory coping strategy in infancy. *Journal of Abnormal Child Psychology, 16,* 585–599.

Cummings, E. M., Vogel, D., Cummings, J. S., & El-Sheikh, M. (1989). Children's responses to different forms of expression of anger between adults. *Child Development, 60,* 1392–1404.

deLissovoy, V. (1979). Toward the definition of "abuse provoking child." *Child Abuse and Neglect, 3,* 341–350.

Dodge, K. A. (1980). Social cognition and children's aggressive behavior. *Child Development, 51,* 162–170.

Dodge, K. A. (1986). A social information processing model of social competence in children. In M. Perlmutter (Ed.), *Minnesota symposia on child psychology.* Hillsdale, NJ: Erlbaum.

Dodge, K. A., & Coie, J. D. (1987). Social-information-processing factors in reactive and proactive aggression in children's peer groups. *Journal of Personality and Social Psychology, 53,* 1146–1158.

Dodge, K. A., & Coie, J. D. (1989, April). *Bully–victim relationships in boys' play groups.* Paper presented at the meeting of the Society for Research in Child Development, Kansas City, MO.

Dodge, K. A., & Feldman, E. (1990). Issues in social cognition and sociometric status. In S. R. Asher & J. D. Coie (Eds.), *Peer rejection in childhood.* Cambridge: Cambridge University Press.

Dodge, K. A., Pettit, G. S., McClaskey, C. L, & Brown, M. M. (1986). Social competence in children. *Monographs of the Society for Research in Child Development, 51*(Serial No. 213).

Dodge, K. A., & Somberg, D. R. (1987). Hostile attributional biases among aggressive boys are exacerbated under conditions of threats to the self. *Child Development, 58,* 213–224.

Eisenberg, A. R., & Garvey, C. (1981). Children's use of verbal strategies in resolving conflicts. *Discourse Processes, 4,* 149–170.

Erikson, M. F., Sroufe, L. A., & Egeland, B. (1985). The relationship between quality of attachment and behavior problems in preschool in a high-risk sample. In I. Bretherton & E. Waters (Eds.), *Growing points of attachment theory and research. Monographs of the Society for Research in Child Development, 50*(1–2, Serial No. 209).

Fagot, B. I., & Kavanagh, K. (1990). The prediction of antisocial behavior from avoidant attachment classifications. *Child Development, 61,* 864–873.

Forehand, R. (1977). Child noncompliance to parental requests: Behavioral analysis and treatment. In M. Hersen, R. M. Eisler, & P. M. Miller (Eds.), *Progress in behavior modification* (Vol. 5). New York: Academic Press.

Garvey, C. (1984). *Children's talk.* Cambridge, MA: Harvard University Press.

George, C., & Main M. (1979). Social interactions of young abused children. *Child Development, 50,* 306–318.

Gil, D. G. (1970). *Violence against children: Physical child abuse in the United States.* Cambridge, MA: Harvard University Press.

Gottman, J. M., & Katz, L. F. (1989). Effects of marital discord on young children's peer interaction and health. *Developmental Psychology, 25,* 373–381.

Hart, C. H., Ladd, G. W., & Burleson, B. R. (1990). Children's expectations of the outcomes of social strategies: Relations with sociometric status and maternal disciplinary style. *Child Development, 61,* 127–137.

Hartup, W. W. (1974). Aggression in childhood: Developmental perspectives. *American Psychologist, 29,* 336–341.

Hartup, W. W., Laursen, B., Stewart, M. I., & Eastenson, A. (1988). Conflict and the friendship relations of young children. *Child Development, 59,* 1590–1600.

Holden, G. W. (1983). Avoiding conflict: Mothers as tacticians in the supermarket. *Child Development, 54,* 233–244.

Howes, P., & Markman, H. J. (1989). Marital quality and child functioning: A longitudinal investigation. *Child Development, 60,* 1044–1051.

Humphreys, A. P., & Smith, P. K. (1987). Rough and tumble, friendship, and dominance in schoolchildren: Evidence for continuity and change with age. *Child Development, 58,* 201–212.

Hymel, S. (1986). Interpretations of peer behavior: Affective bias in childhood and adolescence. *Child Development, 57,* 431–445.

Jacobson, J. L., & Wille, D. E. (1986). The influence of attachment pattern on developmental changes in peer interaction from the toddler to the preschool period. *Child Development, 57,* 338–347.

Keane, S. P., Brown, K. P., & Crenshaw, T. M. (1990). Children's intention-cue detection as a function of maternal social behavior: Pathways to social rejection. *Developmental Psychology, 26,* 1004–1009.

Kuczynski, L., Kochanska, G., & Maguire, M. (in press). The development of children's noncompliance strategies from toddlerhood to age 5. *Developmental Psychology.*

Kupersmidt J. B., Patterson, C., & Eickholt, C. (1989, April). *Socially rejected children: Bullies, victims, or both?* Paper presented at the meeting of the Society for Research in Child Development, Kansas City, MO.

LaFreniere, P. J., & Sroufe, L. A. (1985). Profiles of peer competence in the preschool: Interrelations between measures, influence of social ecology, and relation to attachment history. *Developmental Psychology, 21,* 56–69.

Leadbeater, B. J., Hellner, I., Allen, J. P., & Aber, J. L. (1989). Assessment of interpersonal negotiation strategies in youth engaged in problem behaviors. *Developmental Psychology, 25,* 465–472.

Lewis, M., Feiring, C., McGuffog, C., & Jaskir, J. (1984). Predicting psychopathology in six-year-olds from early social relations. *Child Development, 55,* 123–136.

Lieberman, A. F. (1977). Preschoolers' competence with a peer: Relations with attachment and peer experience. *Child Development, 48,* 1277–1287.

Loeber, R., & Tengs, T. (1986). The analysis of coercive chains between children, mothers, and siblings. *Journal of Family Violence, 1,* 51–70.

Londerville, S., & Main, M. (1981). Security of attachment, compliance and maternal training methods in the second year of life. *Developmental Psychology, 17,* 289–299.

Lytton, H., & Zwirner, W. (1975). Compliance and its controlling stimuli observed in a natural setting. *Developmental Psychology, 11,* 769–779.

MacKinnon, C. E. (1989). An observational investigation of sibling interactions in married and divorced families. *Developmental Psychology, 25,* 36–44.

Matas, L., Arend, R., & Sroufe, L. A. (1978). Continuity of adaptation in the second year: The relationship between quality of attachment and later competence. *Child Development, 49,* 547–556.

Miller, P. M., Danaher, D. L., & Forbes, D. (1986). Sex-related strategies for coping with interpersonal conflict in children aged five and seven. *Developmental Psychology, 22,* 543–548.

Olweus, D. (1978). *Aggression in the schools: Bullies and whipping boys.* Washington, DC: Hemisphere.

Parkhurst, J. T., & Asher, S. R. (1985). Goals and concerns: Implications for the study of children's social competence. In B. B. Lahey & A. E. Kazdin (Eds.), *Advances in child clinical psychology* (Vol. 8). New York: Guilford Press.

Parpal, M., & Maccoby, E. E. (1985). Maternal responsiveness and subsequent child compliance. *Child Development, 56,* 1326–1334.

Patterson, G. R. (1982). *Coercive family processes*. Eugene, OR: Castalia.

Patterson, G. R., Littman, R. A., & Bricker, W. (1967). Assertive behavior in children: A step toward a theory of aggression. *Monographs of the Society for Research in Child Development, 32*(5, Serial No. 113).

Pellegrini, A. D. (1988). Elementary-school children's rough-and-tumble play and social competence. *Developmental Psychology, 24*, 802–806.

Perry, D. G., & Bussey, K. (1977). Self-reinforcement in high- and low-aggressive boys following acts of aggression. *Child Development, 48*, 653–658.

Perry, D. G., Kusel, S. J., & Perry, L. C. (1988). Victims of peer aggression. *Developmental Psychology, 24*, 807–814.

Perry, D. G., & Perry, L. C. (1974). Denial of suffering in the victim as a stimulus to violence in aggressive boys. *Child Development, 45*, 55–62.

Perry, D. G., Perry, L. C., & Rasmussen, P. (1986). Cognitive social learning mediators of aggression. *Child Development, 57*, 700–711.

Perry, D. G., Perry, L. C., & Weiss, J. R. (1989). Sex differences in the consequences that children anticipate for aggression. *Developmental Psychology, 25*, 312–319.

Perry, D. G., Williard, J., & Perry, L. C. (1990). Peers' perceptions of the consequences that victimized children provide aggressors. *Child Development, 61*, 1310–1325.

Pettit, G. S., & Bates, J. E. (1989). Family interaction patterns and children's behavior problems from infancy to 4 years. *Developmental Psychology, 25*, 413–420.

Pettit, G. S., Dodge, K. A., & Brown, M. M. (1988). Early family experience, social problem solving patterns, and children's social competence. *Child Development, 59*, 107–120.

Pierce, S. (1990). *The behavioral attributes of victimized children*. Unpublished master's thesis, Florida Atlantic University, Boca Raton.

Putallaz, M. (1987). Maternal behavior and children's sociometric status. *Child Development, 58*, 324–340.

Rausch, H. L. (1965). Interaction sequences. *Journal of Personality and Social Psychology, 2*, 487–499.

Renken, B., Egeland, B., Marvinney, D., Mangelsdorf, S., & Sroufe, L. A. (1989). Early childhood antecedents of aggression and passive-withdrawal in early elementary school. *Journal of Personality, 57*, 257–281.

Rocissano, L., Slade, A., & Lynch, V. (1987). Dyadic synchrony and toddler compliance. *Developmental Psychology, 23*, 698–704.

Schwartz, D., & Dodge, K. A. (1990, April). *A behavioral analysis of victims of peer aggression in boys' play groups*. Paper presented at the Southeastern Conference on Human Development, Richmond, VA.

Selman, R. L. (1980). *The growth of interpersonal understanding*. New York: Academic Press.

Selman, R. L., & Demorest, A. P. (1984). Observing troubled children's interpersonal negotiation strategies: Implications of and for a developmental model. *Child Development, 55*, 288–304.

Shantz, C. U. (1987). Conflicts between children. *Child Development, 58*, 283–305.

Shantz, D. W. (1986). Conflict, aggression, and peer status: An observational study. *Child Development, 77*, 1322–1332.

Shantz, D. W., & Shantz, C. U. (1982, August). *Conflicts between children and social-cognitive development*. Paper presented at the meeting of the American Psychological Association, Washington, DC.

Slaby, R. G., & Guerra, N. G. (1988). Cognitive mediators of aggression in adolescent offenders: 1. Assessment. *Developmental Psychology, 24*, 580–588.

Sroufe, L. A. (1983). Infant–caregiver attachment and patterns of adaptation in preschool: The roots of maladaptation and competence. In M. Perlmutter (Ed.), *Minnesota symposia on child psychology* (Vol. 16). Hillsdale, NJ: Erlbaum.

Sroufe, L. A., & Egeland, B. (1989, April). *Early predictors of psychopathology.* Paper presented at the meeting of the Society for Research in Child Development, Kansas City, MO.

Sroufe, L. A., & Fleeson, J. (1988). Relationships within families: Mutual influences. In R. A. Hinde & J. Stevenson-Hinde (Eds.), *The coherence of family relationships.* Oxford: Oxford University Press.

Steinmetz, S. K. (1977). *The cycle of violence: Assertive, aggressive and abusive family interaction.* New York: Praeger.

Troy, M., & Sroufe, L. A. (1987). Victimization among preschoolers: Role of attachment relationship history. *Journal of the American Academy of Child and Adolescent Psychiatry, 2,* 166–172.

Waas, G. A. (1988). Social attributional biases of peer-rejected and aggressive children. *Child Development, 59,* 969–975.

Walker, E., Downey, G., & Bergman, A. (1989). The effects of parental psychopathology and maltreatment on child behavior: A test of the diathesis-stress model. *Child Development, 60,* 15–24.

Walton, M. D., & Sedlak, A. J. (1982). Making amends: A grammar-based analysis of children's social interaction. *Merrill-Palmer Quarterly, 28,* 389–412.

Waters, E., Wippman, J., & Sroufe, L. A. (1979). Attachment, positive affect, and competence in the peer group: Two studies in construct validation. *Child Development, 50,* 821–829.

Westerman, M. A. (1990). Coordination of maternal directives with preschoolers' behavior in compliance-problem and healthy dyads. *Developmental Psychology, 26,* 621–630.

Yeates, K. O., Schultz, L. H., & Selman, R. L. (1991). The development of interpersonal negotiation strategies in thought and action: A social-cognitive link to behavioral adjustment and social status. *Merrill-Palmer Quarterly, 37,* 369–405.

Yeates. K. O., & Selman, R. L. (1989). Social competence in the schools: Toward an integrative developmental model for intervention. *Developmental Review, 9,* 64–100.

Zillmann, D. (1988). Cognition-excitation interdependencies in aggressive behavior. *Aggressive Behavior, 14,* 51–64.

Martha Putallaz and Blair H. Sheppard

Despite its wide usage and theoretical appeal, social competence remains a construct lacking a universally accepted definition (Wine & Smye, 1982; Zigler & Trickett, 1978). Two considerations now dominate research on social competence in children. First, social competence is increasingly studied in ᴛ ᴉe context of particular social tasks (e.g., group entry, peer provocation, conflict management) rather than in a more general sense. Second, children's social competence is increasingly identified with peer sociometric status. Children who experience poor relationships with their peers appear to be at risk for the development of a variety of negative consequences in later life including academic, behavioral, and psychological difficulties (Parker & Asher, 1987).

We will follow these trends in this chapter. First, research on the relation between social status and conflict behavior will be reviewed. Utilizing social status (e.g., standing in a social group) as a criterion of social competence will permit an initial assessment of socially effective methods of approaching and managing conflict. Second, research relating social status and behavior in three problematic social situations (group entry, limited resources, and peer provocation) will be considered. In this section, situation-specific competent and incompetent behaviors will also be addressed. Third, the responses of high- and low-sociometric-status children to hypothetical social dilemmas will be discussed. Finally, the chapter will conclude with an integration of the research reviewed and a discussion of what the research tells us about the relation between social status, social competence, conflict behavior, and cognition about conflict.

The use of the phrase social competence in this introduction is somewhat misleading because this chapter deals separately with competent and incompetent behavior. A theme consistently emerging from this review is that competence and incompetence are not parallel constructs. In particular, social incompetence contains similar elements across situations, whereas competent behavior and thought varies from situation to situation.

330

Social status and conflict behavior

The direct relation between conflict behavior and social status is virtually unstudied. As C. U. Shantz (1987) argued, one reason for this paucity of research on social conflict is that "psychology traditionally has been concerned with the characteristics and behavior of the individual" (p. 285). Conflict is inherently a dyadic or larger group phenomenon.

Historically, research on social status and social behavior assessed the behavior of a single individual in a very global manner, relating measures such as friendliness, sociability, disruptiveness, and aggression to children's social acceptance or rejection (see Hartup, 1983, for a review). Several general findings, however, suggest that conflict behavior might be important in understanding social status. For example, peer-rejected children, regardless of age, engage in more negative interactions with peers (e.g., Gottman, 1977; Hartup, Glazer, & Charlesworth, 1967; Ladd, 1983; Rubin, Daniels-Beirness, & Hayvren, 1982), are more disagreeable (Dodge, Pettit, McClaskey, & Brown, 1986; Putallaz, 1983; Putallaz & Gottman, 1981), are more disruptive (Coie & Kupersmidt, 1983), and exhibit certain forms of aggression more than their nonrejected contemporaries (Coie & Dodge, 1988; Dodge, 1983; Ladd, Price, & Hart, 1988). Given that negativity, aggression, and conflict are related, it can be argued that the frequency and intensity of conflict should be related to social status.

The relation between social status and conflict behavior as well as their separate relations to aggression were studied in one case (D. W. Shantz, 1986). According to Shantz, conflict minimally entails the presence of mutual opposition and efforts to overcome it: Conflict exists when child A attempts to influence B, child B resists, and child A persists. It is this do–resist–redo sequence that specifies the minimal conditions of a conflict. Shantz argued that aggression may or may not be a part of this sequence.

D. W. Shantz's (1986) results showed, first, that conflict and aggression were related. Second, the rate of conflict across all sessions was not correlated with positive nominations, but it was correlated with negative nominations both at the start (time 1: $r = .46$) and at the end (time 2: $r = .61$) of the study. The pattern for aggression was weaker. Finally, conflict was correlated significantly with time 1 and time 2 negative peer nominations with aggression partialled out, but none of the aggression measures remained correlated with negative nominations after conflict was partialled out. Accordingly, Shantz concluded that conflict was more directly related to social rejection than was aggression.

One other study (Dodge, Coie, Pettit, & Price, 1990), although intended as a study of aggression, is relevant, because aggression was examined in terms of aggressive episodes between children rather than as aggressive acts displayed by individuals. The methodology of this study permitted investigation of A–B–A sequences argued by D. W. Shantz (1986) to be the hallmark of conflict episodes. Overall, the pattern of aggression among rejected boys was straightforward: They initiated more aggression, responded aggressively to another's aggression, and escalated aggressive conflict when counteraggression occurred. Rejected boys were involved in more fights, but they also exhibited more nonreciprocated aggression than did nonrejected boys. As Coie (1987) suggested:

It is easy to understand why rejected boys engage in more solitary aggressive acts, acts not responded to by the target. First of all, we saw that when these acts were reciprocated in any way, the rejected boys escalated the level of aggression. They also tended to keep the fight going until the other boy gave in. In short, other boys must have learned that they paid a high price when they responded to the initial aggressive acts of rejected boys. (p. 5)

The results of these two studies may appear somewhat inconsistent. In both studies, the frequency of conflict was higher for disliked than liked boys. However, Dodge et al. (1990) found that both conflict-related and nonconflict-related (nonreciprocated) aggression occurred more frequently among rejected boys. The importance of nonreciprocated aggression in their results suggests that aggression may be more important than conflict in determining status, the opposite of Shantz's results. It is possible, however, that a high frequency of conflict causes others not to reciprocate one's aggression; why respond to aggression if it is only going to escalate into a fight? Shantz's results may explain the results of Dodge et al. Moreover, Dodge et al. did not look at nonaggressive conflicts, as Shantz did.

In summary, two studies indicate that frequency of conflict is inversely related to sociometric status. In particular, negative nominations or social rejection appear to be most closely related to conflict. Aggression and conflict seem to be distinct constructs. Conflict may be a better predictor of sociometric status than aggression, but the few studies available permit few firm conclusions. More research is needed, especially research examining conflict processes in a sequential, microanalytic fashion. To conclude that frequency of conflict is related to status is only a first step in an effort to tease out the particular forms, sequences, and patterns of conflict that are problematic.

Potential conflict situations

A second approach to understanding the relation between conflict and social competence involves studying children's social behavior as assessed in specific conflict situations. At least three such situations have been employed, specifically, those involving group entry, limited resources, and ambiguous provocation. These situations appear quite diagnostic because they are difficult for children to manage successfully, and they maximize the probability that conflict will arise. In such a manner, conflict may be studied while keeping the reason for the conflict constant. Each of the three potential conflict situations will be discussed in turn.

Group entry

By far, the most frequently researched of these three situations has been group entry. Researchers are interested in how children approach and attempt to enter the ongoing activities of groups of their peers. A high likelihood that conflict will result exists in these situations because entry is quite difficult to achieve regardless of the child's age or social competence. Garvey (1984) wrote that the task of entering a group "poses a serious problem, not only to the socially inept or relatively unpopular child, but even to the more socially skilled and popular child" (p. 162). And, indeed, Corsaro (1981) found that, among acquainted nursery school groups, 53.9% of all initial entry attempts were rebuffed by the group. Putallaz and Gottman (1981) reported that even the entry attempts of popular second and third graders were rejected or ignored by their classmates 26% of the time.

Although a difficult task, there is a clear consensus as to what constitutes effective entry behavior stemming from over 50 years of research involving entry into unfamiliar groups (Feldbaum, Christenson, & O'Neal, 1980; McGrew, 1972; Phillips, Shenker, & Revitz, 1951; Washburn, 1932; Ziller & Behringer, 1961) as well as familiar ones (Corsaro, 1979, 1981; Forbes, Katz, Paul, & Lubin, 1982; Mallay, 1935). The process of assimilation into an unfamiliar group begins with a period marked by immobility, automanipulation, and passive observation on the part of the newcomer. With time, these behaviors become less frequent and the child is more apt to approach and interact with group members. This initial spectator behavior, whether entering either a familiar or an unfamiliar group, seems to serve the important purpose of permitting the child to learn the behavioral contingencies of the group without directly experiencing them. Through such observation, then, the entry child can learn the group's norms or frame of reference and can then engage in behavior most likely to lead to successful entry (i.e., doing what the group is doing). This behavior appears to convey to the group members that the entering child shares their frame of reference, thereby increasing their receptivity to the entry child.

The proper sequencing of entry bids appears to be critical in terms of attaining group acceptance (Corsaro, 1979, 1981; Forbes et al., 1982; Mallay, 1935). Only after hovering and exhibiting a shared frame of reference with the group should the child be more directive and attempt to influence or redirect the group activity (Phillips et al., 1951). To do so too early in the assimilation process is to risk being rejected or ignored. The importance of persistence also is clear. Entry is a difficult task for all children, and the prospect of acceptance increases with time.

Not surprisingly, children of higher sociometric status are able to achieve group entry more readily than their lower status peers, thus minimizing ensuing conflict. Higher status children require both less time and fewer bids to achieve entry than do lower status children (Putallaz & Gottman, 1981). The entry behavior characteristic of high-status children is consistent with the type of effective entry behavior described thus far. When entering groups, high-status children have been observed to be accommodative, generally positive, likely to imitate or mimic the group members, relevant in their behavior and conversation, and likely to make group-oriented statements, as well as to refrain from being disruptive or trying to exert influence on the group's behavior prematurely. They also seem to engage in an initial period of hovering and passive observation of the group, particularly when entering unfamiliar groups, which would be necessary to ascertain the group's frame of reference (Dodge et al., 1986; Dodge, Schlundt, Schocken, & Delugach, 1983; Putallaz, 1983; Putallaz & Gottman, 1981). In contrast, low-sociometric-status children have been observed to engage in one of two alternative behavioral patterns: First, they engage in protracted, nonstrategic hovering that, while unlikely to result in rejection and/or conflict, maximizes the probability of being ignored by the group. Second, rather than attempt to fit in with the group, their behavior is disruptive, as evidenced by a high incidence of self-statements, disagreeing with the group members, stating feelings and opinions, and being off-task and irrelevant, resulting in being either rejected or ignored by the group (Dodge et al., 1983, 1986; Putallaz, 1983; Putallaz & Gottman, 1981).

An obvious interpretation of these results is that higher status children perform the optimal entry behavior, become accepted by the group relatively easily, and thus reduce the potential for conflict, whereas their lower status counterparts have some skills deficit and, consequently, do not achieve entry easily. Certainly such an explanation is possible and no doubt plays a role in understanding being rejected or ignored in the entry situation. Even when low-status children engage in appropriate entry behavior, however, they experience exclusion (Dodge et al., 1983; Putallaz &

Gottman, 1981). Thus, an array of additional explanations to that of a skills deficit has been offered.

Putallaz (1983), for example, tested whether differences in perceptual accuracy might account in part for the behavioral differences exhibited. Following their attempts to join two unfamiliar children at play, 6-year-olds viewed their entry videotapes and were asked on several occasions to describe what the two group members in the film were "doing here" and "What were you trying to do here?" Results indicated that the subjects' perceptual accuracy improved the prediction of their sociometric status over and above the contribution made by the relevance of their behavior. Thus, the behavioral differences in entry might be explained partially by an inability to read the group's behavior accurately, a necessary prerequisite to performing the appropriate behavior.

In two studies, Dodge and his colleagues (e.g., Dodge et al., 1986) tested a much more sophisticated model of social cognition. Their information-processing model entails five steps: encoding of the social cues present in a situation, mental representation and interpretation of those cues, generation of potential behavioral responses, evaluation and selection of an optimal response, and enactment of that response. In one study, abilities of 5-, 6- and 7-year-olds in these steps were assessed through their responses to a videotaped entry episode and role-playing. The other study involved severely aggressive, rejected 7- and 9-year-olds matched to nonaggressive, average status controls. In the first study, two of the processing steps, proportion of competent solutions generated and enactment skill, were found to add significant unique variance to the prediction of successful group entry behavior. In the other study, only enactment skill uniquely predicted entry success. Interestingly, there were no differences in social information-processing patterns between the higher and lower status children in either study. Dodge et al. (1986) offered two explanations for this result: Perhaps more extreme criteria for determining status might have led to more robust group differences in processing, or alternatively, a global measure such as general entry competence does not differentiate processing patterns within a single situation very well. Thus, these two studies provide some limited evidence that children's social information-processing is predictive of competent entry behavior, although not of broader measures of social competence.

Extending these results, Rabiner and Coie (1989) examined the effects of altering the expectancies of rejected children prior to attempted group entry. Rejected 8-year-old boys and 9- and 10-year-old girls in the positive expectancy condition (i.e., those led to believe prior to the entry attempt that the group members were looking forward to playing with them) were indeed better liked by the group members as reported in postsession interviews. Results suggest that the incompetent entry behavior of some disliked children may not be attributable to a social skills deficit but, rather, to their interpersonal expectations (Dodge et al.'s cue-processing step).

In summary, entry is a difficult task, but especially for less socially competent children. In general, successful entry is related to the same variables to which status is related. The social cognition work of Dodge and his colleagues is the only exception to this observation, and neither of their studies included a pure status variable. (In one study, a composite, teacher and peer rating of prior entry competence was used; in the other, "average" children were contrasted with aggressive, rejected children.)

The consistency of these entry results is impressive. Some work remains to be done, however. We know little about the social goals or motivations of children who are more or less competent at entry. Several authors have postulated recently that goal differences explain some of the effects in entry (Dodge, Asher, & Renshaw, 1989; Putallaz & Wasserman, 1990). These arguments are especially relevant to the study of conflict and competence, as children who are less competent at entry are hypothesized to have goals discordant with children more competent at entry (e.g., prevention of rejection vs. attaining entry). However, no direct empirical test of goal differences has yet been conducted in an entry context. Better clarification of the status–cognition–behavior relation is also needed.

Limited resources

In the second problematic social situation studied, that of limited resources (or resource density), attractive objects (e.g., toys, games) are in short supply, and the children must collectively manage their use. As with group entry, this situation appears to be a difficult one for children to manage, and the potential for conflict is great.

In his careful ethnography of behavior in the preschool setting, Smith (1974; Smith & Connolly, 1980) described the impact of limiting resources on children's social interaction. As the amount of play equipment available decreased, there were significant increases in physical aggression, object conflicts, and agonistic behavior. Increased screaming and crying also were noted. Most of the fights involved possessions, reflecting the increased competition for the few toys available. In addition, there were significant increases in the amount of finger and thumb sucking displayed, interpreted as manifestations of increased anxiety and stress. There also were more instances of children watching other children, playing with room fittings, or not engaging in any activity. Interestingly, decreasing the play equipment available resulted in an increase in the mean subgroup size of children playing together, regardless of whether they were engaged in cooperative or parallel play. Use of popular items decreased with decreasing equipment availability, while engagement in less popular activities increased. Thus, the children seemed to have three primary strategies for dealing with a limited resource dilemma: They either competed for the resource, increased their sharing of objects in larger groups, or chose less optimal toys with which to play.

Using the amount of access to a resource as a measure of competence, Charlesworth and LaFreniere (1983; LaFreniere & Charlesworth, 1987) examined the influence of dominance and friendship on the behavior of preschoolers in the limited resource situation. In both classrooms and experimentally formed playgroups, children were given access to one commercially popular, toy motion picture viewer. In order for a child to be able to see the cartoon in the viewer, however, the assistance of two other children was required.

It was observed that, consistent with Smith's research, the majority of peer interaction involved aggressive and agonistic behavior rather than cooperative or prosocial acts, and this pattern seemed to increase over time. Dominance was a strong and consistent predictor of resource usage, with the more dominant children in the classroom hierarchy situated in the viewing position and actually viewing the film a greater amount of time. Although the number of friends the children had in the classroom was not related to resource usage, the number of friends the children had in the experimentally formed groups was. Groups with friends viewed the film more than did groups with no friends, with friends of high dominance enjoying the greatest usage of the resource.

Recently, we investigated whether children's sociometric status differentiated their behavioral reactions to a limited resource situation (Putallaz & Sheppard, 1990). To examine this possibility, we paired 6-year-old unacquainted children according to their sociometric status and confronted them with three situations in which there was only one toy for the two children. Low-status dyads competed for the resource (i.e., focused on their own interests) more frequently than did high-status dyads, who exhibited orientations focused more frequently on mutual benefit (i.e., compromise or collaboration). Dyadic competition and status were related to dyadic affect in a manner that suggested that the competitive orientation among low-status dyads induced negative feelings in the children. In contrast, the high-status children may have been less focused on the resource and more preoccupied, instead, with a competing goal of developing a positive relationship with the other child, thus resulting in positive feelings between the children.

In summary, too few studies have been conducted on the limited resource situation, but they suggest some promising conclusions. The most effective strategy is to be firm, but inclusive. Friendly dominance works in some situations. Strategies allowing both children to play with the toy are most related to positive affect and are adopted primarily by high-status dyads. Competition (purely firm) and accommodation (purely inclusive) result in negative affect and are used more commonly by low-status than high-status dyads. The microprocesses underlying these broad strategies are not known. In addition, necessary changes in strategy across different types of resource dilemmas need to be studied. Do strategies need to vary, for example, with toys that naturally lend themselves to team play versus role taking versus individual play?

Provocation

The final potential conflict situation used to study children's social competence also involves the simulation of a potentially difficult social scenario, specifically one in which children are required to respond to provocation by a peer. This situation has been most extensively studied by Dodge and his colleagues (e.g., Dodge et al., 1986). Here, children are confronted with a situation in which a peer knocks down their block tower, for example, under one of three conditions: hostile, accidental, or ambiguous intent. Unlike the group entry and limited resource situations, however, research concerning peer provocation has involved primarily children's cognitive responses (to vignette descriptions or videotaped portrayals) rather than behavioral responses.

Only one study (involving severely aggressive, rejected children and nonaggressive average children) included an analogue assessment of the children's actual behavior in the provocation situation with the provocateur (Dodge et al., 1986). The rating of children's competence in this situation revealed no status differences. One difficulty with the provocation situation, however, is that an index of competence is not as clear as it is for the entry situation (i.e., group acceptance) or the limited resource situation (i.e., access to the resource, or affect). For example, it is not clear why, after provocation, a positive reaction (e.g., laughing or joking) is more competent than a neutral reaction, or even a negative one (e.g., displaying anger). Descriptive data are needed concerning the behavioral reactions of popular and rejected children in the actual situation to help researchers arrive at a definition of competence and to see how it might vary across circumstances.

The lack of behavioral results do not detract from the interesting nature of the children's cognitive reactions to peer provocation. The most intriguing findings reveal that rejected children (particularly aggressive boys) are less accurate than high-status children in identifying accidental (or prosocial) intent leading to a negative outcome and ambiguous intent, but more accurate at identifying hostile intent. Moreover, aggressive, rejected children presume the intent in such situations to have been hostile. Dodge and Frame (1982) attempted to discern whether this was a general tendency to ascribe negative intent or whether it was evident only in interpreting others' behaviors toward oneself (i.e., a cynical world view vs. a personalized, paranoid view). Only when the provocation was directed toward the subject did the aggressive, rejected subjects demonstrate the hostile attributional bias, thus supporting the hypothesis of a personalized and paranoid view.

In summary, the notion that less competent children attribute hostile intent more than competent children do is a very promising result. Research with adults shows that assuming a hostile, competitive intent tends to evoke uncooperative behavior in one's partner, resulting in conflict escalation (e.g., Kelley & Stahelski, 1970). Further research is needed to map out the dynamic interplay between provocation, attributions of intent, and subsequent dyadic interaction. But the study of provocation using a combined cognitive–behavioral approach is clearly called for.

Hypothetical conflict situations

The final research area relevant to understanding the relation between conflict and sociometric status is that in which children's cognitive responses to hypothetical conflict situations have been examined. It is notable, first, that many investigators have examined the quality of children's responses to hypothetically posed conflicts, variously labeled "conflict," "social conflict," and "conflict management" situations (Asher & Renshaw, 1981; Kurdek & Lillie, 1985; Renshaw & Asher, 1983; Richard & Dodge, 1982; Shantz & Shantz, 1985). The most commonly used situation, however, has been that involving limited resources. Hypothetical dilemmas have included a child trying to take a toy from a peer (Asher & Renshaw, 1981), two children with different preferences as to which television program to watch (Renshaw & Asher, 1983; Shantz & Shantz, 1985), two brothers both wanting to use a horse (Kurdek & Lillie, 1985), and a child who has kept a library book that another wants to read (Richard & Dodge, 1982). How the results relate to those stemming from other conflict scenarios is unclear. In addition, in some studies that included more than one type of scenario, results have not been examined separately, but rather have been analyzed across situations (e.g., Rabiner, Lenhart, & Lochman, 1990). A competent response to a hypothetical limited resource scenario may differ dramatically from that given to a rule violation scenario. Thus, many investigators in this research domain have adopted a personality orientation as opposed to a situational research focus. As will be argued, this may increase the likelihood of detecting social incompetence (the correlates of rejection) but may cloud the understanding of social competence, which appears to be more situationally dependent.

Much of this research builds on the earlier work of Spivack and Shure (1974; Shure & Spivack, 1972), who concluded that children's thinking concerning hypothetical social dilemmas related to their overall social adjustment. Further, Spivack and Shure reported that it was the quantity of different responses rather than the quality of them that was most predictive of adjustment. Although relation of sociometric status to the quantity of responses generated appears somewhat equivocal (see Krasnor & Rubin, 1981), considerable consensus exists concerning the relation between sociometric status and the quality of responses to these hypothetical conflicts, regardless of the conflict situation involved (see Dodge & Feldman, 1990). The responses generated by rejected children contain a higher use of aggressive strategies (Asher & Renshaw, 1981; Rubin et al., 1982) and adult intervention strategies (Asarnow & Callan, 1985; Rubin et al., 1982) than do the responses of popular children. Conversely, higher status children suggest strategies that are more compromising (Kurdek & Lillie, 1985); more positive, accommodating, and rule oriented (Renshaw & Asher, 1983); and more effective and relationship enhancing (Asher & Renshaw, 1981). Researchers in two studies (Richard & Dodge, 1982; Rubin & Krasnor, 1986) found that the quality of first responses given did not differ across groups. The responses given by isolated and aggressive children, however, tended to degenerate over time and under stress and included higher proportions of aggressive and inept responses. Rubin and Krasnor (1986) wrote, "Average and popular children appear to have a more well-defined strategy hierarchy in which prosocial strategies outnumber agonistic ones by a substantial margin" (p. 41).

Another temporal element (immediate vs. delayed responding) has been studied (Rabiner et al., 1990) using three groups of female subjects (i.e., average, popular, and rejected) and four groups of male subjects (i.e., average, popular, rejected and aggressive, and rejected and nonaggressive). These 9- and 10-year-old children responded to three kinds of hypothetical dilemmas (provocation, group entry, and being frustrated by a peer) under both an immediate condition, in which they were to respond as quickly as possible with their first thoughts, and a delay condition, in which they had to wait 20 seconds, using the intervening time to consider alternatives. Differences were found between the two response conditions for boys, although not for girls. Both groups of rejected boys generated fewer verbally assertive responses (i.e., assertive but nonaggressive verbal statements) and more conflict escalating responses (i.e., those involving verbal or physical aggression, or impulsive physical actions) than did the nonrejected boys. Under the delay condition, however, only the aggressive, rejected boys differed from the nonrejected ones. Thus, the social problem-solving deficiencies of aggressive, rejected boys may be due to a limited repertoire of appropriate problem-solving strategies, whereas those of nonaggressive, rejected boys may be attributable to impulsiveness.

The relation between children's sociometric status and their expectations regarding the behaviors of others in certain social situations also has been investigated (Crick & Ladd, 1990). Popular, average, neglected, and rejected children were presented with two rule violation, conflict scenarios (i.e., a peer cutting in front of the child in line for recess and a second described only as "similar in nature") and were asked to evaluate six strategies for responding to these violations. Rejected children expected commands to lead to instrumentally successful outcomes more frequently than did the other groups but did not differ on their expectations regarding other strategies. They also had a tendency to focus more on instrumental outcomes and less on relational outcomes than did their peers. In a second study, the investigators found that rejected children evaluated physically aggressive and threat strategies as being more friendly than did other children.

In summary, results consistently show that low-status children (especially aggressive, rejected children) generate more aggressive, commanding, and controlling strategies and evaluate such strategies as friendlier and more efficacious than do other children. These differences are most clearly evident after the initial exchanges and in stressful situations (i.e., conflict) rather than in nonstressful ones (i.e., friendship initiation). Low-status children appear to have more limited and less effective response hierarchies or sequences than higher status children. Further, the goals of lower status children appear to be instrumental in nature rather than relationship oriented, as is the case among higher status children.

Developmental and sex differences

Age and conflict behavior

Before beginning our general discussion of results in this area, apparent developmental trends and sex differences require consideration. With regard to developmental changes in conflict behavior, as children get older their disputes seem less object focused and more reflective of an increasing awareness of people (Dawe, 1934; Rubin & Krasnor, 1986; Shantz & Shantz, 1985). In contrast to their younger counterparts, older children are more apt to pursue two or more goals simultaneously (C. U. Shantz, 1987). However, information regarding developmental changes in such conflict behaviors as issues or strategies remains sparse. C. U. Shantz (1987) recently summarized the situation as follows:

> A central question is what developmental changes occur in issues and strategies. No clear answer to the question exists at this point. In many of the studies, age differences have not been examined (rather wide age ranges are summed over), no other developmental markers have been studied, and where age differences have been examined, they are absent or small or inconsistent from one study to another. (p. 294)

She suggested that coding systems insensitive to developmental change, as well as the lack of an articulated developmental theory to guide researchers in this field, may be responsible, in part, for the absence of developmental findings.

A more consistent pattern of results emerges concerning developmental changes in the relation between children's conflict behavior and social competence. Basically, as children develop from early to middle childhood, they demonstrate more effective means of dealing with conflict. In terms of behavior, bullying and overt persuasion attempts associated with popularity in 6-year-old boys were no longer evident 2 years later (Dodge et al., 1990). Observed aggression also decreases in frequency from preschool to elementary school (Hartup, 1983). With regard to entry, older children have been observed to engage in more positive reciprocity with group members (an effective entry strategy) than do younger children (Dodge et al., 1986). Similarly, in a natural setting, younger children seemed less proficient at entry: They attempted entry proportionately more, were alone more often, joined smaller groups, and sustained their interaction with groups a smaller proportion of the time in comparison to older children (Putallaz & Wasserman, 1989). Aside from suggesting that younger children have more difficulty with social interaction, these results also reflect that social structures, such as cliques and membership groups, as well as social reputation become better defined with age (Bierman & Furman, 1984; Horrocks & Buker, 1951). Finally, older children ignore entry attempts more and reject them less than do preschoolers (Corsaro, 1981; Dodge et al., 1983), indicating a greater sensitivity to the impact of their behavior on the entering child or, at least, the capacity to say no in a subtler, less offensive manner. At the same time, older children are more likely to respond negatively to a disruptive entry bid (Putallaz & Wasserman, 1989), reflecting either a greater awareness of social violations or less tolerance for them.

Similar age-related advancements in competence are apparent in the social cognition domain. Older children evidence more sophisticated patterns of social information processing, especially in terms of generating, evaluating, and enacting responses (Feldman & Dodge, 1987). In response to a hypothetical, peer provocation situation, older children generated more responses and were less likely to endorse ineffective withdrawal responses than their younger counterparts. Further, they were more accurate at detecting prosocial intentions and made fewer errors of presumed hostility. Older children were similarly competent in response to a hypothetical entry situation, as they were less likely to endorse ineffective strategies and more likely to endorse competent ones. Interestingly, older children also anticipated peers to be less receptive to their entry than did younger children, a realistic appraisal given the difficulty associated with entry. In response to a hypothetical, limited resource situation (e.g., which television program to watch), older children focused more on prosocial goals (i.e., concern for their relationship with the new child, helping the new child learn the rules), whereas younger children focused on hostile goals, such as defending their right to the television (Renshaw & Asher, 1983). Finally, in response to a hypothetical, rule violation scenario, older children evaluated friendly behaviors more positively and hostile behaviors more negatively than did younger children. In fact, the evaluation results for the older children resembled those of popular children, whereas the pattern of the younger children resembled that of rejected children (Crick & Ladd, 1990).

In summary, the conflict behavior of young elementary school children appears less competent and their cognitions less well developed than those of older elementary school children. That social competence and age appear related suggests the possibility that social incompetence is, in part, a consequence of a developmental lag.

Gender and conflict behavior

Although not an intended focus of researchers in this domain, the pattern of sex differences emerging in the children's conflict literature is striking and difficult to disregard. In fact, one group of investigators moved from describing the emergent sex differences in their early work as "not easily explained.... The differences may be due to a sample error or reflect the greater aggressiveness of boys" (Charlesworth & LaFreniere, 1983, p. 185) to making these differences the focus of an entire study (Charlesworth & Dzur, 1987). Recently, Maccoby (1990) has described boys as more power assertive in their behavior and more concerned with maintaining their status in the male hierarchy and achieving their individual goals in group interactions, in contrast to girls, who are more polite behaviorally and more socially oriented and concerned with relationship enhancement goals, in addition to achieving their individual goals, in social interaction.

The sex differences found in our review of the children's conflict literature mirror these differences. Boys appear to be more concerned with power and status during their interactions with other children, girls with relationships and sustaining harmonious interaction. For example, there is more conflict in boys' groups, and when conflict does occur with girls, they are more likely to use conflict-mitigating strategies, whereas boys more often use threats and force (Miller, Danaher, & Forbes, 1986). Not surprisingly, then, in response to hypothetical, rule violation scenarios, girls evaluate friendly behaviors more positively and hostile behaviors more negatively than do boys (Crick & Ladd, 1990). Further, girls' conflicts more often concern person control, whereas those of boys are more likely to involve object disputes (Shantz & Shantz, 1985).

Consistent with these sex differences, teachers and clinicians have identified the entry situation (a problem of fitting in socially) as being more problematic for girls and the peer provocation situation (a problem of relative power) as more problematic for boys (Dodge, McClaskey, & Feldman, 1985). These opinions hold true in fact. Despite girls' rarer use of the ineffective, redirect strategy to enter groups at play, they were rejected more than boys (Putallaz & Wasserman, 1989). Boys also used attention-getting entry strategies more and group-oriented strategies less than did girls (Dodge et al., 1986). Forbes et al. (1982) described girls as more concerned with attaining group acceptance during entry than were boys, who, in contrast, seem more concerned with their status vis-à-vis the group members. Girls were accommodative and continued in attempts to fit in with the group despite rejection, whereas, following rejection, boys either attempted to elevate their status relative to the group members (by denigrating the group and its activities, boasting about themselves, or calling in an adult authority) or protected themselves from further loss of status by withdrawing from the group.

The difficulty posed by the peer provocation situation for boys (relative to girls) is easy to understand because it maximizes boys' concerns regarding power and status. Not surprisingly, the social information-processing patterns of the two sexes have been found to differ in response to a hypothetical provocation scenario (although no behavioral differences were reported in the analogue situation). Boys were more likely to attribute hostile intentions to the peer provocateur than were girls. Further, they generated fewer responses to the situation, were twice as likely to generate aggressive responses, and were only half as likely to endorse passive responses as were girls. Girls were also more likely to evaluate withdrawal responses more positively than were boys (Feldman & Dodge, 1987). These results suggest that boys process information about peer provocation in a manner likely to escalate into conflict, whereas girls process it in a manner that minimizes conflict. Contrary to girls, boys view the actions of the provocateur more negatively, view aggression as a more reasonable response, see fewer alternatives to an aggressive reaction to the provocateur, and evaluate more negatively such conflict avoidance strategies as withdrawal and passivity. The peer provocation situation, then, draws on boys' increased concerns over status in the male hierarchy.

Thus, it is not surprising that sex differences have been observed in the limited resource situation as well. In mixed sex groups, boys displayed a higher frequency of undesirable behavior (Johnson, 1935) and more competition for the resource, and gained greater access to the resource than did girls, who, in turn, spent more time in the bystander position (Charlesworth & LaFreniere, 1983). Although pairs of friends used the resource more than nonfriends, boyfriends competed more for it than did girlfriends (LaFreniere & Charlesworth, 1987).

Interestingly, in same-sex groups the gender differences regarding amount of access to the resource and time in the bystander position were not evident. Girls were no longer passive in the situation. This is in keeping with Maccoby's (1990) contention that girls appear behaviorally inhibited in the presence of boys due to their aversive reaction to boys' rougher behavior and to their inability to influence boys. Boys were found to engage in more physical behaviors (e.g., touching, grasping, pulling, pushing, and hitting) than did girls, who engaged in more verbal behavior (e.g., negative commands). Girls also were observed to offer each other the various positions accessing resources more than did boys, although more positive affect characterized the boys' groups (Charlesworth & Dzur, 1987). Dominance appeared to have been distributed less equitably among girls than among boys. High-dominant girls (i.e., high-resource-usage girls) spent less time in the bystander position than did high-dominant boys, whereas low-dominant girls spent more time in the bystander position than did low-dominant boys. High-dominant girls displayed a wider range of behavior (especially positive commands) than did low-dominant girls, although no such difference was noted among boys. This result suggests the interesting paradoxical hypothesis that, because of their greater focus on power and a tendency to argue over relative power, discrepancies in power are less stable among boys than among girls.

In conclusion, these results, taken together, suggest that meaningful trends in conflict behavior and the relation between conflict and competence do exist across age and gender. Future research should include both of these issues as primary foci, and not merely delegate them to secondary analyses. As C. U. Shantz (1987) suggested, the proper discerning of developmental trends will require the development of methods and coding schemes sensitive to age-relevant issues. The same is true for gender.

Discussion

Conflict and social rejection

Considering the combined research, the story of incompetent conflict behavior is a simpler one than that of competent conflict behavior. Conflict behavior is more closely related to social rejection than to social acceptance. Moreover, the patterns of ineffective behavior across situations seem quite similar, and they are likewise similar to the behavior of socially rejected children in general. In contrast, competent conflict behavior appears to be somewhat situation specific. Thus, social conflict provides a clear window on the dynamics of social rejection. We will peer through this window before considering competent conflict behavior.

Concerning their actions, socially rejected children engage in more frequent conflicts, adopt more instrumental and controlling strategies during conflict, escalate conflict to a greater extent, and use nonnormative approaches more in situations likely to evoke conflict than do other children. Concerning their thought processes, rejected children cite less skillful strategies for dealing with situations likely to elicit conflict (especially over time, suggesting cognitive representations for conflict that are less mature), have more negative expectations about conflict outcomes, are less accurate in their perceptions of the behavior and intentions of others in problematic situations, and are more likely to attribute hostile intentions in ambiguous provocation situations, as well as to evaluate hostile strategies more positively and friendly and passive strategies more negatively than do less rejected children. The behavioral and cognitive research thus yields remarkably consistent results. Moreover, this thought and behavior pattern tends to result in negative outcomes in the three problematic situations: rejection in group entry efforts, negative affect with limited resources, and conflict escalation in the face of peer provocation. In diagnostic terms, results suggest that social conflict is a critical context for the determination of negative social status.

Why rejected children are rejected. The relation between conflict thought and behavior suggests several reasons why children are rejected. First, interaction with a socially rejected child is likely to reduce access to desired resources or toys, compared to interaction with other children. Rejected children compete more for desirable objects and persist more in their efforts to achieve them. Thus, children come to expect that when interacting with certain children, one is likely to have reduced access to the things one wants. Over time, these children are chosen as play partners less and less often.

Second, rejected children act nonnormatively. In an entry situation, for example, rejected children are less likely to adopt a group's frame of reference than are higher status children. If this view of the rejected child is correct, it is not surprising that these children are rejected. People do not like others who are not like themselves (Byrne & Griffitt, 1966). Rejected children, being less like others than most children, are thus subject to ever increasing isolation.

Third, much of the behavior of rejected children suggests that they are not especially worried about other children and, instead, are more worried about instrumental issues or social power (Asher & Renshaw, 1981; Crick & Ladd, 1990; Putallaz & Wasserman, 1990). Other children interpret this orientation as a lack of concern for or interest in them. In other words, either intentionally or unintentionally, rejected children provide signals that they do not care about or like other children. Moreover, the controlling strategies used by rejected children restrict the freedom of their contemporaries in many ways.

Fourth, conflicts involving rejected children appear significantly more likely to escalate than do conflicts involving higher status children. There is both direct and circumstantial evidence for this thesis. For example, research on hypothetical social dilemmas indicates that rejected children are especially likely to use aggressive, agonistic strategies after initial, unsuccessful attempts to deal with the situation. Putallaz and Gottman (1981) found that sociometric status was related positively to the occurrence of two behaviors following a disagreement: providing a rationale and suggesting an alternative action, two nonescalatory strategies. Given these results, children are likely to confront serious, escalated conflict if they choose to interact with a rejected child.

It is not surprising, then, that children reject others who do not let them have access to desired objects, who are not like themselves, who exert control over their actions, who initiate conflict, who escalate conflicts when they occur, and who appear not to care about them. Given the negative consequences of their behavior, it is surprising that rejected children act as they do. We turn to that question now.

Why rejected children behave as they do. If conflict situations are so diagnostic, it is worth considering why socially rejected children act as they do in conflict situations. One explanation is that socially rejected children, in fact, value object acquisition and social power more than do nonrejected children. The weight of the evidence suggests that this is probably true. Research on parent–child relations is consistent with this direct, motivational explanation: Parents of rejected children are less warm and more controlling than the parents of higher status children (MacDonald & Parke, 1984; Putallaz, 1987), suggesting that rejected children learn quite early to value control over their social relations.

A related, but somewhat more complicated, interpretation also accounts for some of the behavior of rejected children. Experiences with both parents and peers may make certain children especially sensitive to social rejection (Putallaz & Wasserman, 1990; Rabiner & Coie, 1989). If so, such things as interpreting the behavior of others as hostile, shifting goals from attempts to gain entry to attempts to enhance power, and pursuing nonsocial ends may be a consequence of a fear of rejection resulting from continued rejection. Various results described in this chapter support the notion that rejected children are "oversensitive" to rejection by peers. In research on aggression (Coie, 1987), group entry (Putallaz & Wasserman, 1990), and hypothetical conflict (Rubin & Krasnor, 1986), it is the *reactions* of rejected children to aggression or rebuff that are especially problematic. Rejected children may become more aggressive, agonistic, and focused on control issues after rejection or aggression simply because they are especially sensitive to these cues.

Such ego-defensive notions suggest a difficult "Catch-22" for those interested in intervention with socially rejected children. If socially rejected children place a lesser value on social relations than do socially accepted children, efforts should be made to change rejected children's social diffidence. To attempt to heighten rejected children's interest in interacting with others, however, may increase their fear of social rejection. One possible solution to this dilemma is to focus rejected children's attention on the positive elements in social interaction as opposed to the negative ones. In addition, the ego defensive explanation paints a very sad picture of socially rejected children. They are trapped in a tragic cycle in which, because of their sensitivity to social rejection, they are increasingly likely to be disliked: Ironically, children's concerns about rejection partially cause the rejection.

Yet another possibility is that rejected children cognitively represent conflict differently than do nonrejected children. The data described in this chapter strongly support some sort of cognitive explanation. Possible reasons for the cognitive differences identified include different developmental histories and cognitive abilities. Of course, some of these cognitive processes may be motivationally based. For example, the greater propensity to interpret ambiguous behavior as hostile may derive from an ego-defensive orientation as much as it may reflect a cognitive difference of style. Research is badly needed in order to specify the motivational and nonmotivational underpinnings of these differences.

One final explanation is that other children may behave so as to exacerbate the early behaviors that trigger the cycle of rejection. For example, children withdraw from a disliked child's aggression and, additionally, reject that child's entry attempts to a greater extent than they do for other children who are rebuffed. Thus, other children inadvertently may cause the rejected child to adopt less effective behavior than would otherwise be the case. The deficient strategic sequencing found in hypothetical conflict research among rejected children may be the result of being repeatedly ignored in everday social interaction as much as from some cognitive limitation.

Competence and conflict

The findings relating social competence and conflict are less straightforward than those relating incompetence (rejection) and conflict. On the one hand, there are some strong consistencies in research relating conflict behavior and competence. Those conflict behaviors and cognitions in a given situation that are related to status appear also to be related to more situation-specific criteria (such as acceptance, dyadic affect, and access to desired resource). On the other hand, there are some striking inconsistencies. Effective conflict behavior appears to vary between problem situations. What is competent conflict behavior thus depends on the situation. In group entry, competent behavior includes hovering and identifying the group's norms, whereas in the limited resource situation completely different behavior (such as collaborating over the use of the resource) is competent.

These different behaviors, though, may be similarly motivated and entail similar macrolevel abilities. A clue as to how the same general abilities and motives result in quite different behaviors is provided by one finding from the group entry situation: Competent children appear to adopt the frame of the group to which they seek entry and behave in a relevant manner. Relevance is a function of the norms of the group being entered and the situation at hand. Thus, consistent behavior across situations would not be expected of competent children; instead, adaptive behavior would be expected. Thus, relevance is one form of metaprinciple that, although necessary across most settings, implies quite different behaviors from one setting to another.

A second metaprinciple of competent conflict behavior and cognition emerging from this review involves being socially centered. Other-oriented strategies increase the probability of group entry. Strategies built upon developing mutual involvement with a toy are most related to positive affect in limited resource situations and maximize the degree of access to the resource. Popular children adopt more relationship-focused strategies in hypothetical situations. Each of these observations suggests a child who is socially oriented, a child not just interested in object acquisition, control, or responding to the provocation, but also interested in social interaction for its own sake. Such a social orientation is thus incompatible with many of the negative behaviors associated with social rejection. A strong social orientation increases the amount and quality of interaction with other children. As a result, socially oriented children probably come over time to develop greater social skill and social knowledge than do less socially oriented children.

Research on parenting (e.g., Baumrind, 1973) suggests that such a social orientation may be partly a consequence of the level of warmth exhibited by parents. Warm, loving, moderately controlling parents provide a positive first social experience for their children, thus equipping them with a positive general orientation toward social interaction. Children may learn, either through a form of classical conditioning (interaction is a conditioned positive valence stimulus) or operant conditioning (interaction results in positive outcomes), to value social interaction for its own sake. Other factors such as the child's disposition, general social optimism, and past experiences with other children also likely influence the orientation of a child toward others.

Interestingly, it appears that a social orientation more than a visibly egocentric orientation results in greater individual benefit in the situations studied. Finding a way to play a game together results in access to a toy all the time, not just some of the time. Focusing on the group results in having an opportunity to influence the group. Focusing on the other child defuses a provocation. The situations selected for this review may lend themselves to the paradoxical conclusion that, by focusing on others, children achieve what they themselves wish. Each of the situations requires the cooperation of another child (or children) to achieve complete success. Other situations do not require such help. For example, some objects cannot be easily shared, and some situations are entirely competitive. Thus, we must be careful not to extrapolate too far. These results suggest, however, the conclusion that more may be acquired by not focusing on acquisition.

Socially competent conflict behavior and thought appear to entail a third metaprinciple, an effort to balance one's own interests with those of other children. A child who never attempts to enter a group for fear of disturbing other children does not ever succeed in entry and is likely not popular. A child who always provides a toy to other children invites competition from others and tends not to get to play with the toy. A child who completely turns the other cheek to provocation invites continued provocation. Instead of complete accommodation to the concerns of others, socially competent children appear to be concerned with achieving a balance between their own and others' interests. Pruitt (1983), in discussing effective negotiation, suggests two ways in which integrative (win–win) results are not achieved by adults: They are either too competitive, and thus force others to compete in kind, or are too accommodating, and thus do not force others to consider their interests. Integrative bargaining entails achieving a balance between one's own and others' interests. Similarly, socially competent conflict behavior entails a concern for balancing one's own interests with those of other children.

The fourth metaprinciple of competent conflict behavior and cognition emerging from this review entails social perceptiveness. It is difficult to be relevant if one cannot detect the relevant social norms. It is difficult to attend to other's interests if one cannot discover what they are. Aside from being a requirement for relevance and balance, social perceptiveness appears to be an attribute of effective conflict behavior in its own right. A large number of studies indicate that socially effective children have better developed response hierarchies and are more accurate in their appraisal of conflict situations. How does child perceptiveness develop? Again, it is likely a consequence of both parental training and children's aptitude and past experiences with peers and siblings.

Considering these four aspects of competent conflict behavior (relevance, social centeredness, interest balance, and social perceptiveness), it is easy to see why no specific pattern of competent behavior exists that fits all situations. Competence is a consequence of being able to perceive relevant norms, to detect the interests and motives of other children accurately, and to strike a delicate balance between one's own preferences and those of others while behaving in a relevant manner. In other words, competent behavior is highly situation-specific, dependent upon the social group, the social task, and the individual child. That does not mean that efforts to develop a more precise behavioral understanding are unnecessary. Quite the contrary, there are probably a limited number of meaningful social tasks (or families of social tasks) and types of children's groups. If so, then more precise, microanalytic, sequential information related to each task and group type is called for. Although some situational variability will always exist, detailing specific effective behavior and behavioral sequences in each general domain will be extremely helpful. It is easier to coach children if specific behavioral suggestions can be provided, rather than giving somewhat obtuse general instructions such as "be socially oriented and relevant." Moreover, more specific information will allow researchers to better hone their understanding of social competence and its etiology.

Detailed information in some areas already exists, especially about group entry and the behavior and behavioral sequences likely to achieve entry. Far too little situation-specific microanalytic research exists, however. Available research is actually rather narrowly focused: Investigators make finer and finer distinctions in terms of social status and other apects of target children. In fact, the emerging literature could be described as the study of aggressive, rejected boys in middle childhood. Although these and other individual types are important, it behooves us to consider also competent and incompetent behavior across a range of social tasks and groupings. Such research needs to begin with a delineation of the critical social tasks or settings in which conflict is likely as well as the social groupings that may suggest different strategies for competent behavior. Perhaps, even more importantly, researchers must consider how various settings and groups require different socially appropriate and desirable behaviors of children.

References

Asarnow, J. R., & Callan, J. W. (1985). Boys with peer adjustment problems: Social cognitive processes. *Journal of Consulting and Clinical Psychology, 53,* 80–87.

Asher, S. R., & Renshaw, P. D. (1981). Children without friends: Social knowledge and social skills training. In S. R. Asher & J. M. Gottman (Eds.), *The development of children's friendships.* Cambridge: Cambridge University Press.

Baumrind, D. (1973). The development of instrumental competence through socialization. In A. D. Pick (Ed.), *Minnesota symposia on child psychology* (Vol. 7). Minneapolis: University of Minnesota Press.

Bierman, K. L., & Furman, W. (1984). The effect of social skills training and peer involvement on the social adjustment of preadolescents. *Child Development, 55*, 151–162.

Byrne, D., & Griffitt, W. B. (1966). A developmental investigation of the laws of attraction. *Journal of Personality and Social Psychology, 4*, 699–702.

Charlesworth, W. R., & Dzur, C. (1987). Gender comparisons of preschoolers' behavior and resource utilization in group problem solving. *Child Development, 58*, 191–200.

Charlesworth, W. R., & LaFreniere, P. (1983). Dominance, friendship, and resource utilization in preschool children's groups. *Ethology and Sociobiology, 4*, 175–186.

Coie, J. D. (1987, April). *An analysis of aggressive episodes: Age and peer status differences.* Paper presented at the meeting of the Society for Research in Child Development, Baltimore, MD.

Coie, J. D., & Dodge, K. A. (1988). Multiple sources of data on social behavior and social status in the school: A cross-age comparison. *Child Development, 59*, 815–829.

Coie, J. D., & Kupersmidt, J. (1983). A behavioral analysis of emerging social status in boys' groups. *Child Development, 54*, 1400–1416.

Corsaro, W. A. (1979). "We're friends, right?": Children's use of access rituals in a nursery school. *Language in Society, 8*, 315–336.

Corsaro, W. A. (1981). Friendship in the nursery school: Social organization in a peer environment. In S. R. Asher & J. M. Gottman (Eds.), *The development of children's friendships.* Cambridge: Cambridge University Press.

Crick, N. R., & Ladd, G. W. (1990). Children's perceptions of the outcomes of social strategies: Do the ends justify being mean? *Developmental Psychology, 26*, 612–620.

Dawe, H. C. (1934). An analysis of two hundred quarrels of preschool children. *Child Development, 5*, 139–157.

Dodge, K. A. (1983). Behavioral antecedents of peer social status. *Child Development, 54*, 1386–1399.

Dodge, K. A., Asher, S. R., & Renshaw, P. D. (1989). Social life as a goal coordination task. In C. Ames & R. Ames (Eds.), *Research on motivation in education* (Vol. 3). New York: Academic Press.

Dodge, K. A., Coie, J. D., Pettit, G. S., & Price, J. M. (1990). Peer status and aggression in boys groups: Developmental and contextual analyses. *Child Development, 61*, 1289–1309.

Dodge, K. A., & Feldman, E. (1990). Social cognition and sociometric status. In S. R. Asher & J. D. Coie (Eds.), *Peer rejection in childhood.* Cambridge: Cambridge University Press.

Dodge, K. A., & Frame, C. L. (1982). Social cognitive biases and deficits in aggressive boys. *Child Development, 53*, 620–635.

Dodge, K. A., McClaskey, C., & Feldman, E. (1985). A situational approach to the assessment of social competence in children. *Journal of Consulting and Clinical Psychology, 53*, 344–353.

Dodge, K. A., Pettit, G. S., McClaskey, C. L., & Brown, M. (1986). Social competence in children. *Monographs of the Society for Research in Child Development, 51*(2, Serial No. 213).

Dodge, K. A., Schlundt, D. G., Schocken, I., & Delugach, J. D. (1983). Social competence and children's social status: The role of peer group entry strategies. *Merrill-Palmer Quarterly, 29*, 309–336.

Feldbaum, C. L., Christenson, T. E., & O'Neal, E. C. (1980). An observational study of the assimilation of the newcomer to preschool. *Child Development, 51*, 497–507.

Feldman, E., & Dodge, K. A. (1987). Social information processing and sociometric status: Sex, age, and situational effects. *Journal of Abnormal Child Psychology, 15*, 211–227.

Forbes, D. L., Katz, M. M., Paul, B., & Lubin, D. (1982). Children's plans for joining play: An analysis of structure and function. In D. Forbes & M. T. Greenberg (Eds.), *Children's planning strategies: New directions for child development.* San Francisco: Jossey-Bass.

Garvey, C. (1984). *Children's talk*. Cambridge, MA: Harvard University Press.

Gottman, J. M. (1977). Toward a definition of social isolation in childhood. *Child Development, 48*, 513–517.

Hartup, W. W. (1983). Peer relations. In E. M. Hetherington (Ed.), *Handbook of child psychology: Vol. 4. Socialization, personality, and social development* (4th ed.). New York: Wiley.

Hartup, W. W., Glazer, J. A., & Charlesworth, R. (1967). Peer reinforcement and sociometric status. *Child Development, 38*, 1017–1024.

Horrocks, J. E., & Buker, M. E. (1951). A study of the friendship fluctuations of preadolescents. *Journal of Genetic Psychology, 78*, 131–144.

Johnson, M. W. (1935). The effect on behavior of variation in the amount of play equipment. *Child Development, 6*, 56–68.

Kelley, H. H., & Stahelski, A. J. (1970). Errors in perception of intentions in a mixed-motive game. *Journal of Experimental Social Psychology, 6*, 379–400.

Krasnor, L. R., & Rubin, K. H. (1981). The assessment of social problem-solving skills in young children. In T. Merluzzi, C. Glass, & M. Genest (Eds.), *Cognitive assessment*. New York: Guilford Press.

Kurdek, L. A., & Lillie, R. (1985). The relation between classroom social status and classmate likability, compromising skill, temperament, and neighborhood social interactions. *Journal of Applied Developmental Psychology, 6*, 31–41.

Ladd, G. W. (1983). Social networks of popular, average, and rejected children in school settings. *Merrill-Palmer Quarterly, 29*, 283–307.

Ladd, G. W., Price, J. M., & Hart, C. H. (1988). Predicting preschoolers' peer status from their playground behaviors. *Child Development, 59*, 986–992.

LaFreniere, P. J., & Charlesworth, W. R. (1987). Effects of friendship and dominance status on preschoolers' resource utilization in a cooperative/competitive situation. *International Journal of Behavioral Development, 10*, 345–358.

Maccoby, E. E. (1990). Gender and relationships: A developmental account. *American Psychologist, 50*, 513–520.

MacDonald, K., & Parke, R. D. (1984). Bridging the gap: Parent–child play interaction and peer interactive competence. *Child Development, 55*, 1265–1277.

Mallay, H. (1935). A study of some of the techniques underlying the establishment of successful social contacts at the preschool level. *Journal of Genetic Psychology, 47*, 431–457.

McGrew, W. C. (1972). *An ethological study of children's behavior*. New York: Academic Press.

Miller, P., Danaher, D., & Forbes, D. (1986). Sex-related strategies for coping with interpersonal conflict in children aged five and seven. *Developmental Psychology, 22*, 543–548.

Parker, J. G., & Asher, S. R. (1987). Peer relations and later personal adjustment: Are low-accepted children at risk? *Psychological Bulletin, 102*, 357–389.

Phillips, E. L., Shenker, S., & Revitz, P. (1951). The assimilation of the new child into the group. *Psychiatry, 14*, 319–325.

Pruitt, D. (1983). Achieving integrative agreements. In M. Bazerman & R. J. Lewicki (Eds.), *Research on negotiation in organizations*. Beverly Hills, CA: Sage.

Putallaz, M. (1983). Predicting children's sociometric status from their behavior. *Child Development, 54*, 1417–1426.

Putallaz, M. (1987). Maternal behavior and children's sociometric status. *Child Development, 58*, 324–340.

Putallaz, M., & Gottman, J. M. (1981). An interaction model of children's entry into peer groups. *Child Development, 54*, 1417–1426.

Putallaz, M., & Sheppard, B. H. (1990). Children's social status and orientations to limited resources. *Child Development, 61*, 2022–2027.

Putallaz, M., & Wasserman, A. (1989). Children's naturalistic entry behavior and sociometric status: A developmental perspective. *Developmental Psychology, 25*, 1–9.

Putallaz, M., & Wasserman, A. (1990). Children's entry behavior. In S. R. Asher & J. D. Coie (Eds.), *Peer rejection in childhood*. Cambridge: Cambridge University Press.

Rabiner, D., & Coie, J. (1989). Effect of expectancy inductions on rejected children's acceptance by unfamiliar peers. *Developmental Psychology, 25*, 450–457.

Rabiner, D. L., Lenhart, L., & Lochman, J. E. (1990). Automatic versus reflective social problem solving in relation to children's sociometric status. *Developmental Psychology, 26*, 1010–1016.

Renshaw, P. D., & Asher, S. R. (1983). Children's goals and strategies for social interaction. *Merrill-Palmer Quarterly, 29*, 353–374.

Richard, B. A., & Dodge, K. A. (1982). Social maladjustment and problem solving in school-aged children. *Journal of Consulting and Clinical Psychology, 50*, 226–233.

Rubin, K. H., Daniels-Beirness, T., & Hayvren, M. (1982). Social and social-cognitive correlates of sociometric status in preschool and kindergarten children. *Canadian Journal of Behavioural Science, 14*, 338–348.

Rubin, K. H., & Krasnor, L. R. (1986). Social-cognitive and social behavioral perspectives on problem solving. In M. Perlmutter (Ed.), *Minnesota symposia on child psychology* (Vol. 18). Hillsdale, NJ: Erlbaum.

Shantz, C. U. (1987). Conflicts between children. *Child Development, 58,* 283–305.

Shantz, C. U., & Shantz, D. W. (1985). Conflict between children: Social-cognitive and sociometric correlates. In M. W. Berkowitz (Ed.), *Peer conflict and psychological growth: New directions for child development*. San Francisco: Jossey-Bass.

Shantz, D. W. (1986). Conflict, aggression, and peer status: An observational study. *Child Development, 57*, 1322–1332.

Shure, M. B., & Spivack, G. (1972). Means–ends thinking, adjustment, and social class among elementary school-aged children. *Journal of Consulting and Clinical Psychology, 38,* 348–353.

Smith, P. K. (1974). Aggression in a preschool playgroup: Effects of varying physical resources. In J. DeWit & W. W. Hartup (Eds.), *Determinants and origins of aggressive behavior*. The Hague: Mouton.

Smith, P. K., & Connolly, K. J. (1980). *The ecology of preschool behaviour*. Cambridge: Cambridge University Press.

Spivack, G., & Shure, M. B. (1974). *The problem solving approach to adjustment*. San Francisco: Jossey-Bass.

Washburn, R. W. (1932). A scheme for grading the reactions of children in a new social situation. *Journal of Genetic Psychology, 40*, 84–99.

Wine, J. D., & Smye, M. D. (1982). *Social competence*. New York: Guilford Press.

Zigler, E., & Trickett, P. K. (1978). IQ, social competence, and evaluation of early childhood intervention programs. *American Psychologist, 33*, 789–798.

Ziller, R. C., & Behringer, R. D. (1961). A longitudinal study of the assimilation of the new child into the group. *Human Relations, 14*, 121–133.

13   Conflict and group relations

Frances E. Aboud

The focus of this chapter is on conflict as it arises in relations between racial and ethnic groups. Group relations are particularly evident in the schools of a pluralistic society in which children from different racial and ethnic groups come into contact with each other. Such contact provides opportunities not only for acquaintanceship, but also for conflict. Conflicts inevitably arise whenever people interact with one another, regardless of whether they are friends or enemies. However, given the history of racial conflict in North America, current inequities in society, and most children's background of racial isolation and distrust, one might expect particularly high levels of conflict in desegregated schools.

Conflicts between children and adolescents from different racial groups arise on a daily basis because one group makes demands that the other is not willing to satisfy or because of differing views and incompatible styles of behavior. Another possibility is that people are prone to interpret conflicts as racial when they are really interpersonal. Within this broader context, conflicts may be more salient than otherwise and may become burdened with extra meaning that arises not from the conflict per se (which may be about the use of a pencil), but from the group affiliations of the antagonists. Depending on the way conflicts are resolved, they can either facilitate the acquaintanceship process through negotiation or sabotage it through avoidance.

A review of the literature of the past 30 years points to a number of conceptual and methodological limitations that have biased our view of racial conflict, making it appear more detrimental than it is. The conceptual limitation concerns the definition of conflict used by many researchers. For example, the emphasis placed on competition by Sherif (1956) and Deutsch (1973) led many researchers to equate conflict with competition. Although competition is often associated with conflict, it should not be equated with conflict; it is merely one of the precipitating factors, albeit the most common. Many studies focus on competition, which tends to be high in the intergroup

356

context, and only secondarily mention the conflict behavior or hostilities that follow.

A more important limitation stems from the methods used to study conflict. These methods inadvertently facilitate conflict, and so have led both lay and scientific communities to believe that the level of conflict between groups of children is high and that prejudice is exacerbated by such conflicts. The Robbers Cave experiment by Sherif, Harvey, White, Hood, and Sherif (1961) remains in most people's minds as the prototype of how ordinary children placed in a group context generate extreme degrees of conflict and hostility (see also Insko, Schopler, Hoyle, Dardis, & Graetz, 1990; Tajfel, 1970). The implication is that when children from different racial groups interact, conflict and prejudice are aroused.

My major objection to these findings took form only after comparing them with other studies that reported much lower levels of conflict. The latter studies were conducted with children in familiar settings such as schools, where the children had access to relationships outside the groups being examined. That is, they had relationships with teachers and students in the classroom, with extracurricular groups, with friends from school and neighborhood, and with family members. These alternative group affiliations provided alternative norms and sources of self-esteem. Such conditions may dilute the influence of any single reference group. In contrast, subjects in a summer camp or in a laboratory group experiment were forced to limit themselves to one group allegiance that consequently was their only source of norms and social status. This contextual handicap needs to be overcome when researchers are concerned about controlling certain variables in their design.

Another point to note when examining the literature is that conflict inevitably increases when two groups interact. This seems obvious, though it is rarely considered in research reports. Understandably, conflict researchers are interested in conflict per se and its resolution. But the lay reader is again left with the conclusion that conflicts are destructively high in integrated settings. One way to compensate for the amount of contact is to calculate conflict as a proportion of total interactions. However, instances of avoiding interaction do not enter into this formula, although avoidance is more detrimental to intergroup harmony and reflects a higher level of prejudice than does conflict (Patchen, 1982). In order to assess intergroup harmony, one needs to have information on the amounts of both positive interaction and avoidance, in addition to that of conflict. Perhaps the best single index would be the number of conflicts relative to the number of friendly interactions.

Despite these limitations, research on intergroup conflict has progressed substantially since the early studies. New paradigms have emerged to examine the many ways that conflict is expressed, as well as its determinants and consequences. Because the rationale for such research is predominantly its application in school settings, however, theory construction has been slow.

Allport's (1954) contact theory (and the conditions necessary or sufficient for harmonious contact) still serves as the basis for most of the research. According to this theory, the three most important conditions necessary for group harmony are the equal status of groups, cooperative interdependence in achieving a goal, and support for harmonious relations by higher authorities. These conditions describe the social context for contact. To them have been added other conditions that are social-psychological in nature, such as acquaintanceship or friendship between individuals (Schofield & Sagar, 1983) and the breakdown of social stereotypes and categorization (Miller & Brewer, 1986). Currently, the major theoretical debate centers on the importance of the group versus that of the individual. Some see the integrity of the group as a necessary feature of conflict reduction (Hewstone & Brown, 1986), whereas others claim that the breakdown of group categorization is essential (Miller & Brewer, 1986). There is evidence to support both of these claims (Gaertner, Mann, Murrell, & Dovidio, 1989; Miller, Brewer, & Edwards, 1985). Thus, there is currently no resolution of this controversy.

This chapter begins with a discussion of the terms group and conflict, and then introduces the reader to general issues that form the core of the research endeavors and the methodological paradigms used to study these issues. The three major issues concern the nature and level of conflict that arises between groups of children, the group and individual determinants of such conflicts, and positive and negative consequences.

Meaning of the constructs *group* and *conflict*

There are several meanings of the term *group*. Early writers (e.g., Sherif & Sherif, 1953) found it important to differentiate between the actual aggregates to which one belongs (membership group) and those to which one relates psychologically (reference group). In addition to this distinction is the one between interacting groups such as teammates or cliques (three to nine individuals), and social category grouping such as race or ethnicity. An *interacting group* is a confederation of people who interact on a regular basis, with an organization, shared goals, and shared norms. This definition is used by researchers who study peer groups, particularly adolescent cliques (Gavin & Furman, 1989). *Social category groups* consist of people who are perceived by themselves and others to share an important attribute (Tajfel, 1978; Turner, 1982). In the study of race relations, racial or ethnic background is the assumed shared attribute.

The importance of race in the perception of self and others can be gauged empirically in terms of how frequently and how broadly it is applied. Cohen (1984) measured children's expectations about race in behavioral terms as they worked in groups of four on a collective task. Children from racial minority groups were perceived by themselves and others in the group to have lower status such that they tended to talk less, and their suggestions were less influential. Cognitive indexes such as judgments of how smart, aggressive, and helpful are people from different racial groups yield similar results (e.g., Brown & Johnson, 1971; Doyle, Beaudet, & Aboud, 1988; Williams & Morland, 1976). Moreover, racial groups become the reference groups with which children as young as 4 years of age identify. A tendency exists, however, for children under age 7 in white-dominated societies to select whites as a reference group regardless of their actual race (Aboud, 1988; Spencer & Markstrom-Adams, 1990).

What is meant by the term *conflict* when used in an intergroup context? Basically, at the group or dyadic level, conflict is expressed as incompatible behavior or goals between two persons or groups, such that one person does or says something to which a second person objects (Shantz, 1987). Incompatible goals may sometimes involve a rivalry to beat another out of top standing in marks or sports. I prefer to call this *competition* rather than conflict, especially when fair rules of play exist to determine who is the winner. Conflict usually involves actions that are opposed by the target person(s), where there are no prior agreed-upon rules of conduct. More generally, it involves one-upmanship in verbal sparring, physical strength, or possession of desired materials, such as when one child calls another a name or takes his or her pencil and the second child opposes this action.

Group considerations could enter the conflict in a number of different ways. Generally, intergroup conflict means that instead of two individuals in opposition, there are two groups of two or more individuals each. Regardless of the numbers involved, the conflict would be considered racial if it arose because the two participants were from different races and because racial affiliation was at least one of the stimuli being responded to. The problem here is in deciding whether racial affiliation actually determines a person's response or whether one of the participants simply assumes it does. In many cases, educators and researchers claim that a conflict is not racial (e.g., Cohen, 1984; Kochman, 1981; Patchen, 1982; Schofield,

1982), though one of the participants, usually the recipient of an unwanted action, thinks it is provoked by his or her racial affiliation. Consequently, the scope of group conflict encompasses not only conflicts between two or more groups of children, but also conflicts between individuals who subjectively feel that their opposition to each other is due to racial affiliation.

Issues and paradigms

These concepts were operationalized by Sherif and his colleagues (e.g., Sherif, 1956, 1966; Sherif et al., 1961; Sherif & Sherif, 1953), who studied conflict between interacting groups of boys from the same race. Although conflict was the main focus of the studies, no clear definition for conflict was provided to distinguish it from competition. Actions taken by the boys to beat the other team in sports may be a reflection of healthy competition and rivalry, not conflict. Actions taken to interfere with the other group's daily activities and possessions fit our previous definition of conflict.

In a series of quasi-experimental field studies, Sherif (1966) demonstrated that group conflict could be provoked by team competition. The Robbers Cave experiment (Sherif et al., 1961) is most memorable for the amount of intergroup hostility it generated in normal, middle-class boys competing with other boys at a summer camp. The conditions under which this hostility developed included the formation of two separate groups in isolation from one another and a subsequent team competition. Sherif describes the "stage" of group formation as a 1-week period in which the boys played and worked together unaware of the other group's existence. What emerged was a group structure with different status positions and roles, a set of norms to which all boys eventually conformed, and a feeling of pride in the group.

Intergroup conflict was then provoked by bringing together the two groups for a week-long sports competition. According to Sherif, the eliciting condition was the competition for a goal, the winner's prize. Conflict, according to our earlier definition, was manifested by attempts to seize each others' possessions and interfere with the out-group's achievements. In addition, a great deal of hostility was directed toward all members of the out-group, through name calling, fights, raids, and negative evaluations assessed formally by the experimenters. The hostility was accompanied by an increase in in-group cohesion and solidarity, an overestimation of in-group members' achievements, and a reorganization of the group structure such that bullies assumed more influential positions. The conflict became so acrimonious and preoccupying that the experimenters decided to engineer its reduction via a series of events requiring intergroup cooperation to attain a mutual goal.

The first failed attempt at reconciliation was a night at the movies – a pleasant event that both groups were to share. The subsequent, more successful attempt was a rigged breakdown of the truck that was to provide transportation and food to the two groups. The groups worked together to get the truck functioning again. They derived mutual benefit from working together on this task. In the end, positive ratings of out-group members increased slightly as did the number of children choosing a friend from the out-group.

Issues dealt with in current research

The Robbers Cave findings raise a number of issues: The first issue concerns the nature and amount of group conflict observed among children and adolescents. Although no figures were actually given, the campers appeared to be constantly generating conflict with the opposing team, in terms of calling them names, running off with their possessions, and generally interfering with their daily activities. Is this typical of the nature and number of conflicts reported from more open settings such as schools and neighborhoods, where children have access to many alternative group relationships?

The second issue is the social and psychological conditions that provoke conflict. Sherif points to a number of between-group and within-group factors that appear to provoke and exacerbate conflict, such as competition for the status of winner and in-group cohesion. Furthermore, the researchers' description of events suggested that between-group competition alters within-group structure in such a way as to increase conflict. Thus, the relation between within- and between-group characteristics might be important. Added to this are individual determinants such as the age, gender, race, and level of social understanding of the children.

The third issue concerns the consequences of conflict. Sherif et al. (1961) implied that, if left to their own devices, the boys would have remained hostile and avoided further contact with the other group. Given an opportunity to resolve their differences, however, the boys cooperated with each other, and some even became friends. The question then is: What are the potential negative and positive outcomes?

Paradigms in current research

The research paradigms developed to study these issues vary depending on the kind of groups employed (e.g., interacting vs. noninteracting), researchers' control over the conditions precipitating the conflict (field vs.

analogue laboratory studies), and the kind of conflict being measured (opposition vs. competition).

Field studies. To determine whether teaching children from different races in the same school reduces racial hostilities and provides equal opportunities, researchers have used field studies to examine a variety of outcomes including school achievement, self-esteem, racial attitudes, and peer interaction. To no one's surprise, the increase in contact between children of different races generally produces an increase in conflict (Aronson, Blaney, Stephan, Sikes, & Snapp, 1978; Patchen, 1982; Schofield, 1982). This research paradigm, which makes use of a naturally occurring experiment in group contact, combines observational data with rating scale data. One strength of the paradigm is its focus on spontaneously generated conflict. A second strength is its potential to examine a host of associated factors, such as prior experiences, family influences, and child-related characteristics, which vary naturally among children, in addition to manipulated factors such as classroom composition and structure.

Analogue laboratory studies. Games have focused on competitive behavior, which Sherif and others (Deutsch, 1973) identified as the essential condition for conflict. Tajfel's (1978) contribution to this issue was to develop the minimal group paradigm, which demonstrated that the simple awareness of belonging to a group, however randomly formed, leads members to categorize themselves and others, and to maximize the difference in group rewards in favor of the in-group (a form of competition).

By adapting another laboratory game, namely the Prisoner's Dilemma, Insko and colleagues (Insko et al., 1990) found that there was a tenfold increase in competitive responses when the game was played by groups of students rather than by individuals. These researchers have expanded the relevance of games for studying intergroup conflict by examining eliciting conditions such as intragroup consensus. They also noted the effects of competition on in-group interactions and out-group hostility. The paradigm has been used with preschool children and their friends (Matsumoto, Haan, Yabrove, Theodorou, & Carney, 1986) but not with children in interacting groups.

Finally, laboratory analogues of the desegregated classroom have been created to study conditions that reduce intergroup conflict and enhance liking and respect for classmates. Classroom-relevant variables such as team cooperation, peer assistance, and successful outcome, along with individual variables such as prejudice, competence, and race have been studied (Cook, 1985; Miller et al., 1985). Although the classroom analogue appears realistic, only a few such studies have been conducted with elementary school children.

Nature and frequency of conflict

Most researchers agree that racial conflict increases when children from two racial groups come into contact. Schofield reports, however, "extremely few serious and overt racial conflicts" occurred during the course of her year-long observation of classrooms, hallways, playground, and cafeteria at a newly desegregated urban middle school in the United States (1982, p. 156). Patchen (1982) found moderate levels of self-reported initiation of and participation in conflict with the other race among high school students. For example, the following are percentages of students reporting more than three incidents of a conflict provocation by a student from the other race: Being called a bad name was reported by 20% of blacks and 41% of whites; 10% of blacks and 26% of whites said someone purposely blocked them from passing; 6% of blacks and 34% of whites said someone tried to force them to give money; 19% of blacks and 13% of whites said they were pushed or hit and in turn hit back; 17% of blacks and 4% of whites said they pushed or hit an out-group student first.

The best predictor of cross-race overt conflict behavior was being male and having high levels of overt conflict with in-group students (Patchen, 1982). Thus, those who tended to provoke or participate in aggressive racial conflicts were the ones who displayed this pattern in nonracial situations, that is, males with an aggressive predisposition. Also, involvement in these conflicts was associated with holding negative attitudes toward the other race. Furthermore, if one's peers were also prejudiced, the association was stronger, thus revealing a group facilitation effect that could be due to a number of processes such as disinhibition or imitation. To further complicate the issue, however, this type of conflict provocation was not inversely correlated with friendly behavior or with number of other-race friends. In contrast, avoidance was inversely correlated with the number of other-race friends one had. Thus, many of these provocations were initiated by students who also interacted positively and were friends with students from the other race. Avoidance appeared to be more detrimental to cross-race harmony.

The nature of conflict as it is found in the school setting can be gleaned from the behaviors described previously, such as hitting, pushing, blocking, threatening to hurt, demanding money or school materials, derogatory speaking, and name calling. Schofield (1982) categorized these behaviors as "hassling," which refers to annoying provocations, and "intimidation," which refers to frightening provocations aimed at evoking fear itself or gaining compliance to a request.

There are two points to be made about these categories. The first is that children do not always retaliate in kind to these provocations, that is, they do not always hit back. Blacks were more likely than whites to react to these provocations with verbal or physical opposition. Whites were more likely to be afraid, to submit unwillingly to the request or to oppose passively. Passive opposition includes silently withdrawing to another place in the room or ignoring the other's behavior, even though the other child might continue to talk and touch.

The second point is that these behaviors characterize within-race as well as between-race interactions. For example, Schofield and Francis (1982) reported that within-race and cross-race negatively toned interactions in a mixed classroom were equally low at 1% of all interactions. They included physical blows, verbal and nonverbal threats, and insults. In unsupervised areas outside the classroom, however, within-race conflicts were higher. Patchen (1982) reported the following figures for three or more unfriendly contacts with adolescents of one's own race: Being called a bad name was reported by 31% of blacks and 26% of whites; 19% of blacks and 16% of whites said they were pushed or hit but did not retaliate; and 15% of blacks and 9% of whites said they pushed or hit first. Both Patchen (1982) and Schofield (1982) point out that conflict provocation by blacks is directed to both blacks and whites about equally, whereas it was mostly, but not solely, an in-group phenomenon among white students. Thus, these provocations do not characterize racial conflict alone (see also Sagar & Schofield, 1980).

Another form of conflict that is more subtle, but perhaps more aggravating for some, concerns academic conflicts. Schofield (1981) points out that black students in particular feel victims of this kind of conflict. White students' public correction of a black student's answer was seen as a form of control or intrusion. Although the academic strivings of white students are probably not racially motivated, such corrections may be seen by black students as attempts to humiliate them, to control the top academic positions, and to obtain special privileges from the staff. This may be a factor in arousing black students' conflict provocations in an attempt to regain status and control and may partially explain the higher levels of conflict provocation by blacks toward whites. Kochman (1981) also pointed out that styles of conflict differ for blacks and whites; verbal and physical challenges were considered harmless game playing by blacks but were interpreted by whites to be serious provocations.

Factors that provoke conflict

Competition for resources or status was emphasized by Sherif and his colleagues as the spark that ignites conflict. They also pointed out that within-group factors such as leadership style and cohesion interacted with team competition to exacerbate the conflict. For example, when one team lost the day's event, competition intensified and the team reorganized its leadership hierarchy by elevating the status of an aggressive bully, who then put pressure on the team members to pull together and fight harder. Given the influence of between-group factors on within-group factors and vice versa, it may be difficult in field studies to determine their separate effects on conflict. The laboratory studies conducted by Insko and colleagues (Insko et al., 1988, 1990), however, demonstrate that a competitive task enhances within-group cohesion and greed, which in turn provoke between-group mistrust and avoidance. Another set of factors concerns the characteristics of individuals who make up these groups – their race, gender, age, and level of social understanding.

Between-group factors

Competition. A competitive task or a competitive person tends to be associated with outcomes in which the extent of one side's benefit is inversely related to the other side's benefit. Given a clear reward structure, in which the benefits and losses are concrete and immediate, groups seek to benefit themselves. Under these conditions, competition seems almost inevitably to provoke conflict – overt conflict if the two are in contact. Sherif and colleagues (1961) demonstrated that win–loss sports competition between two groups of boys aroused conflict that extended beyond the sports tournament to include many attempts to hassle out-group members and raid their possessions. To distinguish competition from conflict in such a task, I prefer to use *competition* to refer to the actions taken to obtain task-related rewards, and *conflict* to refer to the extra-task actions that interfere with or obstruct others' activities.

Similarly, Tajfel's minimal intergroup paradigm provides a task with a clear payoff structure, which arouses people to maximize their own profit or maximize the profit of individual in-group members at the expense of out-group members. When asked to allocate rewards to in-group and out-group members identified only by their group, approximately 17% of Tajfel's (1970) early adolescent boys gave equal rewards to both groups, whereas 27% maximized the difference in group rewards in favor of their in-group. The rest chose other options such as maximizing their own reward but not penalizing or minimizing others' rewards. In comparison, allocations to two in-group members were such that 34% gave equally, 12% maximized the difference, and the rest chose other options. The findings have been replicated with children as young as 7 years (Vaughan, Tajfel, & Williams, 1981; Wetherell, 1982).

Grouping. This line of research has demonstrated that the simple categorization of people (i.e., the perception of belonging to a group) leads to intergroup competition. Although the percentages choosing the option of maximizing the difference in group rewards were relatively low, Tajfel and colleagues have used this finding to claim that the group context arouses high levels of competition and discrimination. They took great pains to ensure that only the variable of categorization was experimentally manipulated by basing group assignment on random design rather than on personal qualities. Biased attributions about one's group and the other group inevitably follow, however, sometimes as a result of the out-group's competitive actions, but more often as a way of justifying one's own group- or self-serving actions. By varying the number of activities subjects experienced alone with their groups, Insko et al. (1988) found that especially making a joint group decision about strategy substantially enhanced competitiveness over that found both for individuals and for noninteracting groups (the latter group being similar to Tajfel's). There is obviously much more work to be done in uncovering why this feeling of group cohesion enhances competitive actions directed against another group and what kinds of attributions about the self, the in-group, and the out-group follow.

Self-enhancement and mistrust. In addition to the two manipulated variables of belonging and joint decision making that enhance group categorization, other psychological states appear to increase competition in the reward or payoff games. They include the need for self-enhancement or group enhancement (Tajfel, 1978), and defensive mistrust and greed (Insko et al., 1990).

The motivation underlying intergroup competition as described by Tajfel (1978) involves the desire to enhance self-esteem. The desire is fulfilled in a number of ways, one of which is by giving oneself superior outcomes. If the self becomes identified with the group, then self-enhancement takes place by giving superior outcomes to one's group and "basking in its reflected glory" (Cialdini et al., 1976).

Although the self-enhancement motive appears to be best served by competitive interactions that favor the in-group, there is little evidence that superiority over the out-group, in line with Tajfel's explanation, is the motive rather than it simply being self-reward or greed. There is evidence that when self-gain is separated from self-superiority in a Prisoner's Dilemma game, 45% of elementary school children preferred the former strategy and only 15% the latter (Knight, 1981).

Insko and his colleagues (Insko et al., 1990) described this motive as greed when it is taken to extremes in the intergroup context. Among young egocentric children, this form of self-interest is to be expected (Matsumoto et al., 1986); among older children and adolescents, however, it would be considered socially unacceptable. Support for the greed hypothesis comes from the high frequency of competitive responses even when the group's earnings are superior and even after a trial in which the groups have mutually cooperated. The authors propose that greed may be sanctioned and even supported by members of a group who all want to act in a selfish way. This hypothesis is quite consistent with other demonstrations of antisocial group behavior in which the norms of society are replaced with new rules of conduct based on a consensus favoring self-interest (e.g., Zimbardo, 1969). Insko's research (Insko et al., 1990) also demonstrates the mistrust people feel for the out-group, mistrust based on negative experiences or negative stereotypes of the out-group.

Within-group factors

Sherif (1966) discussed a number of structural or organizational factors within his groups of campers that changed during intergroup conflict. These included leadership as well as cohesion among group members. Despite the appearance of cohesion, there was an internal struggle. Bullies took more influential leadership positions, and everyone was pressed to work toward the goal of beating the out-group. With aggressive and competitive individuals in positions of leadership, each group probably initiated more hostile and interfering activities against the other group. Furthermore, any member who wanted to initiate friendly relations with the other group was probably labeled a traitor and forced into line. Thus, conflict outside the tournament that Sherif (1966) exposed the groups to was exacerbated by leaders and pressures to conform.

Disapproval and conformity. Similarly, disapproval from friends and family exerts strong pressures on children and adolescents to avoid cross-race interactions. Moe, Nacoste, and Insko (1981) asked ninth-grade students to rate the approval or disapproval for several cross-race interactions that they expected from friends at school, friends outside of school, and parents. For both white and black students, high disapproval was expected for living in a neighborhood with or accepting as close kin by marriage someone of the other race. Overall, white students expected more disapproval than did black students, particularly concerning the following actions: "Permit this person to do me a favor," "Accept this person as a buddy," and "Accept this person as an intimate friend." Friends outside school and parents were expected to be more disapproving than were friends at school. Statistical associations between disapproval ratings and preference for contact with a person of the same race were high, indicating that within-group social pressure was an important determinant of the racial contacts made.

The fact that children and adolescents belong to a number of different groups and that these groups only partly overlap means that the conformity pressures of any one group are diluted. Interviews with young Canadian adolescents attending a multiethnic school in Montreal revealed that the children saw their schools and classrooms as places where interethnic and interracial friendships were protected from the pressures of a neighborhood gang or a racist parent (Laperriere, 1989). A very similar pattern of "protected" interaction was described by Katz (1955), who observed the weekly meetings of 40 black and white high school students. The adolescents had equal status in the group and formed many cross-racial friendships and cliques. The friends were aware that such relationships must be confined to group meetings or they risked disapproval from schoolmates, family, and the public at large. Conflicts within the group arose because black adolescents in particular were not prepared to lead a double life or to confine cross-race friendships to those of the same sex.

Within-group cohesion and between-group mistrust. It would be useful in this context to know more about the interaction of between- and within-group factors and their combined effects on conflict. A step in this direction was taken by Gavin and Furman (1989), who found that antagonism toward the out-group was enhanced by in-group structural variables such as a clear-cut leadership hierarchy, impermeability of the group, and conformity pressures. In turn, adolescents who were bothered by antagonism from the out-group belonged to (or perhaps created) groups that were internally hierarchical, impermeable, and conforming. Schofield (1982) described a real-life parallel to this pattern of intergroup tension leading to in-group cohesion. White adolescents who felt intimidated by black students formed a clique at school to protect themselves. The presence of this clique provoked the formation of a counterclique of blacks. Both cliques were subsequently disbanded because of the potential for intergroup conflict.

Individual factors

Certain factors reside within the individual or at least are carried around to different groups by the individual (e.g., race and culture, gender, age, and social understanding). These characteristics have not been systematically included in the research on group processes but may be important in determining the individual's perception of between- and within-group factors and the way of resolving conflict.

Race and culture. Differences in intergoup conflict were previously noted among black and white school children. For example, blacks showed equally high levels of conflict provocation toward blacks and whites, whereas whites directed conflict more to whites (Patchen, 1982; Schofield, 1982). Stylistic differences were also noted by Kochman (1981). Some researchers feel that the differences are partly the result of blacks' minority status and their need to compensate for feelings of inferiority.

Minority children have a complex and problematic group identity as a result of being simultaneously a member of a predominantly white society and a member of a minority racial group (Phinney, 1989). Until the age of 7 years, many minority children express the complexity of this dual membership by applying the correct racial label to themselves but perceiving themselves as similar to whites and preferring whites (Aboud, 1988; Spencer & Markstrom-Adams, 1990). Because of their multiple group membership, minority children may experience many inconsistent pressures to conform (e.g., Moe, Nacoste, & Insko, 1981). They also may be involved unwillingly in racial conflict instigated by white children who categorize them in an out-group.

Gender. Gender is another characteristic that plays an important role in group conflict. It has been noted often that girls associate with their own race more exclusively than do boys (e.g., Schofield & Francis, 1982). Schofield (1982) explains this sex difference in the amount of interaction by pointing to the interpersonal goals of early adolescent girls who are preparing for dating and mating in a society in which same-race marriages are the overwhelming norm. Consequently, they rehearse with same-race females. Boys, however, initiate rule-bound physical games that require large numbers of people and for which the criterion for selection is not race but athletic skills and toughness. Despite these behavioral differences, Patchen (1982) found that high school girls expressed more favorable attitudes toward the other race, though this difference is not a reliable finding. Boys, particularly aggressive boys, consistently show more conflict with the other race.

The explanation of these sex differences rests more with style of inter-action than with racial conflict per se.

Age and social understanding. Extrafamilial groups begin to be important for children some time around the age of 4 when they become aware of their membership in category groups defined by race, language, and religion. Such social categories are used spontaneously in the self-descriptions of kindergarteners and occur even more frequently and are considered more important by second graders (Aboud & Skerry, 1983). Thus, a number of reference groups exist for the preschooler, and it is clear that some of them, such as gender and race, influence observational learning, playmate selection, and behavior.

Adolescent groups and cliques have been regarded as qualitatively different from preadolescent groups in the complexity of their structure and norms, as well as in the value placed on them. Gavin and Furman (1989) found that 13- to 16-year-olds assigned much greater value to being in a popular group and experienced more dynamic relations (both positive and negative behaviors) within the group than did younger children. These adolescents, however, rated the peer group as less important than family, friends, school, religion, and extracurricular activities. In terms of group structure, the 13- to 16-year-olds perceived a more clear-cut status hierarchy, although pressures to conform were rated highest in preadolescence and declined thereafter. The decline in conformity pressure and a correspond-ing increase in both the permeability of the group and positive relations with out-groups suggest that, with age, adolescents acquire a broader net-work of relationships and a more mature view of themselves vis-à-vis others (Phinney, 1989). This, in turn, loosens them from the negative and con-straining pressures of a single group, and presumably reduces the likeli-hood of acrimonious conflict.

Although there is currently little research to document this hypothesis, it can be argued that those who possess multiple social relations are less likely to be involved in intergroup conflict than those who possess only one influence group. In certain settings in which intergroup conflict has been observed to be high, such as a laboratory (e.g., Insko et al., 1990) or summer camp (e.g., Savin-Williams, 1979; Sherif et al., 1961), we find that the researchers have engineered one predominant group affiliation. Turner (1978) claims that when a single reference group exists, it will be the only source of social self-definition. Similarly, a single group will be the only source of norms and will override more prosocial norms existing in other relationships and groups. Thus, it appears that a single all-encompassing group relationship tends to exacerbate intergroup competition and conflict by restricting the range of behavior and relationships available.

Prejudice. A final characteristic that sets the stage for interracial conflict in most schools is prejudice. Because prejudice begins around 4 years of age in majority white children (Aboud, 1988), it is usually an antecedent of conflict as well as a consequence. In the school yard, prejudice is more consistently associated with avoidance than with conflict (Patchen, 1982). This implies that those interested in reducing prejudice should be less concerned with eliminating conflict and more concerned with increasing contact, friendly interactions, and the kind of two-way communication that resolves conflict. Although longitudinal analyses have been used, most of the relations are correlational, and only a few laboratory studies have examined the effects of prejudice (Cook, 1985). The role of prejudice will therefore be discussed more thoroughly in the following section on the consequences of conflict.

Negative and positive consequences of intergroup conflict

Prejudice

Prejudice and discrimination are the major negative consequences of inter-group conflict. *Prejudice* typically refers to a predisposition to react unfavorably to people of another group because of their group membership. *Discrimination* refers to behavior, that is, treating someone unfairly because of group membership. Changes in prejudice appear to be affected by three time dimensions: cohort changes, specifically here the pre– versus post–civil rights eras; changes that take place with age; and short intervals of time in which contact and other conditions bring about changes in prejudice.

Cohort and age changes. Research conducted before the 1960s showed high levels of prejudice, often referred to as *normative prejudice* (Adorno, Frenkel-Brunswick, Levinson, & Sanford, 1950) because prejudice was an expected and accepted reaction to racial differences. The prevailing view held for the past 40 years was that prejudice increases with age. Most of the research cited by Brand, Ruiz, and Padilla (1974) shows such an increase, and at this point, we can only speculate that pre–civil rights conditions facilitated such an increase.

A review of the literature of the past 20 years, however, reveals that, among whites, prejudice increases between ages 4 and 7 years and then either remains constant or declines from age 8 to 12 years (Aboud, 1988). Prejudice among racial and ethnic minority children appears to begin around 7 years of age when they start to prefer the in-group; it increases thereafter but does not become more widespread than white prejudice (Aboud, 1988;

Spencer & Markstrom-Adams, 1990). Prejudice appears to continue declining in adolescence or to remain constant (e.g., Carlson & Iovini, 1985; Kalin, 1979).

There is little evidence to show that the prejudice of children under age 7 results from their parents' prejudice or racial conflict. Rather, it seems to result from a combination of two factors: children's awareness of the status hierarchy in the larger society, which places racial minorities at the bottom, and cognitive immaturity. The first has been difficult to study in young children because they egocentrically and sociocentrically place themselves and their group at the top. Even minority children, whose preferences lean toward whites, place their group at the top (Rosenberg & Simmons, 1971). Thus, it is not clear how the hierarchy gets perceived, but it does.

Cognitive immaturity has been studied somewhat more, and it appears that when concrete-operational skills are not available, children's attitudes are dichotomized in line with their perceptions of difference (Aboud, 1981, 1988). Actually, a decline in prejudice is predicted by a cognitive-developmental perspective. The ability to coordinate two or more different aspects of a situation is one of the skills that develops during the concrete-operational stage of thought. This skill manifests itself in the ability to consider simultaneously two different perspectives. In the interracial setting, it has been found that following the ability to conserve, children begin to accept that the racial preferences of a child from another racial group are not wrong but valid given that they arise from one's personal attachments (Aboud, 1981). This ability to reconcile racial differences is associated with lower levels of prejudice in children over age 7 years who have higher racial role-taking skills, moral judgment, and conservation (Clark, Hocevar, & Dembo, 1980; Davidson, 1976; Doyle & Aboud, 1991).

Changes due to contact. Although preschoolers may play with children from another racial group, their experience seems to have no effect on diminishing prejudice toward others of the same group (Aronson et al., 1978). From the time children enter school, their playmates are predominantly of the same racial or ethnic group, although they are by no means from only their group (e.g., Davey, 1983; Singleton & Asher, 1979). For example, in 26 kindergarten classes with a 30% black population, 33% of the white children's group play at recess included blacks (Finkelstein & Haskins, 1983). Although young children thus appear overwhelmingly prejudiced in test situations, they do not necessarily avoid children from other races when interacting in the schoolyard. The discrepancy is presumably due to aspects of the context that make personal characteristics other than race salient.

Contact and conflict in a desegregated middle school lead to many changes in prejudice and the stereotypes that maintain prejudice. *Stereotypes* are usually defined as shared beliefs about the common characteristics of a racial group. Schofield (1982) found that, over time, many white children became more confident in their stereotypes of black students. Consequently, the content of their stereotypes did not change; however, it was applied in a more differentiated manner to only some blacks. Although the direct conflict with blacks led whites to be fearful and to withdraw or submit, they became less afraid over time and were more willing to talk and interact. Thus, in the short-term, contact and conflict can lead to an increase in prejudice and negative stereotyping; with time, however, the emotion becomes less fearful and angry, and the stereotype becomes more differentiated.

Positive consequences

The overall effect of contact in desegregated schools appears to be positive. The tendency to associate exclusively with in-group members dissipates, cross-racial friendships develop, racial attitudes and understanding become more positive, and children become less afraid and anxious (Patchen, 1982; Sagar, Schofield, & Snyder, 1983; Schofield, 1982; Stephan & Rosenfield, 1978a, b; Stephan & Stephan, 1985; Whitley, Schofield, & Snyder, 1984). As a result of numerous conflicts experienced over the course of the year, white children in Schofield's (1982) study learned to cope with them by asking the student council to monitor disruptive behavior, avoiding derogatory remarks that provoked blacks, avoiding unsupervised areas where conflict was more prevalent, and getting a black friend to defend them verbally.

Most researchers agree that such positive outcomes will follow contact only if certain previously discussed conditions are met: the groups have equal status, cooperative interdependence exists among students, and school authorities support such encounters. Such conditions may prove effective, not because they minimize the likelihood of conflict, but because they provide a setting in which conflicts can be resolved positively.

Cooperative interdependence in the group setting can be manipulated by establishing learning groups of four to six students. Generally, grades are still given to individual students (reward independence), but privileges are given to the group as a whole for its performance (reward interdependence). The cooperative groups consist of students who are heterogeneous with respect to race and competence level. The motivation to help in-group members is enhanced through out-group competition – comparative rather than interactive competition (deVries, Edwards, & Slavin, 1978; Johnson, Johnson, & Maruyama, 1984; Weigel, Wiser, & Cook, 1975).

Observational data show that conflict, but not interracial conflict, is higher in the small group classes than in the traditionally taught classrooms (Aronson et al., 1978; Weigel et al., 1975). Teachers, however, have said that the small group situation facilitates better resolution of interracial conflicts. There is more cross-racial helping (e.g., Weigel et al., 1975) and more liking of individual group members (e.g., Aronson et al., 1978; DeVries et al., 1978; Weigel et al., 1975), but these positive attitudes do not extend beyond the classroom. This is a common finding, and as mentioned previously, it suggests that in the classroom or play context, children respond to more than simply the racial characteristics of their peers. In the attitude test context, children are asked to respond only to the racial features of other children's photographs. Thus, prejudice is more likely to be expressed to photographed peers when no interaction is allowed than to peers in an interacting group.

Some investigators believe that only contact between groups that maintains their group distinctiveness will lead to a reduction in racial prejudice beyond the classroom (Hewstone & Brown, 1986). In contrast to this emphasis on grouping, the trend in North America is to personalize individuals within the group, thereby reducing social categorization and intergroup competition. In an analogue of the desegregated classroom, Miller et al. (1985) compared the typical category-based assignment to groups (race and gender) with individuated assignment (random or based on skills or personality); the latter produced much lower bias. Miller and Brewer (1986) also provide evidence that when members act to crosscut social category boundaries (as when an out-group member voluntarily takes a stand different from the group), competitive behavior breaks down. Furthermore, when the interaction allows for the perception of similarity between self and others, intergroup hostility is reduced and generalizes to out-group members.

The laboratory analogues of desegregated classrooms appear to recreate in a controlled setting many of the important features of cross-racial interaction (Brewer, 1985). The two main problems with this, as with the previously described laboratory research, is the lack of alternative group affiliations available to members and the predominant research focus on young adult subjects.

Developmental adaptations

In conclusion, we might want to pull back from the conflict situation itself and ask if conflict provides a setting for the development of positive social skills or if the developmental outcome is generally negative. Do children who experience intergroup conflict learn a new set of skills that benefit their future group interactions or do they simply learn new competitive strategies for winning future conflicts?

If the conflict remains at the group level, as is the case with racial gangs or cliques, it appears to be dysfunctional. As described previously, many conflicts are instigated by boys who are predisposed to engage in aggressive encounters; they tend to be the ones who have high levels of aggressive conflicts with members of their own racial group. They also tend to associate with peers who are prejudiced and who therefore support and facilitate their racial hostility (Patchen, 1982). Thus, racial gangs are made up of boys who have a particular personality and are not representative of most children or adolescents.

Another type of dysfunctional adaptation to conflict is found among children and adolescents who choose to avoid members of the other group. This is found predominantly among white children who passively oppose the instigator of a conflict by ignoring or withdrawing (Schofield, 1982). It is also found among Hispanic students who evidence a great deal of intergroup anxiety (Stephan & Stephan, 1985). Children who avoid conflicts are unlikely to have any friendly contacts with members of the other race. Thus, they do not have the opportunity to acquire a more personalized view of those of the other race or to learn about their similarities.

Most conflicts, however, are between individuals who interact positively with members of the other race and who have friends among them. Thus, conflicts do not disrupt normal peer relations. Children acquire mature strategies for reducing and resolving hostile conflicts. They learn to avoid derogatory remarks that might be hurtful and not to interpret verbal comments as threatening when they are meant to be playful (Sagar & Schofield, 1980). When another-race friend comes to one's defense, the outcome is often a more supportive and understanding friendship. Although the long-term functional adaptations have only recently been addressed, interracial contact and conflict appear to lead to social skills that help minorities find jobs and help majorities work effectively with minority members. A few key skills have been identified, namely expanding one's social network, improving communication, being less categorical in judgment, and reducing social anxiety.

The positive consequences of contact and conflict do not fully offset the negative findings described earlier in the chapter. The conflict, competition, prejudice, and stereotypes that seem an inherent part of intergroup relations need to be considered in light of the context in which they were studied. In the laboratory analogue and summer camp settings, there is no opportunity to look at changes that take place over the long term. In the desegregated school setting, contact and conflict result in the development of beneficial social skills.

Certain limitations of the analogue settings need to be examined more carefully to determine whether they inadvertently lead to higher levels of competition and conflict. One limitation is the tendency to restrict children's social relationships to the single group in which they have been placed for study purposes. The number of group affiliations available to a child or adolescent may be directly related to their dependence on the group's status and, therefore, to intergroup conflict. As well, conflict inevitably rises with the amount of contact between groups, but so does the opportunity for conflict resolution and friendship. The ratio between conflict and friendly interaction is a more relevant index of harmony, and is more likely to reveal the benefits of contact. Finally, because more researchers of intergroup conflict use young adult subjects, there is a need to examine the effect of group contact on children. Children have a less sophisticated understanding of racial differences, but are perhaps more susceptible to the changes envisioned by those who seek a more integrated society.

References

Aboud, F. E. (1981). Egocentrism, conformity, and agreeing to disagree. *Developmental Psychology, 17*, 791–799.

Aboud, F. E. (1988). *Children and prejudice.* New York: Blackwell.

Aboud, F. E., & Skerry, S. A. (1983). Self and ethnic concepts in relation to ethnic constancy. *Canadian Journal of Behavioural Science, 15*, 14–26.

Adorno, T. W., Frenkel-Brunswick, E., Levinson, D. J., & Sanford, R. N. (1950). *The authoritarian personality.* New York: Harper & Row.

Allport, G. W. (1954). *The nature of prejudice.* Reading, MA: Addison-Wesley.

Aronson, E., Blaney, N., Stephan, C., Sikes, J., & Snapp, M. (1978). *The jigsaw classroom.* Beverly Hills, CA: Sage.

Brand, E. S., Ruiz, R. A., & Padilla, A. M. (1974). Ethnic identification and preference: A review. *Psychological Bulletin, 81*, 860–890.

Brewer, M. B. (1985). Experimental research and social policy: Must it be rigor versus relevance? *Journal of Social Issues, 41*, 159–176.

Brown, G., & Johnson, S. P. (1971). The attribution of behavioral connotations to shaded and white figures by Caucasian children. *British Journal of Social and Clinical Psychology, 10*, 306–312.

Carlson, J. M., & Iovini, J. (1985). The transmission of racial attitudes from fathers to sons: A study of blacks and whites. *Adolescence, 20*, 233–237.

Cialdini, R. B., Borden, R. J., Thorne, A., Walker, M. R., Freeman, S., & Sloan, L. R. (1976). Basking in reflected glory: Three (football) field studies. *Journal of Personality and Social Psychology, 34*, 366–375.

Clark, A., Hocevar, D., & Dembo, M. H. (1980). The role of cognitive development in children's explanations and preference for skin color. *Developmental Psychology, 16*, 332–339.

Cohen, E. G. (1984). The desegregated school: Problems in status, power and interethnic climate. In N. Miller & M. B. Brewer (Eds.), *Groups in contact: The psychology of desegregation*. New York: Academic Press.

Cook, S. W. (1985). Experimenting on social issues: The case of school desegregation. *American Psychologist, 40*, 452–460.

Davey, A. G. (1983). *Learning to be prejudiced: Growing up in multi-ethnic Britain*. London: Arnold.

Davidson, F. N. (1976). Ability to respect persons compared to ethnic prejudice in childhood. *Journal of Personality & Social Psychology, 34*, 1256–1267.

Deutsch, M. (1973). *The resolution of conflict*. New Haven, CT: Yale University Press.

DeVries, D. L., Edwards, K. J., & Slavin, R. E. (1978). Biracial learning teams and race relations in the classroom: Four field experiments on Teams-Games-Tournament. *Journal of Educational Psychology, 70*, 356–362.

Doyle, A. B., & Aboud, F. E. (1991). *Prejudice as a social-cognitive development*. Manuscript submitted for publication.

Doyle, A. B., Beaudet, J., & Aboud, F. E. (1988). Developmental patterns in the flexibility of children's ethnic attitudes. *Journal of Cross-Cultural Psychology, 19*, 3–18.

Finkelstein, W., & Haskins R. (1983). Kindergarten children prefer same-color peers. *Child Development, 54*, 502–508.

Gaertner, S. L., Mann, J., Murrell, A., & Dovidio, J. F. (1989). Reducing intergroup bias: The benefits of recategorization. *Journal of Personality & Social Psychology, 57*, 239–249.

Gavin, L. A., & Furman, W. (1989). Age differences in adolescents' perceptions of their peer groups. *Developmental Psychology, 25*, 827–834.

Hewstone, M., & Brown, R. (1986). Contact is not enough: An intergroup perspective on the contact hypothesis. In M. Hewstone & R. Brown (Eds.), *Contact and conflict in intergroup encounters*. New York: Blackwell.

Insko, C. A., Hoyle, R. H., Pinkley, R. L., Hong, G. Y., Slim, R. M., Dalton, B., Ruffin, P. P., Dardis, G. J., Bernthal, P. R., & Schopler, J. (1988). Individual–group discontinuity: The role of a consensus rule. *Journal of Experimental Social Psychology, 24*, 505–519.

Insko, C. A., Schopler, J., Hoyle R. H., Dardis, G. J., & Graetz, K. A. (1990). Individual–group discontinuity as a function of fear and greed. *Journal of Personality & Social Psychology, 58*, 68–79.

Johnson, D. W., Johnson, R., & Maruyama, G. (1984). Goal interdependence and interpersonal attraction in heterogeneous classrooms: A metanalysis. In N. Miller & M. B. Brewer (Eds.), *Groups in contact: The psychology of desegregation*. New York: Academic Press.

Kalin, R. (1979). Ethnic and multicultural attitudes among children in a Canadian city. *Canadian Ethnic Studies, 11*, 69–81.

Katz, I. (1955). *Conflict and harmony in an adolescent interracial group*. New York: New York University Press.

Knight, G. P. (1981). Behavioral and sociometric methods of identifying cooperators, competitors, and individualists: Support for the validity of the social orientation construct. *Developmental Psychology, 17*, 430–433.

Kochman, T. (1981). *Black and white styles in conflict*. Chicago: University of Chicago Press.

Laperrière, A. (1989). *La construction sociale des relations interethniques et interraciales chez les adolescent(e)s*. Unpublished manuscript. Université du Québec à Montréal.

Matsumoto, D., Haan, N., Yabrove, G., Theodorou, P., & Carney, C. C. (1986). Preschoolers' moral actions and emotions in prisoner's dilemma. *Developmental Psychology, 22*, 663–670.

Miller, N., & Brewer, M. B. (1986). Categorization effects on ingroup and outgroup perception. In J. F. Dovidio & S. L. Gaertner (Eds.), *Prejudice, discrimination and racism*. New York: Academic Press.

Miller, N., Brewer, M. B., & Edwards, K. (1985). Cooperative interaction in desegregated settings: A laboratory analogue. *Journal of Social Issues, 41*, 63–79.

Moe, J. L., Nacoste, R. W., & Insko, C. A. (1981). Belief versus race as determinants of discrimination: A study of southern adolescents in 1966 and 1979. *Journal of Personality & Social Psychology, 41*, 1031–1050.

Patchen, M. (1982). *Black–white contact in schools: Its social and academic effects.* West Lafayette, IN: Purdue University Press.

Phinney, J. S. (1989). Stages of ethnic identity in minoirty group adolescents. *Journal of Early Adolescence, 9*, 34–49.

Rosenberg, M., & Simmons, R. G. (1971). *Black and White self-esteem: The urban school child.* Washington, DC: American Sociological Association.

Sagar, H. A., & Schofield, J. W. (1980). Racial and behavioral cues in black and white children's perceptions of ambiguously aggressive acts. *Journal of Personality & Social Psychology, 39*, 590–598.

Sagar, H. A., Schofield, J. W., & Snyder, H. N. (1983). Race and gender barriers: Preadolescent peer behavior in academic classrooms. *Child Development, 54*, 1032–1040.

Savin-Williams, R. C. (1979). Dominance hierarchies in groups of early adolescents. *Child Development, 50*, 142–151.

Schofield, J. W. (1981). Complementary and conflicting identities: Images and interaction in an interracial school. In S. R. Asher & J. M. Gottman (Eds.), *The development of children's friendships.* Cambridge: Cambridge University Press.

Schofield, J. W. (1982). *Black and white in school: Trust, tension or tolerance?* New York: Praeger.

Schofield, J. W., & Francis, W. D. (1982). An observational study of peer interaction in racially mixed "accelerated" classrooms. *Journal of Educational Psychology, 74*, 722–732.

Schofield, J. W., & Sagar, H. A. (1983). Desegregation, school practices, and student race relations. In C. H. Rossell & W. D. Hawley (Eds.), *The consequences of school desegregation.* Philadelphia: Temple University Press.

Shantz, C. U. (1987). Conflicts between children. *Child Development, 58*, 283–305.

Sherif, M. (1956). Experiments in group conflict. *Scientific American, 195*, 54–58.

Sherif, M. (1966). *Group conflict and cooperation*, London: Routledge & Kegan Paul.

Sherif, M., Harvey O. J., White, B. J., Hood, W. R., & Sherif, C. W. (1961). *Intergroup conflict and cooperation: The Robbers Cave experiment.* Norman: University of Oklahoma Press.

Sherif, M., & Sherif, C. (1953). *Groups in harmony and tension: An integration of studies on intergroup relations.* New York: Harper & Row.

Singleton, L. C., & Asher, S. R. (1979). Racial integration and children's peer preferences: An investigation of developmental and cohort differences. *Child Development, 50*, 936–941.

Spencer, M. B., & Markstrom-Adams, C. (1990). Identity processes among racial and ethnic minority children in America. *Child Development, 61*, 290–310.

Stephan, W. G., & Rosenfield, D. (1978a). The effects of desegregation on race relations and self-esteem. *Journal of Educational Psychology, 70*, 670–679.

Stephan, W. G., & Rosenfield, D. (1978b). Effects of desegregation on racial attitudes. *Journal of Personality and Social Psychology, 36*, 795–804.

Stephan, W. G., & Stephan, G. W. (1985). Intergroup anxiety. *Journal of Social Issues, 41*, 157–175.

Tajfel, H. (1970). Experiments in intergroup discrimination. *Scientific American, 223*, 96–102.

Tajfel, H. (1978). Social categorization, social identity and social comparison. In H. Tajfel (Ed.), *Differentiation between social groups.* New York: Academic Press.

Turner, J. C. (1978). Social categorization and social discrimination in the minimal group paradigm. In H. Tajfel (Ed.), *Differentiation between social groups.* New York: Academic Press.

Turner, J. C. (1982). Towards a cognitive redefinition of the social group. In H. Tajfel (Ed.), *Social identity and intergroup relations*. Cambridge: Cambridge University Press.

Vaughan, G. M., Tajfel, H., & Williams, J. (1981). Bias in reward allocation in an intergroup and an interpersonal context. *Social Psychology Quarterly, 44*, 37–42.

Weigel, R. H., Wiser, P. I., & Cook, S. W. (1975). The impact of cooperative learning experiences on cross-ethnic relations and attitudes. *Journal of Social Issues, 31*, 219–244.

Wetherell, M. (1982). Cross-cultural studies of minimal groups: Implications for the social identity theory of intergroup relations. In H. Tajfel (Ed.), *Social identity and intergroup relations*. Cambridge: Cambridge University Press.

Whitley, B. F., Schofield, J. W., & Snyder, H. N. (1984). Peer preferences in a desegregated school: A round robin analysis. *Journal of Personality & Social Psychology, 46*, 799–810.

Williams, J. E., & Morland, J. K. (1976). *Race, color, and the young child*. Chapel Hill: University of North Carolina Press.

Zimbardo, P. G. (1969). The human choice: Individuation, reason, and order versus de-individuation, impulse, and chaos. In W. J. Arnold & D. Levine (Eds.), *Nebraska symposium on motivation*. Lincoln: University of Nebraska Press.

14   Conflict and child maltreatment

Patricia Minuchin

In an enlightened culture, such as our own, it should be possible to concentrate on the optimal conditions for raising children and assuring their healthy growth. Since the early 1960s, however, when Kempe and his colleagues published material on the "battered child" (Kempe, Silverman, Steele, Droegenmueller, & Silver, 1962), we have become increasingly alert to the alarming problem of child maltreatment. The need to ensure basic safety has given rise to legislation, social policies, and efforts to understand abuse and ameliorate its effects. There are, as yet, few certainties in this area. Theories have been partial, research flawed, and neither the causes nor the effects are thoroughly documented. More integrative theories are emerging and the quality of research is improving, but the field still requires considerable exploration.

In this chapter, we focus particularly on the role of conflict in maltreatment, limiting the discussion to physical abuse and neglect and to parent–child abuse within the family. We approach *conflict* as an interpersonal phenomenon, defined as an oppositional interchange involving two or more people, and we are concerned particularly with destructive conflict. As Shantz (1987) has noted, it is important to separate the concept of conflict from that of aggression; they are not necessarily associated. When conflict leads to abuse, however, it is aggressive by definition. In this chapter, therefore, we explore the role of destructive conflict in abuse, considering the conditions under which it occurs, the impact, and possibilities for positive change.

The parameters of neglect and physical abuse are not totally clear. The Child Abuse Prevention and Treatment Act of 1974 established the National Center on Child Abuse and Neglect, which was to provide a uniform definition, facilitate research, and suggest standards for prevention and treatment (Daro, 1988). The center's definition is broad, covering physical, sexual, and mental maltreatment that harms the health and welfare of a child under age 18. "Neglect" is inadequate attention to health, safety, food,

380

shelter, and so forth; "physical abuse" is nonaccidental physical injury. It is evident that the definitions do not solve the problems of judgment and reporting. There are different points of view on major issues: the relative importance of parental intent versus extent of injury; and the balance between protecting the child and protecting parental rights. The latter is an issue of particular complexity when judging neglect in the context of family poverty. States vary in their criteria for reporting abuse, and actual practice depends, in the end, on professional workers. Because investigators draw samples from designated cases of abuse or neglect, this situation affects the clarity and consistency of research findings. In subsequent sections, we consider theories of maltreatment, the role of destructive conflict, the impact on development, and interventions to treat or prevent abuse.

Explaining child maltreatment: Principal theories

To understand the context of maltreatment it is necessary to summarize the more general theories in the field, in which *social-ecological* factors have been emphasized, on the one hand, and *psychological* factors, on the other. The two perspectives have generally been investigated separately, but they are not mutually exclusive. In current reviews, child abuse is seen as a multidetermined phenomenon, in which a variety of factors interact to prepare the context for maltreatment (see Cicchetti & Carlson, 1989; Wolfe, 1987).

Social-ecological theories of abuse

Social-ecological theories appeared in the 1970s and have been championed and documented by Gelles (1973) and Gil (1970), among others. They implicate the characteristics of U.S. culture, established traditions in child rearing, and the realities of life for the poor. From this perspective, the current level of violence in society provides the basic context for child maltreatment because it presents an aggressive model for expressing anger and settling differences. In addition, child-rearing traditions often include a high tolerance for corporal punishment. Many people hit their children with hands, belt, or other objects (Gil, 1970; Parke & Collmer, 1975), basing their actions on long established warnings about sparing the rod and on the acceptability of corporal punishment in their reference group. Against the force of tradition and the model of violence in the culture, professional efforts to promote rational, noncorporal forms of discipline have been only partially successful.

The most thoroughly documented aspect of social-ecological theory is the relationship between abuse and poverty. Though child abuse occurs at all levels of society, the correlation between socioeconomic status and child maltreatment has been clearly established (Daro, 1988; Gil, 1970; Wolfe, 1987). However, many people who live in poverty do not abuse their children, and it is important to seek differentiated data. In this respect, the research of Garbarino and his colleagues is particularly useful (e.g., Garbarino & Sherman, 1980). They documented such environmental correlates of maltreatment as low income, high mobility, and single parent status, but they also compared the characteristics of equally poor neighborhoods in which the risk of child abuse was statistically different. They found a pattern of greater social impoverishment in the high-risk area. Families in this area had fewer practical and social resources for child care and for dealing with life crises. The investigators suggest that the clustering of needy families in areas where social resources are least available increases the level of stress and the likelihood of abuse. Homelessness and drugs compound the problem, as these conditions are accompanied by a decrease in social resources and an increase in erratic behavior.

Social and ecological explanations do not deal directly with the role of conflict in relation to abuse. They suggest, however, that the stress of difficult life conditions among the poor and the scarcity of resources and social supports in some neighborhoods make it more likely that conflict will arise within families; the model of violence in the culture and the acceptability of corporal punishment in child-rearing traditions make it more likely that such conflict will eventuate in abuse.

Psychological theories of abuse

Psychological explanations of maltreatment have been prominent in the field, and much research has focused on the personality and childhood experiences of the abusing adult. It has been established that the vast majority of abusing adults are not psychotic (Justice & Justice, 1990; Spinetta & Rigler, 1972; Wolfe, 1987), but correlational research has produced a long list of dysfunctional characteristics, including low self-esteem, poor impulse control, inadequate skills for handling pressure, and unrealistic expectations of children. Although plausible, the list is not very different from descriptions of people who have other troubles but do not abuse children, and this approach has yielded little predictive power.

The importance of personal history is more clearly established. It is an axiom in the field that people who were abused in childhood are apt to become abusing parents (Parke & Collmer, 1975; Spinetta & Rigler, 1972).

The generalization has been challenged by some investigators who note, with reason, that there is little information about people who were abused in childhood but do not abuse their children (Daro, 1988; Kadushin & Martin, 1981; Kaufman & Zigler, 1987). Granting the validity of both points, two questions invite further investigation: What enables people with a history of maltreatment to become adequate, nonabusing parents? And what aspects of childhood experience and development are relevant to the later syndrome of child maltreatment? Answers to the first question may involve resilience and support systems, and will be discussed in a later section. Answers to the second may lie not only in the experience of abuse but in the derailment, for whatever reason, of optimal social development, including social cognition, empathy, and mechanisms for controlling aggression.

In exploring the relationship between social cognition and child maltreatment, Newberger and White (1989) describe aspects of interpersonal awareness that evolve through childhood and are part of the repertoire that people bring to parenting. These include the capacity to take the perspective of another (e.g., the child), to understand how rules are made and conflict resolved (e.g., in family life and parent–child interchange), and to balance the needs of the self with a responsibility for others. In studies of abusing mothers, Newberger and her colleagues applied these ideas to interview data, assessing the complexity of parental awareness through a specially constructed coding scheme. They found that the social cognition of abusing mothers was less mature in response to parental issues than that of controls.

In a similar vein, Feshbach (1989) has focused on empathy, noting that the research is sparse but that physically abusive parents are generally found to be less empathic than are controls. Her definition and measure of "empathy" include both the cognitive skills for understanding another perspective and the capacity to read emotion and respond with affect. In a comparative study, she found that the abusing mothers of young children were significantly less empathic than the control group and suggestively distinguished from the mothers of disturbed, nonabused children by a lower score on empathic distress. This affective factor may have an important role in inhibiting abuse, if further data support the suggestion that abusing parents are less sensitive than others to the child's pain. The question is complex, however. There is some evidence that abusive parents may react with anger to the distress they perceive. If they are impulsive or under pressure, empathic distress may lead not to the inhibition of abuse but to remorse after the fact.

These studies are promising. They suggest that the prosocial orientation and affect of abusive parents is limited, in comparison with parents who do not abuse their children. However, the studies are few, and they do not establish a clear link between social development in childhood and adult abusive behavior, nor do they explore the stressful conditions and immediate stimuli that trigger abusive propensities in the adult. This is a fertile area for research.

While the search for the psychological roots of maltreatment has concentrated, understandably, on the adult, there also has been some effort to describe the characteristics of children who are abused. Investigators are wary of blaming the victim, but current formulations see the child as a participant, by virtue of characteristics that range from physical attributes to functioning style. Some children have special needs that require patience and extra care: premature babies, babies who are slow to respond, babies who are hyperactive or born drug addicted, and children of any age who have physical or mental handicaps. Some factors are objectively describable, but the perception of the adult is often crucial. What one parent sees as defiant, another might enjoy as strong minded, and the perception of a child as "slow to respond" depends partly on the parent's own style. As the child grows older and more complex, a variety of behaviors can trigger an abusive reaction from the adult.

Not all adults react in this way, however, and the characteristics of the child are not a sufficient explanation. Most child abuse is an interactional event. Adult and child elicit responses from each other, producing patterns that may become consistent and that may be implicitly supported by other family members. We consider interactive theories and data in the next section, which is focused on conflict in relation to maltreatment.

Conflict and child maltreatment

In considering the particular role of conflict, we will be dealing with the maltreatment of children beyond infancy. The exclusion of infant abuse follows from the definition of conflict as an oppositional interchange. Abusive mothers tend to interpret child behavior more negatively than do other mothers (Newberger & White, 1989) and may well attribute defiant intentions to an infant, but babies who do not eat or will not stop crying are not challenging the adult. Until the child is able to say, "No!" or act out intentional resistance, parent–child conflict is not established. In our discussion, therefore, we set a lower age limit, starting some time in the second year.

We also will deal separately with neglect and physical abuse, because the role of conflict in these two forms of maltreatment is not equivalent.

Neglect is the most commonly reported form of maltreatment (Wolfe, 1987), covering inadequate parental attention to the child's basic needs. If we look at the profile of the most typical situation, it is a recapitulation of the ecological and psychological features that prepare the groundwork for maltreatment. Neglect occurs primarily among the poor, and the neglectful parent is usually female. She is apt to be young, unmarried, poorly educated, living on welfare, and socially isolated. She also may use drugs, at least intermittently. Her background has seldom included the formative experiences that create mature social cognition, and there are few social or practical forces in the current situation to ease her stress.

Is conflict a direct factor in the parental neglect of children? It does not seem so. Neglect is the absence of action rather than the presence of an oppositional exchange. However, conflict and conflict avoidance may be indirect factors.

There may be conflict elsewhere in the family system, for instance. The young mothers so often implicated in neglect offer an example. We know from clinical work that there is often unresolved conflict between the mother and her family. The result is a cutting of contact, contributing to the mother's sense of inadequacy and, potentially, to the neglect of her children. The neglect may even be a message to the family, conveying the mother's anger and implicit appeal for help. If the conflict is addressed, the family may become part of the solution, rather than part of the problem, offering backup care for the children and a network of social support for the mother.

Parental neglect may also occur in the service of conflict avoidance. The point is speculative but worth considering. We know from contact with the inner-city poor that parents love their children, even in the midst of distress, disorder, and drugs, and they do not want to harm them. An angry, impotent parent, facing difficult life conditions and a pileup of stress, may be avoiding conflict and physical abuse of the children by reducing contact. The result is still child maltreatment, but the implications are different. A broader range of interventions becomes possible if neglect is seen as the result of an active effort to avoid conflict and abuse, rather than a self-centered indifference to the children.

Physical abuse, in contrast to neglect, involves direct aggressive action. It can arise without apparent provocation, and we cannot assume that it always stems from conflict. However, an oppositional interchange often precedes, accompanies, and/or follows abuse. We need, therefore, to examine the conditions that move a normal, potentially manageable phenomenon to this destructive level. In the following sections, we consider destructive conflict in the parent–child dyad, destructive conflict in the family system, and the relation of developmental factors to abuse.

Destructive conflict between parent and child

Reports of physical abuse usually focus on establishing adult intent and the extent of injury, but more detailed material suggests that conflict between parent and child is often involved. Reports from a Wisconsin agency describe a range in the quality of disagreement and reaction (Kadushin & Martin, 1981). Some cite sustained violent behavior on the part of the parent, such as a mother who reacted to her 2-year-old's refusal to eat by throwing him across the room and beating him with a shoe, so that he required medical treatment. In another example, a caseworker reported the following:

Rosemarie, 13, was taping a song that was on the radio and told her mother to be quiet. When she wasn't, Rosemarie swore at her, which made Mrs. B. angry. She threw her tea at Rosemarie, pushed her to the floor, kicked her in the back and hit her with a belt. (pp. 118–119)

Other reports indicate a less sustained and violent loss of parental control:

Mother requested that daughter, 13, stay at home. Daughter argued and swung at mother, missing mother, who then struck back at daughter, hitting her in the face and leaving bruise to her lower left cheek. (p. 117)

Despite the range, all these incidents involve parent–child conflict and physical abuse, and it is important to understand how they come about.

Destructive dyadic interactions have been analyzed by Kadushin and Martin (1981) and by Patterson (1982). The former interviewed 66 parents who had abused their children, ranging in age from infancy through adolescence. They recorded the parent's perception of the child's behavior and description of the incident. Patterson, a social learning theorist, based his analysis on observations, tests, and treatment of families with aggressive, preadolescent children. The main points of their combined analyses can be summarized as follows:

- A prolonged sequence of interaction is typical, involving several steps in the interchange and an escalation in intensity to the point of physical abuse. As an example: "Do it"; "No"; "I said do it!"; "I don't care"; "If you don't do it right now, I'll show you!"; no response; parent strikes child.
- Over time, the interaction may escalate faster and more sharply, and the conflict may start at a higher point. Patterson explains this in terms of negative reinforcement, which increases the likelihood that abusive behavior effective in stopping previous incidents will recur. As a parent explains, "I've tried to reason, ground him . . . but I know it doesn't work."
- In these situations, the adult is often carrying an emotional load, which Patterson diagrams in terms of arousal and anger. Parents predisposed to aggressive behavior strike out when they are under stress and perceive

the child as intentionally disobedient. In interview, parents describe the pressures of economic problems, large families, and the shame of criticism from others.

- The child's aversive behavior is an important part of the interaction. The situation arises in the context of rules and expectations for acceptable behavior, the child's violation or direct challenge, and the parent's effort to control. Though such conflicts are normal, they escalate, in these situations, with both parent and child as participants.

- The participants have poor skills for resolving conflict and terminating the incident. This point is crucial. Conflict that is not resolved is likely to escalate and invoke violence.

In general, these points emphasize a dysfunctional process: coercive behavior, escalation, poor mechanisms for conflict resolution, and negative reinforcement. Social and psychological factors create the predisposition for parental aggression, but a conflict situation is often the flash point. Management of the conflict determines whether a disagreement between parent and child will be resolved constructively or terminate in violence.

Destructive conflict in the family system

Most child abuse is seen as a dyadic event. For theorists with a systemic perspective, however, that is a limited view of causality. They see the interaction of parent and child as embedded in the structure of the larger family, and in the patterns that govern behavior within and across subsystems (P. Minuchin, 1985). When a parent abuses a child, it is assumed that more than two people are involved, either because tension elsewhere in the system targets the child or because members of the family are helping to maintain the pattern, albeit unwittingly. A spouse may stand passively by while a child is beaten because he or she is afraid to intervene, enacting a pattern of conflict avoidance in this triangle that holds as well between husband and wife. For this reason, Justice and Justice (1990) bring the "abusing couple" into therapy, though only one parent has mistreated the child.

Conflict is a primary concern of family therapists. They have described triangulating and detouring mechanisms by which parents involve children in their disagreements, the spread of conflict from the interaction of spouses to parent–child units, and the efforts of children to deflect their parents' conflict through psychosomatic illness or acting out (Christensen & Margolin, 1988; S. Minuchin, Rosman, & Baker, 1978). There are different patterns of abuse, however, and they suggest different underlying family dynamics. If all the children in the family are mistreated, principal factors may include predisposing adult characteristics and the use of violence as the prepotent mode of conflict resolution. If one child is targeted, likely factors include the child's characteristics, the parent's perception of this child, and the patterns of interaction they have established, as well as family coalitions that include the child and stress the parent (e.g., a grandmother who is fond of this child, critical of the way the parent handles the child, and apt to sabotage parental control by supporting the child's escalation of arguments). The connection between family dynamics and particular patterns of abuse has not been systematically studied.

Research concerning the characteristics of abusive families is sparse, but Silber's (1990) study focused directly on conflict negotiation, comparing families with abusive fathers to matched nonabusing families. Silber asked each family to discuss an area of family disagreement, then coded the videotape for on- and off-task behavior, participation of different family members, and the extent of dyadic interaction. In this situation, where families must negotiate their differences, she found significantly less effective patterns in the abusive families: less verbal interaction and on-task behavior, less sustained dyadic discussion, more disagreements that moved across generations, and less tendency for children to initiate new approaches. She considered her findings consistent with theories of conflict avoidance in dysfunctional families and with findings that point to limitations in the initiative of abused children.

Burgess and Conger (1978) compared the behavior of abusive, neglectful, and control families on a series of tasks, coding each family member for interaction, affect, command, and compliance. They found that maltreating families interacted less than controls and were more negative with their children. Mothers in abusive families differed from controls more than did fathers, and mothers in neglectful families were notable for negative behavior. The authors suggest that it would be useful to study the relative child-rearing participation of mothers and fathers and to document response sequences and conditional probabilities.

The observational studies of Reid, Taplin, and Lorber (1981) confirm the finding of more restricted interaction in abusive families. Also, mothers and children in abusive families were more aggressive than family members in comparison groups, and spouses in the abusive families were significantly more aggressive toward each other than were other couples. The investigators note that abusive families have poor management skills and tend to handle challenge with aggression, but they suggest that parent–child conflict is not a sufficient explanation for abuse. Rather, it is the combination of parent–parent and parent–child conflict, in a family, that produces a high-risk situation.

Together, these studies suggest that interaction in abusive families is relatively constricted and negative in tone, that such families may be characterized by spousal conflict as well as parent–child conflict, that they handle conflict aggressively and tend to avoid it, and that their patterns do not encourage child initiative. They also suggest differences between abusive and neglectful families as well as between mothers and fathers.

The exploration of family patterns in abusive families is at an early stage. In future research, it will be important to focus on process rather than rate of behavior, including sequences, contingencies and the involvement of several people in a unit of interaction. For this purpose, videotapes provide a more flexible source of data than rotating time samples of individuals. They allow for multiple inspections, and it is possible to document the behavior of siblings or of the second parent while one parent is interacting with the child. Other productive directions for research include the following: (a) a study of spouse interaction, in two-parent abusing families, considering their patterns of conflict resolution as a couple, their roles in child rearing and discipline, and the behavior of the spouse when parent–child conflict is escalating toward abuse; (b) a comparison of families in which the father is the primary abuser with families in which the mother is the primary abuser; (c) a comparative study of families with targeted, as opposed to multiple, abuse; (d) a further exploration of differences between abusing and neglectful families; and (e) a more differentiated attention to family patterns in relation to developmental stages. The inclusion of all family members, in the studies cited, is an important step in understanding the context of abuse. However, researchers have not broken down the data to analyze either the behavior of younger and older children, during family tasks, or the specific nature of parent interaction with children of different ages.

Developmental factors in destructive conflict

There are developmental differences in the nature and frequency of conflicts that go out of control. Analyzing over 800 cases that terminated in physical abuse, Kadushin and Martin (1981) found that most incidents involved transgression against parental rules or expectations and that the behavior was significantly related to age. With the youngest children, incidents arose in connection with nurturance and socialization (e.g., eating, crying, sleeping, elimination). Compliance with social standards was primarily implicated in abusive incidents with children between ages 6 and 12 (e.g., lying and stealing). Incidents with adolescents concerned authority, autonomy, and responsibility (e.g., social and sexual behavior, rules for coming and going, and household chores; see also Collins & Laursen, this volume; Libbey & Bybee, 1979). There were no gender differences in child behavior, but the gender of the abusing parent was related to the child's age: Mothers and fathers were equally likely to abuse children under age 13, but fathers were more likely to abuse adolescents. Collins and Laursen indicate that mother–adolescent conflict is more common than conflict between fathers and adolescents. However, the latter may be more intense and more likely to escalate to physical aggression.

According to most reviews, approximately half the cases of reported abuse occur in relation to children 5 years of age or older, and over a quarter concern children ages 12 to 18 (Daro, 1988; Kadushin & Martin, 1981; Libbey & Bybee, 1979; Lourie, 1979). Does physical abuse start at age 6 or at age 13, or does a reported incident at such times bring a pattern to light? In fact, the situation varies; first-time abuse may arise at any point, though in some families abuse has been recurrent.

The abuse of adolescents is a case in point. The particular issues of a family at this developmental stage may precipitate first-time abuse or exacerbate a persistently aggressive style of interaction. The issues, reviewed by Collins and Laursen, this volume, are well known, including the particular drives of the adolescent and the mismatch between the adolescent world and the realities of middle-aged parents. In that context, conflict may escalate to abuse. Lourie (1979) studied 70 cases of abusive families with adolescents ages 12 to 18 and described three patterns: (a) Adults are disorganized and inadequate as parents. Abuse has been continuous, coming to light because the adolescent is independent enough to resist or make a report. The incidence of this pattern is low. (b) Adults have been rigid and disciplinary, exercising corporal punishment at a level acceptable to the community in order to control child behavior. When the adolescent challenges control, punishment changes quality, becoming physically abusive. (c) Adults have been child centered and indulgent. Adolescent challenge is labile, provocative, and experienced by the family as betrayal. Conflict leads to abuse for the first time and does not reflect a pattern of family violence.

Lourie's model of abuse emphasizes stage-specific factors. He maintains that the characteristics of the adult and child are relevant but do not, in themselves, bring about abuse. They interact with developmental demands at particular stages, such as autonomy at adolescence, which may be more difficult for people with certain characteristics to handle than the issues of previous stages. Family members are then unable to resolve their conflicts and the potential for abuse is activated.

The impact on development

Research on the impact of maltreatment is not definitive. There are problems of definition and design, insufficient attention to variables such as continuity and severity, and many obstacles to conducting prospective longitudinal research. In addition, the effects of destructive conflict are difficult to track because many studies focus on very young children. It is possible, however, to summarize the major trends.

Major findings concerning maltreatment

Emerging theories emphasize the idea that abuse interferes with the normal flow of development (Aber, Allen, Carlson, & Cicchetti, 1989; Wolfe, 1987). If abuse is severe, starts early, and is combined with neglect, it affects the physical organism and the process of attachment. Under those conditions, it may have a catastrophic impact, including intellectual deficits, poor motor functioning, social maladjustment, and poor self-image (Daro, 1988). As noted, however, abuse varies in severity and may arise later in development. We know little about the interference with normal development if a child is securely attached and abuse arises in connection with subsequent developmental tasks, such as setting and accepting limits. Such questions await further study.

Abuse that is connected with conflict is most likely to affect social development, including the child's behavior with peers and adults and the evolution of social understanding. Though there are no specific data on the effects of destructive conflict, the recurrent finding about abused children is that they are more aggressive than children who are not maltreated (Erickson, Egeland, & Pianta, 1989; George & Main, 1979; Hoffman-Plotkin & Twentyman, 1984; Mueller & Silverman, 1989; Reidy, 1977), although there are exceptions to this finding (e.g., Jacobson & Straker, 1982). They are more aggressive with peers (Mueller & Silverman, 1989) and more likely to strike out at adults and avoid friendly overtures, both in preschool settings (George & Main, 1979) and at home (Bousha & Twentyman, 1984; Wolfe, 1987). Teachers and parents describe them as difficult to manage, socially immature, and characterized more by behavior problems and low self-esteem than are other children (Hoffman-Plotkin & Twentyman, 1984; Reidy, 1977; Salzinger, Kaplan, Pelcovitz, Samit, & Kreiger, 1984). In adolescence, aggression is defined and studied as antisocial behavior. Abused adolescents have higher delinquency rates than does the general population (Daro, 1988; Wolfe, 1987), but it is unlikely that their behavior is rooted exclusively in abuse.

Investigators who gather data on both social interaction and aggression present mixed findings. In the study of Jacobson and Straker (1982), abused school-age children interacted less and with less enjoyment than did controls but were not more aggressive. In contrast, Hoffman-Plotkin and Twentyman (1984) found that abused preschool children did not interact less with other children, but their contacts were more combative. These investigators also compared abused and neglected children with each other, finding that the behavior of neglected children was socially avoidant, rather than aggressive. Children physically abused in the family may be carrying models of conflict that escalate rapidly and spill over into aggressive control, so that they are not able to negotiate the arguments that arise naturally in peer interaction.

In studies of social cognition, the findings are reminiscent of those concerning abusive parents: Abused children perform more poorly than do controls on measures of affective and cognitive role taking, social sensitivity, and the ability to discriminate emotions (Barahal, Waterman, & Martin, 1981; Main & George, 1985; Straker & Jacobson, 1981; Wolfe, 1987). Smetana, Kelly, and Twentyman (1984) looked at moral development, finding that most of their preschool sample could recognize transgressions and were aware of the difference between social conventions and moral violations, but maltreated children differed from controls. In addition, abused and neglected children differed from each other. Abused children were more alert to psychological distress; neglected children responded more to the injustice of distributing resources unevenly.

The suggestion that some abused children may react to psychological distress is partly supported by Main and George (1985). The young abused children in their sample generally responded with less concern than did other children to distress in their peers, but some children exhibited a mixture of fear, attack, and comforting behavior. With slightly older children (age 3 to 5), Frodi and Smetana (1984) found that abused children were sharper in their social awareness than were neglected children and better able to read the emotions of others. In these few studies, suggestions of indifference and delayed development coexist with indications of heightened sensitivity in abused, if not neglected, children. Clinical experience suggests that this possibility deserves further systematic study. Some children who live in families characterized by substance abuse, unpredictability, and aggressive incidents appear highly attuned to danger, becoming skillful at reading mood, shielding siblings, and protecting one parent from the other. Concern for negative effects in these children centers on their premature responsibility rather than their indifference.

As noted, researchers have begun to identify differences between abused and neglected children. Augoustinos (1987), reviewing recent research, has noted that neglect appears potentially more damaging to psychosocial and language development than does physical abuse, unless abuse starts early and is violent. Data from the Minnesota Mother–Child Interaction Project, a prospective longitudinal study, indicate that the most severe and varied problems, at ages 5 and 6, were manifested by children in the neglected group, as compared with children who were physically or sexually abused or whose mothers were unavailable (Erickson, Egeland, & Pianta, 1989). The trend toward studying the effects of particular forms of maltreatment is promising and important.

Maltreatment and resilience

There are useful findings in these data, but it is good to remember that they are incomplete. The status of the child as abused, neglected, or not maltreated does not predict behavior very well, and abused children do not always become abusing parents. It is important, therefore, that some attention has been paid to the question of resilience. How and why do some abused children develop reasonably well? What are the natural mediators that deflect potential damage, as distinct from programmed interventions? Relevant material comes from studies of adults who were abused as children but do not harm their offspring, and from the study of resilient children. The literature on resilience examines the capacity of some children to overcome handicaps and difficult life situations (Anthony & Cohler, 1987; Garmezy, 1985; Luthar & Zigler, 1991) and includes the specific study of children who have experienced abuse (Farber & Egeland, 1987; Mrazek & Mrazek, 1987).

What seems established as a major factor is the presence of at least one person in the child's life who is loving and supportive (e.g., Egeland, Jacobvitz, & Papatola, 1987; Kaufman & Zigler, 1987). In examining the profiles of children who were relatively well adapted, despite abuse, Farber and Egeland (1987) found that they were securely attached and their mothers were emotionally supportive. In a similar vein, Giblin, Starr, & Agronow (1984) found that abused young children who were contacting, persistent in play, and self-accepting had responsive mothers and lived in homes supplied with toys. Such findings raise interesting questions about the implications of being loved and abused by the same person, a not uncommon situation, or of maintaining a close relationship with a parent who does not intervene when the other parent is abusive.

In considering the components of resilience in children, Mrazek and Mrazek (1987) point to characteristics of the child, such as intelligence, the temperamental ability to maintain a positive sense of self, and the capacity to seek supportive relationships and to reframe negative experience. We may wonder where these characteristics come from, but when present, they allow for psychological survival. If adaptive behavior is to be sustained, however, contemporary realities are important. The point is evident in studies of adults who are adequate parents despite an abusive history. In addition to having supportive figures in childhood and experiencing abuse that was not severe, these people usually have current support systems, including partners who are loving and who participate in parenting (Egeland, Jacobvitz, & Papatola, 1987; Farber & Egeland, 1987). Children who cope adequately in abusive circumstances will probably need positive factors in their family, school, or peer group, as they grow, in order to sustain their adaptation.

Against this background of findings, we can extrapolate to situations in which abuse stems from conflict. We can posit a child who is securely attached and living in a nurturant family but who is jeopardized by family conflict and abuse over issues of control. Development may either be derailed or progress normally. The negative possibility follows from the fact that the child carries a self-defeating model for handling conflict into new systems: child–teacher, child–peers. If the child has poor frustration tolerance, no model or skills for negotiation, and a tendency to quick aggression, he or she may be perceived by teachers as troublesome and avoided or rejected by other children. An interference with progress in learning and social relations may follow.

A positive pattern depends on a combination of factors. Some may reside in the child, but it is likely that alternative models of conflict negotiation are the most important mediators. Such models must come from somewhere in the child's environment. In the family, that would require at least one person who can handle challenge, hold down escalation, and bring conflict to a firm, nonaggressive resolution. The school is also a potential resource. Though they may perceive these children as problematic, teachers may be skillful models of conflict negotiation, both in interchange with the child and in mediating conflicts that arise among children. It would be useful to study teacher mediation and teacher–child sequences in conflict situations that involve abused children. Where that is well handled, abused children may prove resilient and able to incorporate alternative, nondestructive models of conflict negotiation. Positive experiences with conflict resolution are among the natural factors that may facilitate adequate development for children at risk from maltreatment, as long as they are not excessively and continuously damaged by other circumstances.

Intervention and prevention

There is no literature dealing directly with the treatment of conflict that leads to maltreatment. It is possible, however, to draw on material from related areas: interventions to reduce conflict and those to treat or prevent abuse.

Programs for modifying conflict have been reviewed, in this volume, by Furman and McQuaid. Among the programs discussed, parent management and family therapy are particularly relevant for situations of parent–child maltreatment. When these programs are assessed, there is some indication of improved communication and child behavior but little systematic evidence concerning long-term effects or the applicability to severely dysfunctional families. The authors also note the sparsity of programs focused on conflict management, as distinct from conflict reduction. For abusing families, management is probably the essential goal.

Multimodal programs are identified as among the most promising for modifying conflict, and the same generalization holds for child abuse interventions. In evaluating 19 demonstration programs funded by the National Center on Child Abuse and Neglect, Daro (1988) found a comprehensive psychosocial approach to be most effective. Others also have described varied approaches, including family and group therapy, parent–child models, home-based programs, programs tailored for children and adolescents, and informal social supports (Justice & Justice, 1990; Rothery & Cameron, 1990). Daro notes that young children benefited from therapeutic preschools and adolescents gained from group counseling, skill development, and temporary shelter, but the overall prognosis was not good if parents were not responsive and family circumstances did not change. Many families required a combination of therapy and concrete assistance with problems of housing, income, health, and child care.

In Daro's (1988) study, the form of maltreatment was a major consideration in assessing the family and determining services. Neglectful parents, whose isolation, economic problems and poor skills have been discussed, required multiple social services and responded best to concrete interventions that empower them in dealing with the children and that are applicable to the problems of daily life. Physically abusive families did not necessarily require social services, but issues of impulse control and the management of anger under stress were important. These families are candidates for interventions focused on conflict expression and resolution, including work with parent and child, both parents in relation to the child, the adult couple, and systemic therapy.

In assessing the outcome of interventions, available studies have concentrated on the persistence or recurrence of abuse. Figures for continued abuse differ, reflecting a variety of poorly specified conditions, but they are not encouraging, ranging from one fifth to two thirds of the cases (see Daro, 1988; Wolfe, 1987). The prognosis is poorest, of course, when abuse or neglect has been severe and continuous. In view of this situation, there is a particular concern for prevention and for reaching families at risk.

Preventive efforts target young, poor, single, first-time parents especially and often focus on caretaking skills and child development knowledge. There is less attention to issues of autonomy and control that arise in the child's second year, although the development of constructive parent–child patterns for resolving conflict is an important preventive measure against abuse.

When abuse or neglect is reported, the first interventions are conducted by official institutions such as child protective services, whose investigators determine the next steps. They may recommend services or remove the child. In either event, the situation holds potential for conflict between the family and the system. As Kagan and Schlosberg (1989) note, families often feel invaded by multiple social agencies, such as courts and the welfare system, and withdraw or resist help despite their need. These authors have implemented a home-based program, geared to multiproblem families in crisis, and have been successful in preventing child placement in 88% of their cases. Other sources report similar figures if multiple intensive services are provided at a point when the family is at risk of dismemberment (Daro, 1988).

In many cases, investigators remove children from their homes for placement in foster care. The numbers are startling: In 1991, there were over 50,000 children in foster care in New York City alone. It is clear that severely abused or neglected children must be removed for their basic safety, but reported cases vary widely in severity, and the negative effects of maltreatment must be balanced against the trauma of separation. The issues have not been well formulated and research is sparse. The comparative study of Wald, Carlsmith, and Leiderman (1988) found no consistent advantage in either foster placement or remaining at home, and their research underlined the compexity of the variables and the difficulty of drawing generalizations.

An important question for research concerns the developmental effects of the process, as it is usually conducted. Removal is often abrupt, there are few provisions for helping children and families with the shock of transition, and contact between child and parents after placement is controlled and infrequent (P. Minuchin, 1991). If children are attached to their parents, what are the effects of separation, infrequent contact, and the need to relate suddenly to unfamiliar substitutes? How do attachments proceed, not only for young children but for adolescents, whose developmental tasks concern autonomy rather than new family attachments? And how do children process the different expectations of two families and their own mixed loyalties? Some foster children are placed in a series of homes because they are difficult to handle. The assumption that their behavior is the result of the original maltreatment rather than a reaction to separation and placement is unstudied.

Psychological theory suggests that certain conditions would modify the most traumatic effects of separation. In particular, it seems evident that children and parents should maintain contact and that foster and biological families should constitute a network for communication and continuity of care. A program of this kind has proven feasible (see P. Minuchin et al., 1990), but such efforts must be studied in terms of the effect on the child's experience and development, as well as on the growth of competence and adequate parenting in the original family.

In general, programs of intervention and prevention in child maltreatment are growing and take many forms, but research is sparse. Available studies concerning the effects of treatment are not reassuring, but the provision of intensive and varied services to families at risk appears to be a promising approach. The need for more differentiated study is obvious, as is the need for psychologists to participate in formulating issues and programs.

Summary and conclusions

We have dealt with the possible relation between conflict and the physical abuse or neglect of children. In doing so, it has been necessary to infer and extrapolate from related fields, since this question has not been a focus of theory or research. Because conflict is a major factor in advancing or impeding development, however, it is worth exploring the process by which conflict becomes destructive, as well as the roots and impact of parent–child interchanges that go out of control.

Child maltreatment is currently explained by psychosocial theories, which emphasize both the environmental conditions that foster stress and the experiences and characteristics that predispose certain adults to neglect or abuse children. The effects of neglect or abuse depend on severity, time of onset, and continuity. It is likely that maltreatment interferes with the course of normal development and takes different forms, but there is some evidence of an impact on social cognition, empathy, and the control of aggression in relations with peers and adults. The latter may reflect not only a ready state of anger, but the internalization of a negative model for negotiating conflict that includes rapid escalation and poor skills for resolving disagreements. The impact of maltreatment on development certainly requires more study, including a broader range of variables, a careful documentation of the child's experience at different developmental stages, and further investigation of the factors that make for resilience. It also would be important to study the effects of separating children from their families, as a response to neglect or abuse. The decision is difficult for case workers, and they have had little sophisticated input from specialists in child development.

The particular role of conflict in maltreatment is not well studied. Conflict is not an inevitable feature of the situation, but it may be directly involved in physical abuse, when parent–child disagreements take a destructive form, and indirectly involved in neglect, when conflict in the extended family isolates and depowers a parent. It is important to define and study destructive conflict not only in dyads but in the context of the larger family system, which may maintain abusive behavior in ways that are not evident from a focused concern with one parent and child.

Future researchers should also pay attention to variables that have been noted in the field but are insufficiently studied. The gender of the parent is one. Mothers have been studied far more than fathers, although the latter are often the abusers of older children. In addition, the interaction of the adults, when children are abused, is a neglected and necessary direction for research. Age of the child is another major factor. Much of the research is focused on very young children, though maltreatment of children over age 5 is more prevalent than generally assumed. If we are concerned with conflict, it is especially important to study children who are old enough to participate in the escalation that leads to abuse by their parents. Also, it would be instructive to compare situations in which one child in the family is targeted, as distinct from families with generalized violence. Family dynamics, the impact of abuse, and helpful interventions might well be different in these situations.

In every aspect of this field, research has been limited and/or inconclusive. From the available material, however, it is hard to avoid the conclusion that the most useful investigations will be those that encompass families and complex programs. Abusive dyads are embedded in larger units, and conflict is apt to be a family affair. By the same token, the most promising interventions are multimodal, encompassing, but not residing in, specific experiences for abusing adults and abused children. Efforts to pull apart the elements of such programs for purposes of evaluation will probably not prove productive. Even if the task is complex, however, continuing research is essential. Child maltreatment is not an academic topic; it is a profound human problem. Whatever knowledge we can accumulate will provide some direction for practical action in an area that cannot wait for certainty.

References

Aber, J. L., Allen, J. P., Carlson, V., & Cicchetti, D. (1989). The effects of maltreatment on development during early childhood: Recent studies and their theoretical, clinical and policy implications. In D. Cicchetti & V. Carlson (Eds.), *Child maltreatment*. Cambridge: Cambridge University Press.

Anthony, E. J., & Cohler, B. J. (Eds.). (1987). *The invulnerable child*. New York: Guilford Press.

Augoustinos, M. (1987). Developmental effects of child abuse: Recent findings. *Child Abuse and Neglect, 11*, 15–27.

Barahal, R. M., Waterman, J., & Martin, H. P. (1981). The social cognitive development of abused children. *Journal of Consulting and Clinical Psychology, 49*, 508–516.

Bousha, D. M., & Twentyman, C. T. (1984). Mother–child interactional style in abuse, neglect, and control groups: Naturalistic observations in the home. *Journal of Abnormal Psychology, 93*, 106–114.

Burgess, R., & Conger, R. (1978). Family interaction in abusive, neglectful and normal families. *Child Development, 49*, 1163–1173.

Christensen, A., & Margolin, G. (1988). Conflict and alliance in distressed and non-distressed families. In R. A. Hinde & J. Stevenson-Hinde (Eds.), *Relationships within families: Mutual influences*. Oxford: Oxford University Press.

Cicchetti, D., & Carlson, V. (Eds.). (1989). *Child maltreatment*. Cambridge: Cambridge University Press.

Daro, D. (1988). *Confronting child abuse: Research for effective program design*. New York: Free Press.

Egeland, B., Jacobvitz D., & Papatola, K. (1987). Intergenerational continuity of abuse. In R. Gelles & J. Lancaster (Eds.), *Child abuse and neglect*. New York: Aldine de Gruyter.

Erickson, M., Egeland, B., & Pianta, R. (1989). The effects of maltreatment on the development of young children. In D. Cicchetti & V. Carlson (Eds.), *Child maltreatment*. Cambridge: Cambridge University Press.

Farber, E., & Egeland, B. (1987). Invulnerability among abused and neglected children. In E. J. Anthony & B. J. Cohler (Eds.), *The invulnerable child*. New York: Guilford Press.

Feshbach, N. (1989). The construct of empathy and the phenomenon of physical maltreatment of children. In D. Cicchetti & V. Carlson (Eds.), *Child maltreatment*. Cambridge: Cambridge University Press.

Frodi, A., & Smetana, J. (1984). Abused, neglected and nonmaltreated preschoolers' ability to discriminate emotion in others: The effects of IQ. *Child Abuse and Neglect, 8*, 459–465.

Garbarino, J., & Sherman, D. (1980). High-risk neighborhoods and high-risk families: The human ecology of child maltreatment. *Child Development, 51*, 188–198.

Garmezy, N. (1985). Stress-resistant children: The search for protective factors. In J. Stevenson (Ed.), *Recent research in developmental psychopathology*. Oxford: Pergamon Press.

Gelles, R. (1973). Child abuse as psychopathology: A sociological critique and reformulation. *American Journal of Orthopsychiatry, 43*, 611–621.

George, C., & Main, M. (1979). Social interactions of young abused children: Approach, avoidance and aggression. *Child Development, 50*, 306–318.

Giblin, P., Starr, R., & Agronow, S. (1984). Affective behavior of abused and control children: Comparisons of parent–child interactions and the influence of home environment variables. *Journal of Genetic Psychology, 144*, 69–82.

Gil, D. (1970). *Violence against children: Physical child abuse in the United States*. Cambridge, MA: Harvard University Press.

Hoffman-Plotkin, D., & Twentyman, C. (1984). A multimodal assessment of behavioral and cognitive deficits in abused and neglected preschoolers. *Child Development, 55*, 794–802.

Jacobson, R., & Straker, G. (1982). Peer group interaction of physically abused children. *Child Abuse and Neglect, 6*, 321–327.

Justice, B., & Justice, R. (1990). *The abusing family* (rev. ed.). New York: Plenum.

Kadushin, A., & Martin, J. (1981) *Child abuse: An interactional event*. New York: Columbia University Press.

Kagan, R., & Schlosberg, S. (1989). *Families in perpetual crisis*. New York: Norton.

Kaufman, J., & Zigler, E. (1987). Do abused children become abusive parents? *American Journal of Orthopsychiatry, 57*, 186–192.

Kempe, C., Silverman, F., Steele, B., Droegenmueller, W., & Silver, H. (1962). The battered child syndrome. *Journal of the American Medical Association, 181*, 17–24.

Libbey, P., & Bybee, R. (1979). The physical abuse of adolescents. *Journal of Social Issues, 35*, 101–126.

Lourie, I. (1979). Family dynamics and the abuse of adolescents: A case for a developmental phase-specific model of child abuse. *Child Abuse and Neglect, 3*, 967–974.

Luthar, S., & Zigler, E. (1991). Vulnerability and competence: A review of research on resilience in childhood., *American Journal of Orthopsychiatry, 61*, 6–22.

Main, M., & George, C. (1985). Responses of abused and disadvantaged toddlers to distress in agemates: A study in the day care setting. *Developmental Psychology, 21*, 407–412.

Minuchin, P. (1985). Families and individual development: Provocations from the field of family therapy. *Child Development, 56*, 289–302.

Minuchin, P. (1991). When the context changes: A consideration of families in transitional periods. In R. Cohen & A. Siegel (Eds.), *Context and development*. Hillsdale, NJ: Erlbaum.

Minuchin, P., with Brooks, A., Colapinto, J., Genijovich, E., Minuchin, D., & Minuchin, S. (1990). *Training manual for foster parents*. New York: Family Studies.

Minuchin, S., Rosman, B., & Baker, L. (1978). *Psychosomatic families*. Cambridge, MA: Harvard University Press.

Mrazek P., & Mrazek, D. (1987). Resilience in child maltreatment victims: A conceptual exploration. *Child Abuse and Neglect, 11*, 357–366.

Mueller, E., & Silverman, S. (1989). Peer relations in maltreated children. In D. Cicchetti & V. Carlson (Eds.), *Child maltreatment*. Cambridge: Cambridge University Press.

Newberger, C., & White, K. (1989). Cognitive foundations for parental care. In D. Cicchetti & V. Carlson (Eds.), *Child maltreatment*. Cambridge: Cambridge University Press.

Parke, R., & Collmer, C. (1975). Child abuse: An interdisciplinary analysis. In E. M. Hetherington (Ed.), *Review of child development research* (Vol. 5). Chicago: University of Chicago Press.

Patterson, G. R. (1982). *A social learning approach. 3: Coercive family process*. Eugene, OR: Castalia.

Reid, J., Taplin, P., & Lorber, R. (1981). A social interactional approach to the treatment of abusive families. In R. Stuart (Ed.), *Violent behavior*. New York: Brunner/Mazel.

Reidy, T. (1977). The aggressive characteristics of abused and neglected children. *Journal of Clinical Psychology, 33*, 1140–1145.

Rothery, M., & Cameron, G. (Eds). (1990). *Child maltreatment: Expanding our concept of helping*. Hillsdale, NJ: Erlbaum.

Salzinger, S., Kaplan, S., Pelcovitz, D., Samit, C., & Kreiger, R. (1984). Parent and teacher assessment of children's behavior in child maltreating families. *Journal of the American Academy of Child Psychiatry, 23*, 458–464.

Shantz, C. U. (1987). Conflicts between children. *Child Development, 58*, 283–305.

Silber, S. (1990). Conflict negotiation in child abusing and nonabusing families. *Journal of Family Psychology*, *3*, 368–384.

Smetana, J., Kelly, M., & Twentyman, C. (1984). Abused, neglected and nonmaltreated children's judgments of moral and social transgressions. *Child Development*, *55*, 277–287.

Spinetta, J., & Rigler, D. (1972). The child abusing parent: A psychological review. *Psychological Bulletin*, *77*, 1409–14.

Straker, G., & Jacobson, R. (1981). Aggression, emotional maladjustment and empathy in the abused child. *Developmental Psychology*, *17*, 762–765.

Wald, M., Carlsmith, J., & Leiderman, P. (1988). *Protecting abused and neglected children*. Stanford, CA: Stanford University Press.

Wolfe, D. (1987). *Child abuse: Implications for child development and psychopathology*. Beverly Hills, CA: Sage.

15 Intervention programs for the management of conflict

Wyndol Furman and Elizabeth L. McQuaid

Arguments with parents, clashes with siblings, and conflicts with peers are aversive and frustrating to a child. When they are extreme, such conflicts may be destructive, jeopardizing the quality of the child's relationships or depriving a child of important developmental experiences.

In this chapter, we discuss intervention programs designed to manage destructive conflict. We have tried to cast a wide net in several respects. First, we describe programs for managing conflict in a range of relationships, including those with parents, siblings, and peers. Second, we describe not only those programs explicitly designed to reduce destructive conflict, but also those programs that target related phenomena, such as aggression and noncompliance.

Before proceeding, we first need to consider what constitutes destructive conflict. In general, conflict arises from incompatible behaviors or goals within an interpersonal context (C. U. Shantz, 1987). This incompatibility is expressed by one individual's overt opposition to another's actions or statements. This definition includes a wide range of conflicts, from minor disagreements over the best way to play a game to heated fistfights, whereas both children and adults usually think of conflicts as episodes of protracted and aggressive opposition (Selman, 1980).

Social scientists have come to recognize some of the positive functions of conflicts. Piaget (1932) proposed that interpersonal conflicts can foster a better understanding of others and can thus serve to reduce egocentrism. Shantz and Hobart (1989) suggested that an individual's participation in constructive conflict can further social development, through increasing both social connectedness and individuality. Some conflicts yield benefits for interpersonal relationships: Conflicts among peers sometimes serve to mark interpersonal boundaries and clarify group decision-making processes.

Support for the completion of this manuscript was provided by grant No. MH45830 from the National Institute of Mental Health and a W. T. Grant Faculty Scholars Award to Wyndol Furman.

402

Familial conflicts can provide a forum for open communication and lead to the clarification of the rights and obligations of different family members (Vuchinich, 1987).

Of course, not all conflicts lead to such rosy endings. Deutsch (1973) distinguished between two different types of conflict – destructive and constructive. "Destructive conflict" was defined as conflict in which threats and coercion are used and in which there is an expansion and escalation beyond the initial issue. In "constructive conflict," the issue remains focused and is negotiated through mutual problem solving. Hartup and Laursen (in press) further elaborated on Deutsch's (1973) distinction by specifying that, among children, effective conflicts typically result in ongoing social interactions, whereas ineffective conflicts usually end in discontinued interactions and avoidance. Constructive conflict, then, depends on the individuals being able to avoid escalation and expansion of the issue into other domains, to engage in mutual problem solving, and to maintain social interaction.

Although a number of contemporary investigators advocate a differentiation between constructive and destructive conflict, this distinction is not usually evident in empirical research. That is, social scientists do not regularly categorize particular episodes of conflict as constructive or destructive, nor do they try to distinguish between dyads that typically engage in these two types of conflict. Accordingly, we must rely on theoretical propositions concerning what is and is not destructive conflict. Of course, all of us – adults and children alike – engage in some destructive conflict. But if a dyad's conflicts are typically destructive in nature, then we can consider the conflict to be dysfunctional.

We believe that three indexes exist that signal whether conflict is destructive and may be dysfunctional for the dyad members. First, if conflict occurs frequently or constitutes a high proportion of a dyad's interactions, we think it is likely to be destructive in nature. If conflict is frequent, one suspects that problems are not being adequately resolved. Consistent with this idea, families that seek assistance for child behavioral problems have been found to engage in high levels of coercive, conflictual interactions (Patterson, Reid, Jones, & Conger, 1975). The simple frequency of conflict can be misleading, however, unless one takes into account the overall frequency of interactions. For example, several investigators have found that children engage in more conflicts or negative interactions with friends than nonfriends, but the proportions of interactions that were negative are relatively comparable (Hartup, Laursen, Stewart, & Eastenson, 1988; Masters & Furman, 1981). In contrast, Laursen (1990) found that adolescent friends engaged in more conflict than did nonfriends, even when controlling for total time spent together. Perhaps the differing results of these studies reflect developmental changes in the nature of friendships. In any case, it seems important to consider the proportion of interactions that are conflictual, as well as the frequency, although as yet we do not know which of these is more closely associated with dysfunctional exchanges in different kinds of relationships.

Second, if the conflict is extended in nature or is expressed in more marked forms such as aggression, then it would appear that the conflict has escalated and is thus likely to be destructive. The extended conflict or escalation indicates that efforts to resolve the conflict have been unsuccessful. Research on family violence, for example, clearly indicates that intense, marked conflicts have a negative impact across a variety of cognitive and socioemotional domains (Garbarino & Gilliam, 1980). Even when the conflict does not reach abusive levels, we suspect that such interchanges are likely to have a deleterious effect on the relationship.

Third, if the conflicts (even minor ones) between the members of a particular dyad typically end with disengagement, we would consider the conflicts to be destructive. We do not mean to imply that walking away from a heated argument cannot be an effective way of managing some conflicts. Rather, the consistent use of withdrawal or disengagement may serve to curtail constructive resolution of conflict. Unless the dyad subsequently returns to the issue underlying the conflict, the basis of the conflict may not be resolved and may, if anything, become exacerbated.

In the same vein, we believe that it is also undesirable if a dyad avoids conflict consistently. In any relationship, some conflict is inherent and, in fact, healthy (Foot, Chapman, & Smith, 1977; Hartup & Laursen, in press; Shantz & Hobart, 1989). Marked efforts to avoid such conflicts suggest that the individuals involved are unable to resolve their incompatible goals and behavior through mutual problem solving. Although avoidance alone does not distinguish constructive from destructive conflict, we believe that conflict avoidance should be considered a fourth index that the management or occurrence of conflict within relationships may be destructive.

This list may not be exhaustive, of course, and its value can only be determined through research. At the same time, the set of four indexes closely resembles those used by researchers to identify dysfunctional patterns of conflicts among married couples. For example, distressed couples engage in more negative interactions and conflicts than do nondistressed couples (Gottman, 1979; Gottman & Krokoff, 1989; Vincent, Friedman, Nugent, & Messerly, 1979). Similarly, distressed couples are more likely to engage in negative interactions that spiral in intensity (Gottman, 1979; Margolin & Wampold, 1981). In one longitudinal investigation of marital interaction and satisfaction, Gottman and Krokoff (1989) found that withdrawal from interaction and conflict was associated with deterioration of marital satisfaction over time, and they speculated that couples that avoid conflict may be at risk longitudinally. This is because such avoidance is sometimes associated with differing relationship expectations (Krokoff, Gottman, & Roy, 1988). Although the marital literature suggests that these four indexes are thus promising, we clearly need to evaluate their utility in studying children's conflicts.

Conflict and its occurrence

Like Shantz (1987), we regard conflict – constructive or destructive – as a dyadic phenomenon. Conflicts are the property of the dyad, not of a particular individual. At the same time, we believe that destructive and constructive conflict may stem from either individual or relationship characteristics. For example, two children may frequently conflict because one of them is aggressive; alternatively, some dyads may typically engage in conflicts because of certain inherently incompatible goals (such as siblings who constantly argue over which television program to watch). Certainly, the distinction between individual and dyadic bases of dysfunctional conflict is not absolute. Even when one individual seems primarily responsible for the conflicts in a dyad, the other individual may serve as a stimulus for aversive interactions. At the same time, we believe that the monadic–dyadic distinction is a useful heuristic because it has strong implications for the focus of the treatment selected. Thus, in the sections that follow, we discuss both dyadic and individual factors that lead to dysfunctional conflict.

Conflict-prone dyads

Most of the work on conflict-prone dyads has focused on familial relationships. Gerald Patterson and his colleagues (Patterson, 1982; Patterson, et al., 1975) have proposed that coercive interaction patterns within the parent–child relationships foster the recurrence of conflict. Aggressive, noncompliant behaviors are often aversive stimuli to parents, and in an effort to terminate the aversiveness, parents may acquiesce to the child's request. Unfortunately, such parental behavior inadvertently reinforces the child's behavior, increasing the likelihood that the child will use noncompliant or aggressive tactics in the future. Alternatively, parental control tactics may escalate to yelling and other forms of aggression, which may be reinforced by eventual child compliance. Thus, parents and children may become trapped in a coercive cycle in which inappropriate behavior by each is negatively reinforced by the other.

Wahler (1976) suggested that positive reinforcement may also play a role in fostering noncompliance and contributing to parent–child conflict. When children refuse to comply with parental rules such as a certain bedtime, parents may reinforce inadvertently the child's noncompliant behavior by attempting to talk to the child or by reading the child another story. In this way, parental attention positively reinforces the child's noncompliance. Over the course of a decade, Patterson and his colleagues (Patterson, 1982; Patterson et al., 1975) and Wahler (1976) have gathered substantial evidence documenting the presence of such coercive interactions and how they result in increased parent–child conflict.

Patterson (1982) also demonstrated that the coercion model accounts for the reinforcement and maintenance of aggressive, coercive interchanges between siblings. Other investigators have suggested that certain aspects of sibling relationships inherently foster sibling conflict (Reit, 1985; Shantz & Hobart, 1989). Competition for both parental attention and shared possessions, as well social comparison processes and an emerging sense of self, can all contribute to sibling conflict (Reit, 1985; Shantz & Hobart, 1989). Parents' behavior in particular has been implicated. For example, parental responsivity and warmth have been found to be associated with low conflict, whereas parental power assertion has been linked with frequent conflict (Bryant & Crockenberg, 1980; Furman & Giberson, in press). Additionally, differential treatment of siblings has been positively linked to conflict and negatively linked to prosocial behaviors (Brody, Stoneman, & Burke, 1987; Bryant & Crockenberg, 1980; Furman & Giberson, in press; Stocker, Dunn, & Plomin, 1989). It should be noted that these investigators did not differentiate between clinically significant levels of conflict and more normal levels, but our own observations suggest that a number of the highly conflictual dyads are dysfunctional. One general implication of the literature on siblings is that the sources of conflict may lie outside the dyad. For example, marital conflict may lead to conflict in parent–child relationships (Emery, 1982; Furman & Giberson, in press).

Relatively little empirical work has investigated how or why certain peer dyads habitually engage in conflict. Recently, however, Dodge and his colleagues have tried to identify the dyadic contexts in which aggression occurs most frequently (Dodge, Price, Coie, & Christopolous, in press). The authors found two types of dyads who were high in conflict – mutually aggressive dyads and asymmetric ones in which only one member is aggressive. These two conflict dyads differed in the nature of conflictual interaction: Asymmetric dyads showed high rates of proactive bullying, whereas mutually aggressive dyads demonstrated a frequent incidence of angry, reactive aggression. This beginning is promising, but much remains to be specified about conflictual peer dyads.

Conflict-prone individuals

What kind of children are likely to engage in destructive conflict? Unfortunately, investigators have not focused on identifying such children. Accordingly, we must rely on studies of related phenomena, such as aggressiveness, impulsivity, and noncompliance. In his seminal work on conflict and aggression in peer groups, Olweus (1978) identified two distinct subtypes of conflict-prone children – "bullies" and "whipping boys." The "bullies" were characterized by strong aggressive tendencies, weak control of such tendencies when activated, and a generally more positive attitude toward violence. Similarly, D. W. Shantz (1986) found that conflict-prone children use a higher percentage of physically aggressive acts in resolving disputes than do their peers who are less prone to conflict. Aggressive children are likely to be rejected by their peers (Asarnow, 1983; Bierman, Miller, & Stabb, 1987; Coie, Christopulos, Terry, Dodge, & Lochman, 1989; Coie, Dodge, & Kupersmidt, 1990; Price & Dodge, 1989). Moreover, D. W. Shantz (1986) found that the strongest predictor of peer rejection was not the rate of physical aggressiveness per se, but the rate of conflict itself.

Although a great deal of research has examined aspects and potential causes of aggressive behavior in children, much less work has addressed the behavior and characteristics of children who are regularly targets of aggression, the "whipping boys." In Olweus's (1978) original study, the whipping boys were found to be anxious, insecure, and isolated among their peers. Although often involved in episodes of peer conflict, the majority of them were nonviolent, perhaps because of insecurity or a lack of appropriate assertiveness skills. In a study of child victims of peer aggression, Perry, Kusel, and Perry (1988) found a much higher proportion of victims who actively provoked their aggressors than in the original Olweus study. Perry and his colleagues suggested that both types of victims may act in ways that invite aggression, although further research is needed to illuminate the specific dynamics of these interactions.

Aside from the work dealing with aggression, relatively few studies have been concerned with identifying children who are prone to peer conflict. Some studies, however, suggest that children with problems in impulse control may get into frequent conflicts with peers. Milich and Landau (1982) found that hyperactive children were more likely than their less impulsive peers to engage in disruptive, immature, and inappropriate behavior. For example, hyperactive, impulsive children were cited as frequently pulling out the chairs of other children and poking at peers. These disruptive, aversive behaviors may lead to more conflicts with peers, although this relation is not well documented.

Targeting aggressive, submissive, or impulsive behavior may be one strategy to reduce destructive conflict. Alternatively, one could focus on the factors that lead to excessive aggression, submissiveness, or impulsivity. In an earlier article (Furman, 1984b), we proposed that unskillful behavior, which includes poor conflict management, may reflect deficits in any of a number of underlying variables. These include (a) motivation – children's general intentions or goals for social interchanges; (b) social perception – the identification and interpretation of social situations; (c) social knowledge – knowledge about the context, person, or social behavior in general; (d) social processing or problem solving; (e) the behavioral repertoire – the array of available verbal and motor behaviors; and (f) external and internal feedback or evaluation.

Research on aggressive children illustrates how excessive aggression results from a range of deficits. Aggressive children, for example, place more value than their nonaggressive peers on certain outcomes of aggression such as achieving control of others, suggesting that their motivational hierarchies differ (Boldizar, Perry, & Perry, 1989). Aggressive children also perceive social situations differently: Specifically, they are more likely to attribute hostile intent to others than do their less aggressive peers, particularly when the actions are directed toward them (Dodge, 1985; Dodge, Pettit, McClaskey, & Brown, 1986; Lochman, 1987; Sancilio, Plumert, & Hartup, 1989; Waas, 1988). Furthermore, aggressive children are less able to generate alternative strategies for managing conflict (Deluty, 1981).

Dodge, Pettit, McClaskey and Brown (1986) proposed a social information-processing model, which incorporates several of the components delineated previously. Specifically, this model includes the encoding of social cues, the mental representation of those cues, the accessing of potential behavioral responses, the selection of an optimal response, and the enactment of that response. According to the model, skillful processing at each step increases the likelihood that a child will behave in a socially competent manner in interpersonal situations. Relevant research indicates that a child's pattern of processing information indeed predicts not only behavior, but competence and success in social situations such as those requiring peer group entry and response to provocation. Furthermore, various individual components of information processing provide distinct increments in the prediction of competence and sucess (Dodge et al., 1986).

To provide a detailed review of the specific underlying deficits associated with aggressiveness is beyond the scope of this chapter, but this brief overview illustrates how problems in social behavior may reflect underlying deficits. Submissiveness, impulsivity, and destructive conflict have been studied much less, but we suspect that similar underlying deficits could be identified. The important implication for present purposes is that modifying the inappropriate management of conflict by targeting such deficits is possible.

Conflict assessment

Before discussing conflict intervention, it is necessary to provide a brief overview of the various methods used to assess conflict. One general approach, which has roots in industrial-organizational psychology, is to "diagnose the conflict problem" by gathering as much information about the conflict as possible. Metaphoric, dramatic approaches, such as having each participant "build" a live sculpture of the conflict or diagram triangular relations in a conflict, can be useful methods of gaining information about system dynamics. Alternatively, self-report measures, such as the Hocker–Wilmot Assessment Guide (Hocker & Wilmot, 1985) and Wehr's (1979) Conflict Mapping Guide can be used to gather more information regarding the antecedents and dynamics of specific conflicts. The rationale underlying this general approach is that by illuminating the specific dynamics of the conflict, participants can begin to construct creative, productive solutions to the particular conflict. Although this is a worthwhile goal, it is perhaps better suited to solving management problems than identifying whether certain individuals, dyads, or groups are "conflict prone" and whether underlying systemic and/or individual changes are necessary in the prevention of future conflicts.

Another general approach to conflict assessment is to determine the overall level of conflict in a given relationship through the use of self-report measures. Certain scales, such as the Family Environment Scale (Moos & Moos, 1974) and the Family Functioning Scale (Tavitian, Lubiner, Green, Grebstgein, & Velicer, 1987) can be used to assess various dimensions of family functioning, including the extent of conflictual interactions. In our own laboratory, we have developed a set of instruments for assessing conflict and other dimensions of relationships with friends, siblings, parents, and other members of the social network (see Adler & Furman, 1988; Furman & Buhrmester, 1985a, 1985b). With the exception of Straus's (1979) Conflict Tactics Scale, which assesses the methods of conflict resolution used, these self-report measures simply assess the frequency of conflict.

Additionally, these measures have been used primarily as research tools, and their utility in identifying individuals or dyads in need of intervention has not been extensively investigated.

Observational schemes also have been developed for examining patterns of interactions in families (see Grotevant & Carlson, 1989; Touliatos, Perlmutter, & Straus, 1990). Some contain explicit conflict codes, and many contain codes that could be used to examine the sequence of events occurring during negative interchanges. At the same time, it is important to recognize that these measures have not been used for clinical purposes. Normative information rarely exists; in fact, comparisons between dysfunctional and functional families have not been made with many of the measures.

A few intervention programs for child noncompliance (see, e.g., Forehand & McMahon, 1981; Patterson, 1982; Robin & Foster, 1989) include an assessment component as the initial phase of the intervention package. In these programs, parents are taught to chart sequences of behaviors that occur in family interaction to determine the elements of conflictual episodes. Such assessment information is valuable because it can be used to specify appropriate intervention strategies. These assessments, however, are linked closely to specific programs. Thus, there is a great need to develop standardized observational or questionnaire measures that can be used clinically to identify conflict-prone dyads.

Intervention approaches

Interventions designed to decrease conflict in children's and adolescents' relationships differ widely in treatment focus. A number of interventions are constructed so the programmers focus on conflict as a dyadic, familial, or even group phenomenon, to be approached within the context of specific relationships (e.g., Alexander & Parsons, 1973; Patterson et al., 1975; Robin & Foster, 1989). Within these interventions, the focus of treatment becomes the processes within the relationship, such as the arguments that a parent and adolescent may have over a curfew or household chores. These interventions are often geared toward giving the individuals strategies with which to manage relationship conflict constructively, as well as to decrease the overall amount of conflict.

Other programs (Feindler & Ecton, 1986; Feindler & Fremouw, 1983; Goldstein & Glick, 1987; Kendall & Braswell, 1985) target certain individual characteristics of particular children, such as aggressiveness or impulsivity, that may predispose children to frequent conflicts. Although the reduction of conflict is not the primary goal of these treatments, such changes may result from decreases in impulsive or aggressive behavior or general improvement in interpersonal functioning. Still other interventions rest on the assumption that conflict arises out of deficits in conflict resolution strategies, and thus focus on the development of appropriate interpersonal problem-solving skills as a means to reduce conflict (Kazdin, Bass, Siegel, & Thomas, 1989; Spivack & Shure, 1974; Weissberg & Allen, 1986). Each of these different approaches is reviewed subsequently.

Focus on relationships: Families and dyads

Parent management-training programs. Within families, child noncompliance is a common behavior problem that can lead to recurring conflicts between young children and their parents (Forehand & McMahon, 1981). A number of parent management-training (PMT) programs have been designed to alter the patterns of interaction between parent and child so that prosocial behaviors, rather than noncompliance and coercion, are directly reinforced in the family (e.g., Forehand & McMahon, 1981; Patterson et al., 1975). After an intensive period of assessment, the therapists help the parents to redefine and understand problem behavior in terms of social learning principles. Parents then learn behavioral techniques (e.g., positive reinforcement, contingency contracting, time-out) that will serve to reinforce prosocial behavior and decrease noncompliant behavior in the home. Throughout the treatment process, the therapist aids the parents in monitoring the success of the techniques by charting the occurrence of prosocial and aversive behaviors in the home over time.

In their reviews of the research, Forehand and McMahon (1981) and Kazdin (1987) report that PMT programs have been shown to improve target children's behavior, even to bring it within normal limits. A number of the studies indicate that PMT can alter other aspects of family dysfunction. The frequency of compliant behavior of nontargeted siblings has been shown to increase, and indexes of maternal depression have been shown to decrease systematically.

Despite the overall success of PMT that has been demonstrated in numerous therapy outcome studies, various limitations should be noted. To begin with, the research programs using PMT place tremendous demands on the parents outside of the treatment sessions, including charting child behavior, reading treatment manuals, and, in some programs, responding to regular telephone contacts by the therapist (e.g., Patterson et al., 1975). These demands make the program difficult for some parents who are under a great deal of stress or who themselves have significant psychopathology. In fact, families with high levels of dysfunction and low levels of maternal social support have been found to make relatively few gains while receiving PMT (e.g., Dumas & Wahler, 1983; Strain, Young, & Horowitz, 1981).

Many clinicians use such parent-training approaches, but without the extensive record keeping. Clinical reports suggest that such streamlined procedures are useful, but their effectiveness has not been evaluated extensively or systematically. One must also recognize that parent–child conflict may be influenced by factors outside of that dyad, such as family stress, marital discord, and lack of social support (Patterson, 1982). PMT may need to be supplemented by other approaches to address the problems of seriously dysfunctional families (Kazdin, 1987).

Family therapy interventions. When parent–child conflict habitually disrupts familial relationships, families sometimes seek family therapy as a means to improve relations in the home. Whereas PMT programs are most frequently used with families who have preschool or elementary school children, family therapy interventions are typically geared toward families that include older children, particularly adolescents (e.g., Robin & Foster, 1989).

Two family therapy approaches designed to ameliorate parent–child conflict are Alexander and Parson's (1982) Functional Family Therapy (FFT) and Robin and Foster's (1989) Problem Solving Communication Training (PSCT) program. FFT and PSCT are both based on an integration of family systems and cognitive-behavioral approaches. Clinical problems in the family, including parent–child conflict, are understood in terms of the functions that they serve within the family. For example, a child's disruptive behavior, by drawing attention to the child, may allow the family to avoid other critical problems such as marital conflict. Conflictual patterns are maintained by poor communication and problem-solving skills and may be exacerbated by problems in family structure and unreasonable beliefs on the part of family members.

Both the FFT and PSCT programs contain multiple components: (a) training to address communication problems among family members, (b) restructuring to change cognitive distortions, and (c) active interventions to identify and break conflictual cycles. In the treatment sessions, the therapist helps the family members to alter maladaptive communication patterns and to learn more constructive methods of communicating. As the family members become more proficient at communicating, these methods are applied to more conflict-laden topics.

The comprehensiveness of these approaches allows the therapist to address a number of different components of parent–child conflict, ranging from negative verbal behaviors to triangulation and alliance formation within the family. For example, the therapist can address a father's frequent criticisms of a mother's parenting in two ways, by using behavioral techniques to decrease the overall rate of negative statements and by pointing out how the critical statements serve to ally father and son against mother.

One difference between the two programs lies in the sequencing of treatment components: A functional family therapist begins therapy with the relabeling and restructuring of attributions and cognitive distortions and then follows with skill building. In PSCT, these activities are not sequential, but intertwined. Additionally, in FFT the therapist does not specifically focus on altering the functions served by family members' behavior; instead, the emphasis is on how the interactions of family members can be changed so that these functions can be served with less pain and conflict. PSCT therapists, however, may or may not attempt to change the functions served by family members' behavior (Robin & Foster, 1989).

Alexander and his colleagues have conducted a number of empirical evaluations of FFT, principally with delinquent youths and their families (Alexander & Barton, 1976; Alexander & Parsons, 1973, 1982; Barton, Alexander, Waldron, Turner, & Warburton, 1985; Parsons & Alexander, 1973). FFT has proved more effective than no treatment and more effective than client-centered family therapy and psychodynamically oriented counseling in improving family communication at posttreatment. FFT has also proved more effective than the other forms of family treatment studied in reducing recidivism among youth offenders.

The treatment efficacy of PSCT has been assessed as well (Foster, 1978; Robin, 1979, 1981; Stern, 1984). As a whole, these studies demonstrate that PSCT improves the management of parent–adolescent conflict. Robin (1981) and Stern (1984) reported that problem-solving communication training produces greater changes in laboratory communication and results in greater treatment satisfaction than alternative therapies. Indexes of family conflict, however, were comparable across treatment modalities.

Although both programs have demonstrated changes in the communication patterns existing within families at posttreatment, the durability of these changes has not been extensively investigated (Robin & Foster, 1989). Furthermore, the problem of generalizing skills learned in treatment to the home environment has not been fully addressed. Finally, the applicability of FFT and PSCT to different types of families and family problems has yet to be specified. The programs seem to require a certain degree of "psychological mindedness" and self-reflective ability on the part of the clients and, thus, may not be appropriate with severely dysfunctional families.

Nevertheless, FFT and PSCT are among the few programs specifically designed to reduce conflict within a relational context. Other family therapy approaches, such as those proposed by Minuchin (1974) and, more recently, Hoffmann and her colleagues (Boscolo, Cecchin, Hoffmann, & Penn, 1987; Hoffmann, 1981), may also prove to be valuable approaches to the problem. Practicing clinicians regularly use such approaches for treating parent–adolescent conflict, but relatively little empirical work has examined their effectiveness.

Sibling programs. A few programs have been developed to reduce sibling conflict. Several behavioral investigators have demonstrated that reinforcing children for cooperative play and sending them to time-out for fighting effectively reduces conflicts among siblings (Allison & Allison, 1971; Leitenberg, Burchard, Burchard, Fuller, & Lysaught, 1977; O'Leary, O'Leary, & Becker, 1967). However, a few case studies suggest that when parents have been taught to stay out of sibling conflicts, the frequency of conflicts declines (Kelly & Main, 1979; Levi, Buskila, & Gerzi, 1977). These two approaches seem diametrically opposite to one another, but they both may teach parents ways to avoid being caught in the middle of the conflict or inadvertently reinforcing the children for fighting.

The limited number of intervention programs for sibling conflict is somewhat surprising in light of the fact that children report more conflict with their siblings than with other family members or their friends (Furman & Buhrmester, 1985a). However, our anecdotal impression is that parents of school-age children think that sibling conflict is inevitable and not readily changeable. Accordingly, it may not be thought of as a problem that warrants intervention, and in fact, we do not know when sibling conflict is dysfunctional. A significant amount of such conflict, however, involves physical aggression. Sibling aggression is the most common form of family violence, exceeding both parental and spousal abuse (Straus, Gelles, & Steinmetz, 1980). Thus, sibling conflict, at least in its extreme forms, does seem to warrant intervention.

In considering treatment possibilities, it is important to keep in mind our prior comment that sibling conflict is linked to parenting styles and the relative treatment of the siblings (see Furman & Giberson, in press). Hence, we believe that PMT and family therapy approaches described previously could prove to be promising means of treating dysfunctional sibling conflict.

Peer programs. Whereas relational approaches have been used to modify conflict in families, these approaches have not been commonly used to address conflict in peer relations. Two noteworthy exceptions warrant mentioning.

Selman and Schultz (1990) have proposed a new and innovative therapy format – pair therapy – for addressing the friendship problems of emotionally disturbed children. According to their theory of interpersonal understanding, children of different ages are expected to have different skill levels for comprehending and negotiating interpersonal interactions. Emotionally disturbed children display developmental delays or deficits in such interpersonal understanding (Selman, 1980). Pair therapy uses the dyad as a therapeutic format to foster the development of interpersonal reasoning. This approach is believed to enhance the peer relations of these children by helping them learn "what it means and feels like to make and keep a friend."

Two children (not necessarily friends, enemies, or acquaintances) and a pair therapist meet together regularly, typically once a week for an hour. The role of the pair therapist is to facilitate and mediate the pair's social interactions and to provide the pair with a third person's perspective on those interactions. The social relationship between the pair is the vehicle for therapeutic change, for it is through the sharing of experience and the successful negotiation of conflicts, as guided by the therapist, that the growth of interpersonal understanding occurs. By fostering the development of interpersonal understanding in one peer relationship, other peer relations are believed to be enhanced. The approach has been used to treat socially isolated, emotionally disturbed children, but to date, it has not been empirically evaluated. Because the program is not specifically aimed at reducing conflict, it remains particularly unclear whether such change occurs.

Another dyadic or small group approach is to have children participate in cooperative activities. For example, after a series of cooperative games and sports, preschool and kindergarten children have been found to share more and feel happier (Orlick, 1981). When elementary school children have worked together on schoolwork, the number of friendships in the classroom has increased (DeVries & Slavin, 1978). Bierman and Furman (1984) had small groups of unaccepted children and their peers make videos together. Changes were found in peer acceptance and rates of peer interaction, but these were short lived. Changes in partners' ratings of their likability were, however, maintained for the unaccepted children who received social skills training as well. Although cooperative activities seem to be a promising approach, their effects on conflict have not been assessed.

Focus on individuals

The preceding approaches are attempts to treat conflicts within a dyadic, familial, or small group context. Alternatively, one can try to change the behavior of the individual. These approaches do not have the reduction of conflict as a primary goal; nevertheless, reductions in aggressiveness or impulsivity, or improvements in problem-solving skills may lead to reductions in conflict.

Social skills training. This approach (also called "coaching") has been commonly used to improve unpopular children's relations. It is based on the ideas that children with peer relationship problems lack specific social skills and that these skills can be taught to children lacking them (Asher & Renshaw, 1981). In a typical program, a series of social skills is taught over a succession of lessons. In one of our programs, for example, unaccepted fifth- and sixth-grade children are taught three conversational skills – self-expressions, questions, and leadership bids (Bierman & Furman, 1984). In each lesson, the children are first taught the general concept and rationale for the skill and provided specific behavioral examples. The instructor may talk about why it is important to tell people things about oneself and what things one may want to tell the other. The instructor may model the skill, perhaps during a conversation, and then have the child or children practice applying the skill, perhaps in a conversation with another child. Finally, children receive feedback and reinforcement for their performance.

These programs have been found to change both social behaviors and social acceptance, although the specific effects vary somewhat among studies (see Bierman, 1989; Furman, 1984a; Ladd & Asher, 1985). Moreover, most of these programs are designed to promote positive social behaviors and may lead to a reduction in aggression, disruptive behavior, or conflicts if the children learn to substitute positive behaviors for negative ones or if they begin to be treated more positively by others. Evidence establishing changes in negative behaviors is limited, however (Coie & Koeppel, 1990). Bierman, Miller, and Stabb (1987) found that teaching conversational skills resulted in changes in rejected children's positive and negative behaviors. Only a combined treatment of skills training and response cost techniques for negative behaviors, however, resulted in sociometric changes. Even in this case, the only evident change was that treatment partners liked the children more; changes in aggressive behavior were not evident. Thus, the potential impact of conversational skill training on conflict remains unclear.

Assertiveness training. We suggested previously that the tendency to avoid conflict can be seen as a destructive form of conflict. Children who are unassertive may lack the appropriate social skills to stand up for their rights and negotiate conflicts through mutual problem solving. Assertiveness training may help children learn to negotiate conflicts with more interpersonal skill. Such programs have the same format as the social skills programs described in the preceding sections. They have been administered to individual children lacking the appropriate social skills to negotiate conflict successfully (e.g., Bornstein, Bellack, & Hersen, 1977), to groups of children identified as unassertive (e.g., Kirkland, Thelen, & Miller, 1983), and to entire classes of children (e.g., Rotheram, Armstrong, & Booraem, 1982).

Although such programs have not been extensively evaluated, Rotheram et al. (1982) found that children who had received assertiveness training produced responses that were more assertive during problem solving than were children who had not received the treatment. Children in the treatment group were also rated higher on comportment, popularity, and achievement by their teachers 1 year after receiving treatment. This finding is particularly striking because the teachers did not know the prior treatment condition. Although these results are promising, assertiveness training has not been evaluated enough to permit strong conclusions regarding its effectiveness in teaching children the social skills necessary for negotiating difficult interpersonal situations. This is particularly the case because the programs are structured to improve assertive behaviors across a variety of contexts, rather than in conflictual situations per se.

Self-instructional training programs. In cognitive-behavioral therapy, the focus is on cognitions regarding certain events, thoughts, or emotions. By addressing the client's thinking processes directly, the therapist helps the client to change his or her own thoughts and consequent behaviors. Meichenbaum (1975; Meichenbaum & Goodman, 1971) was one of the first to suggest that this approach could be used to teach impulsive children self-control. In his Self-Instructional Training, the child is taught to "stop and think" before acting and to use verbal mediation to help guide subsequent behavior.

The training sequence begins with the child observing a self-verbalizing model perform a simple task such as a maze. Next, the child performs the same task while following the verbal instructions of the model. The child then talks aloud while performing the task, attempting to approximate the verbalizations of the model; in effect, the child learns to substitute his or her own verbalizations for those of the model. Last, the child repeats the task employing covert self-instructions in order to consolidate the internalization process (Meichenbaum, 1975). As the sessions proceed, the child practices a range of different tasks, varying in complexity and difficulty. In subsequent elaborations of the paradigm, behavioral reinforcers and contingency contracting have been added to facilitate self-instruction (Kendall & Braswell, 1985). Camp and her colleagues have combined self-instructional and problem-solving approaches in their "Think Aloud" program (Camp, 1977; Camp, Blom, Herbert, & VanDoorninck, 1977).

Many of the early researchers of self-instructional training assessed effects in terms of changes in cognitive problem-solving skills, rather than changes in the behaviors or relationships of the target children. Nevertheless, self-instructional training has been found to be effective in reducing the frequency of impulsive behaviors of trained children (see Kendall & Braswell, 1985, for a review). Recent studies have addressed what treatment and subject variables are most likely to predict behavioral and cognitive change. Modeling, self-reinforcement, and role playing were, for example, found to effect the most changes. No ethnic or gender differences in ability to benefit from treatment were found, although more aggressive children were less likely to make behavioral gains than were less aggressive children.

Social problem solving. A related procedure has been to teach children social problem-solving skills. This approach is similar to Meichenbaum's (1975) self-instructional training in its emphasis on helping the child learn new ways of managing problem situations. The primary focus in both treatment approaches is on cognitive processes themselves, as opposed to the behavioral outcomes that result. In social problem-solving programs, children are taught thinking skills that will help them systematically negotiate interpersonal problems.

In one of the first efforts of this type, Spivack and Shure (1974) taught preschool children "alternative solutions thinking" and "consequential thinking" in a series of 46 lessons and activities taught by their teacher. Improvements were found in the problem-solving skills and teacher ratings of the adjustment of impulsive (aggressive) and inhibited (withdrawn) children. These effects were still present a year later, and well-adjusted children who had been exposed to the program were less likely to develop behavioral problems during the second year. Efforts to replicate these effects, however, have not been very successful (Rickel, Eshelman, & Loigman, 1983; Sharp, 1981; Winer, Hilpert, Gesten, Cowen, & Schubin, 1982).

Problem-solving programs have been commonly used in elementary school classrooms. Allen and his colleagues (Allen, Chinsky, Larcen, Lochman, & Selinger, 1976) taught third- and fourth-grade children divergent thinking, problem identification skills, alternative solution thinking, consequential thinking, and an elaboration of solutions generated. Changes were found in problem-solving ability, but not in sociometric status or teacher ratings of adjustment. Similarly, in a series of studies, a group of investigators at the University of Rochester have found changes in problem-solving skills, but changes in ratings of peer relations have been inconsistent (Gesten et al., 1982; Weissberg, Gesten, Carnike, et al., 1981; Weissberg, Gesten, Rapkin, et al., 1981). Few studies have included observational assessments of change.

Typically, problem-solving programs have been used to prevent potential problems that normal school-age children may experience. Recently, however, Kazdin et al. (1989) evaluated the effectiveness of problem-solving training (with and without in vivo practice) as well as relationship therapy for treating severe antisocial behavior. Compared to relationship therapy, problem-solving training showed significantly greater reductions in antisocial and other behavioral problems and greater increases in prosocial behavior. These effects were evident at both school and home and at a 1-year follow-up.

Adolescent anger control programs. A number of programs have been designed to reduce adolescents' anger and aggressive behavior (Feindler & Ecton, 1986; Feindler & Fremouw, 1983; Feindler, Marriott, & Iwata, 1984; Goldstein & Glick, 1987). These programs use a range of cognitive-behavioral approaches, including self-instructional and problem-solving training. Two of these programs, Feindler's (Feindler & Ecton, 1986) Adolescent Anger Control program, and Goldstein and Glick's (1987) Aggression Replacement Training (ART) have their origins in the stress inoculation or coping skills approach originated by Meichenbaum (1975) and Novaco (1978). This approach incorporates cognitive-behavioral techniques for arousal reduction into the self-instructional training originally proposed by Meichenbaum and Goodman (1971). An important underlying concept of the stress inoculation approach is that an individual's behavior during a provocation can have an impact on his or her level of affect. Thus, an individual's aggressive response to a provocation can actually increase the respondent's own level of anger because it may escalate the situation and increase the likelihood of further provocation. Preventing such an automatic aggressive response is therefore a major focus for treatment.

Feindler's program for adolescent anger control, which can be administered in either a group or an individual format, begins by educating the adolescent clients about anger, its cognitive, physiological, and its behavioral components. They are also encouraged to examine the antecedents of their own anger. The cognitive component of the anger control program involves training the adolescents to use self-instructional methods to prepare, guide, and direct them through anger-provoking incidents without becoming angry and aggressive. The behavioral aspect of the program involves training the adolescents in relaxation techniques to help them moderate their arousal during a provocation. Clients are also trained in interpersonal problem-solving techniques to facilitate the development of prosocial behavior as an appropriate alternative to aggression.

This multimodal approach has been shown to provide adolescents with effective means of controlling their anger. Feindler and her colleagues (Feindler, Marriott, & Iwata, 1984) found that highly disruptive adolescents who received the treatment had significantly higher change scores than controls on measures of problem-solving ability, self-control, and daily frequencies of disruptive behavior and severe aggression. Further evaluation of the program with more disturbed adolescents in a psychiatric inpatient unit also revealed significant reductions in aggressive and disruptive behaviors, as well as increases in self-control, problem-solving abilities, and social skills (Feindler & Ecton, 1986). One important direction for this and other programs using multimodal approaches is to identify the particular components effecting change.

Goldstein and Glick's (1987) Aggression Replacement Training program has three major components: (a) structured learning to enhance prosocial skills levels, (b) anger control training to teach the inhibition of aggressive behaviors, and (c) moral education in which ethical dilemmas are discussed so as to encourage moral development. Hence, the program is very similar to that of Feindler and her colleagues, except for the inclusion of the moral education component. One would expect such a comprehensive approach to be effective, but to date there are no empirical evaluations of this program.

Finally, Guerra and Slaby (1990) recently developed a 12-session program for aggressive adolescent offenders. The program combines problem-solving training and self-instructional training with efforts to modify beliefs that aggression is a legitimate activity. Participants improved in problem-solving skills, endorsed beliefs supporting aggression less, and showed decreases in staff ratings of aggression, impulsivity, and inflexible behaviors. Changes in recidivism were not apparent.

Conclusion

The preceding sections have described a diversity of programs that may be helpful for reducing conflict and improving the management of conflict. At the same time, these programs are limited.

Perhaps the most noteworthy limitation is that most of the programs have not been designed to focus on conflict reduction per se. In part, this reflects the fact that we know relatively little about what destructive conflict is or how much it needs to occur before it becomes dysfunctional. It is hard to treat a problem when you do not know what it is! This is particularly the case for a variable such as conflict, because some conflict seems inherent and, in fact, healthy. It seems very unlikely that one would want to teach children not to engage in conflict or, for that matter, to be always compliant or assertive.

In the initial section of this chapter, we outlined a series of four criteria that indicate whether the expression or management of conflict in a dyad is dysfunctional. Although we believe these criteria are reasonable, they are primarily based on speculation: Empirical research is desperately needed on this topic.

We believe that such work needs to be guided by two important considerations – the relational context in which conflict occurs and the developmental status of those involved. Some studies show that the form of conflict varies as a function of the relationship involved. For example, dyads composed of friends utilize more mature conflict resolution strategies than nonfriend dyads (Nelson & Aboud, 1985). Differences also occur between parent–child and peer relations, and between peer and sibling relations. Clearly, the definition of a conflict problem needs to be relationship specific.

In the same vein, studies show that the form of conflict varies with age (Shantz, 1987). Many aspects of conflict change, including the reasons for disputes, the negotiation strategies used for conflict resolution, and the interpersonal goals children have in conflict situations (Selman & Demorest, 1985; Shantz, 1987). With a few noteworthy exceptions (e.g., Selman & Schultz, 1988, 1990; Spivack & Shure, 1974), however, the intervention programs reviewed here are rather adevelopmental in conceptualization and approach. Better descriptive information could help us choose among the multitude of potential interventions available.

One must also recognize that the theoretical bases for the different programs are quite different. From a social skills perspective, for example, a child with problems in conflict management may lack necessary social skills, whereas from a social-cognitive perspective, the child may lack the necessary cognitive skills to control impulses. Still others might conceptualize the problem in terms of coercive interchanges between individuals (e.g., Patterson, 1984). We know relatively little, however, about the etiology and nature of conflict in different relationships or different developmental periods that may help us select the most promising intervention approach.

Additionally, to reduce conflict per se, programs may need to be designed differently in several respects. As noted previously, conflict is a dyadic phenomenon. As such, a relational context seems a particularly promising approach. That is, the interveners would not necessarily focus on changing one individual's behaviors but, instead, would focus on changing the pattern of interactions between the two. Such an approach has been used in parent-training programs and family therapy but still remains a relatively new venue in intervention programs with children.

Although dyadic approaches seem promising, it is important to recognize that conflicts may stem from extradyadic sources. For example, we previously observed that parent-child conflict can be exacerbated by family stress, marital discord, and lack of social support (Patterson, 1982). Recent research also suggests that children's expectations and strategies in conflict situations with peers originate in early relationship experiences. For example, children who expect unfriendly assertive methods to be successful in resolving peer conflict tend to have mothers who use power-assertive discipline strategies (Hart, Ladd, & Burleson, 1990), and rejected children and their mothers tend to report more aggressive behavioral responses to nonhostile provocations than do popular children and their mothers (Keane, Brown, & Crenshaw, 1990). Similarly, Dishion (1990) found a relation between inadequate parent management practices and poor peer relationships, a relation that was mediated, in part, by boys' antisocial behavior. So as we learn more about the etiology of conflict, we will want to design programs that address these factors. For example, based on the results described here, components that cover parenting skills should be included in programs for improving peer relations.

Whereas a relational emphasis seems promising, programs that focus on individuals should not be ignored. Often times, one particular individual is primarily responsible for the conflict that occurs or may be involved in many conflict-ridden relationships. The primary recommendation for these programs is simple: Assess changes in the frequency and form of conflict. As noted previously, however, the evidence that these programs affect conflict is mainly inferential.

Most of the individually oriented or relational programs reviewed here are focused on increasing positive behaviors or interchanges. The literature on social skills training, however, suggests that these approaches may not necessarily change conflictual interactions without some supplementation or alteration in the program format. Certain components are needed, in particular, to teach children to control their initial aggressive impulses as well as to engage in more appropriate problem solving.

We are particularly struck by the absence of programs designed to prevent problems in conflict management. The prevalence of conflictual parent–adolescent dyads and distressed marital couples clearly underscores the importance of such programs. Conflict is inherent in relationships, yet most of us perceive it to be very distressing (Selman, 1980). Stated simply, most of us do not know how to fight properly!

The field also could benefit from examining the adult clinical and organizational literatures on the prevention and treatment of conflict (Hocker & Wilmot, 1985; Jacobson & Margolin, 1979). Numerous intervention approaches for the treatment of conflict have been developed within these fields. Some of the existing programs have borrowed ideas from these fields, but much more could be learned from them. Marital researchers have conducted detailed examinations of the sequences of interactions by distressed and nondistressed couples. For example, Gottman (1979) found that nonclinic couples' problem solving was characterized by an initial phase of validating statements followed by a contract phase characterized by problem solutions and agreements. In contrast, clinic couples started with exchanging complaints, tended to enter into a negative exchange loop in which disagreements were reciprocated, and did not reach the contract phase. Similarly, nondistressed couples tend to respond to problem statements with positive statements, whereas distressed couples validated the statement but disagreed (the "yes, but" sequence) (Revenstorf, Hahlweg, Schindler, & Vogel, 1984). These findings give us clues about how conflict may be successfully or unsuccessfully resolved in relationships, suggesting, at the very least, that such sequential analyses are a promising way of examining children's conflicts.

Finally, research on treatment efficacy generally has lacked methodological rigor. Several standard criticisms of treatment research apply, including the need for further work on the generalizability and long-term effects of the interventions. Some of the most promising clinical programs are multimodal in nature, but what specific components are responsible for the observed changes are unknown. Greater specification of the population receiving the intervention also is needed. For example, Hawkins (in press) found that the effects of a primary prevention program for antisocial behavior were greater for Caucasian subjects then for black subjects. We know little about which programs will be effective with populations of different socioeconomic statuses or cultural backgrounds, or why. Such information would assist programmers in tailoring their interventions to a given population (Kazdin, 1987).

Clearly, the work on conflict interventions for children is only beginning. As we develop a better understanding of the nature of destructive conflict, design appropriate programs for its control, and assess impact more rigorously, we should also be able to make children's lives more harmonious.

References

Adler, T., & Furman, W. (1988). A model for close relationships and relationship dysfunctions. In S. W. Duck (Ed.), *Handbook of personal relationships: Theory, research, and interventions*. London: Wiley.

Alexander, J. F., & Barton, C. (1976). Behavioral systems therapy for families. In D. H. L. Olson (Ed.), *Treating relationships*. Lake Mills, IA: Graphic.

Alexander, J. F., & Parsons, B. V. (1973). Short-term behavioral intervention with delinquent families: Impact on family process and recidivism. *Journal of Abnormal Psychology, 81*, 219–225.

Alexander, J. F., & Parsons, B. V. (1982). *Functional family therapy*. Monterey, CA: Brooks/Cole.

Allen, G. J., Chinsky, J. M., Larcen, S. W., Lochman, J. E., & Selinger, H. V. (1976). *Community psychology and the schools: A behaviorally oriented multilevel preventive approach*. Hillsdale, NJ: Erlbaum.

Allison, T. S., & Allison, S. L. (1971). Time out from reinforcement: Effects on sibling aggression. *The Psychological Record, 21*, 81–86.

Asarnow, J. R. (1983). Children with peer adjustment problems: Sequential and nonsequential analyses of school behavior. *Journal of Consulting and Clinical Psychology, 51*, 709–717.

Asher, S. R., & Renshaw, P. D. (1981). Children without friends: Social knowledge and skill training. In S. R. Asher & J. M. Gottman (Eds.), *The development of children's friendships*. Cambridge: Cambridge University Press.

Barton, C., Alexander, J. F., Waldron, H., Turner, C. W., & Warburton, J. (1985). Generalizing treatment effects of functional family therapy: Three replications. *American Journal of Family Therapy, 13*, 16–26.

Bierman, K. L. (1989). Improving the peer relationships of rejected children. In B. B. Lahey & A. E. Kazdin (Eds.), *Advances in child clinical psychology* (Vol. 12). New York: Plenum.

Bierman, K. L., & Furman, W. (1984). The effects of social skills training and peer involvement on the social adjustment of preadolescents. *Child Development, 55*, 151–162.

Bierman, K. L., Miller, C. L., & Stabb, S. D. (1987). Improving the social behavior and peer acceptance of rejected boys: Effects of social skill training with instructions and prohibitions. *Journal of Consulting and Clinical Psychology, 55*, 194–200.

Boldizar, J. P., Perry, D. G., & Perry, L. C. (1989). Outcome values and aggression. *Child Development, 60*, 571–579.

Bornstein, M. R., Bellack, A. S., & Hersen, M. (1977). Social skills training for unassertive children: A multiple baseline analysis. *Journal of Applied Behavior Analysis, 10*, 183–195.

Boscolo, L., Cecchin, G., Hoffmann, L., & Penn, P. (1987). *Milan systemic family therapy: Conversations in theory and practice*. New York: Basic.

Brody, G. H., Stoneman, Z. H., & Burke, M. (1987). Child temperaments, maternal differential behavior, and sibling relationships. *Developmental Psychology, 23*, 354–362.

Bryant, B. K., & Crockenberg, S. B. (1980). Correlates and dimensions of prosocial behavior: A study of female siblings with their mothers. *Child Development, 51*, 529–544.

Camp, B. W. (1977). Verbal mediation in young aggressive boys. *Journal of Abnormal Psychology, 86*(2), 145–153.

Camp, B. W., Blom, G. F., Herbert, F., & van Doorninck, W. J. (1977). "Think Aloud": A program for developing self-control in young aggressive boys. *Journal of Abnormal Child Psychology, 5*, 157–169.

Coie, J. D., Christopoulos, C., Terry, R., Dodge, K. A., & Lochman, J. E. (1989). Types of aggressive relationships, peer rejection, and developmental consequences. In B. H. Schneider, G. Attili, J. Nadel, & R. P. Weissberg (Eds.), *Social competence in developmental perspective*. Dordrecht, The Netherlands: Kluwer Academic Publishers.

Coie, J. D., Dodge, K. A., & Kupersmidt, J. B. (1990). Peer group behavior and social status. In S. R. Asher & J. D. Coie (Eds.), *Peer rejection in childhood*. Cambridge: Cambridge University Press.

Coie, J., & Koeppel, G. K. (1990). Adapting intervention to the problems of aggressive and disruptive rejected children. In S. R. Asher & J. D. Coie (Eds.), *Peer rejection in childhood*. Cambridge: Cambridge University Press.

Deluty, R. H. (1981). Alternative-thinking ability of aggressive, assertive and submissive children. *Cognitive Therapy and Research, 5*, 309–312.

Deutsch, M. (1973). *The resolution of conflict: Constructive and destructive processes*. New Haven, CT: Yale University Press.

DeVries, D. L., & Slavin, R. E. (1978). Teams-Games-Tournament (TGT): Review of ten classroom experiments. *Journal of Research and Development in Education, 12*, 28–38.

Dishion, T. J. (1990). The family ecology of boys' peer relationships in middle childhood. *Child Development, 61*, 874–892.

Dodge, K. A. (1985). Attributional bias in aggressive children. In P.C. Kendall (Ed.), *Advances in cognitive-behavioral research and therapy* (Vol. 4). New York: Academic Press.

Dodge, K. A., Pettit, G. S., McClaskey, C. L., & Brown, M. M. (1986). Social competence in children. *Monographs of the Society for Research in Child Development, 51*(2, Serial No. 213).

Dodge, K. A., Price, J. M., Coie, J. D., & Christopoulos, C. (in press). On the development of aggressive dyadic relationships in boys' peer groups. *Human Development*.

Dumas, J. E., & Wahler, R. G. (1983). Predictors of treatment outcome in parent training: Mother insularity and socioeconomic disadvantage. *Behavioral Assessment, 5*, 301–313.

Emery, R. (1982). Interparental conflict and the children of discord and divorce. *Psychological Bulletin, 92*, 310–330.

Feindler, E. L., & Ecton, R. B. (1986). *Adolescent anger control: Cognitive-behavioral techniques*. Elmsford, NY: Pergamon Press.

Feindler, E. L., & Fremouw, W. J. (1983). Stress inoculation training for adolescent anger problems. In D. Meichenbaum & M. E. Jaremko (Eds.), *Stress reduction and prevention*. New York: Plenum.

Feindler, E. L., Marriott, S. A., & Iwata, M. (1984). Group anger control training for junior high school delinquents. *Cognitive Therapy and Research, 8*, 299–311.

Foot, H. C., Chapman, A. J., & Smith, J. R. (1977). Friendship and social responsiveness in boys and girls. *Journal of Personality and Social Psychology, 35*, 401–411.

Forehand, R., & McMahon, R. J. (1981). *Helping the noncompliant child: A clinician's guide to parent training*. New York: Guilford Press.

Foster, S. L. (1978). *Family conflict management: Skill training and generalization procedures*. Unpublished doctoral dissertation, State University of New York, Stony Brook.

Furman, W. (1984a). Enhancing children's peer relations and friendships. In S. W. Duck (Ed.), *Personal relationships: Vol. 5. Repairing personal relationships*. New York: Academic Press.

Furman, W. (1984b). Issues in the assessment of social skills of normal and handicapped children. In T. Field, M. Siegal, & J. Roopnarine (Eds.), *Friendships of normal and handicapped children*. New York: Ablex.

Furman, W., & Buhrmester, D. (1985a). Children's perceptions of the personal relationships in their social networks. *Developmental Psychology, 21*, 1016–1022.

Furman, W., & Buhrmester, D. (1985b). Children's perceptions of the quality of sibling relationships. *Child Development, 56*, 448–461.

Furman, W., & Giberson, R. (in press). Identifying the links between parents and their children's sibling relationships. In S. Shmuel (Ed.), *Proceedings of the Eighth Annual Workshop on Human Development*.

Garbarino, J., & Gilliam, G. (1980). *Understanding abusive families*. Lexington, MA: Heath.

Gesten, E. L., Rains, M. L., Rapkin, B. D., Weissberg, R. P., Flores de Apodaca, F., Cowen, E. L., & Bowen, R. (1982). Training children in social problem-solving competencies: A first and second look. *American Journal of Community Psychology, 10*, 95–115.

Goldstein, A. P., & Glick, B. (1987). *Aggression replacement training: A comprehensive intervention for aggressive youth.* Champaign, IL: Research Press.

Gottman, J. M. (1979). *Marital interaction: Experimental investigations.* New York: Academic Press.

Gottman, J. M., & Krokoff, L. J. (1989). Marital interaction and satisfaction: A longitudinal view. *Journal of Consulting and Clinical Psychology, 57*, 47–52.

Grotevant, H. D., & Carlson, C. I. (1989). *Family assessment: A guide to methods and measures.* New York: Guilford Press.

Guerra, N. G., & Slaby, R. G. (1990). Cognitive mediators of aggression in adolescent offenders: Intervention. *Developmental Psychology, 26*, 269–277.

Hart, C. H., Ladd, G. W., & Burleson, B. R. (1990). Children's expectations of the outcomes of social strategies: Relations with sociometric status and maternal disciplinary styles. *Child Development, 61*, 127–137.

Hartup, W. W., & Laursen, B. (in press). Conflict and context in peer relations. In C. Hart (Ed.), *Children on playgrounds: Research perspectives and applications.* Ithaca: SUNY Press.

Hartup, W. W., Laursen, B., Stewart, M. I., & Eastenson, A. (1988). Conflict and the friendship relations of young children. *Child Development, 59*, 1590–1600.

Hawkins, J. (in press). Reducing early childhood aggression. *Journal of American Academy of Child and Adolescent Psychiatry.*

Hocker, J. L., & Wilmot, W. W. (1985). *Interpersonal conflict* (2d ed.). Dubuque, IA: Brown.

Hoffmann, L. (1981). *Foundations of family therapy.* New York: Basic.

Jacobson, N. S., & Margolin, G. (1979). *Marital therapy.* New York: Brunner/Mazel.

Kazdin, A. E. (1987). Treatment of antisocial behavior in children: Current status and future directions. *Psychological Bulletin, 102*, 187–203.

Kazdin, A. E., Bass, D., Siegel, T., & Thomas, C. (1989). Cognitive-behavioral therapy and relationship therapy in the treatment of children referred for antisocial behavior. *Journal of Consulting and Clinical Psychology, 57*, 522–535.

Keane, S. P., Brown, K. B., & Crenshaw, T. M. (1990). Children's intention-cue detection as a function of maternal social behavior: Pathways to social rejection. *Developmental Psychology, 26*, 1004–1009.

Kelly, F. D., & Main, F. O. (1979). Sibling conflict in a single-parent family: An empirical case study. *American Journal of Family Therapy, 7*, 39–47.

Kendall, P. C., & Braswell, L. (1985). *Cognitive-behavioral therapy for impulsive children.* New York: Guilford Press.

Kirkland, K. D., Thelen, M. H., & Miller, D. J. (1983). Group assertion training with adolescents. *Child and Family Behavior Therapy, 4*, 1–12.

Krokoff, L. J., Gottman, J. M., & Roy, A. K. (1988). Blue-collar marital interaction and a companionate philosophy of marriage. *Journal of Personal and Social Relationship, 5*, 201–222.

Ladd, G. W., & Asher, S. R. (1985). Social skill training and children's peer relations. In L. L'Abate & M. Milan (Eds.), *Handbook of social skills training and research.* New York: Wiley.

Laursen, B. (1990). *Relationships and conflict during adolescence.* Unpublished manuscript, University of Maine, Orono.

Leitenberg, H., Burchard, J. D., Burchard, S. M., & Fuller, E. J., & Lysaught, T. V. (1977). Using positive reinforcement to suppress behavior: Some experimental comparisons with sibling conflict. *Behavior Therapy, 8*, 168–182.

Levi, A. M., Buskila, M., & Gerzi, S. (1977). Benign neglect: Reducing fights among siblings. *Journal of Individual Psychology, 33,* 240–245.

Lochman, J. E. (1987). Self- and peer perceptions and attributional biases of aggressive and nonaggressive boys in dyadic interactions. *Journal of Consulting and Clinical Psychology, 55,* 404–410.

Margolin, G., & Wampold, B. E. (1981). Sequential analysis of conflict and accord in distressed and nondistressed marital partners. *Journal of Consulting and Clinical Psychology, 49,* 554–567.

Masters, J. C., & Furman, W. (1981). Popularity, individual friendship selections, and specific peer interactions among children. *Developmental Psychology, 17,* 344–350.

Meichenbaum, D. (1975). Self-instructional methods. In A. Goldstein & F. Kanfer (Eds.), *Helping people change: Methods and materials.* New York: Pergamon Press.

Meichenbaum, D., & Goodman, J. (1971, April). *The nature and modification of impulsive children: Training impulsive children to talk to themselves.* Paper presented at the meeting of the Society for Research in Child Development, Minneapolis, MN.

Milich, R., & Landau, S. (1982). Socialization and peer relations in hyperactive children. *Advances in Learning and Behavioral Disabilities, 1,* 283–339.

Minuchin, S. (1974). *Families and family therapy.* Cambridge, MA: Harvard University Press.

Moos, R., & Moos, B. (1974). *Family environment scale.* Palo Alto, CA: Consulting Psychologists Press.

Nelson, J., & Aboud, F. E. (1985). The resolution of social conflict between friends. *Child Development, 56,* 1009–1017.

Novaco, R. W. (1978). Anger and coping with stress: Cognitive-behavioral intervention. In J. P. Foreyet & D. P. Rathjen (Eds.), *Cognitive behavioral therapy: Research and application.* New York: Plenum.

O'Leary, K., O'Leary, D., & Becker, B. (1967). Modification of a deviant sibling interaction pattern in the home. *Behavior Research and Therapy, 5,* 113–126.

Olweus, D. (1978). *Aggression in the schools: Bullies and whipping boys.* Washington, DC: Hemisphere.

Orlick, T. D. (1981). Positive socialization via cooperative games. *Developmental Psychology, 17,* 426–429.

Parsons, B. V., & Alexander, J. F. (1973). Short-term family intervention: A therapy outcome study. *Journal of Consulting and Clinical Psychology, 41,* 195–201.

Patterson, G. R. (1982). *Coercive family process.* Eugene, OR: Castalia.

Patterson, G. R. (1984). Siblings: Fellow travelers in coercive family processes. In R. J. Blanchard & D. C. Blanchard (Eds.), *Advances in the study of aggression* (Vol. 1). New York: Academic Press.

Patterson, G. R., Reid, J. B., Jones, R. R., & Conger, R. C. (1975). *A social learning approach to family intervention: Vol. 1. Families with aggressive children.* Eugene, OR: Castalia.

Perry, D. G., Kusel, S. J., & Perry, L. C. (1988). Victims of peer aggression. *Developmental Psychology, 24,* 807–814.

Piaget, J. (1932). *The moral judgment of the child.* London: Kegan Paul.

Price, J. M., & Dodge, K. A. (1989). Reactive and proactive aggression in childhood: Relations to peer status and social context dimensions. *Journal of Abnormal Child Psychology, 17,* 455–471.

Reit, S. V. (1985). *Sibling rivalry.* New York: Ballantine.

Revenstorf, D., Hahlweg, K., Schindler, L., & Vogel, B. (1984). Interaction analysis of marital conflict. In K. Hahlweg & N. S. Jacobson (Eds.), *Marital interaction: Analysis and modification.* New York: Guilford Press.

Rickel, A. U., Eshelman, A. K., & Loigman, G. A. (1983). Social problem solving training: A follow-up study of cognitive and behavioral effects. *Journal of Abnormal and Child Psychology, 11,* 15–28.

Robin, A. L. (1979). Problem-solving communication training: A behavioral approach to the treatment of parent–adolescent conflict. *American Journal of Family Therapy, 7,* 69–82.

Robin, A. L. (1981). A controlled evaluation of problem-solving communication training with parent–adolescent conflict. *Behavior therapy, 12,* 593–609.

Robin, A. L., & Foster, S. L. (1989). *Negotiating parent–adolescent conflict.* New York: Guilford Press.

Rotheram, M. J., Armstrong, M., & Booraem, C. (1982). Assertiveness training in fourth- and fifth-grade children. *American Journal of Community Psychology, 10,* 567–582.

Sancilio, M. F., Plumert, J. M., & Hartup, W. W. (1989). Friendship and aggressiveness as determinants of conflict outcomes in middle childhood. *Developmental Psychology, 25,* 812–819.

Selman, R. L. (1980). *The growth of interpersonal understanding.* New York: Academic Press.

Selman, R. L., & Demorest, A. P. (1985). Putting thoughts and feelings into perspective: A developmental view on how children deal with interpersonal disequilibrium. In D. Bearison & H. Zimilies (Eds.), *Thinking and emotions: Developmental perspectives.* Hillsdale, NJ: Erlbaum.

Selman, R. L., & Schultz, L. H. (1988). Interpersonal thought and action in the case of a troubled early adolescent. In S. R. Shirk (Ed.), *Cognitive development and child psychotherapy.* New York: Plenum.

Selman, R. L., & Schultz, L. H. (1990). *Making a friend in youth.* Chicago: University of Chicago Press.

Shantz, C. U. (1987). Conflict between children. *Child Development, 58,* 283–305.

Shantz, C. U., & Hobart, C. J. (1989). Social conflict and development: Peers and siblings. In T. J. Berndt & G. W. Ladd (Eds.), *Peer relationships in child development.* New York: Wiley.

Shantz, D. W. (1986). Conflict, aggression, and peer status: An observational study. *Child Development, 57,* 1322–1332.

Sharp, K. C. (1981). The importance of interpersonal problem solving training on preschoolers' social competency. *Journal of Applied Developmental Psychology, 2,* 129–143.

Spivack, G., & Shure, M. B. (1974). *Social adjustment of young children: A cognitive approach to solving real-life problems.* San Francisco: Jossey-Bass.

Stern, S. (1984). *A group cognitive-behavioral approach to the management and resolution of parent–adolescent conflict.* Unpublished doctoral dissertation, University of Chicago.

Stocker, C., Dunn, J., & Plomin, R. (1989). Sibling relationships: Links with child temperament, maternal behavior, and family structure. *Child Development, 60,* 715–727.

Strain, P. S., Young, C. C., & Horowitz, J. (1981). Generalized behavior change during oppositional child training: An examination of child and family demographic variables. *Behavior Modification, 5,* 15–26.

Straus, M. A. (1979). Measuring intrafamily conflict and violence: The Conflict Tactics (C.T.) Scales. *Journal of Marriage and the Family, 41,* 75–88.

Straus, M. A., Gelles, R. J., & Steinmetz, S. K. (1980). *Behind closed doors: Violence in the American family.* New York: Doubleday.

Tavitian, M. L., Lubiner, J., Green, L., Grebstgein, L. C., & Velicer, W. F. (1987). Dimensions of family functioning. *Journal of Social Behavior and Personality, 2,* 191–204.

Touliatos, J., Perlmutter, B. F., & Straus, M. A. (Eds.). (1990). *Handbook of family measurement techniques.* Beverly Hills, CA: Sage.

Vincent, J. P., Friedman, L. C., Nugent, J., & Messerly, L. (1979). Demand characteristics in observations of marital interactions. *Journal of Consulting and Clinical Psychology, 47,* 557–566.

Vuchinich, S. (1987). Starting and stopping spontaneous family conflicts. *Journal of Marriage and the Family, 49,* 591–601.

Waas, G. A. (1988). Social attributional biases of peer-rejected and aggressive children. *Child Development, 59*, 969–975.

Wahler, R. G. (1976). Deviant child behavior within the family: Developmental speculations and behavior change strategies. In H. Leitenberg (Ed.), *Handbook of behavior modification and behavior therapy.* Englewood Cliffs, NJ: Prentice-Hall.

Wehr, P. (1979). *Conflict resolution.* Boulder, CO: Westview Press.

Weissberg, R. P., & Allen, J. P. (1986). Promoting children's social skills and adaptive interpersonal behavior. In B. H. Schneider, K. H. Rubin, & J. E. Ledingham (Eds.), *Children's peer relations: Issues in assessment and intervention.* New York: Springer-Verlag.

Weissberg, R. P., Gesten, E. L., Carnike, C. L., Toro, P. A., Rapkin, B. D., Davidson, E., & Cowen, E. L. (1981). Social problem-solving skills training: A competence-building intervention to second- to fourth-grade children. *American Journal of Community Psychology, 9*, 411–424.

Weissberg, R. P., Gesten, E. L., Rapkin, B. P., Cowen, E. L., Davidson, E., Flores de Apodaca, R., & McKim, B. J. (1981). Evaluation of a social problem solving training program for suburban and inner-city third-grade children. *Journal of Consulting and Clinical Psychology, 49*, 251–261.

Winer, J. I., Hilpert, P. L., Gesten, E. L., Cowen, E. L., & Schubin, W. E. (1982). The evaluation of a kindergarten social problem-solving program. *Journal of Primary Prevention, 2*, 205–216.

Author index

Subject index